The Cricketer Who's Who 2017

Foreword by
MARCUS TRESCOTHICK

Editor
BENJ MOOREHEAD

Compiled by
HENRY COWEN, JO HARMAN,
ED KEMP & PHIL WALKER

Design
JOE PROVIS & ROB WHITEHOUSE

The
Cricketers'
Who's Who
2017

This edition first published in the UK by All Out Cricket Ltd

© All Out Cricket Ltd 2017
www.alloutcricket.com

ISBN: 978-1-909811-34-8

Published by Jellyfish Publishing
www.jellyfishsolutions.co.uk

Editor: *Benj Moorehead;* Research and editorial: *Henry Cowen, George Dabby, Benedict Gardner, Jo Harman, Ed Kemp, Phil Walker*
Design: *Joe Provis, Rob Whitehouse;* Images: *Getty Images unless stated;*
Print: *Jellyfish Print Solutions*

Acknowledgements
The publishers would like to thank the county clubs, the Professional Cricketers' Association and the players for their assistance in helping to put together this book. Additional information has been gathered from espncricinfo.com and cricketarchive.com. Thanks also to George Franks and Roger Ockenden for providing images

Openers

FOREWORD

By Marcus Trescothick

Welcome to the 2017 edition of *The Cricketers' Who's Who*. I remember picking up the book as a kid and sifting through all the different players. It was exciting when I first appeared in it – which was all the way back in 1993! As a player, I return to *The Cricketers' Who's Who* to look up the guys I am playing against. It's an iconic book.

This season will be my 25th as a professional cricketer. I haven't got any celebrations planned, but perhaps Somerset will have something to celebrate come the end of the season. The club makes no bones about the fact that we've not won the County Championship before and how much we want to change that. I've had the pleasure of playing in some good teams, both with Somerset and England, and obviously the 2005 Ashes is the current highlight of my career. I'd love to put the County Championship next to it.

From a neutral point of view, the end of the 2016 season was thrilling, with three teams vying for the Championship on the last day. But it was pretty tough for all of us at Somerset to just sit there waiting to see what would happen in the match between Middlesex and Yorkshire at Lord's. I also had a stinking hangover from the end-of-season party we'd had the previous night after winning our game at Taunton with a day to spare. It was all so close, but it wasn't to be.

This year will be a good learning curve for our new 23-year-old captain, Tom Abell. Tom's got a sharp cricket brain and a good general approach to the game. It might take him some time to deal with the pressure of the job, but that's where the senior players like myself can help out. We also have Matt Maynard, our coach, and it will be great for Tom to have Chris Rogers back as a batting coach and team mentor.

It's fantastic that Taunton will host its first men's international match this summer, with England playing a Twenty20 against South Africa. Everyone at the club is really excited about it.

Later in the summer The Oval will host its hundredth Test when England play South Africa. I made my highest Test score of 219 in the same fixture at the same ground back in 2003. That was Alec Stewart's last Test match. We hadn't lost a series at home for a long time but were 2–1 down going into that final Test. South Africa won the toss and made around 460, but we managed to get ahead of the game by scoring 600 and then bowled them out pretty cheaply. To be able to come from behind like that was a massive step for the team.

There is also the Champions Trophy to look forward to this summer. I still can't understand how we lost the Champions Trophy final at The Oval in 2004, no matter how many times I watch the highlights. It was of course nice to get a hundred in the final but we should have won

that game. West Indies were eight down and still needed 70-odd runs, yet suddenly they were closing in on victory. As hosts, you have the extra support from the home crowd, you feel more comfortable, and you might even be able to go home between games to get away from it all. But it does also bring the expectation that you should win on home soil.

Saying that, the team that England have at the moment is very special. They must be close to being favourites and I think this could be the first time that we win a trophy on our patch. The batting is very strong, so if they can get their bowling right they'll be tough to beat. Fingers crossed!

Marcus Trescothick
March 2017

Nothing can make it *better*. I take medication, but that just manages to suppress things. Usually you have an operation to make yourself better, but in my case it was done just to look after me if I need it.

My life has been turned upside down but I've tried to view it as positively as possible and that's probably saved me. I don't know what I would have done without my girlfriend's support. In the last few years, she and I were used to spending six months at a time apart. But I've spent the last year in her pocket. She's become my safety net; I'm so used to having her there.

As soon as the incident happened, we said to each other: "Well, we might as well make the best of a bad situation." And that's the way we've handled it.

* * *

I took straight to social media. Cricket has taught me that if you bottle things up, it will make them 10 times worse. With my heart condition, the last thing I needed was a battle with my own mind – it was going to be hard enough anyway. So I thought that I could help others and myself by sharing my feelings about my experience, and I've had lots of people contacting me through social media and I've spoken to hundreds of people. They feel they can speak to me because I've been so open about it.

This might be a strange thing to say, but occasionally I used to lie in bed and think, 'If I died, I wonder who would miss me?' That was a negative, insecure mindset. But the reaction to what happened to me *was* like I had died. I spent four days in hospital after the news came out, just reading all the amazing things people said and wrote. There were 26 million tweets about me in the first two hours after it was announced, and ultimately around 60 million. Some of them were private messages to me, and I replied to every one. It was a saving grace for me. People say words can't make a difference, but they really got me through the worst four days of my life. When you're low, you need a bit of love. I got that and it saved me.

The NHS saved me too. People complain about the NHS because you might have to wait a few hours if you've got a broken finger – but that's due to someone's life being saved. When you really need them, they're there.

My agent, Luke Sutton, has been amazing. I've spent my whole career getting the right people around me to help my cricket. Yes, they helped with my cricket, but when I really needed them it was to do with my life.

Three months on from the heart attack, I'd battled through everything and was doing really well. Then came a moment in the car on the way back from watching the rugby at Twickenham when I realised that I wasn't invincible. I'd always been the best at something. I had always been fit and strong. Not anymore. That was tough to take.

Everything is different from my previous life, apart from walking into the same house. Spicy food affects my heart, and caffeine or chocolate is off limits. I can't drive anymore.

I had been so looking forward to going into the last year of my contract with Notts because I knew I'd have a few counties trying to sign me – which is great, because you're good at something that you do. When you've lost that thing you're good at, it's a lonely world. I still don't know where the next contract is coming from. It's daunting.

I'd already considered going into the media or coaching. I enjoy giving insight, and media and coaching is my avenue into that. I love the game too much to stay away from it. Besides, I've got to forge a career. My financial situation is fairly insecure right now.

That's why I was rushing around following my retirement, busting a gut to fulfil any media opportunity that came my way. But my body couldn't take the stress. I had another attack – and it was even worse than the first episode. I hadn't realised how fragile my body was. Once more I had to take a step back and learn about my parameters, about my new body.

Of course I would have liked to have played until my late 30s, so in that sense I'm retired a dozen years too early. But I'm also a decade ahead of everyone else in terms of starting a new career.

* * *

People assume that my favourite moments as a cricketer were the times when I scored hundreds, for instance when I was Man of the Match against Australia in the Old Trafford ODI in 2015. But for me it was taking all those close catches in South Africa and winning games for England – and winning what turned out to be my final series as an international cricketer. I'm so glad I did that before I finished. I finished on a high.

This England team are a good bunch. They stuck by me, and raised £25,000 for my charity. I still speak to them all a lot.

I love watching them play and it's great to be part of the media and analysing the performance of my mates. If they're rubbish, I'll say so. But I'll do it the right way – the same way as if I was telling it to their face. It's good to be honest. Life is tough when you lie.

COMING FULL CIRCLE

Forty-four years since the late Rachael Heyhoe Flint beat the men to the punch and organised cricket's first World Cup, the tournament returns to England this summer. Isabelle Duncan, *author of* Skirting The Boundary, *a critically acclaimed history of women's cricket, looks back at England's triumph of 1973 and forward to what promises to be a wonderful advert for the progress made since*

THEN

Well, the women got there first: the inaugural cricket World Cup was held in 1973, two years before the first men's tournament. We have the Wolverhampton duo of Rachael Heyhoe Flint and Sir Jack Hayward to thank for this stroke of genius. With a bushy tailed and unique approach to the game, Rachael, the then England captain, and Jack, the millionaire philanthropist, made it happen. Hayward, a successful businessman and property developer, stumped up £40,000 to finance the entire tournament and is quoted as saying: "I love women and I love cricket, so what better than to support something that combines both."

South Africa were kept out in the cold due to their government's apartheid laws. Australia and New Zealand, both Test-playing nations, were invited, and Jamaica and Trinidad and Tobago were included following tours by England's women to the West Indies. To beef up the tournament, an 'International XI' and 'Young England' side also featured to bring the number of competing teams up to seven.

It was played entirely as a round-robin tournament with no knockout stages, and the last scheduled match between England and Australia could not have been poised more perfectly with the latter leading the table by a solitary point going into the final game. These were heady times for England, with Heyhoe Flint leading her team to a 92-run victory over the Aussies. A match-winning knock of 118 by the supremely talented allrounder Enid Bakewell, with a useful 64 from Heyhoe Flint in support, set the tone for a dominant victory. The press embraced the occasion, as Brian Marshall of the *Sunday Telegraph* reported:

They put on 101 for the first wicket and, following the dismissal of Thomas for 40, she [Bakewell] found an admirable partner in her captain Flint. Scoring almost at will for a spell, Enid Bakewell failed by only two runs to obtain her century before lunch. The feature of the second-wicket partnership of 117 was Heyhoe Flint's aggressive 64. She made a hesitant start but later made amends with powerful leg shots as Australia began to wilt in the face of such belligerent opposition.

HRH Princess Anne enjoyed the spectacle and presented the cup in front of an elated grandstand. Next stop was 10 Downing Street for the victorious team as prime minister Edward Heath hosted a reception.

Heyhoe Flint sadly died earlier this year, and Bakewell was one of hundreds who attended the funeral in Wolverhampton. She had learnt her trade on the rustic, hand-cut (hedge shears), uncovered pitches of her mining village near Nottingham. She mucked in with the local boys and faced fast bowling on unpredictable surfaces, forcing her to concentrate hard and be nimble on her feet. This served her well in her international career. Bakewell's world-record opening stand of 246 with Lynne Thomas at Hove against the International XI in the 1973 World Cup was a record for 25 years. Both scored unbeaten centuries. It was one of many big stands she shared with her dear friend, and the bond they have is enduring. Bakewell named her youngest daughter, Lynne, after her old partner in crime.

Motherhood did not always blend well with international cricket for these young women. Feeding babies on the boundary and pinning down babysitters during the hours of play was not an easy task. When asked if she thought the inaugural World Cup was a turning point for women's cricket, Bakewell replied: "I had these young children and I didn't have time to be philosophical about cricket back then," she told me. "I took each game as it went."

These women also had jobs to hold down with employers who were not always understanding. There were husbands to placate and money was tight since no financial help came from the men's game. They had to fend for themselves. "We were not allowed to claim expenses or be paid," said Bakewell. "Rachael vowed and declared that she was going to change things, as it was only players who could afford to play for England and go on tour who were chosen. I had to go back to work to raise the £603 airfare for the 1968/69 tour of Australia and New Zealand."

This was a four-and-a-half-month trip and players were expected to have deep pockets and sympathetic employers. Rachael kept her word and the 1973 World Cup was born with full sponsorship.

There were many firsts for England's women cricketers in the Seventies: the 1973 World Cup itself, the maiden official ODI series between England and Australia in 1976, and then the icing on the cake – their first appearance at Lord's later that year. A combination of winning the first World Cup and the Equal Opportunities Commission breathing down the neck of MCC had paved the way for England's women to fulfil their ambition of playing at the home of cricket.

NOW

The World Cup will make the full circle back to Lord's with the 2017 final to be played there on July 23. This will be the 11th women's World Cup, featuring eight teams playing at four intimate county grounds: Derby, Bristol, Leicester and Taunton.

The road to this World Cup began in earnest in 2014 with the first structured bilateral tournament in the women's game, the ICC Women's Championship, featuring the top eight ranked teams playing each other over a two-and-a-half-year period. Each country was guaranteed at least 21 ODIs and the top four sides gained automatic qualification for the 2017 World Cup.

The bottom four teams, plus six other nations, battled it out at February's World Cup Qualifier in Sri Lanka for the remaining four places. The drive behind this Women's Championship is to ensure a sustainable volume of cricket and an attempt to narrow the gap between England and Australia and the rest of the world. The two powerhouses are streets ahead in terms of financial investment, and there is a danger of other countries being left behind. This structured bilateral cricket also brings context and meaning to every game. Surely this is something the men's game should look at.

In the 10 World Cups played to date, Australia are by far the most successful team, having lifted the trophy six times and failed to appear in the final on only two occasions. England have three titles to their name and New Zealand tasted victory on home soil in 2000.

STUDY THE FORM

The advent of professionalism in women's cricket, coupled with the razzmatazz of new global T20 tournaments such as the Women's Big Bash in Australia and the Kia Super League in England, will no doubt lift the quality at this 2017 World Cup.

We will feast on the artistry and flair of the best elite female players the world has to offer. Suzie Bates, 2016 *Wisden* Cricketer of the Year and New Zealand captain, is an exceptional player, and look out for the explosive batting of her veteran teammate, Sara McGlashan. Australia have the indomitable Ellyse Perry, a brilliant allrounder and pin-up girl of the women's game. England's very own Tammy Beaumont is in the form of her life with the blade and in 2016 hard-hitting allrounder Nat Sciver hit the fastest half-century in ODIs.

Hayley Matthews, the rising star of West Indies, stole the show in last year's World T20 final, while her senior colleagues Stafanie Taylor and Deandra Dottin are two of the world's most destructive batters. For South Africa, premier allrounder Marizanne Kapp is one to watch out for, as is Shabnim Ismail, possibly the fastest women's bowler on the planet. Mithali Raj, India's captain, will want to make amends for her country's first-round exit in the 2013 World Cup at home, and towering seamer Jhulan Goswami could be lethal on English pitches. Pakistan, despite being in the doldrums of late, can take comfort in their captain, Sana Mir, and her fizzing off-breaks.

MEDIA EXPOSURE

This will be the first World Cup for England as full professionals and that will bring unprecedented media scrutiny. While we cannot expect professionalism to instantly translate into on-pitch results and we must be patient, these players are being judged by different standards now. The 2017 World Cup will be a thorough examination of their talent.

Fingers crossed that Sky, who hold the broadcasting rights on all English cricket until the end of 2019, will do the right thing and cover the majority of the event. There has been a stark contrast in broadcasting between women's cricket in England and the free-to-air broadcaster, Channel Ten, used in Australia for the women's game.

The Women's Big Bash in Australia in early 2016 blew everyone away by drawing unprecedented audiences on Ten's second digital channel, thus earning an upgrade to their main channel for some of the more high-profile matches. The crowds flocked to the grounds, the mainstream media were enamoured, and the next generation of cricket-lovers were inspired as participation numbers shot up. Just ask the Australian Matt Dwyer, now employed as the ECB's director of participation and growth, about the importance of free-to-air television. He has a proven track record at Cricket Australia where he got behind the Big Bash and free-to-air TV, culminating in rocketing participation numbers and spectator interest.

By contrast, in this country not a single match during the 2016 Kia Super League was televised. Small consolation came in the shape of Sky's behind-the-scenes feature programme. Thank goodness that *Test Match Special* decided to broadcast seven of the games on BBC radio. The women obviously impressed in 2016 as Sky have now taken the plunge and announced live coverage of six Super League group matches and both games on Finals Day for 2017. Progress. So, come on Sky, give these women the exposure they deserve, and showcase this parade of female cricketing talent in the 2017 World Cup.

THE COUNTY CHAMPIONSHIP'S MOST THRILLING FINISHES

A whole winter has passed but county cricket is still buzzing with the extraordinary denouement to the 2016 season. Elgan Alderman *picks out the most hair-raising climaxes in the County Championship's 126-year history*

1 **Warwickshire** 1911

In one of the Championship's hottest summers, Warwickshire became the first side outside the Big Six (Yorkshire, Lancashire, Notts, Surrey, Middlesex and Kent) to win the title. The champions were inspired by their 22-year-old debonair captain Frank Foster, who scored 1,383 runs at 44.61 and took 116 wickets at 19.15 with his left-arm seam. They went into their final match at Northampton needing a win to usurp leaders Kent, who had won the Championship two seasons running. Foster, in tandem with veteran fast bowler Frank Field, skittled Northamptonshire for 73 and 175, despite delays for rain. This was the first season to award points for drawn matches; under the previous rules Warwickshire would not have come out on top.

2 **Middlesex** 1920

Aged 46, Pelham 'Plum' Warner had wanted to relinquish the Middlesex captaincy but was persuaded to have one last hurrah. By the end of July, Warner's unfancied side trailed Lancashire at the top by a distance, before eight wins on the bounce brought Middlesex back into the reckoning. They still had to win their last game at Lord's against Surrey, who along with Lancashire were also in contention. By the final day it looked as if Warner would be denied his fairytale finish. Lancashire were strolling to victory at Old Trafford, while Middlesex trailed Surrey by 46 runs having just begun their second innings. They declared at 316-7, setting their opponents 244 in three hours. Jack Hobbs went cheaply but Andy Sandham threatened before Patsy Hendren took "the best catch of my career" at long-on to precipitate a collapse to 188 all out. The Grand Old Man of English cricket was carried off the field for the last time with a second Championship title and 29,028 runs to his name.

3 **Lancashire** 1927

Having gone unbeaten for 26 matches, Lancashire were rumbled by Sussex in their penultimate game and then could only draw at Leicester. It left Nottinghamshire wanting only a draw from their final match at Swansea against winless Glamorgan to become champions for the second time in 37 years of Championship cricket. Notts won the toss and posted 233 before Glamorgan replied with 375 thanks to 163 from opener Eddie Bates. The champions-elect collapsed on the third morning, losing seven wickets for 14 runs as they were dismissed for 61 to lose by an innings. William 'Dodger' Whysall, George Gunn and Wilfred Payton had scored almost 5,000 runs between them in the campaign but in the decisive fixture they were no match for Jack Mercer, the Glamorgan seamer taking 6-31 to give the Welshmen something to sing about. Lancashire completed a hat-trick of Championships the following summer.

4 **Yorkshire** 1959

Surrey were looking for their eighth title on the bounce but their ageing side was beginning to creak and Yorkshire, among others, were waiting to pounce. Warwickshire and Gloucestershire had also mounted challenges during a hot, dry summer but it all came down to Yorkshire's exhilarating final-day chase at Hove. Sussex stubbornly held on until after tea before they were dismissed to set Yorkshire 215 in 105 minutes. Inspired by a partnership of 141 between Bryan Stott and Doug Padgett, they reached their target in just 28.3 overs, and Surrey's failure to beat Middlesex at The Oval handed Yorkshire their first outright title in 13 years – and one of seven they would win over the next decade.

5 **Worcestershire** 1974

Hampshire, the defending champions, went into their final home match at Bournemouth two points ahead of Worcestershire. It was a surprise that they had not settled the matter earlier, having gone 31 points clear at the top after beating Worcestershire by an innings in early August. But rain denied Hampshire near-certain victories in their penultimate two home games, while Worcestershire took advantage of better weather with three wins in a row. What happened next? Well, nothing much beyond a deluge of rain and some wild winds which meant that Hampshire's final game against Yorkshire was abandoned without a ball being bowled. The last two days of Worcestershire's drawn match at Chelmsford were also lost to the weather, but the four bonus points they accrued on the first day were enough to pinch the pennant.

6 **Middlesex and Kent** 1977

Exactly 100 years had passed since WG Grace's Gloucestershire last won the Championship – albeit in the 'unofficial' era. And now, under the captaincy of South Africa's Mike Procter, they were five points clear of Middlesex and Kent at the top of the table entering the final round of games. The two chasing teams were both playing away from home, while Gloucestershire hosted Hampshire at Bristol. An expectant crowd of around 5,000 turned up for the final day, with Hampshire chasing 271. To much relief Barry Richards was dismissed early, but that was as good as it got. Gordon Greenidge hit 94 as the visitors marched to their target for the loss of four wickets. Procter, the only bowler to snaffle more than 100 victims in the season, bowled 22 wicketless overs. Thus Gloucestershire were leapfrogged by Middlesex and Kent, who won their matches to finish the season level on points. Forty years later, and Gloucestershire are still waiting.

7 **Essex** 1984

A two-horse race between Essex and Nottinghamshire was decided by the penultimate ball of the season in surely the Championship's greatest ever finish. Notts had a four-point lead going into the final round of fixtures, in which they made the trip to Taunton while their pursuers were at Old Trafford. Essex wrapped up a 10-wicket victory inside two days, and with it a full complement of bonus points, meaning Notts had to win. Set 297 in 60 overs, they were going well at 258-5 only for Clive Rice (98) to become the first of three wickets to fall for two runs. It came down to 14 required from the final over with Notts' last-wicket pair in the middle. Mike Bore hit 10 of them and then launched the fifth ball back over the bowler's head – and into the hands of Richard Ollis, a substitute fielder, at long-on. Pandemonium broke out in the Chelmsford pavilion, where the Essex players had been gathered around a radio all day.

8 **Worcestershire** 1988

Kent were aggrieved when they were controversially denied a bowling point during the mid-season victory at Edgbaston because two members of the opposition were unfit to bat. Come the last round of matches, Kent trailed Worcestershire at the top of the table by... one point. They made short work of Surrey at Canterbury, but Worcestershire were well on course for victory against Glamorgan at New Road until the teams turned up on the final morning to find that vandals had poured engine oil over the wicket. A feverish attempt to dry the pitch ensued, and Worcestershire were able to complete an innings victory by the afternoon. With both sides taking maximum bonus points, Worcestershire finished champions by that single point.

9 **Lancashire** 2011

Warwickshire sat atop the table. Three points adrift, and 77 years since they last won the title outright, Lancashire lay in wait. Both were well placed for victory on the final day of the season. At Taunton, Lancashire had reduced Somerset to 105-5 – a lead of just five – inspired by their veteran captain Glen Chapple, who shrugged off a hamstring injury to bowl with pace. Meanwhile Warwickshire had Hampshire 43-3 after enforcing the follow-on at Southampton. They were denied the win by dogged centuries from Michael Carberry and Neil McKenzie, and Peter Trego threatened to do the same at Taunton. But Gary Keedy ran the last Somerset man out with the first direct hit of his 17-year career to give Lancashire 34 overs to chase down 211. They were up to the task, Steven Croft and Karl Brown steering Lancashire to victory, and the long-awaited title, with five overs to spare.

10 **Middlesex** 2016

Last year's finale was a humdinger, with first and second in the table meeting for a showdown at Lord's – and third-placed Somerset waiting in the wings. Leaders Middlesex knew they had to beat Yorkshire once Somerset had wrapped up a 325-run win inside three days at Taunton. On the final day Yorkshire chased an agreed target of 240 runs in 40 overs. That came down to 87 in 10 with six wickets in hand, with Tim Bresnan leading the charge. But Bresnan's dismissal for 55 prompted a collapse as the Yorkshire batsmen threw the bat in pursuit of quick runs. The end was as swift as it was dramatic, Toby Roland-Jones clean-bowling Ryan Sidebottom to complete a hat-trick and give Middlesex their first title for 23 years. For Somerset, never before champions, it was another agonising brush with glory.

KEY

RHB LB R1 W1 MVP2

R – 1,000 or more first-class runs in an English season (the number next to 'R' denotes how many times the player has achieved this feat)

W – 50 or more first-class wickets in an English season (the number next to 'W' denotes how many times the player has achieved this feat)

MVP – Denotes a player's presence in the top 100 places of the 2016 Overall MVP Points (the number next to 'MVP' denotes the player's specific placing)

---

* – Not out innings (e.g. 137*)

(s) – A competition has been shared between two or more winners

CB40 – Clydesdale Bank 40 (English domestic 40-over competition, 2010-2012)

CC1/CC2 – County Championship Division One/County Championship Division Two

LB – Leg break bowler

LF – Left-arm fast bowler

LFM – Left-arm fast-medium bowler

LHB – Left-hand batsman

LM – Left-arm medium bowler

LMF – Left-arm medium-fast bowler

MCCU – Marylebone Cricket Club University

NWT20 – NatWest T20 Blast (English domestic 20-over competition, 2014-17)

OB – Off-break bowler

ODI – One-Day International

RF – Right-arm fast bowler

RFM – Right-arm fast-medium bowler

RHB – Right-hand batsman

RL50 – Royal London One-Day Cup (English domestic 50-over competition, 2014-17)

RM – Right-arm medium bowler

RMF – Right-arm medium-fast bowler

SLA – Slow left-arm orthodox bowler

SLC – Slow left-arm Chinaman bowler

T20/T20I – Twenty20/Twenty20 International

UCCE – University Centre of Cricketing Excellence

WK – Wicketkeeper

YB40 –Yorkshire Bank 40 (English domestic 40-over competition, 2013)

NOTES: The statistics given for a player's best batting and best bowling performance are limited to first-class cricket. If a field within a player's career statistics is left blank then the record for that particular statistic is incomplete, e.g. there is no record for how many balls a player has faced in first-class cricket. An '-' indicates that a particular statistic is inapplicable, e.g. a player has never bowled a ball in first-class cricket. All stats correct as of March 8, 2017.

The
Teams

DERBYSHIRE

FORMED: 1870
HOME GROUND: The 3aaa County Ground, Derby
ONE-DAY NAME: Derbyshire Falcons
CAPTAIN: Billy Godleman (Championship and RL50), TBC (NWT20)
2016 RESULTS: CC2: 9/9; RL50: 7/9 North Group; NWT20: 7/9 North Group
HONOURS: Championship: 1936; Gillette/NatWest/C&G/FP Trophy: 1981; Benson & Hedges Cup: 1993; Sunday League: 1990

THE LOWDOWN

Derbyshire are in a state of flux after a difficult 2016 in which they finished bottom of Division Two without a single victory. The coaching structure has been overhauled, with Kim Barnett now director of cricket and New Zealander John Wright the county's new specialist T20 coach. Chesney Hughes, prolific last summer, departed after failing to agree terms so another glut of runs are required from Billy Godleman, in his second season as four-day captain, and Wayne Madsen, who has hit 1,000 first-class runs in each of the last four seasons. Wickets have been harder to come by, with much of the burden on the shoulders of veteran Tony Palladino (now a player-coach). South Africa's Hardus Viljoen, signed on a Kolpak deal, will add genuine pace, while 21-year-old Will Davis showed great promise in his breakthrough year. A dash of mystery comes from Sri Lankan leg-spinner Jeevan Mendis (with the club until June) and South Africa's Imran Tahir (thereafter).

DIRECTOR OF CRICKET: KIM BARNETT

A batsman for Derbyshire between 1979 and 1998, Barnett captained the club for more than a decade and also played four Tests for England. He leaves his role as club president as part of a revamped coaching restructure in which former opener Steve Stubbings returns as first XI support coach and ex-Northants batsman Mal Loye takes on a development role. The most eye-catching appointment was that of John Wright as a specialist T20 coach. A former New Zealand and Derbyshire batsman, Wright won the IPL with Mumbai Indians in 2013.

Batting

	Mat	Inns	NO	Runs	HS	Ave	SR	100	50	4s	6s
HR Hosein	4	8	4	423	108	105.75	45.43	1	4	44	0
SJ Thakor	9	13	4	606	130	67.33	69.02	2	2	74	3
WL Madsen	15	26	4	1292	163	58.72	52.79	6	3	171	2
CM MacDonell	1	2	1	56	35*	56.00	41.79	0	0	8	0
CF Hughes	11	19	4	806	137*	53.73	52.85	3	4	114	7
BA Godleman	13	24	0	934	204	38.91	53.18	3	2	124	6
AL Hughes	5	9	0	299	140	33.22	45.85	1	1	38	1
BT Slater	9	15	1	393	110	28.07	47.92	1	1	44	1
HD Rutherford	10	17	1	441	78	27.56	51.16	0	3	69	1
GTG Cork	1	2	0	53	49	26.50	51.45	0	0	7	1
NT Broom	14	22	1	530	96	25.23	50.04	0	2	53	4
TAI Taylor	3	6	0	147	80	24.50	55.68	0	1	20	0
MJJ Critchley	7	12	1	263	70*	23.90	54.90	0	1	36	1
AJ Mellor	2	3	0	71	44	23.66	39.01	0	0	9	0
A Carter	4	4	1	68	39	22.66	98.55	0	0	8	3
TP Milnes	5	9	0	188	56	20.88	65.05	0	1	27	1
T Poynton	9	11	2	167	53	18.55	36.46	0	1	20	0
AP Palladino	14	20	5	268	49	17.86	50.37	0	0	35	2
CF Parkinson	4	7	2	80	48*	16.00	42.78	0	0	7	1
WJ Durston	4	4	0	63	43	15.75	61.76	0	0	9	0
BD Cotton	8	11	3	102	26	12.75	58.28	0	0	14	1
LJ Fletcher	4	4	0	34	14	8.50	47.22	0	0	4	0
TA Wood	2	4	0	32	14	8.00	33.33	0	0	5	0
WS Davis	6	8	1	34	15	4.85	48.57	0	0	7	0

Bowling

	Overs	Mdns	Runs	Wkts	BBI	BBM	Ave	Econ	SR	5w	10w
NT Broom	17.0	2	64	3	1/9	2/20	21.33	3.76	34.0	0	0
AP Palladino	453.5	110	1201	39	5/74	7/91	30.79	2.64	69.8	2	0
SJ Thakor	188.0	24	687	22	5/63	5/78	31.22	3.65	51.2	1	0
TP Milnes	172.0	37	509	15	6/93	6/93	33.93	2.95	68.8	1	0
WS Davis	170.2	20	733	21	7/146	8/204	34.90	4.30	48.6	1	0
CF Parkinson	170.4	28	531	14	4/90	7/178	37.92	3.11	73.1	0	0
WJ Durston	101.4	14	397	9	3/149	3/43	44.11	3.90	67.7	0	0
BD Cotton	202.3	50	661	14	4/28	6/62	47.21	3.26	86.7	0	0
CF Hughes	106.3	11	430	9	3/87	3/87	47.77	4.03	71.0	0	0
TAI Taylor	63.0	13	250	4	2/103	2/80	62.50	3.96	94.5	0	0
LJ Fletcher	99.0	25	276	4	1/18	2/71	69.00	2.78	148.5	0	0
A Carter	101.0	12	440	6	3/114	3/114	73.33	4.35	101.0	0	0
WL Madsen	165.1	21	527	7	2/24	2/59	75.28	3.19	141.5	0	0
MJJ Critchley	122.2	3	639	4	2/101	2/101	159.75	5.22	183.5	0	0
AL Hughes	53.0	10	169	1	1/34	1/60	169.00	3.18	318.0	0	0

Catches/Stumpings:
16 Poynton (inc 1st), 11 Madsen, Mellor, 9 Hosein, 8 C Hughes, Rutherford, 7 Broom, A Hughes, Mellor, 6 Godleman, 3 Critchley, Durston, Slater, 2 Carter, Palladino, 1 Cotton, Fletcher, Hemmings, Milnes, Wood

Batting

	Mat	Inns	NO	Runs	HS	Ave	SR	100	50	4s	6s
BT Slater	6	6	2	328	148*	82.00	84.97	2	1	39	2
BA Godleman	6	6	1	298	91	59.60	82.32	0	3	29	5
NT Broom	6	5	2	177	90	59.00	97.25	0	1	13	2
HD Rutherford	5	4	0	195	104	48.75	101.56	1	0	15	8
WL Madsen	7	6	2	168	69*	42.00	80.00	0	1	15	1
HR Hosein	2	2	1	42	40	42.00	110.52	0	0	6	0
MJJ Critchley	6	3	1	60	43	30.00	120.00	0	0	4	4
JDS Neesham	2	2	1	26	26*	26.00	123.80	0	0	2	1
AL Hughes	7	4	0	65	30	16.25	87.83	0	0	5	0
SJ Thakor	7	4	1	46	29	15.33	83.63	0	0	4	1
WJ Durston	4	4	0	52	30	13.00	61.90	0	0	3	0
AP Palladino	2	2	0	16	15	8.00	114.28	0	0	1	1
CF Hughes	1	1	0	7	7	7.00	20.58	0	0	0	0
BD Cotton	7	2	2	15	14*	-	78.94	0	0	1	0
A Carter	3	-	-	-	-	-	-	-	-	-	-
WS Davis	1	-	-	-	-	-	-	-	-	-	-
AJ Mellor	2	-	-	-	-	-	-	-	-	-	-
T Poynton	3	-	-	-	-	-	-	-	-	-	-

Bowling

	Overs	Mdns	Runs	Wkts	BBI	Ave	Econ	SR	4w	5w
JDS Neesham	8.0	2	35	1	1/35	35.00	4.37	48.0	0	0
WJ Durston	11.0	0	53	1	1/28	53.00	4.81	66.0	0	0
AL Hughes	41.0	2	202	3	1/29	67.33	4.92	82.0	0	0
A Carter	19.1	0	97	5	3/59	19.40	5.06	23.0	0	0
WL Madsen	3.0	0	16	0	-	-	5.33	-	0	0
BD Cotton	47.2	4	258	10	4/43	25.80	5.45	28.4	1	0
AP Palladino	20.0	0	112	0	-	-	5.60	-	0	0
SJ Thakor	41.0	2	268	10	3/36	26.80	6.53	24.6	0	0
MJJ Critchley	48.0	1	350	6	2/53	58.33	7.29	48.0	0	0

Catches/Stumpings:
7 Madsen, 3 Broom, A Hughes, 2 Cotton, 1 Hosein, Palladino, Poynton, Rutherford

	Mat	Inns	NO	Runs	HS	Ave	SR	100	50	4s	6s
WL Madsen	12	11	3	257	59*	32.12	134.55	0	2	18	10
HD Rutherford	12	12	1	343	71*	31.18	142.91	0	2	36	12
T Poynton	6	4	2	57	37*	28.50	132.55	0	0	2	1
WJ Durston	8	8	0	223	51	27.87	162.77	0	1	24	10
JDS Neesham	12	10	2	199	45	24.87	135.37	0	0	19	5
CF Hughes	12	11	1	244	46	24.40	127.74	0	0	18	10
SJ Thakor	12	9	3	127	30	21.16	149.41	0	0	10	6
NT Broom	12	12	1	232	68	21.09	118.36	0	2	16	5
AL Hughes	12	8	1	88	27	12.57	91.66	0	0	6	1
MJJ Critchley	12	5	2	31	10	10.33	140.90	0	0	1	2
BD Cotton	4	3	2	7	4	7.00	63.63	0	0	0	0
BA Godleman	2	2	0	6	4	3.00	50.00	0	0	0	0
A Carter	9	1	0	0	0	0.00	0.00	0	0	0	0
TP Milnes	1	1	0	0	0	0.00	0.00	0	0	0	0
AJ Mellor	1	1	1	10	10*	-	142.85	0	0	0	0
HR Hosein	5	2	2	0	0*	-	-	0	0	0	0

Batting

	Overs	Mdns	Runs	Wkts	BBI	Ave	Econ	SR	4w	5w
MJJ Critchley	37.5	0	259	11	3/36	23.54	6.84	20.6	0	0
AL Hughes	38.0	0	287	6	3/23	47.83	7.55	38.0	0	0
WL Madsen	8.0	0	61	3	1/7	20.33	7.62	16.0	0	0
SJ Thakor	33.5	0	268	11	3/17	24.36	7.92	18.4	0	0
WJ Durston	15.0	0	123	5	2/17	24.60	8.20	18.0	0	0
A Carter	29.4	0	266	9	3/34	29.55	8.96	19.7	0	0
JDS Neesham	40.3	0	381	15	4/35	25.40	9.40	16.2	1	0
TP Milnes	3.0	0	30	0	-	-	10.00	-	0	0
BD Cotton	10.0	0	106	3	2/24	35.33	10.60	20.0	0	0

Bowling

Catches/Stumpings:
8 C Hughes, 7 Hosein, 5 Madsen, 4 A Hughes, Neesham, 3 Broom, Critchley, Durston, 2 Carter, Thakor, 1 Cotton

TEAM PROFILE

FORMED: 1882
HOME GROUND: Emirates Riverside
T20 BLAST NAME: Durham Jets
CAPTAIN: Paul Collingwood
(Championship), Keaton Jennings
(RL50), TBC (NWT20)
2016 RESULTS: CC1: 4/9; RL50: 5/9
North Group; NWT20: Runners-up
HONOURS: Championship: (3) 2008,
2009, 2013; Gillette/NatWest/C&G/
FP Trophy: 2007; Pro40/National
League/CB40/YB40/RL50: 2014

THE LOWDOWN

Back-to-back wins at the end of last season meant that Durham finished just 30 points behind champions Middlesex to cap an encouraging summer in which they made their first T20 final. Then the roof fell in. Durham's financial problems forced them to accept a £3.8m ECB bailout, and the conditions that came with it: relegation from Division One, a 48-point deduction in 2017 (and further handicaps in the short formats) and the removal of Emirates Riverside's Test-match status. Durham loyalists rallied to the cause, including new chairman Ian Botham, and the club's debts were eased by a deal with the local council. Nevertheless, Durham are in a hole, made deeper by the departure of Mark Stoneman and Scott Borthwick, two of their most prolific batsmen. Much will depend on the new 50-over captain Keaton Jennings – when not required by England – and the contributions of overseas batsmen Stephen Cook and Tom Latham.

HEAD COACH: JON LEWIS

A solid opening batsman who made 16 first-class centuries in a playing career spent at Essex and later Durham, Lewis took over as head coach in June 2013 after Geoff Cook stepped down to recover from a heart attack, immediately leading the side to the County Championship title and then to victory in the Royal London One-Day Cup the following year. Lewis guided the club to its first T20 Finals Day in 2016.

Batting

	Mat	Inns	NO	Runs	HS	Ave	SR	100	50	4s	6s
KK Jennings	16	28	4	1548	221*	64.50	53.93	7	2	215	2
MD Stoneman	16	28	1	1234	141*	45.70	64.57	2	5	166	6
SG Borthwick	16	28	2	1060	188*	40.76	53.02	3	5	147	2
U Arshad	2	3	0	119	84	39.66	54.58	0	1	13	2
PD Collingwood	14	24	6	595	106*	33.05	49.50	1	3	63	7
BA Carse	8	8	2	176	47	29.33	50.86	0	0	28	2
G Clark	3	6	0	170	58	28.33	49.27	0	2	24	1
BA Stokes	6	9	1	226	51	28.25	62.25	0	2	25	4
JTA Burnham	14	24	1	630	135	27.39	43.90	1	3	86	4
RD Pringle	10	12	2	243	57*	24.30	69.03	0	1	32	4
G Onions	16	19	7	282	65	23.50	51.17	0	1	35	1
MJ Richardson	15	24	2	510	99*	23.18	45.29	0	3	60	1
BJ McCarthy	7	10	2	176	51*	22.00	56.41	0	1	23	4
MA Wood	3	6	0	130	36	21.66	76.92	0	0	21	2
AJ Hickey	3	6	3	64	36*	21.33	41.02	0	0	6	2
P Coughlin	6	10	0	198	39	19.80	50.25	0	0	29	0
WJ Weighell	3	4	1	53	22	17.66	50.96	0	0	7	2
SW Poynter	4	7	0	119	42	17.00	54.09	0	0	19	0
GJ Muchall	1	2	0	30	17	15.00	51.72	0	0	5	0
C Rushworth	13	16	5	114	31*	10.36	55.33	0	0	18	0

Bowling

	Overs	Mdns	Runs	Wkts	BBI	BBM	Ave	Econ	SR	5w	10w
WJ Weighell	112.5	22	329	16	5/33	9/130	20.56	2.91	42.3	1	0
AJ Hickey	47.5	6	143	6	2/19	2/19	23.83	2.98	47.8	0	0
MA Wood	78.0	7	275	11	3/24	5/75	25.00	3.52	42.5	0	0
KK Jennings	55.0	14	159	6	2/26	2/26	26.50	2.89	55.0	0	0
BA Stokes	183.3	36	560	18	4/54	7/186	31.11	3.05	61.1	0	0
G Onions	544.0	95	1688	54	5/90	8/152	31.25	3.10	60.4	1	0
BJ McCarthy	177.1	25	632	20	5/70	6/121	31.60	3.56	53.1	1	0
C Rushworth	343.2	68	1049	32	5/93	5/75	32.78	3.05	64.3	1	0
BA Carse	148.2	21	569	17	3/38	4/86	33.47	3.83	52.3	0	0
P Coughlin	137.3	26	395	10	2/31	3/87	39.50	2.87	82.5	0	0
RD Pringle	201.2	24	804	19	7/107	10/260	42.31	3.99	63.5	1	1
SG Borthwick	310.3	33	1194	23	5/79	8/152	51.91	3.84	81.0	1	0
PD Collingwood	39.1	6	127	1	1/39	1/39	127.00	3.24	235.0	0	0
MD Stoneman	5.0	1	28	0	-	-	-	5.60	-	0	0
U Arshad	30.0	4	103	0	-	-	-	3.43	-	0	0

Catches/Stumpings:
34 Richardson (inc 1st), 25 Borthwick, 18 Jennings, 12 Collingwood, Poynter, 9 Pringle, 8 Stoneman, 6 Burnham, 3 Coughlin, Rushworth, 2 Carse, McCarthy, Onions, 1 Hickey, Muchall, Stokes, Weighell

ROYAL LONDON ONE-DAY CUP AVERAGES 2016

Batting

	Mat	Inns	NO	Runs	HS	Ave	SR	100	50	4s	6s
MJ Richardson	5	4	1	156	64	52.00	96.29	0	2	7	2
GJ Muchall	2	1	0	42	42	42.00	110.52	0	0	3	1
MD Stoneman	8	7	0	247	93	35.28	85.17	0	2	33	1
SG Borthwick	8	7	0	238	84	34.00	88.14	0	3	26	2
P Mustard	5	5	0	161	88	32.20	99.38	0	1	17	4
RD Pringle	8	7	0	209	125	29.85	119.42	1	0	24	6
PD Collingwood	6	6	0	168	69	28.00	105.66	0	2	15	3
U Arshad	7	4	3	24	15	24.00	46.15	0	0	0	0
CS MacLeod	3	3	1	46	29*	23.00	80.70	0	0	5	0
KK Jennings	8	7	2	104	24	20.80	74.28	0	0	8	1
JTA Burnham	5	4	0	69	26	17.25	66.34	0	0	7	1
P Coughlin	5	3	0	31	17	10.33	91.17	0	0	1	0
G Clark	3	3	0	28	19	9.33	71.79	0	0	1	0
C Rushworth	8	3	1	12	8	6.00	42.85	0	0	1	0
J Harrison	3	2	1	1	1	1.00	16.66	0	0	0	0
SW Poynter	3	2	2	35	27*	-	184.21	0	0	4	1
MA Wood	1	-	-	-	-	-	-	-	-	-	-

Bowling

	Overs	Mdns	Runs	Wkts	BBI	Ave	Econ	SR	4w	5w
MA Wood	10.0	0	43	2	2/43	21.50	4.30	30.0	0	0
KK Jennings	29.0	0	157	2	1/34	78.50	5.41	87.0	0	0
PD Collingwood	12.0	0	65	0	-	-	5.41	-	0	0
J Harrison	26.0	2	145	6	4/40	24.16	5.57	26.0	1	0
RD Pringle	38.0	0	212	4	2/39	53.00	5.57	57.0	0	0
U Arshad	40.1	0	226	5	3/50	45.20	5.62	48.2	0	0
P Coughlin	29.0	0	175	2	1/56	87.50	6.03	87.0	0	0
C Rushworth	62.0	4	389	12	3/19	32.41	6.27	31.0	0	0
SG Borthwick	63.0	1	404	4	1/48	101.00	6.41	94.5	0	0
MD Stoneman	0.4	0	8	1	1/8	8.00	12.00	4.0	0	0

Catches/Stumpings:
5 Borthwick, 3 Poynter, Pringle, 2 Arshad, Jennings, Mustard, Stoneman, 1 Collingwood, Muchall, Rushworth, Wood

Batting

	Mat	Inns	NO	Runs	HS	Ave	SR	100	50	4s	6s
PD Collingwood	8	6	4	139	44*	69.50	134.95	0	0	11	4
KK Jennings	17	13	5	348	88	43.50	126.54	0	1	24	7
U Arshad	14	6	4	70	43	35.00	140.00	0	0	6	2
CS MacLeod	5	5	0	165	83	33.00	142.24	0	1	14	3
P Mustard	13	11	1	290	75*	29.00	131.81	0	2	28	8
GJ Muchall	9	6	2	103	32	25.75	111.95	0	0	4	3
MD Stoneman	17	15	1	356	82*	25.42	137.45	0	2	37	8
P Coughlin	12	6	2	87	26*	21.75	147.45	0	0	4	3
SG Borthwick	17	7	3	82	29	20.50	101.23	0	0	2	0
MJ Richardson	17	12	2	188	37	18.80	109.94	0	0	16	5
BA Stokes	7	5	0	91	56	18.20	151.66	0	1	11	3
G Clark	5	5	0	89	36	17.80	128.98	0	0	11	3
RD Pringle	17	14	2	139	33	11.58	129.90	0	0	15	4
JTA Burnham	4	4	0	27	17	6.75	87.09	0	0	1	2
BJ McCarthy	6	3	1	2	2*	1.00	40.00	0	0	0	0
MA Wood	5	1	1	5	5*	-	166.66	0	0	1	0
C Rushworth	13	2	2	0	0*	-	0.00	0	0	0	0
J Harrison	1	-	-	-	-	-	-	-	-	-	-

Bowling

	Overs	Mdns	Runs	Wkts	BBI	Ave	Econ	SR	4w	5w
MA Wood	20.0	0	122	9	4/25	13.55	6.10	13.3	1	0
C Rushworth	46.0	1	297	19	3/14	15.63	6.45	14.5	0	0
KK Jennings	50.0	0	368	9	2/18	40.88	7.36	33.3	0	0
SG Borthwick	50.4	0	373	18	4/18	20.72	7.36	16.8	1	0
PD Collingwood	12.3	0	102	2	1/21	51.00	8.16	37.5	0	0
P Coughlin	37.5	1	328	17	5/42	19.29	8.66	13.3	0	1
BJ McCarthy	18.3	0	166	7	3/23	23.71	8.97	15.8	0	0
RD Pringle	17.0	0	163	2	1/14	81.50	9.58	51.0	0	0
U Arshad	48.5	0	476	12	3/30	39.66	9.74	24.4	0	0
J Harrison	4.0	0	47	2	2/47	23.50	11.75	12.0	0	0

Catches/Stumpings:
12 Mustard (inc 1st), 10 Richardson, 8 Borthwick, 7 Stoneman, 6 Pringle, 5 Collingwood, Muchall, Rushworth, 3 Coughlin, Jennings, MacLeod, 2 Arshad, Clark, Richardson, Stokes, 1 Burnham, Wood

ESSEX

FORMED: 1876
HOME GROUND: The Cloudfm County Ground, Chelmsford
ONE-DAY NAME: Essex Eagles
CAPTAIN: Ryan ten Doeschate
2016 RESULTS: CC2: Winners; RL50: Quarter-finalists; NWT20: Quarter-finalists
HONOURS: Championship: (6) 1979, 1983, 1984, 1986, 1991, 1992; Gillette/NatWest/C&G/FP Trophy: (3) 1985, 1997, 2008; Benson & Hedges Cup: (2) 1979, 1998; Pro40/National League/CB40/YB40/RL50: (2) 2005, 2006; Sunday League: (3) 1981, 1984, 1985

THE LOWDOWN

Essex are back in the top flight of the Championship for the first time in seven years, although they will be without cult heroes David Masters and Graham Napier, who retired after helping the club to the Division Two title last season. Replacing 1,069 games of experience – not to mention 1,893 wickets – will not be easy. Jamie Porter, 23, is to lead the attack, with the wily Kiwi Neil Wagner a valuable asset in the opening months. The arrival of Mohammad Amir later in the season whets the appetite, but the shrewdest signing may be South African off-spinner Simon Harmer on a Kolpak. Essex are blessed with an array of talented allrounders, led by Ryan ten Doeschate, who will take charge in all formats following Ravi Bopara's decision to relinquish the limited-overs captaincy. Their batting line-up, strengthened by the return of Varun Chopra and Adam Wheater, is one of the most exciting in the country, with Nick Browne, Tom Westley and Dan Lawrence all tipped for England.

HEAD COACH: CHRIS SILVERWOOD

After taking over temporarily from Paul Grayson in 2015, Silverwood lifted Essex from sixth to third in Division Two to earn the job on a permanent basis. It was a well-judged appointment, as he guided Essex to promotion last summer. In his playing days Silverwood took 577 first-class wickets for Yorkshire, Middlesex and Essex, and made six Test appearances for England, as well as playing seven ODIs. He retired in 2009, after which he briefly worked with England Lions.

COUNTY CHAMPIONSHIP AVERAGES 2016

Batting

	Mat	Inns	NO	Runs	HS	Ave	SR	100	50	4s	6s
AN Cook	7	11	4	643	142	91.85	49.12	3	2	88	1
RN ten Doeschate	15	21	3	1157	145	64.27	71.86	4	6	125	7
T Westley	16	23	0	1217	254	52.91	56.16	3	7	188	1
NLJ Browne	16	25	3	1046	255	47.54	53.36	2	5	139	4
DW Lawrence	15	21	0	902	154	42.95	54.37	3	4	112	5
JS Foster	15	20	3	677	113	39.82	65.41	1	3	76	13
RS Bopara	15	21	1	750	99	37.50	45.89	0	6	93	2
PI Walter	2	2	0	75	47	37.50	67.56	0	0	12	0
V Chopra	2	3	0	105	79	35.00	59.65	0	1	15	0
AJA Wheater	2	3	0	98	59	32.66	45.37	0	1	11	0
JC Mickleburgh	8	12	0	314	103	26.16	42.26	1	1	45	0
JD Ryder	7	10	1	234	51	26.00	48.14	0	2	28	1
Ashar Zaidi	3	5	0	120	37	24.00	60.60	0	0	17	1
GR Napier	14	15	2	298	124	22.92	62.08	1	0	36	8
DD Masters	9	10	5	105	47*	21.00	34.53	0	0	13	2
KS Velani	2	2	0	41	22	20.50	58.57	0	0	8	0
JA Porter	14	12	7	56	20*	11.20	27.58	0	0	5	0
MW Dixon	3	3	0	23	14	7.66	43.39	0	0	3	0
MR Quinn	4	6	1	29	10	5.80	30.20	0	0	3	0
TC Moore	1	2	1	4	4*	4.00	12.90	0	0	1	0
WMH Rhodes	4	3	0	4	3	1.33	23.52	0	0	0	0
AP Beard	2	1	1	0	0*	-	0.00	0	0	0	0

Bowling

	Overs	Mdns	Runs	Wkts	BBI	BBM	Ave	Econ	SR	5w	10w
DD Masters	325.1	92	824	40	7/52	9/113	20.60	2.53	48.7	1	0
MR Quinn	142.0	24	473	22	7/76	11/163	21.50	3.33	38.7	1	1
GR Napier	451.3	96	1460	63	5/59	8/78	23.17	3.23	43.0	4	0
RS Bopara	336.3	65	1110	42	5/49	7/120	26.42	3.29	48.0	2	0
JA Porter	456.2	74	1613	55	5/46	8/99	29.32	3.53	49.7	2	0
Ashar Zaidi	19.5	3	61	2	1/0	2/27	30.50	3.07	59.5	0	0
WMH Rhodes	87.0	23	278	9	2/34	4/114	30.88	3.19	58.0	0	0
RN ten Doeschate	118.0	14	430	11	4/31	4/31	39.09	3.64	64.3	0	0
MW Dixon	84.1	12	386	9	5/124	6/189	42.88	4.58	56.1	1	0
DW Lawrence	25.0	2	129	3	1/5	1/16	43.00	5.16	50.0	0	0
T Westley	109.5	18	351	8	2/13	2/13	43.87	3.19	82.3	0	0
PI Walter	50.0	7	214	4	3/44	4/112	53.50	4.28	75.0	0	0
AP Beard	54.2	6	219	4	2/67	3/126	54.75	4.03	81.5	0	0
TC Moore	24.0	7	73	1	1/73	1/73	73.00	3.04	144.0	0	0
JD Ryder	75.0	15	254	1	1/36	1/67	254.00	3.38	450.0	0	0
NLJ Browne	1.0	0	8	0	-	-	-	8.00	-	0	0
KS Velani	3.0	0	41	0	-	-	-	13.66	-	0	0

Catches/Stumpings:
49 Foster (inc 1st), 17 Westley, 13 Browne, 12 Lawrence, ten Doeschate, 9 Mickleburgh, 8 Cook, 7 Porter, 6 Wheater, 4 Bopara, Chopra, Ryder, 3 Moore, 2 Napier, 1 Beard, Quinn, Rhodes

Batting

	Mat	Inns	NO	Runs	HS	Ave	SR	100	50	4s	6s
JD Ryder	9	8	0	435	131	54.37	92.16	2	3	43	8
JS Foster	9	6	3	160	75*	53.33	141.59	0	1	19	3
NLJ Browne	9	8	0	358	99	44.75	93.96	0	2	46	2
RN ten Doeschate	9	8	2	217	53	36.16	109.59	0	1	17	3
T Westley	9	8	0	274	110	34.25	81.30	1	1	26	2
RS Bopara	9	8	1	219	74*	31.28	73.98	0	2	11	0
Ashar Zaidi	9	8	2	144	41	24.00	109.92	0	0	12	4
DW Lawrence	8	7	0	93	35	13.28	76.22	0	0	4	2
DD Masters	9	5	2	25	12*	8.33	62.50	0	0	3	0
GR Napier	6	4	0	32	17	8.00	65.30	0	0	2	0
JC Mickleburgh	1	1	0	3	3	3.00	75.00	0	0	0	0
MR Quinn	6	3	3	11	10*	-	61.11	0	0	1	0
JA Porter	4	1	1	0	0*	-	0.00	0	0	0	0
MW Dixon	2	-	-	-	-	-	-	-	-	-	-

Bowling

	Overs	Mdns	Runs	Wkts	BBI	Ave	Econ	SR	4w	5w
DD Masters	76.0	5	299	8	2/16	37.37	3.93	57.0	0	0
Ashar Zaidi	44.0	1	223	6	3/33	37.16	5.06	44.0	0	0
T Westley	14.0	0	72	0	-	-	5.14	-	0	0
JA Porter	23.0	0	122	0	-	-	5.30	-	0	0
DW Lawrence	46.0	0	255	6	3/35	42.50	5.54	46.0	0	0
GR Napier	45.0	2	280	12	3/50	23.33	6.22	22.5	0	0
MR Quinn	48.0	1	308	9	4/71	34.22	6.41	32.0	1	0
RN ten Doeschate	26.0	0	184	8	2/25	23.00	7.07	19.5	0	0
MW Dixon	10.0	0	71	0	-	-	7.10	-	0	0
RS Bopara	47.0	0	334	10	3/33	33.40	7.10	28.2	0	0

Catches/Stumpings:
13 Foster (inc 6st), 8 Bopara, 5 Browne, 4 Lawrence, Ryder, 3 Zaidi, 2 ten Doeschate, Westley, 1 Napier

	Mat	Inns	NO	Runs	HS	Ave	SR	100	50	4s	6s
Ashar Zaidi	15	11	2	363	59*	40.33	168.83	0	3	21	23
RN ten Doeschate	15	11	4	233	58*	33.28	116.50	0	1	17	7
T Westley	15	14	1	403	74*	31.00	126.72	0	1	53	3
RS Bopara	15	14	3	283	81*	25.72	115.51	0	2	18	10
DW Lawrence	15	12	3	229	36	25.44	119.27	0	0	24	4
JD Ryder	12	11	1	214	52*	21.40	129.69	0	1	31	3
NLJ Browne	6	5	0	84	27	16.80	97.67	0	0	7	1
GR Napier	12	5	2	48	21*	16.00	150.00	0	0	2	4
MR Quinn	14	2	1	14	8*	14.00	155.55	0	0	1	1
KS Velani	6	6	0	62	19	10.33	108.77	0	0	9	2
JS Foster	15	7	0	54	27	7.71	110.20	0	0	4	1
CJ Taylor	5	3	1	15	14	7.50	93.75	0	0	1	1
PI Walter	7	3	1	15	8	7.50	136.36	0	0	0	1
MW Dixon	1	1	0	1	1	1.00	50.00	0	0	0	0
Wahab Riaz	5	4	4	25	14*	-	156.25	0	0	0	2
DD Masters	7	1	1	0	0*	-	0.00	0	0	0	0

Batting

	Overs	Mdns	Runs	Wkts	BBI	Ave	Econ	SR	4w	5w
T Westley	9.0	0	58	1	1/11	58.00	6.44	54.0	0	0
RN ten Doeschate	18.0	1	125	8	3/19	15.62	6.94	13.5	0	0
Ashar Zaidi	27.0	0	190	5	2/16	38.00	7.03	32.4	0	0
DW Lawrence	26.0	0	185	10	2/11	18.50	7.11	15.6	0	0
RS Bopara	48.0	0	361	11	2/15	32.81	7.52	26.1	0	0
DD Masters	24.0	0	193	5	2/29	38.60	8.04	28.8	0	0
GR Napier	43.2	0	369	22	3/28	16.77	8.51	11.8	0	0
MW Dixon	4.0	0	35	1	1/35	35.00	8.75	24.0	0	0
MR Quinn	52.0	0	470	16	4/35	29.37	9.03	19.5	1	0
Wahab Riaz	19.4	0	186	4	1/29	46.50	9.45	29.5	0	0
PI Walter	18.0	0	178	4	3/26	44.50	9.88	27.0	0	0
CJ Taylor	1.0	0	19	0	-	-	19.00	-	0	0

Bowling

Catches/Stumpings:
9 Westley, 8 Bopara, 7 Foster (inc 1st), ten Doeschate, 6 Lawrence, Napier, 3 Browne, Quinn, Ryder, 2 Masters, Zaidi, 1 Riaz, Taylor, Velani, Walter

GLAMORGAN

FORMED: 1888
HOME GROUND: The SSE SWALEC, Cardiff
CAPTAIN: Jacques Rudolph
2016 RESULTS: CC2: 8/9; RL50: 7/9 South Group; NWT20: Quarter-finalists
HONOURS: Championship: (3) 1948, 1969, 1997; Pro40/National League/ CB40/YB40/RL50: (2) 2002, 2004; Sunday League: 1993

THE LOWDOWN

Glamorgan continue to put their faith in a raft of young, local talent, so the inconsistencies that plague the side should come as no surprise. Last summer they made the T20 quarter-finals only to capitulate against Yorkshire. They finished eighth in Division Two of the Championship, often throwing away the advantage with batting collapses. Aneurin Donald, the most exciting of the Welsh young guns, hit an astonishing 234 off 136 balls at Colwyn Bay, but no batsman averaged over 40 in four-day cricket. Greater support from the seniors would help. South African Jacques Rudolph enters his third season as captain on the back of a disappointing 2016, while the return of his compatriot Colin Ingram to Championship action is keenly awaited. Ingram made 502 runs in the 2016 T20 Blast but was unavailable in red-ball cricket due to a knee injury. The ever-reliable Michael Hogan leads the bowling attack, while Aussie-born Dutch seamer Timm van der Gugten was a revelation last summer. The scheduled signing of South African quick Marchant de Lange will further bolster their pace attack.

HEAD COACH: ROBERT CROFT

Croft took over from Toby Radford after a management restructure following the 2015 season. During his 23 years as a Glamorgan player the off-spinner played 21 Tests and 50 ODIs between 1996 and 2001. He was given an MBE in 2013 for services to cricket after finally hanging up his boots with 903 senior appearances to his name. In all Croft took 1,175 first-class wickets, including 51 five-wicket hauls.

Batting

	Mat	Inns	NO	Runs	HS	Ave	SR	100	50	4s	6s
CB Cooke	7	13	2	421	63	38.27	53.90	0	3	60	0
GG Wagg	13	22	3	693	106	36.47	61.65	1	5	79	13
WD Bragg	16	31	1	1088	161*	36.26	49.77	2	8	127	0
AHT Donald	16	30	1	983	234	33.89	74.92	1	5	135	16
KS Carlson	4	8	1	227	119	32.42	54.83	1	1	31	0
AO Morgan	9	17	3	406	103*	29.00	43.79	1	1	60	1
MA Wallace	14	26	4	611	78	27.77	61.71	0	5	84	1
NJ Selman	10	19	2	470	122*	27.64	46.67	2	2	53	0
DL Lloyd	15	27	1	712	107	28.30	59.83	2	2	106	5
JA Rudolph	15	29	2	659	87	24.40	42.13	0	3	96	0
CAJ Meschede	13	22	4	431	78	23.94	70.88	0	3	59	8
AG Salter	7	11	3	171	45*	21.37	50.89	0	0	20	2
JM Kettleborough	3	6	0	107	42	17.83	43.14	0	0	16	0
RAJ Smith	1	2	0	25	25	12.50	49.01	0	0	4	0
MG Hogan	15	22	6	191	30	11.93	71.80	0	0	26	3
T van der Gugten	13	20	4	159	36	9.93	42.74	0	0	19	3
HW Podmore	2	4	1	24	16*	8.00	35.29	0	0	2	0
LJ Carey	3	5	1	12	11	3.00	37.50	0	0	2	0

Bowling

	Overs	Mdns	Runs	Wkts	BBI	BBM	Ave	Econ	SR	5w	10w
LJ Carey	84.4	13	330	13	4/92	7/151	25.38	3.89	39.0	0	0
T van der Gugten	450.0	72	1458	56	5/52	9/133	26.03	3.24	48.2	5	0
MG Hogan	500.4	139	1287	49	5/36	6/106	26.26	2.57	61.3	2	0
JA Rudolph	25.5	4	58	2	1/5	1/9	29.00	2.24	77.5	0	0
KS Carlson	45.0	7	178	6	5/28	5/78	29.66	3.95	45.0	1	0
HW Podmore	54.3	5	225	6	3/59	4/123	37.50	4.12	54.5	0	0
GG Wagg	421.0	69	1397	37	5/90	7/127	37.75	3.31	68.2	1	0
CAJ Meschede	351.5	65	1168	27	5/84	6/162	43.25	3.31	78.1	1	0
RAJ Smith	14.0	3	51	1	1/51	1/51	51.00	3.64	84.0	0	0
AO Morgan	232.0	34	740	13	2/37	3/57	56.92	3.18	107.0	0	0
DL Lloyd	149.1	17	583	10	3/36	3/53	58.30	3.90	89.5	0	0
AG Salter	136.0	13	492	7	3/56	4/137	70.28	3.61	116.5	0	0
NJ Selman	3.0	1	8	0	-	-	-	2.66	-	0	0
WD Bragg	9.0	1	29	0	-	-	-	3.22	-	0	0

Catches/Stumpings:
54 Wallace (inc 1st), 12 Donald, 10 Bragg, Rudolph, 8 Hogan, 7 Selman, 6 Cooke, 5 Lloyd, Salter, Wagg, 3 Meschede, Morgan, 2 Kettleborough, van der Gugten, 1 Carlson, Carey, Smith

GLAMORGAN

Batting

	Mat	Inns	NO	Runs	HS	Ave	SR	100	50	4s	6s
CA Ingram	8	7	1	367	107	61.16	126.55	1	2	19	19
JA Rudolph	8	7	1	233	53	38.83	67.14	0	1	22	2
CB Cooke	4	4	0	150	80	37.50	113.63	0	1	10	5
WD Bragg	8	7	0	260	75	37.14	90.90	0	2	27	2
DL Lloyd	8	7	0	253	65	36.14	93.01	0	2	36	1
T van der Gugten	5	5	2	71	21	23.66	112.69	0	0	9	1
GG Wagg	8	7	0	152	52	21.71	107.04	0	1	13	3
AG Salter	5	5	2	60	42	20.00	125.00	0	0	2	3
AHT Donald	8	7	0	109	53	15.57	77.30	0	1	8	1
MA Wallace	4	3	0	44	21	14.66	67.69	0	0	4	0
CAJ Meschede	8	7	1	70	45	11.66	79.54	0	0	9	1
DA Cosker	4	2	0	4	2	2.00	57.14	0	0	0	0
MG Hogan	8	4	4	26	14*	-	96.29	0	0	4	0
AO Morgan	1	-	-	-	-	-	-	-	-	-	-
RAJ Smith	1	-	-	-	-	-	-	-	-	-	-

Bowling

	Overs	Mdns	Runs	Wkts	BBI	Ave	Econ	SR	4w	5w
CA Ingram	33.0	0	165	6	3/38	27.50	5.00	33.0	0	0
CAJ Meschede	65.0	1	337	7	2/30	48.14	5.18	55.7	0	0
JA Rudolph	4.0	0	23	0	-	-	5.75	-	0	0
MG Hogan	71.4	1	430	11	4/41	39.09	6.00	39.0	1	0
AG Salter	24.0	0	147	1	1/38	147.00	6.12	144.0	0	0
GG Wagg	65.1	2	411	11	2/48	37.36	6.30	35.5	0	0
T van der Gugten	47.1	2	304	7	3/33	43.42	6.44	40.4	0	0
DA Cosker	28.0	0	181	2	2/45	90.50	6.46	84.0	0	0
AO Morgan	2.0	0	18	0	-	-	9.00	-	0	0
DL Lloyd	7.0	0	71	0	-	-	10.14	-	0	0
RAJ Smith	3.0	1	32	0	-	-	10.66	-	0	0

Catches/Stumpings:
6 Wagg, 4 Cooke, Donald, Ingram, 3 Hogan, Lloyd, Salter, Wallace, 1 Bragg, Meschede, Rudolph

www.glamorgancricket.com / tel: 029 2040 9380

GLAMORGAN

Batting

	Mat	Inns	NO	Runs	HS	Ave	SR	100	50	4s	6s
CA Ingram	14	14	2	502	101	41.83	164.59	1	4	42	29
CB Cooke	6	4	2	65	24*	32.50	118.18	0	0	4	3
DL Lloyd	14	14	1	382	97*	29.38	129.49	0	2	47	8
AHT Donald	14	12	3	235	55	26.11	128.41	0	2	27	7
MA Wallace	8	8	1	180	69*	25.71	108.43	0	1	19	1
JA Rudolph	14	13	3	210	40*	21.00	99.05	0	0	19	2
GG Wagg	14	10	4	91	32*	15.16	101.11	0	0	6	2
MG Hogan	13	3	1	28	13	14.00	133.33	0	0	2	2
AG Salter	6	4	2	28	16*	14.00	112.00	0	0	1	1
T van der Gugten	14	5	2	35	13	11.66	152.17	0	0	5	1
CAJ Meschede	14	7	1	48	17	8.00	81.35	0	0	2	2
SW Tait	8	2	2	12	12*	-	171.42	0	0	2	0
DW Steyn	5	1	1	7	7*	-	140.00	0	0	1	0
DA Cosker	9	1	1	6	6*	-	75.00	0	0	0	0
NJ Selman	1	-	-	-	-	-	-	-	-	-	-

Bowling

	Overs	Mdns	Runs	Wkts	BBI	Ave	Econ	SR	4w	5w
DW Steyn	18.3	0	113	11	4/18	10.27	6.10	10.0	1	0
MG Hogan	40.3	0	276	16	4/28	17.25	6.81	15.1	1	0
DA Cosker	24.2	0	166	8	2/19	20.75	6.82	18.2	0	0
T van der Gugten	39.0	2	268	19	4/14	14.10	6.87	12.3	2	0
JA Rudolph	3.0	0	22	0	-	-	7.33	-	0	0
CAJ Meschede	28.1	0	207	9	2/16	23.00	7.34	18.7	0	0
CA Ingram	21.0	1	163	9	4/32	18.11	7.76	14.0	1	0
SW Tait	19.0	0	153	6	2/17	25.50	8.05	19.0	0	0
GG Wagg	31.1	0	265	13	3/38	20.38	8.50	14.3	0	0
AG Salter	1.0	0	15	0	-	-	15.00	-	0	0

Catches/Stumpings:
12 Cooke (inc 2st), 10 Ingram, 7 Hogan, Wagg, 6 Donald, Rudolph, 5 Lloyd, 4 Meschede, Wallace (inc 1st), 3 van der Gugten, 2 Cosker, Steyn, 1 Tait

TEAM PROFILE

FORMED: 1871
HOME GROUND: The Brightside Ground, Bristol
CAPTAIN: Gareth Roderick (Championship), Michael Klinger (RL50, NWT20)
2016 RESULTS: CC2: 6/9; RL50: 8/9 South Group; NWT20: Quarter-finalists
HONOURS: Gillette/NatWest/C&G/FP Trophy: (5) 1973, 1999, 2000, 2003, 2004; Benson & Hedges Cup: (3) 1977, 1999, 2000; Pro40/National League/CB40/YB40/RL50: (2) 2000, 2015

THE LOWDOWN

Gloucestershire spent most of the off-season keeping what they have, with half the squad signing new deals. Many of them are coming into their prime, and the county are particularly spoilt for seamers. Matt Taylor and Craig Miles, both 22, impressed last summer, with Liam Norwell offering excellent support to the seasoned left-armer David Payne. Batting will be the greater worry. New Zealander Hamish Marshall has left after 11 seasons at Bristol, while the prolific Michael Klinger will be playing mostly white-ball cricket in 2017. Gloucestershire will hope for another good year for Chris Dent and a better one for Australian Cameron Bancroft, who disappointed on a two-month spell last summer. Phil Mustard has signed a two-year deal after impressing on loan last summer. Gloucestershire's best chance of success may come in the shorter formats. Klinger (548 runs) and Benny Howell (24 wickets) were the leading performers in last year's T20 Blast in which Gloucestershire showed blistering form before losing in the quarter-finals.

HEAD COACH: RICHARD DAWSON

Dawson was appointed in early 2015 after gaining some coaching experience with Yorkshire's Second XI and inspired Gloucestershire to win the Royal London One-Day Cup in his first season. A former Yorkshire and Gloucestershire off-spinner who played seven Tests, he had worked as a spin-bowling and one-day coach at Bristol following his retirement in 2011. His assistant, Ian Harvey, has extended his contract until 2019.

Batting

	Mat	Inns	NO	Runs	HS	Ave	SR	100	50	4s	6s
M Klinger	7	12	4	589	140	73.62	51.08	3	2	66	8
P Mustard	6	10	2	447	107*	55.87	47.55	1	3	60	0
CDJ Dent	16	29	3	1243	180	47.80	51.74	3	7	164	6
GL van Buuren	7	12	2	459	172*	45.90	60.07	2	0	60	2
HJH Marshall	16	26	0	1022	135	39.30	54.97	4	5	134	4
JMR Taylor	16	26	2	860	107*	35.83	72.08	2	4	112	19
GH Roderick	14	25	3	725	102	32.95	49.18	1	6	82	3
DA Payne	14	18	4	389	67*	27.78	50.45	0	3	55	0
CN Miles	13	20	4	407	60*	25.43	48.62	0	3	57	1
GT Hankins	9	15	0	374	116	24.93	49.08	1	1	52	0
CT Bancroft	5	9	0	192	70	21.33	41.46	0	1	26	0
IA Cockbain	4	7	0	147	67	21.00	50.17	0	1	22	1
K Noema-Barnett	8	12	0	245	84	20.41	50.72	0	2	32	5
BAC Howell	5	7	1	113	41	18.83	69.75	0	0	13	4
LC Norwell	11	15	3	224	102	18.66	51.73	1	0	31	4
MD Taylor	5	8	5	42	9*	14.00	41.17	0	0	7	0
WA Tavare	6	10	0	112	36	11.20	29.94	0	0	16	0
J Shaw	12	16	4	125	29	10.41	37.76	0	0	17	0
JR Bracey	1	2	0	14	12	7.00	24.56	0	0	1	0
TRG Hampton	1	2	1	0	0*	0.00	0.00	0	0	0	0

Bowling

	Overs	Mdns	Runs	Wkts	BBI	BBM	Ave	Econ	SR	5w	10w
LC Norwell	377.5	87	1167	39	4/65	8/140	29.92	3.08	58.1	0	0
CN Miles	381.0	55	1581	52	5/54	8/112	30.40	4.14	43.9	2	0
GL van Buuren	84.0	17	219	7	3/15	4/62	31.28	2.60	72.0	0	0
DA Payne	451.4	83	1380	43	5/36	8/132	32.09	3.05	63.0	1	0
J Shaw	326.5	59	1258	34	5/79	5/79	37.00	3.84	57.6	1	0
MD Taylor	143.0	15	543	13	4/56	5/101	41.76	3.79	66.0	0	0
JMR Taylor	293.5	52	998	22	4/16	5/140	45.36	3.39	80.1	0	0
K Noema-Barnett	192.4	43	551	11	3/56	3/56	50.09	2.85	105.0	0	0
CDJ Dent	48.4	8	543	3	2/21	2/21	50.33	3.10	97.3	0	0
TRG Hampton	21.0	1	107	1	1/73	1/107	107.00	5.09	126.0	0	0
BAC Howell	46.1	11	150	1	1/97	1/97	150.00	3.24	277.0	0	0
IA Cockbain	2.5	0	20	0	-	-	-	7.05	-	0	0
HJH Marshall	9.0	0	58	0	-	-	-	6.44	-	0	0

Catches/Stumpings:
27 Roderick (inc 2st), 23 Mustard, 17 Dent, 13 Marshall, 10 J Taylor, 9 Payne, 8 Klinger, 6 Hankins, Noema-Barnett, Tavaré, 4 van Buuren, 3 Bancroft, Miles, Shaw, 1 Cockbain, Norwell, M Taylor

Batting

	Mat	Inns	NO	Runs	HS	Ave	SR	100	50	4s	6s
M Klinger	8	7	1	337	166*	56.16	83.83	1	1	37	6
CDJ Dent	6	6	0	278	142	46.33	97.88	2	0	36	3
TMJ Smith	8	6	3	124	43*	41.33	68.13	0	0	6	0
HJH Marshall	8	6	0	208	74	34.66	83.53	0	2	18	3
GH Roderick	4	3	0	75	64	25.00	83.33	0	1	10	1
MD Taylor	8	4	3	25	16	25.00	113.63	0	0	3	0
GL van Buuren	4	3	0	70	38	23.33	60.86	0	0	4	1
BAC Howell	8	7	0	157	77	22.42	82.19	0	1	12	3
K Noema-Barnett	3	3	1	44	29	22.00	68.75	0	0	2	2
PJ Grieshaber	1	1	0	20	20	20.00	111.11	0	0	1	0
JMR Taylor	4	3	0	52	43	17.33	89.65	0	0	3	1
IA Cockbain	8	7	0	119	35	17.00	69.59	0	0	10	2
DA Payne	3	2	0	26	23	13.00	66.66	0	0	3	0
LC Norwell	4	3	1	21	10	10.50	63.63	0	0	2	0
CN Miles	8	5	0	41	16	8.20	71.92	0	0	2	1
P Mustard	3	2	0	5	5	2.50	62.50	0	0	1	0

Bowling

	Overs	Mdns	Runs	Wkts	BBI	Ave	Econ	SR	4w	5w
GL van Buuren	23.2	1	107	1	1/33	107.00	4.58	140.0	0	0
BAC Howell	56.1	1	276	10	2/32	27.60	4.91	33.7	0	0
K Noema-Barnett	22.0	0	115	3	2/56	38.33	5.22	44.0	0	0
LC Norwell	36.0	5	200	7	3/56	28.57	5.55	30.8	0	0
DA Payne	18.0	1	101	3	2/56	33.66	5.61	36.0	0	0
MD Taylor	57.0	2	322	6	2/33	53.66	5.64	57.0	0	0
TMJ Smith	46.0	1	266	6	4/26	44.33	5.78	46.0	1	0
CN Miles	53.2	0	356	8	2/54	44.50	6.67	40.0	0	0
CDJ Dent	6.0	0	45	2	1/14	22.50	7.50	18.0	0	0

Catches/Stumpings:
5 Cockbain, 4 Roderick, 3 Mustard, Smith, 2 Dent, Grieshaber, Howell, Klinger, Marshall, van Buuren, 1 Miles, Noema-Barnett, Norwell, Payne, J Taylor

GLOUCESTERSHIRE
COUNTY CRICKET CLUB

Batting

	Mat	Inns	NO	Runs	HS	Ave	SR	100	50	4s	6s
IA Cockbain	15	14	5	499	73*	55.44	132.36	0	3	43	13
JMR Taylor	6	4	1	161	80	53.66	167.70	0	1	14	9
M Klinger	15	14	3	548	101	49.81	134.64	1	4	58	16
CDJ Dent	13	9	4	193	45	38.60	112.20	0	0	15	2
GH Roderick	12	5	3	53	22*	26.50	160.60	0	0	5	2
HJH Marshall	15	14	0	298	90	21.28	131.27	0	2	32	5
AJ Tye	14	5	3	41	18*	20.50	151.85	0	0	0	3
BAC Howell	15	10	2	150	37	18.75	128.20	0	0	10	5
GL van Buuren	6	3	1	27	14	13.50	87.09	0	0	2	1
K Noema-Barnett	9	5	1	44	37	11.00	115.78	0	0	3	2
PJ Grieshaber	1	1	0	9	9	9.00	81.81	0	0	0	0
TMJ Smith	14	2	1	9	8*	9.00	112.50	0	0	0	0
P Mustard	1	1	0	5	5	5.00	41.66	0	0	0	0
LC Norwell	12	2	2	2	2*	-	100.00	0	0	0	0
MD Taylor	13	1	1	1	1*	-	100.00	0	0	0	0
CT Bancroft	1	-	-	-	-	-	-	-	-	-	-
CJ Liddle	1	-	-	-	-	-	-	-	-	-	-
CN Miles	1	-	-	-	-	-	-	-	-	-	-
DA Payne	1	-	-	-	-	-	-	-	-	-	-

Bowling

	Overs	Mdns	Runs	Wkts	BBI	Ave	Econ	SR	4w	5w
BAC Howell	56.0	1	385	24	3/18	16.04	6.87	14.0	0	0
MD Taylor	43.0	1	315	15	3/16	21.00	7.32	17.2	0	0
TMJ Smith	44.0	0	327	12	2/13	27.25	7.43	22.0	0	0
GL van Buuren	18.0	0	138	6	3/19	23.00	7.66	18.0	0	0
JMR Taylor	5.0	0	40	0	-	-	8.00	-	0	0
AJ Tye	49.1	0	421	18	3/16	23.38	8.56	16.3	0	0
K Noema-Barnett	19.0	0	171	3	1/17	57.00	9.00	38.0	0	0
LC Norwell	33.5	0	310	3	1/32	103.33	9.16	67.6	0	0
CN Miles	3.0	0	29	2	2/29	14.50	9.66	9.0	0	0
CDJ Dent	1.5	0	22	1	1/14	22.00	12.00	11.0	0	0
DA Payne	4.0	0	62	0	-	-	15.50	-	0	0
CJ Liddle	2.0	0	35	0	-	-	17.50	-	0	0

Catches/Stumpings:
9 Cockbain, 8 Norwell, 7 Klinger, 5 Dent, Marshall, Roderick (inc 1st), Smith, 4 Howell, 3 van Buuren, 2 Mustard (inc 1st), J Taylor, M Taylor, Tye, 1 Bancroft (inc 1st), Miles, Noema-Barnett

TEAM PROFILE

HAMPSHIRE
CRICKET

FORMED: 1863
HOME GROUND: The Ageas Bowl, Southampton
CAPTAIN: James Vince
2016 RESULTS: CC1: 8/9; RL50: 5/9 South Group; NWT20: 8/9 South Group
HONOURS: Championship: (2) 1961, 1973; Gillette/NatWest/C&G/FP Trophy: (3) 1991, 2005, 2009; Benson & Hedges Cup: (2) 1988, 1992; Pro40/National League/CB40/YB40/RL50: 2012; Sunday League: (3) 1975, 1978, 1986; T20 Cup: (2) 2010, 2012

THE LOWDOWN

A disappointing season in all formats was rescued when Durham's financial problems saved Hampshire from Championship relegation. But it could not hide the shortcomings of a side which won just 10 of 38 matches last summer. The seam-bowling department, plagued by injury, relied heavily on the now-departed Ryan McLaren. To that end South African paceman Kyle Abbott arrives on a Kolpak deal, having called a halt to his international career, and West Indies' Fidel Edwards has been re-signed after missing most of last season with a broken ankle. Left-armer Reece Topley would make for a potent trio of quicks but ongoing injury problems restricted him to just one appearance in his first year with the county. Adam Wheater has returned to Essex but George Bailey (Australia, overseas) and Rilee Rossouw (South Africa, Kolpak) should provide plenty of runs. It is hoped that opener Michael Carberry will return to action after undergoing a successful operation to remove a tumour in December.

FIRST-TEAM COACH: CRAIG WHITE

White was appointed in November to replace Dale Benkenstein, who left the club for family reasons last summer after two-and-a-half years in charge. The former England and Yorkshire allrounder has been on the Hampshire staff since 2012, taking up the roles of assistant coach and bowling specialist, and took charge for six Championship matches at the end of last season. "I was thrust into the job and really enjoyed it," he said. White had a distinguished playing career which included 30 Tests and 51 ODIs.

	Mat	Inns	NO	Runs	HS	Ave	SR	100	50	4s	6s
SM Ervine	12	21	4	1050	158*	61.76	55.32	4	5	122	11
R McLaren	15	24	9	832	100	55.46	50.82	1	6	110	6
AJA Wheater	12	21	4	802	204*	47.17	61.36	2	3	105	5
JHK Adams	14	25	2	897	99	35.88	42.83	0	8	136	0
LD McManus	10	13	1	425	132*	35.41	52.21	1	2	64	3
LA Dawson	12	20	1	644	116	33.89	51.31	1	5	76	1
JM Vince	8	14	0	473	119	33.78	54.87	1	2	69	2
TP Alsop	12	20	0	655	117	32.75	48.41	1	5	88	1
WR Smith	16	28	0	827	210	29.53	37.40	1	3	103	0
MA Carberry	8	15	1	411	107	29.35	45.97	1	1	53	0
GK Berg	10	13	3	288	56	28.80	75.98	0	1	36	5
CP Wood	2	2	0	37	31	18.50	54.41	0	0	4	0
JA Tomlinson	6	9	4	75	23*	15.00	41.43	0	0	8	0
RJW Topley	1	1	0	15	15	15.00	22.05	0	0	1	0
GM Andrew	6	7	1	85	25	14.16	48.02	0	0	9	3
MS Crane	12	17	4	101	22	7.76	29.27	0	0	12	0
BTJ Wheal	8	9	4	37	14	7.40	19.27	0	0	5	1
TL Best	6	8	1	49	23*	7.00	49.49	0	0	4	2
JJ Weatherley	1	2	0	13	9	6.50	21.31	0	0	1	0
A Carter	2	2	0	8	4	4.00	100.00	0	0	2	0
FH Edwards	2	1	0	4	4	4.00	66.66	0	0	1	0
DJ Wainwright	1	2	2	36	35*	-	57.14	0	0	3	0

Batting

	Overs	Mdns	Runs	Wkts	BBI	BBM	Ave	Econ	SR	5w	10w
A Carter	42.0	8	126	6	4/52	5/76	21.00	3.00	42.0	0	0
TP Alsop	10.0	0	66	2	2/59	2/59	33.00	6.60	30.0	0	0
JA Tomlinson	151.3	40	483	14	4/74	5/87	34.50	3.18	64.9	0	0
BTJ Wheal	211.0	36	720	20	6/51	7/71	36.00	3.41	63.3	1	0
JM Vince	15.2	1	72	2	1/14	1/14	36.00	4.69	46.0	0	0
GK Berg	251.2	73	694	19	6/56	7/116	36.52	2.76	79.3	1	0
R McLaren	382.0	81	1242	32	5/104	5/61	38.81	3.25	71.6	1	0
TL Best	136.5	20	554	14	5/90	6/91	39.57	4.04	58.6	1	0
LA Dawson	306.5	56	877	20	4/100	6/85	43.85	2.85	92.0	0	0
MS Crane	372.0	49	1409	31	3/19	6/89	45.45	3.78	72.0	0	0
CP Wood	51.0	19	139	3	2/79	3/100	46.33	2.72	102.0	0	0
DJ Wainwright	31.0	4	112	2	2/112	2/112	56.00	3.61	93.0	0	0
GM Andrew	129.0	25	439	7	3/104	3/104	62.71	3.40	110.5	0	0
WR Smith	126.1	20	401	5	1/0	2/121	80.20	3.17	151.4	0	0
FH Edwards	45.0	6	247	3	3/102	3/102	82.33	5.48	90.0	0	0
SM Ervine	61.0	10	216	2	1/11	1/24	108.00	3.54	183.0	0	0

Bowling

Catches/Stumpings:

26 McManus (inc 6st), 17 Wheater (inc 1st), 13 Adams, 12 Alsop, 11 Smith, 9 Ervine, 6 McLaren, 5 Vince, 4 Carberry, Crane, 3 Berg, Best, 2 Andrew, Dawson, Tomlinson, 1 Carter, Wheal

HAMPSHIRE
CRICKET

Batting

	Mat	Inns	NO	Runs	HS	Ave	SR	100	50	4s	6s
LA Dawson	8	8	3	359	100*	71.80	118.87	1	3	23	6
TP Alsop	7	7	1	327	116	54.50	86.50	1	2	31	2
AJA Wheater	5	5	0	238	90	47.60	88.14	0	2	22	2
R McLaren	4	4	1	136	46*	45.33	106.25	0	0	13	3
JM Vince	1	1	0	41	41	41.00	107.89	0	0	7	0
SM Ervine	6	6	0	219	53	36.50	102.81	0	2	18	5
WR Smith	8	8	1	225	84	32.14	73.77	0	2	11	0
JHK Adams	7	7	0	221	92	31.57	84.35	0	2	25	3
GM Andrew	8	8	3	152	70*	30.40	138.18	0	1	10	7
BTJ Wheal	4	3	2	19	13	19.00	126.66	0	0	1	1
LD McManus	8	5	0	90	35	18.00	90.90	0	0	5	2
JJ Weatherley	2	2	0	29	27	14.50	76.31	0	0	1	1
GK Berg	7	4	1	42	23	14.00	85.71	0	0	1	1
MS Crane	7	3	2	12	7*	12.00	54.54	0	0	0	0
Shahid Afridi	1	1	0	4	4	4.00	40.00	0	0	0	0
RA Stevenson	3	1	0	0	0	0.00	0.00	0	0	0	0
TL Best	2	1	1	0	0*	-	0.00	0	0	0	0

Bowling

	Overs	Mdns	Runs	Wkts	BBI	Ave	Econ	SR	4w	5w
LA Dawson	71.0	0	302	8	2/42	37.75	4.25	53.2	0	0
Shahid Afridi	10.0	0	44	0	-	-	4.40	-	0	0
R McLaren	37.0	2	182	10	4/42	18.20	4.91	22.2	1	0
BTJ Wheal	28.3	2	143	7	4/38	20.42	5.01	24.4	1	0
GK Berg	58.0	1	305	11	4/25	27.72	5.25	31.6	2	0
SM Ervine	15.0	1	84	1	1/34	84.00	5.60	90.0	0	0
JJ Weatherley	3.0	0	17	0	-	-	5.66	-	0	0
TL Best	20.0	0	122	1	1/47	122.00	6.10	120.0	0	0
MS Crane	55.0	0	349	9	4/80	38.77	6.34	36.6	1	0
GM Andrew	47.3	1	315	7	2/32	45.00	6.63	40.7	0	0
WR Smith	10.0	0	70	0	-	-	7.00	-	0	0
RA Stevenson	20.0	0	142	2	1/28	71.00	7.10	60.0	0	0

Catches/Stumpings:
9 McManus (inc 3st), 5 Crane, Dawson, 4 Ervine, 3 Adams, Andrew, Berg, Smith, Wheater
(inc 1st), 2 Alsop, 1 Afridi

HAMPSHIRE
CRICKET

	Mat	Inns	NO	Runs	HS	Ave	SR	100	50	4s	6s	
J Goodwin	1	1	0	32	32	32.00	110.34	0	0	5	0	
LA Dawson	13	12	2	299	76*	29.90	126.16	0	1	18	7	
JM Vince	5	4	0	106	62	26.50	116.48	0	1	15	0	
MA Carberry	7	6	0	154	54	25.66	120.31	0	1	16	4	
TP Alsop	8	7	0	143	85	20.42	117.21	0	1	15	5	
JJ Weatherley	5	4	0	81	43	20.25	132.78	0	0	6	2	
R McLaren	3	3	1	39	23	19.50	150.00	0	0	4	1	
Shahid Afridi	12	11	0	191	35	17.36	160.50	0	0	18	9	
AJA Wheater	9	9	0	148	39	16.44	116.53	0	0	20	2	Batting
GM Andrew	9	8	4	64	31	16.00	128.00	0	0	6	2	
DJG Sammy	7	6	1	70	30	14.00	132.07	0	0	4	4	
SM Ervine	12	11	0	127	56	11.54	117.59	0	1	10	4	
LD McManus	9	7	0	78	41	11.14	109.85	0	0	5	2	
BJ Taylor	5	3	1	21	9*	10.50	84.00	0	0	3	0	
JHK Adams	6	5	0	47	18	9.40	123.68	0	0	5	2	
BTJ Wheal	6	2	0	18	16	9.00	100.00	0	0	3	0	
GK Berg	6	5	3	14	5*	7.00	73.68	0	0	0	0	
TL Best	9	6	3	16	8	5.33	88.88	0	0	2	0	
WR Smith	4	4	0	14	9	3.50	73.68	0	0	0	0	
RA Stevenson	1	1	0	3	3	3.00	60.00	0	0	0	0	
GT Griffiths	4	2	2	6	4*	-	85.71	0	0	0	0	
MS Crane	2	2	2	2	2*	-	40.00	0	0	0	0	

	Overs	Mdns	Runs	Wkts	BBI	Ave	Econ	SR	4w	5w	
Shahid Afridi	44.0	0	274	9	3/33	30.44	6.22	29.3	0	0	
BJ Taylor	10.2	0	68	3	2/20	22.66	6.58	20.6	0	0	
LA Dawson	44.0	0	296	19	5/17	15.57	6.72	13.8	1	1	
BTJ Wheal	16.0	0	129	5	3/43	25.80	8.06	19.2	0	0	
R McLaren	9.0	0	73	5	2/14	14.60	8.11	10.8	0	0	
GT Griffiths	12.0	0	101	5	3/33	20.20	8.41	14.4	0	0	Bowling
GM Andrew	20.0	0	178	8	2/19	22.25	8.90	15.0	0	0	
JJ Weatherley	1.0	0	9	0	-	-	9.00	-	0	0	
GK Berg	14.1	0	129	5	2/13	25.80	9.10	17.0	0	0	
DJG Sammy	13.5	0	126	6	2/20	21.00	9.10	13.8	0	0	
TL Best	27.1	0	258	4	2/38	64.50	9.49	40.7	0	0	
RA Stevenson	4.0	0	40	2	2/40	20.00	10.00	12.0	0	0	
MS Crane	4.0	0	41	0	-	-	10.25	-	0	0	
WR Smith	6.0	0	69	1	1/14	69.00	11.50	36.0	0	0	

Catches/Stumpings:
7 Dawson, 5 McManus (inc 1st), Wheater (inc 2st), 4 Vince, 3 Afridi, Alsop, Andrew, Weatherley,
2 Best, Ervine, Griffiths, 1 Carberry, Crane, McLaren, Sammy, Smith, Stevenson, Taylor

TEAM PROFILE

FORMED: 1870
HOME GROUND: The Spitfire Ground, Canterbury
ONE-DAY NAME: Kent Spitfires
CAPTAIN: Sam Northeast
2016 RESULTS: CC2: Runners-up; RL50: Quarter-finalists; NWT20: 7/9 South Group
HONOURS: Championship: (7) 1906, 1909, 1910, 1913, 1970, 1977(s), 1978; Gillette/NatWest/C&G/FP Trophy: (2) 1967, 1974; Pro40/National League/CB40/RL50: 2001; Benson & Hedges Cup: (3) 1973, 1976, 1978; Sunday League: (4) 1972, 1973, 1976, 1995; T20 Cup: 2007

THE LOWDOWN

Denied Championship promotion because of a one-off season in which second place was not enough, Kent look in good shape. They have an outstanding captain in 27-year-old captain Sam Northeast, who hit more than 2,000 runs across all formats last summer, including five Championship hundreds. Daniel Bell-Drummond is also starting to show the consistency to back up his many admirers. At the other end of the spectrum, 40-year-old Darren Stevens goes into his 20th season in fine fettle, having averaged nearly 50 with the bat and 30 with the ball in 2016. Mitchell Claydon, another senior, leads an attack featuring Will Gidman and the brilliant but enigmatic Matt Coles, who will be aiming for more of the form that made him the leading wicket-taker in last season's Royal London One-Day Cup.

HEAD COACH: MATT WALKER

Walker takes over after three years as assistant coach under Jimmy Adams, who has become West Indies' director of cricket following five years at Canterbury. Walker, who has worked with Essex and England Lions, scored nearly 20,000 runs for Kent and Essex between 1992 and 2011. He scored 275* against Somerset in 1996, which is the fourth-highest score by a Kent batsman. His high-profile assistant is due to be former South Africa fast bowler Allan Donald, whose arrival was delayed by visa complications.

	Mat	Inns	NO	Runs	HS	Ave	SR	100	50	4s	6s
WRS Gidman	5	7	4	362	99*	120.66	52.38	0	5	41	1
SA Northeast	15	22	6	1337	191	83.56	67.35	5	3	156	7
DJ Bell-Drummond	12	19	5	747	124	53.35	54.76	1	6	101	1
DI Stevens	14	16	0	782	140	48.87	73.77	2	5	94	17
SW Billings	7	7	0	329	171	47.00	73.11	1	1	54	1
TWM Latham	6	9	1	374	90	46.75	48.38	0	4	55	0
SR Dickson	14	20	3	675	207*	39.70	47.30	1	4	77	6
JL Denly	15	21	2	733	206*	38.57	49.79	1	4	94	3
AJ Blake	7	10	3	268	89*	38.28	63.20	0	2	33	5
MD Hunn	4	3	2	35	32*	35.00	44.30	0	0	1	3
MT Coles	10	9	0	273	70	30.33	75.00	0	2	30	6
JC Tredwell	11	12	2	291	124	29.10	42.66	1	0	39	1
AP Rouse	6	6	0	164	65	27.33	53.42	0	1	27	1
AJ Ball	4	6	0	141	66	23.50	49.64	0	1	16	1
CJ Haggett	6	5	1	87	33*	21.75	33.85	0	0	13	0
GC Viljoen	4	4	0	80	63	20.00	54.42	0	1	9	0
ME Claydon	14	15	3	187	55	15.58	58.25	0	1	29	1
CF Jackson	3	4	0	61	38	15.25	41.78	0	0	5	0
HR Bernard	1	1	0	14	14	14.00	53.84	0	0	2	0
FK Cowdrey	1	2	0	18	15	9.00	50.00	0	0	3	0
K Rabada	2	3	0	25	14	8.33	49.01	0	0	4	0
Imran Qayyum	2	2	1	0	0*	0.00	0.00	0	0	0	0
AEN Riley	3	2	2	37	32*	-	50.68	0	0	5	0

Batting

	Overs	Mdns	Runs	Wkts	BBI	BBM	Ave	Econ	SR	5w	10w
GC Viljoen	103.5	12	385	20	5/55	8/121	19.25	3.70	31.1	1	0
MT Coles	291.5	51	1059	37	5/116	7/150	28.62	3.62	47.3	1	0
DI Stevens	401.1	104	1131	37	4/74	5/77	30.56	2.81	65.0	0	0
WRS Gidman	44.0	15	123	4	2/21	3/57	30.75	2.79	66.0	0	0
ME Claydon	399.4	75	1519	48	5/42	8/156	31.64	3.80	49.9	2	0
K Rabada	77.0	21	232	7	4/118	4/118	33.14	3.01	66.0	0	0
HR Bernard	22.0	3	105	3	2/68	3/105	35.00	4.77	44.0	0	0
CJ Haggett	158.4	30	529	15	4/15	6/93	35.26	3.33	63.4	0	0
JC Tredwell	299.0	61	921	22	4/45	6/134	41.86	3.08	81.5	0	0
MD Hunn	87.0	8	335	8	2/33	3/115	41.87	3.85	65.2	0	0
Imran Qayyum	78.2	14	283	6	3/158	3/125	47.16	3.61	78.3	0	0
AJ Ball	42.0	2	159	3	2/46	2/46	53.00	3.78	84.0	0	0
JL Denly	66.3	4	222	3	2/31	2/31	74.00	3.33	133.0	0	0
SA Northeast	1.4	0	2	0	-	-	-	1.20	-	0	0
SR Dickson	1.0	0	4	0	-	-	-	4.00	-	0	0
TWM Latham	2.0	0	5	0	-	-	-	2.50	-	0	0
AEN Riley	26.0	1	146	0	-	-	-	5.61	-	0	0

Bowling

Catches/Stumpings:
29 Rouse (inc 1st), 26 Billings (inc 1st), 14 Tredwell, 9 Jackson, Latham, 8 Dickson, Stevens, 7 Denly, 5 Coles, Gidman, Northeast, 4 Blake, 2 Ball, Hunn, 1 Bell-Drummond, Claydon, Haggett, Qayyum, Viljoen

Batting

	Mat	Inns	NO	Runs	HS	Ave	SR	100	50	4s	6s
SR Dickson	1	1	0	99	99	99.00	78.57	0	1	9	2
AJ Blake	9	6	3	202	66*	67.33	106.31	0	2	24	4
JL Denly	9	9	2	428	105	61.14	77.81	2	1	41	7
DJ Bell-Drummond	8	8	0	332	91	41.50	86.23	0	3	37	1
JC Tredwell	9	4	2	76	47*	38.00	80.85	0	0	6	0
SA Northeast	9	9	1	274	66*	34.25	83.03	0	2	17	5
DI Stevens	9	8	2	195	61	32.50	82.27	0	2	15	7
SW Billings	8	8	1	218	106*	31.14	117.20	1	1	24	5
MT Coles	9	4	0	114	91	28.50	156.16	0	1	11	7
CF Hartley	2	1	0	15	15	15.00	71.42	0	0	0	0
WRS Gidman	5	3	1	24	19	12.00	57.14	0	0	1	1
TWM Latham	2	2	0	16	9	8.00	48.48	0	0	1	0
FK Cowdrey	3	3	0	14	9	4.66	46.66	0	0	2	0
CF Jackson	1	1	1	28	28*	-	116.66	0	0	2	1
ME Claydon	8	2	2	10	8*	-	142.85	0	0	1	0
DA Griffiths	5	1	1	0	0*	-	-	0	0	0	0
IAA Thomas	2	-	-	-	-	-	-	-	-	-	-

Bowling

	Overs	Mdns	Runs	Wkts	BBI	Ave	Econ	SR	4w	5w
JL Denly	4.0	0	16	1	1/16	16.00	4.00	24.0	0	0
DI Stevens	61.0	2	247	7	2/14	35.28	4.04	52.2	0	0
CF Hartley	16.0	0	65	4	2/23	16.25	4.06	24.0	0	0
WRS Gidman	34.0	1	160	6	3/28	26.66	4.70	34.0	0	0
JC Tredwell	67.0	1	345	8	3/55	43.12	5.14	50.2	0	0
MT Coles	80.1	4	418	24	6/56	17.41	5.21	20.0	1	1
ME Claydon	63.1	2	344	6	2/42	57.33	5.44	63.1	0	0
FK Cowdrey	26.0	0	147	4	2/38	36.75	5.65	39.0	0	0
DA Griffiths	34.0	0	209	3	2/44	69.66	6.14	68.0	0	0
IAA Thomas	14.0	0	88	3	3/31	29.33	6.28	28.0	0	0

Catches/Stumpings:
11 Billings (inc 1st), 8 Blake, 5 Cole, Northeast, 3 Stevens, 2 Jackson, Latham, Tredwell, 1 Cowdrey, Denly, Gidman, Thomas

	Mat	Inns	NO	Runs	HS	Ave	SR	100	50	4s	6s
DJ Bell-Drummond	9	9	2	379	112*	54.14	148.04	1	2	47	4
SA Northeast	14	14	0	462	75	33.00	145.28	0	4	40	15
JL Denly	14	14	0	378	75	27.00	129.89	0	3	32	16
AJ Blake	14	12	4	198	37	24.75	115.11	0	0	10	7
TWM Latham	7	6	0	128	48	21.33	120.75	0	0	9	5
ME Claydon	11	5	4	21	15*	21.00	70.00	0	0	1	0
FK Cowdrey	9	8	2	121	71	20.16	134.44	0	1	11	2
DI Stevens	14	12	1	168	33	15.27	137.70	0	0	14	8
SW Billings	13	13	2	164	55*	14.90	115.49	0	1	8	4
MT Coles	8	6	0	49	31	8.16	132.43	0	0	4	2
DA Griffiths	13	4	1	16	8	5.33	100.00	0	0	1	1
JC Tredwell	14	8	2	28	10*	4.66	71.79	0	0	0	0
K Rabada	6	4	2	3	3*	1.50	37.50	0	0	0	0
WRS Gidman	1	1	1	30	30*	-	150.00	0	0	4	0
IAA Thomas	4	2	2	3	3*	-	75.00	0	0	0	0
AJ Ball	1	-	-	-	-	-	-	-	-	-	-
MD Hunn	1	-	-	-	-	-	-	-	-	-	-
AP Rouse	1	-	-	-	-	-	-	-	-	-	-

	Overs	Mdns	Runs	Wkts	BBI	Ave	Econ	SR	4w	5w
K Rabada	24.0	0	162	6	2/31	27.00	6.75	24.0	0	0
FK Cowdrey	23.0	0	178	8	3/18	22.25	7.73	17.2	0	0
MT Coles	30.0	0	235	8	4/27	29.37	7.83	22.5	1	0
JC Tredwell	48.0	0	414	8	3/32	51.75	8.62	36.0	0	0
IAA Thomas	15.0	0	132	4	2/42	33.00	8.80	22.5	0	0
AJ Ball	1.0	0	9	0	-	-	9.00	-	0	0
ME Claydon	42.0	0	384	10	3/25	38.40	9.14	25.2	0	0
DI Stevens	39.2	0	372	11	4/31	33.81	9.45	21.4	1	0
DA Griffiths	45.3	0	437	13	2/22	33.61	9.60	21.0	0	0
MD Hunn	3.0	0	35	1	1/35	35.00	11.66	18.0	0	0
WRS Gidman	4.0	0	55	0	-	-	13.75	-	0	0

Catches/Stumpings:
8 Blake, 7 Billings (inc 2st), Tredwell, 6 Denly, 3 Latham, Northeast, Rabada, Cowdrey, Griffiths, Stevens, 1 Bell-Drummond, Coles

TEAM PROFILE

Lancashire County Cricket Club

TM

FORMED: 1864
HOME GROUND: Emirates Old Trafford, Manchester
ONE-DAY NAME: Lancashire Lightning
CAPTAIN: Steven Croft
2016 RESULTS: CC1: 7/9, RL50: 9/9 North Group, NWT20: 5/9 North Group
HONOURS: Championship: (9) 1897, 1904, 1926, 1927, 1928, 1930, 1934, 1950(s), 2011; Gillette/NatWest/C&G/FP Trophy: (7) 1970, 1971, 1972, 1985, 1990, 1996, 1998; Benson & Hedges Cup: (4) 1984, 1990, 1995, 1996; Pro40/National League/CB40/YB40/RL50: 1999; Sunday League: (4) 1969, 1970, 1989, 1998; T20 Cup: 2015

THE LOWDOWN

After a bright start Lancashire flirted dangerously with relegation at the end of a season in which they failed to make the T20 quarter-finals and finished bottom of their 50-over group. Yet there were some individual triumphs, notably 23-year-old Liam Livingstone, who made 815 runs at 50.93 and was also effective in the shorter formats. Haseeb Hameed, 20, passed 1,000 runs in his first full season but so swift has been his ascent to the Test team that Lancashire are likely to see less of him in 2017. Alviro Petersen is serving a two-year ban for failing to report match-fixing but Lancashire hope to recoup his runs with the signing of 42-year-old Shivnarine Chanderpaul. Another Kolpak arrival is South African wicketkeeper Dane Vilas, leaving space for his compatriot Ryan McLaren as an overseas player in all formats, to be supported by Junaid Khan in the T20 Blast. Persistent back problems forced Tom Smith to retire aged 31.

HEAD COACH: GLEN CHAPPLE

With Ashley Giles returning to Warwickshire, Lancashire have turned to a recently retired local legend to replace him. Chapple took 1,373 wickets in 664 appearances during a 23-year playing career at Old Trafford, leading the club to the County Championship in 2011. He had worked as assistant to Giles and coached Lancashire to the Second XI Trophy last year. Former Lancashire skipper Mark Chilton has been appointed assistant coach.

www.lccc.co.uk / tel: 0161 282 4000

Batting

	Mat	Inns	NO	Runs	HS	Ave	SR	100	50	4s	6s
LS Livingstone	15	23	7	815	108*	50.93	58.00	2	6	89	8
H Hameed	16	27	3	1198	122	49.91	39.01	4	7	143	1
AN Petersen	15	24	1	1134	191	49.30	64.39	3	6	125	10
RP Jones	4	7	2	212	106*	42.40	32.61	1	0	27	2
LA Procter	16	25	1	822	137	34.25	42.19	2	3	101	2
TC Smith	8	13	0	417	87	32.07	40.09	0	4	51	2
NL Buck	3	4	2	63	27*	31.50	50.40	0	0	5	2
AL Davies	5	6	0	187	55	31.16	58.80	0	1	28	0
SJ Croft	16	25	1	713	100	29.70	40.60	1	4	73	8
TJ Moores	2	3	0	78	35	26.00	43.33	0	0	8	2
J Clark	7	10	1	225	84*	25.00	48.49	0	2	28	2
AM Lilley	4	7	1	129	45	21.50	94.16	0	0	16	5
JC Buttler	1	2	0	42	26	21.00	144.82	0	0	6	1
SC Kerrigan	13	18	7	225	48	20.45	41.13	0	0	26	1
KR Brown	10	17	0	337	61	19.82	44.34	0	2	47	0
KM Jarvis	16	23	4	338	57	17.78	53.14	0	1	47	3
TE Bailey	6	9	1	91	53	11.37	35.68	0	1	14	0
N Wagner	9	12	0	111	37	9.25	59.35	0	0	14	1
JM Anderson	4	4	1	14	8	4.66	46.66	0	0	2	0
MW Parkinson	4	5	1	16	9	4.00	25.00	0	0	1	0
TJ Lester	2	2	1	1	1	1.00	6.66	0	0	0	0
S Mahmood	1	1	1	0	0*	-	0.00	0	0	0	0

Bowling

	Overs	Mdns	Runs	Wkts	BBI	BBM	Ave	Econ	SR	5w	10w
JM Anderson	137.5	46	307	15	3/29	6/71	20.46	2.22	55.1	0	0
TC Smith	133.0	31	374	15	5/25	5/53	24.93	2.81	53.2	1	0
TE Bailey	215.4	51	592	22	5/110	6/167	26.90	2.74	58.8	2	0
N Wagner	286.4	52	937	32	6/66	11/111	29.28	3.26	53.7	2	1
KM Jarvis	545.2	130	1673	51	6/70	11/119	32.80	3.06	64.1	2	1
MW Parkinson	114.1	23	363	10	5/49	6/123	36.30	3.17	68.5	1	0
SC Kerrigan	498.4	106	1326	35	6/86	10/166	37.88	2.65	85.4	2	1
J Clark	132.0	23	456	11	3/20	4/50	41.45	3.45	72.0	0	0
AM Lilley	105.3	21	333	8	5/130	5/150	41.62	3.15	79.1	1	0
LA Procter	152.5	28	505	10	3/14	3/31	50.50	3.30	91.7	0	0
SJ Croft	46.0	7	155	2	1/19	1/44	77.50	3.36	138.0	0	0
NL Buck	63.0	12	210	2	1/65	1/76	105.00	3.33	189.0	0	0
S Mahmood	33.0	5	121	1	1/121	1/121	121.00	3.66	198.0	0	0
LS Livingstone	51.0	7	166	1	1/19	1/19	166.00	3.25	306.0	0	0
H Hameed	2.0	0	3	0	-	-	-	1.50	-	0	0
TJ Lester	29.0	3	119	0	-	-	-	4.10	-	0	0

Catches/Stumpings:
26 Livingstone, 19 Croft, 18 Davies (inc 1st), 11 Croft, 9 Smith, 8 Petersen, 7 Moores, 6 Brown, Kerrigan, Hameed, 5 Procter, 3 Jarvis, Jones, 2 Wagner, 1 Anderson, Buttler, Clark, Lilley, Parkinson

Batting

	Mat	Inns	NO	Runs	HS	Ave	SR	100	50	4s	6s
MJ Guptill	2	2	0	95	50	47.50	115.85	0	1	9	4
SJ Croft	8	6	0	249	78	41.50	81.63	0	3	12	5
LA Procter	7	6	1	198	63*	39.60	85.34	0	2	14	2
LS Livingstone	8	6	0	189	98	31.50	88.31	0	1	13	5
JC Buttler	4	3	0	93	91	31.00	113.41	0	1	10	1
AN Petersen	8	8	2	177	73*	29.50	70.80	0	1	21	0
KR Brown	8	7	1	149	51	24.83	76.41	0	1	19	0
TC Smith	6	6	0	130	56	21.66	64.03	0	1	13	0
J Clark	8	6	1	80	29	16.00	101.26	0	0	5	1
TJ Moores	4	3	1	22	10	11.00	81.48	0	0	3	0
SD Parry	8	6	2	27	9	6.75	69.23	0	0	2	0
NL Buck	6	4	2	11	7	5.50	40.74	0	0	2	0
KM Jarvis	3	2	1	1	1*	1.00	33.33	0	0	0	0
S Mahmood	7	2	2	6	6*	-	46.15	0	0	0	0
AM Lilley	1	-	-	-	-	-	-	-	-	-	-

Bowling

	Overs	Mdns	Runs	Wkts	BBI	Ave	Econ	SR	4w	5w
KM Jarvis	23.4	0	121	6	4/31	20.16	5.11	23.6	1	0
SD Parry	55.0	1	285	9	3/43	31.66	5.18	36.6	0	0
SJ Croft	34.0	0	183	2	1/28	91.50	5.38	102.0	0	0
TC Smith	35.0	1	191	7	3/45	27.28	5.45	30.0	0	0
J Clark	39.0	0	220	6	2/37	36.66	5.64	39.0	0	0
S Mahmood	44.0	3	260	5	3/55	52.00	5.90	52.8	0	0
NL Buck	36.0	3	214	8	3/45	26.75	5.94	27.0	0	0
LA Procter	13.0	0	83	0	-	-	6.38	-	0	0
LS Livingstone	15.0	0	99	3	3/51	33.00	6.60	30.0	0	0

Catches/Stumpings:
6 Croft, 3 Brown, Buck, Mahmood, Moores (inc 1st), 2 Buttler, Parry, Petersen, Smith, 1 Clark, Livingstone

	Mat	Inns	NO	Runs	HS	Ave	SR	100	50	4s	6s
AN Petersen	12	12	2	455	103*	45.50	140.43	1	2	32	13
JC Buttler	6	6	2	166	57	41.50	204.93	0	2	16	10
TJ Moores	6	4	2	62	39*	31.00	110.71	0	0	5	1
SJ Croft	13	12	5	199	36	28.42	112.42	0	0	9	4
LS Livingstone	12	11	2	247	55	27.44	144.44	0	1	16	12
KR Brown	13	12	1	289	62*	26.27	124.56	0	2	27	8
MJ Guptill	5	5	0	125	72	25.00	131.57	0	1	17	2
J Clark	11	7	2	111	31*	22.20	146.05	0	0	6	5
LM Reece	4	3	0	48	32	16.00	114.28	0	0	7	1
TC Smith	3	3	1	24	9*	12.00	80.00	0	0	3	0
AL Davies	2	2	0	21	15	10.50	91.30	0	0	2	0
SD Parry	13	3	1	21	15	10.50	123.52	0	0	3	0
N Wagner	5	3	1	18	9	9.00	150.00	0	0	1	1
LA Procter	5	2	0	17	16	8.50	100.00	0	0	2	0
AM Lilley	10	3	0	14	10	4.66	127.27	0	0	2	0
NL Buck	8	2	1	0	0*	0.00	0.00	0	0	0	0
KM Jarvis	1	1	1	9	9*	-	112.50	0	0	1	0
GA Edwards	11	1	1	2	2*	-	100.00	0	0	0	0
GT Griffiths	1	-	-	-	-	-	-	-	-	-	-
S Mahmood	2	-	-	-	-	-	-	-	-	-	-

Batting

	Overs	Mdns	Runs	Wkts	BBI	Ave	Econ	SR	4w	5w
GT Griffiths	0.1	0	0	0	-	-	0.00	-	0	0
LS Livingstone	2.0	0	9	1	1/9	9.00	4.50	12.0	0	0
S Mahmood	8.0	1	43	6	3/12	7.16	5.37	8.0	0	0
TC Smith	4.5	0	31	0	-	-	6.41	-	0	0
SJ Croft	26.0	0	180	6	2/24	30.00	6.92	26.0	0	0
NL Buck	28.0	0	206	12	4/26	17.16	7.35	14.0	1	0
AM Lilley	26.3	0	206	8	2/21	25.75	7.77	19.8	0	0
SD Parry	43.0	0	349	12	5/13	29.08	8.11	21.5	0	1
J Clark	35.0	0	302	9	2/28	33.55	8.62	23.3	0	0
GA Edwards	35.0	0	335	16	3/33	20.93	9.57	13.1	0	0
N Wagner	17.0	0	168	4	2/25	42.00	9.88	25.5	0	0
LM Reece	6.0	0	65	2	2/29	32.50	10.83	18.0	0	0
KM Jarvis	1.0	0	20	0	-	-	20.00	-	0	0

Bowling

Catches/Stumpings:
6 Buttler (inc 1st), Croft, Moores (inc 1st), 5 Clark, Guptill, Livingstone, 4 Parry, Petersen, 3 Brown, Edwards, 2 Lilley, Procter, 1 Davies, Jarvis, Reece, Smith, Wagner

LEICESTERSHIRE
COUNTY CRICKET CLUB

FORMED: 1879

HOME GROUND: Fischer County Ground, Leicester

ONE-DAY NAME: Leicestershire Foxes

CAPTAIN: Mark Cosgrove (Championship), Clint McKay (RL50, NWT20)

2016 RESULTS: CC2: 7/9; RL50: 8/9 North Group; NWT20: 9/9 North Group

HONOURS: Championship: (3) 1975, 1996, 1998; Benson & Hedges Cup: (3) 1972, 1975, 1985; Sunday League: (2) 1974, 1977; T20 Cup: (3) 2004, 2006, 2011

THE LOWDOWN

Leicestershire have made modest gains as they enter the middle of CEO Wasim Khan's five-year plan to put the Foxes on an even footing. In September profits were announced for the second year running and the team avoided the wooden spoon for the first time since 2012. But seventh in Division Two and six wins from 22 limited-overs matches was no cause to rejoice. New coach Pierre de Bruyn says "it is time to take a look at ourselves" – a message aimed at the batsmen, of whom only captain Mark Cosgrove passed 1,000 Championship runs last summer. Colin Ackermann, 25, arrives on a European passport with well over 4,000 first-class runs under his belt. Australian Clint McKay, who replaces Mark Pettini as limited-overs captain, will again lead an impressive seam attack bolstered by the arrivals of Richard Jones (Warwickshire) and Gavin Griffiths (Lancashire).

HEAD COACH: PIERRE DE BRUYN

The tough-talking de Bruyn takes over from Andrew McDonald, who has returned home to take charge of the Melbourne Renegades and Victoria. An allrounder who played the majority of his cricket in his native South Africa before retiring in 2010, de Bruyn was a successful coach at the University of Pretoria before joining Leicestershire a year ago as second XI and assistant skills coach, working closely with McDonald. "The club has underperformed massively," he said. "We owe the supporters better."

COUNTY CHAMPIONSHIP AVERAGES 2016

Batting

	Mat	Inns	NO	Runs	HS	Ave	SR	100	50	4s	6s
WA White	4	4	2	103	58	51.50	62.80	0	1	13	1
MJ Cosgrove	16	27	1	1279	146	49.19	61.54	5	5	182	5
NJ O'Brien	9	14	3	432	93	39.27	50.17	0	2	41	3
EJH Eckersley	11	18	2	624	117	39.00	48.97	3	1	73	2
NJ Dexter	16	27	1	958	136	36.84	48.92	3	4	125	2
PJ Horton	16	28	2	908	117*	34.92	51.21	2	6	123	1
ML Pettini	16	26	2	694	142*	28.91	46.29	2	1	91	3
AJ Robson	16	28	1	732	84	27.11	43.72	0	9	92	1
RA Jones	6	9	2	127	33	18.14	39.56	0	0	11	1
RJ Sayer	2	4	2	36	32*	18.00	34.95	0	0	4	0
BA Raine	14	19	1	321	64	17.83	50.07	0	1	41	2
CJ McKay	15	20	1	300	65	15.78	59.28	0	2	39	4
RML Taylor	3	4	0	50	21	12.50	37.59	0	0	5	0
LJ Hill	2	4	0	46	36	11.50	42.99	0	0	5	0
D Klein	2	4	1	31	16*	10.33	63.26	0	0	5	0
AM Ali	4	7	0	71	30	10.14	32.42	0	0	7	1
HE Dearden	2	4	0	36	16	9.00	40.90	0	0	3	0
TJ Wells	1	2	0	18	18	9.00	40.90	0	0	2	0
CE Shreck	16	20	12	51	20	6.37	31.48	0	0	8	0
ZJ Chappell	2	3	0	17	10	5.66	48.57	0	0	3	0
JKH Naik	2	2	2	34	26*	-	24.63	0	0	1	0
JS Sykes	1	1	1	12	12*	-	54.54	0	0	2	0

Bowling

	Overs	Mdns	Runs	Wkts	BBI	BBM	Ave	Econ	SR	5w	10w
PJ Horton	13.0	3	43	2	2/6	2/6	21.50	3.30	39.0	0	0
CJ McKay	411.1	78	1260	56	6/73	8/84	22.50	3.06	44.0	1	0
WA White	64.1	13	225	10	4/24	4/24	22.50	3.50	38.5	0	0
D Klein	44.0	5	211	9	4/107	5/104	23.44	4.79	29.3	0	0
NJ Dexter	261.5	50	824	29	5/52	5/52	28.41	3.14	54.1	1	0
BA Raine	338.0	77	1108	35	5/66	7/111	31.65	3.27	57.9	1	0
ZJ Chappell	20.2	2	98	3	2/44	2/46	32.66	4.81	40.6	0	0
CE Shreck	442.3	85	1455	44	4/33	6/92	33.06	3.28	60.3	0	0
MJ Cosgrove	29.4	2	112	3	2/14	2/28	37.33	3.77	59.3	0	0
RA Jones	115.0	20	446	7	2/41	2/69	63.71	3.87	98.5	0	0
RJ Sayer	67.0	6	273	4	2/113	2/112	68.25	4.07	100.5	0	0
RML Taylor	48.3	9	187	2	2/34	2/97	93.50	3.85	145.5	0	0
EJH Eckersley	2.0	0	7	0	-	-	-	3.50	-	0	0
AM Ali	3.0	1	21	0	-	-	-	7.00	-	0	0
AJ Robson	8.0	1	32	0	-	-	-	4.00	-	0	0
JKH Naik	30.0	6	67	0	-	-	-	2.23	-	0	0

Catches/Stumpings:
30 N O'Brien, 29 Eckersley, 14 Robson, 10 Cosgrove, 8 Horton, 6 Shreck, 4 Dexter, 3 Pettini, 2 Dearden, Jones, Naik, Raine, Taylor, 1 Ali, White

Batting

	Mat	Inns	NO	Runs	HS	Ave	SR	100	50	4s	6s
RML Taylor	3	2	1	74	62	74.00	101.36	0	1	3	4
NJ O'Brien	6	5	2	164	82	54.66	100.00	0	1	18	5
KJ O'Brien	6	4	0	203	89	50.75	105.72	0	2	22	4
MJ Cosgrove	6	4	0	194	91	48.50	97.48	0	2	21	1
CS Delport	4	2	0	71	46	35.50	98.61	0	0	11	0
ML Pettini	7	6	1	165	92	33.00	73.00	0	2	15	1
LJ Hill	7	5	0	112	55	22.40	95.72	0	1	10	3
RJ Sayer	4	3	1	39	26	19.50	114.70	0	0	4	1
MGK Burgess	2	2	0	37	36	18.50	105.71	0	0	3	1
TJ Wells	3	2	0	33	31	16.50	82.50	0	0	1	2
AJ Robson	1	1	0	16	16	16.00	55.17	0	0	2	0
PJ Horton	4	4	1	42	32	14.00	73.68	0	0	6	0
BA Raine	6	4	0	47	20	11.75	85.45	0	0	2	2
CJ McKay	5	3	0	29	14	9.66	78.37	0	0	1	1
NJ Dexter	5	4	0	36	21	9.00	70.58	0	0	2	2
JS Sykes	2	2	1	5	4*	5.00	35.71	0	0	0	0
OH Freckingham	2	2	2	5	5*	-	166.66	0	0	1	0
JKH Naik	1	1	1	1	1*	-	100.00	0	0	0	0
AM Ali	1	-	-	-	-	-	-	-	-	-	-
D Klein	2	-	-	-	-	-	-	-	-	-	-

Bowling

	Overs	Mdns	Runs	Wkts	BBI	Ave	Econ	SR	4w	5w
PJ Horton	2.0	0	7	1	1/7	7.00	3.50	12.0	0	0
RJ Sayer	35.0	3	159	4	1/31	39.75	4.54	52.5	0	0
CS Delport	19.0	0	91	4	2/41	22.75	4.78	28.5	0	0
D Klein	17.3	0	90	2	2/38	45.00	5.14	52.5	0	0
CJ McKay	38.0	3	209	2	1/53	104.50	5.50	114.0	0	0
NJ Dexter	30.0	0	169	4	4/22	42.25	5.63	45.0	1	0
RML Taylor	16.0	0	94	5	4/58	18.80	5.87	19.2	1	0
OH Freckingham	16.0	1	96	2	2/60	48.00	6.00	48.0	0	0
KJ O'Brien	32.0	0	194	5	2/48	38.80	6.06	38.4	0	0
BA Raine	47.0	1	299	5	3/62	59.80	6.36	56.4	0	0
JKH Naik	7.0	0	52	0	-	-	7.42	-	0	0
JS Sykes	12.0	0	90	0	-	-	7.50	-	0	0
MJ Cosgrove	9.0	0	73	0	-	-	8.11	-	0	0
TJ Wells	2.0	0	25	0	-	-	12.50	-	0	0

Catches/Stumpings:
5 N O'Brien (inc 2st), 3 Cosgrove, 2 Delport, Hill, Taylor, 1 Freckingham, Horton, McKay, Pettini, Sayer

	Mat	Inns	NO	Runs	HS	Ave	SR	100	50	4s	6s
F Behardien	5	4	2	108	48*	54.00	138.46	0	0	10	2
LJ Hill	11	8	3	187	31*	37.40	155.83	0	0	13	9
Umar Akmal	6	6	2	134	52*	33.50	121.81	0	1	11	5
ML Pettini	12	12	1	331	76	30.09	124.43	0	3	43	5
CS Delport	8	8	2	178	68	29.66	142.40	0	1	10	12
MJ Cosgrove	12	12	1	294	66*	26.72	141.34	0	3	34	8
NJ Dexter	10	4	2	53	34	26.50	110.41	0	0	3	1
RML Taylor	5	3	2	26	17*	26.00	173.33	0	0	1	2
BA Raine	10	6	2	101	48	25.25	99.01	0	0	7	2
NJ O'Brien	6	5	1	98	39	24.50	128.94	0	0	5	5
KJ O'Brien	9	8	1	115	29	16.42	111.65	0	0	12	1
CJ McKay	12	2	1	15	15*	15.00	75.00	0	0	0	0
TJ Wells	10	7	2	60	26*	12.00	107.14	0	0	4	1
JKH Naik	7	1	0	5	5	5.00	100.00	0	0	0	0
PJ Horton	1	1	1	29	29*	-	116.00	0	0	3	0
RJ Sayer	5	1	1	1	1*	-	100.00	0	0	0	0
MGK Burgess	1	-	-	-	-	-	-	-	-	-	-
RA Jones	2	-	-	-	-	-	-	-	-	-	-

	Overs	Mdns	Runs	Wkts	BBI	Ave	Econ	SR	4w	5w
CJ McKay	42.2	0	267	13	3/20	20.53	6.30	19.5	0	0
NJ Dexter	29.0	0	212	6	2/16	35.33	7.31	29.0	0	0
JKH Naik	13.0	0	101	3	1/15	33.66	7.76	26.0	0	0
KJ O'Brien	22.3	0	176	7	3/27	25.14	7.82	19.2	0	0
BA Raine	35.4	1	310	13	3/7	23.84	8.69	16.4	0	0
TJ Wells	9.0	0	80	1	1/19	80.00	8.88	54.0	0	0
CS Delport	8.5	0	81	4	2/21	20.25	9.16	13.2	0	0
MJ Cosgrove	2.0	0	19	1	1/19	19.00	9.50	12.0	0	0
RML Taylor	15.3	0	151	3	1/19	50.33	9.74	31.0	0	0
F Behardien	10.0	0	104	2	2/35	52.00	10.40	30.0	0	0
RA Jones	6.0	0	77	2	2/37	38.50	12.83	18.0	0	0
RJ Sayer	9.0	0	116	3	2/20	38.66	12.88	18.0	0	0

Catches/Stumpings:
5 Pettini, Raine, 4 K O'Brien, N O'Brien, 3 Cosgrove, Dexter, Hill, Wells, 2 Akmal, McKay, Taylor, 1 Delport, Naik, Sayer

TEAM PROFILE

FORMED: 1864
HOME GROUND: Lord's Cricket Ground, London
CAPTAIN: James Franklin (Championship, RL50), Dawid Malan (NWT20)
2016 RESULTS: CC1: Champions; RL50: 6/9 South Group; NWT20: Quarter-finalists
HONOURS: Championship: (13) 1903, 1920, 1921, 1947, 1949(s), 1976, 1977(s), 1980, 1982, 1985, 1990, 1993, 2016; Gillette/NatWest/C&G/FP Trophy: (4) 1977, 1980, 1984, 1998; Benson & Hedges Cup: (2) 1983, 1986; Sunday League: 1992; T20 Cup: 2008

THE LOWDOWN

How do you top that? After the euphoria of their first Championship title in 23 years, achieved in the most dramatic circumstances, the challenge now is to retain the trophy. The club have understandably kept their hands in their pockets over the winter, content with a squad which, despite the individual brilliance of Nick Gubbins (1,409 Championship runs) and Toby Roland-Jones (Middlesex's leading wicket-taker in all three formats), thrived most as a collective. Only Gubbins passed 1,000 runs yet most of the regular top six averaged 40 or more, while eight bowlers reached double-figures in the wicket-taking tally. A string of players have been tied up on new deals, including the understated Kiwi captain James Franklin. Australia's George Bailey has defected to Hampshire but compatriot Adam Voges returns for his fourth summer with the club. An increasing focus on the shorter formats was evident in the appointment of Daniel Vettori as T20 coach, while Brendon McCullum will return for another wallop at the top of the order.

HEAD COACH: RICHARD SCOTT

Scott had an eight-year county career with Hampshire and Gloucestershire – as well as turning out for Middlesex Second XI, whom he coached for two seasons before his promotion to the top role in 2009. Former New Zealand spinner Daniel Vettori has been appointed T20 coach as Middlesex seek to replicate their four-day success in the shorter formats.

	Mat	Inns	NO	Runs	HS	Ave	SR	100	50	4s	6s
AC Voges	6	6	1	388	160*	77.60	49.87	1	2	39	0
GJ Bailey	3	5	1	284	110*	71.00	53.68	1	2	43	1
JK Fuller	3	2	0	129	93	64.50	89.58	0	1	9	5
NRT Gubbins	16	24	1	1409	201*	61.26	52.30	4	9	187	10
SD Robson	14	21	1	899	231	44.95	51.10	3	4	121	3
SS Eskinazi	9	15	1	609	157	43.50	50.96	2	2	85	5
JA Simpson	16	23	5	779	100*	43.27	50.45	1	7	105	12
DJ Malan	15	23	1	951	147	43.22	56.84	3	5	130	4
JEC Franklin	14	19	4	641	99	42.73	52.07	0	4	79	6
JAR Harris	7	9	3	203	78	33.83	44.71	0	2	24	1
PR Stirling	9	7	1	199	85	33.16	55.43	0	1	24	1
TS Roland-Jones	15	14	3	319	79*	29.00	79.35	0	2	27	16
NRD Compton	10	17	1	436	131	27.25	38.44	1	2	48	1
HW Podmore	3	2	1	23	21	23.00	52.27	0	0	3	0
TJ Murtagh	14	12	4	168	47	21.00	76.36	0	0	16	3
OP Rayner	13	13	3	100	26	10.00	34.12	0	0	11	0
ST Finn	8	7	1	50	22*	8.33	66.66	0	0	5	1
RH Patel	1	1	1	4	4*	-	21.05	0	0	0	0

Batting

	Overs	Mdns	Runs	Wkts	BBI	BBM	Ave	Econ	SR	5w	10w
HW Podmore	90.0	21	240	11	4/54	7/143	21.81	2.66	49.0	0	0
OP Rayner	444.5	108	1202	51	6/79	9/102	23.56	2.70	52.3	3	0
TS Roland-Jones	482.2	95	1524	54	6/54	10/127	28.22	3.15	53.5	2	1
TJ Murtagh	457.2	116	1227	43	5/53	7/86	28.53	2.68	63.8	1	0
ST Finn	259.0	41	912	31	4/54	7/111	29.41	3.52	50.1	0	0
RH Patel	37.0	7	94	3	2/54	3/94	31.33	2.54	74.0	0	0
JK Fuller	100.0	17	393	12	5/70	6/104	32.75	3.93	50.0	1	0
DJ Malan	29.0	4	87	2	1/5	1/10	43.50	3.00	87.0	0	0
JAR Harris	228.2	34	807	16	3/67	5/181	50.43	3.53	85.6	0	0
JEC Franklin	205.0	39	646	11	3/26	4/47	58.72	3.15	111.8	0	0
NRT Gubbins	7.0	0	38	0	-	-	-	5.42	-	0	0
AC Voges	15.0	0	65	0	-	-	-	4.33	-	0	0
PR Stirling	53.0	6	138	0	-	-	-	2.60	-	0	0

Bowling

Catches/Stumpings:

46 Simpson (inc 1st), 18 Rayner, 16 Robson, 10 Franklin, 9 Compton, 6 Gubbins, Malan, 5 Voges, 4 Eskinazi, Murtagh, Roland-Jones, 3 Fuller, Stirling, 2 Bailey, Harris, 1 Finn, Podmore

Batting

	Mat	Inns	NO	Runs	HS	Ave	SR	100	50	4s	6s
BB McCullum	3	3	0	228	110	76.00	128.08	1	1	25	10
PR Stirling	8	8	1	348	125*	49.71	91.33	2	1	37	7
EJG Morgan	6	6	1	219	103*	43.80	85.54	1	1	27	2
SD Robson	1	1	0	41	41	41.00	66.12	0	0	1	0
JK Fuller	6	3	1	61	42*	30.50	148.78	0	0	3	2
NRT Gubbins	8	8	0	227	89	28.37	93.03	0	1	15	7
JEC Franklin	8	6	0	149	55	24.83	94.90	0	1	8	4
DJ Malan	5	5	0	124	70	24.80	72.09	0	1	12	0
RF Higgins	4	4	1	67	39	22.33	73.62	0	0	5	0
JA Simpson	8	7	1	124	33	20.66	64.58	0	0	9	0
TS Roland-Jones	6	5	2	62	30*	20.66	106.89	0	0	4	1
OP Rayner	6	4	2	38	21*	19.00	108.57	0	0	2	1
GJ Bailey	4	4	0	28	12	7.00	54.90	0	0	1	1
JAR Harris	3	2	1	2	2*	2.00	100.00	0	0	0	0
NA Sowter	2	1	0	0	0	0.00	0.00	0	0	0	0
TG Helm	3	2	2	14	10*	-	73.68	0	0	0	0
AC Voges	1	1	1	2	2*	-	50.00	0	0	0	0
ST Finn	1	-	-	-	-	-	-	-	-	-	-
TJ Murtagh	4	-	-	-	-	-	-	-	-	-	-
RH Patel	1	-	-	-	-	-	-	-	-	-	-

Bowling

	Overs	Mdns	Runs	Wkts	BBI	Ave	Econ	SR	4w	5w
ST Finn	10.0	2	31	2	2/31	15.50	3.10	30.0	0	0
OP Rayner	53.0	0	246	6	2/40	41.00	4.64	53.0	0	0
JEC Franklin	52.3	0	250	12	3/25	20.83	4.76	26.2	0	0
TS Roland-Jones	42.2	3	214	13	4/40	16.46	5.05	19.5	1	0
TG Helm	18.0	0	91	2	1/30	45.50	5.05	54.0	0	0
TJ Murtagh	38.0	3	202	4	2/28	50.50	5.31	57.0	0	0
JAR Harris	21.0	2	119	4	2/19	29.75	5.66	31.5	0	0
RF Higgins	15.0	0	97	1	1/53	97.00	6.46	90.0	0	0
JK Fuller	38.2	0	258	6	3/53	43.00	6.73	38.3	0	0
AC Voges	3.0	0	23	0	-	-	7.66	-	0	0
NA Sowter	8.0	0	62	0	-	-	7.75	-	0	0
PR Stirling	14.0	0	109	3	1/30	36.33	7.78	28.0	0	0
DJ Malan	3.0	0	24	2	2/24	12.00	8.00	9.0	0	0
RH Patel	4.0	0	35	0	-	-	8.75	-	0	0

Catches/Stumpings:
8 Simpson (inc 2st), 6 Rayner, 3 Gubbins, Roland-Jones, Sowter, 2 Franklin, Fuller, Morgan, 1 Finn, Harris, Higgins, Murtagh, Stirling

	Mat	Inns	NO	Runs	HS	Ave	SR	100	50	4s	6s
AC Voges	2	2	1	75	52*	75.00	127.11	0	1	7	0
DJ Malan	13	12	2	368	93	36.80	147.79	0	4	37	15
EJG Morgan	8	7	1	220	59*	36.66	122.90	0	2	18	8
BB McCullum	6	5	1	132	87*	33.00	148.31	0	1	8	8
SS Eskinazi	1	1	0	29	29	29.00	107.40	0	0	3	0
GJ Bailey	8	8	0	225	76	28.12	109.75	0	2	26	1
PR Stirling	10	10	0	266	60	26.60	154.65	0	2	31	12
JA Simpson	15	14	3	243	54	22.09	142.10	0	1	19	11
RF Higgins	12	10	4	121	57*	20.16	118.62	0	1	12	3
TS Roland-Jones	13	9	4	93	18*	18.60	152.45	0	0	7	3
NRT Gubbins	11	9	0	119	32	13.22	117.82	0	0	9	4
JEC Franklin	15	14	3	116	39	10.54	101.75	0	0	6	2
OP Rayner	5	3	1	15	13	7.50	93.75	0	0	1	0
JK Fuller	12	6	2	27	14	6.75	158.82	0	0	1	2
NA Sowter	12	2	1	6	4	6.00	66.66	0	0	0	0
MJ McClenaghan	3	2	1	5	4	5.00	100.00	0	0	1	0
HW Podmore	7	2	0	3	2	1.50	60.00	0	0	0	0
ST Finn	6	1	0	0	0	0.00	-	0	0	0	0
JAR Harris	2	-	-	-	-	-	-	-	-	-	-
TG Helm	1	-	-	-	-	-	-	-	-	-	-
TJ Murtagh	1	-	-	-	-	-	-	-	-	-	-
RH Patel	2	-	-	-	-	-	-	-	-	-	-

Batting

	Overs	Mdns	Runs	Wkts	BBI	Ave	Econ	SR	4w	5w
RF Higgins	14.0	0	98	7	5/13	14.00	7.00	12.0	0	1
OP Rayner	15.4	0	113	5	3/23	22.60	7.21	18.8	0	0
NA Sowter	36.0	0	260	11	2/29	23.63	7.22	19.6	0	0
TG Helm	4.0	0	29	1	1/29	29.00	7.25	24.0	0	0
TS Roland-Jones	39.0	0	287	17	3/24	16.88	7.35	13.7	0	0
JEC Franklin	28.2	0	211	6	1/3	35.16	7.44	28.3	0	0
RH Patel	8.0	0	61	3	2/27	20.33	7.62	16.0	0	0
JK Fuller	39.1	0	320	14	3/24	22.85	8.17	16.7	0	0
ST Finn	16.0	0	132	4	2/24	33.00	8.25	24.0	0	0
MJ McClenaghan	8.0	0	78	6	4/33	13.00	9.75	8.0	1	0
PR Stirling	13.0	0	128	3	1/17	42.66	9.84	26.0	0	0
HW Podmore	21.3	0	217	5	2/27	43.40	10.09	25.8	0	0
TJ Murtagh	2.0	0	22	0	-	-	11.00	-	0	0
JAR Harris	4.0	0	48	0	-	-	12.00	-	0	0
DJ Malan	2.0	0	26	0	-	-	13.00	-	0	0

Bowling

Catches/Stumpings:

11 Simpson (inc 3st), 6 Franklin, Fuller, Morgan, 5 Bailey, Stirling, 4 Finn, Podmore, 3
Gubbins, Malan, McCullum, 2 Higgins, Patel, Roland-Jones, Sowter, 1 McClenaghan, Rayner

M

NORTHAMPTONSHIRE

FORMED: 1878
HOME GROUND: County Ground, Northampton
ONE-DAY NAME: Northamptonshire Steelbacks
CAPTAIN: Alex Wakely
2016 RESULTS: CC2: 5/9; RL50: Quarter-finalists; NWT20: Champions
HONOURS: Gillette/NatWest/C&G/FP Trophy: (2) 1976, 1992; Benson & Hedges Cup: 1980; T20 Cup: (2) 2013, 2016

THE LOWDOWN

Champions in 2013, finalists in 2015, champions again in 2016: Northamptonshire are T20 kings. Short of star names, the club once again showed the benefits of a small, tight-knit squad. Their ingenuity was summed up in the figure of Richard Gleeson, a Minor Counties player transformed at the age of 28 into Northants' leading short-format seamer last summer. The county's impressive white-ball form extended to the 50-over competition in which they topped their group, and it took a Kumar Sangakkara special to knock them out in the quarter-finals. A late spike in their Championship form showed that promotion might be possible in 2017. They were galvanised by a phenomenal output from Ben Duckett – 2,258 runs across all formats. Nathan Buck has signed from Lancashire to cover the loss of fast bowler Olly Stone to Warwickshire, and England U19 captain Max Holden arrives on loan from Middlesex.

HEAD COACH: DAVID RIPLEY

A Northamptonshire stalwart, Ripley led the club to their maiden T20 title in 2013 – their first trophy in two decades – and repeated the trick last season. The challenge now is to push for promotion in the Championship. In a 17-year career Ripley scored over 10,000 runs for the county with more than 1,000 dismissals as a wicketkeeper. After retiring in 2001 he moved on to become second XI coach before his promotion to the top job in 2012.

Batting

	Mat	Inns	NO	Runs	HS	Ave	SR	100	50	4s	6s
LJ Evans	1	2	0	147	74	73.50	56.32	0	2	16	0
BM Duckett	14	24	2	1338	282*	60.81	79.45	4	5	190	7
RI Newton	10	19	3	810	202*	50.62	54.18	3	2	112	2
JD Libby	5	7	1	293	102	48.83	42.96	1	1	31	1
AM Rossington	12	17	4	556	138*	42.76	77.11	1	3	67	15
SP Crook	10	15	3	484	145	40.33	64.79	2	1	63	0
AG Wakely	12	19	3	630	104	39.37	47.15	1	4	76	7
SA Zaib	3	5	1	127	65*	31.75	45.84	0	1	17	1
SP Terry	2	3	0	95	54	31.66	68.84	0	1	12	1
RI Keogh	11	17	0	519	154	30.52	53.78	1	2	69	3
RE Levi	10	14	0	427	104	30.50	67.88	1	1	61	0
RK Kleinveldt	11	15	2	391	97	30.07	99.74	0	3	47	12
OP Stone	3	3	0	83	60	27.66	64.84	0	1	12	0
D Murphy	11	17	4	355	60*	27.30	43.66	0	1	35	1
RJ Gleeson	6	6	2	89	31	22.25	33.20	0	0	13	0
JJ Cobb	6	8	0	160	49	20.00	43.59	0	0	26	0
S Prasanna	2	4	0	70	31	17.50	106.06	0	0	11	2
GG White	5	5	0	73	33	14.60	58.40	0	0	3	3
MS Panesar	3	4	2	28	17*	14.00	32.55	0	0	3	0
Azharullah	12	15	3	72	14*	6.00	28.23	0	0	9	1
BW Sanderson	14	15	3	58	19	4.83	29.74	0	0	9	0
CA Barrett	2	2	2	118	114*	-	65.92	1	0	15	1

Bowling

	Overs	Mdns	Runs	Wkts	BBI	BBM	Ave	Econ	SR	5w	10w
S Prasanna	53.2	13	165	9	5/97	5/97	18.33	3.09	35.5	1	0
BW Sanderson	408.5	95	1157	55	8/73	10/89	21.03	2.83	44.6	4	1
GG White	107.0	24	281	13	6/44	7/91	21.61	2.62	49.3	1	0
RI Keogh	242.2	42	828	31	9/52	13/125	26.70	3.41	46.9	1	1
SA Zaib	32.0	2	174	5	5/148	5/174	34.80	5.43	38.4	1	0
JD Libby	21.0	3	71	2	1/13	1/22	35.50	3.38	63.0	0	0
RK Kleinveldt	302.1	60	930	26	5/53	8/123	35.76	3.07	69.7	1	0
Azharullah	277.2	46	987	25	6/68	6/80	39.48	3.55	66.5	1	0
D Murphy	5.0	0	40	1	1/40	1/40	40.00	8.00	30.0	0	0
OP Stone	87.4	8	282	6	4/56	5/95	47.00	3.21	87.6	0	0
CA Barrett	20.0	0	100	2	1/29	2/100	50.00	5.00	60.0	0	0
RJ Gleeson	147.5	25	505	10	4/105	4/105	50.50	3.41	88.7	0	0
SP Crook	139.2	18	578	10	2/7	4/31	57.80	4.14	83.6	0	0
MS Panesar	112.0	16	425	5	3/122	4/182	85.00	3.79	134.4	0	0
BM Duckett	0.5	0	8	0	-	-	-	9.60	-	0	0
AM Rossington	2.0	0	12	0	-	-	-	6.00	-	0	0
AG Wakely	5.0	1	12	0	-	-	-	2.40	-	0	0
JJ Cobb	39.0	6	94	0	-	-	-	2.41	-	0	0

Catches/Stumpings:
35 Murphy (inc 2st), 14 Rossington (inc 3st), 11 Kleinveldt, Levi, Wakely, 10 Duckett (inc 1st), 4 Keogh, Newton, 3 Barrett, Stone, White, Zaib, 2 Evans, Panesar, Prasanna, 1 Azharullah, Crook, Gleeson, Libby, Sanderson, Terry

Batting

	Mat	Inns	NO	Runs	HS	Ave	SR	100	50	4s	6s
RK Kleinveldt	6	5	2	285	128	95.00	160.11	1	1	28	14
BM Duckett	8	7	0	443	121	63.28	98.88	1	3	56	5
SP Crook	8	6	2	207	52*	51.75	107.25	0	1	14	3
RI Keogh	9	8	1	321	134	45.85	103.54	1	2	34	2
JJ Cobb	9	9	1	337	88	42.12	91.32	0	4	35	12
AM Rossington	9	9	2	287	97	41.00	100.34	0	2	29	6
S Prasanna	2	1	0	30	30	30.00	176.47	0	0	2	2
AG Wakely	9	8	0	235	71	29.37	84.83	0	2	19	7
RI Newton	7	6	0	144	65	24.00	105.88	0	1	8	6
GG White	9	6	3	69	40	23.00	113.11	0	0	4	2
RE Levi	2	2	0	27	20	13.50	100.00	0	0	3	1
Azharullah	9	3	1	15	8*	7.50	46.87	0	0	2	0
RJ Gleeson	8	4	2	7	4*	3.50	43.75	0	0	0	0
BW Sanderson	3	1	1	4	4*	-	80.00	0	0	0	0
D Murphy	1	-	-	-	-	-	-	-	-	-	-

Bowling

	Overs	Mdns	Runs	Wkts	BBI	Ave	Econ	SR	4w	5w
S Prasanna	8.0	0	31	1	1/31	31.00	3.87	48.0	0	0
GG White	66.0	3	315	18	6/37	17.50	4.77	22.0	0	1
RJ Gleeson	55.1	2	292	13	5/47	22.46	5.29	25.4	1	1
RK Kleinveldt	46.0	1	257	4	1/18	64.25	5.58	69.0	0	0
JJ Cobb	38.0	0	222	7	3/53	31.71	5.84	32.5	0	0
RI Keogh	39.0	0	230	0	-	-	5.89	-	0	0
Azharullah	70.0	0	440	12	5/43	36.66	6.28	35.0	0	1
SP Crook	37.3	0	258	2	1/68	129.00	6.88	112.5	0	0
BW Sanderson	14.0	0	132	1	1/94	132.00	9.42	84.0	0	0
AG Wakely	0.4	0	24	0	-	-	36.00	-	0	0

Catches/Stumpings:
6 Rossington (inc 2st), 4 Murphy (inc 1st), Wakely, 3 Cobb, Newton, White, 2 Azharullah, Keogh, Sanderson, 1 Crook, Gleeson

	Mat	Inns	NO	Runs	HS	Ave	SR	100	50	4s	6s
BM Duckett	14	14	3	477	84	43.36	141.54	0	3	64	7
AG Wakely	14	11	3	286	64	35.75	134.90	0	3	24	11
JJ Cobb	15	15	2	464	80	35.69	128.17	0	5	43	18
RE Levi	12	11	0	269	61	24.45	151.97	0	2	28	12
AM Rossington	15	15	1	317	85	22.64	140.26	0	3	38	11
SP Crook	15	13	3	163	43	16.30	113.98	0	0	18	4
GG White	15	7	4	46	22*	15.33	106.97	0	0	1	4
RI Keogh	9	6	1	73	28	14.60	125.86	0	0	8	0
RK Kleinveldt	10	7	2	53	23	10.60	123.25	0	0	4	2
RI Newton	1	1	0	7	7	7.00	140.00	0	0	1	0
RJ Gleeson	10	4	1	14	7*	4.66	93.33	0	0	2	0
S Prasanna	10	7	2	14	6*	2.80	60.86	0	0	0	1
MA Ashraf	7	2	1	1	1	1.00	25.00	0	0	0	0
Azharullah	12	2	2	6	6*	-	66.66	0	0	1	0
BW Sanderson	3	1	1	1	1*	-	100.00	0	0	0	0
OP Stone	3	-	-	-	-	-	-	-	-	-	-

Batting

	Overs	Mdns	Runs	Wkts	BBI	Ave	Econ	SR	4w	5w
RJ Gleeson	37.3	0	224	14	3/12	16.00	5.97	16.0	0	0
S Prasanna	37.0	0	257	12	3/24	21.41	6.94	18.5	0	0
MA Ashraf	22.0	0	165	7	3/17	23.57	7.50	18.8	0	0
GG White	42.0	0	318	13	4/20	24.46	7.57	19.3	1	0
BW Sanderson	11.0	0	86	8	3/31	10.75	7.81	8.2	0	0
RK Kleinveldt	37.5	0	296	15	3/14	19.73	7.82	15.1	0	0
JJ Cobb	23.1	0	196	6	2/21	32.66	8.46	23.1	0	0
Azharullah	39.3	0	335	8	2/27	41.87	8.48	29.6	0	0
SP Crook	30.0	0	266	9	3/28	29.55	8.86	20.0	0	0
OP Stone	8.5	0	90	3	1/11	30.00	10.18	17.6	0	0

Bowling

Catches/Stumpings:
12 Rossington (inc 5st), 10 Crook, 9 Keogh, 8 White, 7 Cobb, 6 Levi, 4 Wakely, 3 Duckett, Prasanna, 1 Azharullah, Gleeson, Kleinveldt

TEAM PROFILE

NOTTINGHAMSHIRE
COUNTY CRICKET CLUB ®

FORMED: 1841
HOME GROUND: Trent Bridge, Nottingham
ONE-DAY NAME: Notts Outlaws
CAPTAIN: Chris Read (Championship, RL50), Dan Christian (NWT20)
2016 RESULTS: CC1: 9/9; RL50: 6/9 North Group; NWT20: Semi-finalists
HONOURS: County Championship: (6) 1907, 1929, 1981, 1987, 2005, 2010; Gillette/NatWest/C&G/FP Trophy: 1987; Pro40/National League/CB40/YB40/RL50: 2013; Benson & Hedges Cup: 1989; Sunday League: 1991

THE LOWDOWN

Last summer was a tale of two formats for Nottinghamshire. They thundered to T20 Finals Day with a string of virtually flawless performances that produced eight wins in the group stages, only to be beaten by eventual champions Northants in the semi-finals. In the Championship they crashed to nine losses after a solitary victory in April, and will be playing in Division Two for the first time in a decade. The same batsmen who shone in the T20 Blast were part of a collective failure in four-day cricket; none of the regular batsmen averaged 40. Alex Hales, who was available for only two Championship matches, has a point to prove after losing his Test place, while Riki Wessels will hope he can replicate his outstanding short-format form in the first-class game. Australian fast bowler Peter Siddle is again sidelined by injury but compatriot James Pattinson will be a handy replacement. Left-arm Harry Gurney, outstanding across all formats last summer, will again be the trump card.

HEAD COACH: PETER MOORES

Notts have shuffled the pack following relegation last season. After 14 years as head coach, Mick Newell makes way for Moores, who has been working at Notts as a coaching consultant since 2015, but remains director of cricket. Moores had two spells as England head coach and won the Championship with Sussex in 2003 and Lancashire in 2011. Paul Franks will act as his deputy, with South African Ant Botha becoming assistant coach in place of Wayne Noon.

www.trentbridge.co.uk / tel: 0115 982 3000

	Mat	Inns	NO	Runs	HS	Ave	SR	100	50	4s	6s
WT Root	1	2	1	76	66*	76.00	70.37	0	1	11	1
AD Hales	2	3	0	143	73	47.66	48.97	0	1	23	1
SJ Mullaney	16	30	2	1009	165	36.03	59.00	3	3	149	10
BRM Taylor	13	24	2	759	114	34.50	51.21	2	3	103	10
SR Patel	16	28	0	957	124	34.17	59.92	2	6	120	15
SCJ Broad	4	6	0	191	55	31.83	88.42	0	1	29	1
JD Libby	11	21	0	627	144	29.85	41.25	1	3	64	0
CMW Read	12	21	4	492	101	28.94	49.39	1	3	62	5
MJ Lumb	16	29	0	817	108	28.17	48.74	1	3	107	2
MH Wessels	12	21	2	489	159*	25.73	52.41	1	3	67	1
DT Christian	3	5	1	96	31	24.00	44.85	0	0	12	1
GP Smith	7	12	0	257	54	21.41	39.72	0	1	36	0
BA Hutton	12	19	3	337	74	21.06	41.24	0	2	41	0
TJ Moores	4	7	0	123	41	17.57	41.27	0	0	21	0
Imran Tahir	7	12	4	127	25	15.87	53.36	0	0	12	4
L Wood	3	5	1	55	27	13.75	73.33	0	0	9	0
LJ Fletcher	6	10	2	88	32	11.00	36.06	0	0	11	0
JT Ball	11	17	1	153	33	9.56	69.86	0	0	20	5
JM Bird	5	8	0	51	23	6.37	50.00	0	0	8	0
M Carter	3	5	1	20	8	5.00	33.89	0	0	4	0
HF Gurney	13	21	9	56	16	4.66	51.37	0	0	5	2

Batting

	Overs	Mdns	Runs	Wkts	BBI	BBM	Ave	Econ	SR	5w	10w
JT Ball	343.0	64	1133	49	6/57	9/120	23.12	3.30	42.0	3	0
SCJ Broad	116.0	35	312	10	3/50	5/95	31.20	2.68	69.6	0	0
LJ Fletcher	183.1	48	469	15	4/25	7/95	31.26	2.56	73.2	0	0
HF Gurney	412.5	76	1304	41	6/61	9/136	31.80	3.15	60.4	2	0
SR Patel	351.5	64	1147	32	4/71	5/100	35.84	3.26	65.9	0	0
Imran Tahir	288.4	51	930	25	7/112	7/154	37.20	3.22	69.2	1	0
JM Bird	157.3	27	558	15	4/56	5/119	37.20	3.54	63.0	0	0
BA Hutton	268.3	47	1027	26	3/54	4/113	39.50	3.82	61.9	0	0
SJ Mullaney	139.5	36	430	10	3/54	3/94	43.00	3.07	83.9	0	0
L Wood	80.0	13	297	4	3/53	3/109	74.25	3.71	120.0	0	0
DT Christian	15.0	1	80	1	1/22	1/22	80.00	5.33	90.0	0	0
M Carter	76.0	8	316	3	1/46	1/46	105.33	4.15	152.0	0	0
WT Root	2.0	0	5	0	-	-	-	2.50	-	0	0
JD Libby	4.0	1	8	0	-	-	-	2.00	-	0	0

Bowling

Catches/Stumpings:
35 Read (inc 2st), 23 Wessels (inc 2st), 19 Mullaney, 12 Patel, 10 Taylor, 6 Lumb, 3 Ball, Broad, Fletcher, Hutton, Libby, Smith, Tahir, 2 Carter, Christian, Wood, 1 Bird, Gurney

Batting

	Mat	Inns	NO	Runs	HS	Ave	SR	100	50	4s	6s
MJ Lumb	8	7	0	482	184	68.85	107.82	3	0	54	11
MH Wessels	8	7	0	453	146	64.71	110.48	2	2	54	15
SJ Mullaney	8	6	3	189	89*	63.00	106.77	0	1	12	8
L Wood	2	2	1	56	52	56.00	160.00	0	1	5	2
DT Christian	8	7	0	328	94	46.85	117.14	0	4	23	14
LJ Fletcher	8	4	3	38	21*	38.00	82.60	0	0	2	1
JT Ball	5	3	2	34	27	34.00	161.90	0	0	2	3
CMW Read	4	4	0	119	59	29.75	125.26	0	1	8	6
SR Patel	8	7	1	176	55	29.33	104.76	0	1	13	3
GP Smith	8	7	0	171	73	24.42	81.42	0	1	10	3
BRM Taylor	8	7	1	136	44	22.66	84.47	0	0	16	2
SKW Wood	4	1	0	1	1	1.00	50.00	0	0	0	0
HF Gurney	8	2	2	3	2*	-	50.00	0	0	0	0
BA Hutton	1	-	-	-	-	-	-	-	-	-	-

Bowling

	Overs	Mdns	Runs	Wkts	BBI	Ave	Econ	SR	4w	5w
HF Gurney	64.3	0	376	19	5/51	19.78	5.82	20.3	0	1
L Wood	13.0	1	76	3	2/44	25.33	5.84	26.0	0	0
DT Christian	29.0	0	174	6	3/44	29.00	6.00	29.0	0	0
LJ Fletcher	59.4	1	371	6	2/52	61.83	6.21	59.6	0	0
SJ Mullaney	54.3	0	346	8	3/81	43.25	6.34	40.8	0	0
JT Ball	38.0	0	245	6	2/47	40.83	6.44	38.0	0	0
SR Patel	61.0	1	401	6	2/51	66.83	6.57	61.0	0	0
SKW Wood	7.0	0	48	1	1/38	48.00	6.85	42.0	0	0
BA Hutton	10.0	0	72	1	1/72	72.00	7.20	60.0	0	0

Catches/Stumpings:
7 Read, 5 Fletcher, 3 Ball, Christian, Mullaney, Patel, Taylor, Wessels, Wood, 2 Smith, 1 Gurney, Lumb

OUTLAWS

	Mat	Inns	NO	Runs	HS	Ave	SR	100	50	4s	6s
CMW Read	8	4	3	88	35*	88.00	179.59	0	0	10	2
MH Wessels	13	12	2	420	80*	42.00	139.53	0	3	43	15
DT Christian	13	11	3	327	56	40.87	159.51	0	3	17	23
AD Russell	3	3	0	95	41	31.66	186.27	0	0	5	8
GP Smith	12	11	2	264	52*	29.33	125.11	0	2	27	6
MJ Lumb	13	12	1	269	69*	24.45	141.57	0	2	34	10
SR Patel	13	9	1	143	58	17.87	106.71	0	1	9	3
SKW Wood	5	3	1	26	17	13.00	108.33	0	0	2	1
SCJ Broad	2	1	0	11	11	11.00	100.00	0	0	1	0
SJ Mullaney	13	7	1	51	16	8.50	141.66	0	0	3	3
HF Gurney	12	2	1	5	5*	5.00	100.00	0	0	1	0
BRM Taylor	9	5	2	14	5	4.66	53.84	0	0	0	0
JT Ball	11	4	2	4	2*	2.00	44.44	0	0	0	0
AD Hales	2	2	0	4	4	2.00	50.00	0	0	1	0
L Wood	1	1	0	0	0	0.00	0.00	0	0	0	0
LJ Fletcher	5	3	3	6	3*	-	75.00	0	0	0	0
BA Hutton	1	1	0	4	4*	-	133.33	0	0	0	0
Imran Tahir	7	-	-	-	-	-	-	-	-	-	-

Batting

	Overs	Mdns	Runs	Wkts	BBI	Ave	Econ	SR	4w	5w
SR Patel	48.0	0	312	16	4/20	19.50	6.50	18.0	1	0
AD Russell	12.0	0	82	7	3/20	11.71	6.83	10.2	0	0
Imran Tahir	23.0	0	160	6	3/13	26.66	6.95	23.0	0	0
SJ Mullaney	36.2	0	278	12	3/12	23.16	7.65	18.1	0	0
JT Ball	36.0	0	288	9	2/18	32.00	8.00	24.0	0	0
LJ Fletcher	18.4	0	153	2	1/30	76.50	8.19	56.0	0	0
HF Gurney	41.1	1	342	17	4/20	20.11	8.30	14.5	1	0
SCJ Broad	2.0	0	18	0	-	-	9.00	-	0	0
SKW Wood	2.0	0	19	1	1/9	19.00	9.50	12.0	0	0
L Wood	2.0	0	22	0	-	-	11.00	-	0	0
DT Christian	11.0	0	132	2	1/4	66.00	12.00	33.0	0	0
BA Hutton	2.0	0	24	1	1/24	24.00	12.00	12.0	0	0

Bowling

Catches/Stumpings:
11 Wessels, 9 Read (inc 3st), 6 Mullaney, 5 Ball, 3 Christian, Patel, Smith, Tahir, 2 Hales, 1 Russell

SOMERSET
CRICKET CLUB

FORMED: 1875
HOME GROUND: The Cooper Associates County Ground, Taunton
CAPTAIN: Tom Abell (Championship), Jim Allenby (RL50, NWT20)
2016 RESULTS: CC1: Runners-up; RL50: Semi-finalists; NWT20: 9/9 South Group
HONOURS: Gillette/NatWest/C&G/FP Trophy: (3) 1979, 1983, 2001; Benson & Hedges Cup: (2) 1981, 1982; Sunday League: 1979; T20 Cup: 2005

THE LOWDOWN

It all ended with crushing disappointment when Somerset were denied their first Championship title by the last-gasp events at Lord's, yet these are rosy times at Taunton. The club announced an increase in profits last November and host their first men's international T20 match this summer. The squad has a mix of precocious talent and classy experience, from the Overton twins and spin revelation Jack Leach, to the evergreen trio of James Hildreth, Peter Trego and Marcus Trescothick. Tom Abell, 23, has become the youngest four-day captain in Somerset's history after taking over from the retired Chris Rogers, who returns as batting coach. South African Test opener Dean Elgar will be Rogers' replacement, and the arrival of Steven Davies from Surrey completes one of the most fearsome batting line-ups in the country. Somerset showed their 50-over pedigree by reaching the semi-finals of the Royal London One-Day Cup, but will want to an improved T20 campaign after finishing bottom of their group last year.

DIRECTOR OF CRICKET: MATTHEW MAYNARD

A dashing batsman for Glamorgan during a 20-year career, Maynard played four Tests and 14 ODIs for England. He made 54 centuries for the Welsh county, which is a Glamorgan record, and was a key figure when the club won the County Championship in 1997. Maynard was England's assistant coach during the 2005 Ashes and more recently he has coached Glamorgan, Titans and St Lucia Zouks. This will be his third season at Taunton.

Batting

	Mat	Inns	NO	Runs	HS	Ave	SR	100	50	4s	6s
JG Myburgh	3	5	1	234	110	58.50	75.00	1	2	38	3
ME Trescothick	16	27	3	1239	218	51.62	57.07	4	4	193	5
JC Hildreth	16	23	2	1012	166	48.19	64.78	4	2	131	2
PD Trego	16	24	2	1047	154*	47.59	70.74	2	6	127	12
CJL Rogers	16	25	2	1010	132	43.91	51.45	3	6	124	0
TD Groenewald	12	16	12	138	26*	34.50	49.11	0	0	14	4
L Gregory	12	16	4	329	73*	27.41	55.38	0	2	49	0
J Allenby	12	17	0	446	63	26.23	51.32	0	5	52	1
TB Abell	13	22	1	538	135	25.61	45.59	2	1	70	1
C Overton	13	19	2	435	138	25.58	70.38	1	0	56	12
DM Bess	2	3	0	75	41	25.00	53.57	0	0	8	1
J Overton	6	9	2	161	51	23.00	58.75	0	1	15	5
RC Davies	15	19	1	380	86	21.11	67.61	0	3	43	10
RE van der Merwe	7	10	1	180	102*	20.00	65.69	1	0	14	2
AWR Barrow	1	2	0	31	21	15.50	29.80	0	0	3	0
MJ Leach	15	16	4	121	27*	10.08	28.33	0	0	16	0
JH Davey	1	1	0	10	10	10.00	125.00	0	0	2	0

Bowling

	Overs	Mdns	Runs	Wkts	BBI	BBM	Ave	Econ	SR	5w	10w
DM Bess	59.5	20	136	13	6/28	8/59	10.46	2.27	27.6	2	0
MJ Leach	526.3	117	1422	65	6/42	9/115	21.87	2.70	48.6	5	0
J Overton	133.3	27	382	17	5/42	5/77	22.47	2.86	47.1	1	0
TD Groenewald	347.2	85	1005	37	5/90	7/187	27.16	2.89	56.3	2	0
RE van der Merwe	203.4	40	614	22	4/45	8/104	27.90	3.01	55.5	0	0
J Allenby	243.2	57	598	21	4/67	5/67	28.47	2.45	69.5	0	0
L Gregory	276.5	61	894	29	4/58	6/112	30.82	3.22	57.2	0	0
C Overton	380.5	83	1168	34	4/54	6/91	34.35	3.06	67.2	0	0
JH Davey	20.0	3	79	2	2/39	2/79	39.50	3.95	60.0	0	0
PD Trego	149.3	35	429	5	1/14	1/14	85.80	2.86	179.4	0	0
CJL Rogers	1.0	0	4	0	-	-	-	4.00	-	0	0
TB Abell	1.0	0	11	0	-	-	-	11.00	-	0	0
JG Myburgh	5.0	1	22	0	-	-	-	4.40	-	0	0

Catches/Stumpings:
33 Davies (inc 6st), Trescothick, 20 Allenby, 11 C Overton, 10 Abell, 9 Hildreth, 8 Rogers, 5 Leach, Trego, 4 Bess, 3 Gregory, van der Merwe, 2 Barrow, 1 Davey, Groenewald, J Overton

SOMERSET CRICKET CLUB

Batting

	Mat	Inns	NO	Runs	HS	Ave	SR	100	50	4s	6s
DPMD Jayawardene	5	5	1	240	117*	60.00	96.00	1	1	26	2
TB Abell	5	3	0	141	106	47.00	80.57	1	0	12	1
J Overton	2	2	1	47	40*	47.00	117.50	0	0	4	1
J Allenby	10	10	0	423	81	42.30	93.79	0	5	44	7
PD Trego	10	10	2	321	104	40.12	86.29	1	2	25	6
JG Myburgh	7	7	1	240	81	40.00	102.12	0	2	29	7
TD Groenewald	9	5	3	72	34*	36.00	116.12	0	0	3	3
AJ Hose	4	3	0	95	77	31.66	84.07	0	1	12	0
RC Davies	6	4	1	76	46	25.33	113.43	0	0	6	1
JC Hildreth	10	9	1	194	48	24.25	78.86	0	0	10	2
JH Davey	3	2	1	22	13*	22.00	73.33	0	0	2	0
MTC Waller	7	4	3	20	10*	20.00	54.05	0	0	0	0
L Gregory	9	8	0	152	69	19.00	80.85	0	1	9	0
RE van der Merwe	9	7	1	110	41	18.33	113.40	0	0	8	2
AWR Barrow	4	2	0	29	27	14.50	116.00	0	0	1	1
C Overton	9	7	2	72	37*	14.40	97.29	0	0	4	2
PA van Meekeren	1	1	1	2	2*	-	40.00	0	0	0	0

Bowling

	Overs	Mdns	Runs	Wkts	BBI	Ave	Econ	SR	4w	5w
JG Myburgh	1.0	0	4	0	-	-	4.00	-	0	0
J Allenby	33.0	2	149	1	1/22	149.00	4.51	198.0	0	0
JH Davey	21.0	0	105	3	2/28	35.00	5.00	42.0	0	0
PD Trego	48.0	2	246	8	3/33	30.75	5.12	36.0	0	0
RE van der Merwe	61.5	1	323	14	3/51	23.07	5.22	26.5	0	0
C Overton	72.0	2	391	8	3/60	48.87	5.43	54.0	0	0
L Gregory	66.0	1	376	17	4/23	22.11	5.69	23.2	1	0
TD Groenewald	61.2	2	366	15	3/30	24.40	5.96	24.5	0	0
MTC Waller	39.0	0	241	5	2/36	48.20	6.17	46.8	0	0
J Overton	15.0	1	101	4	2/47	25.25	6.73	22.5	0	0
PA van Meekeren	3.0	0	21	0	-	-	7.00	-	0	0

Catches/Stumpings:
9 Davies (inc 1st), 7 van der Merwe, 6 Waller, 3 Allenby, Gregory, Groenewald, Hose, Trego, 2 Abell, Barrow, Davey, Hildreth, Jayawardene, Myburgh, C Overton, J Overton

www.somersetcountycc.co.uk / tel: 0845 337 1875

SOMERSET
CRICKET CLUB

Batting

	Mat	Inns	NO	Runs	HS	Ave	SR	100	50	4s	6s
RE van der Merwe	12	10	5	190	59	38.00	155.73	0	1	14	10
CH Gayle	5	5	0	177	52	35.40	166.98	0	1	17	13
J Allenby	13	13	1	328	91	27.33	117.14	0	2	36	6
DPMD Jayawardene	10	10	1	239	51	26.55	131.31	0	1	28	6
L Gregory	11	11	3	196	37*	24.50	128.10	0	0	17	3
JG Myburgh	10	10	1	218	86*	24.22	139.74	0	1	21	8
PD Trego	13	13	0	257	63	19.76	158.64	0	2	32	10
JC Hildreth	4	4	1	59	39	19.66	128.26	0	0	7	1
JH Davey	4	3	1	31	23*	15.50	124.00	0	0	4	0
MTC Waller	12	5	3	28	11*	14.00	73.68	0	0	2	0
MA Leask	4	4	1	33	12	11.00	137.50	0	0	2	2
TD Rouse	1	1	0	9	9	9.00	90.00	0	0	1	0
Yasir Arafat	5	2	1	8	8*	8.00	133.33	0	0	1	0
J Overton	10	5	0	38	14	7.60	135.71	0	0	2	2
TB Abell	1	1	0	7	7	7.00	70.00	0	0	1	0
AJ Hose	1	1	0	4	4	4.00	100.00	0	0	0	0
RC Davies	12	6	0	14	5	2.33	82.35	0	0	2	0
TD Groenewald	5	1	0	2	2	2.00	50.00	0	0	0	0
PA van Meekeren	2	2	0	2	1	1.00	50.00	0	0	0	0
DM Bess	1	1	0	1	1	1.00	50.00	0	0	0	0
ORT Sale	1	1	0	1	1	1.00	33.33	0	0	0	0
AWR Barrow	1	1	1	17	17*	-	89.47	0	0	1	0
BGF Green	1	1	1	12	12*	-	92.30	0	0	1	0
C Overton	4	2	2	5	3*	-	83.33	0	0	0	0

Bowling

	Overs	Mdns	Runs	Wkts	BBI	Ave	Econ	SR	4w	5w
JH Davey	14.0	0	103	6	3/20	17.16	7.35	14.0	0	0
RE van der Merwe	38.0	0	282	6	3/16	47.00	7.42	38.0	0	0
PD Trego	5.0	0	38	2	1/8	19.00	7.60	15.0	0	0
DM Bess	4.0	0	31	1	1/31	31.00	7.75	24.0	0	0
MTC Waller	36.3	0	290	12	4/33	24.16	7.94	18.2	1	0
L Gregory	38.2	0	328	9	2/25	36.44	8.55	25.5	0	0
J Overton	34.3	0	321	14	4/22	22.92	9.30	14.7	1	0
J Allenby	13.0	0	122	0	-	-	9.38	-	0	0
C Overton	13.0	0	133	2	1/30	66.50	10.23	39.0	0	0
TD Groenewald	13.0	0	137	2	1/38	68.50	10.53	39.0	0	0
PA van Meekeren	6.0	0	64	1	1/45	64.00	10.66	36.0	0	0
Yasir Arafat	18.5	0	205	3	1/35	68.33	10.88	37.6	0	0

Catches/Stumpings:
7 Davies (inc 3st), Waller, 6 van der Merwe, 4 Allenby, Gregory, J Overton,
3 C Overton, Trego, 2 Gayle, Groenewald, 1 Davey, Jayawardene, Leask, Rouse

SURREY
COUNTY CRICKET CLUB

FORMED: 1845
GROUND: The Kia Oval, London
CAPTAIN: Gareth Batty
2016 RESULTS: CC1: 5/9; RL50: Runners-up;
NWT20: 5/9 South Group
HONOURS: Championship: (19) 1890, 1891, 1892,
1894, 1895, 1899, 1914, 1950, 1952, 1953, 1954, 1955,
1956, 1957, 1958, 1971, 1999, 2000, 2002; Gillette/
NatWest/C&G/FP Trophy: 1982; Benson & Hedges
Cup: (3) 1974, 1997, 2001; Pro40/National League/
CB40/YB40/RL50: (2) 2003, 2011; Sunday League:
1996; T20 Cup: 2003

THE LOWDOWN

Surrey would seem to be on the cusp of good things. Only Yorkshire can rival the depth, youth and talent at the Kia Oval – from opener Rory Burns to wicketkeeper Ben Foakes, not forgetting the unstoppable rise of the Curran brothers. In his 40th year, Gareth Batty provides a steady hand at the helm, while the glue in the middle is the great Kumar Sangakkara, free of international distractions. And now the prolific Durham batting pair of Mark Stoneman and Scott Borthwick have been added to the fold, with Steven Davies joining Somerset. As always, the question for Surrey is whether they will add up to the considerable sum of their parts. Consistency eluded them in the Championship last year, and an exhilarating cup run took them to a Lord's final against Warwickshire, where they "fell off a cliff", in the captain's words. Australian opener Aaron Finch returns this summer to form a potent T20 pairing with Jason Roy. They are contenders across all formats.

HEAD COACH: MICHAEL DI VENUTO

Di Venuto took over from Graham Ford when the latter left to become head coach of Sri Lanka ahead of last season. The Australian has strong coaching pedigree, having been his national team's batting coach for three years and acted as temporary head coach when Darren Lehmann was ill. He has plenty of experience in county cricket as a batsman for Sussex, Derbyshire and Durham during a decorated playing career which included nine ODIs.

COUNTY CHAMPIONSHIP AVERAGES 2016

	Mat	Inns	NO	Runs	HS	Ave	SR	100	50	4s	6s
KC Sangakkara	12	22	1	1039	171	49.47	66.94	1	7	142	9
AJ Finch	4	6	0	292	110	48.66	90.68	1	2	39	5
BT Foakes	15	24	6	759	141*	42.16	44.56	1	3	90	2
RJ Burns	16	30	2	1144	122	40.85	49.71	2	7	160	2
SM Curran	9	14	2	472	96	39.33	60.20	0	5	66	6
JJ Roy	11	19	0	745	120	39.21	72.96	2	3	115	0
SM Davies	15	26	2	923	117	38.45	57.68	1	5	124	3
A Harinath	11	21	1	707	137	35.35	47.22	1	4	97	1
DP Sibley	7	13	2	377	99	34.27	35.06	0	3	46	0
ZS Ansari	10	17	1	439	53	27.43	37.45	0	2	51	3
GJ Batty	16	25	4	478	110*	22.76	55.32	1	0	61	5
TK Curran	15	26	1	427	54	17.08	48.74	0	3	61	0
MW Pillans	4	6	1	73	34*	14.60	57.48	0	0	11	0
SC Meaker	11	15	6	126	41	14.00	30.36	0	0	15	1
MP Dunn	2	3	2	13	6*	13.00	29.54	0	0	2	0
R Rampaul	5	7	4	33	13*	11.00	32.35	0	0	5	1
JE Burke	3	5	0	38	31	7.60	30.40	0	0	6	0
GC Wilson	2	4	0	27	12	6.75	29.34	0	0	5	0
MHA Footitt	8	11	3	49	16	6.12	61.25	0	0	5	2

Batting

	Overs	Mdns	Runs	Wkts	BBI	BBM	Ave	Econ	SR	5w	10w
R Rampaul	128.5	13	510	21	5/85	8/150	24.28	3.95	36.8	2	0
MHA Footitt	248.3	44	913	34	7/62	8/118	26.85	3.67	43.8	3	0
SM Curran	215.0	49	752	27	7/58	7/113	27.85	3.49	47.7	2	0
SC Meaker	298.5	42	1145	37	4/40	7/118	30.94	3.83	48.4	0	0
GJ Batty	434.1	93	1280	41	7/32	10/115	31.21	2.94	63.5	2	1
ZS Ansari	236.4	39	691	22	6/36	7/79	31.40	2.91	64.5	1	0
TK Curran	445.4	87	1494	33	4/58	7/156	45.27	3.35	81.0	0	0
JE Burke	37.3	4	184	4	3/65	3/65	46.00	4.90	56.2	0	0
DP Sibley	36.0	6	133	2	2/103	2/117	66.50	3.69	108.0	0	0
MP Dunn	39.0	5	188	1	1/109	1/109	188.00	4.82	234.0	0	0
RJ Burns	3.0	1	7	0	-	-	-	2.33	-	0	0
AJ Finch	3.0	1	10	0	-	-	-	3.33	-	0	0
A Harinath	18.2	1	59	0	-	-	-	3.21	-	0	0
MW Pillans	93.0	15	332	0	-	-	-	3.56	-	0	0

Bowling

Catches/Stumpings:
46 Foakes (inc 3st), 15 Burns, 10 Davies, Sangakkara, 9 Roy, 6 Sibley, 5 Ansari, T Curran, Harinath, Meaker, 4 Batty, 3 S Curran, Footitt, 2 Finch, Rampaul, 1 Pillans, Wilson

Batting

	Mat	Inns	NO	Runs	HS	Ave	SR	100	50	4s	6s
BT Foakes	9	8	1	330	90	47.14	101.53	0	3	28	5
KC Sangakkara	7	7	1	278	130*	46.33	90.84	1	1	23	3
RJ Burns	10	9	2	311	70*	44.42	84.97	0	4	24	4
JJ Roy	10	10	1	387	93*	43	102.65	0	2	52	5
SM Davies	11	11	1	396	104	39.6	91.45	1	2	39	5
MW Pillans	4	3	2	34	17*	34	125.92	0	0	0	2
SM Curran	9	6	0	178	57	29.66	94.17	0	1	19	2
ZS Ansari	6	6	1	129	62	25.8	78.18	0	1	5	0
AJ Finch	4	4	0	83	41	20.75	98.8	0	0	6	6
OJ Pope	1	1	0	20	20	20	86.95	0	0	1	0
TK Curran	10	8	2	94	39	15.66	80.34	0	0	5	0
JW Dernbach	7	2	1	15	8*	15	100	0	0	1	1
DP Sibley	5	3	0	42	27	14	66.66	0	0	2	0
GC Wilson	2	2	0	24	13	12	60	0	0	1	0
GJ Batty	10	6	2	33	13*	8.25	100	0	0	0	2
SC Meaker	11	5	4	5	2*	5	23.8	0	0	0	0
JE Burke	1	1	0	4	4	4	44.44	0	0	0	0
A Harinath	1	1	0	3	3	3	60	0	0	0	0
R Rampaul	2	1	1	2	2*	-	100	0	0	0	0

Batting

	Overs	Mdns	Runs	Wkts	BBI	Ave	Econ	SR	4w	5w
JW Dernbach	44.5	1	205	15	4/39	13.66	4.57	17.9	2	0
MHA Footitt	7.0	1	33	1	1/33	33.00	4.71	42.0	0	0
ZS Ansari	41.0	0	195	3	1/33	65.00	4.75	82.0	0	0
JE Burke	6.0	0	29	1	1/29	29.00	4.83	36.0	0	0
GJ Batty	62.4	1	311	14	5/41	22.21	4.96	26.8	0	1
SM Curran	52.2	0	273	5	1/34	54.60	5.21	62.8	0	0
TK Curran	62.0	2	332	12	3/26	27.66	5.35	31.0	0	0
R Rampaul	18.3	0	100	6	4/47	16.66	5.40	18.5	1	0
SC Meaker	66.0	1	413	17	3/47	24.29	6.25	23.2	0	0
DP Sibley	8.0	0	53	1	1/20	53.00	6.62	48.0	0	0
MW Pillans	16.0	0	109	2	1/41	54.50	6.81	48.0	0	0
AJ Finch	1.0	0	16	0	-	-	16.00	-	0	0

Catches/Stumpings:
14 Foakes (inc 1st), 8 Roy, 5 Sangakkara, 4 Burns, 3 S Curran, T Curran, Davies, Dernbach, Meaker, Sibley, 2 Burke, 1 Ansari, Batty, Finch, Rampaul, Wilson (inc 1st)

SURREY
COUNTY CRICKET CLUB

	Mat	Inns	NO	Runs	HS	Ave	SR	100	50	4s	6s
DP Sibley	8	6	1	247	74*	49.40	119.90	0	2	17	7
JJ Roy	12	12	1	495	120*	45.00	164.45	2	2	66	13
Azhar Mahmood	5	3	2	45	42	45.00	160.71	0	0	4	2
AJ Finch	6	6	0	259	79	43.16	144.69	0	3	20	10
KC Sangakkara	8	8	0	227	72	28.37	165.69	0	2	30	4
MW Pillans	3	2	1	24	13	24.00	88.88	0	0	2	1
ZS Ansari	10	9	4	104	34*	20.80	115.55	0	0	5	2
CH Morris	6	6	1	96	25	19.20	126.31	0	0	4	4
TK Curran	13	11	3	145	32	18.12	126.08	0	0	18	1
DJ Bravo	6	6	0	95	30	15.83	120.25	0	0	2	7
BT Foakes	10	7	3	58	22*	14.50	109.43	0	0	4	0
SM Curran	14	10	0	134	32	13.40	100.75	0	0	12	3
GJ Batty	14	6	5	12	5*	12.00	80.00	0	0	0	0
RJ Burns	13	11	1	105	22	10.50	109.37	0	0	8	2
SM Davies	8	8	0	76	23	9.50	118.75	0	0	10	1
GC Wilson	5	5	1	32	17	8.00	61.53	0	0	2	0
R Rampaul	5	1	0	6	6	6.00	100.00	0	0	1	0
JE Burke	2	2	1	1	1*	1.00	25.00	0	0	0	0
JW Dernbach	6	1	1	1	1*	-	100.00	0	0	0	0

Batting

	Overs	Mdns	Runs	Wkts	BBI	Ave	Econ	SR	4w	5w
ZS Ansari	30.0	0	219	8	2/12	27.37	7.30	22.5	0	0
TK Curran	41.5	0	325	8	3/21	40.62	7.76	31.3	0	0
DJ Bravo	19.5	0	156	5	2/3	31.20	7.86	23.8	0	0
SM Curran	39.0	0	308	11	2/23	28.00	7.89	21.2	0	0
JW Dernbach	24.0	1	192	9	3/32	21.33	8.00	16.0	0	0
GJ Batty	33.1	0	270	6	2/25	45.00	8.14	33.1	0	0
CH Morris	22.0	0	180	5	2/21	36.00	8.18	26.4	0	0
R Rampaul	15.0	0	124	7	3/21	17.71	8.26	12.8	0	0
MW Pillans	8.2	0	71	1	1/21	71.00	8.52	50.0	0	0
JE Burke	3.0	0	26	1	1/8	26.00	8.66	18.0	0	0
Azhar Mahmood	15.4	0	139	7	4/38	19.85	8.87	13.4	1	0
DP Sibley	6.0	0	57	3	2/33	19.00	9.50	12.0	0	0

Bowling

Catches/Stumpings:
11 Foakes (inc 2st), 8 Roy, 5 Bravo, T Curran, 3 Burns, S Curran, Finch, Wilson (inc 1st), 2 Burke, Mahmood, Morris, 1 Ansari, Batty, Davies, Pillans, Sangakkara, Sibley

TEAM PROFILE

FORMED: 1839
HOME GROUND: The 1st Central County Ground, Hove
ONE-DAY NAME: Sussex Sharks
CAPTAIN: Luke Wright
2016 RESULTS: CC2: 4/9; RL50: 9/9 South Group; NWT20: 6/9 South Group
HONOURS: Championship: (3) 2003, 2006, 2007; Gillette/NatWest/C&G/FP Trophy: (5) 1963, 1964, 1978, 1986, 2006; Pro40/National League/CB40/YB40/RL50: (2) 2008, 2009; Sunday League: 1982; T20 Cup: 2009

THE LOWDOWN

Last year was tough for Sussex. If their Championship and T20 campaigns were marked by mediocrity, their 50-over form was more clear-cut, Sussex finishing bottom of their group. Injury and loss of form led to an unsettled team: 24 players were used in four-day cricket, 22 in the Royal London One-Day Cup. A more credible bid for Championship promotion may hinge on better support for the brilliant Australian seamer Steve Magoffin, whose 62 wickets were 39 more than any other bowler managed. Vernon Philander has been signed for the first half of the campaign, and 22-year-old Barbadian fast bowler Jofra Archer is available on a UK passport after impressing at the end of last season. The Kolpak captures of allrounders David Wiese and Stiaan van Zyl add further depth, although leading batsman Ed Joyce has signed a central contract with Ireland and will make only fleeting appearances. Craig Cachopa (released) and Lewis Hatchett (retired) both depart, but batsman Laurie Evans has joined from Warwickshire. New Zealand batsman Ross Taylor returns for the NatWest T20 Blast.

HEAD COACH: MARK DAVIS

Davis was appointed coach following Mark Robinson's switch to England Women in November 2015. A South African allrounder who made his Sussex debut in 2001, Davis took 188 wickets and scored more than 2,000 runs for the county. He previously worked as the club's Second XI coach. Sussex sprung a surprise by appointing former England rugby union star Rob Andrew to replace outgoing chief executive Zac Toumazi, while Hove favourite Michael Yardy is the new batting coach.

Batting

	Mat	Inns	NO	Runs	HS	Ave	SR	100	50	4s	6s
CJ Jordan	5	7	2	323	131	64.60	59.37	1	3	39	3
EC Joyce	12	17	1	1026	250	64.12	55.73	3	6	131	5
CD Nash	15	24	1	1256	144	54.60	52.18	3	9	188	0
BC Brown	16	22	5	854	159*	50.23	69.82	3	4	109	4
LRPL Taylor	8	11	1	478	142*	47.80	61.36	1	4	58	2
LWP Wells	15	21	1	859	181	42.95	43.69	4	1	101	3
OE Robinson	11	14	4	389	81	38.90	63.56	0	3	64	0
MW Machan	7	9	0	249	66	27.66	74.10	0	1	24	3
LJ Wright	6	8	0	213	60	26.62	46.30	0	2	25	1
HZ Finch	7	9	2	175	66	25.00	39.32	0	2	25	0
JC Archer	6	8	0	195	73	24.37	55.71	0	1	28	1
D Wiese	6	9	2	153	70*	21.85	78.06	0	1	23	2
DR Briggs	11	13	3	197	49	19.70	51.16	0	0	33	0
WAT Beer	2	2	1	17	12*	17.00	31.48	0	0	2	0
A Shahzad	7	8	1	109	26	15.57	39.35	0	0	12	0
PD Salt	3	4	0	61	42	15.25	38.12	0	0	5	0
Craig Cachopa	3	5	0	68	34	13.60	45.03	0	0	6	0
GHS Garton	4	5	2	36	18*	12.00	37.50	0	0	3	0
FJ Hudson-Prentice	4	6	0	69	20	11.50	71.13	0	0	12	0
SJ Magoffin	16	16	4	122	23*	10.16	57.81	0	0	19	1
LJ Hatchett	2	2	0	20	17	10.00	28.98	0	0	3	0
SG Whittingham	6	4	2	20	8*	10.00	28.98	0	0	4	0
CAL Davis	2	3	0	14	12	4.66	25.00	0	0	1	0
TJ Haines	2	3	0	12	11	4.00	27.27	0	0	1	0

Bowling

	Overs	Mdns	Runs	Wkts	BBI	BBM	Ave	Econ	SR	5w	10w
SJ Magoffin	523.1	144	1249	62	5/32	10/70	20.14	2.38	50.6	5	1
D Wiese	152.2	34	456	19	4/18	5/50	24.00	2.99	48.1	0	0
LJ Hatchett	41.0	6	182	6	5/58	5/79	30.33	4.43	41.0	1	0
JC Archer	212.1	45	705	23	4/31	7/62	30.65	3.32	55.3	0	0
SG Whittingham	153.4	18	576	18	4/58	5/116	32.00	3.74	51.2	0	0
GHS Garton	88.1	9	352	10	3/93	3/75	35.20	3.99	52.9	0	0
CJ Jordan	201.0	38	678	17	4/36	7/187	39.88	3.37	70.9	0	0
A Shahzad	184.5	25	673	16	3/34	5/134	42.06	3.64	69.3	0	0
HZ Finch	11.0	1	44	1	1/30	1/30	44.00	4.00	66.0	0	0
DR Briggs	345.5	64	1061	23	5/93	5/108	46.13	3.06	90.2	2	0
OE Robinson	267.3	46	910	19	4/110	4/136	47.89	3.40	84.4	0	0
BC Brown	3.0	0	48	1	1/48	1/48	48.00	16.00	18.0	0	0
LWP Wells	153.0	13	558	9	3/105	3/105	62.00	3.64	102.0	0	0
WAT Beer	48.3	5	164	1	1/39	1/85	164.00	3.38	291.0	0	0
MW Machan	1.0	0	3	0	-	-	-	3.00	-	0	0
TJ Haines	4.0	1	8	0	-	-	-	2.00	-	0	0
CD Nash	6.0	0	24	0	-	-	-	4.00	-	0	0

Catches/Stumpings:
40 Brown, 20 Nash, 7 Wiese, 6 Jordan, Machan, Taylor, Wells, 5 Briggs, Finch, 4 Archer, Magoffin, Robinson, 3 Cachopa, Joyce, 2 Davis, Beer, 1 Garton, Haines, Hatchett, Shahzad, Whittingham

SUSSEX
SHARKS

	Mat	Inns	NO	Runs	HS	Ave	SR	100	50	4s	6s
DR Briggs	6	5	4	51	23*	51.00	110.86	0	0	5	1
FJ Hudson-Prentice	1	1	0	48	48	48.00	88.88	0	0	3	0
D Wiese	1	1	0	41	41	41.00	132.25	0	0	6	1
HZ Finch	7	7	1	236	87*	39.33	66.29	0	2	24	1
LRPL Taylor	3	3	0	113	54	37.66	94.95	0	2	8	2
BC Brown	7	7	1	207	62	34.50	82.80	0	1	13	2
Craig Cachopa	1	1	0	32	32	32.00	71.11	0	0	6	0
EC Joyce	6	6	0	187	73	31.16	72.76	0	1	23	3
LJ Wright	8	8	0	249	65	31.12	96.51	0	2	24	5
PD Salt	5	5	0	127	81	25.40	85.23	0	1	16	2
JC Archer	3	3	0	46	35	23.00	83.63	0	0	3	2
CJ Jordan	7	7	0	154	55	22.00	94.47	0	1	13	4
CD Nash	7	7	1	107	69*	17.83	72.29	0	1	7	3
A Shahzad	8	7	1	62	39	10.33	65.95	0	0	2	1
WAT Beer	7	6	1	40	33*	8.00	67.79	0	0	2	0
GHS Garton	5	3	1	6	4	3.00	66.66	0	0	1	0
LWP Wells	1	1	0	3	3	3.00	27.27	0	0	0	0
MW Machan	1	1	0	2	2	2.00	66.66	0	0	0	0
SJ Magoffin	1	1	0	1	1	1.00	20.00	0	0	0	0
CAL Davis	1	1	0	0	0	0.00	0.00	0	0	0	0
OE Robinson	1	1	1	22	22*	-	84.61	0	0	2	0
A Sakande	1	-	-	-	-	-	-	-	-	-	-

Batting

	Overs	Mdns	Runs	Wkts	BBI	Ave	Econ	SR	4w	5w
MW Machan	2.0	0	9	0	-	-	4.50	-	0	0
JC Archer	29.1	3	136	7	5/42	19.42	4.66	25.0	0	1
DR Briggs	48.0	0	235	6	2/45	39.16	4.89	48.0	0	0
LWP Wells	2.0	0	10	0	-	-	5.00	-	0	0
WAT Beer	58.0	1	296	7	2/34	42.28	5.10	49.7	0	0
CJ Jordan	58.4	3	308	13	5/28	23.69	5.25	27.0	0	1
SJ Magoffin	8.0	0	43	1	1/43	43.00	5.37	48.0	0	0
OE Robinson	6.0	0	34	1	1/34	34.00	5.66	36.0	0	0
A Shahzad	62.0	2	359	6	2/34	59.83	5.79	62.0	0	0
A Sakande	7.5	0	46	1	1/46	46.00	5.87	47.0	0	0
GHS Garton	42.0	0	269	10	3/40	26.90	6.40	25.2	0	0
CD Nash	9.0	0	58	0	-	-	6.44	-	0	0
D Wiese	6.0	0	40	0	-	-	6.66	-	0	0
CAL Davis	3.0	0	25	1	1/25	25.00	8.33	18.0	0	0
HZ Finch	1.4	0	22	0	-	-	13.20	-	0	0

Bowling

Catches/Stumpings:
10 Brown (inc 1st), 5 Jordan, 3 Briggs, Garton, Joyce, 2 Finch, Wright, 1 Cachopa, Salt

SUSSEX
SHARKS

	Mat	Inns	NO	Runs	HS	Ave	SR	100	50	4s	6s
LRPL Taylor	10	10	3	394	93*	56.28	133.10	0	3	30	17
MW Machan	11	10	2	247	41*	30.87	149.69	0	0	15	13
LJ Wright	12	11	1	285	83	28.50	131.94	0	2	27	10
CD Nash	13	12	1	308	112*	28.00	133.91	1	0	34	10
CJ Jordan	10	7	3	110	45*	27.50	135.80	0	0	7	5
BC Brown	6	4	0	85	43	21.25	130.76	0	0	6	3
JC Archer	4	3	2	21	12*	21.00	161.53	0	0	3	0
Craig Cachopa	9	6	1	95	45	19.00	126.66	0	0	10	2
PD Salt	10	9	1	151	33	18.87	123.77	0	0	15	3
DR Briggs	10	2	0	24	13	12.00	160.00	0	0	4	0
WAT Beer	12	5	2	29	18	9.66	116.00	0	0	3	0
HZ Finch	3	2	1	2	2	2.00	50.00	0	0	0	0
KMDN Kulasekara	3	1	0	0	0	0.00	0.00	0	0	0	0
A Shahzad	9	1	0	0	0	0.00	0.00	0	0	0	0
D Wiese	4	2	2	26	16*	-	216.66	0	0	3	1
TS Mills	12	2	2	8	7*	-	160.00	0	0	0	1
GHS Garton	2	1	1	2	2*	-	100.00	0	0	0	0
Mustafizur Rahman	2	-	-	-	-	-	-	-	-	-	-
OE Robinson	1	-	-	-	-	-	-	-	-	-	-

	Overs	Mdns	Runs	Wkts	BBI	Ave	Econ	SR	4w	5w
CJ Jordan	30.2	0	220	12	3/18	18.33	7.25	15.1	0	0
Mustafizur Rahman	7.2	0	54	4	4/23	13.50	7.36	11.0	1	0
KMDN Kulasekara	10.4	0	80	7	4/28	11.42	7.50	9.1	1	0
GHS Garton	6.0	0	45	4	4/16	11.25	7.50	9.0	1	0
WAT Beer	35.3	0	271	9	2/23	30.11	7.63	23.6	0	0
TS Mills	38.4	1	296	15	3/15	19.73	7.65	15.4	0	0
A Shahzad	25.0	0	203	11	3/26	18.45	8.12	13.6	0	0
CD Nash	12.0	0	99	1	1/16	99.00	8.25	72.0	0	0
JC Archer	15.0	0	139	5	2/39	27.80	9.26	18.0	0	0
DR Briggs	25.0	0	242	7	3/24	34.57	9.68	21.4	1	0
D Wiese	10.0	0	103	6	4/38	17.16	10.30	10.0	1	0
OE Robinson	1.0	0	17	0	-	-	17.00	-	0	0

Catches/Stumpings:
12 Machan, 6 Taylor, Wright, 5 Jordan, 4 Cachopa, Kulasekara, 3 Beer, Mills, Nash, Salt, 2 Briggs, Mustafizur, Wiese, 1 Archer, Brown, Garton, Finch

TEAM PROFILE

FORMED: 1882
HOME GROUND: Edgbaston Stadium,
Birmingham
T20 BLAST NAME: Birmingham Bears
CAPTAIN: Ian Bell
2015 RESULTS: CC1: 6/9; RL50: Champions;
NWT20: 6/9 North Group
HONOURS: Championship: (7) 1911, 1951, 1972,
1994, 1995, 2004, 2012; Gillette/NatWest/C&G/FP
Trophy: (5) 1966, 1968, 1989, 1993, 1995; Benson
& Hedges Cup: (2) 1994, 2002; Pro40/National
League/CB40/YB40/RL50: (2) 2010, 2016; Sunday
League: (3) 1980, 1994, 1997; T20 Cup: 2014

THE LOWDOWN

A wobbly 2016 was ultimately triumphant after two victories at the end of the season. First
Warwickshire dispatched Surrey at Lord's to win the 50-over trophy, then beat Lancashire
in the Championship to preserve their status in Division One. Their brush with relegation
could be partially blamed on their much-touted top order, none of whom made it to 1,000
runs. Former captain Varun Chopra has returned to Essex, while his successor Ian Bell,
free of England duty, made just one Championship hundred, although his T20 form was
excellent. It was a similar story for England prospect Sam Hain, who averaged 23 in the
Championship but was leading run-scorer in the Royal London Cup. By contrast Jonathan
Trott (2,005 runs) and Jeetan Patel (102 wickets) were masters of all formats. Spearheaded
by the much-underrated allrounder Keith Barker, it was business as usual for the seamers,
and Warwickshire have since added the extra pace of Olly Stone, signed from Northants.

SPORT DIRECTOR: ASHLEY GILES

After leaving Lancashire to be closer to his family, Giles returns for a
second spell in charge of the club where he spent his entire 14-year
playing career. The former England off-spinner takes over from Dougie
Brown, who had succeeded Giles in 2013. As director of cricket, Giles
helped Warwickshire lift the CB40 in 2010 and the Championship title
in 2012 before a brief spell as England's limited-overs coach. Former
captain Jim Troughton will work under Giles as first-team coach.

	Mat	Inns	NO	Runs	HS	Ave	SR	100	50	4s	6s
IJL Trott	16	24	2	975	219*	44.31	56.06	2	6	132	1
CR Woakes	5	7	1	252	121	42.00	48.64	1	1	30	1
TR Ambrose	14	19	4	599	104	39.93	44.33	1	6	68	1
V Chopra	14	22	2	694	107	34.70	54.13	1	5	94	1
IR Bell	15	22	2	678	174	33.90	43.18	1	3	83	0
KHD Barker	16	22	3	608	113	32.00	66.96	1	4	76	3
MR Adair	1	1	0	32	32	32.00	57.14	0	0	3	1
IJ Westwood	10	16	1	367	127	24.46	41.56	1	1	51	0
AJ Mellor	3	5	1	93	27	23.25	48.18	0	0	13	0
SR Hain	15	21	1	455	135	22.75	51.06	1	1	57	1
R Clarke	15	20	3	384	74	22.58	49.54	0	4	49	5
JS Patel	16	21	5	298	31	18.62	67.42	0	0	35	5
ARI Umeed	6	10	1	165	101	18.33	42.52	1	0	18	0
CJC Wright	9	15	2	207	45	15.92	47.26	0	0	28	2
OJ Hannon-Dalby	7	9	3	39	30	6.50	33.33	0	0	5	1
LJ Evans	2	4	0	26	9	6.50	20.47	0	0	4	0
WB Rankin	7	6	1	22	16*	4.40	52.38	0	0	1	1
JE Poysden	5	4	2	8	7*	4.00	32.00	0	0	1	0
M Lamb	1	2	0	2	1	1.00	15.38	0	0	0	0

Batting

	Overs	Mdns	Runs	Wkts	BBI	BBM	Ave	Econ	SR	5w	10w
TR Ambrose	1.5	1	0	1	1/0	1/0	0.00	0.00	11.0	0	0
CR Woakes	128.1	30	409	23	9/36	9/36	17.78	3.19	33.4	1	0
JE Poysden	80.4	7	323	15	5/53	8/133	21.53	4.00	32.2	1	0
KHD Barker	522.1	153	1365	59	5/53	7/86	23.13	2.61	53.1	1	0
JS Patel	616.4	168	1658	69	5/32	10/123	24.02	2.68	53.6	4	1
CJC Wright	265.2	51	776	30	4/41	5/125	25.86	2.92	53.0	0	0
R Clarke	415.3	99	1179	42	4/20	5/44	28.07	2.83	59.3	0	0
WB Rankin	169.2	23	514	18	3/33	5/76	28.55	3.03	56.4	0	0
OJ Hannon-Dalby	153.0	26	524	8	2/39	2/41	65.50	3.42	114.7	0	0
IJL Trott	58.0	7	203	3	2/26	2/26	67.66	3.50	116.0	0	0
V Chopra	2.0	0	12	0	-	-	-	6.00	-	0	0
IJ Westwood	5.0	0	16	0	-	-	-	3.20	-	0	0
IR Bell	8.0	2	17	0	-	-	-	2.12	-	0	0
SR Hain	6.0	0	24	0	-	-	-	4.00	-	0	0
MR Adair	15.0	4	47	0	-	-	-	3.13	-	0	0

Bowling

Catches/Stumpings:
57 Ambrose (inc 4st), 30 Clarke, 19 Hain, 18 Chopra, 8 Patel, 7 Barker, Bell, 4 Mellor, Umeed, 3 Evans, Trott, Westwood, 2 Rankin, Wright, 1 Woakes

Batting

	Mat	Inns	NO	Runs	HS	Ave	SR	100	50	4s	6s
IJL Trott	8	7	1	515	118	85.83	86.12	3	2	50	1
LJ Evans	10	8	4	257	70*	64.25	116.81	0	1	21	9
SR Hain	10	10	1	540	107	60.00	84.24	2	3	54	5
TR Ambrose	10	8	2	357	86	59.50	98.89	0	4	32	6
IR Bell	10	8	2	310	94*	51.66	94.22	0	3	23	4
WTS Porterfield	7	7	1	269	92	44.83	71.73	0	2	36	5
RA Jones	1	1	0	26	26	26.00	200.00	0	0	5	0
R Clarke	10	6	2	83	27	20.75	138.33	0	0	8	1
A Javid	7	4	1	33	20	11.00	103.12	0	0	1	0
CR Woakes	2	1	0	4	4	4.00	66.66	0	0	0	0
WB Rankin	2	1	0	2	2	2.00	40.00	0	0	0	0
JS Patel	10	4	1	5	5*	1.66	55.55	0	0	0	0
OJ Hannon-Dalby	8	2	2	6	5*	-	100.00	0	0	0	0
JE Poysden	3	1	1	2	2*	-	100.00	0	0	0	0
RO Gordon	4	1	1	1	1*	-	100.00	0	0	0	0
KHD Barker	1	-	-	-	-	-	-	-	-	-	-
CJC Wright	7	-	-	-	-	-	-	-	-	-	-

Bowling

	Overs	Mdns	Runs	Wkts	BBI	Ave	Econ	SR	4w	5w
KHD Barker	10.0	4	29	1	1/29	29.00	2.90	60.0	0	0
CR Woakes	16.1	2	71	2	2/24	35.50	4.39	48.5	0	0
JS Patel	92.1	3	447	22	5/43	20.31	4.84	25.1	0	1
R Clarke	83.0	8	404	13	5/26	31.07	4.86	38.3	0	1
A Javid	42.0	0	212	10	4/42	21.20	5.04	25.2	1	0
WB Rankin	20.0	1	103	6	4/66	17.16	5.15	20.0	1	0
RO Gordon	28.4	0	151	6	2/49	25.16	5.26	28.6	0	0
CJC Wright	52.0	2	276	8	2/61	34.50	5.30	39.0	0	0
JE Poysden	29.0	0	154	4	3/46	38.50	5.31	43.5	0	0
OJ Hannon-Dalby	67.0	3	375	9	2/27	41.66	5.59	44.6	0	0
IJL Trott	6.0	0	51	0	-	-	8.50	-	0	0
RA Jones	8.0	0	85	1	1/85	85.00	10.62	48.0	0	0
LJ Evans	1.0	0	12	0	-	-	12.00	-	0	0

Catches/Stumpings:
8 Ambrose (inc 3st), 7 Evans, 5 Patel, 4 Bell, Clarke, Hain, Porterfield, 3 Gordon, Trott, 2 Poysden, 1 Barker, Hannon-Dalby

Batting

	Mat	Inns	NO	Runs	HS	Ave	SR	100	50	4s	6s
IR Bell	14	13	1	489	80	40.75	130.74	0	5	46	16
SR Hain	13	12	1	371	92*	33.72	120.84	0	2	45	5
WTS Porterfield	10	9	2	190	61*	27.14	109.82	0	1	17	3
L Ronchi	8	5	0	112	53	22.40	149.33	0	1	10	6
MS Wade	6	6	1	108	74	21.60	158.82	0	1	7	4
LJ Evans	14	11	1	179	52*	17.90	111.87	0	1	20	4
CR Woakes	4	3	1	31	16*	15.50	119.23	0	0	1	1
A Javid	13	7	2	66	34*	13.20	110.00	0	0	5	0
JE Poysden	9	5	4	12	9*	12.00	150.00	0	0	1	0
R Clarke	12	8	2	67	24*	11.16	97.10	0	0	7	1
OJ Hannon-Dalby	14	5	3	15	5*	7.50	55.55	0	0	0	0
KHD Barker	3	2	1	5	4*	5.00	62.50	0	0	0	0
AD Thomason	5	3	0	12	6	4.00	70.58	0	0	0	0
MR Adair	6	3	0	11	7	3.66	78.57	0	0	1	0
RO Gordon	6	4	1	10	7	3.33	83.33	0	0	0	0
JS Patel	14	7	2	14	7	2.80	53.84	0	0	0	0
V Chopra	1	1	1	97	97*	-	167.24	0	1	8	5
WB Rankin	1	-	-	-	-	-	-	-	-	-	-
CJC Wright	1	-	-	-	-	-	-	-	-	-	-

Bowling

	Overs	Mdns	Runs	Wkts	BBI	Ave	Econ	SR	4w	5w
R Clarke	41.3	1	268	15	3/22	17.86	6.45	16.6	0	0
MR Adair	13.0	0	86	5	2/18	17.20	6.61	15.6	0	0
CR Woakes	13.0	0	89	4	3/25	22.25	6.84	19.5	0	0
JS Patel	44.3	0	310	11	3/23	28.18	6.96	24.2	0	0
CJC Wright	4.0	0	32	2	2/32	16.00	8.00	12.0	0	0
A Javid	19.0	0	156	4	1/12	39.00	8.21	28.5	0	0
OJ Hannon-Dalby	42.4	0	352	12	2/29	29.33	8.25	21.3	0	0
JE Poysden	16.0	0	133	3	2/21	44.33	8.31	32.0	0	0
KHD Barker	12.0	0	103	4	3/34	25.75	8.58	18.0	0	0
RO Gordon	22.0	0	197	6	2/21	32.83	8.95	22.0	0	0
AD Thomason	6.0	0	68	2	2/24	34.00	11.33	18.0	0	0
WB Rankin	3.0	0	35	1	1/35	35.00	11.66	18.0	0	0

Catches/Stumpings:
9 Hain, 7 Patel, 6 Bell, Clarke, 5 Evans, Ronchi, 4 Javid, 3 Porterfield, Poysden, 2 Barker, Wade (inc 1st), 1 Hannon-Dalby, Thomason, Wright

FORMED: 1865
HOME GROUND: County Ground, New Road, Worcester
ONE-DAY NAME: Worcestershire Rapids
CAPTAIN: Joe Leach
2016 RESULTS: CC2: 3/9; RL50: Quarter-finalists; NWT20: 8/9 North Group
HONOURS: Championship: (5) 1964, 1965, 1974, 1988, 1989; Gillette/NatWest/C&G/FP Trophy: 1994; Benson & Hedges Cup: 1991; Pro40/National League/CB40/YB40/RL50: 2007; Sunday League: (3) 1971, 1987, 1988

THE LOWDOWN

Worcestershire finished third in Division Two without ever looking like serious contenders for promotion. Daryl Mitchell, the new PCA chairman, was relieved of the captaincy in September and 26-year-old allrounder Joe Leach will lead the team in all formats following an outstanding season in which he did the 'mini-double' (583 runs and 65 wickets in the Championship), took 20 wickets in the T20 Blast and did some damage with the bat in the shorter formats. Leach carried a bowling attack which will be significantly enhanced if Australia's John Hastings is fully recovered from recent knee surgery. Consistency is the watchword for the batsmen, although in 20-year-old Joe Clarke, who made five Championship hundreds last summer, Worcestershire have one of the country's hottest talents. Kiwi spinner Mitchell Santner will hope to play a more substantial part in the T20 Blast after injury restricted him to one appearance in 2016.

DIRECTOR OF CRICKET: STEVE RHODES

Now in his 12th season in charge at New Road, Rhodes has become a Worcestershire institution. He joined the club as a player in 1985 after beginning his career at his home county Yorkshire. Rhodes played 11 Tests for England, earning a reputation as a skilful wicketkeeper and nuggety batsman. He assisted the England Lions over the 2015/16 winter and had a three-week spell with the senior side during England's tour of Bangladesh last autumn.

Batting

	Mat	Inns	NO	Runs	HS	Ave	SR	100	50	4s	6s
MM Ali	3	4	1	273	136*	91.00	72.41	1	2	43	5
JM Clarke	15	26	1	1206	194	48.24	61.12	5	4	164	2
MJ Henry	6	6	2	180	49*	45.00	75.94	0	0	22	5
J Leach	15	21	5	583	107*	36.43	71.88	1	4	74	3
OB Cox	15	23	2	757	75	36.04	65.94	0	6	108	10
TC Fell	8	16	1	530	85	35.33	55.84	0	4	83	1
DKH Mitchell	15	27	2	873	107*	34.92	51.81	2	5	103	0
BL D'Oliveira	14	25	1	763	202*	31.79	54.46	2	2	104	0
GH Rhodes	6	11	2	274	59	30.44	44.77	0	2	38	0
T Kohler-Cadmore	13	21	1	561	169	28.05	50.76	2	1	80	3
RA Whiteley	13	22	2	542	71	27.10	51.66	0	4	69	15
EG Barnard	14	20	4	430	73	26.87	53.15	0	2	55	0
JD Shantry	11	12	4	210	106	26.25	58.65	1	0	23	8
AN Kervezee	4	7	1	151	41	25.16	48.24	0	0	15	2
CAJ Morris	7	9	6	32	11	10.66	31.06	0	0	4	0
ML Cummins	3	4	1	29	25	9.66	69.04	0	0	4	1
KJ Abbott	2	3	0	18	10	6.00	56.25	0	0	2	0
MJ Santner	1	1	1	23	23*	-	65.71	0	0	3	0

Bowling

	Overs	Mdns	Runs	Wkts	BBI	BBM	Ave	Econ	SR	5w	10w
ML Cummins	96.2	12	377	15	7/84	12/166	25.13	3.91	38.5	2	1
MJ Henry	234.0	48	716	27	5/36	8/88	26.51	3.05	52.0	1	0
J Leach	495.4	74	1786	65	5/60	9/109	27.47	3.60	45.7	5	0
DKH Mitchell	30.5	6	92	3	2/5	2/11	30.66	2.98	61.6	0	0
EG Barnard	358.2	66	1351	31	4/62	4/93	43.58	3.77	69.3	0	0
BL D'Oliveira	259.1	30	761	16	4/80	4/158	47.56	2.93	97.1	0	0
CAJ Morris	144.1	26	563	11	2/35	3/64	51.18	3.90	78.6	0	0
JD Shantry	358.2	87	1039	18	4/89	4/171	57.72	2.89	119.4	0	0
GH Rhodes	64.5	5	263	3	2/83	2/83	87.66	4.05	129.6	0	0
AN Kervezee	33.0	9	89	1	1/12	1/24	89.00	2.69	198.0	0	0
MM Ali	42.0	5	161	1	1/28	1/80	161.00	3.83	252.0	0	0
KJ Abbott	75.0	17	249	1	1/93	1/93	249.00	3.32	450.0	0	0
TC Fell	2.2	1	10	0	-	-	-	4.28	-	0	0
JM Clarke	2.0	0	22	0	-	-	-	11.00	-	0	0

Catches/Stumpings:
34 Cox (inc 2st), 18 Kohler-Cadmore, 13 Mitchell, 12 Whiteley, 8 D'Oliveira, 6 Clarke, 5 Barnard, 4 Fell, Leach, Shantry, 2 Rhodes, 1 Henry, Kervezee, Morris

Batting

	Mat	Inns	NO	Runs	HS	Ave	SR	100	50	4s	6s
TC Fell	5	5	2	252	116*	84.00	95.09	1	2	32	0
MM Ali	1	1	0	81	81	81.00	106.57	0	1	10	1
AN Kervezee	5	5	2	138	77	46.00	104.54	0	1	14	3
DKH Mitchell	7	7	2	215	64	43.00	72.88	0	2	21	1
J Leach	8	6	0	162	63	27.00	100.62	0	1	18	5
T Kohler-Cadmore	8	8	0	209	119	26.12	91.26	1	0	26	3
RA Whiteley	8	5	0	121	61	24.20	93.79	0	1	11	4
EG Barnard	8	4	1	66	38	22.00	67.34	0	0	9	0
JM Clarke	6	5	0	102	44	20.40	75.00	0	0	9	1
OB Cox	8	5	0	84	31	16.80	74.33	0	0	8	1
BL D'Oliveira	7	5	1	58	21	14.50	59.79	0	0	2	0
GH Rhodes	5	2	1	5	5*	5.00	71.42	0	0	1	0
JD Shantry	6	4	1	12	8*	4.00	38.70	0	0	0	0
CJ Russell	2	1	0	2	2	2.00	40.00	0	0	0	0
CAJ Morris	2	2	2	6	6*	-	50.00	0	0	0	0
KJ Abbott	2	-	-	-	-	-	-	-	-	-	-

Bowling

	Overs	Mdns	Runs	Wkts	BBI	Ave	Econ	SR	4w	5w
JD Shantry	40.5	5	163	4	2/10	40.75	3.99	61.2	0	0
BL D'Oliveira	50.5	1	236	5	2/9	47.20	4.64	61.0	0	0
MM Ali	10.0	0	53	1	1/53	53.00	5.30	60.0	0	0
DKH Mitchell	34.2	0	185	4	1/15	46.25	5.38	51.5	0	0
KJ Abbott	20.0	3	112	4	3/56	28.00	5.60	30.0	0	0
J Leach	61.1	3	345	9	3/79	38.33	5.64	40.7	0	0
EG Barnard	54.0	2	307	9	3/45	34.11	5.68	36.0	0	0
GH Rhodes	28.0	1	162	5	2/34	32.40	5.78	33.6	0	0
CAJ Morris	14.0	0	84	3	2/30	28.00	6.00	28.0	0	0
AN Kervezee	3.0	0	19	0	-	-	6.33	-	0	0
CJ Russell	8.0	0	67	2	2/23	33.50	8.37	24.0	0	0

Catches/Stumpings:
8 Cox, 5 Barnard, Leach, 4 D'Oliveira, 3 Rhodes, 2 Clarke, Fell, Mitchell, 1 Abbott, Kohler-Cadmore, Russell, Whiteley

Batting

	Mat	Inns	NO	Runs	HS	Ave	SR	100	50	4s	6s
OB Cox	13	12	8	234	59*	58.50	156.00	0	1	28	6
BL D'Oliveira	13	13	3	353	62*	35.30	126.97	0	1	25	10
T Kohler-Cadmore	13	13	0	323	127	24.84	148.16	1	1	33	15
MM Ali	2	2	0	49	40	24.50	125.64	0	0	5	1
RA Whiteley	13	12	2	226	42*	22.60	141.25	0	0	12	15
DKH Mitchell	12	11	1	215	61	21.50	132.71	0	1	23	2
JM Clarke	12	12	1	227	69*	20.63	120.10	0	1	23	4
AN Kervezee	9	9	1	122	52*	15.25	107.96	0	1	11	0
J Leach	13	8	1	96	18	13.71	120.00	0	0	11	3
MJ Henry	11	4	1	39	35*	13.00	169.56	0	0	3	2
EG Barnard	10	5	3	23	9	11.50	121.05	0	0	1	1
GH Rhodes	4	3	0	16	8	5.33	100.00	0	0	2	0
JD Shantry	11	3	1	7	5	3.50	77.77	0	0	1	0
CAJ Morris	1	1	0	3	3	3.00	150.00	0	0	0	0
MJ Santner	1	1	0	1	1	1.00	33.33	0	0	0	0
KJ Abbott	3	1	1	0	0*	-	-	0	0	0	0
CJ Russell	2	-	-	-	-	-	-	-	-	-	-

Bowling

	Overs	Mdns	Runs	Wkts	BBI	Ave	Econ	SR	4w	5w
GH Rhodes	7.0	0	43	5	4/13	8.60	6.14	8.4	1	0
MJ Santner	4.0	0	29	2	2/29	14.50	7.25	12.0	0	0
DKH Mitchell	18.2	0	136	3	1/15	45.33	7.41	36.6	0	0
MM Ali	8.0	0	60	3	2/44	20.00	7.50	16.0	0	0
CAJ Morris	4.0	0	30	2	2/30	15.00	7.50	12.0	0	0
BL D'Oliveira	30.0	0	251	6	2/20	41.83	8.36	30.0	0	0
JD Shantry	34.0	0	291	4	1/22	72.75	8.55	51.0	0	0
EG Barnard	28.1	0	250	7	2/43	35.71	8.87	24.1	0	0
CJ Russell	6.0	0	54	1	1/33	54.00	9.00	36.0	0	0
J Leach	43.2	0	402	20	5/33	20.10	9.27	13.0	0	1
MJ Henry	33.3	0	325	7	3/15	46.42	9.70	28.7	0	0
KJ Abbott	7.5	0	109	1	1/52	109.00	13.91	47.0	0	0

Catches/Stumpings:
7 Kohler-Cadmore, 6 Cox, D'Oliveira, 4 Barnard, Henry, Kervezee, Mitchell, Whiteley, 3 Shantry, 2 Clarke, 1 Abbott, Ali, Rhodes

TEAM PROFILE

THE YORKSHIRE
COUNTY CRICKET CLUB

FORMED: 1863
HOME GROUND: Headingley Carnegie, Leeds
ONE-DAY NAME: Yorkshire Vikings
CAPTAIN: Gary Ballance
2016 RESULTS: CC1: 3/9; RL50: Semi-finalists;
NWT20: Semi-finalists
HONOURS: County Championship: (33) 1893,
1896, 1898, 1900, 1901, 1902, 1905, 1908, 1912,
1919, 1922, 1923, 1924, 1925, 1931, 1932, 1933,
1935, 1937, 1938, 1939, 1946, 1949, 1959, 1960,
1962, 1963, 1966, 1967, 1968, 2001, 2014, 2015
Gillette/NatWest/C&G/FP Trophy: (3) 1965,
1969, 2002; Benson & Hedges Cup: 1987; Sunday
League: 1983

THE LOWDOWN

Coming within 62 runs of a third successive Championship crown – not to mention two cup semi-finals – is not a bad year for most, but not good enough for Yorkshire, who go into the 2017 season with a new captain for the first time in eight years. Gary Ballance will lead in all formats, with the retired Andrew Gale replacing Jason Gillespie as head coach. Ballance inherits a squad with an abundance of talent. New overseas signing Peter Handscomb is relishing the challenge of the swinging Duke to help cement his place in Australia's Test side. In the bowling department the fitness of 39-year-old Ryan Sidebottom, entering his 21st and final season, and Jack Brooks, who took 60 Championship wickets in 2016, will be crucial. David Willey is recovering from a shoulder operation after a stop-start first season. Azeem Rafiq, brought in from the cold last summer, forms a potent spin partnership with Adil Rashid, which could be the key to a first limited-overs trophy in 15 years.

HEAD COACH: ANDREW GALE

After coaching one of the most successful County Championship teams in modern history, Jason Gillespie has returned to Australia to be with his family and Gale makes the immediate transition from captain to coach after ending a 14-year career – eight of them as skipper – which brought more than 8,000 first-class runs and 20 centuries. "I was planning on coming back for pre-season but once I was offered the job it just felt right," said Gale. "I don't think it works when people try to play and coach."

COUNTY CHAMPIONSHIP AVERAGES 2016

	Mat	Inns	NO	Runs	HS	Ave	SR	100	50	4s	6s
JM Bairstow	4	6	0	533	246	88.83	88.39	2	0	62	4
JE Root	2	3	0	240	213	80.00	87.91	1	0	25	1
JS Lehmann	5	8	1	384	116	54.85	66.09	1	2	51	0
TT Bresnan	11	19	4	722	142*	48.13	47.71	1	5	83	4
LE Plunkett	8	13	3	449	126	44.90	81.04	1	3	54	8
A Lyth	16	30	2	1133	202	40.46	56.84	4	3	142	13
AZ Lees	16	30	1	1165	132	40.17	50.02	3	7	136	6
GS Ballance	13	25	2	780	132	33.91	49.08	2	4	106	1
Azeem Rafiq	6	8	2	201	74	33.50	67.67	0	2	28	1
AU Rashid	10	16	2	393	88	28.07	47.46	0	3	54	0
TM Head	1	2	0	56	54	28.00	57.14	0	1	10	0
JA Brooks	14	20	11	250	48	27.77	62.65	0	0	36	4
AJ Hodd	12	18	3	391	96*	26.06	50.00	0	2	44	1
J Shaw	1	1	0	24	24	24.00	36.92	0	0	2	0
AW Gale	15	26	1	525	83	21.00	41.93	0	2	68	0
WMH Rhodes	2	4	0	73	20	18.25	32.88	0	0	8	0
JA Leaning	9	15	2	233	51	17.92	33.42	0	1	29	1
SA Patterson	15	20	1	300	63*	15.78	44.84	0	2	41	1
DJ Willey	4	5	0	58	22	11.60	62.36	0	0	7	2
KS Williamson	2	4	0	42	28	10.50	33.33	0	0	4	0
RJ Sidebottom	9	11	3	75	23	9.37	26.04	0	0	10	0
BO Coad	1	1	1	17	17*	-	48.57	0	0	3	0

	Overs	Mdns	Runs	Wkts	BBI	BBM	Ave	Econ	SR	5w	10w
RJ Sidebottom	245.0	63	657	31	5/51	6/89	21.19	2.68	47.4	1	0
JE Root	18.0	3	49	2	2/23	2/40	24.50	2.72	54.0	0	0
JA Brooks	432.2	105	1501	60	6/65	8/77	25.01	3.47	43.2	3	0
AZ Lees	4.0	0	51	2	2/51	2/51	25.50	12.75	12.0	0	0
SA Patterson	440.5	138	1146	39	6/56	8/133	29.38	2.59	67.8	1	0
KS Williamson	18.0	2	59	2	1/19	1/19	29.50	3.27	54.0	0	0
TT Bresnan	297.1	71	934	31	5/36	8/51	30.12	3.14	57.5	1	0
AU Rashid	293.2	36	1083	32	4/17	7/54	33.84	3.69	55.0	0	0
DJ Willey	102.0	23	334	9	3/55	3/55	37.11	3.27	68.0	0	0
WMH Rhodes	41.0	5	137	3	2/67	2/67	45.66	3.34	82.0	0	0
A Lyth	79.0	10	322	7	2/9	2/9	46.00	4.07	67.7	0	0
J Shaw	29.0	3	119	2	2/38	2/119	59.50	4.10	87.0	0	0
LE Plunkett	172.1	23	602	10	2/46	4/123	60.20	3.49	103.3	0	0
Azeem Rafiq	99.3	24	275	3	1/12	2/58	91.66	2.76	199.0	0	0
BO Coad	35.0	10	108	1	1/70	1/108	108.00	3.08	210.0	0	0
GS Ballance	1.0	0	11	0	-	-	-	11.00	-	0	0
AJ Hodd	1.0	0	14	0	-	-	-	14.00	-	0	0
TM Head	4.0	1	16	0	-	-	-	4.00	-	0	0
JA Leaning	10.0	2	27	0	-	-	-	2.70	-	0	0

Catches/Stumpings:
38 Hodd (inc 3st), 25 Lyth, 12 Bresnan, Lees, 9 Ballance, Leaning, 7 Rashid, 6 Bairstow (inc 1st), 5 Rafiq, Root, 4 Brooks, 3 Plunkett, Williamson, 2 Gale, Lehmann, 1 Rhodes, Shaw, Sidebottom

Batting

	Mat	Inns	NO	Runs	HS	Ave	SR	100	50	4s	6s
TM Head	4	4	0	277	175	69.25	105.32	1	1	29	4
TT Bresnan	9	8	2	361	95*	60.16	81.85	0	3	21	8
A Lyth	10	9	0	439	136	48.77	114.92	2	1	41	18
JE Root	1	1	0	45	45	45.00	81.81	0	0	3	0
GS Ballance	6	5	0	213	80	42.60	80.68	0	1	18	0
MJ Waite	1	1	0	38	38	38.00	80.85	0	0	3	0
JA Leaning	8	7	1	195	131*	32.50	94.20	1	0	12	5
KS Williamson	3	2	0	50	40	25.00	80.64	0	0	1	0
AU Rashid	6	5	1	88	41	22.00	72.72	0	0	5	2
DJ Willey	9	7	1	123	27	20.50	83.67	0	0	10	7
WMH Rhodes	3	3	0	57	23	19.00	67.05	0	0	5	0
LE Plunkett	9	7	1	91	25*	15.16	98.91	0	0	9	0
AZ Lees	10	9	0	134	32	14.88	62.91	0	0	18	0
AJ Hodd	8	6	2	58	14	14.50	84.05	0	0	2	1
JM Bairstow	2	2	0	22	13	11.00	62.85	0	0	4	0
Azeem Rafiq	6	5	2	28	17*	9.33	77.77	0	0	2	0
SA Patterson	10	5	3	18	8*	9.00	58.06	0	0	2	0
K Carver	4	1	1	12	12*	-	85.71	0	0	0	1
JA Brooks	1	1	1	1	1*	-	50.00	0	0	0	0

Bowling

	Overs	Mdns	Runs	Wkts	BBI	Ave	Econ	SR	4w	5w
JA Brooks	10.0	1	42	1	1/42	42.00	4.20	60.0	0	0
K Carver	13.0	0	55	5	3/5	11.00	4.23	15.6	0	0
LE Plunkett	61.0	1	279	12	4/52	23.25	4.57	30.5	1	0
MJ Waite	10.0	1	48	3	3/48	16.00	4.80	20.0	0	0
SA Patterson	61.0	1	315	9	2/30	35.00	5.16	40.6	0	0
TT Bresnan	62.0	6	335	10	2/22	33.50	5.40	37.2	0	0
AU Rashid	41.3	1	230	10	3/23	23.00	5.54	24.9	0	0
WMH Rhodes	10.0	0	56	0	-	-	5.60	-	0	0
DJ Willey	62.5	5	361	11	3/34	32.81	5.74	34.2	0	0
Azeem Rafiq	40.0	0	269	6	2/46	44.83	6.72	40.0	0	0
A Lyth	4.0	0	29	1	1/29	29.00	7.25	24.0	0	0

Catches/Stumpings:
11 Hodd (inc 4st), 7 Lees, 6 Plunkett, 3 Lyth, Patterson, Rafiq, 2 Bairstow (inc 1st), Ballance, Bresnan, Leaning, Rhodes, Willey, Williamson, 1 Brooks, Head, Rashid

	Mat	Inns	NO	Runs	HS	Ave	SR	100	50	4s	6s
JE Root	3	3	2	104	92*	104.00	155.22	0	1	9	3
KS Williamson	7	6	0	209	65	34.83	121.51	0	1	19	4
TM Head	4	4	0	113	40	28.25	134.52	0	0	5	8
JA Leaning	12	11	1	272	64	27.20	145.45	0	1	19	13
DJ Willey	11	10	0	272	79	27.20	148.63	0	2	23	16
A Lyth	12	12	0	312	87	26.00	152.19	0	2	39	12
AZ Lees	14	13	0	294	59	22.61	123.01	0	1	40	3
TT Bresnan	15	13	4	180	29*	20.00	138.46	0	0	6	11
LE Plunkett	13	11	5	94	34*	15.66	167.85	0	0	7	5
WMH Rhodes	10	9	3	89	45	14.83	125.35	0	0	7	2
GS Ballance	9	7	0	96	33	13.71	104.34	0	0	9	1
Azeem Rafiq	11	3	2	13	6*	13.00	86.66	0	0	1	0
JM Bairstow	3	3	1	24	18	12.00	92.30	0	0	1	1
AU Rashid	11	6	3	16	5*	5.33	72.72	0	0	0	0
SA Patterson	6	1	0	3	3	3.00	42.85	0	0	0	0
AJ Hodd	12	4	1	5	2	1.66	45.45	0	0	0	0
BO Coad	3	1	0	1	1	1.00	50.00	0	0	0	0
J Shaw	1	1	0	1	1	1.00	50.00	0	0	0	0
MJ Waite	1	1	1	19	19*	-	126.66	0	0	2	0
JC Wainman	2	1	1	12	12*	-	100.00	0	0	1	0
K Carver	5	1	1	0	0*	-	-	0	0	0	0

Batting

	Overs	Mdns	Runs	Wkts	BBI	Ave	Econ	SR	4w	5w
MJ Waite	2.0	0	6	1	1/6	6.00	3.00	12.0	0	0
A Lyth	6.0	0	32	1	1/2	32.00	5.33	36.0	0	0
Azeem Rafiq	39.1	0	277	15	2/21	18.46	7.07	15.6	0	0
SA Patterson	15.4	0	117	7	3/23	16.71	7.46	13.4	0	0
DJ Willey	27.5	0	214	9	2/28	23.77	7.68	18.5	0	0
TT Bresnan	44.0	2	353	21	3/15	16.80	8.02	12.5	0	0
LE Plunkett	40.4	0	330	13	2/22	25.38	8.11	18.7	0	0
AU Rashid	35.0	0	286	15	4/26	19.06	8.17	14.0	1	0
K Carver	12.0	0	102	6	3/40	17.00	8.50	12.0	0	0
JC Wainman	5.0	0	49	1	1/27	49.00	9.80	30.0	0	0
J Shaw	1.0	0	10	0	-	-	10.00	-	0	0
WMH Rhodes	14.0	0	143	6	2/18	23.83	10.21	14.0	0	0
JE Root	4.0	0	45	0	-	-	11.25	-	0	0
BO Coad	8.1	0	100	2	1/34	50.00	12.24	24.5	0	0
TM Head	0.1	0	4	0	-	-	24.00	-	0	0

Bowling

Catches/Stumpings:
10 Lyth, 8 Bresnan, Hodd (inc 5st), 7 Ballance, 5 Bairstow (inc 1st), Plunkett, Willey, 4 Leaning, Lees, Rafiq, 3 Coad, Rashid, 2 Carver, Rhodes, Williamson, 1 Root, Shaw, Waite

County
Ins and Outs

DERBYSHIRE
▶IN: Gary Wilson (Sur), Luis Reece (Lan), Daryn Smit (SA, UK passport), Hardus Viljoen (SA, Kolpak), Jeevan Mendis (SL, until June), Imran Tahir (SA, June onwards), Matt Henry (NZ, T20)

◀OUT: Callum Parkinson (Lei), Chesney Hughes, Wes Durston, Harry White, Neil Broom (all REL)

DURHAM
▶IN: Cameron Steel (Mid), Stephen Cook (SA, until July), Tom Latham (NZ, July onwards)

◀OUT: Scott Borthwick (Sur), Mark Stoneman (Sur), Asher Hart (Ham), Phil Mustard (Glo), Jamie Harrison, Calum MacLeod, Gurman Randhawa (all REL), Gordon Muchall (RET)

ESSEX
▶IN: Varun Chopra (War), Adam Wheater (Ham), Simon Harmer (SA, Kolpak), Neil Wagner (NZ, until June), Mohammad Amir (Pak, June onwards)

◀OUT: Jaik Mickleburgh, Tom Moore (both REL), Graham Napier, David Masters (both RET)

GLAMORGAN
▶IN: Marchant de Lange (SA, UK passport)

◀OUT: James Kettleborough, Dewi Penrhyn Jones (both REL), Mark Wallace (RET)

GLOUCESTERSHIRE
▶IN: Phil Mustard (Dur), Cameron Bancroft (Aus), Andrew Tye (Aus, T20)

◀OUT: Tom Hampton, Hamish Marshall (both REL)

HAMPSHIRE
▶IN: Asher Hart (Dur), Kyle Abbott (SA, Kolpak), Rilee Rossouw (SA, Kolpak), George Bailey (Aus)

◀OUT: Adam Wheater (Ess), James Tomlinson, Andy Carter (both RET), Joe Weatherley (Ken, loan)

KENT
▶IN: Will Gidman (Not), Joe Weatherley (Ham, loan)

◀OUT: David Griffith, Sam Weller (both REL)

LANCASHIRE
▶IN: Shivnarine Chanderpaul (WI, Kolpak), Dane Vilas (SA, Kolpak), Ryan McLaren (SA), Junaid Khan (Pak, T20)

◀OUT: Nathan Buck (Nor), Gavin Griffiths (Lei), Luis Reece (Der), George Edwards, Alviro Petersen (both REL), Tom Smith (RET)

LEICESTERSHIRE
▶IN: Gavin Griffiths (Lan), Callum Parkinson (Der), Richard Jones (War), Colin Ackermann (SA, EU passport), Luke Ronchi (NZ, T20), Cameron Delport (SA, T20), James Burke (Sur, loan)

◀OUT: Jigar Naik, Ollie Freckingham, Michael Burgess, Atif Sheikh, Rob Taylor, Niall O'Brien (all REL)

MIDDLESEX
▶IN: Adam Voges (Aus), Brendon McCullum (NZ, T20)
◀OUT: Cameron Steel (Dur), Andrew Balbirnie (REL), Max Holden (Nor, loan, until June)

NORTHAMPTONSHIRE
▶IN: Nathan Buck (Lan), Seekkuge Prasanna (SL, T20), Max Holden (Mid, loan, until June)
◀OUT: Olly Stone (War)

NOTTINGHAMSHIRE
▶IN: Dan Christian (Aus, T20), Ish Sodhi (NZ, T20), James Pattinson (Aus)
◀OUT: Will Gidman (Ken), Sam Wood (REL), Peter Siddle (Aus, REL)

SOMERSET
▶IN: Steven Davies (Sur), Dean Elgar (SA)
◀OUT: Alex Barrow (REL)

SURREY
▶IN: Scott Borthwick, Mark Stoneman (both Dur), Aaron Finch (Aus, T20), Kevin Pietersen (T20)
◀OUT: Steven Davies (Som), Gary Wilson (Der), Azhar Mahmood (REL), James Burke (Lei, loan)

SUSSEX
▶IN: Laurie Evans (War), David Wiese (SA, Kolpak), Stiaan van Zyl (SA, Kolpak), Vernon Philander
       (SA, until June), Ross Taylor (NZ, T20)
◀OUT: Craig Cachopa, Flynn Hudson-Prentice (both REL), Lewis Hatchett (RET)

WARWICKSHIRE
▶IN: Olly Stone (Nor), Colin de Grandhomme (NZ, T20)
◀OUT: Varun Chopra (Ess), Richard Jones (Lei), Laurie Evans (Sus), Recordo Gordon, Jonathan Webb,
       Freddie Coleman (all REL)

WORCESTERSHIRE
▶IN: John Hastings (Aus), Mitchell Santner (NZ, T20)
◀OUT: Chris Russell (REL)

YORKSHIRE
▶IN: Peter Handscomb (Aus), Travis Head (Aus, T20)
◀OUT: Andrew Gale (RET)

CRICVIZ

CRICKET INTELLIGENCE
Available to download now

CricViz allows the user to understand cricket in greater detail than ever before. The unique CricViz computer model enables the prediction of match outcome, the interpretation of team and player performance and the anticipation of what is likely to happen next; cricket intelligence at the next level.

WINVIZ

WinViz probabilities are generated by CricViz's unique computer model of Test cricket. This utilises a database of the last 500 Test matches played, using past and current data to estimate the probability of each result outcome.

PREDICTVIZ

The PredictViz function forecasts the most likely course the match will follow from its current position. The remainder of the game is simulated thousands of times, with the average predicted outcome for innings plotted across the game's remaining timeline.

PLAYVIZ

PlayViz evaluates each team's batting, bowling and fielding against what is expected by the CricViz model. Each of those disciplines is given a positive or negative score in runs, measuring the performance against that of an average Test team in the conditions present at that time.

BATVIZ

BatViz gives a measure of how difficult batting has been in the last 30 minutes of play. The ball tracking data from every ball bowled in the match is compared to a database of over 300,000 deliveries, with runs and wickets from the 1,000 most similar balls in this database averaged to rate the current bowling spells.

FOR MORE INFORMATION

✉ ENQUIRIES@CRICVIZ.COM   🏠 CRICVIZ.COM   🐦 @CRICVIZ   🐦 @CRICPROF   f CRICVIZ

The
Players

KYLE ABBOTT RHB / RFM / R0 / W0

FULL NAME: Kyle John Abbott
BORN: June 18, 1987, Empangeni, KwaZulu-Natal, South Africa
SQUAD NO: 87
NICKNAME: Jimmy
EDUCATION: Kearsney College, KwaZulu-Natal
TEAMS: South Africa, Hampshire, Dolphins, Kings XI Punjab, KwaZulu-Natal, Middlesex, Warriors, Worcestershire
ROLE: Bowler
DEBUT: Test: 2013; ODI: 2013; T20I: 2013; First-class: 2009; List A: 2009; T20: 2011

BEST BATTING: 80 Dolphins vs Titans, Benoni, 2011
BEST BOWLING: 8-45 Dolphins vs Cape Cobras, Cape Town, 2013

TWITTER: @Kyle_Abbott87
NOTES: A well-built South African fast bowler, Abbott interrupted his international career to sign a four-year Kolpak deal with Hampshire in January 2017. He will be available to play across all formats. His Test debut figures of 7-29 are the second-best for South Africa, behind Lance Klusener's 8-64 at Eden Gardens in 1996. This will be Abbott's third stint in county cricket, and his second for Hampshire, who he played for as an overseas player in 2014, impressing with 36 wickets at an average of 20.33 in nine Championship matches

Batting	Mat	Inns	NO	Runs	HS	Ave	SR	100	50	Ct	St
Tests	11	14	0	95	17	6.78	28.10	0	0	4	0
ODIs	28	13	4	76	23	8.44	60.31	0	0	7	0
T20Is	21	6	4	23	9*	11.50	115.00	0	0	7	0
First-class	71	99	17	1344	80	16.39	43.04	0	4	16	0
List A	88	41	17	391	45*	16.29	88.66	0	0	24	0
Twenty20	94	30	20	130	16*	13.00	108.33	0	0	25	0

Bowling	Mat	Balls	Runs	Wkts	BBI	BBM	Ave	Econ	SR	5w	10
Tests	11	2081	886	39	7/29	9/68	22.71	2.55	53.3	3	0
ODIs	28	1303	1051	34	4/21	4/21	30.91	4.83	38.3	0	0
T20Is	21	436	579	26	3/20	3/20	22.26	7.96	16.7	0	0
First-class	71	12818	5819	259	8/45	12/96	22.46	2.72	49.4	16	2
List A	88	3903	3327	114	4/21	4/21	29.18	5.11	34.2	0	0
Twenty20	94	1953	2589	88	5/14	5/14	29.42	7.95	22.1	1	0

TOM ABELL

RHB / RM / R0 / W0

FULL NAME: Thomas Benjamin Abell
BORN: March 5, 1994, Taunton
SQUAD NO: 28
HEIGHT: 5ft 11in
NICKNAME: Tabes
EDUCATION: Taunton School; Exeter University
TEAMS: Somerset
ROLE: Batsman
DEBUT: First-class: 2014; List A: 2015; T20: 2016

SOMERSET

BEST BATTING: 135 Somerset vs Lancashire, Old Trafford, 2016
BEST BOWLING: 1-11 Somerset vs Yorkshire, Taunton, 2015

STRANGEST THING SEEN IN A GAME? A bloke chasing after a ball to the boundary, flying over the advertising boards and into a bonfire
BEST MOMENT IN CRICKET? Beating Durham in 2016 – an incredible game and to win from that position gave me the best feeling I have experienced
HOW WOULD YOUR TEAM-MATES DESCRIBE YOU IN THREE WORDS? Keen, passionate, hilarious
BEST PLAYER IN COUNTY CRICKET? James Hildreth (Som)
MOST UNDERRATED PLAYER IN COUNTY CRICKET? Craig Overton (Som)
TIP FOR THE TOP? Tim Rouse (Som)
CRICKETING HEROES? Brian Lara, Marcus Trescothick
NON-CRICKETING HEROES? Jonny Wilkinson – he won us a World Cup and is such a humble guy. Sonny Bill Williams – similar reasons
SURPRISING FACT? I have a French degree and go to the same hairdesser as Keith Parsons
UNUSUAL OBJECT AT HOME? A pogo stick
TWITTER: @tomabell1

Batting	Mat	Inns	NO	Runs	HS	Ave	SR	100	50	Ct	St
First-class	32	56	5	1600	135	31.37	47.50	3	9	21	0
List A	12	10	1	343	106	38.11	70.86	1	1	4	0
Twenty20	1	1	0	7	7	7.00	70.00	0	0	0	0

Bowling	Mat	Balls	Runs	Wkts	BBI	BBM	Ave	Econ	SR	5w	10
First-class	32	46	33	1	1/11	1/11	33.00	4.30	46.0	0	0
List A	12	-	-	-	-	-	-	-	-	-	-
Twenty20	1	-	-	-	-	-	-	-	-	-	-

COLIN ACKERMANN

RHB / OB / R0 / W0

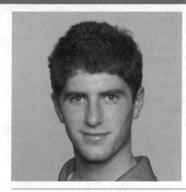

FULL NAME: Colin Niel Ackermann
BORN: April 4, 1991, George, Cape Province, South Africa
SQUAD NO: 84
HEIGHT: 6ft 1in
NICKNAME: Ackers
EDUCATION: Grey High School, Port Elizabeth; University of South Africa
TEAMS: Leicestershire, Eastern Province, Warriors
ROLE: Batsman
DEBUT: First-class: 2010; List A: 2010; T20: 2011

BEST BATTING: 150 Warriors vs Titans, Benoni, 2017
BEST BOWLING: 3-85 Eastern Province vs Free State, Bloemfontein, 2013

WHAT FIRST GOT YOU INTO CRICKET? My dad played a bit and by the age of three I had a bat in my hands
STRANGEST THING SEEN IN A GAME? On a couple of occasions I've seen the groundstaff make a fire on the pitch to dry the wicket so that we can get a game on
BEST MOMENT IN CRICKET? Walking onto the field at Centurion for the 2016 T20 Challenge final in South Africa
HOW WOULD YOUR TEAM-MATES DESCRIBE YOU IN THREE WORDS? Organised, ambitious, enthusiastic
BEST PLAYER IN COUNTY CRICKET? Colin Ingram (Gla)
CRICKETING HEROES? Jacques Kallis
IF YOU WEREN'T A CRICKETER? I'd be involved in property
DESERT ISLAND DISC? Swedish House Mafia – Don't You Worry Child
FANTASY SLIP CORDON? Keeper: Donald Trump, 1st: Me, 2nd: Jacques Kallis, 3rd: Trevor Noah, Gully: David White. Politics, cricket, comedy and my best mate – got it all covered
TWITTER: @Ackers48

Batting	Mat	Inns	NO	Runs	HS	Ave	SR	100	50	Ct	St
First-class	71	124	11	4563	150	40.38	47.28	9	31	63	0
List A	47	43	9	1059	92	31.14	70.50	0	8	32	0
Twenty20	43	41	6	1003	79*	28.65	111.44	0	5	28	0
Bowling	Mat	Balls	Runs	Wkts	BBI	BBM	Ave	Econ	SR	5w	10
First-class	71	2762	1342	33	3/85	4/54	40.66	2.91	83.6	0	0
List A	47	1166	857	23	3/35	3/35	37.26	4.40	50.6	0	0
Twenty20	43	534	575	19	3/23	3/23	30.26	6.46	28.1	0	0

MARK ADAIR

RHB / RFM / R0 / W0

FULL NAME: Mark Richard Adair
BORN: March 27, 1996, Belfast, Northern Ireland
SQUAD NO: 27
HEIGHT: 6ft 3in
NICKNAME: Sparky, Beefy, Dairy
EDUCATION: Sullivan Upper School, Holywood, County Down, Northern Ireland
TEAMS: Warwickshire
ROLE: Allrounder
DEBUT: First-class: 2015; T20: 2016

BEST BATTING: 32 Warwickshire vs Nottinghamshire, Edgbaston, 2016
BEST BOWLING: 1-61 Warwickshire vs Somerset, Taunton, 2015

FAMILY TIES? My brother Ross played for Ireland at youth level
STRANGEST THING SEEN IN A GAME? Sam Hain off his long run
BEST MOMENT IN CRICKET? Making my first-class debut and getting my first wicket
SUPERSTITIONS? I like to walk across the rope with my cap off, then put it on after
HOW WOULD YOUR TEAM-MATES DESCRIBE YOU IN THREE WORDS? A loose cannon
BEST PLAYER IN COUNTY CRICKET? Jeetan Patel (War)
TIP FOR THE TOP? Matthew Lamb (War)
CRICKETING HEROES? Apart from Pete McKay, my brother and Sam Hain, I'd probably say Andrew Flintoff because he was class and very sociable
NON-CRICKETING HEROES? My mum – she makes the best lasagna ever
SURPRISING FACT? I love musicals
UNUSUAL OBJECT AT HOME? A church pew
DESERT ISLAND DISC? Les Misérables (London cast version)
FANTASY SLIP CORDON? Keeper: Conor McGregor (a great chirper behind the stumps), 1st: Andrea Pirlo (no Pirlo, no party), 2nd: Barack Obama, 3rd: Bruce Wayne, Gully: Richard Branson (to sweet-talk him for my life after cricket)
TWITTER: @MarkkAdairr

Batting	Mat	Inns	NO	Runs	HS	Ave	SR	100	50	Ct	St
First-class	2	3	2	66	32	66.00	61.11	0	0	0	0
Twenty20	6	3	0	11	7	3.66	78.57	0	0	0	0

Bowling	Mat	Balls	Runs	Wkts	BBI	BBM	Ave	Econ	SR	5w	10
First-class	2	180	108	1	1/61	1/61	108.00	3.60	180.0	0	0
Twenty20	6	78	86	5	2/18	2/18	17.20	6.61	15.6	0	0

JIMMY ADAMS

LHB / LM / R5 / W0

HAMPSHIRE

FULL NAME: James Henry Kenneth Adams
BORN: September 23, 1980, Winchester
SQUAD NO: 4
HEIGHT: 6ft 1in
NICKNAME: Bison
EDUCATION: Twyford School, Hampshire; Sherborne School, Dorset; Loughborough University
TEAMS: Hampshire, Auckland, England Lions
ROLE: Batsman
DEBUT: First-class: 2002; List A: 2002; T20: 2005

BEST BATTING: 262* Hampshire vs Nottingham, Trent Bridge, 2006
BEST BOWLING: 2-16 Hampshire vs Durham, Chester-le-Street, 2004
COUNTY CAP: 2006 BENEFIT: 2015

WHAT FIRST GOT YOU INTO CRICKET? Watching Robin Smith on the telly
STRANGEST THING SEEN IN A GAME? James Tomlinson taking a one-handed catch at fine-leg while holding a half-eaten banana in his other hand
BEST MOMENT IN CRICKET? Winning at Lord's in the 2009 one-day final. (I wish I'd also been able to enjoy batting with Robin Smith on my debut but I was too busy bricking myself)
MOST UNDERRATED PLAYER IN COUNTY CRICKET? Any opening batsman in April
TIP FOR THE TOP? Max Holden (Mid), Joe Weatherley (Ham)
NON-CRICKETING HEROES? Rorschach, Wolverine, Jimmy Page, Keith Moon
FANTASY SLIP CORDON? Keeper: Me (got to be easier with gloves on, right?), 1st: Father Christmas (worth getting into his good books), 2nd: Fireman Sam (he's always cool, calm and there to help you out – and he's on the telly as I write), Gully: Dad (he always tells me how good he was in the gully)
TWITTER: @Jhkadams

Batting	Mat	Inns	NO	Runs	HS	Ave	SR	100	50	Ct	St
First-class	205	364	28	12791	262*	38.06		21	71	158	0
List A	106	100	12	3547	131	40.30	85.84	2	27	43	0
Twenty20	135	124	14	2643	101*	24.02	123.44	2	9	36	0
Bowling	Mat	Balls	Runs	Wkts	BBI	BBM	Ave	Econ	SR	5w	10
First-class	205	1063	718	13	2/16		55.23	4.05	81.7	0	0
List A	106	79	105	1	1/34	1/34	105.00	7.97	79.0	0	0
Twenty20	135	36	60	0	-	-	-	10.00	-	0	0

AADIL ALI

RHB / OB / R0 / W0

FULL NAME: Aadil Masud Ali
BORN: December 29, 1994, Leicester
SQUAD NO: 14
HEIGHT: 6ft
NICKNAME: Dil
EDUCATION: Lancaster School, Leicester; Wyggeston & Queen Elizabeth I College, Leicester
TEAMS: Leicestershire
ROLE: Batsman
DEBUT: First-class: 2015; List A: 2015; T20: 2015

BEST BATTING: 80 Leicestershire vs Gloucestershire, Leicester, 2015

WHAT FIRST GOT YOU INTO CRICKET? One day my dad's team were a player short so I was made to field. And watching Sachin Tendulkar

FAMILY TIES? My dad came over 25 years ago to play as an overseas player and then settled down. Biggest cricket badger around

BEST MOMENT IN CRICKET? Making my debut in the Championship and then scoring my first fifty

BEST PLAYER IN COUNTY CRICKET? Ravi Bopara (Ess)

MOST UNDERRATED PLAYER IN COUNTY CRICKET? Tom Wells (Lei)

TIP FOR THE TOP? Rob Sayer (Lei)

CRICKETING HEROES? Sachin Tendulkar, Virat Kohli

SURPRISING FACT? I dropped out of Cambridge to live the dream

DESERT ISLAND DISC? An old-school R&B CD

FANTASY SLIP CORDON? Keeper: Kevin Hart, 1st: Me, 2nd: Beyoncé, 3rd: Mesut Özil, Gully: Russell Spiers

TWITTER: @aadilali1

Batting	Mat	Inns	NO	Runs	HS	Ave	SR	100	50	Ct	St
First-class	12	20	1	529	80	27.84	38.13	0	3	4	0
List A	9	8	0	155	84	19.37	68.88	0	1	5	0
Twenty20	2	2	0	30	26	15.00	125.00	0	0	1	0

Bowling	Mat	Balls	Runs	Wkts	BBI	BBM	Ave	Econ	SR	5w	10
First-class	12	42	40	0	-	-	-	5.71	-	0	0
List A	9	72	62	0	-	-	-	5.16	-	0	0
Twenty20	2	-	-	-	-	-	-	-	-	-	-

MOEEN ALI

LHB / OB / R2 / W0

FULL NAME: Moeen Munir Ali
BORN: June 18, 1987, Birmingham
SQUAD NO: 8
HEIGHT: 6ft
NICKNAME: Brother Mo
EDUCATION: Moseley School, Birmingham
TEAMS: England, Worcestershire, Duronto Rajshahi, Matabeleland Tuskers, Moors Sports Club, Warwickshire
ROLE: Allrounder
DEBUT: Test: 2014; ODI: 2014; T20I: 2014; First-class: 2005; List A: 2006; T20: 2007

BEST BATTING: 250 Worcestershire vs Glamorgan, Worcester, 2013
BEST BOWLING: 6-29 Worcestershire vs Lancashire, Old Trafford, 2012
COUNTY CAP: 2007 (Worcestershire)

FAMILY TIES? My cousin Kabir played for England and my brother Kadeer played for Worcestershire, Gloucestershire and Leicestershire
BEST MOMENT IN CRICKET? Playing for England
CRICKETING HEROES? Saeed Anwar and Brian Lara
NON-CRICKETING HEROES? Muhammad Ali
IF YOU WEREN'T A CRICKETER? I'd be working in a chippy
DESERT ISLAND DISC? The Quran
FANTASY SLIP CORDON? Keeper: Muhammad Ali, 1st: Me, 2nd: Chris Jordan, 3rd: Ravi Bopara, Gully: Sachin Tendulkar

Batting	Mat	Inns	NO	Runs	HS	Ave	SR	100	50	Ct	St
Tests	37	62	7	1927	155*	35.03	50.73	5	9	19	0
ODIs	52	48	7	1061	128	25.87	99.71	2	4	18	0
T20Is	22	19	5	202	72*	14.42	112.84	0	1	6	0
First-class	162	275	26	9625	250	38.65	54.27	19	59	95	0
List A	157	148	9	4022	158	28.93	100.57	9	18	49	0
Twenty20	109	103	8	2139	90	22.51	128.85	0	11	33	0

Bowling	Mat	Balls	Runs	Wkts	BBI	BBM	Ave	Econ	SR	5w	10
Tests	37	6666	4138	98	6/67	8/129	42.22	3.72	68.0	2	0
ODIs	52	2549	2137	44	3/32	3/32	48.56	5.03	57.9	0	0
T20Is	22	312	400	14	2/21	2/21	28.57	7.69	22.2	0	0
First-class	162	17882	10642	255	6/29	12/96	41.73	3.57	70.1	7	1
List A	157	4982	4432	100	3/28	3/28	44.32	5.33	49.8	0	0
Twenty20	109	1502	1849	69	5/34	5/34	26.79	7.38	21.7	1	0

JIM ALLENBY   RHB / RM / R0 / W1 / MVP23

FULL NAME: James Allenby
BORN: September 12, 1982, Perth, Australia
SQUAD NO: 6
HEIGHT: 6ft
NICKNAME: Hank
EDUCATION: Christ Church Grammar School
TEAMS: Somerset, Glamorgan, Leicestershire, Peshawar Zalmi, Western Australia
ROLE: Allrounder
DEBUT: First-class: 2006; List A: 2003; T20: 2005

BEST BATTING: 138* Leicestershire vs Bangladesh A, Leicester, 2008
BEST BOWLING: 6-54 Glamorgan vs Hampshire, Cardiff, 2014
COUNTY CAP: 2010 (Glamorgan)

FAMILY TIES? My father was CEO of the WACA in the late '90s and my great-grandfather played for Yorkshire and Hampshire
BEST MOMENT IN CRICKET? Winning the T20 Cup in 2006 with Leicestershire, scoring a hundred on Championship debut in 2006, scoring two T20 hundreds, taking a double hat-trick in the T20 Cup
BEST PLAYER IN COUNTY CRICKET? Jeetan Patel (War)
CRICKETING HEROES? Steve Waugh – had an amazing ability to win games from tough situations. Dean Jones – extraordinary self-belief. Paul Nixon – for playing with high standards for so long and helping anyone he could. Matt Maynard – he helped change how I play and think
SURPRISING FACT? I was a gardener and then a short-order chef in my first five years in England while I was trialling. Loved both of those jobs, and still back my egg-cooking ability
UNUSUAL OBJECT AT HOME? A treadmill
TWITTER: @jimallenby

Batting	Mat	Inns	NO	Runs	HS	Ave	SR	100	50	Ct	St
First-class	151	238	30	7756	138*	37.28	58.75	10	56	160	0
List A	113	107	12	2658	91*	27.97	87.66	0	16	44	0
Twenty20	124	115	16	3068	110	30.98	124.36	2	20	31	0

Bowling	Mat	Balls	Runs	Wkts	BBI	BBM	Ave	Econ	SR	5w	10
First-class	151	17973	7877	298	6/54	10/128	26.43	2.62	60.3	5	1
List A	113	3516	2870	83	5/43	5/43	34.57	4.89	42.3	1	0
Twenty20	124	1540	2026	60	5/21	5/21	33.76	7.89	25.6	2	0

TOM ALSOP

LHB / WK / R0 / W0

FULL NAME: Thomas Philip Alsop
BORN: November 27, 1995, High Wycombe, Buckinghamshire
SQUAD NO: 9
HEIGHT: 5ft 11in
NICKNAME: Deeney, Alsop, Sloppy, T
EDUCATION: Lavington School; The John Bentley School, Wiltshire
TEAMS: Hampshire, England Lions
ROLE: Batsman
DEBUT: First-class: 2014; List A: 2014; T20: 2016

BEST BATTING: 117 Hampshire vs Surrey, The Oval, 2016

FAMILY TIES? Dad played for Merchant Taylors' School and my older brother Owen played for Wiltshire CCC and was in the Hampshire Academy. My little (not so little) brother plays for Wiltshire age-groups
STRANGEST THING SEEN IN A GAME? Tino Best trying to hold an end up
BEST MOMENT IN CRICKET? Scoring my maiden first-class hundred at The Oval in 2016
HOW WOULD YOUR TEAM-MATES DESCRIBE YOU IN THREE WORDS? Reserved, quiet, confident
BEST PLAYER IN COUNTY CRICKET? James Vince (Ham)
MOST UNDERRATED PLAYER IN COUNTY CRICKET? John Simpson (Mid)
TIP FOR THE TOP? Mason Crane (Ham)
CRICKETING HEROES? Virat Kohli, David Warner
NON-CRICKETING HEROES? My mum – she's a nurse on the intensive care unit
IF YOU WEREN'T A CRICKETER? Something within the watch industry. I love my watches
SURPRISING FACT? I adopt tigers, and I used to play international hockey for England
UNUSUAL OBJECT AT HOME? A watch-winder
TWITTER: @TAlsop9

Batting	Mat	Inns	NO	Runs	HS	Ave	SR	100	50	Ct	St
First-class	17	29	0	850	117	29.31	49.38	1	6	15	0
List A	16	16	1	551	116	36.73	80.55	1	3	10	0
Twenty20	8	7	0	143	85	20.42	117.21	0	1	3	0

Bowling	Mat	Balls	Runs	Wkts	BBI	BBM	Ave	Econ	SR	5w	10
First-class	17	60	66	2	2/59	2/59	33.00	6.60	30.0	0	0
List A	16	-	-	-	-	-	-	-	-	-	-
Twenty20	8	-	-	-	-	-	-	-	-	-	-

FULL NAME: Timothy Raymond Ambrose
BORN: December 1, 1982, Newcastle, New South Wales, Australia
SQUAD NO: 11
HEIGHT: 5ft 7in
NICKNAME: Amby, Shambrose
EDUCATION: Merewether Selective High, NSW; Training and Further Education College, NSW
TEAMS: England, Warwickshire, Sussex
ROLE: Wicketkeeper
DEBUT: Test: 2008; ODI: 2008; T20I: 2008; First-class: 2001; List A: 2001; T20: 2003

BEST BATTING: 251* Warwickshire vs Worcestershire, Worcester, 2007
COUNTY CAPS: 2003 (Sussex); 2007 (Warwickshire) **BENEFIT:** 2016 (Warwickshire)

HOW WOULD YOUR TEAM-MATES DESCRIBE YOU IN THREE WORDS? Grumpy, smelly, baldy
BEST MOMENT IN CRICKET? County Championship wins in 2003 and 2012 and a T20 win in 2014. Anytime playing for England
BEST PLAYER IN COUNTY CRICKET? Chris Woakes (War)
TIP FOR THE TOP? Sam Hain (War), Joe Clarke (Wor)
CRICKETING HEROES? Ian Healy for his attention to detail in wicketkeeping
NON-CRICKETING HEROES? Michael Jordan for his ability to deliver under pressure
SURPRISING FACT? I have a Puggle named Frank
TWITTER: @timambrose2016

Batting	Mat	Inns	NO	Runs	HS	Ave	SR	100	50	Ct	St
Tests	11	16	1	447	102	29.80	46.41	1	3	31	0
ODIs	5	5	1	10	6	2.50	29.41	0	0	3	0
T20Is	1	-	-	-	-	-	-	-	-	1	1
First-class	210	316	30	9742	251*	34.06	52.21	15	60	553	37
List A	162	132	20	3586	135	32.01	77.90	3	20	156	32
Twenty20	84	58	16	1060	77	25.23	113.24	0	3	49	23

Bowling	Mat	Balls	Runs	Wkts	BBI	BBM	Ave	Econ	SR	5w	10
Tests	11	-	-	-	-	-	-	-	-	-	-
ODIs	5	-	-	-	-	-	-	-	-	-	-
T20Is	1	-	-	-	-	-	-	-	-	-	-
First-class	210	17	1	1	1/0	1/0	1.00	0.35	17.0	0	0
List A	162	-	-	-	-	-	-	-	-	-	-
Twenty20	84	-	-	-	-	-	-	-	-	-	-

MOHAMMAD AMIR
LHB / LFM / R0 / W0

FULL NAME: Mohammad Amir
BORN: April 13, 1992, Gujjar Khan, Pakistan
SQUAD NO: 5
HEIGHT: 6ft 2in
TEAMS: Pakistan, Essex, Chittagong Vikings, Federal Areas, Karachi Kings, National Bank of Pakistan, Rawalpindi, Sindh, Sui Southern Gas Corperation
ROLE: Bowler
DEBUT: Test: 2009; ODI: 2009; T20I: 2009; First-class: 2008; List A: 2008; T20: 2008

BEST BATTING: 66 Sui Southern Gas Corporation vs Lahore Blues, Lahore, 2015
BEST BOWLING: 7-61 National Bank of Pakistan vs Lahore Shalimar, Lahore, 2009

TWITTER: @iamamirofficial
NOTES: Once the most exciting teenage fast bowler in the world; then the scandal, the fall, and the humbling. The sight of Mohammad Amir being whisked away from Southwark Crown Court after being found guilty of spot-fixing at Lord's in 2010 remains one of cricket's darkest images. Repentant and now rehabilitated, he is back at the heart of Pakistan's attack, producing spells of ferocious speed and prodigious movement that recall the brilliance of those early years. Although only sporadically successful since his return to international cricket, he was a key part of the Pakistan team that snatched a 2-2 draw in last summer's Test series against England. A stint at Essex from mid-season onwards will assist with Amir's reintegration into the cricket family

Batting	Mat	Inns	NO	Runs	HS	Ave	SR	100	50	Ct	St
Tests	25	48	8	546	48	13.65	35.85	0	0	1	0
ODIs	29	21	6	269	73*	17.93	91.18	0	2	6	0
T20Is	31	8	3	41	21*	8.20	80.39	0	0	4	0
First-class	45	71	11	941	66	15.68	41.38	0	2	7	0
List A	48	27	10	308	73*	18.11	87.50	0	2	11	0
Twenty20	74	28	13	146	21*	9.73	93.58	0	0	7	0

Bowling	Mat	Balls	Runs	Wkts	BBI	BBM	Ave	Econ	SR	5w	10
Tests	25	5293	2732	81	6/84	7/106	33.72	3.09	65.3	3	0
ODIs	29	1512	1221	45	4/28	4/28	27.13	4.84	33.6	0	0
T20Is	31	690	809	34	3/18	3/18	23.79	7.03	20.2	0	0
First-class	45	8243	4175	175	7/61	10/97	23.85	3.03	47.1	8	1
List A	48	2547	1958	81	5/36	5/36	24.17	4.61	31.4	1	0
Twenty20	74	1644	1855	84	4/30	4/30	22.08	6.77	19.5	0	0

JAMES ANDERSON

LHB / RFM / R0 / W2

FULL NAME: James Michael Anderson
BORN: July 30, 1982, Burnley, Lancashire
SQUAD NO: 9
HEIGHT: 6ft 2in
NICKNAME: Jimmy, Jimbo, Jimbob
EDUCATION: St Theodore's Roman Catholic High School, Burnley
TEAMS: England, Lancashire, Auckland
ROLE: Bowler
DEBUT: Test: 2003; ODI: 2002; T20I: 2007; First-class: 2002; List A: 2000; T20: 2004

LANCASHIRE

BEST BATTING: 81 England vs India, Trent Bridge, 2014
BEST BOWLING: 7-43 England vs New Zealand, Trent Bridge, 2008
COUNTY CAP: 2003 BENEFIT: 2012

FAMILY TIES? My dad played for Burnley and uncle and cousin still play club cricket
BEST MOMENT IN CRICKET? Ashes wins, County Championship winners' medal
CRICKETING HEROES? Allan Donald, Peter Martin, Glen Chapple
NON-CRICKETING HEROES? Ian Wright, Steve Davis (ex-Burnley FC), Boris Becker
IF YOU WEREN'T A CRICKETER? I'd be busking with my recorder
SURPRISING FACT? I can peel a potato in 2.4 seconds. I have a personality. I'm allergic to mushrooms
DESERT ISLAND DISC? James – Runaground
TWITTER: @jimmy9

Batting	Mat	Inns	NO	Runs	HS	Ave	SR	100	50	Ct	St
Tests	122	168	61	1093	81	10.21	41.15	0	1	77	0
ODIs	194	79	43	273	28	7.58	48.66	0	0	53	0
T20Is	19	4	3	1	1*	1.00	50.00	0	0	3	0
First-class	203	256	94	1658	81	10.23		0	1	121	0
List A	247	100	60	366	28	9.15		0	0	62	0
Twenty20	44	10	6	23	16	5.75	88.46	0	0	8	0

Bowling	Mat	Balls	Runs	Wkts	BBI	BBM	Ave	Econ	SR	5w	10
Tests	122	26840	13310	467	7/43	11/71	28.50	2.97	57.4	21	3
ODIs	194	9584	7861	269	5/23	5/23	29.22	4.92	35.6	2	0
T20Is	19	422	552	18	3/23	3/23	30.66	7.84	23.4	0	0
First-class	203	41180	20556	777	7/43		26.45	2.99	52.9	38	6
List A	247	11994	9657	343	5/23	5/23	28.15	4.83	34.9	2	0
Twenty20	44	933	1318	41	3/23	3/23	32.14	8.47	22.7	0	0

MARTIN ANDERSSON

RHB / RM / R0 / W0

FULL NAME: Martin Kristoffer Andersson
BORN: September 6, 1996, Reading
SQUAD NO: 24
HEIGHT: 6ft 1in
NICKNAME: Tino, Pasty
EDUCATION: Reading Blue Coat School; University of Leeds
TEAMS: Berkshire, Middlesex 2nd XI
ROLE: Allrounder
DEBUT: Yet to make first-team debut

WHAT FIRST GOT YOU INTO CRICKET? The 2005 Ashes
STRANGEST THING SEEN IN A GAME? A fielder clotheslined by a washing line hanging between two trees while he was chasing the ball over the boundary
BEST MOMENT IN CRICKET? Hitting a six off the penultimate ball to win the Second XI T20 final in 2016
HOW WOULD YOUR TEAM-MATES DESCRIBE YOU IN THREE WORDS? Committed, motivated, unconventional
BEST PLAYER IN COUNTY CRICKET? Ben Duckett (Nor)
MOST UNDERRATED PLAYER IN COUNTY CRICKET? Paul Stirling (Mid)
TIP FOR THE TOP? Stevie Eskinazi (Mid)
CRICKETING HEROES? Jacques Kallis, Andrew Flintoff
NON-CRICKETING HEROES? David Attenborough
IF YOU WEREN'T A CRICKETER? Walking the Appalachian Trail
SURPRISING FACT? I have 90% of my middle finger left. The other 10% was left in a door frame in a building at school
UNUSUAL OBJECT AT HOME? Didgeridoo
DESERT ISLAND DISC? The xx – Coexist
FANTASY SLIP CORDON? Keeper: Morgan Freeman (for his great voice), 1st: Michael McIntyre (for entertainment), 2nd: Me, 3rd: Neo (from The Matrix – he will catch anything), Gully: Jennifer Aniston
TWITTER: @MartinAnderss11

ZAFAR ANSARI LHB / SLA / R1 / W0 / MVP93

FULL NAME: Zafar Shahaan Ansari
BORN: December 10, 1991, Ascot, Berkshire
SQUAD NO: 22
HEIGHT: 6ft
NICKNAME: PM, Zaf
EDUCATION: Hampton School; University of Cambridge; Royal Holloway, University of London
TEAMS: England, Surrey
ROLE: Allrounder
DEBUT: Test: 2016; ODI: 2015; First-class: 2011; List A: 2010; T20: 2011

SURREY

BEST BATTING: 112 Surrey vs Glamorgan, Colwyn Bay, 2014
BEST BOWLING: 6-30 Surrey vs Gloucestershire, The Oval, 2015
COUNTY CAP: 2014

FAMILY TIES? My father played a couple of first-class games in Pakistan. My brother Akbar captained Cambridge Blues, played first-class cricket for Cambridge MCCU
STRANGEST THING SEEN IN A GAME? In India, during the Test match in Vizag, a dog ran around the pitch and did a poo after the steward threw a shoe at it
SUPERSTITIONS? Arrive at the ground as late as possible
HOW WOULD YOUR TEAM-MATES DESCRIBE YOU IN THREE WORDS? Bookish, calm, detached
BEST PLAYER IN COUNTY CRICKET? Haseeb Hameed (Lan)
MOST UNDERRATED PLAYER IN COUNTY CRICKET? James Hildreth (Som)
TIP FOR THE TOP? Amar Virdi (Sur)
UNUSUAL OBJECT AT HOME? Lots of Atlanta Falcons merchandise

Batting	Mat	Inns	NO	Runs	HS	Ave	SR	100	50	Ct	St
Tests	3	5	0	49	32	9.80	36.02	0	0	1	0
ODIs	1	-	-	-	-	-	-	-	-	0	0
First-class	69	113	15	2957	112	30.17	36.75	3	15	31	0
List A	42	36	12	819	66*	34.12	91.10	0	4	21	0
Twenty20	69	51	23	768	67*	27.42	119.25	0	1	16	0

Bowling	Mat	Balls	Runs	Wkts	BBI	BBM	Ave	Econ	SR	5w	10
Tests	3	408	275	5	2/76	3/118	55.00	4.04	81.6	0	0
ODIs	1	-	-	-	-	-	-	-	-	-	-
First-class	69	8615	4479	127	6/30	8/236	35.26	3.11	67.8	6	0
List A	42	1289	1215	38	4/42	4/42	31.97	5.65	33.9	0	0
Twenty20	69	948	1215	39	3/17	3/17	31.15	7.68	24.3	0	0

JOFRA ARCHER — RHB / RFM / R0 / W0

SUSSEX

FULL NAME: Jofra Chioke Archer
BORN: April 1, 1995, Bridgetown, Barbados
SQUAD NO: 22
HEIGHT: 6ft 2in
NICKNAME: Regi
EDUCATION: Christ Church Foundation School, Barbados
TEAMS: Sussex
ROLE: Bowler
DEBUT: First-class: 2016; List A: 2016; T20: 2016

BEST BATTING: 73 Sussex vs Essex, Colchester, 2016
BEST BOWLING: 4-31 Sussex vs Leicestershire, Leicester, 2016

STRANGEST THING SEEN IN A GAME? A seagull being hit by the ball
BEST MOMENT IN CRICKET? My five-wicket haul for Sussex against Somerset at Taunton in the Royal London One-Day Cup in July 2016
HOW WOULD YOUR TEAM-MATES DESCRIBE YOU IN THREE WORDS? Quiet, funny, competitive
BEST PLAYER IN COUNTY CRICKET? Batsman: Ed Joyce (Sus). Bowler: Steve Magoffin (Sus)
MOST UNDERRATED PLAYER IN COUNTY CRICKET? Will Beer (Sus)
TIP FOR THE TOP? Delray Rawlins, Stuart Whittingham, George Garton (all Sus)
CRICKETING HEROES? Curtly Ambrose
NON-CRICKETING HEROES? Nelson Mandela, my mother
SURPRISING FACT? I'm both left- and right-handed
FANTASY SLIP CORDON? Keeper: Jerome Jones, 1st: Corey Collymore, 2nd: Chris Jordan, 3rd: Me. Those are the three people I'm most comfortable with
TWITTER: @craig_arch

Batting	Mat	Inns	NO	Runs	HS	Ave	SR	100	50	Ct	St
First-class	7	8	0	195	73	24.37	55.71	0	1	4	0
List A	3	3	1	46	35	23.00	83.63	0	0	0	0
Twenty20	4	3	2	21	12*	21.00	161.53	0	0	1	0

Bowling	Mat	Balls	Runs	Wkts	BBI	BBM	Ave	Econ	SR	5w	10
First-class	7	1459	778	28	4/31	7/62	27.78	3.19	52.1	0	0
List A	3	175	136	7	5/42	5/42	19.42	4.66	25.0	1	0
Twenty20	4	90	139	5	2/39	2/39	27.80	9.26	18.0	0	0

USMAN ARSHAD RHB / RMF / R0 / W0

FULL NAME: Usman Arshad
BORN: January 9, 1993, Bradford
SQUAD NO: 78
HEIGHT: 5ft 11in
NICKNAME: Benny
EDUCATION: Beckfoot Grammar School
TEAMS: Durham
ROLE: Bowler
DEBUT: First-class: 2013; List A: 2013; T20: 2014

BEST BATTING: 84 Durham vs Yorkshire, Chester-le-Street, 2016
BEST BOWLING: 4-78 Durham vs Northamptonshire, Northampton, 2014

WHAT FIRST GOT YOU INTO CRICKET? Playing with my brothers in the garden
BEST MOMENT IN CRICKET? Playing in T20 Finals Day at Edgbaston in 2016
HOW WOULD YOUR TEAM-MATES DESCRIBE YOU IN THREE WORDS? Genuine top lad
BEST PLAYER IN COUNTY CRICKET? Keaton Jennings (Dur)
TIP FOR THE TOP? Graham Clark (Dur)
CRICKETING HEROES? Chris Martin – because he swings it all over and has left-handers in his pocket
IF YOU WEREN'T A CRICKETER? I'd be a property developer or a handyman
SURPRISING FACT? I can throw left-handed. I didn't start bowling until I was 16
DESERT ISLAND DISC? Drake – Take Care
TWITTER: @usman_arshad65

Batting	Mat	Inns	NO	Runs	HS	Ave	SR	100	50	Ct	St
First-class	17	21	1	548	84	27.40	53.10	0	3	6	0
List A	14	7	4	56	25	18.66	58.94	0	0	2	0
Twenty20	37	18	7	152	43	13.81	119.68	0	0	8	0

Bowling	Mat	Balls	Runs	Wkts	BBI	BBM	Ave	Econ	SR	5w	10
First-class	17	1624	955	36	4/78	6/34	26.52	3.52	45.1	0	0
List A	14	453	471	9	3/50	3/50	52.33	6.23	50.3	0	0
Twenty20	37	678	990	42	3/18	3/18	23.57	8.76	16.1	0	0

MUHAMMAD AZHARULLAH RHB / RFM / R0 / W0

NORTHAMPTONSHIRE

FULL NAME: Muhammad Azharullah
BORN: December 25, 1983, Burewala, Pakistan
SQUAD NO: 92
HEIGHT: 5ft 8in
NICKNAME: Amazerulla, Azza, Azz
EDUCATION: Government College, Burewala; Bahauddin Zakariya University, Multan
TEAMS: Northamptonshire, Baluchistan, Multan, Quetta, Punjab
ROLE: Bowler
DEBUT: First-class: 2004; List A: 2005; T20: 2005

BEST BATTING: 58* Northamptonshire vs Kent, Canterbury, 2015
BEST BOWLING: 7-74 Quetta vs Lahore Ravi, Quetta, 2005
COUNTY CAP: 2015

WHAT FIRST GOT YOU INTO CRICKET? My eldest brother Mazhar Ullah was a fast bowler and played junior level of regional cricket but, unlike me, he was a good student and decided to become a doctor. I'm trying to fulfill his cricket dream
STRANGEST THING SEEN IN A GAME? A five-ball over when a team needed one run to win off the last ball
BEST MOMENT IN CRICKET? Winning the 2013 T20 Cup
HOW WOULD YOUR TEAM-MATES DESCRIBE YOU IN THREE WORDS? Cheeky, genius, bhai
BEST PLAYER IN COUNTY CRICKET? Rory Kleinveldt (Nor)
MOST UNDERRATED PLAYER IN COUNTY CRICKET? David Murphy (Nor)
TIP FOR THE TOP? Gareth Wade (Nor)
CRICKETING HEROES? Waqar Younis, Nadeem Iqbal, Mohammad Zahid – great fast bowlers
NON-CRICKETING HEROES? Holy Prophet PBUH
SURPRISING FACT? Whenever I don't bowl well I have a spicy curry. I don't listen to music
TWITTER: @azhar_ullah

Batting	Mat	Inns	NO	Runs	HS	Ave	SR	100	50	Ct	St
First-class	104	139	71	895	58*	13.16		0	1	23	0
List A	57	23	10	84	9	6.46	50.29	0	0	11	0
Twenty20	59	12	11	22	6*	22.00	68.75	0	0	9	0

Bowling	Mat	Balls	Runs	Wkts	BBI	BBM	Ave	Econ	SR	5w	10
First-class	104	16922	9648	331	7/74		29.14	3.42	51.1	15	2
List A	57	2527	2361	84	5/38	5/38	28.10	5.60	30.0	3	0
Twenty20	59	1134	1582	64	4/14	4/14	24.71	8.37	17.7	0	0

GEORGE BAILEY

RHB / RM / RO / WO

FULL NAME: George John Bailey
BORN: September 7, 1982, Tasmania
HEIGHT: 5ft 10in
NICKNAME: Hector
EDUCATION: University of Tasmania
TEAMS: Australia, Scotland, Hampshire,
Chennai Super Kings, Hobart Hurricanes,
Kings XI Punjab, Melbourne Stars,
Middlesex, Rising Pune Supergiants,
Sussex, Tasmania
ROLE: Batsman
DEBUT: Test: 2013; ODI: 2012; T20I: 2012;
First-class: 2004; List A: 2002; T20: 2006

BEST BATTING: 200* Tasmania vs New South Wales, Wollongong, 2017

NOTES: The Australian middle-order batsman signed with Hampshire for the second time, having first represented the club in 2013. Bailey has previously played for Middlesex and Sussex. He is available to play in all three formats, although may miss some games due to international commitments. In 2012 Bailey became the first man to captain Australia on international debut since Dave Gregory in the first-ever Test match. He was part of the team that whitewashed England in the 2013/14 Ashes, equalling Brian Lara's record by taking James Anderson for 28 runs in a single over

Batting	Mat	Inns	NO	Runs	HS	Ave	SR	100	50	Ct	St
Tests	5	8	1	183	53	26.14	58.84	0	1	10	0
ODIs	90	85	10	3044	156	40.58	83.51	3	22	48	0
T20Is	29	25	7	470	63	26.11	140.71	0	2	10	0
First-class	127	226	21	8322	200*	40.59	54.14	20	42	112	0
List A	249	231	25	7349	156	35.67	83.91	9	46	113	0
Twenty20	156	140	35	3085	76	29.38	131.16	0	19	62	0

Bowling	Mat	Balls	Runs	Wkts	BBI	BBM	Ave	Econ	SR	5w	10
Tests	5	-	-	-	-	-	-	-	-	-	-
ODIs	90	-	-	-	-	-	-	-	-	-	-
T20Is	29	-	-	-	-	-	-	-	-	-	-
First-class	127	84	46	0	-	-	-	3.28	-	0	0
List A	249	53	40	1	1/19	1/19	40.00	4.52	53.0	0	0
Twenty20	156	12	24	0	-	-	-	12.00	-	0	0

TOM BAILEY

RHB / RFM / R0 / W0

LANCASHIRE

FULL NAME: Thomas Ernest Bailey
BORN: April 21, 1991, Preston, Lancashire
SQUAD NO: 8
HEIGHT: 6ft 4in
NICKNAME: Jebby, Bails
EDUCATION: Myerscough College, Lancashire
TEAMS: Lancashire
ROLE: Bowler
DEBUT: First-class: 2012; List A: 2014; T20: 2015

BEST BATTING: 53 Lancashire vs Middlesex, Old Trafford, 2016
BEST BOWLING: 5-12 Lancashire vs Leicestershire, Leicester, 2015

FAMILY TIES? My dad played for a local side and I used to watch him every weekend as a kid
STRANGEST THING SEEN IN A GAME? A magpie colliding with a fielder at deep square-leg
BEST MOMENT IN CRICKET? Winning the NatWest T20 Blast in 2015
HOW WOULD YOUR TEAM-MATES DESCRIBE YOU IN THREE WORDS? Interesting, hilarious, gentle
BEST PLAYER IN COUNTY CRICKET? Marcus Trescothick (Som)
TIP FOR THE TOP? Danny Lamb (Lan)
CRICKETING HEROES? Steve Harmison – I just wanted to bowl fast
NON-CRICKETING HEROES? Tom Webster
IF YOU WEREN'T A CRICKETER? I'd be a nuclear scientist
SURPRISING FACT? I'm actually really smart
DESERT ISLAND DISC? Fugees – Greatest Hits
FANTASY SLIP CORDON? Keeper: Tom Webster, 1st: Danny Lamb, 2nd: Jack the Ripper, 3rd: Me
TWITTER: @TomBailDog

Batting	Mat	Inns	NO	Runs	HS	Ave	SR	100	50	Ct	St
First-class	22	30	7	370	53	16.08	45.28	0	1	2	0
List A	7	3	3	12	5*	-	60.00	0	0	1	0
Twenty20	9	2	1	0	0*	0.00	0.00	0	0	5	0

Bowling	Mat	Balls	Runs	Wkts	BBI	BBM	Ave	Econ	SR	5w	10
First-class	22	3991	2123	64	5/12	6/65	33.17	3.19	62.3	3	0
List A	7	329	290	10	3/31	3/31	29.00	5.28	32.9	0	0
Twenty20	9	138	246	7	2/24	2/24	35.14	10.69	19.7	0	0

JONNY BAIRSTOW   RHB / WK / R3 / W0

FULL NAME: Jonathan Marc Bairstow
BORN: September 26, 1989, Bradford
SQUAD NO: 21
NICKNAME: Bluey
EDUCATION: St Peter's School, York; Leeds Metropolitan University
TEAMS: England, Yorkshire, Peshawar Zalmi
ROLE: Batsman/wicketkeeper
DEBUT: Test: 2012; ODI: 2011; T20I: 2011; First-class: 2009; List A: 2009; T20: 2010

BEST BATTING: 246 Yorkshire vs Hampshire, Headingley, 2016
COUNTY CAP: 2011

FAMILY TIES? My father David played for Yorkshire and England
CRICKETING HEROES? Sachin Tendulkar
NON-CRICKETING HEROES? Jonny Wilkinson and Steve Irwin
IF YOU WEREN'T A CRICKETER? I'd be a rugby player
SURPRISING FACT? I played football for the Leeds United Academy for seven years
DESERT ISLAND DISC? Vengaboys or David Guetta
FANTASY SLIP CORDON? Keeper: Dad, 1st: Me, 2nd: David Beckham, 3rd: Mila Kunis, 4th: Ray Mears, Gully: Elisha Cuthbert
TWITTER: @jbairstow21

Batting	Mat	Inns	NO	Runs	HS	Ave	SR	100	50	Ct	St
Tests	38	65	6	2435	167*	41.27	55.04	3	14	93	5
ODIs	23	19	3	514	83*	32.12	86.67	0	3	16	2
T20Is	20	15	4	195	60*	17.72	107.73	0	1	23	0
First-class	142	230	31	9621	246	48.34		21	51	357	16
List A	85	75	9	2165	123	32.80	96.78	2	13	61	7
Twenty20	89	77	15	1448	102*	23.35	123.76	1	5	56	10
Bowling	Mat	Balls	Runs	Wkts	BBI	BBM	Ave	Econ	SR	5w	10
Tests	38	-	-	-	-	-	-	-	-	-	-
ODIs	23	-	-	-	-	-	-	-	-	-	-
T20Is	20	-	-	-	-	-	-	-	-	-	-
First-class	142	6	1	0	-	-	-	1.00	-	0	0
List A	85	-	-	-	-	-	-	-	-	-	-
Twenty20	89	-	-	-	-	-	-	-	-	-	-

ADAM BALL

RHB / LMF / R0 / W0

FULL NAME: Adam James Ball
BORN: March 1, 1993, Greenwich, London
SQUAD NO: 24
HEIGHT: 6ft 2in
NICKNAME: Bally
EDUCATION: Beths Grammar School, Bexley
TEAMS: Kent
ROLE: Allrounder
DEBUT: First-class: 2011; List A: 2010;
T20: 2011

BEST BATTING: 69 Kent vs Lancashire, Canterbury, 2013
BEST BOWLING: 3-36 Kent vs Leicestershire, Leicester, 2011

BEST MOMENT IN CRICKET? Signing my first professional contract with Kent and being
named as England U19 captain
CRICKETING HEROES? Andrew Flintoff
DESERT ISLAND DISC? Taio Cruz
TWITTER: @AdamBall2
NOTES: Left-armer and lower-order batsman who joined Kent ahead of the 2010 season as a
16-year-old. Captained England in the 2012 U19 World Cup and shone in T20 cricket for his
county but has been a bit-part player over recent seasons

Batting	Mat	Inns	NO	Runs	HS	Ave	SR	100	50	Ct	St
First-class	29	42	3	800	69	20.51	44.59	0	3	17	0
List A	31	23	8	232	40*	15.46	81.97	0	0	10	0
Twenty20	37	18	6	142	18	11.83	105.97	0	0	22	0

Bowling	Mat	Balls	Runs	Wkts	BBI	BBM	Ave	Econ	SR	5w	10
First-class	29	2112	1434	29	3/36	3/45	49.44	4.07	72.8	0	0
List A	31	873	810	22	3/36	3/36	36.81	5.56	39.6	0	0
Twenty20	37	588	810	27	2/18	2/18	30.00	8.26	21.7	0	0

JAKE BALL

RHB / RFM / R0 / W1 / MVP25

FULL NAME: Jacob Timothy Ball
BORN: March 14, 1991, Mansfield, Nottinghamshire
SQUAD NO: 28
HEIGHT: 6ft 3in
NICKNAME: Yak
EDUCATION: Meden School, Mansfield
TEAMS: England, Nottinghamshire
ROLE: Bowler
DEBUT: Test: 2016; ODI: 2016; First-class: 2011; List A: 2009; T20: 2011

BEST BATTING: 49* Nottinghamshire vs Warwickshire, Trent Bridge, 2015
BEST BOWLING: 6-49 Nottinghamshire vs Sussex, Trent Bridge, 2015

FAMILY TIES? My uncle Bruce French played for England. My older brother Jonathan has played Minor Counties for Lincolnshire
BEST MOMENT IN CRICKET? Taking my first five-wicket haul against Sussex
HOW WOULD YOUR TEAM-MATES DESCRIBE YOU IN THREE WORDS? Funny and laid-back
SUPERSTITIONS? I always turn the same way at the end of my mark
TIP FOR THE TOP? Luke Wood (Not)
IF YOU WEREN'T A CRICKETER? I'd be working in property
SURPRISING FACT? I was a batter till the age of 15
DESERT ISLAND DISC? The Beatles – 1
FANTASY SLIP CORDON? Keeper: Me, 1st: Jennifer Aniston, 2nd: Ross Barkley, 3rd: Jack Whitehall, Gully: David Beckham
TWITTER: @Jakeball30

Batting	Mat	Inns	NO	Runs	HS	Ave	SR	100	50	Ct	St
Tests	3	6	0	52	31	8.66	47.70	0	0	1	0
ODIs	6	1	0	28	28	28.00	127.27	0	0	1	0
First-class	37	57	6	574	49*	11.25	72.75	0	0	5	0
List A	62	23	11	150	28	12.50	117.18	0	0	10	0
Twenty20	38	9	7	20	8*	10.00	90.90	0	0	9	0

Bowling	Mat	Balls	Runs	Wkts	BBI	BBM	Ave	Econ	SR	5w	10
Tests	3	456	228	2	1/47	1/47	114.00	3.00	228.0	0	0
ODIs	6	335	342	12	5/51	5/51	28.50	6.12	27.9	1	0
First-class	37	5541	3112	116	6/49	9/67	26.82	3.36	47.7	4	0
List A	62	2440	2302	76	5/51	5/51	30.28	5.66	32.1	1	0
Twenty20	38	753	1052	39	3/36	3/36	26.97	8.38	19.3	0	0

GARY BALLANCE

LHB / LB / R2 / W0

FULL NAME: Gary Simon Ballance
BORN: November 22, 1989, Harare, Zimbabwe
SQUAD NO: 19
NICKNAME: Gazza, Gaz
EDUCATION: Peterhouse School, Marondera, Zimbabwe; Harrow School, London
TEAMS: England, Yorkshire, Derbyshire, Mid West Rhinos
ROLE: Batsman
DEBUT: Test: 2014; ODI: 2013; First-class: 2008; List A: 2006; T20: 2010

BEST BATTING: 210 Mid West Rhinos vs Southern Rocks, Masvingo, 2011
COUNTY CAP: 2012 (Yorkshire)

NOTES: A close family friend of former Zimbabwe skipper David Houghton, Ballance signed for Derbyshire at 16 before joining the Yorkshire Academy in 2008. He played for Zimbabwe U19 at the World Cup in 2006 before qualifying to play for England. He made his ODI debut in 2013 before making his Test bow at Sydney in the 2013/14 Ashes. He had an exceptional summer in Test cricket in 2014, hitting three centuries to cement his place at No.3. He lost his Test place during the 2015 Ashes but was recalled last summer, only to be jettisoned again after struggling in Bangladesh last October. Ballance captains Yorkshire across all formats in 2017 after the retirement of Andrew Gale

Batting	Mat	Inns	NO	Runs	HS	Ave	SR	100	50	Ct	St
Tests	21	38	2	1413	156	39.25	47.02	4	7	20	0
ODIs	16	15	1	297	79	21.21	67.04	0	2	8	0
First-class	117	191	18	8198	210	47.38	51.35	29	38	107	0
List A	88	82	12	3336	139	47.65	86.35	6	20	39	0
Twenty20	69	62	8	1322	68	24.48	119.96	0	5	39	0

Bowling	Mat	Balls	Runs	Wkts	BBI	BBM	Ave	Econ	SR	5w	10
Tests	21	12	5	0	-	-	-	2.50	-	0	0
ODIs	16	-	-	-	-	-	-	-	-	-	-
First-class	117	162	154	0	-	-	-	5.70	-	0	0
List A	88	-	-	-	-	-	-	-	-	-	-
Twenty20	69	-	-	-	-	-	-	-	-	-	-

CAMERON BANCROFT　　　RHB / WK / R0 / W0

FULL NAME: Cameron Timothy Bancroft
BORN: November 19, 1992, Perth, Australia
SQUAD NO: 43
HEIGHT: 5ft 10in
EDUCATION: Aquinas College, Perth
TEAMS: Australia, Gloucestershire, Perth Scorchers, Western Australia
ROLE: Batsman/wicketkeeper
DEBUT: T20I: 2016; First-class: 2013; List A: 2011; T20: 2014

BEST BATTING: 211 Western Australia vs New South Wales, Perth, 2015

TWITTER: @cbancroft4
NOTES: Came close to a Test debut for Australia after an impressive 2014/15 Sheffield Shield season in which he averaged 47 and scored a double hundred in the final game of the season. Made his international debut in January 2016, in a T20 against India at Sydney. An opening batsman, he joined Gloucestershire for the first two months of the 2016 season and found the going tough, with just one fifty in nine Championship innings. Has re-signed for the 2017 season to play across all formats

Batting	Mat	Inns	NO	Runs	HS	Ave	SR	100	50	Ct	St
T20Is	1	1	1	0	0*	-	-	0	0	1	0
First-class	51	92	4	3159	211	35.89	40.71	8	11	64	1
List A	34	33	4	959	176	33.06	72.76	1	6	25	0
Twenty20	14	9	3	159	72	26.50	124.21	0	1	9	3

Bowling	Mat	Balls	Runs	Wkts	BBI	BBM	Ave	Econ	SR	5w	10
T20Is	1	-	-	-	-	-	-	-	-	-	-
First-class	51	6	0	0	-	-	-	0.00	-	0	0
List A	34	-	-	-	-	-	-	-	-	-	-
Twenty20	14	-	-	-	-	-	-	-	-	-	-

LIAM BANKS

RHB / RM / RO / WO

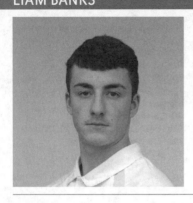

FULL NAME: Liam Banks
BORN: March 27, 1999, Stoke-on-Trent
SQUAD NO: 8
HEIGHT: 5ft 11in
NICKNAME: Banksy
EDUCATION: Newcastle-under-Lyme School and Sixth Form College
TEAMS: Staffordshire
ROLE: Batsman
DEBUT: Yet to make first-team debut

WHAT FIRST GOT YOU INTO CRICKET? Living close to a cricket club
STRANGEST THING SEEN IN A GAME? A cow on a cricket field
BEST MOMENT IN CRICKET? Scoring a hundred after my grandad died
HOW WOULD YOUR TEAM-MATES DESCRIBE YOU IN THREE WORDS? Leader, honest, fun
BEST PLAYER IN COUNTY CRICKET? Ben Duckett (Nor)
TIP FOR THE TOP? Dom Bess (Som), Matt Parkinson (Lan), Matthew Lamb (War)
CRICKETING HEROES? Joe Root, Ricky Ponting
IF YOU WEREN'T A CRICKETER? I'd be a cricket coach or labour worker
SURPRISING FACT? I love animals and fishing
UNUSUAL OBJECT AT HOME? A piece of rock from Lanzarote
DESERT ISLAND DISC? Noel Gallagher
FANTASY SLIP CORDON? Keeper: Grandad, 1st: Luke (my best mate), 2nd: My brother, 3rd: Joe Root, Gully: Jack Wood (a friend)

KEITH BARKER

LHB / LFM / R0 / W3 / MVP12

FULL NAME: Keith Hubert Douglas Barker
BORN: October 21, 1986, Manchester
SQUAD NO: 13
HEIGHT: 6ft 2in
NICKNAME: Barks, Barky, Barksy
EDUCATION: Moorhead High School, Accrington; Preston College
TEAMS: Warwickshire
ROLE: Allrounder
DEBUT: First-class: 2009; List A: 2009; T20: 2009

WARWICKSHIRE

BEST BATTING: 125 Warwickshire vs Surrey, Guildford, 2013
BEST BOWLING: 6-40 Warwickshire vs Somerset, Taunton, 2012
COUNTY CAP: 2013

FAMILY TIES? Father, godfather and brothers all played various levels of cricket
STRANGEST THING SEEN IN A GAME? Neil Carter falling over three times in one over
BEST MOMENT IN CRICKET? Winning the County Championship at Worcester in 2012
HOW WOULD YOUR TEAM-MATES DESCRIBE YOU IN THREE WORDS? Loud, prankster, car-addict
BEST PLAYER IN COUNTY CRICKET? Jeetan Patel (War)
MOST UNDERRATED PLAYER IN COUNTY CRICKET? Jack Leach (Som)
TIP FOR THE TOP? Alex Mellor (War)
NON-CRICKETING HEROES? Lewis Hamilton – confident in his ability and backs himself in any situation
IF YOU WEREN'T A CRICKETER? I'd be a lower-league footballer or a policeman
SURPRISING FACT? I never scored a hundred in an innings for Enfield CC First XI
FANTASY SLIP CORDON? Keeper: Dean Barker, 1st: Me, 2nd: Keith Barker Snr, 3rd: Gary Barker, Gully: Andy Barker

Batting	Mat	Inns	NO	Runs	HS	Ave	SR	100	50	Ct	St
First-class	89	113	18	2784	125	29.30	60.42	6	9	30	0
List A	49	33	8	440	56	17.60	88.88	0	1	11	0
Twenty20	59	31	6	316	46	12.64	104.98	0	0	17	0
Bowling	Mat	Balls	Runs	Wkts	BBI	BBM	Ave	Econ	SR	5w	10
First-class	89	14991	7446	289	6/40	10/70	25.76	2.98	51.8	12	1
List A	49	1714	1639	53	4/33	4/33	30.92	5.73	32.3	0	0
Twenty20	59	1074	1395	62	4/19	4/19	22.50	7.79	17.3	0	0

ED BARNARD

RHB / RFM / RO / WO

FULL NAME: Edward George Barnard
BORN: November 20, 1995, Shrewsbury
SQUAD NO: 30
HEIGHT: 6ft
NICKNAME: Test-tube, Barndoor, Earthworm Jim
EDUCATION: Meole Brace School, Shrewsbury; Shrewsbury School
TEAMS: Worcestershire
ROLE: Bowler
DEBUT: First-class: 2015; List A: 2015; T20: 2015

BEST BATTING: 73 Worcestershire vs Derbyshire, Derby, 2016
BEST BOWLING: 4-62 Worcestershire vs Leicestershire, Worcester, 2016

FAMILY TIES? Dad (Andy) played for Shropshire; brother (Mike) played for Shropshire and first-class cricket for Oxford MCCU; brother (Steve) played for Shropshire
STRANGEST THING SEEN IN A GAME? Circling swan stops play
BEST MOMENT IN CRICKET? Beating India in the 2014 U19 World Cup quarter-final
BEST PLAYER IN COUNTY CRICKET? Jeetan Patel (War)
MOST UNDERRATED PLAYER IN COUNTY CRICKET? Wayne Madsen (Der)
TIP FOR THE TOP? Josh Tongue, Ollie Westbury (both Wor)
CRICKETING HEROES? Andrew Flintoff in the 2005 Ashes
NON-CRICKETING HEROES? Nelson Mandela and Alan Shearer
DESERT ISLAND DISC? Ashton Kutcher
FANTASY SLIP CORDON? Keeper: Tim Vine, 1st: Ed Sheeran, 2nd: Angelina Jolie, 3rd: Me, Gully: Ricky Gervais
TWITTER: @EdBarn95

Batting	Mat	Inns	NO	Runs	HS	Ave	SR	100	50	Ct	St
First-class	19	25	6	503	73	26.47	54.73	0	2	7	0
List A	15	10	1	168	51	18.66	92.30	0	1	8	0
Twenty20	24	9	3	38	10	6.33	88.37	0	0	13	0

Bowling	Mat	Balls	Runs	Wkts	BBI	BBM	Ave	Econ	SR	5w	10
First-class	19	2895	1768	47	4/62	4/72	37.61	3.66	61.5	0	0
List A	15	690	658	21	3/45	3/45	31.33	5.72	32.8	0	0
Twenty20	24	385	559	13	2/18	2/18	43.00	8.71	29.6	0	0

GEORGE BARTLETT

RHB / OB / R0 / W0

FULL NAME: George Anthony Bartlett
BORN: March 14, 1998, Frimley, Surrey
SQUAD NO: 14
EDUCATION: Millfield School, Somerset
TEAMS: England U19, Somerset 2nd XI
ROLE: Batsman
DEBUT: Yet to make first-team debut

SOMERSET

TWITTER: @georgebartlett9
NOTES: A batsman who bowls off-spin, Bartlett is a product of the Somerset Academy and signed a one-year contract with the club in October 2016. Earlier this year he made 179 for England U19 against India U19 in a four-day 'Test' at Nagpur, taking Nasser Hussain's record for the highest score by an England U19 batsman overseas. Bartlett made his debut for Somerset Second XI in 2014 and featured in the 2016 U19 World Cup. He made a hundred in the U19 Test against Sri Lanka last summer and earned a senior contract on the back of consistent performances for Somerset seconds in 2016, making appearances in the finals of both the Second XI T20 and Second XI Trophy competitions

GARETH BATTY — RHB / OB / R0 / W2 / MVP20

SURREY

FULL NAME: Gareth Jon Batty
BORN: October 13, 1977, Bradford
SQUAD NO: 13
HEIGHT: 5ft 11in
NICKNAME: Bats, Stuta
EDUCATION: Bingley Grammar School
TEAMS: England, Surrey, Worcestershire, Yorkshire
ROLE: Bowler
DEBUT: Test: 2003; ODI: 2002; T20I: 2009; First-class: 1997; List A: 1998; T20: 2003

BEST BATTING: 133 Worcestershire vs Surrey, The Oval, 2004
BEST BOWLING: 8-68 Surrey vs Essex, Chelmsford, 2014
COUNTY CAP: 2011 (Surrey) **TESTIMONIAL:** 2017 (Surrey)

FAMILY TIES? Dad played for Yorkshire seconds, brother Jeremy for Yorkshire and Somerset
HOW WOULD YOUR TEAM-MATES DESCRIBE YOU IN THREE WORDS? Stubborn, passionate, ginger
BEST PLAYER IN COUNTY CRICKET? Kumar Sangakkara (Sur)
NON-CRICKETING HEROES? Winston Churchill and Maggie Thatcher – people who had the courage to make decisions
IF YOU WEREN'T A CRICKETER? I'd be a fireman
SURPRISING FACT? This is my 21st year as a pro and also my testimonial year
TWITTER: @Garethbatty2017

Batting	Mat	Inns	NO	Runs	HS	Ave	SR	100	50	Ct	St
Tests	9	12	2	149	38	14.90	25.68	0	0	3	0
ODIs	10	8	2	30	17	5.00	41.09	0	0	4	0
T20Is	1	1	0	4	4	4.00	57.14	0	0	0	0
First-class	240	359	60	7100	133	23.74		3	30	161	0
List A	247	184	37	2279	83*	15.50		0	5	80	0
Twenty20	133	80	27	595	87	11.22	103.83	0	1	38	0

Bowling	Mat	Balls	Runs	Wkts	BBI	BBM	Ave	Econ	SR	5w	10
Tests	9	1714	914	15	3/55	5/153	60.93	3.19	114.2	0	0
ODIs	10	440	366	5	2/40	2/40	73.20	4.99	88.0	0	0
T20Is	1	18	17	0	-	-	-	5.66	-	0	0
First-class	240	42903	20819	629	8/68		33.09	2.91	68.2	26	3
List A	247	9585	7350	232	5/35	5/35	31.68	4.60	41.3	2	0
Twenty20	133	2335	2853	99	4/13	4/13	28.81	7.33	23.5	0	0

AARON BEARD

LHB / RMF / RO / WO

FULL NAME: Aaron Paul Beard
BORN: October 15, 1997, Chelmsford
SQUAD NO: 14
HEIGHT: 5ft 11in
NICKNAME: Beardo
EDUCATION: The Boswells School, Chelmsford; Great Baddow High School, Chelmsford
TEAMS: Essex
ROLE: Bowler
DEBUT: First-class: 2016

ESSEX

BEST BATTING: 0* Essex vs Northamptonshire, Northampton, 2016
BEST BOWLING: 4-62 Essex vs Sri Lankans, Chelmsford, 2016

WHAT FIRST GOT YOU INTO CRICKET? My dad and uncle both played and I used to go along and watch
BEST MOMENT IN CRICKET? Taking 4-62 against Sri Lanka on my first-class debut in 2016
TIP FOR THE TOP? Dan Lawrence (Ess)
CRICKETING HEROES? Andrew Flintoff – I want to play cricket with the confidence he had
NON-CRICKETING HEROES? David Beckham, Cristiano Ronaldo
IF YOU WEREN'T A CRICKETER? I'd be a footballer
SURPRISING FACT? When playing golf I putt right-handed and play the rest of my shots left-handed
DESERT ISLAND DISC? Jax Jones – You Don't Know Me
FANTASY SLIP CORDON? Keeper: Del Boy, 1st: James Corden, 2nd: Andrew Flintoff, 3rd: Margot Robbie, Gully: Me
TWITTER: @aaronbeard_14

Batting	Mat	Inns	NO	Runs	HS	Ave	SR	100	50	Ct	St
First-class	3	1	1	0	0*	-	0.00	0	0	1	0

Bowling	Mat	Balls	Runs	Wkts	BBI	BBM	Ave	Econ	SR	5w	10
First-class	3	458	300	9	4/62	5/81	33.33	3.93	50.8	0	0

WILL BEER RHB / LB / RO / WO

SUSSEX

FULL NAME: William Andrew Thomas Beer
BORN: October 8, 1988, Crawley, Sussex
SQUAD NO: 18
HEIGHT: 5ft 9.5in
NICKNAME: Beery
EDUCATION: Reigate Grammar School;
Collyer's Sixth Form College, Horsham
TEAMS: Sussex
ROLE: Bowler
DEBUT: First-class: 2008; List A: 2009;
T20: 2008

BEST BATTING: 39 Sussex vs Middlesex, Lord's, 2013
BEST BOWLING: 3-31 Sussex vs Worcestershire, Worcester, 2010

FAMILY TIES? My dad played for Sussex Second XI and Horsham
STRANGEST THING SEEN IN A GAME? A seagull famously stopped a delivery of mine going
for six – instead it cost me only two runs! Pretty sure the seagull survived too
BEST MOMENT IN CRICKET? Winning the T20 domestic tournament in 2009 alongside my
first-class debut at Lord's
BEST PLAYER IN COUNTY CRICKET? Jeetan Patel (War) – brilliant in all three formats
MOST UNDERRATED PLAYER IN COUNTY CRICKET? Ben Brown (Sus)
TIP FOR THE TOP? Jofra Archer, Stuart Whittingham (both Sus)
CRICKETING HEROES? Shane Warne, Michael Yardy
SURPRISING FACT? I am a big horse-racing fan – I never miss a Final Furlong podcast. I have
an orange belt in judo
DESERT ISLAND DISC? Good Old Sussex By The Sea
FANTASY SLIP CORDON? Keeper: James Corden, 1st: Shane Warne, 2nd: Me, 3rd: Cameron
Diaz, Gully: David Beckham
TWITTER: @willbeer18

Batting	Mat	Inns	NO	Runs	HS	Ave	SR	100	50	Ct	St
First-class	12	14	3	236	39	21.45	30.93	0	0	5	0
List A	50	30	9	334	45*	15.90	82.46	0	0	10	0
Twenty20	90	50	16	316	37	9.29	125.89	0	0	19	0
Bowling	Mat	Balls	Runs	Wkts	BBI	BBM	Ave	Econ	SR	5w	10
First-class	12	1231	719	14	3/31	3/36	51.35	3.50	87.9	0	0
List A	50	2070	1780	44	3/27	3/27	40.45	5.15	47.0	0	0
Twenty20	90	1644	1981	70	3/14	3/14	28.30	7.22	23.4	0	0

IAN BELL — RHB / RM / R4 / W0 / MVP43

FULL NAME: Ian Ronald Bell
BORN: April 11, 1982, Walsgrave, Coventry, Warwickshire
SQUAD NO: 4
HEIGHT: 5ft 10in
NICKNAME: Belly
EDUCATION: Princethorpe College, Rugby
TEAMS: England, Warwickshire, Perth Scorchers
ROLE: Batsman
DEBUT: Test: 2004; ODI: 2004; T20I: 2006; First-class: 1999; List A: 1999; T20: 2003

WARWICKSHIRE

BEST BATTING: 262* Warwickshire vs Sussex, Horsham, 2004
BEST BOWLING: 4-4 Warwickshire vs Middlesex, Lord's, 2004
COUNTY CAP: 2001 BENEFIT: 2011

BEST MOMENT IN CRICKET? Winning the County Championship with Warwickshire and Ashes victories
CRICKETING HEROES? Ricky Ponting, Dominic Ostler, Jeetan Patel
NON-CRICKETING HEROES? Gary Shaw, Gordon Cowans
IF YOU WEREN'T A CRICKETER? I'd be sitting at the Holte End watching the Villa
SURPRISING FACT? I have an honorary doctorate at Coventry University
TWITTER: @Ian_Bell

Batting	Mat	Inns	NO	Runs	HS	Ave	SR	100	50	Ct	St
Tests	118	205	24	7727	235	42.69	49.46	22	46	100	0
ODIs	161	157	14	5416	141	37.87	77.16	4	35	54	0
T20Is	8	8	1	188	60*	26.85	115.33	0	1	4	0
First-class	278	467	50	18500	262*	44.36		51	96	211	0
List A	302	289	30	10494	158	40.51		11	76	106	0
Twenty20	77	74	9	1864	90	28.67	122.06	0	11	26	0

Bowling	Mat	Balls	Runs	Wkts	BBI	BBM	Ave	Econ	SR	5w	10
Tests	118	108	76	1	1/33	1/33	76.00	4.22	108.0	0	0
ODIs	161	88	88	6	3/9	3/9	14.66	6.00	14.6	0	0
T20Is	8	-	-	-	-	-	-	-	-	-	-
First-class	278	2875	1615	47	4/4		34.36	3.37	61.1	0	0
List A	302	1290	1138	33	5/41	5/41	34.48	5.29	39.0	1	0
Twenty20	77	132	186	3	1/12	1/12	62.00	8.45	44.0	0	0

DANIEL BELL-DRUMMOND RHB/RM/R1/W0/MVP56

FULL NAME: Daniel James Bell-Drummond
BORN: August 4, 1993, Lewisham, London
SQUAD NO: 23
HEIGHT: 5ft 11in
NICKNAME: DBD, Deebz
EDUCATION: Millfield School, Somerset;
Anglia Ruskin University
TEAMS: Kent, England Lions
ROLE: Batsman
DEBUT: First-class: 2011; List A: 2011;
T20: 2011

BEST BATTING: 206* Kent vs Loughborough MCCU, Canterbury, 2016
COUNTY CAP: 2015

FAMILY TIES? My father got me into cricket. I've always really enjoyed spending time at my local club Catford Wanderers CC
BEST MOMENT IN CRICKET? Making my first-class debut
MOST UNDERRATED PLAYER IN COUNTY CRICKET? Will Gidman (Ken)
TIP FOR THE TOP? Tom Alsop (Ham), Tom Helm (Mid)
CRICKETING HEROES? Brian Lara, Kevin Pietersen, Chris Gayle, Marcus Trescothick
NON-CRICKETING HEROES? Nelson Mandela, Muhammad Ali, Thierry Henry
IF YOU WEREN'T A CRICKETER? I'd be a musician
FANTASY SLIP CORDON? Keeper: Floyd Mayweather Jr, 1st: Me, 2nd: Robin van Persie,
3rd: Lee Evans, Gully: Brian Lara
TWITTER: @deebzz23

Batting	Mat	Inns	NO	Runs	HS	Ave	SR	100	50	Ct	St
First-class	68	114	11	3824	206*	37.12	50.36	9	20	27	0
List A	49	48	3	1613	171*	35.84	79.81	2	11	16	0
Twenty20	45	45	2	1095	112*	25.46	128.97	1	6	11	0

Bowling	Mat	Balls	Runs	Wkts	BBI	BBM	Ave	Econ	SR	5w	10
First-class	68	41	54	0	-	-	-	7.90	-	0	0
List A	49	12	15	0	-	-	-	7.50	-	0	0
Twenty20	45	-	-	-	-	-	-	-	-	-	-

GARETH BERG

RHB / RMF / RO / WO

FULL NAME: Gareth Kyle Berg
BORN: January 18, 1981, Cape Town,
South Africa
SQUAD NO: 13
HEIGHT: 6ft
NICKNAME: Ice, Bergy, Ford
EDUCATION: South African College School,
Cape Town
TEAMS: Italy, Hampshire, Middlesex
ROLE: Allrounder
DEBUT: First-class: 2008; List A: 2008;
T20: 2009

BEST BATTING: 130* Middlesex vs Leicestershire, Leicester, 2011
BEST BOWLING: 6-56 Hampshire vs Yorkshire, Southampton, 2016
COUNTY CAP: 2010 (Middlesex)

TWITTER: @Bergy646
NOTES: Joined Hampshire for the start of the 2015 season after seven years at Middlesex and had a highly successful first season with his new county, hitting 674 first-class runs and picking up 43 wickets – his best haul in England. Less effective in 2016, scoring one fifty in 13 Championship innings, although he was Hampshire's leading wicket-taker in the RL Cup

Batting	Mat	Inns	NO	Runs	HS	Ave	SR	100	50	Ct	St
First-class	98	150	18	3942	130*	29.86	65.38	2	23	58	0
List A	70	53	8	1114	75	24.75	91.76	0	5	25	0
Twenty20	66	53	18	915	90	26.14	127.97	0	3	15	0

Bowling	Mat	Balls	Runs	Wkts	BBI	BBM	Ave	Econ	SR	5w	10
First-class	98	12479	6416	202	6/56	7/90	31.76	3.08	61.7	4	0
List A	70	2001	1834	51	4/24	4/24	35.96	5.49	39.2	0	0
Twenty20	66	1146	1452	55	4/20	4/20	26.40	7.60	20.8	0	0

HUGH BERNARD

RHB / RMF / R0 / W0

FULL NAME: Hugh Robert Bernard
BORN: September 14, 1996, Canterbury
SQUAD NO: 27
HEIGHT: 5ft 11in
NICKNAME: Bernie, Hughsey, HB
EDUCATION: Archbishop's School, Canterbury
TEAMS: Kent
ROLE: Bowler
DEBUT: First-class: 2016; List A: 2017

BEST BATTING: 14 Kent vs Glamorgan, Canterbury, 2016
BEST BOWLING: 2-68 Kent vs Glamorgan, Canterbury, 2016

WHAT FIRST GOT YOU INTO CRICKET? Playing with my dad in the back garden
BEST MOMENT IN CRICKET? Taking a five-fer for England U19 in Australia
HOW WOULD YOUR TEAM-MATES DESCRIBE YOU IN THREE WORDS? A little strange
BEST PLAYER IN COUNTY CRICKET? Sam Northeast (Ken)
MOST UNDERRATED PLAYER IN COUNTY CRICKET? Steven Mullaney (Not)
TIP FOR THE TOP? Adam Hickey (Dur), Matt Hunn, Charlie Hartley, Ivan Thomas (all Ken)
CRICKETING HEROES? James Anderson, Malcolm Marshall
IF YOU WEREN'T A CRICKETER? I'd be a professional footballer
UNUSUAL OBJECT AT HOME? A left-handed screwdriver and a long weight
DESERT ISLAND DISC? Rick Astley – Never Gonna Give You Up
FANTASY SLIP CORDON? Keeper: David Beckham, 1st: Martin Luther King, 2nd: Jack Whitehall, 3rd: Me
TWITTER: @HughBernard1996

Batting	Mat	Inns	NO	Runs	HS	Ave	SR	100	50	Ct	St
First-class	1	1	0	14	14	14.00	53.84	0	0	0	0
List A	2	2	1	7	7	7.00	46.66	0	0	0	0

Bowling	Mat	Balls	Runs	Wkts	BBI	BBM	Ave	Econ	SR	5w	10
First-class	1	132	105	3	2/68	3/105	35.00	4.77	44.0	0	0
List A	2	96	90	1	1/40	1/40	90.00	5.62	96.0	0	0

DOM BESS
RHB / OB / R0 / W0

FULL NAME: Dominic Mark Bess
BORN: July 22, 1997, Exeter, Devon
SQUAD NO: 38
HEIGHT: 5ft 11in
NICKNAME: Calf, Bessy
EDUCATION: Blundell's School, Tiverton, Devon
TEAMS: Somerset
ROLE: Bowler
DEBUT: First-class: 2016; T20: 2016

BEST BATTING: 41 Somerset vs Nottinghamshire, Taunton, 2016
BEST BOWLING: 6-28 Somerset vs Warwickshire, Taunton, 2016

WHAT FIRST GOT YOU INTO CRICKET? Playing with my grandad in his garden
FAMILY TIES? My grandad, dad, uncle and cousins all played for Sidmouth CC
BEST MOMENT IN CRICKET? Making my first-class debut against Pakistan in 2016 and then taking 6-28 on my Championship debut later in the summer
BEST PLAYER IN COUNTY CRICKET? Jack Leach (Som)
MOST UNDERRATED PLAYER IN COUNTY CRICKET? Tom Abell (Som) – having grown up playing with him, I can say that he is going to be a seriously good player. Becoming Somerset captain aged 22 just shows he's got something very special about him
TIP FOR THE TOP? George Hankins (Glo), Mason Crane (Ham)
CRICKETING HEROES? Nathon Lyon, AB de Villiers, Ian Bell, Jack Leach
NON-CRICKETING HEROES? My parents – I can't thank them enough for what they've done for me
IF YOU WEREN'T A CRICKETER? I'd be working for my old man as an electrician
SURPRISING FACT? I have the biggest head in the south-west, unofficially
DESERT ISLAND DISC? Ed Sheeran – Divide
TWITTER: @dombess99

Batting	Mat	Inns	NO	Runs	HS	Ave	SR	100	50	Ct	St
First-class	3	5	0	100	41	20.00	53.47	0	0	5	0
Twenty20	1	1	0	1	1	1.00	50.00	0	0	0	0

Bowling	Mat	Balls	Runs	Wkts	BBI	BBM	Ave	Econ	SR	5w	10
First-class	3	539	264	13	6/28	8/59	20.30	2.93	41.4	2	0
Twenty20	1	24	31	1	1/31	1/31	31.00	7.75	24.0	0	0

SAM BILLINGS

RHB / WK / R0 / W0

FULL NAME: Samuel William Billings
BORN: June 15, 1991, Pembury, Kent
SQUAD NO: 7
HEIGHT: 6ft
NICKNAME: Bilbo, Skittles
EDUCATION: Haileybury and Imperial College, Hertfordshire; Loughborough University
TEAMS: England, Kent, Delhi Daredevils, Islamabad United, Sydney Sixers
ROLE: Batsman/wicketkeeper
DEBUT: ODI: 2015; T20I: 2015; First-class: 2011; List A: 2011; T20: 2011

BEST BATTING: 171 Kent vs Gloucestershire, Bristol, 2016
COUNTY CAP: 2015

BEST MOMENT IN CRICKET? Making my England debut
CRICKETING HEROES? Sachin Tendulkar and Adam Gilchrist – both phenomenal players. One is the best-ever in my opinion and the other single-handedly changed the role of a wicketkeeper in any team
NON-CRICKETING HEROES? Lewis Hamilton, David Beckham and Cristiano Ronaldo – all unbelievable athletes who have excelled in their fields
IF YOU WEREN'T A CRICKETER? Working for the family business or in the City. I'm very driven – if I want something I'll work tirelessly to get it
DESERT ISLAND DISC? Tinie Tempah
FANTASY SLIP CORDON? Keeper: Me, 1st: Michael McIntyre, 2nd: Candice Swanepoel, 3rd: Aristotle, 4th: Sachin Tendulkar, Gully: David Beckham
TWITTER: @sambillings

Batting	Mat	Inns	NO	Runs	HS	Ave	SR	100	50	Ct	St
ODIs	9	8	0	239	62	29.87	94.84	0	2	6	0
T20Is	10	9	0	133	53	14.77	154.65	0	1	6	1
First-class	45	65	5	1982	171	33.03	59.04	3	10	124	9
List A	71	65	12	2342	175	44.18	109.08	5	16	61	7
Twenty20	99	93	11	1714	78*	20.90	123.93	0	7	60	7

Bowling	Mat	Balls	Runs	Wkts	BBI	BBM	Ave	Econ	SR	5w	10
ODIs	9	-	-	-	-	-	-	-	-	-	-
T20Is	10	-	-	-	-	-	-	-	-	-	-
First-class	45	1	4	0	-	-	-	24.00	-	0	0
List A	71	-	-	-	-	-	-	-	-	-	-
Twenty20	99	-	-	-	-	-	-	-	-	-	-

ALEX BLAKE

LHB / RM / RO / WO

FULL NAME: Alexander James Blake
BORN: January 25, 1989, Farnborough, Kent
SQUAD NO: 10
HEIGHT: 6ft 2in
NICKNAME: Blakey, Butler, TS
EDUCATION: Hayes Secondary School, Kent;
Leeds Metropolitan University
TEAMS: Kent
ROLE: Batsman
DEBUT: First-class: 2008; List A: 2007;
T20: 2010

KENT

BEST BATTING: 105* Kent vs Yorkshire, Headingley, 2010
BEST BOWLING: 2-9 Kent vs Pakistanis, Canterbury, 2010

WHAT FIRST GOT YOU INTO CRICKET? Watching my dad play club cricket for Bromley Town CC on Saturdays
BEST MOMENT IN CRICKET? My maiden first-class century vs Yorkshire in 2010
HOW WOULD YOUR TEAM-MATES DESCRIBE YOU IN THREE WORDS? Reckless, indecisive, handsome
SUPERSTITIONS? Wearing the same pair of gloves that I've scored runs in previously
BEST PLAYER IN COUNTY CRICKET? Matt Coles (Ken)
TIP FOR THE TOP? Sam Curran (Sur)
CRICKETING HEROES? Brian Lara and Graham Thorpe – two of the best left-handers when I was growing up
NON-CRICKETING HEROES? Gary Barlow – lyrical genius
IF YOU WEREN'T A CRICKETER? I'd be doing something that requires a suit in London
DESERT ISLAND DISC? One Direction – Night Changes
TWITTER: @aj_blake10

Batting	Mat	Inns	NO	Runs	HS	Ave	SR	100	50	Ct	St
First-class	37	58	5	1278	105*	24.11	58.01	1	6	22	0
List A	69	56	14	1183	89	28.16	93.00	0	7	39	0
Twenty20	78	69	18	1120	71*	21.96	133.01	0	5	39	0

Bowling	Mat	Balls	Runs	Wkts	BBI	BBM	Ave	Econ	SR	5w	10
First-class	37	204	129	3	2/9	2/9	43.00	3.79	68.0	0	0
List A	69	84	74	3	2/13	2/13	24.66	5.28	28.0	0	0
Twenty20	78	-	-	-	-	-	-	-	-	-	-

RAVI BOPARA RHB / RM / R1 / W0 / MVP16

ESSEX

FULL NAME: Ravinder Singh Bopara
BORN: May 4, 1985, Forest Gate, London
SQUAD NO: 25
HEIGHT: 5ft 10in
EDUCATION: Brampton Manor, London
TEAMS: England, Essex, Auckland, Chittagong Kings, Dhaka Dynamites, Dolphins, Gloucestershire, Karachi Kings, Kings XI Punjab, Sunrisers Hyderabad, Sydney Sixers, Sylhet Super Stars
ROLE: Allrounder
DEBUT: Test: 2007; ODI: 2007; T20I: 2008; First-class: 2002; List A: 2002; T20: 2003

BEST BATTING: 229 Essex vs Northamptonshire, Chelmsford, 2007
BEST BOWLING: 5-49 Essex vs Derbyshire, Chelmsford, 2016
COUNTY CAP: 2005 (Essex) **BENEFIT:** 2015

FAMILY TIES? Brother played Essex age-group cricket
BEST MOMENT IN CRICKET? Playing for England, scoring 201* against Leicestershire in a one-day match, playing in the IPL and BPL, and scoring three centuries in a row for England
CRICKETING HEROES? Sachin Tendulkar
SURPRISING FACT? I have a fast-food business
DESERT ISLAND DISC? A Drake or Jay Z album
FANTASY SLIP CORDON? Keeper: Robert De Niro, 1st: Ronnie Kray, 2nd: Reggie Kray, 3rd: Me, Gully: Sachin Tendulkar
TWITTER: @ravibopara

Batting	Mat	Inns	NO	Runs	HS	Ave	SR	100	50	Ct	St
Tests	13	19	1	575	143	31.94	52.89	3	0	6	0
ODIs	120	109	21	2695	101*	30.62	77.84	1	14	35	0
T20Is	38	35	10	711	65*	28.44	118.69	0	3	7	0
First-class	181	296	32	10785	229	40.85	51.89	26	45	93	0
List A	298	277	53	8936	201*	39.89			14	53	95	0
Twenty20	249	231	43	4964	105*	26.40	118.47	1	26	82	0

Bowling	Mat	Balls	Runs	Wkts	BBI	BBM	Ave	Econ	SR	5w	10
Tests	13	434	290	1	1/39	1/39	290.00	4.00	434.0	0	0
ODIs	120	1860	1523	40	4/38	4/38	38.07	4.91	46.5	0	0
T20Is	38	322	387	16	4/10	4/10	24.18	7.21	20.1	0	0
First-class	181	13604	8278	226	5/49		36.62	3.65	60.1	3	0
List A	298	7015	6179	220	5/63	5/63	28.08	5.28	31.8	1	0
Twenty20	249	3418	4199	170	6/16	6/16	24.70	7.37	20.1	1	0

SCOTT BORTHWICK   LHB / LB / R3 / W0 / MVP9

FULL NAME: Scott George Borthwick
BORN: April 19, 1990, Sunderland, County Durham
SQUAD NO: 6
HEIGHT: 5ft 10in
NICKNAME: Badger
EDUCATION: Farringdon Community Sports College, Sunderland
TEAMS: England, Surrey, Chilaw Marians, Durham, Wellington
ROLE: Allrounder
DEBUT: Test: 2014; ODI: 2011; T20I: 2011; First-class 2009; List A: 2009; T20: 2008

SURREY

BEST BATTING: 216 Durham vs Middlesex, Chester-le-Street, 2014
BEST BOWLING: 6-70 Durham vs Surrey, The Oval, 2013

STRANGEST THING SEEN IN A GAME? Steve Harmison bowling a bouncer at Tony Frost and hitting him on the head and his glasses falling to me at short-leg
HOW WOULD YOUR TEAM-MATES DESCRIBE YOU IN THREE WORDS? Badger, energetic, likeable
BEST PLAYER IN COUNTY CRICKET? Kumar Sangakkara (Sur)
MOST UNDERRATED PLAYER IN COUNTY CRICKET? Mark Stoneman (Sur)
TIP FOR THE TOP? Brydon Carse (Dur)
NON-CRICKETING HEROES? Niall Quinn
SURPRISING FACT? I know Only Fools And Horses word for word
TWITTER: @Borthwick16

Batting	Mat	Inns	NO	Runs	HS	Ave	SR	100	50	Ct	St
Tests	1	2	0	5	4	2.50	26.31	0	0	2	0
ODIs	2	2	0	18	15	9.00	112.50	0	0	0	0
T20Is	1	1	0	14	14	14.00	87.50	0	0	1	0
First-class	128	217	22	7256	216	37.21	55.44	15	40	164	0
List A	86	63	10	1133	87	21.37	79.50	0	7	30	0
Twenty20	80	44	13	508	62	16.38	96.94	0	1	33	0

Bowling	Mat	Balls	Runs	Wkts	BBI	BBM	Ave	Econ	SR	5w	10
Tests	1	78	82	4	3/33	4/82	20.50	6.30	19.5	0	0
ODIs	2	54	72	0	-	-	-	8.00	-	0	0
T20Is	1	24	15	1	1/15	1/15	15.00	3.75	24.0	0	0
First-class	128	11015	7230	195	6/70	8/84	37.07	3.93	56.4	3	0
List A	86	2450	2456	63	5/38	5/38	38.98	6.01	38.8	1	0
Twenty20	80	1031	1359	61	4/18	4/18	22.27	7.90	16.9	0	0

WILL BRAGG

LHB / RM / R3 / W0

GLAMORGAN

FULL NAME: William David Bragg
BORN: October 24, 1986, Newport, Wales
SQUAD NO: 22
HEIGHT: 5ft 10in
NICKNAME: BPOT, Shelf
EDUCATION: Rougemont School, Newport; University of Wales Institute
TEAMS: Glamorgan
ROLE: Batsman
DEBUT: First-class 2007; List A: 2005; T20: 2010

BEST BATTING: 161* Glamorgan vs Essex, Cardiff, 2016
BEST BOWLING: 2-10 Glamorgan vs Worcestershire, Cardiff, 2013
COUNTY CAP: 2015

FAMILY TIES? Dad played club cricket in the South Wales League
BEST MOMENT IN CRICKET? Scoring 1,000 runs in my first full season in 2011
SUPERSTITIONS? Always go to the toilet before batting
CRICKETING HEROES? Herschelle Gibbs, Brian Lara, Daryll Cullinan
NON-CRICKETING HEROES? Kenny Powers, Ricky Gervais
IF YOU WEREN'T A CRICKETER? I'd be working abroad in finance
SURPRISING FACT? I play acoustic guitar
FANTASY SLIP CORDON? Keeper: Ricky Gervais, 1st: Karl Pilkington, 2nd: Piers Morgan, 3rd: Britney Spears, Gully: Peggy Mitchell
TWITTER: @WDBragg22

Batting	Mat	Inns	NO	Runs	HS	Ave	SR	100	50	Ct	St
First-class	108	190	7	5608	161*	30.64	49.10	6	35	44	1
List A	41	37	2	1070	88	30.57	77.53	0	8	4	0
Twenty20	2	2	0	21	15	10.50	75.00	0	0	0	0

Bowling	Mat	Balls	Runs	Wkts	BBI	BBM	Ave	Econ	SR	5w	10
First-class	108	698	459	5	2/10	2/10	91.80	3.94	139.6	0	0
List A	41	44	54	1	1/11	1/11	54.00	7.36	44.0	0	0
Twenty20	2	-	-	-	-	-	-	-	-	-	-

FULL NAME: Timothy Thomas Bresnan
BORN: February 28, 1985, Pontefract, Yorkshire
SQUAD NO: 16
HEIGHT: 6ft
NICKNAME: Brez, Brezzylad
EDUCATION: Castleford High School, West Yorkshire; New College Pontefract
TEAMS: England, Yorkshire, Hobart Hurricanes, Perth Scorchers
ROLE: Allrounder
DEBUT: Test: 2009; ODI: 2006; T20I: 2006; First-class: 2003; List A: 2001; T20: 2003

BEST BATTING: 169* Yorkshire vs Durham, Chester-le-Street, 2015
BEST BOWLING: 5-36 Yorkshire vs Nottinghamshire, Scarborough, 2016
COUNTY CAP: 2006 **BENEFIT:** 2014

BEST MOMENT IN CRICKET? The MCG on Boxing Day in the 2010/11 Ashes, with 96,000 people in the ground at 11am singing the national anthem
TIP FOR THE TOP? Matthew Fisher, Mathew Waite (both Yor)
CRICKETING HEROES? Shaun Pollock, Jacques Kallis
NON-CRICKETING HEROES? Anyone in the armed forces – fighting to protect our rights and way of life while endangering themselves
IF YOU WEREN'T A CRICKETER? I'd be a builder
SURPRISING FACT? I'm a fully qualified scuba-diver
TWITTER: @timbresnan

Batting	Mat	Inns	NO	Runs	HS	Ave	SR	100	50	Ct	St
Tests	23	26	4	575	91	26.13	39.43	0	3	8	0
ODIs	85	64	20	871	80	19.79	90.25	0	1	20	0
T20Is	34	22	9	216	47*	16.61	127.05	0	0	10	0
First-class	170	226	38	5741	169*	30.53	47.98	6	30	83	0
List A	255	182	51	2677	95*	20.43	89.95	0	7	66	0
Twenty20	131	94	36	1196	51	20.62	129.15	0	1	48	0

Bowling	Mat	Balls	Runs	Wkts	BBI	BBM	Ave	Econ	SR	5w	10
Tests	23	4674	2357	72	5/48	8/141	32.73	3.02	64.9	1	0
ODIs	85	4221	3813	109	5/48	5/48	34.98	5.42	38.7	1	0
T20Is	34	663	887	24	3/10	3/10	36.95	8.02	27.6	0	0
First-class	170	29105	14927	481	5/36		31.03	3.07	60.5	8	0
List A	255	11240	9726	290	5/48	5/48	33.53	5.19	38.7	1	0
Twenty20	131	2540	3295	123	3/10	3/10	26.78	7.78	20.6	0	0

DANNY BRIGGS — RHB / SLA / RO / WO

FULL NAME: Danny Richard Briggs
BORN: April 30, 1991, Newport, Isle of Wight
SQUAD NO: 21
HEIGHT: 6ft 2in
NICKNAME: Briggsy
EDUCATION: Carisbrooke High School
TEAMS: England, Sussex, Hampshire
ROLE: Bowler
DEBUT: ODI: 2012; T20I: 2012; First-class: 2009; List A: 2009; T20: 2010

BEST BATTING: 54 Hampshire vs Gloucestershire, Bristol, 2011
BEST BOWLING: 6-45 England Lions vs Windward Islands, Roseau, 2011
COUNTY CAP: 2012 (Hampshire)

BEST MOMENT IN CRICKET? Making my England debut in ODI and T20I cricket
HOW WOULD YOUR TEAM-MATES DESCRIBE YOU IN THREE WORDS? Relaxed, very chilled
BEST PLAYER IN COUNTY CRICKET? James Vince (Ham)
TIP FOR THE TOP? Joe Clarke (Wor)
CRICKETING HEROES? Daniel Vettori – he was the best left-arm spinner in the world and survived a long career doing very basic things well
IF YOU WEREN'T A CRICKETER? I'd be coaching a club or school
DESERT ISLAND DISC? Ed Sheeran
FANTASY SLIP CORDON? Keeper: Karl Pilkington, 1st: James Tomlinson, 2nd: David Beckham, 3rd: Shane Warne
TWITTER: @DannyBriggs19

Batting	Mat	Inns	NO	Runs	HS	Ave	SR	100	50	Ct	St
ODIs	1	-	-	-	-	-	-	-	-	0	0
T20Is	7	1	1	0	0*	-	-	0	0	1	0
First-class	80	95	22	1184	54	16.21		0	1	26	0
List A	74	34	15	252	25	13.26	93.33	0	0	22	0
Twenty20	113	23	15	77	13	9.62	110.00	0	0	21	0

Bowling	Mat	Balls	Runs	Wkts	BBI	BBM	Ave	Econ	SR	5w	10
ODIs	1	60	39	2	2/39	2/39	19.50	3.90	30.0	0	0
T20Is	7	108	199	5	2/25	2/25	39.80	11.05	21.6	0	0
First-class	80	14472	7315	217	6/45	9/96	33.70	3.03	66.6	8	0
List A	74	3236	2751	77	4/32	4/32	35.72	5.10	42.0	0	0
Twenty20	113	2323	2799	133	5/19	5/19	21.04	7.22	17.4	1	0

STUART BROAD

LHB / RFM / R0 / W0

FULL NAME: Stuart Christopher John Broad
BORN: June 24, 1986, Nottingham
SQUAD NO: 8
HEIGHT: 6ft 5in
NICKNAME: Broady
EDUCATION: Oakham School, Rutland
TEAMS: England, Nottinghamshire, Hobart Hurricanes, Kings XI Punjab, Leicestershire
ROLE: Bowler
DEBUT: Test: 2007; ODI: 2006; T20I: 2006; First-class: 2005; List A: 2005; T20: 2006

NOTTINGHAMSHIRE

BEST BATTING: 169 England vs Pakistan, Lord's, 2010
BEST BOWLING: 8-15 England vs Australia, Trent Bridge, 2015
COUNTY CAP: 2007 (Leicestershire)

FAMILY TIES? My father Chris played for England, Nottinghamshire and Gloucestershire and is now an ICC match official
CRICKETING HEROES? Glenn McGrath, Shaun Pollock
NON-CRICKETING HEROES? Brian Clough, Lewis Hamilton
IF YOU WEREN'T A CRICKETER? I'd be a traffic warden
SURPRISING FACT? I often dream in French
FANTASY SLIP CORDON? Keeper: Mark Crossley, 1st: Des Lyttle, 2nd: Steve Chettle, 3rd: Des Walker, 4th: Stuart Pearce
TWITTER: @StuartBroad8

Batting	Mat	Inns	NO	Runs	HS	Ave	SR	100	50	Ct	St
Tests	102	145	19	2691	169	21.35	64.98	1	10	32	0
ODIs	121	68	25	529	45*	12.30	74.61	0	0	27	0
T20Is	56	26	10	118	18*	7.37	100.00	0	0	21	0
First-class	166	227	34	4215	169	21.83	62.59	1	19	56	0
List A	140	76	27	578	45*	11.79	73.44	0	0	30	0
Twenty20	85	32	12	152	18*	7.60	102.01	0	0	26	0

Bowling	Mat	Balls	Runs	Wkts	BBI	BBM	Ave	Econ	SR	5w	10
Tests	102	21000	10503	368	8/15	11/121	28.54	3.00	57.0	15	2
ODIs	121	6109	5364	178	5/23	5/23	30.13	5.26	34.3	1	0
T20Is	56	1173	1491	65	4/24	4/24	22.93	7.62	18.0	0	0
First-class	166	31842	16627	603	8/15		27.57	3.13	52.8	26	3
List A	140	6981	6121	206	5/23	5/23	29.71	5.26	33.8	1	0
Twenty20	85	1788	2144	100	4/24	4/24	21.44	7.19	17.8	0	0

YORKSHIRE

JACK BROOKS RHB / RFM / R0 / W3 / MVP55

FULL NAME: Jack Alexander Brooks
BORN: June 4, 1984, Oxford
SQUAD NO: 70
HEIGHT: 6ft 2in
NICKNAME: Animal, Ferret, SuBo, Headband Warrior, King of Oxford, Therapist
EDUCATION: Wheatley Park School, South Oxfordshire
TEAMS: Yorkshire, England Lions, Northamptonshire
ROLE: Bowler
DEBUT: First-class: 2009; List A: 2009; T20: 2010

BEST BATTING: 53* England Lions vs South Africa A, Paarl, 2015
BEST BOWLING: 6-65 Yorkshire vs Middlesex, Lord's, 2016
COUNTY CAPS: 2012 (Northamptonshire); 2013 (Yorkshire)

BEST MOMENT IN CRICKET? First-class debut vs Australia in 2009, winning the County Championship with Yorkshire in 2014 and 2015
CRICKETING HEROES? Curtly Ambrose, Allan Donald, Darren Gough, Dennis Lillee – all characters I admired for ability, personality and aggression
IF YOU WEREN'T A CRICKETER? I was a salesman before I signed my first pro-contract as a 24-year-old. But perhaps I'd be a farmer instead. Or travelling the world feeding my soul and having fun
SURPRISING FACT? I chose my middle name. Official Susan Boyle lookalike
DESERT ISLAND DISC? Oasis (any of the early stuff)
TWITTER: @brooksyferret

Batting	Mat	Inns	NO	Runs	HS	Ave	SR	100	50	Ct	St
First-class	98	112	44	1128	53*	16.58	54.57	0	3	26	0
List A	36	15	5	49	10	4.90	52.12	0	0	4	0
Twenty20	46	10	6	59	33*	14.75	134.09	0	0	9	0

Bowling	Mat	Balls	Runs	Wkts	BBI	BBM	Ave	Econ	SR	5w	10
First-class	98	16770	9574	360	6/65	9/84	26.59	3.42	46.5	13	0
List A	36	1584	1276	37	3/30	3/30	34.48	4.83	42.8	0	0
Twenty20	46	822	1014	38	5/21	5/21	26.68	7.40	21.6	1	0

BEN BROWN

RHB / WK / R0 / W0

FULL NAME: Ben Christopher Brown
BORN: November 23, 1988, Crawley, Sussex
SQUAD NO: 26
HEIGHT: 5ft 8in
NICKNAME: Brownie, Goblin
EDUCATION: Ardingly College
TEAMS: Sussex
ROLE: Wicketkeeper
DEBUT: First-class: 2007; List A: 2007; T20: 2008

SUSSEX

BEST BATTING: 163 Sussex vs Durham, Hove, 2014
BEST BOWLING: 1-48 Sussex vs Essex, Colchester, 2016
COUNTY CAP: 2014

BEST MOMENT IN CRICKET? Being capped at Sussex
CRICKETING HEROES? Adam Gilchrist – he changed the modern game and made standards for wicketkeepers improve
NON-CRICKETING HEROES? All my family for supporting me through my career, and José Mourinho!
IF YOU WEREN'T A CRICKETER? I'd be trying my hand in journalism or media
DESERT ISLAND DISC? Rod Stewart
FANTASY SLIP CORDON? Keeper: Me, 1st: Frank Lampard, 2nd: Jack Bauer, 3rd: 'Rocket' Rod Stewart, Gully: Henry VIII
TWITTER: @Ben_brown26

Batting	Mat	Inns	NO	Runs	HS	Ave	SR	100	50	Ct	St
First-class	102	156	25	4981	163	38.02	61.23	13	24	266	15
List A	54	41	10	720	62	23.22	90.22	0	4	52	10
Twenty20	60	51	7	612	68	13.90	109.48	0	1	23	7

Bowling	Mat	Balls	Runs	Wkts	BBI	BBM	Ave	Econ	SR	5w	10
First-class	102	90	93	1	1/48	1/48	93.00	6.20	90.0	0	0
List A	54	-	-	-	-	-	-	-	-	-	-
Twenty20	60	-	-	-	-	-	-	-	-	-	-

KARL BROWN

RHB / RM / RO / WO

FULL NAME: Karl Robert Brown
BORN: May 17, 1988, Bolton, Lancashire
SQUAD NO: 14
HEIGHT: 5ft 10in
NICKNAME: Browny, Charlie
EDUCATION: Hesketh Fletcher CofE High School, Greater Manchester
TEAMS: Lancashire, Moors Sports Club
ROLE: Batsman
DEBUT: First-class: 2006; List A: 2007; T20: 2011

BEST BATTING: 132 Lancashire vs Glamorgan, Old Trafford, 2015
BEST BOWLING: 2-30 Lancashire vs Nottinghamshire, Trent Bridge, 2009
COUNTY CAP: 2015

FAMILY TIES? My dad played league cricket for Atherton CC and was the professional for Clifton CC
BEST MOMENT IN CRICKET? Scoring my maiden first-class and one-day hundreds and playing for England U19
CRICKETING HEROES? Andrew Flintoff, Stuart Law
NON-CRICKETING HEROES? Kevin Davies, Lionel Messi, Ronnie O'Sullivan, Phil Taylor, Sergio García
SURPRISING FACT? I played football for Wigan Athletic
TWITTER: @karlos173

Batting	Mat	Inns	NO	Runs	HS	Ave	SR	100	50	Ct	St
First-class	83	136	6	3505	132	26.96	46.46	2	22	51	0
List A	68	64	11	2016	129	38.03	82.79	2	11	19	0
Twenty20	74	71	9	1763	69	28.43	126.74	0	13	26	0

Bowling	Mat	Balls	Runs	Wkts	BBI	BBM	Ave	Econ	SR	5w	10
First-class	83	90	65	2	2/30	2/37	32.50	4.33	45.0	0	0
List A	68	6	17	0	-	-	-	17.00	-	0	0
Twenty20	74	-	-	-	-	-	-	-	-	-	-

NICK BROWNE LHB / LB / R2 / W0 / MVP89

FULL NAME: Nicholas Laurence Joseph Browne

BORN: March 24, 1991, Leytonstone, Essex

SQUAD NO: 10

HEIGHT: 6ft 3in

NICKNAME: Brownie, Orse

EDUCATION: Trinity Catholic High School, London

TEAMS: Essex

ROLE: Batsman

DEBUT: First-class: 2013; List A: 2015; T20: 2015

ESSEX

BEST BATTING: 255 Essex vs Derbyshire, Chelmsford, 2016

COUNTY CAP: 2015

WHAT FIRST GOT YOU INTO CRICKET? I was practically born into South Woodford CC, where there weren't enough hours in the day for me to play cricket

STRANGEST THING SEEN IN A GAME? When a certain ex-England left-arm spinner lay stretched out on all fours without even noticing that the ball had flown passed him towards the boundary

BEST MOMENT IN CRICKET? Scoring my maiden first-class hundred. I was lucky enough to have my family there at the ground, and to see my mother and father so emotional was a moment I'll never forget

BEST PLAYER IN COUNTY CRICKET? Tom Westley (Ess)

TIP FOR THE TOP? Dan Lawrence (Ess)

CRICKETING HEROES? Alastair Cook, Graham Gooch, Marcus Trescothick

FANTASY SLIP CORDON? Keeper: Anthony Kiedis (Red Hot Chili Peppers), 1st: Me, 2nd: Anthony McGrath, 3rd: Micky Flanagan, 4th: Jaik Mickleburgh, Gully: Tom Westley

TWITTER: @NickBrowne4

Batting	Mat	Inns	NO	Runs	HS	Ave	SR	100	50	Ct	St
First-class	48	79	9	3110	255	44.42	51.85	11	11	41	0
List A	17	14	0	511	99	36.50	90.28	0	3	7	0
Twenty20	14	12	2	165	38	16.50	114.58	0	0	6	0

Bowling	Mat	Balls	Runs	Wkts	BBI	BBM	Ave	Econ	SR	5w	10
First-class	48	262	171	0	-	-	-	3.91	-	0	0
List A	17	-	-	-	-	-	-	-	-	-	-
Twenty20	14	-	-	-	-	-	-	-	-	-	-

NATHAN BUCK

RHB / RFM / R0 / W0

NORTHAMPTONSHIRE

FULL NAME: Nathan Liam Buck
BORN: April 26, 1991, Leicester
SQUAD NO: 11
HEIGHT: 6ft 3in
NICKNAME: Bucky
EDUCATION: Ashby Grammar School,
Ashby-de-la-Zouch
TEAMS: Northamptonshire, England Lions,
Lancashire, Leicestershire
ROLE: Bowler
DEBUT: First-class: 2009; List A: 2009;
T20: 2010

BEST BATTING: 29* Leicestershire vs Worcestershire, Worcester, 2014
BEST BOWLING: 5-76 Leicestershire vs Essex, Chelmsford, 2014
COUNTY CAP: 2011 (Leicestershire)

WHAT FIRST GOT YOU INTO CRICKET? My older brother Mitchell played, so I joined in with him at the age of 12 and it went from there
STRANGEST THING SEEN IN A GAME? Josh Cobb running a three with Adam Rossington, and Liam Livingstone's hairline
BEST MOMENT IN CRICKET? Finding three £2 coins at third man during a Championship match in 2013
BEST PLAYER IN COUNTY CRICKET? Jeetan Patel (War)
MOST UNDERRATED PLAYER IN COUNTY CRICKET? Liam Livingstone (Lan)
TIP FOR THE TOP? Saqib Mahmood, Danny Lamb (both Lan)
NON-CRICKETING HEROES? Peter Griffin, Ronald McDonald
SURPRISING FACT? I once cooked one-minute noodles in 58 seconds. I got seven A-stars and three As at GCSE
UNUSUAL OBJECT AT HOME? A grip cone beside my bed
TWITTER: @nathanbuck17

Batting	Mat	Inns	NO	Runs	HS	Ave	SR	100	50	Ct	St
First-class	65	89	26	722	29*	11.46		0	0	9	0
List A	42	19	8	91	21	8.27	61.48	0	0	10	0
Twenty20	32	7	5	19	8*	9.50	79.16	0	0	5	0

Bowling	Mat	Balls	Runs	Wkts	BBI	BBM	Ave	Econ	SR	5w	10
First-class	65	10310	6087	158	5/76	7/79	38.52	3.54	65.2	4	0
List A	42	1741	1786	51	4/39	4/39	35.01	6.15	34.1	0	0
Twenty20	32	663	929	41	4/26	4/26	22.65	8.40	16.1	0	0

KIERAN BULL

RHB / OB / R0 / W0

FULL NAME: Kieran Andrew Bull
BORN: April 5, 1995, Haverfordwest, Pembrokeshire, Wales
SQUAD NO: 11
HEIGHT: 6ft 1in
NICKNAME: Bully
EDUCATION: Queen Elizabeth High School, Haverfordwest; Cardiff Metropolitan University
TEAMS: Glamorgan
ROLE: Bowler
DEBUT: First-class: 2014; List A: 2015

BEST BATTING: 31 Glamorgan vs Gloucestershire, Swansea, 2015
BEST BOWLING: 4-62 Glamorgan vs Kent, Canterbury, 2014

WHAT FIRST GOT YOU INTO CRICKET? Watching my brother play at our local club
STRANGEST THING SEEN IN A GAME? Play being suspended due to a helicopter landing on the field
BEST MOMENT IN CRICKET? Making my first-class debut at Canterbury
BEST PLAYER IN COUNTY CRICKET? Colin Ingram (Gla)
MOST UNDERRATED PLAYER IN COUNTY CRICKET? Jake Libby (Not)
TIP FOR THE TOP? Lukas Carey, Kiran Carlson (both Gla)
CRICKETING HEROES? Darren Gough, Graeme Swann
NON-CRICKETING HEROES? Steven Gerrard, Ron Burgundy
SURPRISING FACT? I set off an alarm every time I walk into a shop due to the metal screw in my back. Aged 10 I moved to Spain to take up a place in a tennis academy and lived there for two years, representing Spain at age-group level. I was also ball boy for Rafael Nadal
UNUSUAL OBJECT AT HOME? A singing fish on the wall
DESERT ISLAND DISC? Arctic Monkeys – AM
FANTASY SLIP CORDON? Keeper: Will Ferrell, 1st: James Corden, 2nd: Me, 3rd: Chris Coleman, Gully: Dwayne Leverock
TWITTER: @Kieran_Bull89

Batting	Mat	Inns	NO	Runs	HS	Ave	SR	100	50	Ct	St
First-class	7	10	3	69	31	9.85	23.15	0	0	1	0
List A	2	-	-	-	-	-	-	-	-	0	0

Bowling	Mat	Balls	Runs	Wkts	BBI	BBM	Ave	Econ	SR	5w	10
First-class	7	744	483	9	4/62	4/62	53.66	3.89	82.6	0	0
List A	2	52	48	1	1/40	1/40	48.00	5.53	52.0	0	0

JAMES BURKE

RHB / RMF / RO / WO

FULL NAME: James Edward Burke
BORN: January 25, 1991, Plymouth, Devon
SQUAD NO: 8
HEIGHT: 6ft 3in
NICKNAME: Burkey
EDUCATION: Plymouth College School; Open University, Milton Keynes
TEAMS: Surrey, Leicestershire, Somerset
ROLE: Allrounder
DEBUT: First-class: 2012; List A: 2015; T20: 2014

BEST BATTING: 79 Surrey vs Derbyshire, The Oval, 2015
BEST BOWLING: 4-19 Surrey vs Leicestershire, Leicester, 2015

WHAT FIRST GOT YOU INTO CRICKET? The Ashes
STRANGEST THING SEEN IN A GAME? The collision of Rory Burns and Moises Henriques
BEST MOMENT IN CRICKET? Winning Division Two of the County Championship
HOW WOULD YOUR TEAM-MATES DESCRIBE YOU IN THREE WORDS? Carefree, weird, different
BEST PLAYER IN COUNTY CRICKET? Jason Roy (Sur)
MOST UNDERRATED PLAYER IN COUNTY CRICKET? Rory Burns (Sur)
TIP FOR THE TOP? Sam Curran (Sur)
CRICKETING HEROES? Brett Lee
NON-CRICKETING HEROES? Lawrence Krauss – my favourite physicist
IF YOU WEREN'T A CRICKETER? I'd be working in virtual reality
SURPRISING FACT? I'm doing a Physics degree and I love classical music
DESERT ISLAND DISC? Lord Of The Rings Soundtrack
NOTES: Burke joined Leicestershire on a one-year loan ahead of the 2017 season

Batting	Mat	Inns	NO	Runs	HS	Ave	SR	100	50	Ct	St
First-class	12	16	1	274	79	18.26	43.76	0	2	6	0
List A	10	10	2	94	26*	11.75	85.45	0	0	3	0
Twenty20	14	9	2	30	8	4.28	71.42	0	0	6	0

Bowling	Mat	Balls	Runs	Wkts	BBI	BBM	Ave	Econ	SR	5w	10
First-class	12	1023	647	23	4/19	6/54	28.13	3.79	44.4	0	0
List A	10	357	350	17	5/28	5/28	20.58	5.88	21.0	1	0
Twenty20	14	147	225	10	3/23	3/23	22.50	9.18	14.7	0	0

JACK BURNHAM   RHB / RM / R0 / W0

FULL NAME: Jack Tony Arthur Burnham
BORN: January 18, 1997, Durham
SQUAD NO: 8
HEIGHT: 6ft 3in
NICKNAME: Erny
EDUCATION: Deerness Valley
Comprehensive School, Durham;
The Durham Federation
TEAMS: Durham
ROLE: Batsman
DEBUT: First-class: 2015; List A: 2016;
T20: 2016

DURHAM

BEST BATTING: 135 Durham vs Surrey, The Oval, 2016

FAMILY TIES? My mum and dad coached the U13 team at Esh Winning CC for three years
STRANGEST THING SEEN IN A GAME? When we turned up to Evenwood CC to find 25 horses on the pitch (match abandoned)
BEST MOMENT IN CRICKET? My maiden hundred for the Durham at The Oval in 2016
HOW WOULD YOUR TEAM-MATES DESCRIBE YOU IN THREE WORDS? Funny, outrageous, numpty
BEST PLAYER IN COUNTY CRICKET? Jason Roy (Sur)
MOST UNDERRATED PLAYER IN COUNTY CRICKET? Mark Stoneman (Sur)
TIP FOR THE TOP? Dan Lawrence (Ess), Joe Clarke (Wor)
CRICKETING HEROES? Andrew Flintoff, Stephen Harmison
NON-CRICKETING HEROES? Cristiano Ronaldo, Alan Shearer
IF YOU WEREN'T A CRICKETER? I'd be a coach or plumber
SURPRISING FACT? I scored my first hundred aged nine
TWITTER: @BurnhamMorton

Batting	Mat	Inns	NO	Runs	HS	Ave	SR	100	50	Ct	St
First-class	19	33	2	795	135	25.64	45.11	1	5	8	0
List A	5	4	0	69	26	17.25	66.34	0	0	0	0
Twenty20	4	4	0	27	17	6.75	87.09	0	0	1	0
Bowling	Mat	Balls	Runs	Wkts	BBI	BBM	Ave	Econ	SR	5w	10
First-class	19	-	-	-	-	-	-	-	-	-	-
List A	5	-	-	-	-	-	-	-	-	-	-
Twenty20	4	-	-	-	-	-	-	-	-	-	-

RORY BURNS — LHB / RM / WK / R3 / W0 / MVP47

FULL NAME: Rory Joseph Burns
BORN: August 26, 1990, Epsom, Surrey
SQUAD NO: 17
HEIGHT: 5ft 10in
NICKNAME: Fong, The Cat (goalkeeper)
EDUCATION: Whitgift School; City of London Freemen's; Cardiff Metropolitan University
TEAMS: Surrey
ROLE: Batsman
DEBUT: First-class: 2011; List A: 2012; T20: 2012

BEST BATTING: 199 Surrey vs Gloucestershire, Bristol, 2014
BEST BOWLING: 1-18 Surrey vs Middlesex, Lord's, 2013
COUNTY CAP: 2014

STRANGEST THING SEEN IN A GAME? Didn't see him… Moises Henriques
BEST MOMENT IN CRICKET? Any time I share the crease with Arun Harinath
HOW WOULD YOUR TEAM-MATES DESCRIBE YOU IN THREE WORDS? Niggly, entertaining, humble
BEST PLAYER IN COUNTY CRICKET? Kumar Sangakkara (Sur)
MOST UNDERRATED PLAYER IN COUNTY CRICKET? Arun Harinath (Sur)
TIP FOR THE TOP? Sam Curran, Dominic Sibley (both Sur)
CRICKETING HEROES? Kumar Sangakkara – his batting and keeping are a pleasure to watch. Brian Lara – that backlift and the entertainment value. Mark Butcher – again, that backlift!
NON-CRICKETING HEROES? Jonny Wilkinson – that drop goal and humility in abundance
SURPRISING FACT? I can play the saxophone and I love dachshunds
UNUSUAL OBJECT AT HOME? A strong whisky collection
DESERT ISLAND DISC? Fall Out Boy – From Under The Cork Tree
TWITTER: @roryburns17

Batting	Mat	Inns	NO	Runs	HS	Ave	SR	100	50	Ct	St
First-class	77	136	12	5093	199	41.07	49.00	10	27	73	0
List A	32	31	3	1062	95	37.92	88.79	0	9	14	0
Twenty20	27	23	3	254	46*	12.70	107.17	0	0	7	1

Bowling	Mat	Balls	Runs	Wkts	BBI	BBM	Ave	Econ	SR	5w	10
First-class	77	180	127	2	1/18	1/18	63.50	4.23	90.0	0	0
List A	32	-	-	-	-	-	-	-	-	-	-
Twenty20	27	-	-	-	-	-	-	-	-	-	-

JOS BUTTLER

RHB / WK / R0 / W0

FULL NAME: Joseph Charles Buttler
BORN: September 8, 1990, Taunton
SQUAD NO: 6
NICKNAME: Jose
EDUCATION: King's College, Taunton
TEAMS: England, Lancashire, Melbourne Renegades, Mumbai Indians, Somerset
ROLE: Wicketkeeper/batsman
DEBUT: Test: 2014; ODI: 2012; T20I: 2011; First-class: 2009; List A: 2009; T20: 2009

LANCASHIRE

BEST BATTING: 144 Somerset vs Hampshire, Southampton, 2013
COUNTY CAP: 2013 (Somerset)

TWITTER: @josbuttler
NOTES: Signed for Lancashire in September 2013 to pursue more opportunities as a keeper after sharing duties with Craig Kieswetter at Somerset. Came to prominence after scoring 55 from just 25 balls in the 2010 T20 Cup semi-final between Somerset and Notts. A successful tour with England Lions to Sri Lanka in early 2012 led to a call-up for England's limited-overs squads for the series against Pakistan in UAE. Usurped Matt Prior as England's No.1 Test wicketkeeper in 2014, scoring 85 on Test debut against India at Southampton. Lost his place to Jonny Bairstow following a poor Ashes series but returned to the Test side on the 2016/17 tour of India. Hit England's three fastest ODI hundreds, the quickest coming off 46 balls against Pakistan at Dubai in 2015. Retained by Mumbai Indians for the 2017 IPL season

Batting	Mat	Inns	NO	Runs	HS	Ave	SR	100	50	Ct	St
Tests	18	30	5	784	85	31.36	55.52	0	6	54	0
ODIs	87	75	12	2290	129	36.34	118.40	4	12	110	13
T20Is	53	46	11	943	73*	26.94	139.91	0	5	15	3
First-class	77	120	12	3490	144	32.31	58.76	4	20	165	2
List A	157	135	32	4456	129	43.26	119.62	6	28	162	18
Twenty20	163	144	34	3081	73*	28.00	147.06	0	17	86	17

Bowling	Mat	Balls	Runs	Wkts	BBI	BBM	Ave	Econ	SR	5w	10
Tests	18	-	-	-	-	-	-	-	-	-	-
ODIs	87	-	-	-	-	-	-	-	-	-	-
T20Is	53	-	-	-	-	-	-	-	-	-	-
First-class	77	12	11	0	-	-	-	5.50	-	0	0
List A	157	-	-	-	-	-	-	-	-	-	-
Twenty20	163	-	-	-	-	-	-	-	-	-	-

MICHAEL CARBERRY   LHB / OB / R4 / W0

FULL NAME: Michael Alexander Carberry
BORN: September 29, 1980, Croydon, Surrey
SQUAD NO: 15
HEIGHT: 5ft 11in
NICKNAME: Carbs
EDUCATION: St John Rigby College, Wigan
TEAMS: England, Hampshire, Kent, Perth Scorchers, Surrey
ROLE: Batsman
DEBUT: Test: 2010; ODI: 2013; T20I: 2014; First-class: 2001; List A: 1999; T20: 2003

BEST BATTING: 300* Hampshire vs Yorkshire, Southampton, 2011
BEST BOWLING: 2-85 Hampshire vs Durham, Chester-le-Street, 2006
COUNTY CAP: 2006 (Hampshire)

TWITTER: @carbs646
NOTES: An opening batsman, Carberry made his Test debut against Bangladesh in 2010, scoring 30 and 34. It was three years until his next chance, when he was drafted in for the doomed tour of Australia in 2013/14. He was England's second-highest runscorer overall in the series but hasn't played a Test since. Scored 300* against Yorkshire at Southampton in 2011. Helped Hampshire to two titles, the T20 Cup and CB40, in 2012. Hit over 1,000 first-class runs in 2015. Having survived a blood clot on the lung in 2010, Carberry was diagnosed with a cancerous tumour midway through the 2016 season but he returned to training in January following a successful operation

Batting	Mat	Inns	NO	Runs	HS	Ave	SR	100	50	Ct	St
Tests	6	12	0	345	60	28.75	41.31	0	1	7	0
ODIs	6	6	0	114	63	19.00	63.33	0	1	2	0
T20Is	1	1	0	7	7	7.00	100.00	0	0	1	0
First-class	192	337	25	13244	300*	42.44	51.22	34	64	90	0
List A	168	157	16	4650	150*	32.97		6	34	60	0
Twenty20	138	129	16	3496	100*	30.93	123.05	1	28	43	0

Bowling	Mat	Balls	Runs	Wkts	BBI	BBM	Ave	Econ	SR	5w	10
Tests	6	-	-	-	-	-	-	-	-	-	-
ODIs	6	6	12	0	-	-	-	12.00	-	0	0
T20Is	1	-	-	-	-	-	-	-	-	-	-
First-class	192	1535	1069	17	2/85		62.88	4.17	90.2	0	0
List A	168	322	297	11	3/37	3/37	27.00	5.53	29.2	0	0
Twenty20	138	18	19	1	1/16	1/16	19.00	6.33	18.0	0	0

LUKAS CAREY

RHB / RFM / R0 / W0

FULL NAME: Lukas John Carey
BORN: July 17, 1997, Carmarthen, Wales
SQUAD NO: 17
EDUCATION: Pontarddulais Comprehensive
School, Swansea; Gower College Swansea
TEAMS: Glamorgan
ROLE: Bowler
DEBUT: First-class: 2016

GLAMORGAN

BEST BATTING: 11 Glamorgan vs Worcestershire, Worcester, 2016
BEST BOWLING: 4-92 Glamorgan vs Northamptonshire, Swansea, 2016

NOTES: Hailing from Robert Croft's club Pontarddulais, Carey made a promising start to his Glamorgan career in August 2016, picking up seven wickets against Northants with his skiddy fast-medium seamers. Another graduate from Glamorgan's academy, he joins Aneurin Donald and Kiran Carlson in the ranks of talented local products looking to reinvigorate the Welsh club

Batting	Mat	Inns	NO	Runs	HS	Ave	SR	100	50	Ct	St
First-class	3	5	1	12	11	3.00	37.50	0	0	1	0

Bowling	Mat	Balls	Runs	Wkts	BBI	BBM	Ave	Econ	SR	5w	10
First-class	3	508	330	13	4/92	7/151	25.38	3.89	39.0	0	0

KIRAN CARLSON

RHB / OB / R0 / W0

GLAMORGAN

FULL NAME: Kiran Shah Carlson
BORN: May 16, 1998, Cardiff, Wales
SQUAD NO: 11
HEIGHT: 5ft 8in
EDUCATION: Whitchurch High School, Cardiff
TEAMS: Glamorgan
ROLE: Allrounder
DEBUT: First-class: 2016; List A: 2016

BEST BATTING: 119 Glamorgan vs Essex, Chelmsford, 2016
BEST BOWLING: 5-28 Glamorgan vs Northamptonshire, Northampton, 2016

WHAT FIRST GOT YOU INTO CRICKET? I always loved playing ball games and loved cricket since my first training session when I was seven years old
BEST MOMENT IN CRICKET? Scoring my first hundred for Glamorgan against Essex at Chelmsford in 2016
BEST PLAYER IN COUNTY CRICKET? Ben Duckett (Nor)
IF YOU WEREN'T A CRICKETER? I'd be a civil engineer
TWITTER: @kirancarlson
NOTES: Another from the Glamorgan conveyor belt, Carlson will line up alongside Aneurin Donald in the Welsh county's middle order this summer, and after becoming the club's youngest ever centurion in 2016 – following hot on the heels of a debut five-wicket haul – much is expected of this off-spinning allrounder. As a schoolboy he attended Whitchurch High School – from where Gareth Bale, Sam Warburton and Geraint Jones all graduated – and was a talented fly-half before choosing to concentrate on cricket

Batting	Mat	Inns	NO	Runs	HS	Ave	SR	100	50	Ct	St
First-class	4	8	1	227	119	32.42	54.83	1	1	1	0
List A	1	1	0	17	17	17.00	94.44	0	0	1	0

Bowling	Mat	Balls	Runs	Wkts	BBI	BBM	Ave	Econ	SR	5w	10
First-class	4	270	178	6	5/28	5/78	29.66	3.95	45.0	1	0
List A	1	-	-	-	-	-	-	-	-	-	-

BRYDON CARSE

RHB / RFM / RO / WO

FULL NAME: Brydon Alexander Carse
BORN: July 31, 1995, Port Elizabeth, South Africa
SQUAD NO: 99
HEIGHT: 6ft 2in
NICKNAME: Cheesy
EDUCATION: Pearson High School, Port Elizabeth
TEAMS: Durham, Eastern Province
ROLE: Bowler
DEBUT: First-class: 2016; T20: 2014

DURHAM

BEST BATTING: 47 Durham vs Nottinghamshire, Trent Bridge, 2016
BEST BOWLING: 3-38 Durham vs Lancashire, Chester-le-Street, 2016

FAMILY TIES? My dad played for Northamptonshire, Rhodesia, Eastern Province, Border and Western Province
STRANGEST THING SEEN IN A GAME? Snow falling during a County Championship game
BEST MOMENT IN CRICKET? My maiden first-class wickets on the way to a victory
BEST PLAYER IN COUNTY CRICKET? Keaton Jennings (Dur)
MOST UNDERRATED PLAYER IN COUNTY CRICKET? Ben Raine (Lei)
TIP FOR THE TOP? Brad Wheal (Ham)
CRICKETING HEROES? Mark Boucher, Brett Lee
NON-CRICKETING HEROES? Roger Federer
SURPRISING FACT? I'm outstanding at table-tennis
UNUSUAL OBJECT AT HOME? Buddha ornaments
DESERT ISLAND DISC? Chunda Munki – For Real
FANTASY SLIP CORDON? Keeper: Mark Boucher, 1st: Wiz Khalifa, 2nd: Donald Trump, 3rd: Me, Gully: Shrek
TWITTER: @CarseBrydon

Batting	Mat	Inns	NO	Runs	HS	Ave	SR	100	50	Ct	St
First-class	9	8	2	176	47	29.33	50.86	0	0	2	0
Twenty20	1	1	0	1	1	1.00	50.00	0	0	0	0

Bowling	Mat	Balls	Runs	Wkts	BBI	BBM	Ave	Econ	SR	5w	10
First-class	9	950	607	17	3/38	4/86	35.70	3.83	55.8	0	0
Twenty20	1	18	11	1	1/11	1/11	11.00	3.66	18.0	0	0

MATT CARTER

RHB / OB / R0 / W0

NOTTINGHAMSHIRE

FULL NAME: Matthew Carter
BORN: May 26, 1996, Lincoln
SQUAD NO: 20
HEIGHT: 6ft 6in
NICKNAME: Carts
EDUCATION: Branston Community Academy, Lincolnshire
TEAMS: Nottinghamshire
ROLE: Bowler
DEBUT: First-class: 2015

BEST BATTING: 11 Nottinghamshire vs Somerset, Taunton, 2015
BEST BOWLING: 7-56 Nottinghamshire vs Somerset, Taunton, 2015

FAMILY TIES? My dad and oldest brother played at village level. Brother Andrew played for Notts, Derby and Hampshire before retiring in 2016
STRANGEST THING SEEN IN A GAME? The Notts Second XI strength and conditioning coach having to bat for us, turning down a single, and then getting caught when short-leg took a worldie
BEST MOMENT IN CRICKET? Taking seven wickets in the first innings on my first-class debut
HOW WOULD YOUR TEAM-MATES DESCRIBE YOU IN THREE WORDS? Loud, annoying, stupid
BEST PLAYER IN COUNTY CRICKET? Tim Bresnan (Yor)
MOST UNDERRATED PLAYER IN COUNTY CRICKET? Tom Westley (Ess)
TIP FOR THE TOP? Matthew Fisher (Yor)
CRICKETING HEROES? Andrew Flintoff in the 2005 Ashes
IF YOU WEREN'T A CRICKETER? I'd be doing a lot of shooting (see below)
SURPRISING FACT? Any chance I get, whether for an hour or a full day, it's spent with the dog in the middle of a field shooting
UNUSUAL OBJECT AT HOME? A cabinet full of guns
DESERT ISLAND DISC? Sia – This Is Acting

Batting	Mat	Inns	NO	Runs	HS	Ave	SR	100	50	Ct	St
First-class	4	7	1	31	11	5.16	39.24	0	0	3	0

Bowling	Mat	Balls	Runs	Wkts	BBI	BBM	Ave	Econ	SR	5w	10
First-class	4	754	511	13	7/56	10/195	39.30	4.06	58.0	1	1

FULL NAME: Karl Carver
BORN: March 26, 1996, Northallerton, Yorkshire
SQUAD NO: 29
HEIGHT: 5ft 11in
NICKNAME: Keith, Carves , Curly
EDUCATION: Thirsk School and Sixth Form College, North Yorkshire
TEAMS: Yorkshire
ROLE: Bowler
DEBUT: First-class: 2014; List A: 2015; T20: 2015

YORKSHIRE

BEST BATTING: 16 Yorkshire vs Leeds/Bradford MCCU, Headingley, 2015
BEST BOWLING: 4-106 Yorkshire vs MCC, Abu Dhabi, 2016

STRANGEST THING SEEN IN A GAME? Our fine-leg fielder at Sheriff Hutton Bridge having his lunch stolen and his coffee knocked over by a bird
BEST MOMENT IN CRICKET? Making my full debuts in all formats for my home county Yorkshire. Getting the wicket of Kumar Sangakkara on my List A debut against Surrey in 2015
SUPERSTITIONS? Wearing my sunglasses to bowl in. Often bat in a long-sleeved shirt
HOW WOULD YOUR TEAM-MATES DESCRIBE YOU IN THREE WORDS? Quiet, team-man, smiley
BEST PLAYER IN COUNTY CRICKET? Keaton Jennings (Dur)
MOST UNDERRATED PLAYER IN COUNTY CRICKET? Ben Foakes (Sur)
TIP FOR THE TOP? Matthew Fisher, Matthew Waite (both Yor), Rob Jones (Lan)
CRICKETING HEROES? Joe Root – because even though he's the best player in the world he's still a good bloke
SURPRISING FACT? I went on tour to India in February 2016 and ended up playing for Hong Kong in a T20 because they were short on numbers
TWITTER: Carver_Karl

Batting	Mat	Inns	NO	Runs	HS	Ave	SR	100	50	Ct	St
First-class	5	7	4	59	16	19.66	46.82	0	0	2	0
List A	9	2	2	47	35*	-	75.80	0	0	1	0
Twenty20	8	2	1	2	2	2.00	50.00	0	0	3	0

Bowling	Mat	Balls	Runs	Wkts	BBI	BBM	Ave	Econ	SR	5w	10
First-class	5	734	425	14	4/106	6/194	30.35	3.47	52.4	0	0
List A	9	210	163	7	3/5	3/5	23.28	4.65	30.0	0	0
Twenty20	8	96	132	6	3/40	3/40	22.00	8.25	16.0	0	0

SHIVNARINE CHANDERPAUL — LHB / LB / R1 / W0

LANCASHIRE

FULL NAME: Shivnarine Chanderpaul
BORN: August 16, 1974, Unity Village, Demerara, Guyana
NICKNAME: Shiv, Tiger
EDUCATION: Gibson School, Guyana; Cove and John High School, Guyana
TEAMS: West Indies, Lancashire, Derbyshire, Durham, Guyana, Khulna Royal Bengals, Royal Challengers Bangalore, Sylhet Royals, Uva Next, Warwickshire
ROLE: Batsman
DEBUT: Test: 1994; ODI: 1994; T20I: 2006; First-class: 1992; List A: 1992; T20: 2006

BEST BATTING: 303* Guyana vs Jamaica, Kingston, 1996
BEST BOWLING: 4-48 Guyana vs Leeward Islands, Basseterre, 1993
COUNTY CAPS: 2010 (Lancashire); 2014 (Derbyshire)

TWITTER: @chanderpaulshiv
NOTES: The middle-order left-hander is West Indies' most capped Test cricketer and sits at No.7 on the all-time Test runscorers list. Having retired from international cricket, he joined Lancashire in 2017 at the age of 42 as a Kolpak player available in all formats. He played eight matches for Lancashire as an overseas player in 2010, in which he scored two hundreds and five fifties. He has represented four county sides, with a combined tally of 3,815 Championship runs at 52.99

Batting	Mat	Inns	NO	Runs	HS	Ave	SR	100	50	Ct	St
Tests	164	280	49	11867	203*	51.37	43.31	30	66	66	0
ODIs	268	251	40	8778	150	41.60	70.74	11	59	73	0
T20Is	22	22	5	343	41	20.17	98.84	0	0	7	0
First-class	355	579	105	25919	303*	54.68		73	135	187	0
List A	414	385	72	13230	150	42.26		13	97	114	0
Twenty20	81	78	11	1576	87*	23.52	105.77	0	8	24	0

Bowling	Mat	Balls	Runs	Wkts	BBI	BBM	Ave	Econ	SR	5w	10
Tests	164	1740	883	9	1/2	1/2	98.11	3.04	193.3	0	0
ODIs	268	740	636	14	3/18	3/18	45.42	5.15	52.8	0	0
T20Is	22	-	-	-	-	-	-	-	-	-	-
First-class	355	4812	2532	60	4/48		42.20	3.15	80.2	0	0
List A	414	1681	1388	56	4/22	4/22	24.78	4.95	30.0	0	0
Twenty20	81	-	-	-	-	-	-	-	-	-	-

ZAK CHAPPELL

RHB / RFM / R0 / W0

FULL NAME: Zachariah John Chappell
BORN: August 21, 1996, Grantham, Lincolnshire
SQUAD NO: 32
HEIGHT: 6ft 5in
NICKNAME: Chappy, Chappelly
EDUCATION: Stamford School, Lincolnshire
TEAMS: Leicestershire
ROLE: Bowler
DEBUT: First-class: 2015; List A: 2015; T20: 2015

BEST BATTING: 96 Leicestershire vs Derbyshire, Derby, 2015
BEST BOWLING: 2-44 Leicestershire vs Kent, Leicester, 2015

BEST MOMENT IN CRICKET? Scoring 96 on my Championship debut batting at No.10
HOW WOULD YOUR TEAM-MATES DESCRIBE YOU IN THREE WORDS? Not very clever
BEST PLAYER IN COUNTY CRICKET? Charlie Shreck (Lei)
TIP FOR THE TOP? Aadil Ali, Rob Sayer (both Lei)
CRICKETING HEROES? Brett Lee – he bowled rockets
NON-CRICKETING HEROES? Muhammad Ali
IF YOU WEREN'T A CRICKETER? I'd be a PE teacher
SURPRISING FACT? I can walk on my hands
TWITTER: @ZakkChappell

Batting	Mat	Inns	NO	Runs	HS	Ave	SR	100	50	Ct	St
First-class	3	5	0	120	96	24.00	68.57	0	1	0	0
List A	2	2	1	32	31	32.00	46.37	0	0	0	0
Twenty20	1	-	-	-	-	-	-	-	-	0	0

Bowling	Mat	Balls	Runs	Wkts	BBI	BBM	Ave	Econ	SR	5w	10
First-class	3	278	204	5	2/44	2/46	40.80	4.40	55.6	0	0
List A	2	65	53	1	1/28	1/28	53.00	4.89	65.0	0	0
Twenty20	1	12	25	0	-	-	-	12.50	-	0	0

VARUN CHOPRA

RHB / LB / R3 / W0

ESSEX

FULL NAME: Varun Chopra
BORN: June 21, 1987, Barking, Essex
SQUAD NO: 6
HEIGHT: 6ft 1in
NICKNAME: Tiddles, Chops
EDUCATION: Ilford County High School
TEAMS: Essex, Tamil Union Cricket and Athletic Club, Warwickshire
ROLE: Batsman
DEBUT: First-class: 2006; List A: 2006; T20: 2006

BEST BATTING: 233* Tamil Union vs Sinhalese Sports Club, Colombo, 2012
COUNTY CAP: 2012 (Warwickshire)

WHAT FIRST GOT YOU INTO CRICKET? Dad taking me to Joe Hussain's Ilford Cricket School
STRANGEST THING SEEN IN A GAME? Chris Wright's celebrations
BEST MOMENT IN CRICKET? Winning the T20 competition in 2014 off the last ball in front of a packed house at Edgbaston
BEST PLAYER IN COUNTY CRICKET? Keith Barker (War)
TIP FOR THE TOP? Sam Hain (War), Dan Lawrence (Ess)
CRICKETING HEROES? Sachin Tedulkar – he was pure class and dealt with the pressure of a whole nation on his shoulders. Shane Warne – a wizard with the ball who transformed spin bowling and left a massive influence on the game with his character and skill
NON-CRICKETING HEROES? Roger Federer – he oozes class and makes things look simple
IF YOU WEREN'T A CRICKETER? I'd be an architect
UNUSUAL OBJECT AT HOME? A chin-up bar
FANTASY SLIP CORDON? Keeper: MS Dhoni, 1st: Me, 2nd: The Rock, 3rd: Tiger Woods, Gully: José Mourinho
TWITTER FEED: @vchops3

Batting	Mat	Inns	NO	Runs	HS	Ave	SR	100	50	Ct	St
First-class	168	275	19	9358	233*	36.55	50.72	19	48	195	0
List A	91	88	6	3506	115	42.75	74.59	7	24	33	0
Twenty20	79	77	10	1824	97*	27.22	110.61	0	14	18	0

Bowling	Mat	Balls	Runs	Wkts	BBI	BBM	Ave	Econ	SR	5w	10
First-class	168	204	128	0	-	-	-	3.76	-	0	0
List A	91	18	18	0	-	-	-	6.00	-	0	0
Twenty20	79	-	-	-	-	-	-	-	-	-	-

DAN CHRISTIAN

RHB / RFM / RO / WO

FULL NAME: Daniel Trevor Christian
BORN: May 4, 1983, Sydney, Australia
SQUAD NO: 54
HEIGHT: 6ft
EDUCATION: St Gregory's College, Sydney
TEAMS: Australia, Nottinghamshire, Brisbane Heat, Deccan Chargers, Gloucestershire, Hampshire, Hobart Hurricanes, Middlesex, New South Wales, RC Bangalore, South Australia, Victoria
ROLE: Allrounder
DEBUT: ODI: 2012; T20I: 2010; First-class: 2008; List A: 2006; T20: 2006

NOTTINGHAMSHIRE

BEST BATTING: 131* South Australia vs New South Wales, Adelaide, 2011
BEST BOWLING: 5-24 South Australia vs Western Australia, Perth, 2010
COUNTY CAP: 2013 (Gloucestershire)

TWITTER: @danchristian54
NOTES: A veteran of the IPL and the Big Bash, the Australian allrounder captained Nottinghamshire to nine straight wins in last year's T20 Blast and returns in 2017. It will be his third consecutive summer at Trent Bridge, having also played for Hampshire, Gloucestershire and Middlesex. He struggled to cement a regular place in either of Australia's limited-overs sides, and last played for his country in 2014

Batting	Mat	Inns	NO	Runs	HS	Ave	SR	100	50	Ct	St
ODIs	19	18	5	273	39	21.00	88.92	0	0	10	0
T20Is	15	6	3	18	6*	6.00	120.00	0	0	5	0
First-class	74	126	17	3377	131*	30.98	55.18	5	14	80	0
List A	117	106	21	2804	117	32.98	101.74	2	14	42	0
Twenty20	182	156	33	2636	129	21.43	132.06	1	9	71	0

Bowling	Mat	Balls	Runs	Wkts	BBI	BBM	Ave	Econ	SR	5w	10
ODIs	19	727	595	20	5/31	5/31	29.75	4.91	36.3	1	0
T20Is	15	210	310	11	3/27	3/27	28.18	8.85	19.0	0	0
First-class	74	9380	5161	151	5/24	9/87	34.17	3.30	62.1	3	0
List A	117	3776	3453	105	6/48	6/48	32.88	5.48	35.9	3	0
Twenty20	182	2924	4024	139	5/14	5/14	28.94	8.25	21.0	2	0

GRAHAM CLARK

RHB / RM / R0 / W0

DURHAM

FULL NAME: Graham Clark
BORN: March 16, 1993, Whitehaven, Cumbria
SQUAD NO: 7
HEIGHT: 6ft 1in
NICKNAME: Sparky, Schnoz
EDUCATION: St Benedict's Catholic High School, Whitehaven
TEAMS: Durham
ROLE: Batsman
DEBUT: First-class: 2015; List A: 2015; T20: 2015

BEST BATTING: 58 Durham vs Hampshire, Southampton, 2016

FAMILY TIES? My older brother Jordan plays for Lancashire, while both my eldest brother Darren and my dad have represented Cumbria at Minor Counties level. My dad is a Level 3 coach and my mam is a Level 2 coach
STRANGEST THING SEEN IN A GAME? Thousands of bees stopping play for about five minutes while everyone lay on the floor motionless
BEST MOMENT IN CRICKET? Scoring 91*in a T20 against Yorkshire at a packed Headingley
HOW WOULD YOUR TEAM-MATES DESCRIBE YOU IN THREE WORDS? Awkward, sweaty, white
BEST PLAYER IN COUNTY CRICKET? Keaton Jennings (Dur)
TIP FOR THE TOP? Brydon Carse, James Weighell (both Dur)
CRICKETING HEROES? Michael Vaughan, Marcus Trescothick, Ricky Ponting
IF YOU WEREN'T A CRICKETER? I'd be working at Sellafield in Cumbria
SURPRISING FACT? I started out as a wicketkeeper, then bowled leg-spin for years and I'm now trying my hand at medium-pace
UNUSUAL OBJECT AT HOME? Turntables. I'm a DJ in my spare time
TWITTER: @GrahamClark16

Batting	Mat	Inns	NO	Runs	HS	Ave	SR	100	50	Ct	St
First-class	6	12	0	235	58	19.58	44.17	0	2	2	0
List A	10	10	0	170	42	17.00	88.08	0	0	0	0
Twenty20	9	9	2	185	91*	26.42	138.05	0	1	2	0

Bowling	Mat	Balls	Runs	Wkts	BBI	BBM	Ave	Econ	SR	5w	10
First-class	6	-	-	-	-	-	-	-	-	-	-
List A	10	-	-	-	-	-	-	-	-	-	-
Twenty20	9	12	21	0	-	-	-	10.50	-	0	0

JORDAN CLARK

RHB / RM / RO / WO

FULL NAME: Jordan Clark
BORN: October 14, 1990, Whitehaven, Cumbria
SQUAD NO: 16
HEIGHT: 6ft 4in
NICKNAME: Clarky
EDUCATION: Sedbergh School, Cumbria
TEAMS: Lancashire
ROLE: Allounder
DEBUT: First-class: 2015; List A: 2010; T20: 2011

LANCASHIRE

BEST BATTING: 84* Lancashire vs Yorkshire, Old Trafford, 2016
BEST BOWLING: 4-101 Lancashire vs Northamptonshire, Northampton, 2015

FAMILY TIES? My younger brother Graham plays for Durham. My older brother Darren has played Minor Counties with Cumberland and together with dad won the National Village Cup with Cleator CC in 2013
SUPERSTITIONS? I keep my bat in a jumper
CRICKETING HEROES? Adam Gilchrist, Andrew Flintoff
NON-CRICKETING HEROES? Jeremy Piven
IF YOU WEREN'T A CRICKETER? I'd be writing books and poetry, or I'd be a newsreader
SURPRISING FACT? I have an arm of tattoos
DESERT ISLAND DISC? Anything by Drake
TWITTER: @Clarksy16

Batting	Mat	Inns	NO	Runs	HS	Ave	SR	100	50	Ct	St
First-class	19	27	3	644	84*	26.83	52.31	0	3	4	0
List A	32	22	4	416	72	23.11	86.12	0	1	5	0
Twenty20	47	33	12	448	44	21.33	131.37	0	0	15	0

Bowling	Mat	Balls	Runs	Wkts	BBI	BBM	Ave	Econ	SR	5w	10
First-class	19	2260	1336	30	4/101	6/159	44.53	3.54	75.3	0	0
List A	32	810	817	19	2/27	2/27	43.00	6.05	42.6	0	0
Twenty20	47	558	821	30	4/22	4/22	27.36	8.82	18.6	0	0

JOE CLARKE

RHB / WK / R1 / W0

FULL NAME: Joseph Michael Clarke
BORN: May 26, 1996, Shrewsbury, Shropshire
SQUAD NO: 33
HEIGHT: 5ft 11in
NICKNAME: Clarkey
EDUCATION: Llanfyllin High School, Powys
TEAMS: Worcestershire, England Lions
ROLE: Batsman
DEBUT: First-class: 2015; List A: 2015; T20: 2015

BEST BATTING: 194 Worcestershire vs Derbyshire, Worcester, 2016

WHAT FIRST GOT YOU INTO CRICKET? My older brother and the 2005 Ashes
STRANGEST THING SEEN IN A GAME? Joe Leach's head
BEST MOMENT IN CRICKET? Beating India in the quarter-final of the U19 World Cup
HOW WOULD YOUR TEAM-MATES DESCRIBE YOU IN THREE WORDS? Cheeky, confident, funny
BEST PLAYER IN COUNTY CRICKET? Jack Leach (Som)
TIP FOR THE TOP? Matthew Fisher (Yor)
CRICKETING HEROES? Adam Gilchrist – he inspired me to play cricket
NON-CRICKETING HEROES? Cristiano Ronaldo, David Beckham, Roger Federer
IF YOU WEREN'T A CRICKETER? I'd be a plumber or an actor
SURPRISING FACT? I can speak (some) Welsh
DESERT ISLAND DISC? Justin Bieber – Purpose
FANTASY SLIP CORDON? Keeper: Me, 1st: Margot Robbie, 2nd: Nicole Scherzinger, 3rd: Emily Ratajkowski, Gully: Notorious B.I.G.
TWITTER: @joeclarke10

Batting	Mat	Inns	NO	Runs	HS	Ave	SR	100	50	Ct	St
First-class	28	45	2	1856	194	43.16	59.75	7	8	10	0
List A	24	23	4	526	131*	27.68	81.55	1	2	13	0
Twenty20	14	13	1	243	69*	20.25	120.29	0	1	2	0

Bowling	Mat	Balls	Runs	Wkts	BBI	BBM	Ave	Econ	SR	5w	10
First-class	28	12	22	0	-	-	-	11.00	-	0	0
List A	24	-	-	-	-	-	-	-	-	-	-
Twenty20	14	-	-	-	-	-	-	-	-	-	-

RIKKI CLARKE — RHB / RFM / R1 / W0 / MVP8

FULL NAME: Rikki Clarke
BORN: September 29, 1981, Orsett, Essex
SQUAD NO: 81
HEIGHT: 6ft 4in
NICKNAME: Clarkey, Crouchy, Rock
EDUCATION: Broadwater Secondary; Godalming College
TEAMS: England, Warwickshire, Derbyshire, Surrey
ROLE: Allrounder
DEBUT: Test: 2003; ODI: 2003; First-class: 2002; List A: 2001; T20: 2003

WARWICKSHIRE

BEST BATTING: 214 Surrey vs Somerset, Guildford, 2006
BEST BOWLING: 6-63 Warwickshire vs Kent, Canterbury, 2010
COUNTY CAPS: 2005 (Surrey); 2011 (Warwickshire)

FAMILY TIES? My dad who played club cricket and my three-year-old son Max who smokes it to all parts of the lounge
BEST MOMENT IN CRICKET? My England Test and ODI debuts, winning the County Championship with Surrey and Warwickshire, winning the first-ever T20 Cup with Surrey, becoming joint world-record holder for catches by an outfielder in a first-class innings
BEST PLAYER IN COUNTY CRICKET? Jeetan Patel (War)
MOST UNDERRATED PLAYER IN COUNTY CRICKET? Laurie Evans (Sus)
TIP FOR THE TOP? Sam Curran (Sur), Aaron Thomason (War)
SURPRISING FACT? I was named after Ricky Villa, who scored the winning FA Cup goal for Spurs in 1981, the year I was born
TWITTER: @rikkiclarke81

Batting	Mat	Inns	NO	Runs	HS	Ave	SR	100	50	Ct	St
Tests	2	3	0	96	55	32.00	37.94	0	1	1	0
ODIs	20	13	0	144	39	11.07	62.06	0	0	11	0
First-class	210	319	38	9488	214	33.76		16	49	323	0
List A	213	175	24	3762	98*	24.91		0	19	98	0
Twenty20	137	124	32	1930	79*	20.97	119.95	0	5	66	0

Bowling	Mat	Balls	Runs	Wkts	BBI	BBM	Ave	Econ	SR	5w	10
Tests	2	174	60	4	2/7	3/11	15.00	2.06	43.5	0	0
ODIs	20	469	415	11	2/28	2/28	37.72	5.30	42.6	0	0
First-class	210	21676	12352	375	6/63		32.93	3.41	57.8	3	0
List A	213	5480	4919	129	5/26	5/26	38.13	5.38	42.4	1	0
Twenty20	137	1695	2041	83	3/11	3/11	24.59	7.22	20.4	0	0

MITCHELL CLAYDON

LHB / RMF / RO / W2

FULL NAME: Mitchell Eric Claydon
BORN: November 25, 1982, Fairfield, New South Wales, Australia
SQUAD NO: 8
HEIGHT: 6ft 3in
NICKNAME: Ellen, Precious, Lips
EDUCATION: Westfield Sports High School, Sydney
TEAMS: Kent, Canterbury, Central Districts, Durham, Yorkshire
ROLE: Bowler
DEBUT: First-class: 2005; List A: 2006; T20: 2006

BEST BATTING: 77 Kent vs Leicestershire, Leicester, 2014
BEST BOWLING: 6-104 Durham vs Somerset, Taunton, 2011
COUNTY CAP: 2016 (Kent)

BEST MOMENT IN CRICKET? Winning three County Championship titles with Durham and being voted as the Players' Player of the Year at Kent in 2014
CRICKETING HEROES? Ricky Ponting
NON-CRICKETING HEROES? Tiger Woods
IF YOU WEREN'T A CRICKETER? I'd be a policeman
SURPRISING FACT? I'm a magician, a keen surfer and I love to play a prank or two
DESERT ISLAND DISC? Foo Fighters
TWITTER: @mitchellclaydon

Batting	Mat	Inns	NO	Runs	HS	Ave	SR	100	50	Ct	St
First-class	91	115	23	1445	77	15.70	59.80	0	4	10	0
List A	92	43	12	228	19	7.35	81.42	0	0	5	0
Twenty20	122	42	23	175	19	9.21	92.10	0	0	24	0

Bowling	Mat	Balls	Runs	Wkts	BBI	BBM	Ave	Econ	SR	5w	10
First-class	91	13594	8166	252	6/104		32.40	3.60	53.9	7	0
List A	92	3966	3656	118	4/39	4/39	30.98	5.53	33.6	0	0
Twenty20	122	2509	3452	139	5/26	5/26	24.83	8.25	18.0	2	0

BEN COAD

RHB / RFM / R0 / W0

FULL NAME: Benjamin Oliver Coad
BORN: January 10, 1994, Harrogate, Yorkshire
SQUAD NO: 10
HEIGHT: 6ft 3in
NICKNAME: Coady, Hench
EDUCATION: Thirsk School and Sixth Form College, North Yorkshire
TEAMS: Yorkshire
ROLE: Bowler
DEBUT: First-class: 2016; List A: 2013; T20: 2015

BEST BATTING: 17* Yorkshire vs Durham, Chester-le-Street, 2016
BEST BOWLING: 1-57 Yorkshire vs Pakistan A, Headingley, 2016

FAMILY TIES? My brothers played representative cricket at junior levels. My dad played Minor Counties for Suffolk
BEST MOMENT IN CRICKET? My second T20 game in 2015, playing against Warwickshire at home in front of a very good crowd and managing to take two wickets and winning the game against the defending champions
SUPERSTITIONS? At Headingley I touch the White Rose on the stairs as I walk out
BEST PLAYER IN COUNTY CRICKET? Joe Root (Yor)
TIP FOR THE TOP? Matthew Fisher (Yor)
SURPRISING FACT? I'm a Newcastle United fan
DESERT ISLAND DISC? Arctic Monkeys – Whatever People Say I Am, That's What I'm Not
FANTASY SLIP CORDON? Keeper: Kevin Hart, 1st: Me, 2nd: Will Smith, 3rd: Alan Shearer, Gully: Usain Bolt
TWITTER: @bencoad10

Batting	Mat	Inns	NO	Runs	HS	Ave	SR	100	50	Ct	St
First-class	2	2	1	18	17*	18.00	41.86	0	0	0	0
List A	7	3	3	3	2*	-	27.27	0	0	3	0
Twenty20	5	2	1	3	2*	3.00	60.00	0	0	3	0

Bowling	Mat	Balls	Runs	Wkts	BBI	BBM	Ave	Econ	SR	5w	10
First-class	2	318	165	2	1/57	1/57	82.50	3.11	159.0	0	0
List A	7	260	282	3	1/34	1/34	94.00	6.50	86.6	0	0
Twenty20	5	91	154	6	2/24	2/24	25.66	10.15	15.1	0	0

JOSH COBB RHB / LB / R0 / W0 / MVP96

FULL NAME: Joshua James Cobb
BORN: August 17, 1990, Leicester
SQUAD NO: 4
HEIGHT: 6ft
NICKNAME: Cobby, Tuck Shop, Lord
EDUCATION: Oakham School, Rutland
TEAMS: Northamptonshire, Barisal Bulls, Central Districts, Dhaka Gladiators, Leicestershire, Prime Doleshwar Sporting Club, Sylhet Superstars
ROLE: Batsman
DEBUT: First-class: 2007; List A: 2008; T20: 2008

BEST BATTING: 148* Leicestershire vs Middlesex, Lord's, 2008
BEST BOWLING: 2-11 Leicestershire vs Gloucestershire, Leicester, 2011

FAMILY TIES? My dad Russell played for Leicestershire
BEST MOMENT IN CRICKET? Being Man of the Match in two T20-winning finals
HOW WOULD YOUR TEAM-MATES DESCRIBE YOU IN THREE WORDS? Massive gym freak
BEST PLAYER IN COUNTY CRICKET? Ben Duckett (Nor)
MOST UNDERRATED PLAYER IN COUNTY CRICKET? Sam Northeast (Ken)
CRICKETING HEROES? Former fast bowler Steve Kirby. He used to give me throw-downs in front of the green dustbin as a young kid at Kibworth CC back in the '90s
IF YOU WEREN'T A CRICKETER? At Oakham I was a member of the debating society and took an active interest in historical and modern British politics, so most likely I would be involved in local politics and government. I take a number of book and papers with me to away games which keep me busy during rain delays, much to the dismay of my team-mates
SURPRISING FACT? I was once a childhood model for Next… where did it all go wrong?
DESERT ISLAND DISC? Gina G – Ooh Aah Just A Little Bit. One of my favourite dancefloor anthems and I know all the moves
TWITTER: @cobby24

Batting	Mat	Inns	NO	Runs	HS	Ave	SR	100	50	Ct	St
First-class	102	174	17	4030	148*	25.66	47.57	3	24	46	0
List A	77	73	6	2576	137	38.44	93.74	6	15	24	0
Twenty20	116	110	12	2350	84	23.97	132.76	0	13	57	0

Bowling	Mat	Balls	Runs	Wkts	BBI	BBM	Ave	Econ	SR	5w	10
First-class	102	2190	1292	14	2/11	2/11	92.28	3.53	156.4	0	0
List A	77	1446	1413	31	3/34	3/34	45.58	5.86	46.6	0	0
Twenty20	116	1071	1459	52	4/22	4/22	28.05	8.17	20.5	0	0

IAN COCKBAIN RHB / RM / R0 / W0

FULL NAME: Ian Andrew Cockbain
BORN: February 17, 1987, Liverpool
SQUAD NO: 28
HEIGHT: 6ft
NICKNAME: Coey, Bird's Nest
EDUCATION: Maghull High School, Sefton; Liverpool John Moores University
TEAMS: Gloucestershire
ROLE: Batsman
DEBUT: First-class: 2011; List A: 2011; T20: 2011

BEST BATTING: 151* Gloucestershire vs Surrey, Bristol, 2014
BEST BOWLING: 1-23 Gloucestershire vs Durham MCCU, Bristol, 2016
COUNTY CAP: 2011

FAMILY TIES? My dad, Ian, played for Lancashire
BEST MOMENT IN CRICKET? Scoring my maiden first-class century
HOW WOULD YOUR TEAM-MATES DESCRIBE YOU IN THREE WORDS? Old, weathered, annoying
BEST PLAYER IN COUNTY CRICKET? Michael Klinger (Glo)
MOST UNDERRATED PLAYER IN COUNTY CRICKET? Liam 'The Viking' Norwell (Glo)
TIP FOR THE TOP? Craig Miles, Matt Taylor (both Glo)
CRICKETING HEROES? Shane Warne, AB de Villiers, Ricky Ponting
NON-CRICKETING HEROES? Roger Federer, Duncan Ferguson
IF YOU WEREN'T A CRICKETER? Working as an independent financial advisor with my old man for Ian Cockbain Wealth Management
UNUSUAL OBJECT AT HOME? Some random spiritual stones which my partner places around our home
DESERT ISLAND DISC? Straight Outta Compton Soundtrack

Batting	Mat	Inns	NO	Runs	HS	Ave	SR	100	50	Ct	St
First-class	49	84	6	2355	151*	30.19	42.91	4	13	34	0
List A	52	45	8	1036	98*	28.00	88.09	0	7	37	0
Twenty20	71	67	12	1774	91*	32.25	125.81	0	12	38	0

Bowling	Mat	Balls	Runs	Wkts	BBI	BBM	Ave	Econ	SR	5w	10
First-class	49	47	44	1	1/23	1/23	44.00	5.61	47.0	0	0
List A	52	-	-	-	-	-	-	-	-	-	-
Twenty20	71	-	-	-	-	-	-	-	-	-	-

MATT COLES

LHB / RFM / R0 / W2 / MVP29

KENT

FULL NAME: Matthew Thomas Coles
BORN: May 26, 1990, Maidstone, Kent
SQUAD NO: 26
HEIGHT: 6ft 3in
NICKNAME: Colesy
EDUCATION: Maplesden Noakes School, Maidstone; MidKent College
TEAMS: Kent, Dhaka Dynamites, England Lions, Hampshire
ROLE: Allrounder
DEBUT: First-class: 2009; List A: 2009; T20: 2010

BEST BATTING: 103* Kent vs Yorkshire, Headingley, 2012
BEST BOWLING: 6-51 Kent vs Northamptonshire, Northampton, 2012
COUNTY CAP: 2012 (Kent)

TWITTER: @MattColes_90
NOTES: A powerful allrounder, Coles caught the eye with a maiden Championship century against Yorkshire at Headingley in 2012, a season in which he also took 59 first-class wickets at 22.72. In 2012/13 he was picked for the England Lions tour of Australia but was sent home with Ben Stokes after twice breaching discipline rules. In 2013 he moved to Hampshire on loan and picked up 24 wickets in five matches. Coles signed permanently in 2014 but, despite taking 41 wickets at 28.41 to help Hampshire get promoted, he left the county and returned to Kent in March 2015, taking 67 Championship wickets. He was impressive across all formats in 2016, finishing as the leading wicket-taker (24) in the RL Cup

Batting	Mat	Inns	NO	Runs	HS	Ave	SR	100	50	Ct	St
First-class	95	124	16	2157	103*	19.97	66.61	1	11	44	0
List A	66	36	5	465	100	15.00	112.04	1	1	27	0
Twenty20	73	53	9	455	54	10.34	136.63	0	1	25	0

Bowling	Mat	Balls	Runs	Wkts	BBI	BBM	Ave	Econ	SR	5w	10
First-class	95	14206	8457	302	6/51	10/98	28.00	3.57	47.0	10	2
List A	66	2612	2459	113	6/32	6/32	21.76	5.64	23.1	2	0
Twenty20	73	1445	2108	73	4/27	4/27	28.87	8.75	19.7	0	0

PAUL COLLINGWOOD RHB / RM / R2 / W0

FULL NAME: Paul David Collingwood
BORN: May 26, 1976, Shotley Bridge, County Durham
SQUAD NO: 5
HEIGHT: 5ft 11in
NICKNAME: Colly, Weed, Wobbles
EDUCATION: Blackfyne Comprehensive School; Derwentside College, Consett
TEAMS: England, Durham, Delhi Daredevils, Impi, Perth Scorchers, Rajasthan Royals
ROLE: Allrounder
DEBUT: Test: 2003; ODI: 2001; T20I: 2005; First-class: 1996; List A: 1995; T20: 2005

DURHAM

BEST BATTING: 206 England vs Australia, Adelaide, 2006
BEST BOWLING: 5-52 Durham vs Somerset, Grangefield Road, 2005
BENEFIT: 2007

FAMILY TIES? My dad and brother played for Shotley Bridge
BEST MOMENT IN CRICKET? Playing for England, winning the World T20 in 2010 and the three Ashes wins
SUPERSTITIONS? A little jig as I walk out to bat, but it's getting harder as it involves squatting three times
FANTASY SLIP CORDON? Keeper: Phil Mustard (to provide the one-liners), 1st: Me, 2nd: Candice Swanepoel, 3rd: Graeme Swann (I can wind him up about his beloved Newcastle Utd), Gully: Keith Lemon
TWITTER: @Colly622

Batting	Mat	Inns	NO	Runs	HS	Ave	SR	100	50	Ct	St
Tests	68	115	10	4259	206	40.56	46.44	10	20	96	0
ODIs	197	181	37	5092	120*	35.36	76.98	5	26	108	0
T20Is	35	33	2	583	79	18.80	127.01	0	3	14	0
First-class	280	482	50	15507	206	35.89		32	80	317	0
List A	417	391	69	10997	132	34.15		10	62	201	0
Twenty20	124	108	12	1875	79	19.53	119.80	0	7	40	0

Bowling	Mat	Balls	Runs	Wkts	BBI	BBM	Ave	Econ	SR	5w	10
Tests	68	1905	1018	17	3/23	3/35	59.88	3.20	112.0	0	0
ODIs	197	5186	4294	111	6/31	6/31	38.68	4.96	46.7	1	0
T20Is	35	222	329	16	4/22	4/22	20.56	8.89	13.8	0	0
First-class	280	11882	6070	155	5/52		39.16	3.06	76.6	2	0
List A	417	10960	8800	264	6/31	6/31	33.33	4.81	41.5	1	0
Twenty20	124	1372	1622	81	5/6	5/6	20.02	7.09	16.9	2	0

MIDDLESEX

FULL NAME: Nicholas Richard Denis Compton
BORN: June 26, 1983, Durban, South Africa
SQUAD NO: 3
HEIGHT: 6ft 2in
NICKNAME: Compdog, Compo
EDUCATION: Hilton College, KwaZulu-Natal; Harrow School, London; Durham University
TEAMS: England, Middlesex, Mashonaland Eagles, Somerset, Worcestershire
ROLE: Batsman
DEBUT: Test: 2012; First-class: 2004; List A: 2001; T20: 2004

BEST BATTING: 254* Somerset vs Durham, Chester-le-Street, 2011
BEST BOWLING: 1-1 Somerset vs Hampshire, Southampton, 2010
COUNTY CAPS: 2006 (Middlesex); 2011 (Somerset)

FAMILY TIES? My dad Richard played club cricket in Durban. Grandfather (Denis) played a bit of cricket and football in England during the 1940s and 1950s. He had a cool hairstyle
BEST MOMENT IN CRICKET? Winning an away Test series in India with England for the first time in 28 years
HOW WOULD YOUR TEAM-MATES DESCRIBE YOU IN THREE WORDS? Charismatic, chiseled, cultured
CRICKETING HEROES? Jacques Kallis – he was a master of his emotions. Brian Lara – for his arrogance. Jos Buttler – for his large shnozz. James Taylor – he had more strengths as a cricketer than anyone I know
SURPRISING FACT? I broke my arm when I was five, which is why I give the impression that I am carrying large Persian carpets under my arm
TWITTER: @thecompdog

Batting	Mat	Inns	NO	Runs	HS	Ave	SR	100	50	Ct	St
Tests	16	30	3	775	117	28.70	36.04	2	2	7	0
First-class	175	306	35	11169	254*	41.21	46.48	25	54	88	0
List A	114	104	20	3045	131	36.25	78.86	6	19	46	0
Twenty20	87	74	7	1318	78	19.67	114.21	0	7	31	0

Bowling	Mat	Balls	Runs	Wkts	BBI	BBM	Ave	Econ	SR	5w	10
Tests	16	-	-	-	-	-	-	-	-	-	-
First-class	175	176	227	3	1/1	1/1	75.66	7.73	58.6	0	0
List A	114	61	53	1	1/0	1/0	53.00	5.21	61.0	0	0
Twenty20	87	-	-	-	-	-	-	-	-	-	-

ALASTAIR COOK
LHB / OB / R6 / W0

FULL NAME: Alastair Nathan Cook
BORN: December 25, 1984, Gloucester
SQUAD NO: 26
HEIGHT: 6ft 2in
NICKNAME: Cookie, Chef
EDUCATION: Bedford School
TEAMS: England, Essex
ROLE: Batsman
DEBUT: Test: 2006; ODI: 2006; T20I: 2007;
First-class: 2003; List A: 2003; T20: 2005

ESSEX

BEST BATTING: 294 England vs India, Edgbaston, 2011
BEST BOWLING: 3-13 Essex vs Northamptonshire, Chelmsford, 2005
COUNTY CAP: 2005 BENEFIT: 2014

FAMILY TIES? Dad played for the local club side and was a very good opening bat, while my mum made the teas. My brothers played for Maldon CC
BEST MOMENT IN CRICKET? Ashes wins home and away, becoming the world No.1 Test team, Essex winning the 50-over competition, making my England debut
CRICKETING HEROES? Graham Gooch – as a boy I watched him playing for Essex at the County Ground
IF YOU WEREN'T A CRICKETER? I'd be a farmer
FANTASY SLIP CORDON? Keeper: Mark Pettini, 1st: Me, 2nd: Charlize Theron

Batting	Mat	Inns	NO	Runs	HS	Ave	SR	100	50	Ct	St
Tests	140	253	15	11057	294	46.45	46.93	30	53	141	0
ODIs	92	92	4	3204	137	36.40	77.13	5	19	36	0
T20Is	4	4	0	61	26	15.25	112.96	0	0	1	0
First-class	252	449	35	19808	294	47.84	50.77	56	97	252	0
List A	150	148	10	5204	137	37.71	78.95	9	31	63	0
Twenty20	32	30	2	892	100*	31.85	127.61	1	5	13	0

Bowling	Mat	Balls	Runs	Wkts	BBI	BBM	Ave	Econ	SR	5w	10
Tests	140	18	7	1	1/6	1/6	7.00	2.33	18.0	0	0
ODIs	92	-	-	-	-	-	-	-	-	-	-
T20Is	4	-	-	-	-	-	-	-	-	-	-
First-class	252	282	211	7	3/13		30.14	4.48	40.2	0	0
List A	150	18	10	0	-	-		3.33	-	0	0
Twenty20	32	-	-	-	-	-	-	-	-	-	-

SAM COOK

RHB / RFM / R0 / W0

FULL NAME: Samuel James Cook
BORN: August 4, 1997, Chelmsford, Essex
SQUAD NO: 16
HEIGHT: 6ft 2in
NICKNAME: Cookie
EDUCATION: Great Baddow High School,
Chelmsford; Loughborough University
TEAMS: Essex 2nd XI, Loughborough MCCU
ROLE: Bowler
DEBUT: First-class: 2016

BEST BATTING: 0 Loughborough MCCU vs Surrey, The Oval, 2016
BEST BOWLING: 3-64 Loughborough MCCU vs Kent, Canterbury, 2016

WHAT FIRST GOT YOU INTO CRICKET? The 2005 Ashes
STRANGEST THING SEEN IN A GAME? Coming off the field for snow
BEST MOMENT IN CRICKET? Taking four wickets in a spell for Loughborough MCCU against Leicestershire last season – it made it even more special that these were the top four batsmen
SUPERSTITIONS? I always have to give my hat and jumper to the umpire before starting an over – I never let anyone run them to the umpire, even if they are just being helpful and speeding up the over-rate
HOW WOULD YOUR TEAM-MATES DESCRIBE YOU IN THREE WORDS? Gullible, hard-working, tenacious
BEST PLAYER IN COUNTY CRICKET? Ben Duckett (Nor)
MOST UNDERRATED PLAYER IN COUNTY CRICKET? Steve Magoffin (Sus)
TIP FOR THE TOP? Tim van der Gugten (Gla), Tom Abell (Som), Joe Clarke (Wor)
NON-CRICKETING HEROES? Sir Alex Ferguson, Leonardo da Vinci
IF YOU WEREN'T A CRICKETER? I'd be running a dogs kennel
SURPRISING FACT? I'm currently taking a degree in History
UNUSUAL OBJECT AT HOME? DJ decks
TWITTER: @samcook09

Batting	Mat	Inns	NO	Runs	HS	Ave	SR	100	50	Ct	St
First-class	2	1	0	0	0	0.00	0.00	0	0	0	0

Bowling	Mat	Balls	Runs	Wkts	BBI	BBM	Ave	Econ	SR	5w	10
First-class	2	265	178	4	3/64	3/64	44.50	4.03	66.2	0	0

FULL NAME: Stephen Craig Cook
BORN: November 29, 1982, Johannesburg, South Africa
SQUAD NO: 6
TEAMS: South Africa, Durham, Gauteng, Lions, North West
ROLE: Batsman
DEBUT: Test: 2016; First-class: 2001; List A: 2001; T20: 2004

DURHAM

BEST BATTING: 390 Lions vs Warriors, East London, 2009
BEST BOWLING: 3-42 Lions vs Dolphins, Durban, 2008

TWITTER: @StephenCookSA
NOTES: The South African opening batsman has joined Durham as an overseas player for the first half of the season. The son of former Proteas international Jimmy Cook, he hade his international bow at the age of 33 in January 2016, against England at Centurion, and became the sixth South African to score a century on Test debut. He scored consecutive Test centuries against Australia and Sri Lanka at the end of last year. His innings of 390 for Lions against Warriors in 2009 is the highest first-class score by a South African and the 12th-highest of all time. That knock included a sixth-wicket partnership of 365 with Thami Tsolekile, also a South African record

Batting	Mat	Inns	NO	Runs	HS	Ave	SR	100	50	Ct	St
Tests	10	17	0	618	117	36.35	45.10	3	2	6	0
First-class	189	347	29	12969	390	40.78		40	52	123	0
List A	150	145	12	5182	127*	38.96	78.36	9	38	25	0
Twenty20	20	20	0	477	66	23.85	122.62	0	2	3	0

Bowling	Mat	Balls	Runs	Wkts	BBI	BBM	Ave	Econ	SR	5w	10
Tests	10	12	16	0	-	-	-	8.00	-	0	0
First-class	189	792	450	11	3/42	3/42	40.90	3.40	72.0	0	0
List A	150	231	230	5	1/2	1/2	46.00	5.97	46.2	0	0
Twenty20	20	-	-	-	-	-	-	-	-	-	-

CHRIS COOKE RHB / WK / R0 / W0

FULL NAME: Christopher Barry Cooke
BORN: May 30, 1986, Johannesburg, South Africa
SQUAD NO: 46
HEIGHT: 5ft 11in
NICKNAME: Chris Jelly, Dough, Beans, Minty, Shapeless, Cookie
EDUCATION: Bishops School, Cape Town; University of Cape Town
TEAMS: Glamorgan, Western Province
ROLE: Batsman/wicketkeeper
DEBUT: First-class: 2009; List A: 2009; T20: 2011

BEST BATTING: 171 Glamorgan vs Kent, Canterbury, 2014

FAMILY TIES? I grew up watching my old man and two big brothers playing cricket – and must have copied them as they were both keeper-batters
STRANGEST THING SEEN IN A GAME? Snow stops play at Derby in 2016
BEST MOMENT IN CRICKET? Winning the YB40 semi-final in 2013 to get to Lord's
HOW WOULD YOUR TEAM-MATES DESCRIBE YOU IN THREE WORDS? A terrible swiller
BEST PLAYER IN COUNTY CRICKET? Colin Ingram (Gla)
MOST UNDERRATED PLAYER IN COUNTY CRICKET? Will Bragg (Gla)
TIP FOR THE TOP? Aneurin Donald, David Lloyd (both Gla)
CRICKETING HEROES? Adam Gilchrist, Hylton Ackerman
NON-CRICKETING HEROES? Nelson Mandela
SURPRISING FACT? I'm allergic to shellfish, I'm a decent leggie, and I have to have the volume on an even number
UNUSUAL OBJECT AT HOME? A couple of Puggles
DESERT ISLAND DISC? Bob Marley
TWITTER: @Cooky_24

Batting	Mat	Inns	NO	Runs	HS	Ave	SR	100	50	Ct	St
First-class	50	85	10	2799	171	37.32	52.43	3	19	42	1
List A	64	58	8	1849	137*	36.98	100.10	2	11	26	2
Twenty20	65	55	11	1053	65*	23.93	140.58	0	3	37	2
Bowling	Mat	Balls	Runs	Wkts	BBI	BBM	Ave	Econ	SR	5w	10
First-class	50	-	-	-	-	-	-	-	-	-	-
List A	64	-	-	-	-	-	-	-	-	-	-
Twenty20	65	-	-	-	-	-	-	-	-	-	-

GREG CORK

RHB / LMF / R0 / W0

FULL NAME: Gregory Teodor Gerald Cork
BORN: September 29, 1994, Derby
SQUAD NO: 14
HEIGHT: 6ft 2in
NICKNAME: Corky
EDUCATION: Denstone College, Staffordshire; Leeds Metropolitan University
TEAMS: Derbyshire
ROLE: Allrounder
DEBUT: First-class: 2016; List A: 2015; T20: 2014

BEST BATTING: 49 Derbyshire vs Worcestershire, Worcester, 2016

FAMILY TIES? My father Dominic played for England
BEST EXPERIENCE ON A CRICKET PITCH? My first-class debut
HOW WOULD YOUR TEAM-MATES DESCRIBE YOU IN THREE WORDS? Loud, funny, polite
BEST PLAYER IN COUNTY CRICKET? Wayne Madsen (Der)
TIP FOR THE TOP? Shiv Thakor (Der)
CRICKETING HEROES? Andrew Flintoff – he could change the game with bat or ball
NON-CRICKETING HEROES? David Beckham, Alex Mytton (Made In Chelsea)
IF YOU WEREN'T A CRICKETER? I'd be a footballer
SURPRISING FACT? I'm a quarter Italian. I played chess for Derbyshire U17
UNUSUAL OBJECT AT HOME? Pull-up bar
DESERT ISLAND DISC? Justin Bieber – Purpose
FANTASY SLIP CORDON? Keeper: Alex Mytton (safe hands), 1st: Ian 'The Postman' Poulter (will always deliver), 2nd: Peter Kay (to crack us a joke when we have a day in the dirt), 3rd: Drake (to listen to a few beatz), Gully: Me
TWITTER: @Greg_Cork

Batting	Mat	Inns	NO	Runs	HS	Ave	SR	100	50	Ct	St
First-class	1	2	0	53	49	26.50	51.45	0	0	0	0
List A	3	1	0	8	8	8.00	133.33	0	0	0	0
Twenty20	10	6	3	43	13*	14.33	95.55	0	0	4	0
Bowling	Mat	Balls	Runs	Wkts	BBI	BBM	Ave	Econ	SR	5w	10
First-class	1	102	70	0	-	-	-	4.11	-	0	0
List A	3	80	98	5	2/17	2/17	19.60	7.35	16.0	0	0
Twenty20	10	165	277	8	2/36	2/36	34.62	10.07	20.6	0	0

MARK COSGROVE — LHB / RM / R2 / W0 / MVP35

LEICESTERSHIRE

FULL NAME: Mark James Cosgrove
BORN: June 14, 1984, Adelaide, Australia
SQUAD NO: 55
HEIGHT: 5ft 9in
NICKNAME: Cozzie
EDUCATION: Trinity College, Adelaide
TEAMS: Australia, Leicestershire, Glamorgan, Hobart Hurricanes, South Australia, Sydney Sixers, Sydney Thunder, Tasmania
ROLE: Batsman
DEBUT: ODI: 2006; First-class: 2002; List A: 2002; T20: 2006

BEST BATTING: 233 Glamorgan vs Derbyshire, Derby, 2006
BEST BOWLING: 3-3 South Australia vs Tasmania, Adelaide, 2007
COUNTY CAP: 2006 (Glamorgan)

BEST MOMENT IN CRICKET? Receiving the Man of the Match award in my first ODI for Australia in 2006
SUPERSTITIONS? Listening to music before I go out to bat
BEST PLAYER IN COUNTY CRICKET? Wayne Madsen (Der)
MOST UNDERRATED PLAYER IN COUNTY CRICKET? Mark Stoneman (Sur)
CRICKETING HEROES? Brian Lara
NON-CRICKETING HEROES? Steven Gerrard
IF YOU WEREN'T A CRICKETER? I'd be an Aussie Rules player
SURPRISING FACT? I grew up at the same club as Darren Lehmann and Ryan Harris
UNUSUAL OBJECT AT HOME? A swimming pool
DESERT ISLAND DISC? Nelly – Country Grammar
TWITTER: @Cozzie99

Batting	Mat	Inns	NO	Runs	HS	Ave	SR	100	50	Ct	St
ODIs	3	3	0	112	74	37.33	96.55	0	1	0	0
First-class	181	321	18	12678	233	41.84	62.77	33	72	124	0
List A	137	132	4	4043	121	31.58	87.58	4	31	42	0
Twenty20	98	95	6	2126	89	23.88	120.31	0	10	21	0

Bowling	Mat	Balls	Runs	Wkts	BBI	BBM	Ave	Econ	SR	5w	10
ODIs	3	30	13	1	1/1	1/1	13.00	2.60	30.0	0	0
First-class	181	3952	2186	50	3/3		43.72	3.31	79.0	0	0
List A	137	1067	1141	18	2/21	2/21	63.38	6.41	59.2	0	0
Twenty20	98	197	320	10	2/11	2/11	32.00	9.74	19.7	0	0

DERBYSHIRE

FULL NAME: Benjamin David Cotton
BORN: September 13, 1993, Stoke-on-Trent, Staffordshire
SQUAD NO: 36
HEIGHT: 6ft 6in
NICKNAME: Big'un
EDUCATION: Clayton Hall Business and Language College, Newcastle-under-Lyme; Staffordshire University
TEAMS: Derbyshire
ROLE: Bowler
DEBUT: First-class: 2014; List A 2014; T20: 2014

BEST BATTING: 43 Derbyshire vs Leicestershire, Derby, 2015
BEST BOWLING: 4-20 Derbyshire vs Leicestershire, Derby, 2014

STRANGEST THING SEEN IN A GAME? A streaker at Leicester
BEST MOMENT IN CRICKET? Dismissing Virat Kohli
BEST PLAYER IN COUNTY CRICKET? Keaton Jennings (Dur)
MOST UNDERRATED PLAYER IN COUNTY CRICKET? Wayne Madsen (Der) – 1,000 runs in a season for the last four years
TIP FOR THE TOP? Harvey Hosein, Ben Slater (both Der)
CRICKETING HEROES? Glenn McGrath, Andrew Flintoff
NON-CRICKETING HEROES? Ian Poulter – I love his passion to win
IF YOU WEREN'T A CRICKETER? I'd be removing asbestos roofs for my dad's company
SURPRISING FACT? I'm hoping to become a groundsman when I finish cricket
UNUSUAL OBJECT AT HOME? A set of decks for mixing music. Not a clue how to use them
DESERT ISLAND DISC? Oasis (any album)
FANTASY SLIP CORDON? Keeper: James Corden, 1st: Noel Gallagher, 2nd: Andrew Flintoff, 3rd: Me, Gully: Peter Kay
TWITTER: @cotts1993

Batting	Mat	Inns	NO	Runs	HS	Ave	SR	100	50	Ct	St
First-class	18	25	6	264	43	13.89	59.19	0	0	3	0
List A	20	9	7	61	18*	30.50	78.20	0	0	3	0
Twenty20	10	5	3	15	8	7.50	93.75	0	0	1	0

Bowling	Mat	Balls	Runs	Wkts	BBI	BBM	Ave	Econ	SR	5w	10
First-class	18	2789	1517	37	4/20	6/62	41.00	3.26	75.3	0	0
List A	20	863	780	26	4/43	4/43	30.00	5.42	33.1	0	0
Twenty20	10	204	314	11	2/19	2/19	28.54	9.23	18.5	0	0

JOSH COUGHLIN LHB / RM / R0 / W0

FULL NAME: Josh Coughlin
BORN: September 29, 1997, Sunderland
SQUAD NO: 29
HEIGHT: 6ft 4in
NICKNAME: Coggers
EDUCATION: St Robert of Newminster Catholic School, Sunderland
TEAMS: Durham
ROLE: Allrounder
DEBUT: First-class: 2016

BEST BATTING: 0 Durham vs Sri Lanka A, Chester-le-Street, 2016
BEST BOWLING: 1-10 Durham vs Sri Lanka A, Chester-le-Street, 2016

FAMILY TIES? My gran's brother played Minor Counties, and my older brother Paul also plays for Durham
STRANGEST THING SEEN IN A GAME? Sheep on the field of play
BEST MOMENT IN CRICKET? Winning the Second XI Championship at the Riverside in 2016
HOW WOULD YOUR TEAM-MATES DESCRIBE YOU IN THREE WORDS? Tall and gangly
BEST PLAYER IN COUNTY CRICKET? Keaton Jennings (Dur)
TIP FOR THE TOP? James Weighell (Dur)
CRICKETING HEROES? Andrew Flintoff
UNUSUAL OBJECT AT HOME? Nerf guns
DESERT ISLAND DISC? Alan Walker – Faded
FANTASY SLIP CORDON? Keeper: Dale Doback, 1st: Jermain Defoe, 2nd: Me, 3rd: Peter Griffin, Gully: 50 Cent
TWITTER: @Coughlin97

Batting	Mat	Inns	NO	Runs	HS	Ave	SR	100	50	Ct	St
First-class	1	1	0	0	0	0.00	0.00	0	0	0	0

Bowling	Mat	Balls	Runs	Wkts	BBI	BBM	Ave	Econ	SR	5w	10
First-class	1	156	45	2	1/10	2/45	22.50	1.73	78.0	0	0

PAUL COUGHLIN

RHB / RMF / R0 / W0

FULL NAME: Paul Coughlin
BORN: October 23, 1992, Sunderland
SQUAD NO: 29
HEIGHT: 6ft 2in
NICKNAME: Coggers
EDUCATION: St Robert of Newminster
Catholic School, Sunderland
TEAMS: Durham
ROLE: Allrounder
DEBUT: First-class: 2012; List A: 2012;
T20: 2014

DURHAM

BEST BATTING: 85 Durham vs Lancashire, Chester-le-Street, 2014
BEST BOWLING: 4-10 Durham vs Somerset, Chester-le-Street, 2015

WHAT FIRST GOT YOU INTO CRICKET? Playing in my uncle's homemade net in his garden
FAMILY TIES? A different uncle, Tommy Harland, played for Durham as a Minor County. My younger brother Josh is a Durham team-mate
STRANGEST THING SEEN IN A GAME? A fielder placed directly behind the bowler's arm
BEST MOMENT IN CRICKET? Winning the RL Cup at Lord's in 2014
HOW WOULD YOUR TEAM-MATES DESCRIBE YOU IN THREE WORDS? Pretty chilled out
BEST PLAYER IN COUNTY CRICKET? Keaton Jennings (Dur)
TIP FOR THE TOP? Brydon Carse (Dur)
CRICKETING HEROES? Andrew Flintoff – amazing to watch. Kept the crowd entertained in all aspects of the game
SURPRISING FACT? I started out aiming to be a wicketkeeper. Then tried myself as a batter. Ended up being more of a bowler
FANTASY SLIP CORDON? Keeper: Lee Evans (comedy factor), 1st: Thierry Henry (sporting legend), 2nd: Chris Kamara (to provide in-game commentary), 3rd: Me
TWITTER: @Coughlin92

Batting	Mat	Inns	NO	Runs	HS	Ave	SR	100	50	Ct	St
First-class	21	33	5	671	85	23.96	55.27	0	3	10	0
List A	13	6	1	33	17	6.60	76.74	0	0	1	0
Twenty20	16	6	2	87	26*	21.75	147.45	0	0	4	0

Bowling	Mat	Balls	Runs	Wkts	BBI	BBM	Ave	Econ	SR	5w	10
First-class	21	2411	1290	42	4/10	6/53	30.71	3.21	57.4	0	0
List A	13	450	394	4	1/34	1/34	98.50	5.25	112.5	0	0
Twenty20	16	299	445	21	5/42	5/42	21.19	8.92	14.2	1	0

FABIAN COWDREY

RHB / SLA / RO / WO

FULL NAME: Fabian Kruuse Cowdrey
BORN: January 30, 1993, Canterbury
SQUAD NO: 30
HEIGHT: 6ft
NICKNAME: Cow, Fabs, Fabes
EDUCATION: Tonbridge School; Cardiff Metropolitan University
TEAMS: Kent
ROLE: Allrounder
DEBUT: First-class: 2013; List A: 2013; T20: 2013

BEST BATTING: 62 Kent vs Cardiff MCCU, Cardiff, 2013
BEST BOWLING: 3-59 Kent vs Hampshire, Canterbury, 2014

FAMILY TIES? My father Chris, uncle Graham and grandfather Colin played for Kent. My father and grandfather also played for and captained England
BEST MOMENT IN CRICKET? My debuts in all formats for Kent
CRICKETING HEROES? AB de Villiers and Viv Richards – both impossible to tie down and devastating against even the greatest of bowling attacks
NON-CRICKETING HEROES? Phil Taylor, for his mental strength
IF YOU WEREN'T A CRICKETER? I'd be a singer, lyricist, writer
SURPRISING FACT? I always missed out on choir solos between the age of 6-13 due to my brother's vocal abilities
DESERT ISLAND DISC? Imagine Dragons
TWITTER: @fkcowdrey

Batting	Mat	Inns	NO	Runs	HS	Ave	SR	100	50	Ct	St
First-class	12	21	1	372	62	18.60	48.56	0	2	5	0
List A	25	23	3	555	75	27.75	83.58	0	4	11	0
Twenty20	35	33	4	577	71	19.89	119.95	0	3	12	0

Bowling	Mat	Balls	Runs	Wkts	BBI	BBM	Ave	Econ	SR	5w	10
First-class	12	172	129	3	3/59	3/59	43.00	4.50	57.3	0	0
List A	25	648	575	14	3/32	3/32	41.07	5.32	46.2	0	0
Twenty20	35	449	616	20	3/18	3/18	30.80	8.23	22.4	0	0

BEN COX

RHB / WK / R0 / W0

FULL NAME: Oliver Benjamin Cox
BORN: February 2, 1992, Wordsley, Stourbridge, Worcestershire
SQUAD NO: 10
HEIGHT: 5ft 10in
NICKNAME: Cocko, Cockballs, Coxy, Benji
EDUCATION: Bromsgrove School, Worcestershire
TEAMS: Worcestershire
ROLE: Wicketkeeper
DEBUT: First-class: 2009; List A: 2010; T20: 2010

BEST BATTING: 109 Worcestershire vs Somerset, Worcester, 2015

FAMILY TIES? My old man was a wicketkeeper and had pretty decent hands (so I'm told). He was fearless with going up to the stumps for the quick bowlers – it must run in the family!
STRANGEST THING SEEN IN A GAME? Joe Leach taking a hat-trick with the first three balls of a 50-over game at New Road in 2015, immediately followed by a 10-minute stoppage due to a low-flying swan circling the square
BEST MOMENT IN CRICKET? Celebrating promotion in 2010 and 2014
BEST PLAYER IN COUNTY CRICKET? Ben Duckett (Nor)
MOST UNDERRATED PLAYER IN COUNTY CRICKET? Joe Leach (Wor) – unreal stats
TIP FOR THE TOP? Josh Tongue (Wor)
CRICKETING HEROES? I was more into my rugby growing up
NON-CRICKETING HEROES? Jonny Wilkinson – his commitment and work-rate to be the best has changed the game of rugby and sport around the world. He defines professionalism
IF YOU WEREN'T A CRICKETER? I would have liked to have given rugby a good crack
SURPRISING FACT? I played for West Brom Academy at U13 level but I was terrible so I quit to play rugby and had a trial for England U18. I once had a pet rabbit called Cocoa
TWITTER: @bencox10

Batting	Mat	Inns	NO	Runs	HS	Ave	SR	100	50	Ct	St
First-class	74	120	20	2877	109	28.77	61.65	2	18	185	11
List A	48	33	5	460	39	16.42	92.55	0	0	42	6
Twenty20	58	48	26	673	59*	30.59	137.06	0	1	22	12

Bowling	Mat	Balls	Runs	Wkts	BBI	BBM	Ave	Econ	SR	5w	10
First-class	74	-	-	-	-	-	-	-	-	-	-
List A	48	-	-	-	-	-	-	-	-	-	-
Twenty20	58	-	-	-	-	-	-	-	-	-	-

MASON CRANE

RHB / LB / R0 / W0

FULL NAME: Mason Sidney Crane
BORN: February 18, 1997, Shoreham-by-Sea, Sussex
SQUAD NO: 32
HEIGHT: 5ft 9in
EDUCATION: Lancing College, West Sussex
TEAMS: Hampshire, New South Wales
ROLE: Bowler
DEBUT: First-class: 2015; List A: 2015; T20: 2015

BEST BATTING: 24* Hampshire vs Cardiff MCCU, Southampton, 2016
BEST BOWLING: 5-35 Hampshire vs Warwickshire, Southampton, 2015

WHAT FIRST GOT YOU INTO CRICKET? Watching the Ashes in 2005
BEST MOMENT IN CRICKET? My maiden first-class five-fer
SUPERSTITIONS? To walk back to my mark I always go past the stumps the same side I'm bowling and always turn left at my mark
HOW WOULD YOUR TEAM-MATES DESCRIBE YOU IN THREE WORDS? Doesn't shut up
BEST PLAYER IN COUNTY CRICKET? Liam Dawson (Ham)
MOST UNDERRATED PLAYER IN COUNTY CRICKET? Gareth Berg (Ham)
TIP FOR THE TOP? Joe Weatherley (Ham)
CRICKETING HEROES? Shane Warne, Stuart MacGill, Ian Salisbury
IF YOU WEREN'T A CRICKETER? I'd be wishing I'd tried harder at school
SURPRISING FACT? I can lick my elbow
UNUSUAL OBJECT AT HOME? Two tortoises
FANTASY SLIP CORDON? Keeper: Ant and Dec; 1st: David Beckham, 2nd: Me, 3rd: Alexis Sanchez, Gully: Michael Buble
TWITTER: @masoncrane32

Batting	Mat	Inns	NO	Runs	HS	Ave	SR	100	50	Ct	St
First-class	17	24	9	159	24*	10.60	32.78	0	0	5	0
List A	13	6	3	30	16*	10.00	63.82	0	0	7	0
Twenty20	5	2	2	2	2*	-	40.00	0	0	1	0

Bowling	Mat	Balls	Runs	Wkts	BBI	BBM	Ave	Econ	SR	5w	10
First-class	17	3020	1950	50	5/35	6/89	39.00	3.87	60.4	1	0
List A	13	604	631	18	4/30	4/30	35.05	6.26	33.5	0	0
Twenty20	5	90	138	3	2/35	2/35	46.00	9.20	30.0	0	0

FULL NAME: Zak Crawley
BORN: February 3, 1998, Bromley, Kent
SQUAD NO: 16
HEIGHT: 6ft 5in
NICKNAME: Creepy, Orangutan
EDUCATION: Tonbridge School, Kent
TEAMS: Kent 2nd XI
ROLE: Batsman
DEBUT: Yet to make first-team debut

KENT

WHAT FIRST GOT YOU INTO CRICKET? I got given pads and a bat at the age of about four and so played in the garden with my dad

FAMILY TIES? Dad played a bit at school. My great uncle was a good club cricketer

BEST MOMENT IN CRICKET? Scoring hundreds for Kent Second XI

HOW WOULD YOUR TEAM-MATES DESCRIBE YOU IN THREE WORDS? Tall, argumentative, infallible

BEST PLAYER IN COUNTY CRICKET? Joe Root (Yor)

TIP FOR THE TOP? Sam Curran (Sur)

CRICKETING HEROES? Viv Richards – he batted the way we all want to bat. Ricky Ponting – he was the one I most enjoyed watching

NON-CRICKETING HEROES? Tiger Woods – the greatest champion of all time. He just knew how to get over the line and was the most mentally tough sportsman ever

IF YOU WEREN'T A CRICKETER? I'd be a golfer

SURPRISING FACT? I used to eat 50 apples a week before the age of 12

DESERT ISLAND DISC? Frank Sinatra – You And Me. Or Black Eyed Peas – Where Is The Love?

FANTASY SLIP CORDON? Keeper: Abe Lincoln, 1st: Tiger Woods, 2nd: Muhammad Ali, 3rd: Sachin Tendulkar, 4th: Shane Warne

TWITTER: @zakcrawley

MATT CRITCHLEY

RHB / LB / RO / WO

FULL NAME: Matthew James John Critchley
BORN: August 13, 1996, Preston, Lancashire
SQUAD NO: 20
HEIGHT: 6ft 2in
NICKNAME: Critch
EDUCATION: St Michael's CofE High School, Chorley; Cardinal Newman College, Preston, University of Derby
TEAMS: Derbyshire
ROLE: Allrounder
DEBUT: First-class: 2015; List A: 2015; T20: 2016

BEST BATTING: 137* Derbyshire vs Northamptonshire, Derby, 2015
BEST BOWLING: 3-50 Derbyshire vs Lancashire, Southport, 2015

BEST MOMENT IN CRICKET? Scoring a hundred in my first home game for Derbyshire
HOW WOULD YOUR TEAM-MATES DESCRIBE YOU IN THREE WORDS? Messy, hardworking, easy-going
MOST UNDERRATED PLAYER IN COUNTY CRICKET? Wayne Madsen (Der)
TIP FOR THE TOP? Will Davis (Der)
CRICKETING HEROES? Shane Warne, Stuart MacGill, Michael Clarke
NON-CRICKETING HEROES? Steven Gerrard
SURPRISING FACT? I'm currently studying for a Sports Science degree
TWITTER: @mattcritchley96
NOTES: Leg-spinning allrounder Critchley made history in 2015 when he became the youngest Derbyshire player to score a century. In only his second first-class match, he came in at 103-6 and went on the attack, scoring an unbeaten 137 from 179 balls. He signed a two-year deal in September 2015

Batting	Mat	Inns	NO	Runs	HS	Ave	SR	100	50	Ct	St
First-class	13	20	3	509	137*	29.94	58.77	1	1	5	0
List A	14	9	2	99	43	14.14	106.45	0	0	3	0
Twenty20	12	5	2	31	10	10.33	140.90	0	0	3	0

Bowling	Mat	Balls	Runs	Wkts	BBI	BBM	Ave	Econ	SR	5w	10
First-class	13	1191	1002	8	3/50	3/50	125.25	5.04	148.8	0	0
List A	14	570	624	12	4/48	4/48	52.00	6.56	47.5	0	0
Twenty20	12	227	259	11	3/36	3/36	23.54	6.84	20.6	0	0

STEVEN CROFT   RHB / RM / OB / R0 / W0 / MVP87

FULL NAME: Steven John Croft
BORN: October 11, 1984, Blackpool
SQUAD NO: 15
HEIGHT: 5ft 11in
NICKNAME: Crofty
EDUCATION: Highfield High School, Blackpool; Myerscough College, Lancashire
TEAMS: Lancashire, Auckland, Northern Districts
ROLE: Allrounder
DEBUT: First-class: 2005; List A: 2003; T20: 2006

LANCASHIRE

BEST BATTING: 156 Lancashire vs Northamptonshire, Old Trafford, 2014
BEST BOWLING: 6-41 Lancashire vs Worcestershire, Old Trafford, 2012
COUNTY CAP: 2010

WHAT FIRST GOT YOU INTO CRICKET? Living out in Sri Lanka as an eight-year-old
FAMILY TIES? Dad played for his work's team and is a bad leg-spinner
BEST MOMENT IN CRICKET? Lifting the County Championship in 2011 and winning the T20 Cup in 2015
BEST PLAYER IN COUNTY CRICKET? Adil Rashid (Yor)
TIP FOR THE TOP? Alex Davies (Lan), Sam Curran (Sur)
CRICKETING HEROES? Andrew Flintoff – he was from around my area and played in the same league as me
NON-CRICKETING HEROES? Denzel Washington
SURPRISING FACT? I'm a qualified personal trainer
DESERT ISLAND DISC? Kings Of Leon (any album)
TWITTER: @Stevenjcroft

Batting	Mat	Inns	NO	Runs	HS	Ave	SR	100	50	Ct	St
First-class	146	227	21	6880	156	33.39	50.50	11	41	155	0
List A	136	121	21	3449	107	34.49		1	28	70	0
Twenty20	148	139	32	3376	94*	31.55	123.25	0	20	87	0

Bowling	Mat	Balls	Runs	Wkts	BBI	BBM	Ave	Econ	SR	5w	10
First-class	146	5022	2845	71	6/41	9/105	40.07	3.39	70.7	1	0
List A	136	2548	2297	59	4/24	4/24	38.93	5.40	43.1	0	0
Twenty20	148	1383	1729	61	3/6	3/6	28.34	7.50	22.6	0	0

STEVEN CROOK

RHB / RFM / R0 / W0

FULL NAME: Steven Paul Crook
BORN: May 28, 1983, Adelaide, Australia
SQUAD NO: 25
HEIGHT: 5ft 11in
NICKNAME: Crooky
EDUCATION: Rostrevor College, Adelaide;
University of South Australia
TEAMS: Northamptonshire, Lancashire,
Middlesex, Sheikh Jamal Dhanmondi Club
ROLE: Allrounder
DEBUT: First-class: 2003; List A: 2003;
T20: 2004

BEST BATTING: 145 Northamptonshire vs Worcestershire, Worcester, 2016
BEST BOWLING: 5-48 Middlesex vs Lancashire, Lord's, 2012
COUNTY CAP: 2013 (Northamptonshire)

FAMILY TIES? My older brother Andrew played for South Australia, Lancashire and
Northamptonshire. I only ever got hand-me-downs
STRANGEST THING SEEN IN A GAME? David Murphy take a wicket
BEST PLAYER IN COUNTY CRICKET? Ben Duckett (Nor)
MOST UNDERRATED PLAYER IN COUNTY CRICKET? Graeme White (Nor)
TIP FOR THE TOP? Saif Zaib (Nor)
CRICKETING HEROES? Craig McDermott – I loved his zinc-cream tactics
NON-CRICKETING HEROES? Jim Morrison
SURPRISING FACT? I'm frontman for a band called Juliet The Sun, and I starred (briefly)
in Neighbours
DESERT ISLAND DISC? The Very Best of The Doors
FANTASY SLIP CORDON? Keeper: Jim Morrison, 1st: Kurt Cobain. That's it – I normally only
have one slip
TWITTER: @stevecrook25

Batting	Mat	Inns	NO	Runs	HS	Ave	SR	100	50	Ct	St
First-class	95	126	18	3551	145	32.87	77.21	5	19	31	0
List A	80	59	7	1073	100	20.63	101.32	1	5	16	0
Twenty20	110	81	20	1131	63	18.54	130.29	0	3	31	0

Bowling	Mat	Balls	Runs	Wkts	BBI	BBM	Ave	Econ	SR	5w	10
First-class	95	11580	7546	191	5/48		39.50	3.90	60.6	3	0
List A	80	2821	2698	81	5/36	5/36	33.30	5.73	34.8	1	0
Twenty20	110	1453	2010	73	3/19	3/19	27.53	8.30	19.9	0	0

FULL NAME: Samuel Matthew Curran
BORN: June 3, 1998, Northampton
SQUAD NO: 58
HEIGHT: 5ft 11in
NICKNAME: Junior, Sammy
EDUCATION: Wellington College, Berkshire
TEAMS: Surrey, England Lions
ROLE: Allrounder
DEBUT: First-class: 2015; List A: 2015;
T20: 2015

SURREY

BEST BATTING: 96 Surrey vs Lancashire, The Oval, 2016
BEST BOWLING: 7-58 Surrey vs Durham, Chester-le-Street, 2016

FAMILY TIES? My father Kevin played for Zimbabwe, Gloucestershire and Northamptonshire and my brother Tom plays for Surrey. We have always been a competitive family
STRANGEST THING SEEN IN A GAME? A batsman's phone ringing inside his pad
BEST MOMENT IN CRICKET? Winning games for Surrey is incredible – the one that sticks out is when Kumar Sangakkara hit a 150 to beat Nottinghamshire at The Oval
SUPERSTITIONS? I mark my crease every delivery – five times for seamers and three times against spin
HOW WOULD YOUR TEAM-MATES DESCRIBE YOU IN THREE WORDS? Noisy, annoying, young
BEST PLAYER IN COUNTY CRICKET? Kumar Sangakkara (Sur)
MOST UNDERRATED PLAYER IN COUNTY CRICKET? Adam Rossington (Nor)
TIP FOR THE TOP? Dan Lawrence (Ess), Dom Sibley (Sur), Joe Clarke (Wor)
SURPRISING FACT? I flick my hair after every ball I bowl
UNUSUAL OBJECT AT HOME? A big wooden hippo
TWITTER: @CurranSM

Batting	Mat	Inns	NO	Runs	HS	Ave	SR	100	50	Ct	St
First-class	19	30	5	806	96	32.24	60.23	0	6	5	0
List A	25	17	4	342	57	26.30	88.37	0	1	9	0
Twenty20	21	14	3	170	32	15.45	97.14	0	0	7	0

Bowling	Mat	Balls	Runs	Wkts	BBI	BBM	Ave	Econ	SR	5w	10
First-class	19	2487	1502	55	7/58	8/120	27.30	3.62	45.2	4	0
List A	25	1077	961	26	4/32	4/32	36.96	5.35	41.4	0	0
Twenty20	21	354	471	18	3/17	3/17	26.16	7.98	19.6	0	0

TOM CURRAN

RHB / RFM / R0 / W1 / MVP31

FULL NAME: Thomas Kevin Curran
BORN: March 12, 1995, Cape Town, South Africa
SQUAD NO: 59
HEIGHT: 6ft
NICKNAME: TC
EDUCATION: Wellington College, Berkshire
TEAMS: Surrey, England Lions
ROLE: Bowler
DEBUT: First-class: 2014; List A: 2013; T20: 2014

BEST BATTING: 60 Surrey vs Leicestershire, Leicester, 2015
BEST BOWLING: 7-20 Surrey vs Gloucestershire, The Oval, 2015

FAMILY TIES? My father Kevin played for Northants and Zimbabwe and my brother Sam also plays for Surrey
BEST MOMENT IN CRICKET? Gareth Batty getting a hat-trick to win Division Two in 2015
BEST PLAYER IN COUNTY CRICKET? Jason Roy (Sur)
MOST UNDERRATED PLAYER IN COUNTY CRICKET? Rory Burns (Sur)
TIP FOR THE TOP? Joe Clarke (Wor), Dominic Sibley (Sur)
CRICKETING HEROES? Hamilton Masakadza – he smashes it
NON-CRICKETING HEROES? Dan Bilzerian – he lives the dream
IF YOU WEREN'T A CRICKETER? I would be fishing or else playing the guitar in a bar somewhere exotic
UNUSUAL OBJECT AT HOME? A harp
DESERT ISLAND DISC? Some mix you wouldn't know
FANTASY SLIP CORDON? Keeper: Michelangelo the Teenage Mutant Ninja Turtle, 1st: Me, 2nd: Margot Robbie, 3rd: Rey Mysterio
TWITTER: @_TC59

Batting	Mat	Inns	NO	Runs	HS	Ave	SR	100	50	Ct	St
First-class	42	58	7	815	60	15.98	48.86	0	4	17	0
List A	36	26	8	301	44	16.72	89.58	0	0	11	0
Twenty20	35	17	3	235	41	16.78	126.34	0	0	13	0

Bowling	Mat	Balls	Runs	Wkts	BBI	BBM	Ave	Econ	SR	5w	10
First-class	42	7514	4151	147	7/20	10/176	28.23	3.31	51.1	6	1
List A	36	1582	1413	58	5/16	5/16	24.36	5.35	27.2	2	0
Twenty20	35	705	964	34	4/35	4/35	28.35	8.20	20.7	0	0

ANUJ DAL

RHB / RM / RO / WO

FULL NAME: Anuj Kailash Dal
BORN: July 8, 1996, Newcastle-under-Lyme, Staffordshire
SQUAD NO: 65
HEIGHT: 5ft 9in
NICKNAME: Nuj, Nujii
EDUCATION: Durban High School; Nottingham High School
TEAMS: England U19, Nottinghamshire 2nd XI
ROLE: Batsman
DEBUT: Yet to make first-team debut

WHAT FIRST GOT YOU INTO CRICKET? My family. My brother and dad are cricket fanatics so naturally I fell in love with the game too

STRANGEST THING SEEN IN A GAME? Turning up to a Second XI Championship game to find only one umpire

BEST MOMENT IN CRICKET? Fielding in the Ashes on home soil at Trent Bridge in front of a full house

HOW WOULD YOUR TEAM-MATES DESCRIBE YOU IN THREE WORDS? Witty, knowledgeable, quirky

BEST PLAYER IN COUNTY CRICKET? Keaton Jennings (Dur)

MOST UNDERRATED PLAYER IN COUNTY CRICKET? Graeme White (Nor)

TIP FOR THE TOP? Sam Curran (Sur), Matthew Fisher, Josh Shaw (both Yor)

CRICKETING HEROES? Jacques Kallis, AB de Villiers, Brett Lee, Virat Kohli

NON-CRICKETING HEROES? Rafael Nadal, Matt Damon, Tom Cruise

IF YOU WEREN'T A CRICKETER? I'd be a personal trainer or a trader in the stock market

SURPRISING FACT? I'm fluent in Spanish

UNUSUAL OBJECT AT HOME? Several bottles of women's deodorant which are (unashamedly) mine

DESERT ISLAND DISC? Take That – Rule The World

FANTASY SLIP CORDON? Keeper: Michael McIntyre, 1st: Graeme Swann, 2nd: Graham Norton, 3rd: Russell Peters, 4th: Matt Damon, Gully: Jennifer Aniston

TWITTER: @AnujDal

JOSH DAVEY
RHB / RM / RO / WO

FULL NAME: Joshua Henry Davey
BORN: August 3, 1990, Aberdeen, Scotland
SQUAD NO: 38
EDUCATION: Culford School
TEAMS: Scotland, Somerset, Middlesex
ROLE: Allrounder
DEBUT: ODI: 2010; T20I: 2012; First-class: 2010; List A: 2010; T20: 2010

BEST BATTING: 72 Middlesex vs Oxford MCCU, Oxford, 2010
BEST BOWLING: 4-53 Scotland vs Afghanistan, Abu Dhabi, 2013

TWITTER FEED: @JoshDavey38
NOTES: After four years at Middlesex, Davey was released at the end of 2013 and excelled for Somerset Second XI in 2014, which led to a full contract at the county. The seam-bowling allrounder hit an unbeaten 48 and took 3-41 for Scotland against Ireland at Edinburgh in the 2011 Tri-Nation Tournament to help his country to a five-wicket win. Attended the Darren Lehmann Cricket Academy in Adelaide in 2009. Took 5-9 for Scotland against Afghanistan at Ayr in 2010. In January 2015, against the same opponents, he took 6-28 and scored 53*. He played for Scotland in the 2015 World Cup, finishing as his team's highest wicket-taker

Batting	Mat	Inns	NO	Runs	HS	Ave	SR	100	50	Ct	St
ODIs	28	25	5	463	64	23.15	66.23	0	2	9	0
T20Is	14	7	2	55	24	11.00	127.90	0	0	9	0
First-class	12	20	1	362	72	19.05	41.37	0	3	6	0
List A	66	58	11	1122	91	23.87	66.00	0	5	21	0
Twenty20	32	18	7	151	24	13.72	120.80	0	0	21	0

Bowling	Mat	Balls	Runs	Wkts	BBI	BBM	Ave	Econ	SR	5w	10
ODIs	28	1151	998	46	6/28	6/28	21.69	5.20	25.0	2	0
T20Is	14	298	422	14	4/34	4/34	30.14	8.49	21.2	0	0
First-class	12	1077	589	22	4/53	6/79	26.77	3.28	48.9	0	0
List A	66	2273	2068	80	6/28	6/28	25.85	5.45	28.4	2	0
Twenty20	32	478	676	25	4/34	4/34	27.04	8.48	19.1	0	0

ALEX DAVIES   RHB / WK / R0 / W0

FULL NAME: Alexander Luke Davies
BORN: August 23, 1994, Darwen, Lancashire
SQUAD NO: 17
HEIGHT: 5ft 8in
NICKNAME: Davo, Chikwambo, Little Boy
EDUCATION: Queen Elizabeth's Grammar School, Blackburn
TEAMS: Lancashire
ROLE: Wicketkeeper
DEBUT: First-class: 2012; List A: 2011; T20: 2014

BEST BATTING: 99 Lancashire vs Kent, Old Trafford, 2015

FAMILY TIES? Dad played club cricket all his life
BEST MOMENT IN CRICKET? Winning the T20 Blast with Lancashire in 2015
HOW WOULD YOUR TEAM-MATES DESCRIBE YOU IN THREE WORDS? Little-man syndrome
BEST PLAYER IN COUNTY CRICKET? Jos Buttler (Lan)
TIP FOR THE TOP? Gavin Griffiths (Lei)
CRICKETING HEROES? Sachin Tendulkar – he timed the ball amazingly. Adam Gilchrist – the first high-quality aggressive batsman-keeper. AB de Villiers – for his 360-degree gameplay
NON-CRICKETING HEROES? Alan Shearer, David Beckham, my grandad
IF YOU WEREN'T A CRICKETER? I'd be studying or travelling
SURPRISING FACT? Despite being a wicketkeeper, I can bowl with both arms
DESERT ISLAND DISC? Ed Sheeran
FANTASY SLIP CORDON? Keeper: Me, 1st: Denzel Washington, 2nd: Brian Potter, 3rd: Jessica Biel, Gully: Jordan Rhodes
TWITTER: @aldavies23

Batting	Mat	Inns	NO	Runs	HS	Ave	SR	100	50	Ct	St
First-class	33	45	2	1444	99	33.58	53.40	0	11	84	6
List A	16	13	3	380	73*	38.00	102.15	0	3	16	3
Twenty20	25	23	2	274	47	13.04	129.24	0	0	19	4

Bowling	Mat	Balls	Runs	Wkts	BBI	BBM	Ave	Econ	SR	5w	10
First-class	33	-	-	-	-	-	-	-	-	-	-
List A	16	-	-	-	-	-	-	-	-	-	-
Twenty20	25	-	-	-	-	-	-	-	-	-	-

RYAN DAVIES

RHB / WK / R0 / W0

FULL NAME: Ryan Christopher Davies
BORN: November 5, 1996, Thanet, Kent
SQUAD NO: 77
HEIGHT: 5ft 8in
NICKNAME: Rizzlar, Riz, Davo
EDUCATION: Sandwich Technology School; Canterbury Academy
TEAMS: Somerset, Kent
ROLE: Wicketkeeper
DEBUT: First-class: 2015; List A: 2016; T20: 2015

BEST BATTING: 86 Kent vs Lancashire, Old Trafford, 2016

STRANGEST THING SEEN IN A GAME? Chris Read hitting a ball out of the ground and smashing his stumps in the same motion
BEST MOMENT IN CRICKET? Playing at The Oval in front of 24,000
HOW WOULD YOUR TEAM-MATES DESCRIBE YOU IN THREE WORDS? Smelly, grubby, chav
BEST PLAYER IN COUNTY CRICKET? Jeetan Patel (War)
MOST UNDERRATED PLAYER IN COUNTY CRICKET? Sam Northeast (Ken)
TIP FOR THE TOP? Daniel Bell-Drummond (Ken)
CRICKETING HEROES? Marcus Trescothick
NON-CRICKETING HEROES? Who doesn't love Cristiano Ronaldo? He's always challenging himself to break records and be the best in the world
SURPRISING FACT? I have dropped five iPhones in the bath
UNUSUAL OBJECT AT HOME? A drum
DESERT ISLAND DISC? OneRepublic
FANTASY SLIP CORDON? Keeper: Karl Pilkington, 1st: Jack Whitehall, 2nd: Cristiano Ronaldo, 3rd: Daniel Radcliffe, Gully: José Mourinho
TWITTER: @RyanDavies777

Batting	Mat	Inns	NO	Runs	HS	Ave	SR	100	50	Ct	St
First-class	20	25	1	415	86	17.29	65.97	0	3	36	6
List A	6	4	1	76	46	25.33	113.43	0	0	8	1
Twenty20	15	7	0	20	6	2.85	105.26	0	0	8	4

Bowling	Mat	Balls	Runs	Wkts	BBI	BBM	Ave	Econ	SR	5w	10
First-class	20	-	-	-	-	-	-	-	-	-	-
List A	6	-	-	-	-	-	-	-	-	-	-
Twenty20	15	-	-	-	-	-	-	-	-	-	-

STEVE DAVIES

LHB / WK / R6 / W0 / MVP92

FULL NAME: Steven Michael Davies
BORN: June 17, 1986, Bromsgrove, Worcestershire
SQUAD NO: 11
HEIGHT: 5ft 11in
NICKNAME: Dave
EDUCATION: King Charles High School, Kidderminster
TEAMS: England, Somerset, Surrey, Worcestershire
ROLE: Batsman/wicketkeeper
DEBUT: ODI: 2009; T20I: 2009; First-class: 2005; List A: 2003; T20: 2006

BEST BATTING: 200* Surrey vs Glamorgan, Cardiff, 2015
COUNTY CAP: 2011 (Surrey)

BEST MOMENT IN CRICKET? My double hundred against Glamorgan in 2015
SUPERSTITIONS? My area in the dressing room must be tidy and I always play shadow shots in the mirror before batting
HOW WOULD YOUR TEAM-MATES DESCRIBE YOU IN THREE WORDS? Laid-back, calm, loyal
BEST PLAYER IN COUNTY CRICKET? Tom Curran (Sur)
TIP FOR THE TOP? Sam Curran (Sur)
CRICKETING HEROES? Adam Gilchrist
NON-CRICKETING HEROES? Roger Federer
IF YOU WEREN'T A CRICKETER? I'd be a professional tennis player
SURPRISING FACT? I'm a session harp player
DESERT ISLAND DISC? Elton John – Greatest Hits
TWITTER: @SteveDavies43

Batting	Mat	Inns	NO	Runs	HS	Ave	SR	100	50	Ct	St
ODIs	8	8	0	244	87	30.50	105.62	0	1	8	0
T20Is	5	5	0	102	33	20.40	124.39	0	0	2	1
First-class	182	299	30	10878	200*	40.43	62.26	21	50	407	20
List A	170	159	14	5459	127*	37.64		9	34	131	41
Twenty20	116	108	8	2217	99*	22.17	141.03	0	12	55	18

Bowling	Mat	Balls	Runs	Wkts	BBI	BBM	Ave	Econ	SR	5w	10
ODIs	8	-	-	-	-	-	-	-	-	-	-
T20Is	5	-	-	-	-	-	-	-	-	-	-
First-class	182	-	-	-	-	-	-	-	-	-	-
List A	170	-	-	-	-	-	-	-	-	-	-
Twenty20	116	-	-	-	-	-	-	-	-	-	-

WILL DAVIS

RHB / RFM / R0 / W0

FULL NAME: William Samuel Davis
BORN: March 6, 1996, Stafford
SQUAD NO: 44
HEIGHT: 6ft 2in
NICKNAME: Thumb, Spaceman
EDUCATION: Stafford Grammar School
TEAMS: Derbyshire
ROLE: Bowler
DEBUT: First-class: 2015; List A: 2016

BEST BATTING: 15 Derbyshire vs Leicestershire, Derby, 2016
BEST BOWLING: 7-146 Derbyshire vs Glamorgan, Colwyn Bay, 2016

STRANGEST THING SEEN IN A GAME? Greg Cork's field placements
BEST MOMENT IN CRICKET? Taking my maiden five-wicket haul in first-class cricket against Glamorgan at Colwyn Bay in 2016
SUPERSTITIONS? I have to turn at the end of my bowling mark before running in
HOW WOULD YOUR TEAM-MATES DESCRIBE YOU IN THREE WORDS? Switched-on, clever, spaceman
BEST PLAYER IN COUNTY CRICKET? Wayne Madsen (Der)
MOST UNDERRATED PLAYER IN COUNTY CRICKET? Wayne Madsen (Der)
TIP FOR THE TOP? Charlie MacDonell (Der)
CRICKETING HEROES? Andrew Flintoff
NON-CRICKETING HEROES? Cristiano Ronaldo
IF YOU WEREN'T A CRICKETER? I'd be a professional gamer
UNUSUAL OBJECT AT HOME? Slendertone
DESERT ISLAND DISC? Taylor Swift – Love Story
FANTASY SLIP CORDON? Keeper: Jack Whitehall, 1st: Me, 2nd: David Attenborough, 3rd: Conor McGregor, Gully: Floyd Mayweather
TWITTER: @W_Davis44

Batting	Mat	Inns	NO	Runs	HS	Ave	SR	100	50	Ct	St
First-class	7	9	2	42	15	6.00	47.72	0	0	0	0
List A	1	-	-	-	-	-	-	-	-	-	-

Bowling	Mat	Balls	Runs	Wkts	BBI	BBM	Ave	Econ	SR	5w	10
First-class	7	1154	814	24	7/146	8/204	33.91	4.23	48.0	1	0
List A	1	-	-	-	-	-	-	-	-	-	-

LIAM DAWSON   RHB / SLA / R1 / W0 / MVP5

FULL NAME: Liam Andrew Dawson
BORN: March 1, 1990, Swindon
SQUAD NO: 8
HEIGHT: 5ft 8in
NICKNAME: Daws, Lemmy, Chav, Stomper
EDUCATION: The John Bentley School, Wiltshire
TEAMS: England, Hampshire, Essex, Mountaineers, Rangpur Riders
ROLE: Allrounder
DEBUT: Test: 2016; ODI: 2016; T20I: 2016; First-class: 2007; List A: 2007; T20: 2008

HAMPSHIRE

BEST BATTING: 169 Hampshire vs Somerset, Southampton, 2011
BEST BOWLING: 7-51 Mountaineers vs Mashonaland Eagles, Mutare Sports Club, 2011
COUNTY CAP: 2013 (Hampshire)

WHAT FIRST GOT YOU INTO CRICKET? Watching my dad play for Goatacre CC
FAMILY TIES? My brother Brad has played Minor Counties for Wiltshire
BEST MOMENT IN CRICKET? My England debut in 2016
HOW WOULD YOUR TEAM-MATES DESCRIBE YOU IN THREE WORDS? Stubborn, chav, argumentative
BEST PLAYER IN COUNTY CRICKET? Mark Wood (Dur)
MOST UNDERRATED PLAYER IN COUNTY CRICKET? Steven Mullaney (Not)
TIP FOR THE TOP? Mason Crane (Ham), Sam Curran (Sur)
TWITTER: @daws128

Batting	Mat	Inns	NO	Runs	HS	Ave	SR	100	50	Ct	St
Tests	1	2	1	66	66*	66.00	42.58	0	1	0	0
ODIs	1	1	0	10	10	10.00	76.92	0	0	0	0
T20Is	2	-	-	-	-	-	-	-	-	2	0
First-class	118	193	22	5875	169	34.35	48.60	8	32	125	0
List A	128	106	20	2791	113*	32.45	94.00	2	14	61	0
Twenty20	100	70	20	908	76*	18.16	109.92	0	1	49	0

Bowling	Mat	Balls	Runs	Wkts	BBI	BBM	Ave	Econ	SR	5w	10
Tests	1	258	129	2	2/129	2/129	64.50	3.00	129.0	0	0
ODIs	1	48	70	2	2/70	2/70	35.00	8.75	24.0	0	0
T20Is	2	36	47	3	3/27	3/27	15.66	7.83	12.0	0	0
First-class	118	9493	5001	132	7/51	7/84	37.88	3.16	71.9	3	0
List A	128	4490	3696	102	6/47	6/47	36.23	4.93	44.0	1	0
Twenty20	100	1420	1728	68	5/17	5/17	25.41	7.30	20.8	1	0

COLIN DE GRANDHOMME   RHB / RFM / R0 / W0

WARWICKSHIRE

FULL NAME: Colin de Grandhomme
BORN: July 22, 1986, Harare, Zimbabwe
TEAMS: New Zealand, Warwickshire, Auckland, Manicaland, Midlands, Nagenahira Nagas, North Island
ROLE: Allrounder
DEBUT: Test: 2016; ODI: 2012; T20I: 2012; First-class: 2005; List A: 2004; T20: 2007

BEST BATTING: 144* Auckland vs Otago, Auckland, 2016
BEST BOWLING: 6-24 Auckland vs Wellington, Auckland, 2014

NOTES: Warwickshire have signed the seam-bowling allrounder for the duration of the NatWest T20 Blast. De Grandhomme made his New Zealand debut in 2012 against his native Zimbabwe, playing one ODI and four T20Is before being dropped. He returned to the international scene for the 2016 home Test series against Pakistan, taking 6-41 on debut in Christchurch and winning the Man of the Match award. At the time of his writing, his T20 batting strike-rate of 171.04 is the highest of any player in the world (minimum 250 balls faced). "Colin adds the batting firepower that we desire in our middle order, whilst adding depth to our bowling attack as an experienced seam bowler," said Warwickshire sport director Ashley Giles

Batting	Mat	Inns	NO	Runs	HS	Ave	SR	100	50	Ct	St
Tests	4	6	1	145	37	29.00	98.63	0	0	5	0
ODIs	9	7	2	165	36	33.00	97.63	0	0	2	0
T20Is	8	8	4	75	41*	18.75	147.05	0	0	5	0
First-class	87	144	19	4453	144*	35.62	71.24	10	25	89	0
List A	108	98	12	2197	151	25.54		2	6	48	0
Twenty20	100	91	23	1772	72*	26.05	171.04	0	6	46	0

Bowling	Mat	Balls	Runs	Wkts	BBI	BBM	Ave	Econ	SR	5w	10
Tests	4	575	260	10	6/41	7/64	26.00	2.71	57.5	1	0
ODIs	9	300	263	7	2/40	2/40	37.57	5.26	42.8	0	0
T20Is	8	60	82	3	2/22	2/22	27.33	8.20	20.0	0	0
First-class	87	8403	3973	133	6/24	7/64	29.87	2.83	63.1	2	0
List A	108	2804	2463	59	4/37	4/37	41.74	5.27	47.5	0	0
Twenty20	100	745	1140	40	3/22	3/22	28.50	9.18	18.6	0	0

MARCHANT DE LANGE

RHB / RF / RO / WO

FULL NAME: Marchant de Lange
BORN: October 13, 1990, Tzaneen, Transvaal, South Africa
HEIGHT: 6ft 7in
TEAMS: South Africa, Glamorgan, Barbados Tridents, Easterns, Free State, Guyana Amazon Warriors, Knights, Kolkata Knight Riders, Mumbai Indians, Titans
ROLE: Bowler
DEBUT: Test: 2011; ODI: 2012; T20I: 2012; First-class: 2010; List A: 2010; T20: 2011

GLAMORGAN

BEST BATTING: 65 Knights vs Lions, Kimberley, 2016
BEST BOWLING: 7-23 Knights vs Titans, Centurion, 2016

TWITTER: @Marchant90
NOTES: Immensely tall and quick, de Lange took 7-81 in his debut Test match, against Sri Lanka at Durban in 2011. But he has appeared only intermittently for South Africa since then, playing one more Test match and a sprinkling of ODIs and T20Is. Subject to the awarding of a visa and ECB approval, he was due to sign for Glamorgan as a local player because his wife has a British passport

Batting	Mat	Inns	NO	Runs	HS	Ave	SR	100	50	Ct	St
Tests	2	2	0	9	9	4.50	47.36	0	0	1	0
ODIs	4	-	-	-	-	-	-	-	-	0	0
T20Is	6	-	-	-	-	-	-	-	-	1	0
First-class	53	71	9	837	65	13.50	68.88	0	1	26	0
List A	54	35	10	269	29	10.76	86.77	0	0	15	0
Twenty20	54	21	9	107	22	8.91	117.58	0	0	8	0

Bowling	Mat	Balls	Runs	Wkts	BBI	BBM	Ave	Econ	SR	5w	10
Tests	2	448	277	9	7/81	8/126	30.77	3.70	49.7	1	0
ODIs	4	209	198	10	4/46	4/46	19.80	5.68	20.9	0	0
T20Is	6	140	228	7	2/26	2/26	32.57	9.77	20.0	0	0
First-class	53	9647	5802	209	7/23	11/62	27.76	3.60	46.1	8	2
List A	54	2635	2349	105	5/59	5/59	22.37	5.34	25.0	3	0
Twenty20	54	1123	1622	62	4/23	4/23	26.16	8.66	18.1	0	0

HARRY DEARDEN

LHB / OB / R0 / W0

FULL NAME: Harry Edward Dearden
BORN: May 7, 1997, Bury, Lancashire
SQUAD NO: 5
HEIGHT: 5ft 8in
NICKNAME: H, Haz, Deards
EDUCATION: Tottington High School, Bury;
Bury College
TEAMS: Leicestershire
ROLE: Batsman
DEBUT: First-class: 2016

BEST BATTING: 16 Leicestershire vs Glamorgan, Leicester, 2016

WHAT FIRST GOT YOU INTO CRICKET? The 2005 Ashes. I still have the box-set at home and get it out from time to time
FAMILY TIES? Dad played for the Lancashire Cricket Board and still plays now
STRANGEST THING SEEN IN A GAME? It happened during a T20 on a wet Friday night for my club team. The ball was pretty soggy before an opposition batter hit it out the ground, losing the ball. We gave a replacement to the umpire, who wiped it along the wet outfield, claiming the substitute ball had to be in the exact same state as the lost one. Madness
BEST MOMENT IN CRICKET? My first-class debut for Leicestershire in 2016
HOW WOULD YOUR TEAM-MATES DESCRIBE YOU IN THREE WORDS? Hard-working, organised, honest
BEST PLAYER IN COUNTY CRICKET? Tim Bresnan (Yor)
MOST UNDERRATED PLAYER IN COUNTY CRICKET? Joe Leach (Wor)
TIP FOR THE TOP? Rob Sayer, Zak Chappell (both Lei)
CRICKETING HEROES? Brian Lara, Alastair Cook, Shane Warne
NON-CRICKETING HEROES? Paul Scholes, Roy Keane
SURPRISING FACT? I was on a Channel 4 roadshow for the 2001 Ashes series, having a split-screen with Shane Warne
DESERT ISLAND DISC? Bastille – Bad Blood
TWITTER: @HarryDearden97

Batting	Mat	Inns	NO	Runs	HS	Ave	SR	100	50	Ct	St
First-class	2	4	0	36	16	9.00	40.90	0	0	2	0

Bowling	Mat	Balls	Runs	Wkts	BBI	BBM	Ave	Econ	SR	5w	10
First-class	2	-	-	-	-	-	-	-	-	-	-

CAMERON DELPORT

LHB / RM / R0 / W0

FULL NAME: Cameron Scott Delport
BORN: May 12, 1989, Durban, South Africa
SQUAD NO: 89
NICKNAME: Camo
EDUCATION: Kloof Senior School, Durban;
Westville Boys' High School, Durban
TEAMS: Leicestershire, Dolphins, KwaZulu-Natal, Lahore Qalandars, Sydney Thunder,
Trinidad & Tobago Red Steel
ROLE: Allrounder
DEBUT: First-class: 2009; List A: 2009;
T20: 2010

BEST BATTING: 163 KwaZulu-Natal vs Northerns, Centurion, 2011
BEST BOWLING: 2-10 KwaZulu-Natal vs Northern Cape, Chatsworth, 2016

TWITTER: @Cam12Delport
NOTES: A seam-bowling allrounder from South Africa, Delport has had stints in T20 leagues around the world and was recruited by Leicestershire for the NatWest T20 Blast midway through 2016 while playing in the Lancashire League. He made 178 runs in eight innings and took four wickets. In 2014 he shared an unbroken first-wicket stand of 367 with Morne van Wyk for South African side Dolphins – the highest first-wicket partnership in List A cricket and second-highest for any wicket

Batting	Mat	Inns	NO	Runs	HS	Ave	SR	100	50	Ct	St
First-class	60	104	6	3185	163	32.50	88.79	3	19	36	0
List A	93	84	6	2346	169*	30.07	107.51	2	12	33	0
Twenty20	113	107	7	2575	103*	25.75	136.02	1	15	42	0

Bowling	Mat	Balls	Runs	Wkts	BBI	BBM	Ave	Econ	SR	5w	10
First-class	60	1141	693	14	2/10	2/10	49.50	3.64	81.5	0	0
List A	93	1429	1405	36	4/42	4/42	39.02	5.89	39.6	0	0
Twenty20	113	703	907	38	4/17	4/17	23.86	7.74	18.5	0	0

JOE DENLY — RHB / LB / R3 / W0 / MVP67

FULL NAME: Joseph Liam Denly
BORN: March 16, 1986, Canterbury, Kent
SQUAD NO: 6
HEIGHT: 6ft
NICKNAME: JD, Denners, No Pants
EDUCATION: Chaucer Technology School, Canterbury
TEAMS: England, Kent, Barisal Burners, Brothers Union, Middlesex
ROLE: Batsman
DEBUT: ODI: 2009; T20I: 2009; First-class: 2004; List A: 2004; T20: 2004

BEST BATTING: 206* Kent vs Northamptonshire, Northampton, 2016
BEST BOWLING: 3-43 Kent vs Surrey, The Oval, 2011
COUNTY CAPS: 2008 (Kent); 2012 (Middlesex)

BEST MOMENT IN CRICKET? Winning the Twenty20 Cup with Kent in 2007. Playing for England in nine ODIs and five T20Is
IF YOU WEREN'T A CRICKETER? I'd be a footballer
TWITTER: @joed1986
NOTES: Fluent batsman who many thought would play more than just nine ODIs and five T20Is for England after bursting on the scene in 2007. Came up through the Kent ranks and re-joined the county in 2015 after an unsuccessful spell at Middlesex. Made one Championship hundred in 2016 and was outstanding in the shorter formats, hitting 428 runs at 61.14 in the RL Cup as well as three T20 Blast fifties

Batting	Mat	Inns	NO	Runs	HS	Ave	SR	100	50	Ct	St
ODIs	9	9	0	268	67	29.77	65.52	0	2	5	0
T20Is	5	5	0	20	14	4.00	68.96	0	0	1	0
First-class	159	275	19	8766	206*	34.24	55.85	18	46	67	0
List A	128	123	12	3892	115	35.06	74.86	6	20	39	0
Twenty20	142	138	10	3212	100	25.09	117.44	1	21	56	0

Bowling	Mat	Balls	Runs	Wkts	BBI	BBM	Ave	Econ	SR	5w	10
ODIs	9	-	-	-	-	-	-	-	-	-	-
T20Is	5	6	9	1	1/9	1/9	9.00	9.00	6.0	0	0
First-class	159	2878	1616	31	3/43	6/114	52.12	3.36	92.8	0	0
List A	128	434	343	18	3/19	3/19	19.05	4.74	24.1	0	0
Twenty20	142	48	76	1	1/9	1/9	76.00	9.50	48.0	0	0

CHRIS DENT   LHB / SLA / WK / R3 / W0 / MVP58

FULL NAME: Christopher David James Dent
BORN: January 20, 1991, Bristol
SQUAD NO: 15
HEIGHT: 5ft 10in
NICKNAME: Denty, Maggot
EDUCATION: Backwell School, North Somerset; Filton College, Bristol
TEAMS: Gloucestershire
ROLE: Batsman
DEBUT: First-class: 2010; List A: 2009; T20: 2010

GLOUCESTERSHIRE

BEST BATTING: 268 Gloucestershire vs Glamorgan, Bristol, 2015
BEST BOWLING: 2-21 Gloucestershire vs Sussex, Hove, 2016
COUNTY CAP: 2010

STRANGEST THING SEEN IN A GAME? Liam Norwell scoring a first-class hundred
BEST MOMENT IN CRICKET? Winning the RL Cup in 2015
SUPERSTITIONS? Listen to the same song before every innings
HOW WOULD YOUR TEAM-MATES DESCRIBE YOU IN THREE WORDS? Messy, stiff, maggot
BEST PLAYER IN COUNTY CRICKET? Ben Duckett (Nor)
MOST UNDERRATED PLAYER IN COUNTY CRICKET? Matt Taylor (Glo)
TIP FOR THE TOP? Olly Currill (Glo 2nd XI)
CRICKETING HEROES? Brian Lara – I loved watching him when I was growing up
NON-CRICKETING HEROES? My dog Simba
SURPRISING FACT? I tiled my kitchen
UNUSUAL OBJECT AT HOME? A Rhodesian Ridgeback on the sofa
DESERT ISLAND DISC? An Eminem album
TWITTER: @Cdent15

Batting	Mat	Inns	NO	Runs	HS	Ave	SR	100	50	Ct	St
First-class	100	177	16	6013	268	37.34	53.28	11	35	124	0
List A	49	44	4	1221	151*	30.52	95.61	3	2	15	0
Twenty20	49	43	7	725	63*	20.13	116.37	0	3	17	0

Bowling	Mat	Balls	Runs	Wkts	BBI	BBM	Ave	Econ	SR	5w	10
First-class	100	1082	663	7	2/21	2/21	94.71	3.67	154.5	0	0
List A	49	438	412	12	4/43	4/43	34.33	5.64	36.5	0	0
Twenty20	49	120	168	5	1/4	1/4	33.60	8.40	24.0	0	0

JADE DERNBACH

RHB / RFM / R0 / W1

FULL NAME: Jade Winston Dernbach
BORN: March 3, 1986, Johannesburg, South Africa
SQUAD NO: 16
HEIGHT: 6ft 2in
NICKNAME: Dirtbag, DJ Douche
EDUCATION: St John the Baptist School, Woking, Surrey
TEAMS: England, Surrey, Melbourne Stars, Wellington
ROLE: Bowler
DEBUT: ODI: 2011; T20I: 2011; First-class: 2003; List A: 2005; T20: 2005

BEST BATTING: 56* Surrey vs Northamptonshire, Northampton, 2011
BEST BOWLING: 6-47 Surrey vs Leicestershire, Leicester, 2010
COUNTY CAP: 2011

WHAT FIRST GOT YOU INTO CRICKET? It chose me
BEST MOMENT IN CRICKET? Winning the C&G Trophy. Promotion to Division One of the Championship. My England debut
HOW WOULD YOUR TEAM-MATES DESCRIBE YOU IN THREE WORDS? Charismatic, attractive, high-end
BEST PLAYER IN COUNTY CRICKET? Kumar Sangakkara (Sur)
TIP FOR THE TOP? Ollie Pope (Sur)
IF YOU WEREN'T A CRICKETER? I would be Harvey Specter's understudy
SURPRISING FACT? I am the 17th-best 'Pick-up Sticks' player in Surrey
UNUSUAL OBJECT AT HOME? The Great Gatsby
TWITTER: @Jwd_16

Batting	Mat	Inns	NO	Runs	HS	Ave	SR	100	50	Ct	St
ODIs	24	8	1	19	5	2.71	48.71	0	0	5	0
T20Is	34	7	2	24	12	4.80	114.28	0	0	8	0
First-class	97	121	44	725	56*	9.41		0	1	15	0
List A	132	47	19	213	31	7.60	80.37	0	0	26	0
Twenty20	118	29	12	141	24*	8.29	113.70	0	0	27	0

Bowling	Mat	Balls	Runs	Wkts	BBI	BBM	Ave	Econ	SR	5w	10
ODIs	24	1234	1308	31	4/45	4/45	42.19	6.35	39.8	0	0
T20Is	34	702	1020	39	4/22	4/22	26.15	8.71	18.0	0	0
First-class	97	15562	8734	267	6/47		32.71	3.36	58.2	10	0
List A	132	5643	5582	207	6/35	6/35	26.96	5.93	27.2	3	0
Twenty20	118	2377	3349	130	4/22	4/22	25.76	8.45	18.2	0	0

NEIL DEXTER

RHB / RM / RO / WO

FULL NAME: Neil John Dexter
BORN: August 21, 1984, Johannesburg, South Africa
SQUAD NO: 17
HEIGHT: 5ft 11in
NICKNAME: Dexy, Dex, Sexy Dexy
EDUCATION: Northwood School, Durban; University of South Africa
TEAMS: Leicestershire, Essex, Kent, Middlesex
ROLE: Allrounder
DEBUT: First-class: 2005; List A: 2005; T20: 2006

LEICESTERSHIRE

BEST BATTING: 163* Middlesex vs Northamptonshire, Northampton, 2014
BEST BOWLING: 6-63 Middlesex vs Lancashire, Lord's, 2014
COUNTY CAP: 2010 (Middlesex)

BEST MOMENT IN CRICKET? Taking six wickets against Lancashire and reaching my PB with the bat against Northants in 2014
CRICKETING HEROES? Brett Lee – fast and aggressive but played the game in the right spirit. AB de Villiers – the best player in the world in all formats and very humble
NON-CRICKETING HEROES? My family, as they are my No.1 fans
IF YOU WEREN'T A CRICKETER? I'd be a scientist
DESERT ISLAND DISC? The Lonely Island – Motherlover
FANTASY SLIP CORDON? Keeper: Borat, 1st: Barney, 2nd: Cheryl Cole, 3rd: Me, Gully: Albert Einstein
TWITTER: @dexy214

Batting	Mat	Inns	NO	Runs	HS	Ave	SR	100	50	Ct	St
First-class	133	222	25	6990	163*	35.48	51.40	16	34	86	0
List A	100	83	19	1949	135*	30.45	81.47	2	8	26	0
Twenty20	117	94	15	1550	73	19.62	109.92	0	2	44	0

Bowling	Mat	Balls	Runs	Wkts	BBI	BBM	Ave	Econ	SR	5w	10
First-class	133	8608	4435	134	6/63		33.09	3.09	64.2	4	0
List A	100	2293	2144	42	4/22	4/22	51.04	5.61	54.5	0	0
Twenty20	117	1415	1775	64	4/21	4/21	27.73	7.52	22.1	0	0

SEAN DICKSON

RHB / RM / R0 / W0

FULL NAME: Sean Robert Dickson
BORN: September 2, 1991, Johannesburg, South Africa
SQUAD NO: 58
HEIGHT: 5ft 10in
NICKNAME: Dicko
EDUCATION: King Edward VII School, Johannesburg; University of Pretoria
TEAMS: Kent, Northerns
ROLE: Batsman
DEBUT: First-class: 2013; List A: 2013; T20: 2014

BEST BATTING: 207* Kent vs Derbyshire, Derby, 2016
BEST BOWLING: 1-15 Northerns vs Griqualand West, Centurion, 2015

WHAT FIRST GOT YOU INTO CRICKET? Just the interest in playing an incredible sport. Also going to watch live games and watching on the telly
BEST MOMENT IN CRICKET? Signing for Kent and scoring my maiden first-class hundred
CRICKETING HEROES? Hashim Amla
IF YOU WEREN'T A CRICKETER? I'd be a big shot CEO
SURPRISING FACT? I am an unbelievable dancer
UNUSUAL OBJECT AT HOME? A reading book
DESERT ISLAND DISC? The Script
FANTASY SLIP CORDON? Keeper: Jack Whitehall (funny, funny guy), 1st: Iron Man (unbelievable banter), 2nd: Donald Trump (so I can laugh at his ideologies), 3rd: Me, Gully: Trevor Noah (for his accents)
TWITTER: @Seano_146

Batting	Mat	Inns	NO	Runs	HS	Ave	SR	100	50	Ct	St
First-class	27	42	6	1293	207*	35.91	48.88	2	7	12	0
List A	14	13	0	353	99	27.15	71.45	0	3	6	0
Twenty20	4	4	0	114	53	28.50	139.02	0	1	1	0

Bowling	Mat	Balls	Runs	Wkts	BBI	BBM	Ave	Econ	SR	5w	10
First-class	27	72	44	2	1/15	2/40	22.00	3.66	36.0	0	0
List A	14	-	-	-	-	-	-	-	-	-	-
Twenty20	4	6	9	1	1/9	1/9	9.00	9.00	6.0	0	0

MATT DIXON

RHB / RFM / R0 / W0

FULL NAME: Matthew William Dixon
BORN: June 12, 1992, Perth, Australia
SQUAD NO: 30
HEIGHT: 6ft 3in
NICKNAME: Dicko
EDUCATION: Servite College, Perth;
University of Hertfordshire
TEAMS: Essex, Western Australia,
Perth Scorchers
ROLE: Bowler
DEBUT: First-class: 2011; List A: 2010;
T20: 2014

ESSEX

BEST BATTING: 22 Western Australia vs Queensland, Perth, 2011
BEST BOWLING: 5-124 Essex vs Kent, Canterbury, 2016

FAMILY TIES? My dad was my first coach and a player until his mid-20s
STRANGEST THING SEEN IN A GAME? A snake at mid-wicket
BEST MOMENT IN CRICKET? My first five-fer in first-class cricket, against Kent in 2016
HOW WOULD YOUR TEAM-MATES DESCRIBE YOU IN THREE WORDS? Big bogan Australian
BEST PLAYER IN COUNTY CRICKET? Alastair Cook (Ess)
MOST UNDERRATED PLAYER IN COUNTY CRICKET? Tom Westley (Ess)
TIP FOR THE TOP? Dan Lawrence (Ess)
CRICKETING HEROES? Brett Lee
SURPRISING FACT? I have been a Type 1 diabetic for 14 years
FANTASY SLIP CORDON? Keeper: Sam Whiteman (Western Australia), 1st: Me, 2nd: Matt
Quinn (Essex), 3rd: Ricky Ponting
TWITTER: @mattyd_30

Batting	Mat	Inns	NO	Runs	HS	Ave	SR	100	50	Ct	St
First-class	10	10	3	56	22	8.00	45.90	0	0	1	0
List A	11	5	2	17	12	5.66	68.00	0	0	1	0
Twenty20	5	2	0	1	1	0.50	12.50	0	0	0	0

Bowling	Mat	Balls	Runs	Wkts	BBI	BBM	Ave	Econ	SR	5w	10
First-class	10	1330	986	22	5/124	6/189	44.81	4.44	60.4	1	0
List A	11	492	470	7	3/40	3/40	67.14	5.73	70.2	0	0
Twenty20	5	120	167	7	3/32	3/32	23.85	8.35	17.1	0	0

ANEURIN DONALD

RHB / OB / R1 / W0

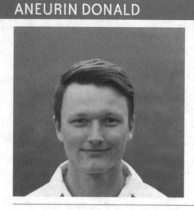

FULL NAME: Aneurin Henry Thomas Donald
BORN: December 20, 1996, Swansea, Wales
SQUAD NO: 12
HEIGHT: 6ft 3in
NICKNAME: Sir Don, The Don
EDUCATION: Pontarddulais Comprehensive School, Swansea; Gower College Swansea
TEAMS: Glamorgan
ROLE: Batsman
DEBUT: First-class: 2014; List A: 2015; T20: 2015

BEST BATTING: 234 Glamorgan vs Derbyshire, Colwyn Bay, 2016

FAMILY TIES? My late grand-uncle, Bernard Hedges, scored the first one-day century for Glamorgan. My brother Gafyn played for the Wales age-groups and plays in the Welsh Premier League for Pontarddulais CC

CRICKETING HEROES? Kevin Pietersen, Jos Buttler

SURPRISING FACT? When I used to net with my brother and father on a Saturday morning, rugby international Leigh Halfpenny would be there every week practising his goal-kicking. I never had the courage to ask him to feed the bowling machine

DESERT ISLAND DISC? Bastille – Bad Blood

FANTASY SLIP CORDON? Keeper: Matt Taylor (Northamptonshire – for general amusement and to make me feel better about myself), 1st: Me, 2nd: Leigh Halfpenny (to run after the ball after it goes through the rest of the cordon), 3rd: Piers Morgan (to add some controversy and to listen to his opinions on just about everything)

TWITTER: @AneurinDonald12

Batting	Mat	Inns	NO	Runs	HS	Ave	SR	100	50	Ct	St
First-class	23	43	2	1439	234	35.09	73.87	2	8	17	0
List A	12	9	0	158	53	17.55	79.39	0	1	6	0
Twenty20	16	13	3	241	55	24.10	126.17	0	2	7	0

Bowling	Mat	Balls	Runs	Wkts	BBI	BBM	Ave	Econ	SR	5w	10
First-class	23	-	-	-	-	-	-	-	-	-	-
List A	12	-	-	-	-	-	-	-	-	-	-
Twenty20	16	-	-	-	-	-	-	-	-	-	-

BEN DUCKETT LHB / OB / WK / R2 / W0 / MVP11

FULL NAME: Ben Matthew Duckett
BORN: October 17, 1994, Farnborough, Kent
SQUAD NO: 17
HEIGHT: 5ft 9in
NICKNAME: Ducky, Toilet
EDUCATION: Millfield School, Somerset; Winchester House School; Stowe School
TEAMS: England, Northamptonshire, Islamabad United
ROLE: Batsman
DEBUT: Test: 2016; ODI: 2016; First-class: 2013; List A: 2013; T20: 2012

BEST BATTING: 282* Northamptonshire vs Sussex, Northampton, 2016

FAMILY TIES? My dad (Graham) was on the Surrey staff and my grandad was an umpire
STRANGEST THING SEEN IN GAME? The TV game against Yorkshire when a streaker ran on the pitch. I won't say what he did but it's worth a watch
BEST MOMENT IN CRICKET? My Test and ODI debuts for England
HOW WOULD YOUR TEAM-MATES DESCRIBE YOU IN THREE WORDS? Toilet, outgoing, loose
BEST PLAYER IN COUNTY CRICKET? Toby Roland-Jones (Mid)
MOST UNDERRATED PLAYER IN COUNTY CRICKET? Rob Keogh (Nor)
TIP FOR THE TOP? Matthew Fisher (Yor), Richard Gleeson (Nor)
CRICKETING HEROES? Brian Lara and Graham Thorpe – two of the best left-handers and most enjoyable to watch
SURPRISING FACT? I have a tattoo of a duck with a cricket bat and the number 17 on the side of my bottom. And I have a big toilet
TWITTER: @benduckett1

Batting	Mat	Inns	NO	Runs	HS	Ave	SR	100	50	Ct	St
Tests	4	7	0	110	56	15.71	57.89	0	1	1	0
ODIs	3	3	0	123	63	41.00	80.92	0	2	0	0
First-class	50	83	6	3213	282*	41.72	70.29	10	15	37	3
List A	41	37	4	1634	220*	49.51	101.55	3	10	25	3
Twenty20	47	43	13	906	84	30.20	128.87	0	3	19	1

Bowling	Mat	Balls	Runs	Wkts	BBI	BBM	Ave	Econ	SR	5w	10
Tests	4	-	-	-	-	-	-	-	-	-	-
ODIs	3	-	-	-	-	-	-	-	-	-	-
First-class	50	5	8	0	-	-	-	9.60	-	0	0
List A	41	-	-	-	-	-	-	-	-	-	-
Twenty20	47	-	-	-	-	-	-	-	-	-	-

MATT DUNN

LHB / RFM / RO / WO

SURREY

FULL NAME: Matthew Peter Dunn
BORN: May 5, 1992, Egham, Surrey
SQUAD NO: 4
HEIGHT: 6ft 1in
NICKNAME: Dunny
EDUCATION: Bishopsgate School; Bearwood College, Wokingham
TEAMS: Surrey
ROLE: Bowler
DEBUT: First-class: 2010; List A: 2011; T20: 2013

BEST BATTING: 31* Surrey vs Kent, Guildford, 2014
BEST BOWLING: 5-48 Surrey vs Gloucestershire, The Oval, 2014

WHAT FIRST GOT YOU INTO CRICKET? Playing in the back garden with my brother
BEST MOMENT IN CRICKET? Taking five wickets on debut for Surrey in 2011
HOW WOULD YOUR TEAM-MATES DESCRIBE YOU IN THREE WORDS? Smiley, upbeat, Viking
BEST PLAYER IN COUNTY CRICKET? Kumar Sangakkara (Sur)
MOST UNDERRATED PLAYER IN COUNTY CRICKET? James Sykes (Lei)
TIP FOR THE TOP? Amar Virdi (Sur)
CRICKETING HEROES? Dale Steyn, Brett Lee
NON-CRICKETING HEROES? The Hairy Bikers
IF YOU WEREN'T A CRICKETER? I'd be a front-end web developer
SURPRISING FACT? I lived in Norway when I was younger, and I can breakdance
UNUSUAL OBJECT AT HOME? A lot of wood
DESERT ISLAND DISC? Mumford And Sons
FANTASY SLIP CORDON? Keeper: Thor, 1st: Me, 2nd: Justin Bieber, 3rd: David Beckham, Gully: James Corden
TWITTER: @MatthewDunn05

Batting	Mat	Inns	NO	Runs	HS	Ave	SR	100	50	Ct	St
First-class	34	35	17	133	31*	7.38	20.62	0	0	5	0
List A	1	-	-	-	-	-	-	-	-	1	0
Twenty20	16	2	0	3	2	1.50	60.00	0	0	4	0

Bowling	Mat	Balls	Runs	Wkts	BBI	BBM	Ave	Econ	SR	5w	10
First-class	34	5062	3405	96	5/48	6/84	35.46	4.03	52.7	3	0
List A	1	36	32	2	2/32	2/32	16.00	5.33	18.0	0	0
Twenty20	16	300	450	22	3/8	3/8	20.45	9.00	13.6	0	0

BRETT D'OLIVEIRA

RHB / LB / RO / WO

FULL NAME: Brett Louis D'Oliveira
BORN: February 28, 1992, Worcester
SQUAD NO: 15
HEIGHT: 5ft 9in
NICKNAME: Dolly
EDUCATION: Blessed Edward Oldcorne Catholic College, Worcester; Worcester Sixth Form College
TEAMS: Worcestershire, England Lions
ROLE: Allrounder
DEBUT: First-class: 2012; List A: 2011; T20: 2012

BEST BATTING: 202* Worcestershire vs Glamorgan, Cardiff, 2016
BEST BOWLING: 5-48 Worcestershire vs Durham, Chester-le-Street, 2015
COUNTY CAP: 2012

WHAT FIRST GOT YOU INTO CRICKET? Watching it live
FAMILY TIES? My grandad Basil played for England and Worcestershire and also went on to coach Worcestershire. My dad Damian played for Worcestershire and went on to be assistant coach and academy director
STRANGEST THING SEEN IN A GAME? Swan stops play
BEST MOMENT IN CRICKET? Playing for England Lions
HOW WOULD YOUR TEAM-MATES DESCRIBE YOU IN THREE WORDS? Short, round, idiot
BEST PLAYER IN COUNTY CRICKET? Jeetan Patel (War)
TIP FOR THE TOP? Tom Fell (Wor)
SURPRISING FACT? I have a coaching level in basketball
DESERT ISLAND DISC? Dr Dre – 2001
FANTASY SLIP CORDON? Keeper: Nelson Mandela, 1st: Michael Jordan, 2nd: Bob Marley, 3rd: Lee Evans
TWITTER: @Bdolly09

Batting	Mat	Inns	NO	Runs	HS	Ave	SR	100	50	Ct	St
First-class	27	47	2	1298	202*	28.84	53.37	3	2	13	0
List A	36	26	8	293	42	16.27	76.30	0	0	13	0
Twenty20	50	32	14	550	62*	30.55	131.26	0	1	11	0

Bowling	Mat	Balls	Runs	Wkts	BBI	BBM	Ave	Econ	SR	5w	10
First-class	27	2682	1502	33	5/48	7/133	45.51	3.36	81.2	1	0
List A	36	1232	1088	24	3/35	3/35	45.33	5.29	51.3	0	0
Twenty20	50	654	843	21	3/20	3/20	40.14	7.73	31.1	0	0

NED ECKERSLEY

RHB / OB / WK / R1 / W0

FULL NAME: Edmund James Holden Eckersley
BORN: August 9, 1989, Oxford
SQUAD NO: 33
HEIGHT: 5ft 11in
NICKNAME: Eckers
EDUCATION: St Benedict's School, Ealing
TEAMS: Leicestershire, Mountaineers
ROLE: Batsman/wicketkeeper
DEBUT: First-class: 2011; List A: 2008; T20: 2011

BEST BATTING: 147 Leicestershire vs Essex, Chelmsford, 2013
BEST BOWLING: 2-29 Leicestershire vs Lancashire, Old Trafford, 2013
COUNTY CAP: 2013

BEST MOMENT IN CRICKET? Back-to-back centuries against Worcestershire in 2013 and being given my county cap during that game
SUPERSTITIONS? I must always do a quick crouch when I enter the pitch to bat
CRICKETING HEROES? Alec Stewart – I always wanted to be a batsman/wicketkeeper and he was England's keeper when I started to watch
IF YOU WEREN'T A CRICKETER? I'd be a sports reporter
FANTASY SLIP CORDON? Keeper: José Mourinho, 1st: Tom Hardy, 2nd: Blake Lively, 3rd: Nelson Mandela
TWITTER: @nedeckersley

Batting	Mat	Inns	NO	Runs	HS	Ave	SR	100	50	Ct	St
First-class	86	153	9	4772	147	33.13	49.55	13	14	132	3
List A	30	29	3	680	108	26.15	84.15	1	3	18	1
Twenty20	49	43	9	530	43	15.58	108.60	0	0	16	3

Bowling	Mat	Balls	Runs	Wkts	BBI	BBM	Ave	Econ	SR	5w	10
First-class	86	82	65	2	2/29	2/29	32.50	4.75	41.0	0	0
List A	30	-	-	-	-	-	-	-	-	-	-
Twenty20	49	-	-	-	-	-	-	-	-	-	-

FIDEL EDWARDS RHB / RF / R0 / W0

FULL NAME: Fidel Henderson Edwards
BORN: February 6, 1982, Barbados
SQUAD NO: 82
HEIGHT: 5ft 4in
NICKNAME: Castro
TEAMS: West Indies, Hampshire, Barbados, Deccan Chargers, Dolphins, Rajasthan Royals, Rangpur Riders, St Lucia Zouks, Sydney Thunder, Sylhet Superstars, Trinidad & Tobago Red Steel
ROLE: Bowler
DEBUT: Test: 2003; ODI: 2003; T20I: 2007; First-class: 2001; List A: 2003; T20: 2007

BEST BATTING: 40 Barbados vs Jamaica, Bridgetown, 2008
BEST BOWLING: 7-87 West Indies vs New Zealand, Napier, 2008

NOTES: Drafted into Hampshire's squad late in the 2015 campaign, Edwards took a remarkable 45 wickets in eight games to help his county stave off relegation from Division One of the Championship. Made just two Championship appearances in 2016 after breaking his ankle playing football in the opening month of the season. Took five wickets on Test debut after playing just one match for Barbados and being spotted in the nets by Brian Lara. Played the last of his 55 Tests in 2012

Batting	Mat	Inns	NO	Runs	HS	Ave	SR	100	50	Ct	St
Tests	55	88	28	394	30	6.56	28.20	0	0	10	0
ODIs	50	22	14	73	13	9.12	45.62	0	0	4	0
T20Is	20	4	2	10	7*	5.00	111.11	0	0	5	0
First-class	97	142	52	639	40	7.10		0	0	19	0
List A	78	32	19	131	21*	10.07		0	0	10	0
Twenty20	89	27	12	87	11*	5.80	83.65	0	0	12	0

Bowling	Mat	Balls	Runs	Wkts	BBI	BBM	Ave	Econ	SR	5w	10
Tests	55	9602	6249	165	7/87	8/132	37.87	3.90	58.1	12	0
ODIs	50	2138	1812	60	6/22	6/22	30.20	5.08	35.6	2	0
T20Is	20	360	497	16	3/23	3/23	31.06	8.28	22.5	0	0
First-class	97	15672	10161	317	7/87		32.05	3.89	49.4	19	2
List A	78	3393	2868	92	6/22	6/22	31.17	5.07	36.8	3	0
Twenty20	89	1778	2247	84	5/22	5/22	26.75	7.58	21.1	1	0

DEAN ELGAR

LHB / SLA / RO / WO

FULL NAME: Dean Elgar
BORN: June 11, 1987, Welkom, Orange Free State, South Africa
SQUAD NO: 64
TEAMS: South Africa, Somerset, Eagles, Free State, Knights, Northerns, Surrey, Titans
ROLE: Batsman
DEBUT: Test: 2012; ODI: 2012; First-class: 2006; List A: 2006; T20: 2008

BEST BATTING: 268 South Africa A vs Australia A, Pretoria, 2013
BEST BOWLING: 4-22 South Africa vs India, Mohali, 2015

TWITTER: @deanelgar
NOTES: Left-handed batsman who has established himself as South Africa's most dependable Test opener. Having played on a short-term contract as cover for Alviro Petersen in 2013, Elgar returns to Somerset in 2017 as their principal overseas player. He will be available for all formats around his international commitments. Gritty and compact, Elgar has been signed to replace the retired Chris Rogers

Batting	Mat	Inns	NO	Runs	HS	Ave	SR	100	50	Ct	St
Tests	33	52	5	1966	140	41.82	45.18	7	6	36	0
ODIs	6	5	1	98	42	24.50	61.25	0	0	3	0
First-class	141	244	21	9832	268	44.08	49.43	29	36	112	0
List A	133	127	20	4223	117	39.46	77.18	4	30	42	0
Twenty20	53	49	14	1302	72	37.20	108.22	0	8	17	0

Bowling	Mat	Balls	Runs	Wkts	BBI	BBM	Ave	Econ	SR	5w	10
Tests	33	899	541	13	4/22	4/56	41.61	3.61	69.1	0	0
ODIs	6	96	67	2	1/11	1/11	33.50	4.18	48.0	0	0
First-class	141	3768	2508	49	4/22	5/141	51.18	3.99	76.8	0	0
List A	133	2699	2435	50	3/43	3/43	48.70	5.41	53.9	0	0
Twenty20	53	579	657	28	4/23	4/23	23.46	6.80	20.6	0	0

FULL NAME: Sean Michael Ervine
BORN: December 6, 1982, Harare, Zimbabwe
SQUAD NO: 7
HEIGHT: 6ft 2in
NICKNAME: Slug, Lion, Siuc
EDUCATION: Lomagundi College, Zimbabwe
TEAMS: Zimbabwe, Hampshire, Duronto
Rajshahi, Matabeleland Tuskers, Midlands,
Mountaineers, Southern Rocks, Western
Australia
ROLE: Allrounder
DEBUT: Test: 2003; ODI: 2001; First-class:
2001; List A: 2001; T20: 2005

HAMPSHIRE

BEST BATTING: 237* Hampshire vs Somerset, Southampton, 2010
BEST BOWLING: 6-82 Midlands vs Mashonaland, Kwekwe Sports Club, 2003
COUNTY CAP: 2005 BENEFIT: 2016

FAMILY TIES? My father Rory played first-class cricket in Zimbabwe. Brother Craig plays for
the current Zimbabwe team. Brother Ryan played for Southern Rocks in Zimbabwe. Uncle
Neil played first-class cricket in Zimbabwe
BEST MOMENT IN CRICKET? Scoring a hundred vs India at Adelaide in the 2004/05 VB
series. Hundreds and Man of the Match in both the semi-final and final of the C&G Trophy
in 2005. Scoring 208 and 160 in the same game for the Southern Rocks in 2010. Playing in the
2003 World Cup in South Africa. Playing with Shane Warne at Hampshire
CRICKETING HEROES? Andy Flower, Shane Warne, Neil McKenzie
IF YOU WEREN'T A CRICKETER? I'd be a golfer, fisherman or African wildlife conservationist
TWITTER: @slug_7

Batting	Mat	Inns	NO	Runs	HS	Ave	SR	100	50	Ct	St
Tests	5	8	0	261	86	32.62	55.41	0	3	7	0
ODIs	42	34	7	698	100	25.85	85.53	1	2	5	0
First-class	210	328	41	10603	237*	36.94		21	53	180	0
List A	236	208	29	5486	167*	30.64		7	26	68	0
Twenty20	174	159	33	3017	82	23.94	129.48	0	10	55	0

Bowling	Mat	Balls	Runs	Wkts	BBI	BBM	Ave	Econ	SR	5w	10
Tests	5	570	388	9	4/146	4/146	43.11	4.08	63.3	0	0
ODIs	42	1649	1561	41	3/29	3/29	38.07	5.67	40.2	0	0
First-class	210	19530	11495	273	6/82		42.10	3.53	71.5	5	0
List A	236	7483	6997	204	5/50	5/50	34.29	5.61	36.6	2	0
Twenty20	174	1404	2074	68	4/12	4/12	30.50	8.86	20.6	0	0

STEVIE ESKINAZI

RHB / WK / R0 / W0

FULL NAME: Stephen Sean Eskinazi
BORN: March 28, 1994, Johannesburg, South Africa
SQUAD NO: 28
HEIGHT: 6ft 2in
NICKNAME: Eski, Esk
EDUCATION: Christ Church Grammar School, Perth; University of Western Australia; University of Hertfordshire
TEAMS: Middlesex
ROLE: Batsman/wicketkeeper
DEBUT: First-class: 2015; T20: 2016

BEST BATTING: 157 Middlesex vs Yorkshire, Scarborough, 2016

WHAT FIRST GOT YOU INTO CRICKET? My parents put a bat in my crib
FAMILY TIES? My dad played a good standard of club cricket in South Africa. My brother Greg played for the first XI at school and my cousin Marc was a talented allrounder
STRANGEST THING SEEN IN A GAME? A couple ran onto the field during a first-class game and stopped in the middle of the pitch to kiss. Tim Murtagh then gave the bloke the ball and he bowled it – after drinking half a bottle of vodka. And I once saw Nathan Sowter take a catch in the slips – that was incredible
BEST MOMENT IN CRICKET? Winning the County Championship in 2016
SUPERSTITIONS? I always walk out to bat with the same routine: jog on, six back-kicks, three side-to-sides (on each side), a squat, and finally a look up at the sky
HOW WOULD YOUR TEAM-MATES DESCRIBE YOU IN THREE WORDS? Absolute wet bag
BEST PLAYER IN COUNTY CRICKET? Toby Roland-Jones (Mid)
MOST UNDERRATED PLAYER IN COUNTY CRICKET? James Hildreth (Som)
TIP FOR THE TOP? Ryan Higgins, Tom Helm, Nathan Sowter (all Mid)
CRICKETING HEROES? Kane Williamson, James Taylor, Jacques Kallis, Ricky Ponting
IF YOU WEREN'T A CRICKETER? I'd be finishing my Commerce degree and playing hockey
SURPRISING FACT? I could have four passports (if that was legal)
TWITTER: @seskinazi

Batting	Mat	Inns	NO	Runs	HS	Ave	SR	100	50	Ct	St
First-class	10	17	1	635	157	39.68	50.55	2	2	5	0
Twenty20	1	1	0	29	29	29.00	107.40	0	0	0	0

Bowling	Mat	Balls	Runs	Wkts	BBI	BBM	Ave	Econ	SR	5w	10
First-class	10	-	-	-	-	-	-	-	-	-	-
Twenty20	1	-	-	-	-	-	-	-	-	-	-

LAURIE EVANS

RHB / RM / RO / WO

FULL NAME: Laurie John Evans
BORN: October 12, 1987, Lambeth, London
SQUAD NO: 32
HEIGHT: 6ft
NICKNAME: Loz
EDUCATION: Whitgift School; The John Fisher School, Purley; Durham University
TEAMS: Sussex, Northamptonshire, Surrey, Warwickshire
ROLE: Batsman
DEBUT: First-class: 2007; List A: 2009; T20: 2009

BEST BATTING: 213* Warwickshire vs Sussex, Edgbaston, 2015
BEST BOWLING: 1-29 Warwickshire vs Sussex, Edgbaston, 2015

WHAT FIRST GOT YOU INTO CRICKET? Started at school as something to play in the summer
BEST MOMENT IN CRICKET? Winning the T20 Cup final
HOW WOULD YOUR TEAM-MATES DESCRIBE YOU IN THREE WORDS? Selfless, confident, hard-working
BEST PLAYER IN COUNTY CRICKET? Joe Root (Yor)
TIP FOR THE TOP? Sam Hain (War)
CRICKETING HEROES? Brian Lara
NON-CRICKETING HEROES? Jonny Wilkinson
IF YOU WEREN'T A CRICKETER? I'd be playing rugby
DESERT ISLAND DISC? Ed Sheeran – X
FANTASY SLIP CORDON? Keeper: James Bond, 1st: Michael Jordan, 2nd: Winston Churchill, 3rd: Margot Robbie
TWITTER: @laurieevans32

Batting	Mat	Inns	NO	Runs	HS	Ave	SR	100	50	Ct	St
First-class	54	92	6	2926	213*	34.02	45.32	5	16	44	0
List A	37	33	8	719	70*	28.76	98.49	0	2	17	0
Twenty20	64	55	12	1000	69*	23.25	126.90	0	6	29	0
Bowling	Mat	Balls	Runs	Wkts	BBI	BBM	Ave	Econ	SR	5w	10
First-class	54	354	259	2	1/29	1/29	129.50	4.38	177.0	0	0
List A	37	36	53	0	-	-	-	8.83	-	0	0
Twenty20	64	22	35	1	1/5	1/5	35.00	9.54	22.0	0	0

WILL FAZAKERLEY

RHB / RFM / R0 / W0

LEICESTERSHIRE

FULL NAME: William Fazakerley
BORN: June 19, 1998, Guernsey
SQUAD NO: 35
HEIGHT: 6ft 3in
NICKNAME: Faz
EDUCATION: Lancing College, West Sussex
TEAMS: Guernsey, Leicestershire 2nd XI
ROLE: Allrounder
DEBUT: Yet to make first-team debut

WHAT FIRST GOT YOU INTO CRICKET? The 2005 Ashes
STRANGEST THING SEEN IN A GAME? I saw a batsman kill an alpaca when clearing the ropes
BEST MOMENT IN CRICKET? Playing with Zak Chappell, my Leicestershire team-mate
HOW WOULD YOUR TEAM-MATES DESCRIBE YOU IN THREE WORDS? Tall, goofy, legend
BEST PLAYER IN COUNTY CRICKET? Kumar Sangakkara (Sur)
MOST UNDERRATED PLAYER IN COUNTY CRICKET? Dawid Malan (Mid)
TIP FOR THE TOP? Sam Curran (Sur), Delray Rawlins (Sus)
CRICKETING HEROES? Jacques Kallis, Ben Stokes
NON-CRICKETING HEROES? Steven Gerrard
IF YOU WEREN'T A CRICKETER? I'd be a footballer
SURPRISING FACT? I was born in Guernsey and have played for their national cricket team
UNUSUAL OBJECT AT HOME? All sorts of hair and beauty products
DESERT ISLAND DISC? PartyNextDoor
FANTASY SLIP CORDON? Keeper: Jack Whitehall, 1st: James Corden, 2nd: Me, 3rd: Steven
Gerrard, Gully: Fernando Torres
TWITTER: @billy_faz

TOM FELL

RHB / OB / WK / R1 / W0

FULL NAME: Thomas Charles Fell
BORN: October 17, 1993, Hillingdon, Middlesex
SQUAD NO: 29
HEIGHT: 6ft
NICKNAME: Lord, Feltch
EDUCATION: Tettenhall College, Wolverhampton; Oakham School, Rutland; Oxford Brookes University
TEAMS: Worcestershire
ROLE: Batsman
DEBUT: First-class: 2013; List A: 2013

WORCESTERSHIRE

BEST BATTING: 171 Worcestershire vs Middlesex, Worcester, 2015
COUNTY CAP: 2013

FAMILY TIES? My dad got a blue at Cambridge University and played in the same team as Mike Atherton

STRANGEST THING SEEN IN A GAME? When I was run-out batting with my flatmate Tom Kohler-Cadmore at Durham. We both thought the ball had gone for four, so stopped to have a chat in the middle. Graham Onions threw the ball in, Tom and I both ran to the keeper's end, and I was ultimately run out at the non-striker's end

BEST MOMENT IN CRICKET? The day we got promoted to Division One in 2014 when Alexei Kervezee's direct hit won us the game

HOW WOULD YOUR TEAM-MATES DESCRIBE YOU IN THREE WORDS? Relaxed, laid-back, sloppy

BEST PLAYER IN COUNTY CRICKET? Joe Leach (Wor)

TIP FOR THE TOP? Tom Kohler-Cadmore (Wor)

NON-CRICKETING HEROES? Andrea Pirlo – I like his attitude towards life

IF YOU WEREN'T A CRICKETER? I'd go skiing in the winter, play a lot of golf, and go on holiday in the summer

SURPRISING FACT? I have a golf handicap of five

DESERT ISLAND DISC? The 1975

Batting	Mat	Inns	NO	Runs	HS	Ave	SR	100	50	Ct	St
First-class	47	79	4	2697	171	35.96	51.31	5	12	42	0
List A	26	26	4	950	116*	43.18	81.47	1	9	7	0

Bowling	Mat	Balls	Runs	Wkts	BBI	BBM	Ave	Econ	SR	5w	10
First-class	47	20	17	0	-	-	-	5.10	-	0	0
List A	26	-	-	-	-	-	-	-	-	-	-

AARON FINCH

RHB / SLA / R0 / W0

SURREY

FULL NAME: Aaron James Finch
BORN: November 17, 1986, Colac, Australia
SQUAD NO: 15
HEIGHT: 5ft 8in
NICKNAME: Finchy
TEAMS: Australia, Surrey, Auckland, Delhi
Daredevils, Gujarat Lions, Melbourne
Renegades, Mumbai Indians, Pune Warriors,
Rajasthan Royals, Ruhuna Royals, Sunrisers
Hyderabad, Victoria, Yorkshire
ROLE: Batsman
DEBUT: ODI: 2013; T20I: 2011; First-class:
2007; List A: 2007; T20: 2009

BEST BATTING: 288* Cricket Australia XI vs New Zealand, Sydney, 2015
BEST BOWLING: 1-0 Victoria vs Western Australia, Perth, 2013

TWITTER: @AaronFinch5
NOTES: Short-format specialist opener for Australia who returns to Surrey in 2017. A
powerful hitter with a simple technique, Finch will be available for the whole of the NatWest
T20 Blast and once again will feature in the Championship when Kumar Sangakkara is
playing in the Caribbean Premier League. He hit three fifties in six T20 appearances for
Surrey last year, also hitting a century and two fifties in first-class cricket. A former Australia
T20 captain, Finch took the reins again in early 2017 when Steve Smith was absent

Batting	Mat	Inns	NO	Runs	HS	Ave	SR	100	50	Ct	St
ODIs	79	75	1	2580	148	34.86	88.96	7	15	36	0
T20Is	31	31	3	1082	156	38.64	149.24	1	7	8	0
First-class	63	104	5	3555	288*	35.90	60.94	6	22	60	0
List A	155	151	6	5337	154	36.80	87.95	11	33	62	0
Twenty20	173	169	15	5407	156	35.11	135.54	2	42	69	0

Bowling	Mat	Balls	Runs	Wkts	BBI	BBM	Ave	Econ	SR	5w	10
ODIs	79	115	95	2	1/2	1/2	47.50	4.95	57.5	0	0
T20Is	31	12	27	0	-	-	-	13.50	-	0	0
First-class	63	350	257	4	1/0	1/0	64.25	4.40	87.5	0	0
List A	155	310	276	7	2/44	2/44	39.42	5.34	44.2	0	0
Twenty20	173	215	335	7	1/9	1/9	47.85	9.34	30.7	0	0

HARRY FINCH

RHB / RM / RO / WO

FULL NAME: Harry Zacariah Finch
BORN: February 10, 1995, Hastings, Sussex
SQUAD NO: 6
HEIGHT: 5ft 9in
NICKNAME: Chozza, Finchy
EDUCATION: St Richard's Catholic College, Bexhill; Eastbourne College
TEAMS: Sussex
ROLE: Batsman
DEBUT: First-class: 2013; List A: 2013; T20: 2014

BEST BATTING: 135* Sussex vs Leeds/Bradford MCCU, Hove, 2016
BEST BOWLING: 1-9 Sussex vs Leeds/Bradford MCCU, Hove, 2016

STRANGEST THING SEEN IN A GAME? A streaker diving head first into the stumps
BEST MOMENT IN CRICKET? My hundred against Pakistan was special. Also a four-day win vs Warwickshire in which Chris Jordan hit a six to win by one wicket
HOW WOULD YOUR TEAM-MATES DESCRIBE YOU IN THREE WORDS? Hard-working, overrated footballer
BEST PLAYER IN COUNTY CRICKET? Tim Bresnan (Yor)
MOST UNDERRATED PLAYER IN COUNTY CRICKET? Ben Brown (Sus)
TIP FOR THE TOP? Stuart Whittingham, George Garton, Jofra Archer (all Sus) – all young seamers to watch out for
CRICKETING HEROES? Michael Yardy – because he is from Hastings like me. Ricky Ponting – I loved watching everything he did
NON-CRICKETING HEROES? Dele Alli – he has no fear!
SURPRISING FACT? I went for a drama scholarship at St Bede's when I was 12, dressed as Harry Potter… I didn't get in
DESERT ISLAND DISC? OneRepublic – Native

Batting	Mat	Inns	NO	Runs	HS	Ave	SR	100	50	Ct	St
First-class	12	17	3	473	135*	33.78	47.92	2	2	9	0
List A	11	10	2	376	92*	47.00	78.00	0	3	2	0
Twenty20	17	12	3	138	35*	15.33	102.22	0	0	3	0

Bowling	Mat	Balls	Runs	Wkts	BBI	BBM	Ave	Econ	SR	5w	10
First-class	12	150	107	2	1/9	1/9	53.50	4.28	75.0	0	0
List A	11	16	24	0	-	-	-	9.00	-	0	0
Twenty20	17	-	-	-	-	-	-	-	-	-	-

STEVEN FINN

RHB / RFM / RO / W2

MIDDLESEX

FULL NAME: Steven Thomas Finn
BORN: April 4, 1989, Watford, Hertfordshire
SQUAD NO: 9
HEIGHT: 6ft 7in
NICKNAME: Finny, Cyril, Finndog
EDUCATION: Parmiter's School, Watford
TEAMS: England, Middlesex, Otago
ROLE: Bowler
DEBUT: Test: 2010; ODI: 2011; T20I: 2011;
First-class: 2005; List A: 2007; T20: 2008

BEST BATTING: 56 England vs New Zealand, Dunedin, 2013
BEST BOWLING: 9-37 Middlesex vs Worcestershire, Worcester, 2010
COUNTY CAP: 2009

FAMILY TIES? My father, Terry, played Minor Counties and my grandad played club cricket
BEST MOMENT IN CRICKET? My Test debut, my first Test five-fer and winning the Ashes in Australia in 2010/11
CRICKETING HEROES? Glenn McGrath – the best seamer in the world as I was growing up
NON-CRICKETING HEROES? Tony Soprano
DESERT ISLAND DISC? Mumford And Sons – Babel
FANTASY SLIP CORDON? Keeper: David Nash, 1st: Me, 2nd: Cara Delevingne, 3rd: Tony Soprano, Gully: Eoin Morgan
TWITTER: @finnysteve

Batting	Mat	Inns	NO	Runs	HS	Ave	SR	100	50	Ct	St
Tests	36	47	22	279	56	11.16	30.96	0	1	8	0
ODIs	68	29	13	133	35	8.31	61.00	0	0	15	0
T20Is	21	3	3	14	8*	-	73.68	0	0	6	0
First-class	134	162	53	966	56	8.86	36.45	0	1	41	0
List A	124	47	19	266	42*	9.50	58.59	0	0	23	0
Twenty20	66	12	9	45	8*	15.00	84.90	0	0	15	0

Bowling	Mat	Balls	Runs	Wkts	BBI	BBM	Ave	Econ	SR	5w	10
Tests	36	6412	3800	125	6/79	9/187	30.40	3.55	51.2	5	0
ODIs	68	3508	2961	102	5/33	5/33	29.02	5.06	34.3	2	0
T20Is	21	480	583	27	3/16	3/16	21.59	7.28	17.7	0	0
First-class	134	24274	13941	488	9/37		28.56	3.44	49.7	12	1
List A	124	5878	4960	177	5/33	5/33	28.02	5.06	33.2	3	0
Twenty20	66	1388	1705	74	4/28	4/28	23.04	7.37	18.7	0	0

MATTHEW FISHER RHB / RFM / R0 / W0

FULL NAME: Matthew David Fisher
BORN: November 9, 1997, York
SQUAD NO: 7
HEIGHT: 6ft 2in
NICKNAME: Fish, Nemo, Pup
EDUCATION: Easingwold School, North Yorkshire
TEAMS: Yorkshire
ROLE: Bowler
DEBUT: First-class: 2015; List A: 2013; T20: 2015

YORKSHIRE

BEST BATTING: 0* Yorkshire vs Warwickshire, Headingley, 2015
BEST BOWLING: 2-61 Yorkshire vs Hampshire, Southampton, 2015

WHAT FIRST GOT YOU INTO CRICKET? Playing with my brothers at our local cricket club, and the 2005 Ashes
BEST MOMENT IN CRICKET? My first-class debut, my five-fer in the T20 Blast, and playing in the U19 World Cup
BEST PLAYER IN COUNTY CRICKET? Jonny Bairstow (Yor)
TIP FOR THE TOP? Joe Clarke, Tom Kohler-Cadmore (both Wor), Dan Lawrence (Ess), Jack Burnham (Dur), Sam Curran (Sur)
CRICKETING HEROES? Andrew Flintoff – the bigger the atmosphere, the better he was
SURPRISING FACT? I completed A-Level studies in PE and Psychology at Easingwold School (near York) in 2016
DESERT ISLAND DISC? Rihanna, Kanye West and Paul McCartney – FourFiveSeconds
TWITTER: @9M_Fisher

Batting	Mat	Inns	NO	Runs	HS	Ave	SR	100	50	Ct	St
First-class	3	2	1	0	0*	0.00	0.00	0	0	1	0
List A	13	5	3	62	34	31.00	81.57	0	0	2	0
Twenty20	13	1	1	0	0*	-	0.00	0	0	5	0

Bowling	Mat	Balls	Runs	Wkts	BBI	BBM	Ave	Econ	SR	5w	10
First-class	3	443	243	5	2/61	2/61	48.60	3.29	88.6	0	0
List A	13	479	431	11	3/32	3/32	39.18	5.39	43.5	0	0
Twenty20	13	245	362	16	5/22	5/22	22.62	8.86	15.3	1	0

LUKE FLETCHER

RHB / RFM / RO / WO

NOTTINGHAMSHIRE

FULL NAME: Luke Jack Fletcher
BORN: September 18, 1988, Nottingham
SQUAD NO: 19
HEIGHT: 6ft 7in
NICKNAME: Fletch
EDUCATION: Henry Mellish Comprehensive School, Nottingham
TEAMS: Nottinghamshire, Derbyshire, Surrey, Wellington
ROLE: Bowler
DEBUT: First-class: 2008; List A: 2008; T20: 2009

BEST BATTING: 92 Nottinghamshire vs Hampshire, Southampton, 2009
BEST BOWLING: 5-52 Nottinghamshire vs Warwickshire, Trent Bridge, 2013
COUNTY CAP: 2014 (Nottinghamshire)

STRANGEST THING SEEN IN A GAME? Snow at Durham. Very strange playing in snow
BEST MOMENT IN CRICKET? When we won the County Championship in 2010. I was 12th man but it was still a great day
SUPERSTITIONS? I always tap my bat in the crease two times when the over is called
HOW WOULD YOUR TEAM-MATES DESCRIBE YOU IN THREE WORDS? Loose, muppet, hungry
BEST PLAYER IN COUNTY CRICKET? Kumar Sangakkara (Sur)
TIP FOR THE TOP? Ben Kitt (Not)
IF YOU WEREN'T A CRICKETER? I applied for the police before I signed for Notts but I'd like to be a bowling coach one day
SURPRISING FACT? My last job was being a chef at Hooters
UNUSUAL OBJECT AT HOME? Loads of stupid love-heart things that my missus hangs on every door. Annoying!
TWITTER: @fletcherluke

Batting	Mat	Inns	NO	Runs	HS	Ave	SR	100	50	Ct	St
First-class	81	118	23	1376	92	14.48	50.29	0	3	20	0
List A	54	26	10	221	40*	13.81	96.92	0	0	9	0
Twenty20	54	16	8	36	8	4.50	80.00	0	0	9	0

Bowling	Mat	Balls	Runs	Wkts	BBI	BBM	Ave	Econ	SR	5w	10
First-class	81	14066	6908	232	5/52	9/108	29.77	2.94	60.6	3	0
List A	54	2199	2055	51	4/44	4/44	40.29	5.60	43.1	0	0
Twenty20	54	1132	1469	60	4/30	4/30	24.48	7.78	18.8	0	0

BEN FOAKES

RHB / WK / R0 / W0

FULL NAME: Benjamin Thomas Foakes
BORN: February 15, 1993, Colchester, Essex
SQUAD NO: 7
HEIGHT: 6ft 2in
NICKNAME: Foakesey
EDUCATION: Tendring Technology College, Essex
TEAMS: Surrey, England Lions, Essex
ROLE: Batsman/wicketkeeper
DEBUT: First-class: 2011; List A: 2013; T20: 2014

BEST BATTING: 141* Surrey vs Hampshire, Southampton, 2016
COUNTY CAP: 2016 (Surrey)

WHAT FIRST GOT YOU INTO CRICKET? Growing up in a small town there wasn't a lot to do so I got involved with all the local sports clubs
FAMILY TIES? My brother plays in the East Anglian Premier League for Frinton-on-Sea
BEST MOMENT IN CRICKET? Getting to a Lord's final in 2016
SUPERSTITIONS? I touch my belly button and top and bottom lip between each ball
HOW WOULD YOUR TEAM-MATES DESCRIBE YOU IN THREE WORDS? Athletic, simple, tight
BEST PLAYER IN COUNTY CRICKET? Kumar Sangakkara (Sur)
MOST UNDERRATED PLAYER IN COUNTY CRICKET? Rory Burns (Sur)
TIP FOR THE TOP? Aaron Beard (Ess)
CRICKETING HEROES? James Foster – made me want to become a keeper when I started watching Essex as a kid
IF YOU WEREN'T A CRICKETER? I'd be exploring Asia
SURPRISING FACT? I had to have a tooth glued back together after a car crash. It came unstuck while I was batting and was dangling, so I had to tear it out at lunch and proceeded to bat with no front teeth

Batting	Mat	Inns	NO	Runs	HS	Ave	SR	100	50	Ct	St
First-class	62	95	19	3051	141*	40.14	53.65	6	16	104	11
List A	36	33	4	715	90	24.65	82.27	0	5	36	4
Twenty20	36	25	6	347	49	18.26	112.29	0	0	19	3

Bowling	Mat	Balls	Runs	Wkts	BBI	BBM	Ave	Econ	SR	5w	10
First-class	62	6	6	0	-	-	-	6.00	-	0	0
List A	36	-	-	-	-	-	-	-	-	-	-
Twenty20	36	-	-	-	-	-	-	-	-	-	-

MARK FOOTITT

RHB / LFM / R0 / W2

FULL NAME: Mark Harold Alan Footitt
BORN: November 25, 1985, Nottingham
SQUAD NO: 9
HEIGHT: 6ft 2in
NICKNAME: Footy
EDUCATION: Carlton Le Willows School, Gedling; West Nottinghamshire College
TEAMS: Surrey, Derbyshire, Nottinghamshire
ROLE: Bowler
DEBUT: First-class: 2005; List A: 2002; T20: 2005

BEST BATTING: 34 Derbyshire vs Leicestershire, Leicester, 2015
BEST BOWLING: 7-62 Surrey vs Lancashire, The Oval, 2016
COUNTY CAP: 2014 (Derbyshire)

WHAT FIRST GOT YOU INTO CRICKET? Watching my dad and grandad playing cricket for the local team
BEST MOMENT IN CRICKET? Getting a seven-fer for Surrey against Lancashire in 2016
TIP FOR THE TOP? Sam Curran (Sur)
CRICKETING HEROES? Brett Lee
NON-CRICKETING HEROES? Adam Sandler and Sir Alex Ferguson
IF YOU WEREN'T A CRICKETER? I'd be a plumber
SURPRISING FACT? I started bowling right-arm then changed to left-arm
UNUSUAL OBJECT AT HOME? Harry Potter wands
DESERT ISLAND DISC? Anything from the 1980s
FANTASY SLIP CORDON? Keeper: Adam Sandler, 1st: Kevin James, 2nd: David Beckham, 3rd: 'Stone Cold' Steve Austin, Gully: Hulk Hogan
TWITTER: @Footitt_mark

Batting	Mat	Inns	NO	Runs	HS	Ave	SR	100	50	Ct	St
First-class	83	109	34	633	34	8.44	61.99	0	0	22	0
List A	36	10	4	28	11*	4.66	68.29	0	0	6	0
Twenty20	14	3	2	2	2*	2.00	66.66	0	0	1	0

Bowling	Mat	Balls	Runs	Wkts	BBI	BBM	Ave	Econ	SR	5w	10
First-class	83	13764	8080	314	7/62		25.73	3.52	43.8	19	1
List A	36	1331	1387	47	5/28	5/28	29.51	6.25	28.3	2	0
Twenty20	14	240	431	12	3/22	3/22	35.91	10.77	20.0	0	0

JAMES FOSTER

RHB / WK / R1 / W0

FULL NAME: James Savin Foster
BORN: April 15, 1980, Whipps Cross, Leytonstone, Essex
SQUAD NO: 7
HEIGHT: 6ft 1in
NICKNAME: Fozzy, Chief, Chiefton
EDUCATION: Forest School, Walthamstow, London; Durham University
TEAMS: England, Essex, Northern Districts
ROLE: Wicketkeeper
DEBUT: Test: 2001; ODI: 2001; T20I: 2009; First-class: 2000; List A: 2000; T20: 2003

BEST BATTING: 212 Essex vs Leicestershire, Chelmsford, 2004
BEST BOWLING: 1-122 Essex vs Northamptonshire, Northampton, 2008
COUNTY CAP: 2001; BENEFIT: 2011

FAMILY TIES? My dad played for Essex Amateurs
BEST MOMENT IN CRICKET? Standing up to a seamer and catching an edge off a full toss
BEST PLAYER IN COUNTY CRICKET? Ryan ten Doeschate (Ess)
MOST UNDERRATED PLAYER IN COUNTY CRICKET? Nick Browne (Ess)
TIP FOR THE TOP? Dan Lawrence (Ess)
CRICKETING HEROES? Nasser Hussain, Jack Russell
IF YOU WEREN'T A CRICKETER? I'd be an architect
TWITTER: @JamesFoster07

Batting	Mat	Inns	NO	Runs	HS	Ave	SR	100	50	Ct	St
Tests	7	12	3	226	48	25.11	34.55	0	0	17	1
ODIs	11	6	3	41	13	13.66	57.74	0	0	13	7
T20Is	5	5	2	37	14*	12.33	115.62	0	0	3	3
First-class	273	406	52	13176	212	37.22		22	68	775	59
List A	219	161	44	3322	83*	28.39		0	16	240	65
Twenty20	164	130	36	2050	65*	21.80	140.60	0	6	69	44

Bowling	Mat	Balls	Runs	Wkts	BBI	BBM	Ave	Econ	SR	5w	10
Tests	7	-	-	-	-	-	-	-	-	-	-
ODIs	11	-	-	-	-	-	-	-	-	-	-
T20Is	5	-	-	-	-	-	-	-	-	-	-
First-class	273	84	128	1	1/122	1/122	128.00	9.14	84.0	0	0
List A	219	-	-	-	-	-	-	-	-	-	-
Twenty20	164	-	-	-	-	-	-	-	-	-	-

JAMES FRANKLIN — LHB / LM / R0 / W0 / MVP48

FULL NAME: James Edward Charles Franklin
BORN: November 7, 1980, Wellington, New Zealand
SQUAD NO: 74
HEIGHT: 6ft 4in
EDUCATION: Victoria University, Wellington
TEAMS: NZ, Middlesex, Adelaide Strikers, Barbados Tridents, Essex, Glamorgan, Gloucestershire, Guyana, Mumbai Indians, Nottinghamshire, Rajshahi Kings, Wellington
ROLE: Allrounder
DEBUT: Test: 2001; ODI: 2001; T20I: 2006; First-class: 1998; List A: 1999; T20: 2004

BEST BATTING: 219 Wellington vs Auckland, Auckland, 2008
BEST BOWLING: 7-14 Gloucestershire vs Derbyshire, Bristol, 2010
COUNTY CAPS: 2006 (Glamorgan); 2014 (Nottinghamshire); 2015 (Middlesex)

FAMILY TIES? An aunt, Jean Coulston, represented New Zealand in the 1950s
BEST MOMENT IN CRICKET? Nothing beats being involved in a team that wins trophies – like Middlesex in 2016!
CRICKETING HEROES? Wasim Akram – a genius
NON-CRICKETING HEROES? Mike Horn – an explorer who has some incredible stories
IF YOU WEREN'T A CRICKETER? I'd be working for NASA on their next space programme
SURPRISING FACT? I can wiggle my ears
TWITTER: @jecfranklin

Batting	Mat	Inns	NO	Runs	HS	Ave	SR	100	50	Ct	St
Tests	31	46	7	808	122*	20.71	37.35	1	2	12	0
ODIs	110	80	27	1270	98*	23.96	76.92	0	4	26	0
T20Is	38	31	8	463	60	20.13	118.41	0	2	13	0
First-class	195	305	45	9484	219	36.47		21	43	102	0
List A	276	229	63	5412	133*	32.60		4	31	87	0
Twenty20	203	183	46	3965	90	28.94	125.59	0	15	69	0

Bowling	Mat	Balls	Runs	Wkts	BBI	BBM	Ave	Econ	SR	5w	10
Tests	31	4767	2786	82	6/119	7/117	33.97	3.50	58.1	3	0
ODIs	110	3848	3354	81	5/42	5/42	41.40	5.22	47.5	1	0
T20Is	38	327	417	20	4/15	4/15	20.85	7.65	16.3	0	0
First-class	195	24819	13148	467	7/14		28.15	3.17	53.1	14	1
List A	276	9263	7610	223	5/42	5/42	34.12	4.92	41.5	2	0
Twenty20	203	2147	2967	97	5/21	5/21	30.58	8.29	22.1	1	0

FULL NAME: James Kerr Fuller
BORN: January 24, 1990, Cape Town, South Africa
SQUAD NO: 26
HEIGHT: 6ft 2in
NICKNAME: Fuller, Foz
EDUCATION: Westlake Boys' High School, Auckland; University of Otago
TEAMS: Middlesex, Auckland, England Lions, Gloucestershire, Otago
ROLE: Bowler
DEBUT: First-class: 2010; List A: 2011; T20: 2011

MIDDLESEX

BEST BATTING: 93 Middlesex vs Somerset, Taunton, 2016
BEST BOWLING: 6-24 Otago vs Wellington, Dunedin, 2013
COUNTY CAP: 2011 (Gloucestershire)

WHAT FIRST GOT YOU INTO CRICKET? Watching the Black Caps play Australia on telly
BEST MOMENT IN CRICKET? Winning the 2015 Lord's one-day final. We were behind for the entire match and only looked like winning it in the final over. It was total euphoria to pull it off and it was special to celebrate with all our families and friends
HOW WOULD YOUR TEAM-MATES DESCRIBE YOU IN THREE WORDS? Hard-working, positive, motivated
BEST PLAYER IN COUNTY CRICKET? Chris Rushworth (Dur)
TIP FOR THE TOP? Sam Curran (Sur)
CRICKETING HEROES? Shane Bond, Brett Lee, Shaun Tait, Allan Donald – I could watch those guys bowl all day. They all have the extra pace factor that could turn a game on its head
NON-CRICKETING HEROES? Sir Edmund Hillary, for achieving the daunting task of climbing Mount Everest in 1953
IF YOU WEREN'T A CRICKETER? I'd be teaching science in a school
TWITTER: @James_Fuller246

Batting	Mat	Inns	NO	Runs	HS	Ave	SR	100	50	Ct	St
First-class	41	48	5	859	93	19.97	66.90	0	4	17	0
List A	49	38	13	566	45	22.64	99.29	0	0	15	0
Twenty20	62	31	11	323	36	16.15	142.92	0	0	25	0

Bowling	Mat	Balls	Runs	Wkts	BBI	BBM	Ave	Econ	SR	5w	10
First-class	41	6494	3817	113	6/24	10/79	33.77	3.52	57.4	5	1
List A	49	2042	1964	70	6/35	6/35	28.05	5.77	29.1	1	0
Twenty20	62	1285	1770	79	4/24	4/24	22.40	8.26	16.2	0	0

GEORGE GARTON

LHB / LMF / R0 / W0

SUSSEX

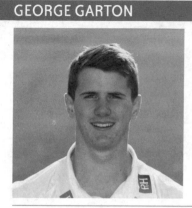

FULL NAME: George Henry Simmons Garton
BORN: April 15, 1997, Brighton
SQUAD NO: 27
EDUCATION: Hurstpierpoint College, West Sussex
TEAMS: Sussex, England Lions
ROLE: Bowler
DEBUT: First-class: 2016; List A: 2016; T20: 2016

BEST BATTING: 18* Sussex vs Glamorgan, Cardiff, 2016
BEST BOWLING: 3-93 Sussex vs Northamptonshire, Northampton, 2016

TWITTER: @george_garton
NOTES: A left-arm seamer with pace and nip who made enough of an impression in his debut season for Sussex to receive a call-up to the England Lions one-day side, culminating in a four-wicket burst against Sri Lanka A in July last year. Garton was already well-known to England's top brass, having represented England U19 with distinction. Despite his inexperience, there is much expected of him in his second full season as the national selectors' search for a left-arm seamer of true international standard continues

Batting	Mat	Inns	NO	Runs	HS	Ave	SR	100	50	Ct	St
First-class	5	5	2	36	18*	12.00	37.50	0	0	1	0
List A	8	3	1	6	4	3.00	66.66	0	0	5	0
Twenty20	2	1	1	2	2*	-	100.00	0	0	1	0

Bowling	Mat	Balls	Runs	Wkts	BBI	BBM	Ave	Econ	SR	5w	10
First-class	5	637	420	11	3/93	3/75	38.18	3.95	57.9	0	0
List A	8	378	395	15	4/43	4/43	26.33	6.26	25.2	0	0
Twenty20	2	36	45	4	4/16	4/16	11.25	7.50	9.0	0	0

RYAN GIBSON

RHB / RM / R0 / W0

FULL NAME: Ryan Gibson
BORN: January 22, 1996, Middlesbrough, Yorkshire
SQUAD NO: 24
NICKNAME: Gibbo
EDUCATION: Fyling Hall School, North Yorkshire
TEAMS: Yorkshire
ROLE: Allrounder
DEBUT: First-class: 2016; List A: 2013; T20: 2015

BEST BATTING: 0 Yorkshire vs Pakistan A, Headingley, 2016
BEST BOWLING: 1-42 Yorkshire vs Pakistan A, Headingley, 2016

NOTES: A young allrounder who made his first-team debut back in 2013 and has continued to impress as a hard-hitting batsman and medium-pacer in second XI cricket. Made his first-class bow last season against Pakistan A. Scored 162* for the Second XI to overcome Leicestershire at York, alongside former captain and new head coach Andrew Gale. Has been at the club since 2008 and made four appearances for England U19 in 2013. Was awarded the Kevin Armitage Scholarship for the best Yorkshire Academy player in 2014, for which the prize was six weeks at the Darren Lehmann Academy

Batting	Mat	Inns	NO	Runs	HS	Ave	SR	100	50	Ct	St
First-class	1	1	0	0	0	0.00	0.00	0	0	0	0
List A	5	4	1	19	9	6.33	76.00	0	0	1	0
Twenty20	3	2	0	32	18	16.00	145.45	0	0	1	0

Bowling	Mat	Balls	Runs	Wkts	BBI	BBM	Ave	Econ	SR	5w	10
First-class	1	72	42	1	1/42	1/42	42.00	3.50	72.0	0	0
List A	5	174	158	5	1/17	1/17	31.60	5.44	34.8	0	0
Twenty20	3	18	30	0	-	-	-	10.00	-	0	0

WILL GIDMAN

LHB / RMF / R1 / W2

KENT

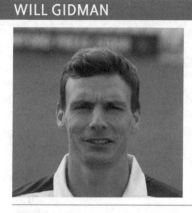

FULL NAME: William Robert Simon Gidman
BORN: February 14, 1985, High Wycombe
SQUAD NO: 42
HEIGHT: 6ft 2in
NICKNAME: Giddo, Willow
EDUCATION: Wycliffe College,
Gloucestershire; Berkshire College of
Agriculture, Maidenhead
TEAMS: Kent, Durham, Gloucestershire,
Nottinghamshire
ROLE: Allrounder
DEBUT: First-class: 2007; List A: 2003;
T20: 2011

BEST BATTING: 143 Gloucestershire vs Leicestershire, Bristol, 2013
BEST BOWLING: 6-15 Gloucestershire vs Leicestershire, Bristol, 2013
COUNTY CAP: 2011 (Nottinghamshire)

WHAT FIRST GOT YOU INTO CRICKET? School, garden games with my brother, and watching it on TV
FAMILY TIES? My brother Alex plays for Worcestershire, and my sister Charlotte is a high-class umpire
BEST MOMENT IN CRICKET? Being on the balcony when England won the Ashes in 2015 was very special
HOW WOULD YOUR TEAM-MATES DESCRIBE YOU IN THREE WORDS? Posh, poor banter
NON-CRICKETING HEROES? Jonny Wilkinson and Muhammad Ali – both changed attitudes
IF YOU WEREN'T A CRICKETER? I'd be running a law firm
SURPRISING FACT? I went to an agricultural college and studied sport
DESERT ISLAND DISC? Meatloaf – Greatest Hits
FANTASY SLIP CORDON? Keeper: James Corden, 1st: Peter Kay, 2nd: Andrew Flintoff, 3rd: Scarlett Johansson, Gully: Muhammad Ali
TWITTER: @wgiddo

Batting	Mat	Inns	NO	Runs	HS	Ave	SR	100	50	Ct	St
First-class	68	104	21	3327	143	40.08	50.88	5	20	22	0
List A	57	39	7	829	94	25.90		0	4	15	0
Twenty20	15	14	6	186	40*	23.25	108.77	0	0	3	0

Bowling	Mat	Balls	Runs	Wkts	BBI	BBM	Ave	Econ	SR	5w	10
First-class	68	9937	4774	202	6/15	10/43	23.63	2.88	49.1	9	1
List A	57	2051	1617	51	4/36	4/36	31.70	4.73	40.2	0	0
Twenty20	15	156	228	6	2/23	2/23	38.00	8.76	26.0	0	0

BRANDON GILMOUR

LHB / RM / R0 / W0

FULL NAME: Brandon Stuart Gilmour
BORN: April 11, 1996, Bulawayo, Zimbabwe
SQUAD NO: 55
HEIGHT: 5ft 11in
NICKNAME: Gilly, Happy, Branny, Leady, Zim
EDUCATION: Park House School, Newbury, Berkshire
TEAMS: Gloucestershire 2nd XI
ROLE: Batsman
DEBUT: Yet to make first-team debut

WHAT FIRST GOT YOU INTO CRICKET? My grandad used to bowl to me in his back garden
BEST PLAYER IN COUNTY CRICKET? Michael Klinger (Glo)
TIP FOR THE TOP? George Hankins (Glo), Graham Clark (Dur), Dom Bess (Som)
CRICKETING HEROES? Ricky Ponting, Brian Lara, Matthew Hayden
NON-CRICKETING HEROES? Richie McCaw
SURPRISING FACT? I look like a llama
DESERT ISLAND DISC? Justin Bieber – Purpose
FANTASY SLIP CORDON? Keeper: Keith Lemon, 1st: Me, 2nd: Ariana Grande, 3rd: James Corden, Gully: Shane Warne
TWITTER: @GilmourBrandon

RICHARD GLEESON

RHB / RFM / RO / WO

FULL NAME: Richard James Gleeson
BORN: December 2, 1987, Blackpool, Lancashire
SQUAD NO: 33
HEIGHT: 6ft 3in
NICKNAME: Gleese
EDUCATION: Carr Head Primary School, Lancashire; Baines High School, Lancashire; University of Cumbria
TEAMS: Northamptonshire, Rangpur Riders
ROLE: Bowler
DEBUT: First-class: 2015; List A: 2016; T20: 2016

BEST BATTING: 31 Northamptonshire vs Gloucestershire, Bristol, 2016
BEST BOWLING: 4-105 Northamptonshire vs Essex, Northampton, 2016

FAMILY TIES? My father ran the bar at our local cricket club, sister ran the kitchen, brother-in-law was the first XI captain
STRANGEST THING SEEN IN A GAME? Someone run straight across the middle of the pitch with the police in pursuit
BEST MOMENT IN CRICKET? Winning the 2016 T20 Blast
HOW WOULD YOUR TEAM-MATES DESCRIBE YOU IN THREE WORDS? Skinny fat man
BEST PLAYER IN COUNTY CRICKET? Ben Duckett (Nor)
MOST UNDERRATED PLAYER IN COUNTY CRICKET? Ben Sanderson (Nor)
CRICKETING HEROES? Darren Gough, Alec Stewart, James Anderson
NON-CRICKETING HEROES? Steven Gerrard
IF YOU WEREN'T A CRICKETER? I'd be coaching cricket
SURPRISING FACT? I did not play any county age-group cricket
UNUSUAL OBJECT AT HOME? A Buddha head
DESERT ISLAND DISC? Oasis – (What's The Story) Morning Glory?
TWITTER: @RicGleeson

Batting	Mat	Inns	NO	Runs	HS	Ave	SR	100	50	Ct	St
First-class	9	8	2	97	31	16.16	32.33	0	0	3	0
List A	8	4	2	7	4*	3.50	43.75	0	0	1	0
Twenty20	13	4	1	14	7*	4.66	93.33	0	0	2	0

Bowling	Mat	Balls	Runs	Wkts	BBI	BBM	Ave	Econ	SR	5w	10
First-class	9	1188	675	17	4/105	4/105	39.70	3.40	69.8	0	0
List A	8	331	292	13	5/47	5/47	22.46	5.29	25.4	1	0
Twenty20	13	262	277	17	3/12	3/12	16.29	6.34	15.4	0	0

BILLY GODLEMAN

LHB / LB / R1 / W0

FULL NAME: Billy Ashley Godleman
BORN: February 11, 1989, Camden, London
SQUAD NO: 1
HEIGHT: 6ft 2in
NICKNAME: G, Chief
EDUCATION: Islington Green School, London
TEAMS: Derbyshire, Essex, Middlesex
ROLE: Batsman
DEBUT: First-class: 2005; List A: 2007; T20: 2006

DERBYSHIRE

BEST BATTING: 204 Derbyshire vs Worcestershire, Derby, 2016

WHAT FIRST GOT YOU INTO CRICKET? My dad played local league cricket and I used to go with him every weekend
BEST MOMENT IN CRICKET? Winning the T20 final vs Kent in 2008 with Middlesex
BEST PLAYER IN COUNTY CRICKET? Kumar Sangakkara (Sur)
TIP FOR THE TOP? Tom Westley (Ess)
CRICKETING HEROES? Graeme Smith, Matthew Hayden
NON-CRICKETING HEROES? Tim Ferriss (American author of self-help books), Robin Sharma (Canadian author specialising in leadership)
SURPRISING FACT? I've studied personal training, sign language and counselling
DESERT ISLAND DISC? Pink Floyd – Wish You Were Here
FANTASY SLIP CORDON? Keeper: Sir Alex Ferguson, 1st: Me, 2nd: David Gilmour (Pink Floyd), 3rd: Tim Ferriss, Gully: Ed Smith

Batting	Mat	Inns	NO	Runs	HS	Ave	SR	100	50	Ct	St
First-class	115	204	9	6210	204	31.84	44.50	12	31	80	0
List A	44	43	6	1228	109*	33.18	71.39	1	6	18	0
Twenty20	42	38	2	622	69	17.27	107.61	0	3	20	0

Bowling	Mat	Balls	Runs	Wkts	BBI	BBM	Ave	Econ	SR	5w	10
First-class	115	30	35	0	-	-	-	7.00	-	0	0
List A	44	-	-	-	-	-	-	-	-	-	-
Twenty20	42	-	-	-	-	-	-	-	-	-	-

BEN GREEN

RHB / RFM / R0 / W0

SOMERSET

FULL NAME: Benjamin George Frederick Green
BORN: September 28, 1997, Exeter, Devon
SQUAD NO: 45
EDUCATION: Exeter School
TEAMS: Somerset
ROLE: Allrounder
DEBUT: T20: 2016

NOTES: Seam-bowling allrounder who signed a three-year contract with Somerset in August 2016. Made his first-team debut in the NatWest T20 Blast against Hampshire last season. A product of the Devon age-group system, Green joined the Somerset Academy in 2013 but continued to play club cricket for Exeter CC, where he was a strong performer in junior and men's cricket. He has represented England at U15, U17 and U19 level. Green made his Somerset Second XI debut in 2014, claiming 3-18 and was a regular in the side throughout 2015 and 2016. He is a "genuine allrounder", according to Somerset director of cricket Matthew Maynard

Batting	Mat	Inns	NO	Runs	HS	Ave	SR	100	50	Ct	St
Twenty20	1	1	1	12	12*	-	92.30	0	0	0	0

Bowling	Mat	Balls	Runs	Wkts	BBI	BBM	Ave	Econ	SR	5w	10
Twenty20	1	12	12	0	-	-	-	6.00	-	0	0

LEWIS GREGORY

RHB / RFM / R0 / W0 / MVP30

FULL NAME: Lewis Gregory
BORN: May 24, 1992, Plymouth, Devon
SQUAD NO: 24
HEIGHT: 6ft
NICKNAME: Mowgli
EDUCATION: Hele's School, Plymouth
TEAMS: Somerset
ROLE: Allrounder
DEBUT: First-class: 2011; List A: 2010; T20: 2011

SOMERSET

BEST BATTING: 73* Somerset vs Yorkshire, Headingley, 2016
BEST BOWLING: 6-47 Somerset vs Northamptonshire, Northampton, 2014

WHAT FIRST GOT YOU INTO CRICKET? I saw it on TV and gave it a go
STRANGEST THING SEEN IN A GAME? Ryan Davies going out to bat in a 50-over game in the wrong shirt
BEST MOMENT IN CRICKET? Taking my maiden first-class five-wicket haul at Lord's
BEST PLAYER IN COUNTY CRICKET? Jeetan Patel (War)
MOST UNDERRATED PLAYER IN COUNTY CRICKET? James Hildreth (Som) – he doesn't get the accolades he deserves
CRICKETING HEROES? Jacques Kallis, Michael Vaughan
NON-CRICKETING HEROES? Tiger Woods, Jonny Wilkinson
SURPRISING FACT? I'm a black belt in taekwondo
DESERT ISLAND DISC? Justin Bieber
TWITTER: @Lewisgregory23

Batting	Mat	Inns	NO	Runs	HS	Ave	SR	100	50	Ct	St
First-class	51	69	9	1164	73*	19.40	53.49	0	4	22	0
List A	45	30	2	557	105*	19.89	90.56	1	2	18	0
Twenty20	47	32	11	410	37*	19.52	119.53	0	0	17	0

Bowling	Mat	Balls	Runs	Wkts	BBI	BBM	Ave	Econ	SR	5w	10
First-class	51	7083	4175	140	6/47	11/122	29.82	3.53	50.5	7	1
List A	45	1599	1610	65	4/23	4/23	24.76	6.04	24.6	0	0
Twenty20	47	773	1064	45	4/15	4/15	23.64	8.25	17.1	0	0

LEICESTERSHIRE

FULL NAME: Gavin Timothy Griffiths
BORN: November 19, 1993, Ormskirk, Lancashire
SQUAD NO: 7
HEIGHT: 6ft 2in
NICKNAME: Gavlar
EDUCATION: St Michael's CofE High School, Chorley, Lancashire; St Mary's College, Crosby, Merseyside
TEAMS: Leicestershire, Hampshire, Lancashire
ROLE: Bowler
DEBUT: List A: 2014; T20: 2015

WHAT FIRST GOT YOU INTO CRICKET? My grandad
BEST MOMENT IN CRICKET? Winning the T20 Blast with Lancashire in 2015
HOW WOULD YOUR TEAM-MATES DESCRIBE YOU IN THREE WORDS? A space man
BEST PLAYER IN COUNTY CRICKET? Chris Woakes (War)
MOST UNDERRATED PLAYER IN COUNTY CRICKET? Gareth Berg (Ham)
TIP FOR THE TOP? Joe Weatherley (Ham)
CRICKETING HEROES? Andrew Flintoff and Allan Donald
IF YOU WEREN'T A CRICKETER? I'd be an umpire
SURPRISING FACT? I once played chess for England
DESERT ISLAND DISC? Justin Bieber – Purpose
FANTASY SLIP CORDON? Keeper: John Bishop, 1st: John Stones, 2nd: Me, 3rd: Jay from The Inbetweeners
TWITTER: @gavvlar

Batting	Mat	Inns	NO	Runs	HS	Ave	SR	100	50	Ct	St
List A	5	2	2	7	5*	-	100.00	0	0	5	0
Twenty20	7	2	2	6	4*	-	85.71	0	0	2	0

Bowling	Mat	Balls	Runs	Wkts	BBI	BBM	Ave	Econ	SR	5w	10
List A	5	226	180	4	3/41	3/41	45.00	4.77	56.5	0	0
Twenty20	7	109	145	7	3/33	3/33	20.71	7.98	15.5	0	0

TIM GROENEWALD RHB / RFM / R0 / W0 / MVP68

FULL NAME: Timothy Duncan Groenewald
BORN: January 10, 1984, Pietermaritzburg, South Africa
SQUAD NO: 5
HEIGHT: 6ft
NICKNAME: Timmy G, Groeners
EDUCATION: Maritzburg College; University of South Africa
TEAMS: Somerset, Derbyshire, Warwickshire
ROLE: Bowler
DEBUT: First-class: 2006; List A: 2006; T20: 2006

BEST BATTING: 78 Warwickshire vs Bangladesh A, Edgbaston, 2008
BEST BOWLING: 6-50 Derbyshire vs Surrey, Croydon, 2009
COUNTY CAP: 2011 (Derbyshire)

WHAT FIRST GOT YOU INTO CRICKET? My dad bought me a cricket set aged four
STRANGEST THING SEEN IN A GAME? A batsman caught in short-leg's pocket
BEST MOMENT IN CRICKET? Together with Jack Leach knocking off the required 31 runs for Somerset to beat Surrey in the Championship when we were nine down – the crowd were incredible, as were the celebrations
HOW WOULD YOUR TEAM-MATES DESCRIBE YOU IN THREE WORDS? Bad cricket watcher
BEST PLAYER IN COUNTY CRICKET? Marcus Trescothick (Som)
MOST UNDERRATED PLAYER IN COUNTY CRICKET? Sam Northeast (Ken)
TIP FOR THE TOP? Dom Bess (Som)
CRICKETING HEROES? Hansie Cronje, Jonty Rhodes, Allan Donald
NON-CRICKETING HEROES? My boys, Jamie and Hayden
IF YOU WEREN'T A CRICKETER? I'd be a coffee-shop owner
SURPRISING FACT? I grow bonsai trees
TWITTER: @timmyg12

Batting	Mat	Inns	NO	Runs	HS	Ave	SR	100	50	Ct	St
First-class	114	162	50	2038	78	18.19	51.11	0	6	39	0
List A	92	54	20	670	57	19.70	112.22	0	2	23	0
Twenty20	92	38	17	383	41	18.23	131.16	0	0	27	0

Bowling	Mat	Balls	Runs	Wkts	BBI	BBM	Ave	Econ	SR	5w	10
First-class	114	19530	10158	336	6/50	9/136	30.23	3.12	58.1	14	0
List A	92	3514	3218	102	4/22	4/22	31.54	5.49	34.4	0	0
Twenty20	92	1667	2254	76	4/21	4/21	29.65	8.11	21.9	0	0

NICK GUBBINS

LHB / LB / R1 / W0 / MVP41

MIDDLESEX

FULL NAME: Nicholas Richard Trail Gubbins
BORN: December 31, 1993, Richmond, Surrey
SQUAD NO: 18
HEIGHT: 6ft 1in
NICKNAME: Gubbs, Gubbo
EDUCATION: Radley College, Oxfordshire;
University of Leeds
TEAMS: Middlesex, England Lions
ROLE: Batsman
DEBUT: First-class: 2013; List A: 2014;
T20: 2015

BEST BATTING: 201* Middlesex vs Lancashire, Lord's, 2016
COUNTY CAP: 2016

FAMILY TIES? My dad played an ODI for Singapore CC against Malaysia
STRANGEST THING SEEN IN A GAME? Tim Murtagh hand the ball to a drunk person during a first-class game vs Oxford MCCU at The Parks. He came on and was allowed a delivery in good spirit. We got a wicket the next ball. Well done, Murts!
BEST MOMENT IN CRICKET? Winning the County Championship in front of our home crowd at Lord's in 2016. That final day…
SUPERSTITIONS? When sweeping bugs off the wicket, get them off safely, avoiding death. I was once bowled by Stuart Broad the over after I killed a bug on the wicket. Never again
BEST PLAYER IN COUNTY CRICKET? Kumar Sangakkara (Sur)
MOST UNDERRATED PLAYER IN COUNTY CRICKET? Harry Podmore (Mid)
TIP FOR THE TOP? Max Holden (Mid)
CRICKETING HEROES? Andrew Strauss – like me, he is an Old-Radleian and ex-Middlesex player. I have been fortunate enough to work with him since I was 17
SURPRISING FACT? I grew up in Singapore and was in the choir when I was 12
TWITTER: @ngubbins18

Batting	Mat	Inns	NO	Runs	HS	Ave	SR	100	50	Ct	St
First-class	35	59	2	2237	201*	39.24	47.67	4	15	12	0
List A	19	19	0	647	141	34.05	90.99	1	3	3	0
Twenty20	17	15	0	240	46	16.00	125.65	0	0	7	0

Bowling	Mat	Balls	Runs	Wkts	BBI	BBM	Ave	Econ	SR	5w	10
First-class	35	60	48	0	-	-	-	4.80	-	0	0
List A	19	-	-	-	-	-	-	-	-	-	-
Twenty20	17	-	-	-	-	-	-	-	-	-	-

BROOKE GUEST

RHB / WK / R0 / W0

FULL NAME: Brooke David Guest
BORN: May 14, 1997, Whitworth Park, Manchester
EDUCATION: Kent Street Senior High School, Perth; Murdoch University, Perth
TEAMS: Australia U19, Lancashire 2nd XI
ROLE: Wicketkeeper
DEBUT: Yet to make first-team debut

NOTES: Born in Manchester, Guest moved to Australia as a young boy and made his Australia U19 debut in 2016. He has also captained Western Australia U19. Guest has since committed his future to England after returning to the UK in 2016 to play for Lancashire, where he turned out for the Second XI, and for Sale CC in the Cheshire County Cricket League. His 803 runs at 53.53, including two hundreds, were more than anyone else in the division. The wicketkeeper will act as cover for both Jos Buttler, whose availability will be restricted by England, and for Alex Davies, who continues to suffer injury problems. "I thoroughly enjoyed my time playing for the second team last summer," said Guest. "Hopefully I can keep contributing in the Second XI and push for a place in the first team"

HARRY GURNEY — RHB / LFM / R0 / W0 / MVP28

NOTTINGHAMSHIRE

FULL NAME: Harry Frederick Gurney
BORN: October 20, 1986, Nottingham
SQUAD NO: 11
HEIGHT: 6ft 3in
NICKNAME: Gramps
EDUCATION: Garendon High School, Loughborough; Loughborough Grammar School; University of Leeds
TEAMS: England, Nottinghamshire, Leicestershire
ROLE: Bowler
DEBUT: ODI: 2014; T20I: 2014; First-class: 2007; List A: 2009; T20: 2009

BEST BATTING: 27* Nottinghamshire vs Cambridge MCCU, Cambridge, 2016
BEST BOWLING: 6-61 Nottinghamshire vs Durham, Chester-le-Street, 2016

STRANGEST THING SEEN IN A GAME? Luke Fletcher with his shirt tucked in
BEST PLAYER IN COUNTY CRICKET? Kumar Sangakkara (Sur)
MOST UNDERRATED PLAYER IN COUNTY CRICKET? Steven Mullaney (Not)
TIP FOR THE TOP? Tom Moores, Luke Wood (both Not)
IF YOU WEREN'T A CRICKETER? I'd be probably still searching for a wife
UNUSUAL OBJECT AT HOME? My name-board from the old scoreboard at Trent Bridge
DESERT ISLAND DISC? Les Misérables 25th Anniversary Edition Soundtrack
FANTASY SLIP CORDON? Keeper: Ricky Gervais (hilarious), 1st: Me, 2nd: David Cameron (I would badger him all day long), 3rd: Michelle Keegan (I would hope that she would see my ungainly action and be overwhelmed with intrigue and love), Gully: Nobody (this is the most over-rated fielding position in cricket)
TWITTER: @gurneyhf

Batting	Mat	Inns	NO	Runs	HS	Ave	SR	100	50	Ct	St
ODIs	10	6	4	15	6*	7.50	45.45	0	0	1	0
T20Is	2	-	-	-	-	-	-	-	-	0	0
First-class	80	102	48	289	27*	5.35	36.30	0	0	10	0
List A	75	21	12	44	13*	4.88	48.88	0	0	6	0
Twenty20	83	9	7	12	5*	6.00	92.30	0	0	9	0

Bowling	Mat	Balls	Runs	Wkts	BBI	BBM	Ave	Econ	SR	5w	10
ODIs	10	455	432	11	4/55	4/55	39.27	5.69	41.3	0	0
T20Is	2	48	55	3	2/26	2/26	18.33	6.87	16.0	0	0
First-class	80	13113	7303	233	6/61	9/136	31.34	3.34	56.2	6	0
List A	75	3141	2950	90	5/24	5/24	32.77	5.63	34.9	3	0
Twenty20	83	1728	2181	93	4/20	4/20	23.45	7.57	18.5	0	0

CALUM HAGGETT

LHB / RM / R0 / W0

FULL NAME: Calum John Haggett
BORN: October 30, 1990, Taunton
SQUAD NO: 25
HEIGHT: 6ft 3in
NICKNAME: Hagg
EDUCATION: Crispin School, Somerset; Millfield School
TEAMS: Kent, Somerset
ROLE: Bowler
DEBUT: First-class: 2013; List A: 2013; T20: 2011

KENT

BEST BATTING: 80 Kent vs Surrey, The Oval, 2015
BEST BOWLING: 4-15 Kent vs Derbyshire, Derby, 2016

WHAT FIRST GOT YOU INTO CRICKET? I lived next to a cricket club
FAMILY TIES? My father played village cricket and my brother played for Somerset seconds
BEST MOMENT IN CRICKET? Making my first-class debut
HOW WOULD YOUR TEAM-MATES DESCRIBE YOU IN THREE WORDS? Tidy, stubborn, unique
MOST UNDERRATED PLAYER IN COUNTY CRICKET? Sam Northeast (Ken)
CRICKETING HEROES? Chris March and Phil Hunt from Ashcott and Shapwick CC. They showed me what to do after the game
NON-CRICKETING HEROES? Mother Teresa, Nelson Mandela, Gandhi
IF YOU WEREN'T A CRICKETER? I'd be a twitcher
SURPRISING FACT? I have a webbed toe
DESERT ISLAND DISC? Queen – Greatest Hits

Batting	Mat	Inns	NO	Runs	HS	Ave	SR	100	50	Ct	St
First-class	33	42	10	800	80	25.00	40.67	0	2	8	0
List A	16	10	0	132	45	13.20	79.51	0	0	5	0
Twenty20	12	7	3	27	11	6.75	100.00	0	0	3	0

Bowling	Mat	Balls	Runs	Wkts	BBI	BBM	Ave	Econ	SR	5w	10
First-class	33	4912	2581	74	4/15	7/97	34.87	3.15	66.3	0	0
List A	16	672	621	19	4/59	4/59	32.68	5.54	35.3	0	0
Twenty20	12	174	291	7	2/12	2/12	41.57	10.03	24.8	0	0

SAM HAIN

RHB / RM / R0 / W0 / MVP63

FULL NAME: Samuel Robert Hain
BORN: July 16, 1995, Hong Kong
SQUAD NO: 16
HEIGHT: 6ft
NICKNAME: Ched, Hainy
EDUCATION: The Southport School,
Queensland, Australia
TEAMS: Warwickshire
ROLE: Batsman
DEBUT: First-class: 2014; List A: 2013;
T20: 2016

BEST BATTING: 208 Warwickshire vs Northamptonshire, Edgbaston, 2014

WHAT FIRST GOT YOU INTO CRICKET? The battles with the brothers in the backyard. Always ended in tears
STRANGEST THING SEEN IN A GAME? When I came on to bowl at Lord's, with my first-ever ball being a head-high full toss. Actually I'd rather not talk about it
BEST MOMENT IN CRICKET? Winning the Royal London One-Day Cup at Lord's in 2016
HOW WOULD YOUR TEAM-MATES DESCRIBE YOU IN THREE WORDS? Ched, drifter, punctual
TIP FOR THE TOP? Mark Adair (War)
NON-CRICKETING HEROES? Bryson DeChambeau – I've tried to copy his golf swing
DESERT ISLAND DISC? Zac Brown Band – The Foundation
FANTASY SLIP CORDON? Keeper: Tiger Woods, 1st: Me, 2nd: Rory McIlroy, 3rd: John Daly, Gully: Jim Jefferies
TWITTER: @Sammiehain

Batting	Mat	Inns	NO	Runs	HS	Ave	SR	100	50	Ct	St
First-class	38	58	5	1827	208	34.47	49.16	7	5	33	0
List A	11	11	1	541	107	54.10	84.00	2	3	4	0
Twenty20	13	12	1	371	92*	33.72	120.84	0	2	9	0

Bowling	Mat	Balls	Runs	Wkts	BBI	BBM	Ave	Econ	SR	5w	10
First-class	38	36	24	0	-	-	-	4.00	-	0	0
List A	11	-	-	-	-	-	-	-	-	-	-
Twenty20	13	-	-	-	-	-	-	-	-	-	-

ALEX HALES

RHB / OB / R3 / W0

FULL NAME: Alexander Daniel Hales
BORN: January 3, 1989, Hillingdon, Middlesex
SQUAD NO: 10
HEIGHT: 6ft 5in
EDUCATION: Chesham High School, Buckinghamshire
TEAMS: England, Nottinghamshire, Adelaide Strikers, Hobart Hurricanes, Melbourne Renegades, Worcestershire
ROLE: Batsman
DEBUT: Test: 2015; ODI: 2014; T20I: 2011; First-class: 2008; List A: 2008; T20: 2009

BEST BATTING: 236 Nottinghamshire vs Yorkshire, Trent Bridge, 2015
BEST BOWLING: 2-63 Nottinghamshire vs Yorkshire, Trent Bridge, 2009
COUNTY CAP: 2011 (Nottinghamshire)

WHAT FIRST GOT YOU INTO CRICKET? Living in the bungalow at Denham CC
HOW WOULD YOUR TEAM-MATES DESCRIBE YOU IN THREE WORDS? Annoying, entertaining, grubby
BEST PLAYER IN COUNTY CRICKET? Kumar Sangakkara (Sur)
TIP FOR THE TOP? Joe Clarke (Wor)
CRICKETING HEROES? Marcus Trescothick, Jacques Kallis, Dominic Cork
DESERT ISLAND DISC? Tupac – Greatest Hits
TWITTER: @AlexHales1

Batting	Mat	Inns	NO	Runs	HS	Ave	SR	100	50	Ct	St
Tests	11	21	0	573	94	27.28	43.84	0	5	8	0
ODIs	41	39	1	1455	171	38.28	94.72	5	6	12	0
T20Is	45	45	5	1257	116*	31.42	133.86	1	7	24	0
First-class	99	171	6	6192	236	37.52	57.93	12	37	83	0
List A	133	129	3	4734	171	37.57	99.47	14	22	45	0
Twenty20	147	146	8	3911	116*	28.34	137.95	1	27	59	0

Bowling	Mat	Balls	Runs	Wkts	BBI	BBM	Ave	Econ	SR	5w	10
Tests	11	18	2	0	-	-	-	0.66	-	0	0
ODIs	41	-	-	-	-	-	-	-	-	-	-
T20Is	45	-	-	-	-	-	-	-	-	-	-
First-class	99	311	173	3	2/63	2/63	57.66	3.33	103.6	0	0
List A	133	4	10	0	-	-	-	15.00	-	0	0
Twenty20	147	3	7	0	-	-	-	14.00	-	0	0

HASEEB HAMEED

RHB / LB / R1 / W0

FULL NAME: Haseeb Hameed
BORN: January 17, 1997, Bolton, Lancashire
SQUAD NO: 23
HEIGHT: 6ft 2in
NICKNAME: Has
EDUCATION: Bolton School
TEAMS: England, Lancashire
ROLE: Batsman
DEBUT: Test: 2016; First-class: 2015

BEST BATTING: 122 Lancashire vs Nottinghamshire, Trent Bridge, 2015
COUNTY CAP: 2016

TWITTER: @HaseebHameed97
NOTES: Tipped as one of the hottest batting prospects in England, Hameed exceeded his reputation in 2016 by making more than 1,000 Championship runs in his first full season at Old Trafford – at 19 years of age becoming the youngest batsman to achieve the feat for Lancashire – and looking immediately at ease when scoring a fifty on his Test debut against India at Rajkot later that year. In August 2014 he hit 389 runs in five matches for England U19 against South Africa U19, an international record for a batsman in a youth bilateral one-day series, with consecutive scores of 97, 97 and 125. Impressed in four Championship matches for Lancashire in 2015, twice passing 50

Batting	Mat	Inns	NO	Runs	HS	Ave	SR	100	50	Ct	St
Tests	3	6	1	219	82	43.80	34.21	0	2	4	0
First-class	25	43	4	1707	122	43.76	38.06	4	11	13	0

Bowling	Mat	Balls	Runs	Wkts	BBI	BBM	Ave	Econ	SR	5w	10
Tests	3	-	-	-	-	-	-	-	-	-	-
First-class	25	18	12	0	-	-	-	4.00	-	0	0

MILES HAMMOND

LHB / OB / R0 / W0

FULL NAME: Miles Arthur Halhead Hammond
BORN: January 11, 1996, Cheltenham, Gloucestershire
SQUAD NO: 88
HEIGHT: 6ft
NICKNAME: Hammo, Wally, Cryles
EDUCATION: St Edward's School, Oxford; University of the Arts London
TEAMS: Gloucestershire
ROLE: Bowler
DEBUT: First-class: 2013; List A: 2013; T20: 2013

BEST BATTING: 30 Gloucestershire vs Glamorgan, Swansea, 2015
BEST BOWLING: 1-96 Gloucestershire vs Glamorgan, Bristol, 2013

WHAT FIRST GOT YOU INTO CRICKET? Dad throwing balls at me when I was two
STRANGEST THING SEEN IN A GAME? An umpire being hit on the backside by a wild throw from a fielder
BEST MOMENT IN CRICKET? Beating Yorkshire at Headingley on my Gloucestershire debut
SUPERSTITIONS? Left sock has to be inside out and I wear my house key around my neck
HOW WOULD YOUR TEAM-MATES DESCRIBE YOU IN THREE WORDS? A space cadet
CRICKETING HEROES? Walter Hammond, Marcus Trescothick, Moeen Ali
NON-CRICKETING HEROES? Jonny Wilkinson, Dan Bilzerian
IF YOU WEREN'T A CRICKETER? I'd be an architect
UNUSUAL OBJECT AT HOME? Solar-illuminating glass cube
DESERT ISLAND DISC? Red Hot Chili Peppers – Greatest Hits
FANTASY SLIP CORDON? Keeper: Norman Foster, 1st: Lee Evans, 2nd: Walter Hammond, 3rd: Dalai Lama, Gully: Jack Whitehall
TWITTER: @hammo125

Batting	Mat	Inns	NO	Runs	HS	Ave	SR	100	50	Ct	St
First-class	3	3	0	34	30	11.33	38.63	0	0	1	0
List A	3	1	0	0	0	0.00	0.00	0	0	0	0
Twenty20	2	-	-	-	-	-	-	-	-	0	0

Bowling	Mat	Balls	Runs	Wkts	BBI	BBM	Ave	Econ	SR	5w	10
First-class	3	294	196	1	1/96	1/155	196.00	4.00	294.0	0	0
List A	3	114	97	5	2/18	2/18	19.40	5.10	22.8	0	0
Twenty20	2	12	17	0	-	-	-	8.50	-	0	0

PETER HANDSCOMB

RHB / WK / R0 / W0

FULL NAME: Peter Stephen Patrick Handscomb
BORN: April 26, 1991, Melbourne, Australia
HEIGHT: 6ft
NICKNAME: Hank
EDUCATION: Mount Waverley Secondary College; Deakin University, Melbourne
TEAMS: Australia, Yorkshire, Gloucestershire, Melbourne Stars, Rising Pune Supergiants, Victoria
ROLE: Batsman/wicketkeeper
DEBUT: Test: 2016; ODI: 2017; First-class: 2011; List A: 2011; T20: 2012

BEST BATTING: 215 Victoria vs New South Wales, Sydney, 2016

TWITTER: @phandscomb54
NOTES: Polished top-order batsman who made a stunning start to his Test career after scoring a fifty on debut against South Africa at Adelaide in November 2016. He made scores of 105, 54 and 110 in his next three Test innings. Born to British parents and raised in Australia, Handscomb spent the 2015 season at Gloucestershire, scoring 401 runs at 44.55 in the Championship. He has signed for Yorkshire as an overseas player and will be available for all three formats in 2017, subject to his international commitments

Batting	Mat	Inns	NO	Runs	HS	Ave	SR	100	50	Ct	St
Tests	6	11	3	480	110	60.00	56.87	2	2	8	0
ODIs	5	4	0	90	82	22.50	94.73	0	1	5	0
First-class	69	115	8	4463	215	41.71	54.41	11	26	104	4
List A	56	50	10	1220	82	30.50	75.49	0	6	49	2
Twenty20	37	31	12	465	103*	24.47	110.97	1	1	19	4

Bowling	Mat	Balls	Runs	Wkts	BBI	BBM	Ave	Econ	SR	5w	10
Tests	6	-	-	-	-	-	-	-	-	-	-
ODIs	5	-	-	-	-	-	-	-	-	-	-
First-class	69	12	21	0	-	-	-	10.50	-	0	0
List A	56	-	-	-	-	-	-	-	-	-	-
Twenty20	37	-	-	-	-	-	-	-	-	-	-

GEORGE HANKINS

RHB / **OB** / **R0** / **W0**

FULL NAME: George Thomas Hankins
BORN: January 4, 1997, Bath
SQUAD NO: 21
HEIGHT: 6ft 1in
NICKNAME: Hanks, Hanko
EDUCATION: Kingswood School, Bath; Millfield School, Somerset
TEAMS: Gloucestershire
ROLE: Batsman
DEBUT: First-class: 2016

BEST BATTING: 116 Gloucestershire vs Northamptonshire, Northampton, 2016

WHAT FIRST GOT YOU INTO CRICKET? My dad used to take me to watch my uncle play every Saturday
BEST MOMENT IN CRICKET? Scoring my maiden first-class hundred in 2016. It was also great when I beat the Millfield School record for the most runs in a season in the last game I played for the school
BEST PLAYER IN COUNTY CRICKET? Michael Klinger (Glo)
TIP FOR THE TOP? Mason Crane (Ham), Aneurin Donald (Gla)
HOW WOULD YOUR TEAM-MATES DESCRIBE YOU IN THREE WORDS? Determined, focused, funny
CRICKETING HEROES? Ricky Ponting
NON-CRICKETING HEROES? Taylor Swift, Ariana Grande
IF YOU WEREN'T A CRICKETER? I'd be a lawyer
SURPRISING FACT? I lack earlobes
DESERT ISLAND DISC? Justin Timberlake – Justified
FANTASY SLIP CORDON? Keeper: Justin Bieber, 1st: Ariana Grande, 2nd: Leonardo DiCaprio, 3rd: David Beckham, Gully: James Corden
TWITTER: @hankins1997

Batting	Mat	Inns	NO	Runs	HS	Ave	SR	100	50	Ct	St
First-class	10	17	0	416	116	24.47	50.36	1	1	6	0
Bowling	Mat	Balls	Runs	Wkts	BBI	BBM	Ave	Econ	SR	5w	10
First-class	10	-	-	-	-	-	-	-	-	-	-

OLIVER HANNON-DALBY

LHB / RMF / RO / WO

FULL NAME: Oliver James Hannon-Dalby
BORN: June 20, 1989, Halifax, Yorkshire
SQUAD NO: 20
HEIGHT: 6ft 8in
NICKNAME: Owl Face, Owl Head, André Schürrle, OHD
EDUCATION: Brooksbank School; Leeds Metropolitan University
TEAMS: Warwickshire, Yorkshire
ROLE: Bowler
DEBUT: First-class: 2008; List A: 2011; T20: 2012

BEST BATTING: 40 Warwickshire vs Somerset, Taunton, 2014
BEST BOWLING: 5-68 Yorkshire vs Somerset, Headingley, 2010

FAMILY TIES? My whole family either play or support local cricket in the Halifax League
STRANGEST THING SEEN IN A GAME? Sam Hain bowling at Lord's
BEST MOMENT IN CRICKET? Winning the T20 Blast in 2014 and the RL Cup in 2016
HOW WOULD YOUR TEAM-MATES DESCRIBE YOU IN THREE WORDS? Big owl face
BEST PLAYER IN COUNTY CRICKET? Jeetan Patel (War)
MOST UNDERRATED PLAYER IN COUNTY CRICKET? Tim Ambrose (War)
TIP FOR THE TOP? Sam Hain, Aaron Thomason, Josh Poysden (all War)
CRICKETING HEROES? Glenn McGrath, Andrew Flintoff, Brett Lee – for any cricketer my age the 2005 Ashes was amazing to watch
NON-CRICKETING HEROES? My labrador Toby
IF YOU WEREN'T A CRICKETER? I'd be impersonating André Schürrle and owls professionally
SURPRISING FACT? Current reigning Warwickshire CCC karaoke champion
UNUSUAL OBJECT AT HOME? A furminator
TWITTER: @ohd20

Batting	Mat	Inns	NO	Runs	HS	Ave	SR	100	50	Ct	St
First-class	48	53	20	218	40	6.60	23.29	0	0	5	0
List A	30	8	5	50	21*	16.66	100.00	0	0	5	0
Twenty20	37	8	4	27	9	6.75	71.05	0	0	6	0

Bowling	Mat	Balls	Runs	Wkts	BBI	BBM	Ave	Econ	SR	5w	10
First-class	48	6654	3781	94	5/68	7/122	40.22	3.40	70.7	2	0
List A	30	1341	1309	44	5/27	5/27	29.75	5.85	30.4	1	0
Twenty20	37	772	1109	43	4/29	4/29	25.79	8.61	17.9	0	0

ARUN HARINATH

LHB / RM / R0 / W0

FULL NAME: Arun Harinath
BORN: April 3, 1987, Sutton, Surrey
SQUAD NO: 10
HEIGHT: 5ft 11in
NICKNAME: Baron
EDUCATION: Tiffin School, Kingston-upon-Thames; Loughborough University
TEAMS: Surrey
ROLE: Batsman
DEBUT: First-class: 2007; List A: 2009

BEST BATTING: 154 Surrey vs Derbyshire, Derby, 2013
BEST BOWLING: 2-1 Surrey vs Middlesex, Lord's, 2013

FAMILY TIES? My dad played club cricket in Sri Lanka and my brother Muhunthan has also played for Surrey
STRANGEST THING SEEN IN A GAME? Solar eclipse stops play
BEST MOMENT IN CRICKET? My maiden first-class hundred for Surrey at The Oval
HOW WOULD YOUR TEAM-MATES DESCRIBE YOU IN THREE WORDS? Hard-working and committed
BEST PLAYER IN COUNTY CRICKET? Ben Stokes (Dur)
MOST UNDERRATED PLAYER IN COUNTY CRICKET? Rory Burns (Sur)
TIP FOR THE TOP? Ben Foakes (Sur)
CRICKETING HEROES? Ricky Ponting – having met and played with him, he is not only one of the greatest cricketers of this generation, but a great person to have in the dressing room too
NON-CRICKETING HEROES? Jonny Wilkinson – a great professional and role model for all aspiring sportsmen
SURPRISING FACT? As of this summer I will have two degrees
UNUSUAL OBJECT AT HOME? An enormous ornamental owl sitting on our balcony to scare the pigeons away
TWITTER: @arunharinath

Batting	Mat	Inns	NO	Runs	HS	Ave	SR	100	50	Ct	St
First-class	70	122	6	3729	154	32.14	44.42	6	21	19	0
List A	7	7	2	108	52	21.60	78.83	0	1	1	0

Bowling	Mat	Balls	Runs	Wkts	BBI	BBM	Ave	Econ	SR	5w	10
First-class	70	345	190	5	2/1	2/1	38.00	3.30	69.0	0	0
List A	7	18	16	0	-	-	-	5.33	-	0	0

SIMON HARMER   RHB / OB / R0 / W0

FULL NAME: Simon Ross Harmer
BORN: February 10, 1989, Pretoria,
South Africa
SQUAD NO: 11
EDUCATION: Nelson Mandela Metropolitan
University, Port Elizabeth
TEAMS: South Africa, Essex, Border, Eastern
Province, Warriors
ROLE: Allrounder
DEBUT: Test: 2015; First-class: 2009; List A:
2010; T20: 2011

BEST BATTING: 100* Eastern Province vs Border, East London, 2011
BEST BOWLING: 8-60 Warriors vs Cape Cobras, Port Elizabeth, 2016

TWITTER: @SimonHarmerRSA
NOTES: Essex have signed Harmer on a one-year Kolpak deal. "Playing county cricket has
always been a boyhood dream of mine and to have the opportunity to fulfil that dream at
Essex is very surreal," he said. The off-spinner played five Tests for South Africa but has
decided his future is best served in county cricket after falling down the national pecking
order. He took seven wickets on Test debut against West Indies at Newlands in 2015 and
claimed 10 in two matches on South Africa's tour of India later that year. He took 34 wickets
at 36.41 for Warriors in the 2016/17 domestic season in South Africa. His best campaign
came in 2011/12 when he claimed 53 first-class wickets at 30.20

Batting	Mat	Inns	NO	Runs	HS	Ave	SR	100	50	Ct	St
Tests	5	6	1	58	13	11.60	33.33	0	0	1	0
First-class	86	134	29	2846	100*	27.10	48.57	1	17	84	0
List A	54	48	12	678	43*	18.83	100.29	0	0	35	0
Twenty20	41	27	11	426	43	26.62	130.27	0	0	14	0
Bowling	Mat	Balls	Runs	Wkts	BBI	BBM	Ave	Econ	SR	5w	10
Tests	5	1148	588	20	4/61	7/153	29.40	3.07	57.4	0	0
First-class	86	20374	10466	317	8/60	11/149	33.01	3.08	64.2	12	1
List A	54	2506	2065	52	4/42	4/42	39.71	4.94	48.1	0	0
Twenty20	41	824	938	26	3/28	3/28	36.07	6.83	31.6	0	0

JAMES HARRIS — RHB / RFM / RO / W2

FULL NAME: James Alexander Russell Harris
BORN: May 16, 1990, Morriston, Swansea
SQUAD NO: 5
HEIGHT: 6ft 1in
NICKNAME: Bones, Jimmy, Harry, Lance
EDUCATION: Pontarddulais Comprehensive School, Swansea; Gorseinon College, Swansea
TEAMS: Middlesex, England Lions, Glamorgan
ROLE: Bowler
DEBUT: First-class: 2007; List A: 2007; T20: 2008

MIDDLESEX

BEST BATTING: 87* Glamorgan vs Nottinghamshire, Swansea, 2007
BEST BOWLING: 9-34 Middlesex vs Durham, Lord's, 2015
COUNTY CAPS: 2010 (Glamorgan); 2015 (Middlesex)

FAMILY TIES? My father played for British Universities
STRANGEST THING SEEN IN A GAME? A drunk couple running onto the field in a game at the Parks vs Oxford MCCU. They had a long snog, he bowled a ball, and then they strolled off
BEST MOMENT IN CRICKET? Taking a nine-fer at Lord's in 2015
HOW WOULD YOUR TEAM-MATES DESCRIBE YOU IN THREE WORDS? Organised, reliable, mad
BEST PLAYER IN COUNTY CRICKET? Toby Roland-Jones (Mid)
TIP FOR THE TOP? Tom Helm, Harry Podmore (both Mid)
NON-CRICKETING HEROES? Eddy Merckx – I'm really into my road cycling and he's easily the greatest ever to throw his leg over a bike
SURPRISING FACT? I'm often clad in Lycra riding around the roads on one of my bikes
UNUSUAL OBJECT AT HOME? Road bike battery charger
TWITTER: @James_Harris9

Batting	Mat	Inns	NO	Runs	HS	Ave	SR	100	50	Ct	St
First-class	110	152	33	2551	87*	21.43		0	12	31	0
List A	56	34	8	295	32	11.34	65.84	0	0	12	0
Twenty20	48	23	10	138	18	10.61	111.29	0	0	5	0

Bowling	Mat	Balls	Runs	Wkts	BBI	BBM	Ave	Econ	SR	5w	10
First-class	110	19373	10755	362	9/34	13/103	29.70	3.33	53.5	12	2
List A	56	2299	2173	75	4/38	4/38	28.97	5.67	30.6	0	0
Twenty20	48	872	1301	41	4/23	4/23	31.73	8.95	21.2	0	0

ASHER HART

FULL NAME: Asher Hale-bopp Joseph Arthur Hart
BORN: March 30, 1997, Carlisle, Cumbria
SQUAD NO: 28
TEAMS: Hampshire
ROLE: Allrounder
DEBUT: Yet to make first-team debut

TWITTER: @asher_hart
NOTES: A seam-bowling allrounder, Hart joined Hampshire in September 2016 after coming up through the ranks at Durham. "He will add both depth and competition to the squad," said Hampshire director of cricket Giles White. Hart enjoyed an impressive 2016 season in Durham's Academy, taking 26 wickets at 16.04 and scoring 441 runs at 36.75, and played a key part in their path to the North East Premier League T20 title, with an economy-rate of just 4.10. He was also a member of the side that won the Second XI Championship in 2016. Though yet to play a first-team game, he did make his way into the squad for one Championship fixture last year as cover for Barry McCarthy, whose return from international duty prevented Hart from making his debut

CHARLIE HARTLEY RHB / RMF / R0 / W0

FULL NAME: Charles Frederick Hartley
BORN: January 4, 1994, Bromsgrove, Worcestershire
SQUAD NO: 22
HEIGHT: 6ft 1in
NICKNAME: Chaz, Chappers, Chaps
EDUCATION: Millfield School, Somerset
TEAMS: Kent
ROLE: Bowler
DEBUT: First-class: 2014; List A: 2014

KENT

BEST BATTING: 2 Kent vs Leicestershire, Leicester, 2014
BEST BOWLING: 2-40 Kent vs Leicestershire, Leicester, 2014

STRANGEST THING SEEN IN A GAME? A dog pick the ball up (in his mouth) and then run off
BEST MOMENT IN CRICKET? Making my Kent debut, closely followed by winning the National Club T20 with Millfield
HOW WOULD YOUR TEAM-MATES DESCRIBE YOU IN THREE WORDS? A Duracell bunny
BEST PLAYER IN COUNTY CRICKET? Daniel Bell-Drummond (Ken)
CRICKETING HEROES? Andrew Flintoff
NON-CRICKETING HEROES? Jonny Wilkinson and Maximus Decimus Meridius from Gladiator. And my grandparents
IF YOU WEREN'T A CRICKETER? I'd be involved in events hospitality, and working hard to get into the property business
SURPRISING FACT? I can put my ankles behind my neck
UNUSUAL OBJECT AT HOME? An ex-policeman's wooden truncheon
DESERT ISLAND DISC? Beach Boys – Pet Sounds
FANTASY SLIP CORDON? Keeper: James Corden, 1st: Andrew Flintoff, 2nd: Mila Kunis, 3rd: Shane Warne, Gully: Michelle Keegan. I'd be listening over the stump mic
TWITTER: @hartcf

Batting	Mat	Inns	NO	Runs	HS	Ave	SR	100	50	Ct	St
First-class	2	3	0	2	2	0.66	4.76	0	0	0	0
List A	4	3	0	24	15	8.00	61.53	0	0	0	0

Bowling	Mat	Balls	Runs	Wkts	BBI	BBM	Ave	Econ	SR	5w	10
First-class	2	288	190	5	2/40	3/91	38.00	3.95	57.6	0	0
List A	4	204	169	6	2/23	2/23	28.16	4.97	34.0	0	0

JOHN HASTINGS
RHB / RFM / R0 / W0

FULL NAME: John Wayne Hastings
BORN: November 4, 1985, Penrith, New South Wales, Australia
SQUAD NO: 2
HEIGHT: 6ft 4in
EDUCATION: Australian College of Physical Education, Sydney
TEAMS: Australia, Worcestershire, Chennai Super Kings, Durham, Kandurata Warriors, Kolkata KR, Melbourne Stars, Victoria
ROLE: Allrounder
DEBUT: Test: 2012; ODI: 2010; T20I: 2010; First-class: 2007; List A: 2007; T20: 2007

BEST BATTING: 93 Victoria vs Tasmania, Hobart, 2010
BEST BOWLING: 7-60 Durham vs Worcestershire, Worcester, 2015

TWITTER: @johnhastings194
NOTES: Powerful and reliable fast-bowling allrounder who is vastly experienced in international and domestic circuit. Previously at Durham before signing for Worcestershire to play for the whole of the 2017 season. Has represented Australia in all three forms of the game, most recently on their white-ball tour of South Africa in October 2016. In recent years he has battled with injury, and underwent surgery on his knee in December. Worcestershire were hopeful that he would be ready for a return to action by the start of the season

Batting	Mat	Inns	NO	Runs	HS	Ave	SR	100	50	Ct	St
Tests	1	2	0	52	32	26.00	59.09	0	0	1	0
ODIs	28	21	11	271	51	27.10	99.26	0	1	5	0
T20Is	9	6	2	46	15	11.50	124.32	0	0	2	0
First-class	69	100	6	2092	93	22.25	54.21	0	10	30	0
List A	104	79	23	1127	69*	20.12	100.26	0	2	33	0
Twenty20	84	56	15	642	80*	15.65	152.13	0	2	20	0

Bowling	Mat	Balls	Runs	Wkts	BBI	BBM	Ave	Econ	SR	5w	10
Tests	1	234	153	1	1/51	1/153	153.00	3.92	234.0	0	0
ODIs	28	1432	1187	40	6/45	6/45	29.67	4.97	35.8	1	0
T20Is	9	186	247	7	3/14	3/14	35.28	7.96	26.5	0	0
First-class	69	12224	5956	223	7/60	9/111	26.70	2.92	54.8	7	0
List A	104	5378	4397	166	6/45	6/45	26.48	4.90	32.3	3	0
Twenty20	84	1718	2169	96	4/26	4/26	22.59	7.57	17.8	0	0

FULL NAME: Thomas George Helm
BORN: May 7, 1994, Aylesbury,
Buckinghamshire
SQUAD NO: 7
HEIGHT: 6ft 4in
NICKNAME: Ched, Helmet, Helmy
EDUCATION: The Misbourne School,
Buckinghamshire
TEAMS: Middlesex, England Lions,
Glamorgan
ROLE: Bowler
DEBUT: First-class: 2013; List A: 2013;
T20: 2016

MIDDLESEX

BEST BATTING: 27 Middlesex vs Oxford MCCU, Oxford, 2015
BEST BOWLING: 3-46 Middlesex vs Yorkshire, Headingley, 2013

FAMILY TIES? My brother Sam plays Minor Counties for Buckinghamshire
BEST MOMENT IN CRICKET? My maiden first-class wicket at Lord's against Nottinghamshire
SUPERSTITIONS? I slide and tap my bat at the end of each over I survive
HOW WOULD YOUR TEAM-MATES DESCRIBE YOU IN THREE WORDS? Really good sort
BEST PLAYER IN COUNTY CRICKET? Toby Roland-Jones (Mid)
MOST UNDERRATED PLAYER IN COUNTY CRICKET? Ryan Higgins (Mid)
TIP FOR THE TOP? Jamie Porter (Ess), Max Holden (Mid)
CRICKETING HEROES? James Anderson – the best swing bowler in the world
NON-CRICKETING HEROES? Frank Lampard, Steph Curry
IF YOU WEREN'T A CRICKETER? I'd be controlling the midfield at Stamford Bridge
UNUSUAL OBJECT AT HOME? 1kg of Jelly Babies
DESERT ISLAND DISC? Red Hot Chili Peppers (any album)
FANTASY SLIP CORDON? Keeper: Lee Mack, 1st: Jennifer Aniston, 2nd: Me, 3rd: Benn
Langdon, Gully: Antonio Conte
TWITTER: @TomHelm7

Batting	Mat	Inns	NO	Runs	HS	Ave	SR	100	50	Ct	St
First-class	9	14	4	129	27	12.90	35.83	0	0	2	0
List A	11	6	4	40	13*	20.00	76.92	0	0	3	0
Twenty20	1	-	-	-	-	-	-	-	-	0	0

Bowling	Mat	Balls	Runs	Wkts	BBI	BBM	Ave	Econ	SR	5w	10
First-class	9	1184	642	22	3/46	5/78	29.18	3.25	53.8	0	0
List A	11	384	292	14	5/33	5/33	20.85	4.56	27.4	1	0
Twenty20	1	24	29	1	1/29	1/29	29.00	7.25	24.0	0	0

ROB HEMMINGS

RHB / RM / R0 / W0

FULL NAME: Robert Phillip Hemmings
BORN: February 28, 1996, Stoke-on-Trent, Staffordshire
SQUAD NO: 24
HEIGHT: 6ft 4in
EDUCATION: Denstone College, Staffordshire
TEAMS: Derbyshire
ROLE: Allrounder
DEBUT: First-class: 2016; List A: 2016

TWITTER: @HemmingsRob
NOTES: Hemmings graduated from the Derbyshire Academy in 2015 and signed his first deal with the county after impressing for the Second XI. The allrounder made his first-team debut last season in a Championship fixture against Worcestershire, returning figures of 0-32 and 0-26 and failing to bat in a rain-affected match. A month later he made his List A debut against Sri Lanka A, scoring 25 not out from 13 deliveries. Hemmings took match figures of 8-105 against Durham in last season's Second XI Championship

Batting	Mat	Inns	NO	Runs	HS	Ave	SR	100	50	Ct	St
First-class	1	-	-	-	-	-	-	-	-	1	0
List A	1	1	1	25	25*	-	192.30	0	0	0	0

Bowling	Mat	Balls	Runs	Wkts	BBI	BBM	Ave	Econ	SR	5w	10
First-class	1	114	58	0	-	-	-	3.05	-	0	0
List A	1	30	35	0	-	-	-	7.00	-	0	0

ALEX HEPBURN

RHB / RM / R0 / W0

FULL NAME: Alex Hepburn
BORN: December 21, 1995, Subiaco, Australia
SQUAD NO: 26
HEIGHT: 5ft 11in
NICKNAME: Audrey, Heppers
EDUCATION: Aquinas College, Perth
TEAMS: Worcestershire
ROLE: Allrounder
DEBUT: List A: 2015

WORCESTERSHIRE

WHAT FIRST GOT YOU INTO CRICKET? A cricket set for my fourth birthday
STRANGEST THING SEEN IN A GAME? An umpire pass out from heat exhaustion during a club game in Perth
BEST MOMENT IN CRICKET? Making my List A debut for Worcestershire at the end of the 2015 season
HOW WOULD YOUR TEAM-MATES DESCRIBE YOU IN THREE WORDS? Up and about
BEST PLAYER IN COUNTY CRICKET? Ben Duckett (Nor)
MOST UNDERRATED PLAYER IN COUNTY CRICKET? Joe Leach (Wor)
TIP FOR THE TOP? Joe Clarke (Wor) – another good summer and he wouldn't be far off higher honours
CRICKETING HEROES? Michael Hussey – he had a very similar role to the one which I want to be able to play in finishing the innings
NON-CRICKETING HEROES? Leonardo DiCaprio and Justin Bieber – they both kill it
IF YOU WEREN'T A CRICKETER? I'd be at university in Australia studying to become a sports teacher or continuing with some landscaping work there
SURPRISING FACT? I'm a massive Harry Potter fan
DESERT ISLAND DISC? Conor Maynard
FANTASY SLIP CORDON? Keeper: Gaz from Geordie Shore, 1st: Me, 2nd: Margot Robbie, 3rd: Justin Bieber, Gully: Michael Hussey
TWITTER: @Alex_Hepburn95

Batting	Mat	Inns	NO	Runs	HS	Ave	SR	100	50	Ct	St
List A	2	1	0	32	32	32.00	94.11	0	0	0	0

Bowling	Mat	Balls	Runs	Wkts	BBI	BBM	Ave	Econ	SR	5w	10
List A	2	113	78	6	4/34	4/34	13.00	4.14	18.8	0	0

ADAM HICKEY

LHB / OB / R0 / W0

DURHAM

FULL NAME: Adam James Hickey
BORN: March 1, 1997, Darlington, County Durham
SQUAD NO: 21
HEIGHT: 6ft 2in
NICKNAME: Hickz
EDUCATION: Biddick School Sports College, Tyne and Wear
TEAMS: Durham
ROLE: Allrounder
DEBUT: First-class 2016

BEST BATTING: 36* Durham vs Somerset, Taunton, 2016
BEST BOWLING: 2-19 Durham vs Somerset, Taunton, 2016

WHAT FIRST GOT YOU INTO CRICKET? The 2005 Ashes
FAMILY TIES? Grandad and Dad both played for local club sides. Dad represented Cumbria in the Minor Counties leagues and played for Durham Second XI
STRANGEST THING SEEN IN A GAME? A flat pitch at Blaydon CC
BEST MOMENT IN CRICKET? Seeing Durham home to win a County Championship game against Lancashire at Southport
HOW WOULD YOUR TEAM-MATES DESCRIBE YOU IN THREE WORDS? Calm, easy-going, determined
BEST PLAYER IN COUNTY CRICKET? Jeetan Patel (War)
MOST UNDERRATED PLAYER IN COUNTY CRICKET? Mark Stoneman (Sur)
TIP FOR THE TOP? Jack Burnham, Brydon Carse (both Dur)
CRICKETING HEROES? Brian Lara
IF YOU WEREN'T A CRICKETER? I'd be hopefully working in the media
SURPRISING FACT? I was born and bred in the North East but support Aston Villa FC
FANTASY SLIP CORDON? Keeper: Morgan Freeman, 1st: Me, 2nd: Michelle Keegan, 3rd: James Corden, Gully: Kendall Jenner
TWITTER: @adamhickey21

Batting	Mat	Inns	NO	Runs	HS	Ave	SR	100	50	Ct	St
First-class	4	7	3	92	36*	23.00	42.39	0	0	1	0

Bowling	Mat	Balls	Runs	Wkts	BBI	BBM	Ave	Econ	SR	5w	10
First-class	4	377	204	6	2/19	2/19	34.00	3.24	62.8	0	0

RYAN HIGGINS
RHB / OB / RO / WO

FULL NAME: Ryan Francis Higgins
BORN: January 6, 1995, Harare, Zimbabwe
SQUAD NO: 11
HEIGHT: 6ft 3in
NICKNAME: Mad Bri, Brian, Higgo, Matchstick
EDUCATION: Peterhouse School, Marondera, Zimbabwe; Bradfield College, Reading
TEAMS: Middlesex
ROLE: Allrounder
DEBUT: List A: 2014; T20: 2014

WHAT FIRST GOT YOU INTO CRICKET? Grandfather and dad
BEST MOMENT IN CRICKET? Watching the boys win the County Championship at Lord's in 2016
HOW WOULD YOUR TEAM-MATES DESCRIBE YOU IN THREE WORDS? Mad, fiery, brian
TIP FOR THE TOP? Max Holden (Mid)
CRICKETING HEROES? Michael Hussey – loved the way he played the game: intensity in his batting and always playing for the team
NON-CRICKETING HEROES? My dad and mum – moved country to get the best for their kids
IF YOU WEREN'T A CRICKETER? I'd be a full-time traveller
SURPRISING FACT? Love a game of chess
UNUSUAL OBJECT AT HOME? A colourful giraffe
DESERT ISLAND DISC? Bryan Adams – Summer Of 69
FANTASY SLIP CORDON? Keeper: Keira Knightley, 1st : Samuel L Jackson, 2nd: Mo Farah, 3rd: Me, 4th: Usain Bolt
TWITTER: @ryanhiggins21

Batting	Mat	Inns	NO	Runs	HS	Ave	SR	100	50	Ct	St
List A	10	9	1	147	39	18.37	75.77	0	0	1	0
Twenty20	22	19	6	279	57*	21.46	114.81	0	1	4	0

Bowling	Mat	Balls	Runs	Wkts	BBI	BBM	Ave	Econ	SR	5w	10
List A	10	90	97	1	1/53	1/53	97.00	6.46	90.0	0	0
Twenty20	22	84	98	7	5/13	5/13	14.00	7.00	12.0	1	0

JAMES HILDRETH RHB / RM / R6 / W0 / MVP95

SOMERSET

FULL NAME: James Charles Hildreth
BORN: September 9, 1984, Milton Keynes, Buckinghamshire
SQUAD NO: 25
HEIGHT: 5ft 10in
NICKNAME: Hildy, Hildz
EDUCATION: Millfield School, Somerset
TEAMS: Somerset, England Lions
ROLE: Batsman
DEBUT: First-class: 2003; List A: 2003; T20: 2004

BEST BATTING: 303* Somerset vs Warwickshire, Taunton, 2009
BEST BOWLING: 2-39 Somerset vs Hampshire, Taunton, 2009
COUNTY CAP: 2007

BEST MOMENT IN CRICKET? Winning the T20 Cup in 2005, captaining England Lions and captaining Somerset
CRICKETING HEROES? Ricky Ponting
IF YOU WEREN'T A CRICKETER? I'd be travelling or on a beach somewhere
SURPRISING FACT? I'm a big MK Dons fan
TWITTER: @dreth25

Batting	Mat	Inns	NO	Runs	HS	Ave	SR	100	50	Ct	St
First-class	220	356	27	14582	303*	44.32		39	66	181	0
List A	186	173	33	4711	151	33.65		6	19	68	0
Twenty20	149	139	26	2663	107*	23.56	119.57	1	11	59	0

Bowling	Mat	Balls	Runs	Wkts	BBI	BBM	Ave	Econ	SR	5w	10
First-class	220	576	492	6	2/39		82.00	5.12	96.0	0	0
List A	186	150	185	6	2/26	2/26	30.83	7.40	25.0	0	0
Twenty20	149	169	247	10	3/24	3/24	24.70	8.76	16.9	0	0

LEWIS HILL

RHB / WK / RO / WO

FULL NAME: Lewis John Hill
BORN: October 5, 1990, Leicester
SQUAD NO: 23
HEIGHT: 5ft 8in
NICKNAME: Lew Show, Lew, Hilly
EDUCATION: Hastings High School, Hinckley; John Cleveland College, Hinckley
TEAMS: Leicestershire
ROLE: Wicketkeeper
DEBUT: First-class: 2015; List A: 2012; T20: 2015

BEST BATTING: 126 Leicestershire vs Surrey, The Oval, 2015

WHAT FIRST GOT YOU INTO CRICKET? Friends played it when we were nine years old, so I joined in at their club

FAMILY TIES? Dad and brother both play for Lutterworth CC

STRANGEST THING SEEN IN A GAME? Turned up to a match to see that somebody overnight had dug holes on a length and along the crease line

BEST MOMENT IN CRICKET? Scoring my maiden first-class century at The Oval and having Kumar Sangakarra and Kevin Pietersen shake my hand at the end of the day

BEST PLAYER IN COUNTY CRICKET? Sam Northeast (Ken)

MOST UNDERRATED PLAYER IN COUNTY CRICKET? Joe Leach (Wor)

TIP FOR THE TOP? Will Fazakerley, Gavin Griffiths (both Lei)

CRICKETING HEROES? Karl Smith and Craig Wilson of Lutterworth CC

IF YOU WEREN'T A CRICKETER? Working for the family sports engineering business

SURPRISING FACT? I was targeted by armed robbers twice while working at a newsagents

DESERT ISLAND DISC? Calum Scott – Dancing On My Own

TWITTER: @ljhill23

Batting	Mat	Inns	NO	Runs	HS	Ave	SR	100	50	Ct	St
First-class	12	23	2	432	126	20.57	55.03	1	1	17	0
List A	22	20	1	395	86	20.78	86.05	0	2	8	1
Twenty20	12	8	3	187	31*	37.40	155.83	0	0	3	0

Bowling	Mat	Balls	Runs	Wkts	BBI	BBM	Ave	Econ	SR	5w	10
First-class	12	12	6	0	-	-	-	3.00	-	0	0
List A	22	-	-	-	-	-	-	-	-	-	-
Twenty20	12	-	-	-	-	-	-	-	-	-	-

ANDY HODD

RHB / WK / R0 / W0

FULL NAME: Andrew John Hodd
BORN: January 12, 1984, Chichester, West Sussex
SQUAD NO: 4
HEIGHT: 6ft
NICKNAME: Hoddfather
EDUCATION: Bexhill High School, East Sussex; Bexhill College; Loughborough University
TEAMS: Yorkshire, Surrey, Sussex
ROLE: Wicketkeeper
DEBUT: First-class: 2003; List A: 2002: T20: 2005

BEST BATTING: 123 Sussex vs Yorkshire, Hove, 2007
COUNTY CAP: 2016 (Yorkshire)

WHAT FIRST GOT YOU INTO CRICKET? Dad throwing balls at me in the back garden and mum dragging me to my local club
SUPERSTITIONS? No! I've been working meticulously on my mental strength – and my mind game is on point!
HOW WOULD YOUR TEAM-MATES DESCRIBE YOU IN THREE WORDS? Over the hill
TIP FOR THE TOP? Will Rhodes, Matthew Fisher (both Yor)
CRICKETING HEROES? My old man for possessing the finest forward D in the business. Brendon McCullum and Adam Gilchrist as fellow wicketkeepers
NON-CRICKETING HEROES? My wife – for putting up with me. Also Giles from Gogglebox
IF YOU WEREN'T A CRICKETER? I'd be the manager of a successful paper merchants
DESERT ISLAND DISC? The Roots – Phrenology
FANTASY SLIP CORDON? Keeper: Me, 1st: George Best (purely for stories), 2nd: Jesus (to turn the drinks into beverages), 3rd: Ricky Gervais (to question everything about Jesus), Gully: DCI John Luther (think we'd be Best Friends Forever)
TWITTER: @Hoddfather

Batting	Mat	Inns	NO	Runs	HS	Ave	SR	100	50	Ct	St
First-class	98	137	23	3198	123	28.05	46.25	4	17	227	22
List A	71	54	13	916	91	22.34		0	2	69	16
Twenty20	73	42	8	400	70	11.76	104.16	0	1	31	16

Bowling	Mat	Balls	Runs	Wkts	BBI	BBM	Ave	Econ	SR	5w	10
First-class	98	16	21	0	-	-	-	7.87	-	0	0
List A	71	-	-	-	-	-	-	-	-	-	-
Twenty20	73	-	-	-	-	-	-	-	-	-	-

MICHAEL HOGAN RHB / RFM / R0 / W2 / MVP38

FULL NAME: Michael Garry Hogan
BORN: May 31, 1981, Newcastle, Australia
SQUAD NO: 31
HEIGHT: 6ft 5in
NICKNAME: Hulk, Hoges
TEAMS: Glamorgan, Hobart Hurricanes, Western Australia
ROLE: Bowler
DEBUT: First-class: 2009; List A: 2009; T20: 2010

BEST BATTING: 57 Glamorgan vs Lancashire, Colwyn Bay, 2015
BEST BOWLING: 7-92 Glamorgan vs Gloucestershire, Bristol, 2013
COUNTY CAP: 2013

BEST MOMENT IN CRICKET? Breaking the 100-wicket mark for Glamorgan was a nice personal achievement
CRICKETING HEROES? Glenn McGrath
IF YOU WEREN'T A CRICKETER? I'd have a career in horticulture
DESERT ISLAND DISC? Jack Johnson – Sitting, Waiting, Wishing
FANTASY SLIP CORDON? Keeper: Billy Connolly, 1st: Me (you don't have to move at 1st), 2nd: James Taylor (the musician not the cricketer), 3rd: Ricky Ponting, Gully: Usain Bolt (to chase anything that goes behind the wicket)
TWITTER: @Hoges31

Batting	Mat	Inns	NO	Runs	HS	Ave	SR	100	50	Ct	St
First-class	118	168	61	1752	57	16.37	84.76	0	2	64	0
List A	57	20	12	141	27	17.62	81.97	0	0	21	0
Twenty20	65	13	7	48	13	8.00	102.12	0	0	28	0

Bowling	Mat	Balls	Runs	Wkts	BBI	BBM	Ave	Econ	SR	5w	10
First-class	118	25162	11289	451	7/92	10/125	25.03	2.69	55.7	17	1
List A	57	2926	2436	93	5/44	5/44	26.19	4.99	31.4	1	0
Twenty20	65	1337	1642	71	4/26	4/26	23.12	7.36	18.8	0	0

MAX HOLDEN — LHB / OB / R0 / W0

MIDDLESEX

FULL NAME: Max David Edward Holden
BORN: December 18, 1997, Cambridge
SQUAD NO: 4
HEIGHT: 6ft 1in
NICKNAME: Texas, Pepsi, Little Chef, Derick
EDUCATION: Sawston Village College, Cambridge; Hills Road Sixth Form College, Cambridge
TEAMS: Northamptonshire, Middlesex 2nd XI
ROLE: Batsman
DEBUT: Yet to make first-team debut

WHAT FIRST GOT YOU INTO CRICKET? Friends played for a local club and they encouraged me to join

FAMILY TIES? Dad was a keen club cricketer

STRANGEST THING SEEN IN A GAME? Essex bowler Aaron Beard open the batting

BEST MOMENT IN CRICKET? Scoring a hundred for England U19 in a youth Test at Northampton

SUPERSTITIONS? I don't like odd numbers so have to tap my bat an even number of times before facing a delivery

HOW WOULD YOUR TEAM-MATES DESCRIBE YOU IN THREE WORDS? Committed, hard-working, determined

BEST PLAYER IN COUNTY CRICKET? Nick Gubbins (Mid)

MOST UNDERRATED PLAYER IN COUNTY CRICKET? John Simpson (Mid)

TIP FOR THE TOP? Mason Crane (Ham), Aaron Beard (Ess)

CRICKETING HEROES? Alastair Cook, Graeme Smith, Brian Lara

NON-CRICKETING HEROES? Thierry Henry

IF YOU WEREN'T A CRICKETER? I'd be training to become a zookeeper

SURPRISING FACT? I played for Cambridge United Youth Academy

UNUSUAL OBJECT AT HOME? A Venus flytrap

DESERT ISLAND DISC? MGMT – Kids

FANTASY SLIP CORDON? Keeper: Ollie Pope, 1st: Me, 2nd: Arsene Wenger, 3rd: James Corden, Gully: Piers Morgan

TWITTER: @maxholden_4

NOTES: England U19 captain. Has joined Northamptonshire on loan but scheduled to return to Middlesex at the end of June

PAUL HORTON

RHB / RM / R3 / W0

FULL NAME: Paul James Horton
BORN: September 20, 1982, Sydney, Australia
SQUAD NO: 2
HEIGHT: 5ft 10in
NICKNAME: Horts, Torts, Aussie, Custard
EDUCATION: Colo High School, Sydney; St Margaret's High School, Liverpool
TEAMS: Leicestershire, Lancashire, Matabeleland Tuskers
ROLE: Batsman
DEBUT: First-class: 2003; List A: 2003; T20: 2005

BEST BATTING: 209 Matabeleland Tuskers vs Southern Rocks, Masvingo, 2011
BEST BOWLING: 2-6 Leicestershire vs Sussex, Leicester, 2016
COUNTY CAP: 2007 (Lancashire)

STRANGEST THING SEEN IN A GAME? A team refuse to take the field because they weren't being paid enough
BEST MOMENT IN CRICKET? Nothing can top winning the County Championship in 2011 with Lancashire. Back-to-back Logan Cup trophies with Matabeleland Tuskers in 2010/11 and 2011/12 was also special
BEST PLAYER IN COUNTY CRICKET? Ben Stokes (Dur)
MOST UNDERRATED PLAYER IN COUNTY CRICKET? Chris Dent (Glo)
TIP FOR THE TOP? Alex Davies (Lan)
CRICKETING HEROES? Mark Waugh, Dean Jones, Brian Lara
NON-CRICKETING HEROES? Roger Federer, Robbie Fowler
SURPRISING FACT? I was a left-handed batsman as a kid. And I was once detained as an illegal immigrant
UNUSUAL OBJECT AT HOME? My French bulldog is pretty unusual at times
TWITTER: @PJHorton20

Batting	Mat	Inns	NO	Runs	HS	Ave	SR	100	50	Ct	St
First-class	180	303	24	10430	209	37.38	48.40	23	57	176	1
List A	107	98	13	2584	111*	30.40		2	13	42	0
Twenty20	82	76	14	1477	71*	23.82	108.52	0	5	32	0

Bowling	Mat	Balls	Runs	Wkts	BBI	BBM	Ave	Econ	SR	5w	10
First-class	180	108	66	2	2/6	2/6	33.00	3.66	54.0	0	0
List A	107	12	7	1	1/7	1/7	7.00	3.50	12.0	0	0
Twenty20	82	-	-	-	-	-	-	-	-	-	-

ADAM HOSE

RHB / RM / R0 / W0

FULL NAME: Adam John Hose
BORN: October 25, 1992, Newport, Isle of Wight
SQUAD NO: 21
HEIGHT: 6ft 5in
NICKNAME: Pipe
EDUCATION: Carisbrooke School, Newport
TEAMS: Somerset
ROLE: Batsman
DEBUT: First-class: 2016; List A: 2015; T20: 2015

BEST BATTING: 10 Somerset vs Pakistanis, Taunton, 2016

WHAT FIRST GOT YOU INTO CRICKET? My dad. Ever since I can remember I was down at my home club (Ventnor CC) on the Isle of Wight, watching and pestering all the players to throw me balls
STRANGEST THING SEEN IN A GAME? The bail landing back on the off stump after the ball clipped it on the way through to the keeper
BEST MOMENT IN CRICKET? My first win in Somerset colours
SUPERSTITIONS? I chew gum when I bat
BEST PLAYER IN COUNTY CRICKET? Marcus Trescothick (Som)
CRICKETING HEROES? Jacques Kallis, Kevin Pietersen, Graeme Hick
NON-CRICKETING HEROES? Grandad
IF YOU WEREN'T A CRICKETER? I'd be doing something in property
SURPRISING FACT? Travelling, dogs and live music are a few of my favourite things
DESERT ISLAND DISC? Red Hot Chili Peppers – Greatest Hits
FANTASY SLIP CORDON? Keeper: Michelle Keegan, 1st: David Beckham, 2nd: Roger Federer, 3rd: James Corden, Gully: David Attenborough
TWITTER: @adamhose21

Batting	Mat	Inns	NO	Runs	HS	Ave	SR	100	50	Ct	St
First-class	1	2	0	18	10	9.00	28.57	0	0	0	0
List A	12	11	0	263	77	23.90	78.27	0	1	7	0
Twenty20	2	2	0	24	20	12.00	126.31	0	0	0	0

Bowling	Mat	Balls	Runs	Wkts	BBI	BBM	Ave	Econ	SR	5w	10
First-class	1	-	-	-	-	-	-	-	-	-	-
List A	12	-	-	-	-	-	-	-	-	-	-
Twenty20	2	-	-	-	-	-	-	-	-	-	-

HARVEY HOSEIN

RHB / WK / R0 / W0

FULL NAME: Harvey Richard Hosein
BORN: August 12, 1996, Chesterfield, Derbyshire
SQUAD NO: 16
HEIGHT: 5ft 11in
NICKNAME: Harv
EDUCATION: Denstone College, Staffordshire
TEAMS: Derbyshire
ROLE: Wicketkeeper
DEBUT: First-class: 2014; List A: 2016; T20: 2016

BEST BATTING: 108 Derbyshire vs Worcestershire, Worcester, 2016

BEST MOMENT IN CRICKET? Scoring my maiden first-class century last year and claiming the world record on my first-class debut after taking 11 catches at The Oval
BEST PLAYER IN COUNTY CRICKET? Haseeb Hameed (Lan)
TIP FOR THE TOP? Shiv Thakor, Matt Critchley (both Der)
CRICKETING HEROES? AB de Villiers, Brian Lara
NON-CRICKETING HEROES? Roger Federer
SURPRISING FACT? I played tennis at county level
DESERT ISLAND DISC? MGMT – Electric Feel
FANTASY SLIP CORDON? Keeper: Me, 1st: Michael McIntyre, 2nd: Frankie Boyle, 3rd: Superman, Gully: AB de Villiers
TWITTER: @HarveyHosein16

Batting	Mat	Inns	NO	Runs	HS	Ave	SR	100	50	Ct	St
First-class	18	28	6	713	108	32.40	42.56	1	5	56	1
List A	3	2	1	42	40	42.00	110.52	0	0	1	1
Twenty20	5	2	2	0	0*	-	-	0	0	7	0

Bowling	Mat	Balls	Runs	Wkts	BBI	BBM	Ave	Econ	SR	5w	10
First-class	18	-	-	-	-	-	-	-	-	-	-
List A	3	-	-	-	-	-	-	-	-	-	-
Twenty20	5	-	-	-	-	-	-	-	-	-	-

BENNY HOWELL

RHB / RM / R0 / W0 / MVP94

GLOUCESTERSHIRE

FULL NAME: Benny Alexander Cameron Howell
BORN: October 5, 1988, Bordeaux, France
SQUAD NO: 13
HEIGHT: 6ft
NICKNAME: Novak, Trowell, Growler
EDUCATION: The Oratory School, Reading
TEAMS: Gloucestershire, Hampshire, Khulna Titans
ROLE: Allrounder
DEBUT: First-class: 2011; List A: 2010; T20: 2011

BEST BATTING: 102 Gloucestershire vs Leicestershire, Cheltenham, 2015
BEST BOWLING: 5-57 Gloucestershire vs Leicestershire, Leicester, 2013
COUNTY CAP: 2012 (Gloucestershire)

WHAT FIRST GOT YOU INTO CRICKET? I started playing French cricket when I was two and was soon playing with my old man's Gray-Nicolls
FAMILY TIES? My dad Jonathan played for Warwickshire for a season
STRANGEST THING SEEN IN A GAME? The playing-field dynamics at Ventnor CC
BEST MOMENT IN CRICKET? Taking a crucial catch to help Gloucestershire win the Lord's one-day final in 2015
HOW WOULD YOUR TEAM-MATES DESCRIBE YOU IN THREE WORDS? Outside the box
MOST UNDERRATED PLAYER IN COUNTY CRICKET? Sam Northeast (Ken)
TIP FOR THE TOP? Matt Taylor (Glo)
NON-CRICKETING HEROES? Jackie Robinson – "Life is not a spectator sport. If you're going to spend your whole life in the grandstand just watching what goes on, in my opinion you're wasting your life."
IF YOU WEREN'T A CRICKETER? I'd be playing Major League Baseball
TWITTER: @BennyHowell510

Batting	Mat	Inns	NO	Runs	HS	Ave	SR	100	50	Ct	St
First-class	60	93	12	2112	102	26.07	52.41	1	11	31	0
List A	63	50	9	1461	122	35.63	89.13	1	8	20	0
Twenty20	77	63	22	928	57	22.63	118.82	0	3	24	0

Bowling	Mat	Balls	Runs	Wkts	BBI	BBM	Ave	Econ	SR	5w	10
First-class	60	5577	2756	84	5/57	8/96	32.80	2.96	66.3	1	0
List A	63	1945	1617	46	3/37	3/37	35.15	4.98	42.2	0	0
Twenty20	77	1260	1490	74	4/26	4/26	20.13	7.09	17.0	0	0

ALEX HUGHES   RHB / RM / RO / WO

FULL NAME: Alex Lloyd Hughes
BORN: September 29, 1991, Wordsley, Staffordshire
SQUAD NO: 18
HEIGHT: 5ft 10in
NICKNAME: Yozza, Barry Horse, Jude Law
EDUCATION: Ounsdale High School, Wolverhampton; University of Worcester
TEAMS: Derbyshire
ROLE: Allrounder
DEBUT: First-class: 2013; List A: 2012; T20: 2011

DERBYSHIRE

BEST BATTING: 140 Derbyshire vs Gloucestershire, Derby, 2016
BEST BOWLING: 4-46 Derbyshire vs Glamorgan, Derby, 2014

BEST MOMENT IN CRICKET? Playing in the same team as Shiv Chanderpaul
HOW WOULD YOUR TEAM-MATES DESCRIBE YOU IN THREE WORDS? Rapper, entrepreneur, motivator
CRICKETING HEROES? Mike Brearley, Dimi Mascarenhas, Mark Ealham
IF YOU WEREN'T A CRICKETER? I'd be an Uber driver or a stuntman
SURPRISING FACT? I got to The X Factor bootcamp in 2012
UNUSUAL OBJECT AT HOME? A samurai sword
DESERT ISLAND DISC? Shrek Soundtrack
FANTASY SLIP CORDON? Keeper: Tom Poynton, 1st: Wes Durston, 2nd: Tom Knight, 3rd: Me, Gully: Chesney Hughes. All Derbyshire legends
TWITTER: @Yozza18

Batting	Mat	Inns	NO	Runs	HS	Ave	SR	100	50	Ct	St
First-class	31	52	7	1162	140	25.82	45.56	2	4	17	0
List A	40	26	5	408	59*	19.42	83.26	0	1	14	0
Twenty20	40	31	6	353	43*	14.12	112.42	0	0	13	0

Bowling	Mat	Balls	Runs	Wkts	BBI	BBM	Ave	Econ	SR	5w	10
First-class	31	2103	1120	22	4/46	4/75	50.90	3.19	95.5	0	0
List A	40	1391	1216	29	3/31	3/31	41.93	5.24	47.9	0	0
Twenty20	40	653	880	19	3/23	3/23	46.31	8.08	34.3	0	0

MATT HUNN

RHB / RFM / R0 / W0

FULL NAME: Matthew David Hunn
BORN: March 22, 1994, Colchester, Essex
SQUAD NO: 14
HEIGHT: 6ft 5in
NICKNAME: Hunny
EDUCATION: St Joseph's College, Ipswich
TEAMS: Kent
ROLE: Bowler
DEBUT: First-class: 2013; List A: 2015; T20: 2015

BEST BATTING: 32* Kent vs Gloucestershire, Canterbury, 2016
BEST BOWLING: 5-99 Kent vs Australians, Canterbury, 2015

STRANGEST THING SEEN IN A GAME? Someone set up a tent and get into it during a professional game
BEST MOMENT IN CRICKET? Signing my first contract and making my debut, and taking five wickets against Australia in 2015
HOW WOULD YOUR TEAM-MATES DESCRIBE YOU IN THREE WORDS? Lanky and quiet
MOST UNDERRATED PLAYER IN COUNTY CRICKET? Daniel Bell-Drummond (Ken)
CRICKETING HEROES? Andrew Flintoff, Morne Morkel
NON-CRICKETING HEROES? Nelson Mandela
SURPRISING FACT? I hold a 24-hour indoor rowing Guinness world record with my school
DESERT ISLAND DISC? Notorious B.I.G.
FANTASY SLIP CORDON? Keeper: Jonny Wilkinson, 1st: Me, 2nd: Jack Whitehall, 3rd: David Beckham, Gully: Nelson Mandela
TWITTER: @MattHunn10

Batting	Mat	Inns	NO	Runs	HS	Ave	SR	100	50	Ct	St
First-class	16	15	10	94	32*	18.80	34.94	0	0	7	0
List A	7	4	3	7	5*	7.00	43.75	0	0	2	0
Twenty20	2	-	-	-	-	-	-	-	-	1	0

Bowling	Mat	Balls	Runs	Wkts	BBI	BBM	Ave	Econ	SR	5w	10
First-class	16	2212	1383	38	5/99	6/125	36.39	3.75	58.2	1	0
List A	7	288	258	6	2/31	2/31	43.00	5.37	48.0	0	0
Twenty20	2	42	65	4	3/30	3/30	16.25	9.28	10.5	0	0

BRETT HUTTON

RHB / RMF / RO / WO

FULL NAME: Brett Alan Hutton
BORN: February 6, 1993, Doncaster, Yorkshire
SQUAD NO: 26
HEIGHT: 6ft 3in
NICKNAME: Bert
EDUCATION: Worksop College, Nottinghamshire
TEAMS: Nottinghamshire
ROLE: Bowler
DEBUT: First-class: 2011; List A: 2011; T20: 2016

BEST BATTING: 74 Nottinghamshire vs Durham, Trent Bridge, 2016
BEST BOWLING: 5-29 Nottinghamshire vs Durham, Trent Bridge, 2015

BEST MOMENT IN CRICKET? Making my County Championship debut for Nottinghamshire
HOW WOULD YOUR TEAM-MATES DESCRIBE YOU IN THREE WORDS? Fat, slow, stiff
TIP FOR THE TOP? Jack Blatherwick (Not)
CRICKETING HEROES? Matthew Hoggard
IF YOU WEREN'T A CRICKETER? I'd be an electrician
DESERT ISLAND DISC? Boys Like Girls – The Great Escape
FANTASY SLIP CORDON? Keeper: Martin Johnson, 1st: Bruno Tonioli, 2nd: Rachel Riley, 3rd: Me
TWITTER: @BrettAH26

Batting	Mat	Inns	NO	Runs	HS	Ave	SR	100	50	Ct	St
First-class	24	38	6	760	74	23.75	44.31	0	3	10	0
List A	9	6	3	66	33*	22.00	88.00	0	0	3	0
Twenty20	1	1	1	4	4*	-	133.33	0	0	0	0

Bowling	Mat	Balls	Runs	Wkts	BBI	BBM	Ave	Econ	SR	5w	10
First-class	24	3472	2138	69	5/29	10/106	30.98	3.69	50.3	2	1
List A	9	414	438	9	3/72	3/72	48.66	6.34	46.0	0	0
Twenty20	1	12	24	1	1/24	1/24	24.00	12.00	12.0	0	0

COLIN INGRAM
LHB / LB / R0 / W0 / MVP57

FULL NAME: Colin Alexander Ingram
BORN: July 3, 1985, Port Elizabeth, South Africa
SQUAD NO: 41
NICKNAME: Bozie, Stingers
EDUCATION: Woodbridge College, Eastern Cape, South Africa
TEAMS: South Africa, Glamorgan, Delhi Daredevils, Eastern Province, Free State, Somerset, Warriors
ROLE: Allrounder
DEBUT: ODI: 2010; T20I: 2010; First-class: 2004; List A: 2005; T20: 2007

BEST BATTING: 190 Eastern Province vs KwaZulu-Natal, Port Elizabeth, 2009
BEST BOWLING: 4-16 Eastern Province vs Boland, Port Elizabeth, 2006

TWITTER: @CAIngram41
NOTES: An aggressive top-order batsman, Ingram joined Glamorgan as a Kolpak on a three-year deal, starting in 2015. He scored 124 on ODI debut for South Africa against Zimbabwe in 2010, putting on 136 with Hashim Amla. He took over as Warriors captain in 2014. He signed for Somerset the same year, playing 12 games across all three formats as a replacement for Alviro Petersen. He had a superb season in white-ball cricket for Glamorgan in 2016 with both bat and ball, striking his maiden T20 hundred. A knee injury prevented him from playing any first-class cricket in 2016

Batting	Mat	Inns	NO	Runs	HS	Ave	SR	100	50	Ct	St
ODIs	31	29	3	843	124	32.42	82.32	3	3	12	0
T20Is	9	9	1	210	78	26.25	129.62	0	1	2	0
First-class	99	175	15	5969	190	37.30		12	29	70	0
List A	164	156	17	6506	130	46.80	88.96	15	42	58	0
Twenty20	129	126	13	3141	101	27.79	133.37	1	21	45	0

Bowling	Mat	Balls	Runs	Wkts	BBI	BBM	Ave	Econ	SR	5w	10
ODIs	31	6	17	0	-	-	-	17.00	-	0	0
T20Is	9	-	-	-	-	-	-	-	-	-	-
First-class	99	3293	1977	48	4/16	5/50	41.18	3.60	68.6	0	0
List A	164	882	763	27	3/38	3/38	28.25	5.19	32.6	0	0
Twenty20	129	356	429	20	4/32	4/32	21.45	7.23	17.8	0	0

KYLE JARVIS

RHB / RFM / R0 / W2 / MVP52

FULL NAME: Kyle Malcolm Jarvis
BORN: February 16, 1989, Harare, Zimbabwe
SQUAD NO: 27
HEIGHT: 6ft 2in
NICKNAME: Jarv
EDUCATION: St John's College, Harare;
University of Pretoria
TEAMS: Zimbabwe, Lancashire, Central
Districts, Mashonaland Eagles, Mid West
Rhinos
ROLE: Bowler
DEBUT: Test: 2011; ODI: 2009; T20I: 2011;
First-class: 2009; List A: 2009; T20: 2011

BEST BATTING: 57 Lancashire vs Yorkshire, Old Trafford, 2016
BEST BOWLING: 7-35 Mashonaland Eagles vs Matabeleland Tuskers, Bulawayo, 2012
COUNTY CAP: 2015

FAMILY TIES? My father Malcolm played for Zimbabwe
BEST MOMENT IN CRICKET? Winning the T20 Blast in 2015
HOW WOULD YOUR TEAM-MATES DESCRIBE YOU IN THREE WORDS? The money team
TIP FOR THE TOP? Alex Davies (Lan), Tom Curran, Sam Curran (both Sur)
NON-CRICKETING HEROES? Floyd Mayweather, Conor McGregor
SURPRISING FACT? I could have been a rugby player
DESERT ISLAND DISC? Bob Marley (any album)
TWITTER: @KyleJarv89

Batting	Mat	Inns	NO	Runs	HS	Ave	SR	100	50	Ct	St
Tests	8	14	6	58	25*	7.25	29.74	0	0	3	0
ODIs	24	15	5	52	13	5.20	40.62	0	0	6	0
T20Is	9	5	2	9	9*	3.00	52.94	0	0	0	0
First-class	63	87	30	871	57	15.28	49.37	0	1	17	0
List A	50	30	14	131	33*	8.18	46.12	0	0	13	0
Twenty20	44	11	5	37	10	6.16	75.51	0	0	15	0

Bowling	Mat	Balls	Runs	Wkts	BBI	BBM	Ave	Econ	SR	5w	10
Tests	8	1569	952	30	5/54	7/115	31.73	3.64	52.3	2	0
ODIs	24	1217	1221	27	3/36	3/36	45.22	6.01	45.0	0	0
T20Is	9	193	270	10	3/15	3/15	27.00	8.39	19.3	0	0
First-class	63	11840	6654	248	7/35	11/119	26.83	3.37	47.7	14	2
List A	50	2260	2098	59	4/31	4/31	35.55	5.56	38.3	0	0
Twenty20	44	901	1267	42	3/15	3/15	30.16	8.43	21.4	0	0

ATEEQ JAVID

RHB / OB / RO / WO

WARWICKSHIRE

FULL NAME: Ateeq Javid
BORN: October 15, 1991, Birmingham
SQUAD NO: 17
HEIGHT: 5ft 7in
NICKNAME: King AJ
EDUCATION: Aston Manor Academy,
Birmingham
TEAMS: Warwickshire
ROLE: Allrounder
DEBUT: First-class: 2009; List A: 2011;
T20: 2013

BEST BATTING: 133 Warwickshire vs Somerset, Edgbaston, 2013
BEST BOWLING: 1-1 Warwickshire vs Lancashire, Old Trafford, 2014

WHAT FIRST GOT YOU INTO CRICKET? While growing up all the kids used to play in the streets so I joined in
BEST MOMENT IN CRICKET? When we celebrated winning the T20 Blast in 2014
HOW WOULD YOUR TEAM-MATES DESCRIBE YOU IN THREE WORDS? Hard-working, smart, intelligent
BEST PLAYER IN COUNTY CRICKET? Ian Bell (War)
TIP FOR THE TOP? Sam Hain (War)
CRICKETING HEROES? Sachin Tendulkar
NON-CRICKETING HEROES? Muhammad Ali
IF YOU WEREN'T A CRICKETER? I'd be a businessman
SURPRISING FACT? I hate going to parties
DESERT ISLAND DISC? Skepta – If You Know Me
TWITTER: @ateeqjavid

Batting	Mat	Inns	NO	Runs	HS	Ave	SR	100	50	Ct	St
First-class	31	49	6	1068	133	24.83	36.08	2	3	16	0
List A	36	29	11	540	43	30.00	86.95	0	0	6	0
Twenty20	52	35	15	449	51*	22.45	118.78	0	1	10	0

Bowling	Mat	Balls	Runs	Wkts	BBI	BBM	Ave	Econ	SR	5w	10
First-class	31	576	340	3	1/1	1/1	113.33	3.54	192.0	0	0
List A	36	1020	972	22	4/42	4/42	44.18	5.71	46.3	0	0
Twenty20	52	675	818	30	4/17	4/17	27.26	7.27	22.5	0	0

KEATON JENNINGS　　　LHB / RM / R1 / W0 / MVP3

FULL NAME: Keaton Kent Jennings
BORN: June 19, 1992, Johannesburg, South Africa
SQUAD NO: 1
HEIGHT: 6ft 4in
EDUCATION: King Edward VII School; University of South Africa
TEAMS: England, Durham, Gauteng
ROLE: Batsman
DEBUT: Test: 2016; First-class: 2011; List A: 2012; T20: 2014

DURHAM

BEST BATTING: 221* Durham vs Yorkshire, Chester-le-Street, 2016
BEST BOWLING: 2-8 Gauteng vs Western Province, Cape Town, 2012

FAMILY TIES? My brother Dylan, my uncle Kenneth and my father Ray have all played first-class cricket
CRICKETING HEROES? Mike Hussey – I loved the way he went about playing the game
IF YOU WEREN'T A CRICKETER? I'd be working in some sort of accountancy job
DESERT ISLAND DISC? U2 – The Joshua Tree
TWITTER: @JetJennings

Batting	Mat	Inns	NO	Runs	HS	Ave	SR	100	50	Ct	St
Tests	2	4	0	167	112	41.75	46.64	1	1	2	0
First-class	76	135	8	4561	221*	35.91	46.53	13	17	41	0
List A	36	35	11	930	101*	38.75	76.35	1	7	7	0
Twenty20	30	18	7	350	88	31.81	125.44	0	1	7	0

Bowling	Mat	Balls	Runs	Wkts	BBI	BBM	Ave	Econ	SR	5w	10
Tests	2	30	20	0	-	-	-	4.00	-	0	0
First-class	76	902	499	14	2/8	2/8	35.64	3.31	64.4	0	0
List A	36	378	389	3	1/9	1/9	129.66	6.17	126.0	0	0
Twenty20	30	456	568	19	4/37	4/37	29.89	7.47	24.0	0	0

RICHARD JONES

RHB / RMF / RO / WO

FULL NAME: Richard Alan Jones
BORN: November 6, 1986, Stourbridge, Worcestershire
SQUAD NO: 25
HEIGHT: 6ft 2in
NICKNAME: Dick, Jonah, Jonesy
EDUCATION: Manchester Metropolitan University
TEAMS: Leicestershire, Matabeleland Tuskers, Warwickshire, Worcestershire
ROLE: Bowler
DEBUT: First-class: 2007; List A: 2008; T20: 2010

BEST BATTING: 62 Matabeleland Tuskers vs Southern Rocks, Bulawayo, 2012
BEST BOWLING: 7-115 Worcestershire vs Sussex, Hove, 2010
COUNTY CAP: 2007 (Worcestershire)

WHAT FIRST GOT YOU INTO CRICKET? When I was nine my best mate started going to nets at a local school. I was sick of him being better than me at football, so I decided to get my own back. My whole career has been an attempt to poke fun at his woeful off-spinners
FAMILY TIES? My dad played for Old Hill CC as a kid, but turned into one of their most loyal bar-frequenting members
BEST MOMENT IN CRICKET? Taking eight wickets in a day for Worcestershire vs Surrey on the same day that my nephew Noah was born
BEST PLAYER IN COUNTY CRICKET? Jonny Bairstow (Yor)
TIP FOR THE TOP? Sam Hain (War), Joe Clarke (Wor)
CRICKETING HEROES? Growing up as a Worcestershire fan, Graeme Hick. To get the chance to play with him was brilliant.
NON-CRICKETING HEROES? Professor Tim Noakes
IF YOU WEREN'T A CRICKETER? I'd be an anthropologist
TWITTER: @richardjones441

Batting	Mat	Inns	NO	Runs	HS	Ave	SR	100	50	Ct	St
First-class	56	85	15	850	62	12.14	40.36	0	2	20	0
List A	13	7	3	49	26	12.25	106.52	0	0	2	0
Twenty20	9	2	1	14	9	14.00	77.77	0	0	7	0

Bowling	Mat	Balls	Runs	Wkts	BBI	BBM	Ave	Econ	SR	5w	10
First-class	56	7418	5048	157	7/115	8/105	32.15	4.08	47.2	5	0
List A	13	453	554	5	1/25	1/25	110.80	7.33	90.6	0	0
Twenty20	9	126	230	9	5/34	5/34	25.55	10.95	14.0	1	0

ROB JONES

RHB / LB / RO / WO

FULL NAME: Robert Peter Jones
BORN: November 3, 1995, Warrington, Cheshire
SQUAD NO: 12
NICKNAME: Jonesy
EDUCATION: Bridgewater High School, Warrington
TEAMS: Lancashire
ROLE: Batsman
DEBUT: First-class: 2016

BEST BATTING: 106* Lancashire vs Middlesex, Old Trafford, 2016

TWITTER: @robpeterjones
NOTES: Opening batsman who impressed with a series of good scores for Lancashire Second XI during the tail-end of the 2015 season, including a century against Scotland A. Also played Minor Counties for Cheshire. Scored his maiden Championship hundred in 2016 in just his third first-class match, carrying his bat against champions Middlesex at Old Trafford after Lancashire had been reduced to 6-4

Batting	Mat	Inns	NO	Runs	HS	Ave	SR	100	50	Ct	St
First-class	4	7	2	212	106*	42.40	32.61	1	0	3	0
Bowling	Mat	Balls	Runs	Wkts	BBI	BBM	Ave	Econ	SR	5w	10
First-class	4	-	-	-	-	-	-	-	-	-	-

CHRIS JORDAN — RHB / RFM / R0 / W1 / MVP100

FULL NAME: Christopher James Jordan
BORN: October 4, 1988, Barbados
SQUAD NO: 8
HEIGHT: 6ft 2in
NICKNAME: CJ
EDUCATION: Combermere School, Barbados;
Dulwich College
TEAMS: England, Sussex, Adelaide
Strikers, Barbados, Peshawar Zalmi, Royal
Challengers Bangalore, Surrey
ROLE: Allrounder
DEBUT: Test: 2014; ODI: 2013; T20I: 2014;
First-class: 2007; List A: 2007; T20: 2008

BEST BATTING: 131 Sussex vs Essex, Colchester, 2016
BEST BOWLING: 7-43 Barbados vs Combined Campuses and Colleges, Bridgetown, 2013
COUNTY CAP: 2014 (Sussex)

TWITTER: @ChrisJordan94
NOTES: Born in Barbados but eligible to represent England through his grandmother. An allrounder known for his brilliant close catching, Jordan is a regular member of England's T20 team but hasn't played a Test since May 2015. Released by Surrey after the 2012 season, he took 61 first-class wickets in his first summer at Hove. Injury has restricted him to 11 Championship appearances over the last two seasons. Scored his maiden first-class hundred in 2016. Won the 2016/17 Pakistan Super League with Peshawar Zalmi. Signed by Sunrisers Hyderabad for the 2017 IPL

Batting	Mat	Inns	NO	Runs	HS	Ave	SR	100	50	Ct	St
Tests	8	11	1	180	35	18.00	56.25	0	0	14	0
ODIs	31	21	7	169	38*	12.07	89.89	0	0	19	0
T20Is	22	14	5	128	27*	14.22	113.27	0	0	11	0
First-class	83	112	18	2262	131	24.06		1	10	101	0
List A	72	50	12	560	55	14.73		0	1	42	0
Twenty20	78	53	19	593	45*	17.44	116.04	0	0	47	0

Bowling	Mat	Balls	Runs	Wkts	BBI	BBM	Ave	Econ	SR	5w	10
Tests	8	1530	752	21	4/18	7/50	35.80	2.94	72.8	0	0
ODIs	31	1532	1521	43	5/29	5/29	35.37	5.95	35.6	1	0
T20Is	22	462	666	26	4/28	4/28	25.61	8.64	17.7	0	0
First-class	83	13850	7978	248	7/43	9/58	32.16	3.45	55.8	8	0
List A	72	3298	3144	109	5/28	5/28	28.84	5.71	30.2	2	0
Twenty20	78	1507	2150	83	4/11	4/11	25.90	8.56	18.1	0	0

ED JOYCE

LHB / RM / R9 / W0

FULL NAME: Edmund Christopher Joyce
BORN: September 22, 1978, Dublin, Ireland
SQUAD NO: 24
HEIGHT: 5ft 10in
NICKNAME: Joycey, Spud, Piece
EDUCATION: Presentation College, Bray;
Trinity College, Dublin
TEAMS: England, Ireland, Sussex, Middlesex
ROLE: Batsman
DEBUT: ODI: 2006; T20I: 2006; First-class:
1997; List A: 1998; T20: 2003

SUSSEX

BEST BATTING: 250 Sussex vs Derbyshire, Derby, 2016
BEST BOWLING: 2-34 Middlesex vs Cambridge UCCE, Cambridge, 2004
COUNTY CAP: 2002 (Middlesex)

TWITTER: @edjoyce24
NOTES: Passed 1,000 first-class runs five English summers in a row between 2002-2006, and has achieved the feat nine times in all. Has represented both Ireland and England in ODI cricket. Scored his one England ODI century against Australia in 2007. His brother, Dom, and sisters, Cecelia and Isobel, have all played international cricket for Ireland. Sussex captain between 2012-15. In 2014 he was named as the No.1 cricketer from non-Test playing nations by All Out Cricket and was the third-leading runscorer in the County Championship with 1,398 runs, including seven hundreds. In 2015 he made 231 – his highest international score – for Ireland against UAE in the Intercontinental Cup. Averaged 64.12 in 12 Championship matches last summer. Signed a central contract with Ireland in December and will be available to Sussex for only a handful of first-class games in 2017

Batting	Mat	Inns	NO	Runs	HS	Ave	SR	100	50	Ct	St
ODIs	63	62	6	2110	160*	37.67	72.03	5	12	22	0
T20Is	18	15	3	405	78*	33.75	93.96	0	1	5	0
First-class	247	406	33	17925	250	48.05		45	92	220	0
List A	292	277	30	9535	160*	38.60		16	55	98	0
Twenty20	91	85	13	1453	78*	20.18	96.35	0	2	29	0

Bowling	Mat	Balls	Runs	Wkts	BBI	BBM	Ave	Econ	SR	5w	10
ODIs	63	-	-	-	-	-	-	-	-	-	-
T20Is	18	-	-	-	-	-	-	-	-	-	-
First-class	247	1311	1033	11	2/34		93.90	4.72	119.1	0	0
List A	292	264	309	6	2/10	2/10	51.50	7.02	44.0	0	0
Twenty20	91	6	12	0	-	-	-	12.00	-	0	0

ROB KEOGH

RHB / OB / R0 / W0

FULL NAME: Robert Ian Keogh
BORN: October 21, 1991, Dunstable, Bedfordshire
SQUAD NO: 14
HEIGHT: 6ft 2in
NICKNAME: Keezy, Key Dog, Chav
EDUCATION: Queensbury Upper School, Dunstable; Dunstable College
TEAMS: Northamptonshire
ROLE: Allrounder
DEBUT: First-class: 2012; List A: 2010; T20: 2011

BEST BATTING: 221 Northamptonshire vs Hampshire, Southampton, 2013
BEST BOWLING: 9-52 Northamptonshire vs Glamorgan, Northampton, 2016

FAMILY TIES? Dad played for Dunstable Town CC
STRANGEST THING SEEN IN A GAME? When a streaker ran on while I was batting in a T20 game on TV against Yorkshire. I don't condone streaking but to be fair it was hilarious
BEST MOMENT IN CRICKET? Hitting the winning runs in the T20 Blast final against Durham in 2016 and celebrating with the boys in the middle
HOW WOULD YOUR TEAM-MATES DESCRIBE YOU IN THREE WORDS? Saggy, tight, chav
BEST PLAYER IN COUNTY CRICKET? Ben Duckett (Nor)
MOST UNDERRATED PLAYER IN COUNTY CRICKET? Sam Northeast (Ken)
TIP FOR THE TOP? Richard Gleeson (Nor)
CRICKETING HEROES? AB de Villiers, Virat Kohli, Michael Clarke, Ian Bell
IF YOU WEREN'T A CRICKETER? I'd be a terrible used-car salesman
UNUSUAL OBJECT AT HOME? A bent nose (Ben Sanderson's) and one of Snow White's seven dwarfs (Ben Duckett)
DESERT ISLAND DISC? Kanye West – The College Dropout
TWITTER: @RobKeogh91

Batting	Mat	Inns	NO	Runs	HS	Ave	SR	100	50	Ct	St
First-class	47	75	5	2296	221	32.80	52.63	6	6	11	0
List A	28	25	2	644	134	28.00	89.19	1	5	5	0
Twenty20	35	15	3	170	28	14.16	116.43	0	0	21	0

Bowling	Mat	Balls	Runs	Wkts	BBI	BBM	Ave	Econ	SR	5w	10
First-class	47	3746	2132	56	9/52	13/125	38.07	3.41	66.8	1	1
List A	28	516	487	1	1/49	1/49	487.00	5.66	516.0	0	0
Twenty20	35	48	61	0	-	-	-	7.62	-	0	0

SIMON KERRIGAN   RHB / SLA / RO / W2

FULL NAME: Simon Christopher Kerrigan
BORN: May 10, 1989, Preston, Lancashire
SQUAD NO: 10
HEIGHT: 5ft 9in
NICKNAME: Kegs, Kegsy, Kegger, Bish
EDUCATION: Corpus Christi High School, Lancashire; Preston College; Edge Hill University, Ormskirk
TEAMS: England, Lancashire
ROLE: Bowler
DEBUT: Test: 2013; First-class: 2010; List A: 2011; T20: 2010

BEST BATTING: 62* Lancashire vs Hampshire, Southport, 2013
BEST BOWLING: 9-51 Lancashire vs Hampshire, Liverpool, 2011
COUNTY CAP: 2013

BEST MOMENT IN CRICKET? Winning the County Championship in 2011
CRICKETING HEROES? Andrew Flintoff, Darren Gough
NON-CRICKETING HEROES? Phil Ivey
TWITTER: @Kegs10
NOTES: Has largely recovered from a nightmare Test debut in 2013, when he took 0-53 from eight nervy overs. Although he has struggled to hold down a place in white-ball cricket, Kerrigan took 44 wickets in the Championship in 2014, 41 in 2015 and 35 in 2016. Signed a two-year contract ahead of the 2017 season

Batting	Mat	Inns	NO	Runs	HS	Ave	SR	100	50	Ct	St
Tests	1	1	1	1	1*	-	8.33	0	0	0	0
First-class	98	115	40	881	62*	11.74	35.35	0	1	33	0
List A	33	14	5	28	10	3.11	49.12	0	0	9	0
Twenty20	24	4	4	9	4*	-	180.00	0	0	11	0

Bowling	Mat	Balls	Runs	Wkts	BBI	BBM	Ave	Econ	SR	5w	10
Tests	1	48	53	0	-	-	-	6.62	-	0	0
First-class	98	19422	9168	305	9/51	12/192	30.05	2.83	63.6	13	3
List A	33	1370	1207	23	3/21	3/21	52.47	5.28	59.5	0	0
Twenty20	24	516	595	20	3/17	3/17	29.75	6.91	25.8	0	0

ALEXEI KERVEZEE

RHB / RM / R1 / W0

WORCESTERSHIRE

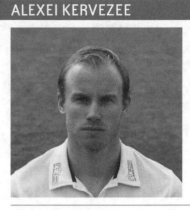

FULL NAME: Alexei Nicolaas Kervezee
BORN: September 11, 1989, Walvis Bay, Namibia
SQUAD NO: 5
HEIGHT: 5ft 9in
NICKNAME: Cubbo, Dexter
EDUCATION: Duneside High, Namibia; Segbroek College, Netherlands
TEAMS: Netherlands, Worcestershire
ROLE: Batsman
DEBUT: ODI: 2006; T20I: 2009; First-class: 2005; List A: 2006; T20: 2009

BEST BATTING: 155 Worcestershire vs Derbyshire, Derby, 2010
BEST BOWLING: 3-72 Worcestershire vs Sussex, Hove, 2015

FAMILY TIES? My uncle played for Netherlands
STRANGEST THING SEEN IN A GAME? Swan stops play
BEST MOMENT IN CRICKET? Walking out to bat in the opening match of the 2009 World T20 against England at Lord's
BEST PLAYER IN COUNTY CRICKET? Kumar Sangakkara (Sur)
TIP FOR THE TOP? Josh Tongue (Wor)
CRICKETING HEROES? AB de Villiers – the way he bats, style and grace combined with sheer brutality at times. I can't think of anyone as dominant in all three formats
NON-CRICKETING HEROES? Dad, Batman
SURPRISING FACT? I'm actually British now
TWITTER: @cubbo455

Batting	Mat	Inns	NO	Runs	HS	Ave	SR	100	50	Ct	St
ODIs	39	36	3	924	92	28.00	73.15	0	4	18	0
T20Is	10	10	1	289	58*	32.11	110.30	0	2	4	0
First-class	97	164	9	4621	155	29.81		6	27	46	0
List A	104	97	9	2632	121*	29.90	79.70	2	13	38	0
Twenty20	87	81	11	1356	58*	19.37	111.88	0	5	36	0

Bowling	Mat	Balls	Runs	Wkts	BBI	BBM	Ave	Econ	SR	5w	10
ODIs	39	24	34	0	-	-	-	8.50	-	0	0
T20Is	10	-	-	-	-	-	-	-	-	-	-
First-class	97	636	378	8	3/72	3/72	47.25	3.56	79.5	0	0
List A	104	78	109	0	-	-	-	8.38	-	0	0
Twenty20	87	12	13	0	-	-	-	6.50	-	0	0

JUNAID KHAN RHB / LFM / R0 / W0

FULL NAME: Mohammad Junaid Khan
BORN: December 24, 1989, Matra, North-West Frontier Province, Pakistan
HEIGHT: 6ft 1in
TEAMS: Pakistan, Lancashire, Abbottabad, Baluchistan, Islamabad Khan Research Laboratories, Khulna Titans, Khyber Pakhtunkhwa Panthers, Middlesex, North West Frontier Province, Peshawar, Water & Power Development Authority
ROLE: Bowler
DEBUT: Test: 2011; ODI: 2011; T20I: 2011; First-class: 2007; List A: 2007; T20: 2006

BEST BATTING: 71 Abbottabad vs Rawalpindi, Abbottabad, 2007
BEST BOWLING: 7-46 Abbottabad vs Peshawar, Peshawar, 2007

TWITTER: @Junaidkhanreal
NOTES: Khan returned to Lancashire ahead of the 2017 season for a third T20 stint with the county. His previous campaigns in 2011 and 2014 both resulted in Lancashire reaching Finals Day, and in 18 games for the club he has taken 31 wickets at an economy of 6.45. The left-armer has represented Pakistan in all three formats, although injury forced him to take an 18-month break from international cricket. His return to the ODI team in January 2017 was a successful one, as Pakistan beat Australia to break a 16-game losing streak Down Under

Batting	Mat	Inns	NO	Runs	HS	Ave	SR	100	50	Ct	St
Tests	22	28	11	122	17	7.17	39.86	0	0	4	0
ODIs	56	25	12	60	25	4.61	55.04	0	0	5	0
T20Is	9	2	2	3	3*	-	75.00	0	0	0	0
First-class	74	100	30	740	71	10.57		0	2	12	0
List A	121	58	25	283	32	8.57		0	0	12	0
Twenty20	97	33	20	124	36	9.53	97.63	0	0	33	0

Bowling	Mat	Balls	Runs	Wkts	BBI	BBM	Ave	Econ	SR	5w	10
Tests	22	4605	2253	71	5/38	8/151	31.73	2.93	64.8	5	0
ODIs	56	2666	2388	83	4/12	4/12	28.77	5.37	32.1	0	0
T20Is	9	162	236	8	3/24	3/24	29.50	8.74	20.2	0	0
First-class	74	14802	7393	302	7/46	13/77	24.48	2.99	49.0	20	3
List A	121	5832	5057	169	5/45	5/45	29.92	5.20	34.5	1	0
Twenty20	97	2139	2442	116	4/12	4/12	21.05	6.84	18.4	0	0

BEN KITT

RHB / RMF / R0 / W0

FULL NAME: Ben Michael Kitt
BORN: January 18, 1995, Plymouth, Devon
SQUAD NO: TBC
HEIGHT: 6ft 3in
NICKNAME: Kitty, BK, Doggers
EDUCATION: Saltash.net Community School, Cornwall; Central College Nottingham
TEAMS: Cornwall, Nottinghamshire 2nd XI
ROLE: Bowler
DEBUT: Yet to make first-team debut

WHAT FIRST GOT YOU INTO CRICKET? My grandad made me a bat in his shed when I was two years old

FAMILY TIES? Pretty much everyone in my family has played for clubs in Cornwall and some of them for the county

STRANGEST THING SEEN IN A GAME? Once at Falmouth CC (Cornwall) we had to lie on the floor for a few minutes as there was a massive swarm of bees flying over the ground. The only reason I was on the floor was because I thought it was part of the warm-up

BEST MOMENT IN CRICKET? Winning the Second XI Championship in 2015

SUPERSTITIONS? I always hold the ball the same way round when I bowl and I always turn the same way at the top of my mark

HOW WOULD YOUR TEAM-MATES DESCRIBE YOU IN THREE WORDS? Aggressive, fun, helpful

BEST PLAYER IN COUNTY CRICKET? Keaton Jennings (Dur)

MOST UNDERRATED PLAYER IN COUNTY CRICKET? Brett Hutton (Not)

TIP FOR THE TOP? Tom Moores (Not)

CRICKETING HEROES? Andrew Flintoff when I was a kid, Jake Ball now

NON-CRICKETING HEROES? Cristiano Ronaldo

SURPRISING FACT? I play darts for about 12 hours a week

UNUSUAL OBJECT AT HOME? Three cuddly toys from my sister

DESERT ISLAND DISC? The Eagles – Greatest Hits

FANTASY SLIP CORDON? Keeper: Cristiano Ronaldo (my idol), 1st: Andrew Flintoff (to hear his stories), 2nd: Me, 3rd: Frankie Boyle (comedy), Gully: Emily Ratajkowski (for obvious reasons)

TWITTER: @benkitt18

DIETER KLEIN

RHB / LFM / RO / WO

FULL NAME: Dieter Klein
BORN: October 31, 1988, Lichtenburg, North West Province, South Africa
SQUAD NO: 77
NICKNAME: The Madman
EDUCATION: Hoërskool Lichtenberg, South Africa
TEAMS: Leicestershire, Lions, North West
ROLE: Bowler
DEBUT: First-class: 2008; List A: 2008; T20: 2013

BEST BATTING: 66 North West vs Border, East London, 2014
BEST BOWLING: 8-72 North West vs Northerns, Potchefstroom, 2014

NOTES: The South African left-armer was signed by Leicestershire for the second half of the 2016 season after impressing for Lowerhouse in the Lancashire League and went on to take nine wickets in two Championship appearances. He qualifies as a non-overseas player due to a German passport, having spent his career in South Africa playing for provincial side North West. His contract runs until the end of 2017

Batting	Mat	Inns	NO	Runs	HS	Ave	SR	100	50	Ct	St
First-class	44	62	12	928	66	18.56	76.50	0	4	12	0
List A	18	8	2	40	17	6.66	66.66	0	0	1	0
Twenty20	8	6	3	46	16	15.33	109.52	0	0	1	0

Bowling	Mat	Balls	Runs	Wkts	BBI	BBM	Ave	Econ	SR	5w	10
First-class	44	6779	4214	163	8/72	10/125	25.85	3.72	41.5	8	1
List A	18	850	644	28	5/35	5/35	23.00	4.54	30.3	1	0
Twenty20	8	124	130	6	3/27	3/27	21.66	6.29	20.6	0	0

RORY KLEINVELDT RHB / RFM / R0 / W1 / MVP39

NORTHAMPTONSHIRE

FULL NAME: Rory Keith Kleinveldt
BORN: March 15, 1983, Cape Town, South Africa
SQUAD NO: 6
NICKNAME: Rors
TEAMS: South Africa, Northamptonshire, Cape Cobras, Hampshire, Western Province
ROLE: Allrounder
DEBUT: Test: 2012; ODI: 2013; T20I: 2008; First-class: 2002; List A: 2002; T20: 2004

BEST BATTING: 115* Western Province vs KwaZulu-Natal, Chatsworth, 2005
BEST BOWLING: 8-47 Cape Cobras vs Warriors, Stellenbosch, 2006

TWITTER: @RoryK_9
NOTES: A powerful, fast-bowling allrounder, Kleinveldt has played four Tests, 10 ODIs and six T20Is for South Africa but hasn't represented his country since 2013. Took over 50 Championship wickets in 2015, his first season as Northants' overseas player, and was the county's leading wicket-taker (15) in the victorious 2016 T20 Blast campaign

Batting	Mat	Inns	NO	Runs	HS	Ave	SR	100	50	Ct	St
Tests	4	5	2	27	17*	9.00	44.26	0	0	2	0
ODIs	10	7	0	105	43	15.00	84.67	0	0	4	0
T20Is	6	3	2	25	22	25.00	250.00	0	0	1	0
First-class	131	181	22	3170	115*	19.93	72.63	1	15	62	0
List A	149	97	20	1577	128	20.48	115.95	1	3	25	0
Twenty20	118	79	24	752	46	13.67	152.22	0	0	24	0

Bowling	Mat	Balls	Runs	Wkts	BBI	BBM	Ave	Econ	SR	5w	10
Tests	4	667	422	10	3/65	4/97	42.20	3.79	66.7	0	0
ODIs	10	513	448	12	4/22	4/22	37.33	5.23	42.7	0	0
T20Is	6	122	173	9	3/18	3/18	19.22	8.50	13.5	0	0
First-class	131	22080	11051	386	8/47		28.62	3.00	57.2	18	1
List A	149	6776	5374	169	4/22	4/22	31.79	4.75	40.0	0	0
Twenty20	118	2370	3042	108	3/14	3/14	28.16	7.70	21.9	0	0

MICHAEL KLINGER RHB / R1 / W0 / MVP34

FULL NAME: Michael Klinger
BORN: July 4, 1980, Melbourne, Australia
SQUAD NO: 2
HEIGHT: 5ft 11in
NICKNAME: Maxy
EDUCATION: Deakin University, Victoria
TEAMS: Australia, Gloucestershire, Adelaide Strikers, Kochi Tuskers Kerala, Perth Scorchers, South Australia, Victoria, Western Australia, Worcestershire
ROLE: Batsman
DEBUT: T20I: 2017; First-class: 1999; List A: 1999; T20: 2006

BEST BATTING: 255 South Australia vs Western Australia, Adelaide, 2008
COUNTY CAPS: 2012 (Worcestershire); 2013 (Gloucestershire)

BEST MOMENT IN CRICKET? Being part of any trophy-winning team: Big Bash and one-day competitions in Australia as well as RL Cup with Gloucestershire in 2015
BEST PLAYER IN COUNTY CRICKET? Adam Lyth (Yor)
TIP FOR THE TOP? Chris Dent, Craig Miles, Liam Norwell (all Glo), Tom Abell (Som)
CRICKETING HEROES? Dean Jones – I had his posters on my wall and he was the best batsman in Victoria where I grew up
NON-CRICKETING HEROES? I loved Australian Rules football. My favourite player was Gary Lyon, from my team Melbourne
IF YOU WEREN'T A CRICKETER? I'd be a director of cricket or head of high performance at a professional cricket organisation
SURPRISING FACT? I sometimes don't sleep the night before a game because I'm thinking about the game too much
TWITTER: @maxyklinger

Batting	Mat	Inns	NO	Runs	HS	Ave	SR	100	50	Ct	St
T20Is	3	3	0	143	62	47.66	127.67	0	1	2	0
First-class	181	319	33	11304	255	39.52	45.89	30	49	175	0
List A	163	161	23	6743	166*	48.86		15	42	60	0
Twenty20	136	133	21	4368	126*	39.00	127.05	6	27	48	0
Bowling	Mat	Balls	Runs	Wkts	BBI	BBM	Ave	Econ	SR	5w	10
T20Is	3	-	-	-	-	-	-	-	-	-	-
First-class	181	6	3	0	-	-	-	3.00	-	0	0
List A	163	-	-	-	-	-	-	-	-	-	-
Twenty20	136	-	-	-	-	-	-	-	-	-	-

TOM KOHLER-CADMORE

RHB / OB / R0 / W0

FULL NAME: Tom Kohler-Cadmore
BORN: August 19, 1994, Chatham, Kent
SQUAD NO: 32
HEIGHT: 6ft 2in
NICKNAME: Pepsi, Herbert, Brother Bilo
EDUCATION: Malvern College, Worcestershire
TEAMS: Worcestershire
ROLE: Batsman
DEBUT: First-class: 2014; List A: 2013; T20: 2014

BEST BATTING: 169 Worcestershire vs Gloucestershire, Worcester, 2016

STRANGEST THING SEEN IN A GAME? Low-flying swan stops play at New Road in 2015
BEST MOMENT IN CRICKET? Getting promoted in 2014
HOW WOULD YOUR TEAM-MATES DESCRIBE YOU IN THREE WORDS? Tall, dark, handsome
BEST PLAYER IN COUNTY CRICKET? Ed Joyce (Sus)
MOST UNDERRATED PLAYER IN COUNTY CRICKET? James Sykes (Lei)
TIP FOR THE TOP? Josh Tongue (Wor)
NON-CRICKETING HEROES? Dale Doback, Brennan Huff (both characters in Step Brothers)
IF YOU WEREN'T A CRICKETER? I would start a business called Prestige Worldwide
UNUSUAL OBJECT AT HOME? A samurai sword signed by Randy Jackson
DESERT ISLAND DISC? Vanilla Ice – Ice Ice Baby
FANTASY SLIP CORDON? Keeper: Me, 1st: The Rock, 2nd: John Cena, 3rd: The Undertaker, 4th: Triple H, Gully: Randy Orton (so he can come out of nowhere)
TWITTER: @tomkohlercadmor

Batting	Mat	Inns	NO	Runs	HS	Ave	SR	100	50	Ct	St
First-class	33	55	4	1521	169	29.82	54.45	3	8	43	0
List A	23	22	0	527	119	23.95	74.54	1	1	5	0
Twenty20	38	38	2	915	127	25.41	138.63	1	5	23	0
Bowling	Mat	Balls	Runs	Wkts	BBI	BBM	Ave	Econ	SR	5w	10
First-class	33	-	-	-	-	-	-	-	-	-	-
List A	23	-	-	-	-	-	-	-	-	-	-
Twenty20	38	-	-	-	-	-	-	-	-	-	-

FULL NAME: Daniel John Lamb
BORN: September 7, 1995, Preston, Lancashire
SQUAD NO: 26
HEIGHT: 6ft 4in
NICKNAME: Lamby, Frank the Tank, The Shermanator
EDUCATION: St Michael's CofE High School, Chorley; Cardinal Newman College, Preston; Edgehill University
TEAMS: Cheshire, Lancashire 2nd XI
ROLE: Allrounder
DEBUT: Yet to make first-team debut

LANCASHIRE

FAMILY TIES? My younger sister Emma plays for Lancashire and we have played together regularly for Bramhall in the Cheshire Premier League
STRANGEST THING SEEN IN A GAME? Burning firework factory stopped play
BEST MOMENT IN CRICKET? Winning the second XI one-day competition with Lancashire in 2016
SUPERSTITIONS? Starbucks vanilla latte before a game
BEST PLAYER IN COUNTY CRICKET? Haseeb Hameed (Lan)
CRICKETING HEROES? Andrew Flintoff
NON-CRICKETING HEROES? Conor McGregor
IF YOU WEREN'T A CRICKETER? I'd be trying to be a professional footballer
SURPRISING FACT? I was Blackburn Rovers FC Academy goalkeeper from U9 to U16 level
FANTASY SLIP CORDON? Keeper: Conor McGregor, 1st: Brad Friedel, 2nd: Raymond Reddington, 3rd: Peter Kay, 4th: Will Ferrell, Gully: Me
TWITTER: @lamby236

MATT LAMB

RHB / RM / RO / WO

WARWICKSHIRE

FULL NAME: Matthew Lamb
BORN: July 19, 1996, Wolverhampton, Staffordshire
SQUAD NO: 7
HEIGHT: 6ft 3in
NICKNAME: Lamby
EDUCATION: North Bromsgrove High School
TEAMS: Warwickshire
ROLE: Batsman
DEBUT: First-class: 2016

BEST BATTING: 1 Warwickshire vs Somerset, Taunton, 2016

FAMILY TIES? My grandad and dad didn't have any interest in cricket. It was my brother who was the only one who played and subsequently got me involved
BEST MOMENT IN CRICKET? Scoring 200 and 167 in one game for Warwickshire Second XI
HOW WOULD YOUR TEAM-MATES DESCRIBE YOU IN THREE WORDS? Quiet, unassuming, chilled
BEST PLAYER IN COUNTY CRICKET? Kumar Sangakkara (Sur)
MOST UNDERRATED PLAYER IN COUNTY CRICKET? Keith Barker (War)
TIP FOR THE TOP? Paul Coughlin (Dur), Joe Clarke (Wor), Sam Hain (War)
CRICKETING HEROES? Andrew Flintoff – he could make things happen from nowhere
NON-CRICKETING HEROES? Steve Bull, Jonny Wilkinson
IF YOU WEREN'T A CRICKETER? I'd be a professional surfer or a plumber
SURPRISING FACT? I was about to quit cricket until I was luckily selected for a second XI game against Worcester in September 2015 and managed to score 142
DESERT ISLAND DISC? The Weeknd – Trilogy
FANTASY SLIP CORDON? Keeper: Emma Watson (she is a dream), 1st: Kevin Hart (he's very funny), 2nd: Jacques Kallis (he's one of my favourite cricketers), 3rd: Justin Bieber (he's a proper geezer)
TWITTER: @Lamb_Matt

Batting	Mat	Inns	NO	Runs	HS	Ave	SR	100	50	Ct	St
First-class	1	2	0	2	1	1.00	15.38	0	0	0	0

Bowling	Mat	Balls	Runs	Wkts	BBI	BBM	Ave	Econ	SR	5w	10
First-class	1	-	-	-	-	-	-	-	-	-	-

TOM LATHAM — LHB / RM / WK / R0 / W0

FULL NAME: Thomas William Maxwell Latham
BORN: April 2, 1992, Christchurch, New Zealand
SQUAD NO: 48
HEIGHT: 5ft 6in
EDUCATION: Christchurch Boys' High School; Lincoln University, Christchurch
TEAMS: New Zealand, Durham, Canterbury, Kent, Scotland, South Island
ROLE: Batsman/wicketkeeper
DEBUT: Test: 2014; ODI: 2012; T20I: 2012; First-class: 2010; List A: 2011; T20: 2012

BEST BATTING: 261 Canterbury vs Central Districs, Napier, 2014
BEST BOWLING: 1-7 New Zealanders vs Cricket Australia XI, Sydney, 2015

FAMILY TIES? My father Rod played cricket for New Zealand in the 1990s
BEST MOMENT IN CRICKET? Making my debut for New Zealand in all three forms
BEST PLAYER IN COUNTY CRICKET? Jeetan Patel (War)
HOW WOULD YOUR TEAM-MATES DESCRIBE YOU IN THREE WORDS? Hard-working, team-first, easy-going
CRICKETING HEROES? Mike Hussey – fellow left-hand top-order batter, always enjoyed how he played and loved cricket so much. Brendon McCullum – admired the way he went out and smashed the ball everywhere, and he was an opening batsman-wicketkeeper like me
IF YOU WEREN'T A CRICKETER? I'd be a builder
TWITTER: @tomlatham2

Batting	Mat	Inns	NO	Runs	HS	Ave	SR	100	50	Ct	St
Tests	30	56	2	2150	177	39.81	46.61	6	12	30	0
ODIs	54	53	7	1367	137	29.71	79.01	2	6	31	4
T20Is	12	9	0	124	26	13.77	102.47	0	0	3	0
First-class	78	138	10	5332	261	41.65	50.54	10	35	94	1
List A	107	100	11	2969	137	33.35	82.47	4	15	74	8
Twenty20	52	43	2	968	82	23.60	127.87	0	5	14	2

Bowling	Mat	Balls	Runs	Wkts	BBI	BBM	Ave	Econ	SR	5w	10
Tests	30	-	-	-	-	-	-	-	-	-	-
ODIs	54	-	-	-	-	-	-	-	-	-	-
T20Is	12	-	-	-	-	-	-	-	-	-	-
First-class	78	26	18	1	1/7	1/7	18.00	4.15	26.0	0	0
List A	107	-	-	-	-	-	-	-	-	-	-
Twenty20	52	-	-	-	-	-	-	-	-	-	-

JEREMY LAWLOR

RHB / OB / R0 / W0

FULL NAME: Jeremy Lloyd Lawlor
BORN: November 4, 1995, Cardiff, Wales
SQUAD NO: 6
HEIGHT: 6ft
NICKNAME: Jez, King
EDUCATION: The Cathedral School, Llandaff;
Cardiff Metropolitan University
TEAMS: Glamorgan
ROLE: Batsman
DEBUT: First-class: 2015

BEST BATTING: 81 Cardiff MCCU vs Hampshire, Southampton, 2016

WHAT FIRST GOT YOU INTO CRICKET? My dad, Peter, taking me down to our local club,
St Fagans CC
FAMILY TIES? My dad played for Glamorgan
SUPERSTITIONS? Always have to touch the crease at the end of an over
HOW WOULD YOUR TEAM-MATES DESCRIBE YOU IN THREE WORDS? Very, very relaxed
TIP FOR THE TOP? Jack Murphy (Gla)
CRICKETING HEROES? Sachin Tendulkar, AB de Villiers
NON-CRICKETING HEROES? Conor McGregor
IF YOU WEREN'T A CRICKETER? I'd be a businessman
DESERT ISLAND DISC? Avicii – Levels

Batting	Mat	Inns	NO	Runs	HS	Ave	SR	100	50	Ct	St
First-class	4	6	1	194	81	38.80	50.00	0	2	2	0

Bowling	Mat	Balls	Runs	Wkts	BBI	BBM	Ave	Econ	SR	5w	10
First-class	4	72	49	0	-	-	-	4.08	-	0	0

DAN LAWRENCE

RHB / OB / R0 / W0

FULL NAME: Daniel William Lawrence
BORN: July 12, 1997, Whipps Cross, Essex
SQUAD NO: 28
EDUCATION: Trinity Catholic High School, London
TEAMS: Essex
ROLE: Batsman
DEBUT: First-class: 2015; List A: 2016; T20: 2015

ESSEX

BEST BATTING: 161 Essex vs Surrey, The Oval, 2015
BEST BOWLING: 1-5 Essex vs Kent, Chelmsford, 2016

FAMILY TIES? My dad is the groundsman at Chingford CC. My great uncle played for England
CRICKETING HEROES? Ricky Ponting, Graeme Smith, AB de Villiers
NON-CRICKETING HEROES? Martin Luther King, David Beckham
DESERT ISLAND DISC? Red Hot Chili Peppers – Dani California
FANTASY SLIP CORDON? Keeper: Sheldon Cooper, 1st: The Rock, 2nd: Rafael Nadal, 3rd: Me, Gully: Viv Richards
TWITTER: @Lawrenc28Daniel

Batting	Mat	Inns	NO	Runs	HS	Ave	SR	100	50	Ct	St
First-class	24	36	3	1479	161	44.81	58.36	4	7	21	0
List A	8	7	0	93	35	13.28	76.22	0	0	4	0
Twenty20	16	13	3	232	36	23.20	118.36	0	0	6	0

Bowling	Mat	Balls	Runs	Wkts	BBI	BBM	Ave	Econ	SR	5w	10
First-class	24	150	129	3	1/5	1/16	43.00	5.16	50.0	0	0
List A	8	276	255	6	3/35	3/35	42.50	5.54	46.0	0	0
Twenty20	16	156	185	10	2/11	2/11	18.50	7.11	15.6	0	0

JACK LEACH

LHB / SLA / RO / W1 / MVP64

SOMERSET

FULL NAME: Matthew Jack Leach
BORN: June 22, 1991, Taunton, Somerset
SQUAD NO: 17
HEIGHT: 6ft
NICKNAME: Nut, Nutter
EDUCATION: Bishop Fox's Community School; Richard Huish College; Cardiff Metropolitan University
TEAMS: Somerset, England Lions
ROLE: Bowler
DEBUT: First-class: 2012; List A: 2012

BEST BATTING: 43 Somerset vs Yorkshire, Headingley, 2014
BEST BOWLING: 7-106 Somerset vs Warwickshire, Taunton, 2015

WHAT FIRST GOT YOU INTO CRICKET? Watching Somerset from a young age
STRANGEST THING SEEN IN A GAME? Marcus Trescothick offering some banter
BEST MOMENT IN CRICKET? Being involved in a last-wicket partnership with Tim Groenewald to beat Surrey in the County Championship
HOW WOULD YOUR TEAM-MATES DESCRIBE YOU IN THREE WORDS? What a nut
BEST PLAYER IN COUNTY CRICKET? Jeetan Patel (War)
MOST UNDERRATED PLAYER IN COUNTY CRICKET? James Hildreth (Som)
TIP FOR THE TOP? Tom Abell (Som)
CRICKETING HEROES? It pains me to say this but it used to be Marcus Trescothick! Now it's Jos Buttler – I like how he keeps his nut down and gets on with it
NON-CRICKETING HEROES? Terry Tibbs from Fonejacker
IF YOU WEREN'T A CRICKETER? I'd work at Sainsbury's
SURPRISING FACT? I wrote a letter to Marcus Trescothick asking for advice when I was about 10 years old. He sent me a long reply and I still have the letter. What a man
UNUSUAL OBJECT AT HOME? Give me a chance – I'm just about to move in
DESERT ISLAND DISC? Coldplay (any album)
TWITTER: @jackleach1991

Batting	Mat	Inns	NO	Runs	HS	Ave	SR	100	50	Ct	St
First-class	35	40	12	321	43	11.46	32.22	0	0	10	0
List A	16	5	2	22	18	7.33	44.00	0	0	9	0

Bowling	Mat	Balls	Runs	Wkts	BBI	BBM	Ave	Econ	SR	5w	10
First-class	35	6548	2928	112	7/106	11/180	26.14	2.68	58.4	7	1
List A	16	824	641	21	3/7	3/7	30.52	4.66	39.2	0	0

JOE LEACH

RHB / RFM / R0 / W2 / MVP4

FULL NAME: Joseph Leach
BORN: October 30, 1990, Stafford
SQUAD NO: 23
HEIGHT: 6ft
NICKNAME: Leachy, Lusty SSSB
EDUCATION: Shrewsbury School;
University of Leeds
TEAMS: Worcestershire
ROLE: Allrounder
DEBUT: First-class: 2012; List A: 2012;
T20: 2013

WORCESTERSHIRE

BEST BATTING: 114 Worcestershire vs Gloucestershire, Cheltenham, 2013
BEST BOWLING: 6-73 Worcestershire vs Warwickshire, Edgbaston, 2015
COUNTY CAP: 2012

FAMILY TIES? Brother (Steve) has played for Oxford MCCU and is captain of Shropshire CCC
STRANGEST THING SEEN IN A GAME? A swan come off the River Severn at New Road before flying at head height around the 30-yard discs (marking the inner ring) for three laps
BEST MOMENT IN CRICKET? Taking a hat-trick with the first three balls of our one-day game with Northants in 2015. But it was bitter-sweet – we still managed to lose the game
HOW WOULD YOUR TEAM-MATES DESCRIBE YOU IN THREE WORDS? Silverspoon, sweaty, belly
MOST UNDERRATED PLAYER IN COUNTY CRICKET? Wayne Madsen (Der)
TIP FOR THE TOP? Joe Clarke, Tom Fell, Ed Barnard (all Wor)
CRICKETING HEROES? Jacques Kallis – one of the greatest cricketers to have played the game. He always found a way to contribute to the team
UNUSUAL OBJECT AT HOME? A garden gnome painted in Wolves colours and with Steve Bull's name on the back
TWITTER: @joeleach230

Batting	Mat	Inns	NO	Runs	HS	Ave	SR	100	50	Ct	St
First-class	56	83	10	2039	114	27.93	61.48	2	14	13	0
List A	22	17	5	388	63	32.33	103.46	0	1	7	0
Twenty20	38	23	7	213	20	13.31	119.66	0	0	6	0

Bowling	Mat	Balls	Runs	Wkts	BBI	BBM	Ave	Econ	SR	5w	10
First-class	56	8359	5134	177	6/73	9/109	29.00	3.68	47.2	8	0
List A	22	954	907	24	4/30	4/30	37.79	5.70	39.7	0	0
Twenty20	38	654	972	46	5/33	5/33	21.13	8.91	14.2	1	0

JACK LEANING

RHB / RM / R0 / W0

YORKSHIRE

FULL NAME: Jack Andrew Leaning
BORN: October 18, 1993, Bristol
SQUAD NO: 34
HEIGHT: 6ft
EDUCATION: Archbishop Holgate's School, York; York College
TEAMS: Yorkshire
ROLE: Batsman
DEBUT: First-class: 2013; List A: 2012; T20: 2013

BEST BATTING: 123 Yorkshire vs Somerset, Taunton, 2015
BEST BOWLING: 2-30 Yorkshire vs MCC, Abu Dhabi, 2016
COUNTY CAP: 2016

TWITTER: @JackLeaning1
NOTES: Son of former York City goalkeeper Andy, Leaning wrote himself into the Yorkshire record books when he hit an unbeaten 164 for the county's U14 side against Cheshire. He was Yorkshire's Academy Player of the Year in 2012 and made his List A debut in the same season. He made his first-class debut in 2013 against Surrey at Headingley and played 10 Championship matches in 2014, top-scoring with 99. Made his maiden Championship century in 2015 and added two more as he compiled 922 runs. Struggled in 2016, with just 233 runs in 15 Championship innings

Batting	Mat	Inns	NO	Runs	HS	Ave	SR	100	50	Ct	St
First-class	40	63	7	1751	123	31.26	44.71	3	8	33	0
List A	32	28	6	786	131*	35.72	86.27	2	4	13	0
Twenty20	30	28	7	624	64	29.71	134.48	0	2	10	0

Bowling	Mat	Balls	Runs	Wkts	BBI	BBM	Ave	Econ	SR	5w	10
First-class	40	304	244	3	2/30	2/30	81.33	4.81	101.3	0	0
List A	32	156	141	7	5/22	5/22	20.14	5.42	22.2	1	0
Twenty20	30	12	30	0	-	-	-	15.00	-	0	0

MICHAEL LEASK   RHB / OB / R0 / W0

FULL NAME: Michael Alexander Leask
BORN: October 29, 1990, Aberdeen, Scotland
SQUAD NO: 29
HEIGHT: 6ft 2in
NICKNAME: Leasky, Noise
EDUCATION: Dyce Academy, Aberdeen
TEAMS: Scotland, Somerset, Northamptonshire
ROLE: Allrounder
DEBUT: ODI: 2014; T20I: 2013; List A: 2013; T20: 2013

SOMERSET

FAMILY TIES? My dad has played at club level for about 40 years
STRANGEST THING SEEN IN A GAME? A bird struck in mid-air by the ball
BEST MOMENT IN CRICKET? My 60 off 40 balls in the semi-final of the World Cup qualifiers in 2014 against Netherlands
HOW WOULD YOUR TEAM-MATES DESCRIBE YOU IN THREE WORDS? Loud, hyper, fun
MOST UNDERRATED PLAYER IN COUNTY CRICKET? Jack Leach (Som)
TIP FOR THE TOP? Tom Abell (Som)
CRICKETING HEROES? Jacques Kallis, Virat Kohli
NON-CRICKETING HEROES? Muhammad Ali
IF YOU WEREN'T A CRICKETER? I worked in the banking industry for five years before becoming a professional cricketer
UNUSUAL OBJECT AT HOME? A slow cooker
DESERT ISLAND DISC? U2 – U218 Singles
FANTASY SLIP CORDON? Keeper: Adam Gilchrist, 1st: Me, 2nd: Keith Lemon, 3rd: Stephen Fry, Gully: David Attenborough
TWITTER: @leasky29

Batting	Mat	Inns	NO	Runs	HS	Ave	SR	100	50	Ct	St
ODIs	16	13	1	215	50	17.91	105.91	0	1	6	0
T20Is	14	9	0	102	58	11.33	106.25	0	1	6	0
List A	34	26	1	328	50	13.12	101.23	0	1	9	0
Twenty20	24	17	2	196	58	13.06	126.45	0	1	10	0

Bowling	Mat	Balls	Runs	Wkts	BBI	BBM	Ave	Econ	SR	5w	10
ODIs	16	368	387	3	1/26	1/26	129.00	6.30	122.6	0	0
T20Is	14	186	217	12	3/20	3/20	18.08	7.00	15.5	0	0
List A	34	787	823	12	2/23	2/23	68.58	6.27	65.5	0	0
Twenty20	24	216	241	14	3/20	3/20	17.21	6.69	15.4	0	0

ALEX LEES

LHB / LB / R2 / W0 / MVP27

FULL NAME: Alexander Zak Lees
BORN: April 14, 1993, Halifax, Yorkshire
SQUAD NO: 14
HEIGHT: 6ft 3in
NICKNAME: Leesy
EDUCATION: Holy Trinity Senior School, Halifax
TEAMS: Yorkshire, England Lions
ROLE: Batsman
DEBUT: First-class: 2010; List A: 2011; T20: 2013

BEST BATTING: 275* Yorkshire vs Derbyshire, Chesterfield, 2013
BEST BOWLING: 2-51 Yorkshire vs Middlesex, Lord's, 2016
COUNTY CAP: 2014

BEST MOMENT IN CRICKET? My 275 not out against Derbyshire in 2013
CRICKETING HEROES? Brian Lara and Matthew Hayden
IF YOU WEREN'T A CRICKETER? I'd be a policeman
SURPRISING FACT? I do a bit of magic on the side
DESERT ISLAND DISC? Drake (anything)
TWITTER: @aleesy14
NOTES: Yorkshire's leading runscorer in the Championship in 2016 (1,165 runs). Captained the side in limited-overs cricket last summer but hands over to Gary Ballance for 2017

Batting	Mat	Inns	NO	Runs	HS	Ave	SR	100	50	Ct	St
First-class	69	116	9	4104	275*	38.35	48.03	10	20	50	0
List A	41	38	2	1095	102	30.41	72.85	1	8	15	0
Twenty20	35	34	2	817	67*	25.53	121.94	0	4	12	0

Bowling	Mat	Balls	Runs	Wkts	BBI	BBM	Ave	Econ	SR	5w	10
First-class	69	54	77	2	2/51	2/51	38.50	8.55	27.0	0	0
List A	41	-	-	-	-	-	-	-	-	-	-
Twenty20	35	-	-	-	-	-	-	-	-	-	-

TOBY LESTER

LHB / LFM / R0 / W0

FULL NAME: Toby James Lester
BORN: April 5, 1993, Blackpool
SQUAD NO: 5
HEIGHT: 6ft 4 in
NICKNAME: Tobs
EDUCATION: Baines High School, Blackpool; Rossall School, Lancashire; Loughborough University
TEAMS: Lancashire
ROLE: Bowler
DEBUT: First-class: 2012

BEST BATTING: 2* Loughborough MCCU vs Sussex, Hove, 2014
BEST BOWLING: 3-50 Lancashire vs Essex, Old Trafford, 2015

TWITTER: @lobylester
NOTES: Left-arm pace bowler who made his first-class debut for Loughborough MCCU in 2014. Lester impressed with his performances in Lancashire's Second XI in 2015, earning him a call-up to the senior side for two matches and a Championship debut against Essex at Old Trafford. Played two more Championship matches in 2016 without taking a wicket

Batting	Mat	Inns	NO	Runs	HS	Ave	SR	100	50	Ct	St
First-class	10	11	7	6	2*	1.50	9.37	0	0	2	0
Bowling	Mat	Balls	Runs	Wkts	BBI	BBM	Ave	Econ	SR	5w	10
First-class	10	1278	821	9	3/50	3/73	91.22	3.85	142.0	0	0

RICHARD LEVI

RHB / R0 / W0

FULL NAME: Richard Ernst Levi
BORN: January 14, 1988, Johannesburg, South Africa
SQUAD NO: 88
HEIGHT: 6ft
EDUCATION: Wynberg Boys' High School, Cape Town; University of South Africa
TEAMS: South Africa, Northamptonshire, Cape Cobras, Mumbai Indians, Somerset, Western Province
ROLE: Batsman
DEBUT: T20I: 2012; First-class: 2006; List A: 2005; T20: 2008

BEST BATTING: 168 Northamptonshire vs Essex, Northampton, 2015

BEST MOMENT IN CRICKET? Making my debuts for my province, South Africa and Northants
CRICKETING HEROES? Gary Kirsten – worked hard to achieve what he did and still does to this day
NON-CRICKETING HEROES? My old man – did everything for me, no questions asked
IF YOU WEREN'T A CRICKETER? I'd be a lumberjack
SURPRISING FACT? I'm not that good at answering questionnaires
DESERT ISLAND DISC? John Mayer – Continuum
TWITTER: @RichardLevi88

Batting	Mat	Inns	NO	Runs	HS	Ave	SR	100	50	Ct	St
T20Is	13	13	2	236	117*	21.45	141.31	1	1	4	0
First-class	78	125	12	4278	168	37.85	65.91	8	26	57	0
List A	115	108	5	3842	166	37.30	105.86	7	23	37	0
Twenty20	174	166	11	4386	117*	28.29	143.85	3	29	49	0

Bowling	Mat	Balls	Runs	Wkts	BBI	BBM	Ave	Econ	SR	5w	10
T20Is	13	-	-	-	-	-	-	-	-	-	-
First-class	78	-	-	-	-	-	-	-	-	-	-
List A	115	-	-	-	-	-	-	-	-	-	-
Twenty20	174	-	-	-	-	-	-	-	-	-	-

JAKE LIBBY

RHB / OB / R0 / W0

FULL NAME: Jacob Daniel Libby
BORN: January 3, 1993, Plymouth, Devon
SQUAD NO: 2
HEIGHT: 5ft 8in
NICKNAME: Libs
EDUCATION: Plymouth College; Truro College, Cornwall; Cardiff Metropolitan University
TEAMS: Nottinghamshire, Northamptonshire
ROLE: Batsman
DEBUT: First-class: 2014

NOTTINGHAMSHIRE

BEST BATTING: 144 Nottinghamshire vs Durham, Chester-le-Street, 2016
BEST BOWLING: 1-13 Northamptonshire vs Leicestershire, Leicester, 2016

WHAT FIRST GOT YOU INTO CRICKET? My dad played for Looe CC and I played with him after his games on a Saturday
FAMILY TIES? My brother plays for and captains Callington CC in the Cornish Premier League
STRANGEST THING SEEN IN A GAME? A bowler tackle a batsman AFL-style as he took off for a single during my first game in Tasmania
SUPERSTITIONS? I always walk onto the pitch after my batting partner
HOW WOULD YOUR TEAM-MATES DESCRIBE YOU IN THREE WORDS? Sarcastic, energetic, calm
BEST PLAYER IN COUNTY CRICKET? Ben Duckett (Nor)
MOST UNDERRATED PLAYER IN COUNTY CRICKET? Brett Hutton (Not)
TIP FOR THE TOP? Ben Kitt (Not)
CRICKETING HEROES? Sachin Tendulkar, Marcus Trescothick, Ricky Ponting
NON-CRICKETING HEROES? The Rock
IF YOU WEREN'T A CRICKETER? I'd love to be a pilot but I am not a great flyer
SURPRISING FACT? I played the lead role in all the school plays
UNUSUAL OBJECT AT HOME? A giant Minion teddy
DESERT ISLAND DISC? ABBA – Mamma Mia
TWITTER: @JakeLibby1

Batting	Mat	Inns	NO	Runs	HS	Ave	SR	100	50	Ct	St
First-class	21	37	2	1158	144	33.08	41.37	3	5	5	0

Bowling	Mat	Balls	Runs	Wkts	BBI	BBM	Ave	Econ	SR	5w	10
First-class	21	305	183	3	1/13	1/22	61.00	3.60	101.6	0	0

CHRIS LIDDLE

RHB / LMF / R0 / W0

FULL NAME: Christopher John Liddle
BORN: February 1, 1984, Middlesbrough, Yorkshire
SQUAD NO: 23
HEIGHT: 6ft 4in
NICKNAME: Lids
EDUCATION: Nunthorpe Comprehensive, Middlesborough; Teeside Tertiary College
TEAMS: Gloucestershire, Dhaka Gladiators, Leicestershire, Sussex
ROLE: Bowler
DEBUT: First-class: 2005; List A: 2006; T20: 2008

BEST BATTING: 53 Sussex vs Worcestershire, Hove, 2007
BEST BOWLING: 3-42 Leicestershire vs Somerset, Leicester, 2006

FAMILY TIES? My brother Andrew plays in the North Yorkshire and South Durham League
BEST MOMENT IN CRICKET? My five-wicket haul in T20 cricket
HOW WOULD YOUR TEAM-MATES DESCRIBE YOU IN THREE WORDS? Very laid-back
BEST PLAYER IN COUNTY CRICKET? Tim Bresnan (Yor)
MOST UNDERRATED PLAYER IN COUNTY CRICKET? Ben Brown (Sus)
TIP FOR THE TOP? Miles Hammond (Glo)
CRICKETING HEROES? Darren Gough, Ryan Sidebottom
NON-CRICKETING HEROES? Jamie Redknapp
IF YOU WEREN'T A CRICKETER? I'd be working off-shore on an oil or gas rig
SURPRISING FACT? I occasionally DJ for friends
DESERT ISLAND DISC? Nas – Get Down
FANTASY SLIP CORDON? Keeper: James Corden, 1st: Dan Bilzerian, 2nd: Jamie Redknapp, 3rd: Me, Gully: Conor McGregor
TWITTER: @chrisliddle11

Batting	Mat	Inns	NO	Runs	HS	Ave	SR	100	50	Ct	St
First-class	25	25	13	143	53	11.91	45.25	0	1	7	0
List A	63	25	7	119	18	6.61	73.45	0	0	18	0
Twenty20	76	16	9	54	16	7.71	71.05	0	0	20	0

Bowling	Mat	Balls	Runs	Wkts	BBI	BBM	Ave	Econ	SR	5w	10
First-class	25	3117	1736	34	3/42	4/82	51.05	3.34	91.6	0	0
List A	63	2363	2309	79	5/18	5/18	29.22	5.86	29.9	1	0
Twenty20	76	1459	1995	82	5/17	5/17	24.32	8.20	17.7	1	0

ARRON LILLEY

RHB / OB / R0 / W0

FULL NAME: Arron Mark Lilley
BORN: April 1, 1991, Tameside, Lancashire
SQUAD NO: 19
HEIGHT: 6ft 2in
NICKNAME: The Bigshow, Lill, Azza
EDUCATION: Mossley Hollins High School, Tameside; Ashton Sixth Form
TEAMS: Lancashire
ROLE: Bowler
DEBUT: First-class: 2013; List A: 2012; T20: 2013

LANCASHIRE

BEST BATTING: 63 Lancashire vs Derbyshire, Southport, 2015
BEST BOWLING: 5-23 Lancashire vs Derbyshire, Southport, 2015

STRANGEST THING SEEN IN A GAME? Liam Livingstone trying to throw the stumps down from slip and hitting Steven Croft on the back of the knee
BEST MOMENT IN CRICKET? Winning the T20 Blast with Lancashire in 2015
HOW WOULD YOUR TEAM-MATES DESCRIBE YOU IN THREE WORDS? Confident, loud, aggressive
BEST PLAYER IN COUNTY CRICKET? Haseeb Hameed (Lan)
TIP FOR THE TOP? Joe Clarke (Wor), Liam Livingstone, Alex Davies (both Lan)
CRICKETING HEROES? Shane Warne, Graeme Swann, Andrew Flintoff
NON-CRICKETING HEROES? Jim Carrey (funny guy), Paul Scholes (aka Sat Nav)
IF YOU WEREN'T A CRICKETER? I'd be a biomechanical scientist
UNUSUAL OBJECT AT HOME? A didgeridoo
DESERT ISLAND DISC? The Courteeners – You're Not 19 Forever
FANTASY SLIP CORDON? Keeper: Jack Whitehall, 1st: Michelle Keegan, 2nd: LeBron James, 3rd: Keith Lemon, 4th: Me, Gully: Pixie Lott
TWITTER: @Arronlilley20

Batting	Mat	Inns	NO	Runs	HS	Ave	SR	100	50	Ct	St
First-class	13	17	5	398	63	33.16	94.31	0	2	4	0
List A	11	4	1	20	10	6.66	111.11	0	0	5	0
Twenty20	43	18	7	76	22*	6.90	135.71	0	0	20	0

Bowling	Mat	Balls	Runs	Wkts	BBI	BBM	Ave	Econ	SR	5w	10
First-class	13	2454	1296	36	5/23	6/151	36.00	3.16	68.1	2	0
List A	11	372	321	15	4/30	4/30	21.40	5.17	24.8	0	0
Twenty20	43	759	903	34	3/31	3/31	26.55	7.13	22.3	0	0

LIAM LIVINGSTONE RHB / LB&OB / R0 / W0 / MVP83

LANCASHIRE

FULL NAME: Liam Stephen Livingstone
BORN: August 4, 1993, Barrow-in-Furness, Cumbria
SQUAD NO: 7
HEIGHT: 6ft 2in
NICKNAME: Livvy, Livvo
EDUCATION: Chetwynde School, Barrow-in-Furness
TEAMS: Lancashire, England Lions
ROLE: Batsman
DEBUT: First-class: 2016; List A: 2015; T20: 2015

BEST BATTING: 140* England Lions vs Sri Lanka A, Dambulla, 2017
BEST BOWLING: 1-19 Lancashire vs Hampshire, Old Trafford, 2016

WHAT FIRST GOT YOU INTO CRICKET? Playing on the outfield at Barrow CC from a very early age
FAMILY TIES? Father and brother played low-level club cricket
BEST MOMENT IN CRICKET? Winning the NatWest T20 Blast in 2015
HOW WOULD YOUR TEAM-MATES DESCRIBE YOU IN THREE WORDS? Maverick, sociable, outgoing
SUPERSTITIONS? Left foot onto the pitch first
BEST PLAYER IN COUNTY CRICKET? Joe Root (Yor)
TIP FOR THE TOP? Mason Crane (Ham)
CRICKETING HEROES? Andrew Flintoff – so good to watch as a young kid. Shane Warne – I was a leg-spinner growing up
NON-CRICKETING HEROES? David Beckham
SURPRISING FACT? I scored 350 in a club game
DESERT ISLAND DISC? One Direction – Greatest Hits
TWITTER: @liaml4893

Batting	Mat	Inns	NO	Runs	HS	Ave	SR	100	50	Ct	St
First-class	18	29	8	1145	140*	54.52	59.88	4	7	31	0
List A	21	16	1	545	98	36.33	90.98	0	4	8	0
Twenty20	28	24	4	384	55	19.20	131.95	0	1	8	0

Bowling	Mat	Balls	Runs	Wkts	BBI	BBM	Ave	Econ	SR	5w	10
First-class	18	384	230	2	1/19	1/19	115.00	3.59	192.0	0	0
List A	21	402	312	11	3/51	3/51	28.36	4.65	36.5	0	0
Twenty20	28	12	9	1	1/9	1/9	9.00	4.50	12.0	0	0

DAVID LLOYD

RHB / OB / R0 / W0

FULL NAME: David Liam Lloyd
BORN: June 15, 1992, St Asaph, Denbighshire, Wales
SQUAD NO: 14
HEIGHT: 6ft
NICKNAME: Ram
EDUCATION: Darland High School, Wrexham; Shrewsbury School
TEAMS: Glamorgan
ROLE: Batsman
DEBUT: First-class: 2012; List A: 2014; T20: 2014

BEST BATTING: 107 Glamorgan vs Kent, Canterbury, 2016
BEST BOWLING: 3-36 Glamorgan vs Northamptonshire, Swansea, 2016

FAMILY TIES? My father and both of my uncles played local cricket and represented Wales Minor Counties
BEST MOMENT IN CRICKET? Scoring my maiden first-class hundred in 2016
HOW WOULD YOUR TEAM-MATES DESCRIBE YOU IN THREE WORDS? Funny, ginger, swiller
MOST UNDERRATED PLAYER IN COUNTY CRICKET? William Bragg (Gla)
TIP FOR THE TOP? Lukas Carey (Gla)
CRICKETING HEROES? Jacques Kallis and Brendon McCullum – both like to play attacking cricket and are great to watch
NON-CRICKETING HEROES? Usain Bolt – trains hard but still has a smile on his face
IF YOU WEREN'T A CRICKETER? I'd be a brewer or solicitor
SURPRISING FACT? I have a degree in Economics
DESERT ISLAND DISC? Tina Turner – Greatest Hits
FANTASY SLIP CORDON? Keeper: Ray Donovan, 1st: Gareth Bale, 2nd: Homer Simpson, 3rd: Me, Gully: Ray Cropper
TWITTER: @lloyddl2010

Batting	Mat	Inns	NO	Runs	HS	Ave	SR	100	50	Ct	St
First-class	36	59	8	1515	107	29.70	62.50	3	5	11	0
List A	22	16	1	342	65	22.80	89.76	0	2	4	0
Twenty20	25	21	1	435	97*	21.75	125.36	0	2	9	0

Bowling	Mat	Balls	Runs	Wkts	BBI	BBM	Ave	Econ	SR	5w	10
First-class	36	2469	1691	36	3/36	3/53	46.97	4.10	68.5	0	0
List A	22	391	368	9	4/10	4/10	40.88	5.64	43.4	0	0
Twenty20	25	24	44	3	2/13	2/13	14.66	11.00	8.0	0	0

MICHAEL LUMB

LHB / RM / R3 / W0 / MVP65

FULL NAME: Michael John Lumb
BORN: February 12, 1980, Johannesburg, South Africa
SQUAD NO: 45
HEIGHT: 6ft
EDUCATION: St Stithians College, Johannesburg
TEAMS: England, Nottinghamshire, Deccan Chargers, Hampshire, Queensland, Rajasthan Royals, Sydney Sixers, Yorkshire
ROLE: Batsman
DEBUT: ODI: 2014; T20I: 2010; First-class: 2000; List A: 2001; T20: 2003

BEST BATTING: 221* Nottinghamshire vs Derbyshire, Trent Bridge, 2013
BEST BOWLING: 2-10 Yorkshire vs Kent, Canterbury, 2001
COUNTY CAPS: 2003 (Yorkshire); 2008 (Hampshire); 2012 (Nottinghamshire)

FAMILY TIES? My father Richard played for Yorkshire and my uncle Tich played for Natal and South Africa
BEST MOMENT IN CRICKET? Playing for England and winning the World T20 in the Caribbean, beating the Aussies in the final
SUPERSTITIONS? Too many to mention – they call me Rain Man
CRICKETING HEROES? Graham Thorpe, Darren Lehmann, Stephen Fleming, Craig White, Shane Warne, Jacques Kallis
NON-CRICKETING HEROES? Nelson Mandela
IF YOU WEREN'T A CRICKETER? I'd be a game ranger

Batting	Mat	Inns	NO	Runs	HS	Ave	SR	100	50	Ct	St
ODIs	3	3	0	165	106	55.00	81.28	1	0	1	0
T20Is	27	27	1	552	63	21.23	133.65	0	3	8	0
First-class	202	343	18	11151	221*	34.31		20	58	116	0
List A	210	203	11	6312	184	32.87	86.77	7	43	70	0
Twenty20	219	217	12	4955	124*	24.17	138.02	1	26	69	0

Bowling	Mat	Balls	Runs	Wkts	BBI	BBM	Ave	Econ	SR	5w	10
ODIs	3	-	-	-	-	-	-	-	-	-	-
T20Is	27	-	-	-	-	-	-	-	-	-	-
First-class	202	330	255	6	2/10		42.50	4.63	55.0	0	0
List A	210	12	28	0	-	-	-	14.00	-	0	0
Twenty20	219	36	65	3	3/32	3/32	21.66	10.83	12.0	0	0

ADAM LYTH

LHB / OB / R3 / W0 / MVP6

FULL NAME: Adam Lyth
BORN: September 25, 1987, Whitby, Yorkshire
SQUAD NO: 9
HEIGHT: 5ft 9in
NICKNAME: Lythy, Budge, Peanut
EDUCATION: Caedmon School; Whitby Community School
TEAMS: England, Yorkshire
ROLE: Batsman
DEBUT: Test: 2015; First-class: 2007; List A: 2006; T20: 2008

BEST BATTING: 251 Yorkshire vs Lancashire, Old Trafford, 2014
BEST BOWLING: 2-9 Yorkshire vs Middlesex, Scarborough, 2016
COUNTY CAP: 2010

FAMILY TIES? My brother and dad played for Scarborough and my grandad played for Whitby
CRICKETING HEROES? Graham Thorpe – I just liked the way he batted
IF YOU WEREN'T A CRICKETER? I'd be playing football
SURPRISING FACT? I had trials with Manchester City before choosing cricket
DESERT ISLAND DISC? Rod Stewart (any album)
FANTASY SLIP CORDON? Keeper: Lee Evans, 1st: David Beckham, 2nd: Tiger Woods, 3rd: Me, Gully: Mila Kunis
TWITTER: @lythy09

Batting	Mat	Inns	NO	Runs	HS	Ave	SR	100	50	Ct	St
Tests	7	13	0	265	107	20.38	50.09	1	0	8	0
First-class	133	219	10	8397	251	40.17		20	46	166	0
List A	97	90	7	2827	136	34.06	91.96	3	13	41	0
Twenty20	73	64	2	1251	87	20.17	129.36	0	4	35	0

Bowling	Mat	Balls	Runs	Wkts	BBI	BBM	Ave	Econ	SR	5w	10
Tests	7	6	0	0	-	-	-	0.00	-	0	0
First-class	133	1796	1115	26	2/9	2/9	42.88	3.72	69.0	0	0
List A	97	204	217	3	1/6	1/6	72.33	6.38	68.0	0	0
Twenty20	73	78	88	4	2/5	2/5	22.00	6.76	19.5	0	0

CHARLIE MACDONELL

DERBYSHIRE

RHB / **OB** / **R0** / **W0**

FULL NAME: Charles Michael MacDonell
BORN: February 23, 1995, Basingstoke, Hampshire
SQUAD NO: 3
HEIGHT: 5ft 9in
NICKNAME: Cmac
EDUCATION: Wellingborough School, Northampton; Durham University
TEAMS: Derbyshire
ROLE: Batsman
DEBUT: First-class: 2015; List A: 2016

BEST BATTING: 91 Durham MCCU vs Gloucestershire, Bristol, 2016

WHAT FIRST GOT YOU INTO CRICKET? It was on the TV and I was taken to Horton House CC aged six
STRANGEST THING SEEN IN A GAME? A drunk man coming onto the pitch to give advice to the players at a Durham MCCU game – he thought he was watching Durham CCC
BEST MOMENT IN CRICKET? Scoring a hundred for Durham MCCU against Warwickshire at Edgbaston in 2015
HOW WOULD YOUR TEAM-MATES DESCRIBE YOU IN THREE WORDS? Unique, different, driven
BEST PLAYER IN COUNTY CRICKET? Ben Duckett (Nor)
MOST UNDERRATED PLAYER IN COUNTY CRICKET? Greg Cork (Der)
TIP FOR THE TOP? Joe Clarke (Wor)
CRICKETING HEROES? AB de Villiers, Ravi Ashwin
NON-CRICKETING HEROES? Roger Federer, Will Smith, Muhammad Ali
SURPRISING FACT? I was a model for the Collingwood College Fashion Show at university
UNUSUAL OBJECT AT HOME? Gravity boots
DESERT ISLAND DISC? Radical Something (featuring Kinetics) – Be Easy

Batting	Mat	Inns	NO	Runs	HS	Ave	SR	100	50	Ct	St
First-class	5	8	2	299	91	49.83	47.76	0	2	1	0
List A	1	1	0	19	19	19.00	59.37	0	0	0	0

Bowling	Mat	Balls	Runs	Wkts	BBI	BBM	Ave	Econ	SR	5w	10
First-class	5	336	248	0	-	-	-	4.42	-	0	0
List A	1	-	-	-	-	-	-	-	-	-	-

MATT MACHAN

LHB / OB / R0 / W0 / MVP87

FULL NAME: Matthew William Machan
BORN: February 15, 1991, Brighton
SQUAD NO: 15
HEIGHT: 5ft 9in
NICKNAME: Meatball, Mach
EDUCATION: Hurstpierpoint College; Brighton College
TEAMS: Scotland, Sussex
ROLE: Batsman
DEBUT: ODI: 2013; T20I: 2013; First-class: 2010; List A: 2010; T20: 2012

SUSSEX

BEST BATTING: 192 Sussex vs Somerset, Taunton, 2015
BEST BOWLING: 1-36 Scotland vs Australia A, Edinburgh, 2013

BEST MOMENT IN CRICKET? Going to the 2015 and 2016 World Cups and my maiden first-class hundred for Sussex
HOW WOULD YOUR TEAM-MATES DESCRIBE YOU IN THREE WORDS? Determined, outgoing, relaxed
BEST PLAYER IN COUNTY CRICKET? Tim Bresnan (Yor)
TIP FOR THE TOP? George Garton, Phil Salt (both Sus)
CRICKETING HEROES? Matthew Hayden
SURPRISING FACT? I have a season ticket at Brighton and Hove Albion
DESERT ISLAND DISC? Now 92
FANTASY SLIP CORDON? Keeper: Dan Bilzerian, 1st: Rihanna, 2nd: Micky Flanagan, 3rd: Me, Gully: James Corden
TWITTER: @Mattmachan

Batting	Mat	Inns	NO	Runs	HS	Ave	SR	100	50	Ct	St
ODIs	23	22	0	734	114	33.36	77.10	1	3	4	0
T20Is	13	13	3	407	67*	40.70	127.98	0	3	7	0
First-class	44	67	4	2089	192	33.15	68.37	5	6	18	0
List A	58	56	5	1810	126*	35.49	87.60	2	9	16	0
Twenty20	72	70	12	1570	90*	27.06	125.29	0	8	40	0

Bowling	Mat	Balls	Runs	Wkts	BBI	BBM	Ave	Econ	SR	5w	10
ODIs	23	402	384	9	3/31	3/31	42.66	5.73	44.6	0	0
T20Is	13	135	156	5	3/23	3/23	31.20	6.93	27.0	0	0
First-class	44	132	103	1	1/36	1/59	103.00	4.68	132.0	0	0
List A	58	640	621	12	3/31	3/31	51.75	5.82	53.3	0	0
Twenty20	72	249	309	9	3/23	3/23	34.33	7.44	27.6	0	0

WAYNE MADSEN
RHB / OB / R4 / W0 / MVP37

DERBYSHIRE

FULL NAME: Wayne Lee Madsen
BORN: January 2, 1984, Durban, South Africa
SQUAD NO: 77
HEIGHT: 5ft 11in
NICKNAME: Madders, Mads
EDUCATION: Highbury Preparatory School; Kearsney College; University of South Africa
TEAMS: Derbyshire, KwaZulu-Natal
ROLE: Batsman
DEBUT: First-class: 2004; List A: 2004; T20: 2010

BEST BATTING: 231* Derbyshire vs Northamptonshire, Northampton, 2012
BEST BOWLING: 3-45 KwaZulu-Natal vs Eastern Province, Port Elizabeth, 2008
COUNTY CAP: 2011

FAMILY TIES? My uncles, Trevor Madsen and Henry Fotheringham, represented South Africa. My other uncle, Mike Madsen, played for Natal and so did my cousin Greg Fotheringham
STRANGEST THING SEEN IN A GAME? Snow stopped play, Derbyshire vs Glamorgan, 2016
BEST MOMENT IN CRICKET? Lifting the Division Two trophy with Derbyshire in 2012. We were tipped to finish bottom at the start of the season
BEST PLAYER IN COUNTY CRICKET? James Hildreth (Som)
MOST UNDERRATED PLAYER IN COUNTY CRICKET? Tim Groenewald (Som)
TIP FOR THE TOP? Callum Parkinson (Lei), Will Davis, Harvey Hosein (both Der)
CRICKETING HEROES? Jonty Rhodes (for his energy), Dale Benkenstein (my first professional captain)
SURPRISING FACT? I hold the Guinness world record for cricket's version of keepy-uppies: the most bat touches in one minute (282)
UNUSUAL OBJECT AT HOME? Biltong maker
TWITTER: @waynemadsen2017

Batting	Mat	Inns	NO	Runs	HS	Ave	SR	100	50	Ct	St
First-class	143	255	22	9364	231*	40.18	49.63	25	46	124	0
List A	80	73	14	2390	138	40.50	86.03	3	15	54	0
Twenty20	72	70	11	1488	65	25.22	125.56	0	8	21	0

Bowling	Mat	Balls	Runs	Wkts	BBI	BBM	Ave	Econ	SR	5w	10
First-class	143	2106	1108	18	3/45		61.55	3.15	117.0	0	0
List A	80	204	153	9	3/27	3/27	17.00	4.50	22.6	0	0
Twenty20	72	60	73	3	1/7	1/7	24.33	7.30	20.0	0	0

STEVE MAGOFFIN

LHB / RFM / RO / W5 / MVP88

FULL NAME: Steven James Magoffin
BORN: December 17, 1979, Corinda, Queensland, Australia
SQUAD NO: 64
HEIGHT: 6ft 4in
NICKNAME: Mal
EDUCATION: Indooroopilly High School; Curtin University, Perth
TEAMS: Sussex, Queensland, Surrey, Western Australia, Worcestershire
ROLE: Bowler
DEBUT: First-class: 2004; List A: 2004; T20: 2006

BEST BATTING: 79 Western Australia vs Tasmania, Perth, 2008
BEST BOWLING: 8-20 Sussex vs Somerset, Horsham, 2013
COUNTY CAP: 2013 (Sussex)

FAMILY TIES? My older brother Chris played grade cricket in Brisbane
BEST MOMENT IN CRICKET? Hitting the winning runs in the 2011/12 Sheffield Shield final for the Queensland Bulls. Touring South Africa for the second Test of Australia's tour in 2009 – I didn't play but it was a great experience
CRICKETING HEROES? Curtly Ambrose, Glenn McGrath, Mike Hussey
NON-CRICKETING HEROES? Tiger Woods, Nathan Buckley (AFL player), Scott Pendlebury (AFL player)
IF YOU WEREN'T A CRICKETER? Not too sure – it's all I've done! But I'd love to be a chef
DESERT ISLAND DISC? Coldplay Live Tour 2012 or The 12th Man Box Set (very popular in Oz)
FANTASY SLIP CORDON? Keeper: Kramer (from Seinfeld), 1st: Me, 2nd: John Bishop, 3rd: Michael McIntyre, Gully: James Corden
TWITTER: @magsy64

Batting	Mat	Inns	NO	Runs	HS	Ave	SR	100	50	Ct	St
First-class	152	205	53	2587	79	17.01	47.60	0	5	35	0
List A	53	31	20	228	24*	20.72	76.25	0	0	12	0
Twenty20	12	3	1	21	11*	10.50	116.66	0	0	3	0

Bowling	Mat	Balls	Runs	Wkts	BBI	BBM	Ave	Econ	SR	5w	10
First-class	152	30385	13429	576	8/20		23.31	2.65	52.7	26	4
List A	53	2646	2084	66	4/58	4/58	31.57	4.72	40.0	0	0
Twenty20	12	246	364	9	2/15	2/15	40.44	8.87	27.3	0	0

SAQIB MAHMOOD

RHB / RFM / R0 / W0

FULL NAME: Saqib Mahmood
BORN: February 25, 1997, Birmingham
SQUAD NO: 25
HEIGHT: 6ft 3in
NICKNAME: Saq
EDUCATION: Matthew Moss High School, Rochdale
TEAMS: Lancashire, England Lions
ROLE: Bowler
DEBUT: First-class: 2016; List A: 2016; T20: 2015

BEST BATTING: 0* Lancashire vs Hampshire, Southampton, 2016
BEST BOWLING: 1-121 Lancashire vs Hampshire, Southampton, 2016

TWITTER: @SaqMahmood25
NOTES: Pace bowler Mahmood joined the Lancashire Academy three years ago. He made his England U19 debut in 2015, taking 3-12 to help rout South Africa for 77 at Northampton. He was part of the Lancashire U17 side that won the 50-over competition and shared the two-day Championship in 2014. Made his full Lancashire debut in 2015, playing in three T20s. Impressed for England at the 2016 U19 World Cup and was a regular member of Lancashire's 50-over side last summer

Batting	Mat	Inns	NO	Runs	HS	Ave	SR	100	50	Ct	St
First-class	1	1	1	0	0*	-	0.00	0	0	0	0
List A	9	2	2	6	6*	-	46.15	0	0	3	0
Twenty20	5	-	-	-	-	-	-	-	-	0	0

Bowling	Mat	Balls	Runs	Wkts	BBI	BBM	Ave	Econ	SR	5w	10
First-class	1	198	121	1	1/121	1/121	121.00	3.66	198.0	0	0
List A	9	354	361	8	3/55	3/55	45.12	6.11	44.2	0	0
Twenty20	5	92	111	8	3/12	3/12	13.87	7.23	11.5	0	0

GAVIN MAIN

RHB / RFM / R0 / W0

FULL NAME: Gavin Thomas Main
BORN: February 28, 1995, Lanark, Scotland
SQUAD NO: 20
HEIGHT: 6ft 1in
NICKNAME: Gav
EDUCATION: The High School of Glasgow;
University of Strathclyde
TEAMS: Scotland, Durham
ROLE: Bowler
DEBUT: T20I: 2015; First-class: 2014;
List A: 2015; T20: 2015

DURHAM

BEST BOWLING: 3-72 Durham vs Nottinghamshire, Trent Bridge, 2014

STRANGEST THING SEEN IN A GAME? A stump being used as a weapon
BEST MOMENT IN CRICKET? Taking a wicket with my first ball at the 2016 World T20
SUPERSTITIONS? I get quite picky about my front foot landing on the crease – the ground has to be firm and I hate craters
HOW WOULD YOUR TEAM-MATES DESCRIBE YOU IN THREE WORDS? Haggis, neeps, tatties
BEST PLAYER IN COUNTY CRICKET? Keaton Jennings (Dur)
MOST UNDERRATED PLAYER IN COUNTY CRICKET? Matt Machan (Sus)
TIP FOR THE TOP? Brydon Carse (Dur), Andrew Umeed (War)
CRICKETING HEROES? Brett Lee – I think every young fast bowler of my generation tried to copy him at some point
IF YOU WEREN'T A CRICKETER? I'd have a job in finance
SURPRISING FACT? I was the Scottish U8 swimming champion
UNUSUAL OBJECT AT HOME? Barry McCarthy
TWITTER: @gmain95

Batting	Mat	Inns	NO	Runs	HS	Ave	SR	100	50	Ct	St
T20Is	4	-	-	-	-	-	-	-	-	1	0
First-class	2	1	1	0	0*	-	0.00	0	0	1	0
List A	2	-	-	-	-	-	-	-	-	0	0
Twenty20	4	-	-	-	-	-	-	-	-	1	0

Bowling	Mat	Balls	Runs	Wkts	BBI	BBM	Ave	Econ	SR	5w	10
T20Is	4	24	34	2	1/13	1/13	17.00	8.50	12.0	0	0
First-class	2	144	100	5	3/72	3/72	20.00	4.16	28.8	0	0
List A	2	102	74	4	2/35	2/35	18.50	4.35	25.5	0	0
Twenty20	4	24	34	2	1/13	1/13	17.00	8.50	12.0	0	0

DAWID MALAN — LHB / LB / R2 / W0 / MVP49

MIDDLESEX

FULL NAME: Dawid Johannes Malan
BORN: September 3, 1987, Roehampton
SQUAD NO: 29
HEIGHT: 6ft
NICKNAME: Mal, Mala
EDUCATION: Paarl Boys' High School; University of South Africa
TEAMS: Middlesex, Barisal Bulls, Boland, England Lions, Peshawar Zalmi, Prime Doleshwar Sporting Club
ROLE: Batsman
DEBUT: First-class: 2006; List A: 2006; T20: 2006

BEST BATTING: 182* Middlesex vs Nottinghamshire, Trent Bridge, 2015
BEST BOWLING: 5-61 Middlesex vs Lancashire, Liverpool, 2012
COUNTY CAP: 2010

FAMILY TIES? My dad Dawid played for Transvaal B and Western Province B and my brother Charl played for MCC Young Cricketers and Loughborough MCCU
STRANGEST THING SEEN IN A GAME? Tim Murtagh getting a random guy – who had decided to walk across the field in the middle of an over – to bowl a ball during a game between Middlesex and Oxford MCCU
BEST MOMENT IN CRICKET? Winning the T20 Cup in 2008 and the Championship in 2016
BEST PLAYER IN COUNTY CRICKET? James Hildreth (Som)
TIP FOR THE TOP? Nick Gubbins (Mid)
CRICKETING HEROES? Gary Kirsten, Matthew Hayden, Mike Hussey
NON-CRICKETING HEROES? My dad – he's always there for me
IF YOU WEREN'T A CRICKETER? I would like to have gone into sports psychology
SURPRISING FACT? I love to go to the cinema by myself
TWITTER: @DJMalan29

Batting	Mat	Inns	NO	Runs	HS	Ave	SR	100	50	Ct	St
First-class	135	227	17	7963	182*	37.91	52.66	17	40	149	0
List A	129	125	18	4356	185*	40.71	82.25	8	21	43	0
Twenty20	133	128	26	3459	115*	33.91	124.60	2	19	45	0

Bowling	Mat	Balls	Runs	Wkts	BBI	BBM	Ave	Econ	SR	5w	10
First-class	135	3019	1910	45	5/61	5/61	42.44	3.79	67.0	1	0
List A	129	1073	1021	33	4/25	4/25	30.93	5.70	32.5	0	0
Twenty20	133	388	464	20	2/10	2/10	23.20	7.17	19.4	0	0

BARRY MCCARTHY

RHB / RMF / RO / WO

FULL NAME: Barry John McCarthy
BORN: September 13, 1992, Dublin, Ireland
SQUAD NO: 60
HEIGHT: 6ft 1in
EDUCATION: St Michael's Catholic Boys College, Dublin; University College Dublin
TEAMS: Ireland, Durham
ROLE: Bowler
DEBUT: ODI: 2016; T20I: 2017; First-class: 2015; List A: 2016; T20: 2016

DURHAM

BEST BATTING: 51* Durham vs Hampshire, Chester-le-Street, 2016
BEST BOWLING: 5-70 Durham vs Lancashire, Chester-le-Street, 2016

FAMILY TIES? My sister (Louise) plays for Ireland and has significantly more caps then me
BEST MOMENT IN CRICKET? My first-class debut for Durham and my first cap for Ireland
HOW WOULD YOUR TEAM-MATES DESCRIBE YOU IN THREE WORDS? Very stiff human
BEST PLAYER IN COUNTY CRICKET? Keaton Jennings (Dur)
MOST UNDERRATED PLAYER IN COUNTY CRICKET? Tim Murtagh (Mid). A lot quicker than he looks
TIP FOR THE TOP? Brydon Carse (Dur)
CRICKETING HEROES? Shane Watson. Both of us have blond hair and are lbw candidates
NON-CRICKETING HEROES? Conor McGregor. The most passionate Irishman to have lived
SURPRISING FACT? I turned down a professional rugby contract and chose cricket
TWITTER: @barrymccarthy2

Batting	Mat	Inns	NO	Runs	HS	Ave	SR	100	50	Ct	St
ODIs	8	6	1	32	13	6.40	46.37	0	0	2	0
T20Is	2	2	0	0	0	0.00	0.00	0	0	0	0
First-class	9	14	4	231	51*	23.10	58.18	0	1	4	0
List A	8	6	1	32	13	6.40	46.37	0	0	2	0
Twenty20	8	5	1	2	2*	0.50	33.33	0	0	0	0

Bowling	Mat	Balls	Runs	Wkts	BBI	BBM	Ave	Econ	SR	5w	10
ODIs	8	398	417	18	4/59	4/59	23.16	6.28	22.1	0	0
T20Is	2	48	102	4	4/33	4/33	25.50	12.75	12.0	0	0
First-class	9	1297	786	24	5/70	6/121	32.75	3.63	54.0	1	0
List A	8	398	417	18	4/59	4/59	23.16	6.28	22.1	0	0
Twenty20	8	159	268	11	4/33	4/33	24.36	10.11	14.4	0	0

BRENDON MCCULLUM

RHB / WK / R0 / W0

FULL NAME: Brendon Barrie McCullum
BORN: September 27, 1981, Dunedin, Otago, New Zealand
SQUAD NO: 42
NICKNAME: Baz
TEAMS: New Zealand, Middlesex, Brisbane Heat, Canterbury, Chennai Super Kings, Glamorgan, Kochi Tuskers Kerala, Kolkata Knight Riders, New South Wales, Otago, Sussex, Warwickshire
ROLE: Batsman
DEBUT: Test: 2004; ODI: 2002; T20I: 2005; First-class: 1999; List A: 2000; T20: 2005

BEST BATTING: 302 New Zealand vs India, Wellington, 2014
BEST BOWLING: 1-1 New Zealand vs Pakistan, Dubai, 2014

TWITTER: @Bazmccullum
NOTES: Middlesex re-signed McCullum for nine matches in the 2017 NatWest T20 Blast. He retired from international cricket in 2016, signing out with the fastest-ever Test century (54 balls) against Australia at Christchurch. In 2014 he became the first New Zealander to score a Test triple century, and also led his side to the World Cup final in 2015. He has previously played for Glamorgan and Sussex, and hit a T20 Blast record of 158* off 64 balls for Birmingham Bears in 2015

Batting	Mat	Inns	NO	Runs	HS	Ave	SR	100	50	Ct	St
Tests	101	176	9	6453	302	38.64	64.60	12	31	198	11
ODIs	260	228	28	6083	166	30.41	96.37	5	32	262	15
T20Is	71	70	10	2140	123	35.66	136.21	2	13	36	8
First-class	150	261	13	9210	302	37.13		17	46	308	19
List A	308	270	32	7368	170	30.95		9	37	305	17
Twenty20	267	262	26	7371	158*	31.23	138.08	7	36	110	14

Bowling	Mat	Balls	Runs	Wkts	BBI	BBM	Ave	Econ	SR	5w	10
Tests	101	175	88	1	1/1	1/13	88.00	3.01	175.0	0	0
ODIs	260	-	-	-	-	-	-	-	-	-	-
T20Is	71	-	-	-	-	-	-	-	-	-	-
First-class	150	259	140	1	1/1	1/13	140.00	3.24	259.0	0	0
List A	308	-	-	-	-	-	-	-	-	-	-
Twenty20	267	6	13	0	-	-	-	13.00	-	0	0

CLINT MCKAY RHB / RFM / R0 / W2 / MVP40

FULL NAME: Clinton James McKay
BORN: February 20, 1983, Melbourne, Australia
SQUAD NO: 27
HEIGHT: 6ft 4in
TEAMS: Australia, Leicestershire, Melbourne Stars, Mumbai Indians, Sydney Thunder, Victoria, Yorkshire
ROLE: Bowler
DEBUT: Test: 2009; ODI: 2009; T20I: 2010; First-class: 2006; List A: 2006; T20: 2008

BEST BATTING: 65 Victoria vs Western Australia, Melbourne, 2012
BEST BOWLING: 6-40 Victoria vs Tasmania, Melbourne, 2011

TWITTER: @clintmckay27
NOTES: The Australian seamer begins his third season as Leicestershire's overseas player. McKay made his ODI debut for Australia in 2009 against India at Hyderabad, taking the wicket of Sachin Tendulkar. His one and only Test appearance came a month later. While lacking express pace, McKay's accuracy helped him become one of Australia's most reliable ODI bowlers, and he was named their One-Day Cricketer of the Year in 2013. Claimed 58 Championship wickets in 2015 and another 56 last summer. Took over from Mark Pettini as Leicestershire's limited-overs captain ahead of the 2017 season

Batting	Mat	Inns	NO	Runs	HS	Ave	SR	100	50	Ct	St
Tests	1	1	0	10	10	10.00	66.66	0	0	1	0
ODIs	59	31	10	190	30	9.04	56.37	0	0	7	0
T20Is	6	4	2	19	7	9.50	86.36	0	0	0	0
First-class	74	104	12	1750	65	19.02	59.18	0	7	16	0
List A	119	62	15	561	57	11.93	69.08	0	1	15	0
Twenty20	103	44	22	285	21*	12.95	119.74	0	0	16	0

Bowling	Mat	Balls	Runs	Wkts	BBI	BBM	Ave	Econ	SR	5w	10
Tests	1	168	101	1	1/56	1/101	101.00	3.60	168.0	0	0
ODIs	59	2965	2364	97	5/28	5/28	24.37	4.78	30.5	2	0
T20Is	6	136	183	4	2/24	2/24	45.75	8.07	34.0	0	0
First-class	74	14655	6978	259	6/40	8/84	26.94	2.85	56.5	7	0
List A	119	6112	4796	172	5/28	5/28	27.88	4.70	35.5	2	0
Twenty20	103	2193	2895	121	4/24	4/24	23.92	7.92	18.1	0	0

SURREY

FULL NAME: Conor McKerr
BORN: January 19, 1998, Johannesburg, South Africa
SQUAD NO: 83
HEIGHT: 6ft 5in
EDUCATION: St John's College, Johannesburg
TEAMS: South Africa U19, Surrey 2nd XI
ROLE: Bowler
DEBUT: Yet to make first-team debut

WHAT FIRST GOT YOU INTO CRICKET? Watching Shaun Pollock as South Africa captain at the World Cup in 2003
BEST MOMENT IN CRICKET? My first wicket for South Africa U19
SUPERSTITIONS? I carry the ball with which I took my first five-fer in my bag
HOW WOULD YOUR TEAM-MATES DESCRIBE YOU IN THREE WORDS? Worst football player
BEST PLAYER IN COUNTY CRICKET? Keaton Jennings (Dur)
MOST UNDERRATED PLAYER IN COUNTY CRICKET? Rory Burns (Sur)
TIP FOR THE TOP? Amar Virdi, Sam Curran (both Sur)
CRICKETING HEROES? Graeme Smith
IF YOU WEREN'T A CRICKETER? I'd be going to university in Johannesburg
SURPRISING FACT? I studied Drama
UNUSUAL OBJECT AT HOME? Mark Footitt
DESERT ISLAND DISC? Jeremy Loops – Down South
FANTASY SLIP CORDON? Keeper: Mark Boucher, 1st: Me, 2nd: Ty Dial, 3rd: Jacques Kallis, Gully: Herschelle Gibbs
TWITTER: @mckerrconor

RYAN MCLAREN LHB / RMF / RO / W1 / MVP21

FULL NAME: Ryan McLaren
BORN: February 9, 1983, Kimberley, South Africa
SQUAD NO: 35
HEIGHT: 6ft 4in
EDUCATION: University of the Free State
TEAMS: South Africa, Lancashire, Dolphins, Eagles, Free State, Hampshire, Kent, Kings XI Punjab, Knights, Kolkata Knight Riders, Middlesex, Mumbai Indians
ROLE: Allrounder
DEBUT: Test: 2010; ODI: 2009; T20I: 2009; First-class: 2003; List A: 2003; T20: 2005

BEST BATTING: 140 Eagles vs Warriors, Bloemfontein, 2006
BEST BOWLING: 8-38 Eagles vs Cape Cobras, Stellenbosch, 2007
COUNTY CAP: 2007 (Kent)

TWITTER: @ryanmac23
NOTES: The South African allrounder signed as Lancashire's overseas player across all formats in 2017 after a successful spell at Hampshire. Has also had stints with Middlesex and Kent. Made headlines in 2007 when he took a hat-trick in the Twenty20 Cup final to help Kent win the tournament. He has not featured for South Africa since 2014

Batting	Mat	Inns	NO	Runs	HS	Ave	SR	100	50	Ct	St
Tests	2	3	1	47	33*	23.50	43.51	0	0	0	0
ODIs	54	41	15	485	71*	18.65	71.32	0	1	13	0
T20Is	12	4	3	9	6*	9.00	69.23	0	0	3	0
First-class	128	191	39	5186	140	34.11		6	27	60	0
List A	190	147	52	2879	88	30.30	84.30	0	13	57	0
Twenty20	156	110	46	1267	51*	19.79	110.94	0	2	59	0

Bowling	Mat	Balls	Runs	Wkts	BBI	BBM	Ave	Econ	SR	5w	10
Tests	2	264	162	3	2/72	2/119	54.00	3.68	88.0	0	0
ODIs	54	2403	2102	77	4/19	4/19	27.29	5.24	31.2	0	0
T20Is	12	263	332	17	5/19	5/19	19.52	7.57	15.4	1	0
First-class	128	20598	10543	380	8/38		27.74	3.07	54.2	14	1
List A	190	7827	6662	243	5/38	5/38	27.41	5.10	32.2	2	0
Twenty20	156	3027	3996	140	5/19	5/19	28.54	7.92	21.6	1	0

LEWIS MCMANUS

RHB / WK / R0 / W0

FULL NAME: Lewis David McManus
BORN: October 9, 1994, Poole, Dorset
SQUAD NO: 18
HEIGHT: 5ft 8in
NICKNAME: Lewy, King
EDUCATION: Claysemore School, Bournemouth; University of Exeter
TEAMS: Hampshire
ROLE: Wicketkeeper
DEBUT: First-class: 2015; List A: 2016; T20: 2016

BEST BATTING: 132* Hampshire vs Surrey, Southampton, 2016

WHAT FIRST GOT YOU INTO CRICKET? It was a sport to play during the football off-season
STRANGEST THING SEEN IN A GAME? James Tomlinson's one-handed catch at fine-leg while holding a banana in the other hand during a first-class game
BEST MOMENT IN CRICKET? My maiden first-class century in 2016
HOW WOULD YOUR TEAM-MATES DESCRIBE YOU IN THREE WORDS? Can't count
BEST PLAYER IN COUNTY CRICKET? Kumar Sangakkara (Sur)
TIP FOR THE TOP? Mason Crane (Ham)
CRICKETING HEROES? Ricky Ponting, Andrew Flintoff
NON-CRICKETING HEROES? Floyd Mayweather, Usain Bolt, Rick Ross, my family
IF YOU WEREN'T A CRICKETER? I'd be a gym junkie
SURPRISING FACT? I play in the same team as Batman
DESERT ISLAND DISC? Floorfillers – 90s Club Classics
FANTASY SLIP CORDON? Keeper: Rick Ross, 1st: David Beckham, 2nd: Leonardo DiCaprio, 3rd: Alan Sugar, Gully: Jonny Wilkinson
TWITTER: @lewis_mcmanus

Batting	Mat	Inns	NO	Runs	HS	Ave	SR	100	50	Ct	St
First-class	13	18	2	613	132*	38.31	48.19	1	4	25	6
List A	8	5	0	90	35	18.00	90.90	0	0	6	3
Twenty20	9	7	0	78	41	11.14	109.85	0	0	4	1

Bowling	Mat	Balls	Runs	Wkts	BBI	BBM	Ave	Econ	SR	5w	10
First-class	13	-	-	-	-	-	-	-	-	-	-
List A	8	-	-	-	-	-	-	-	-	-	-
Twenty20	9	-	-	-	-	-	-	-	-	-	-

STUART MEAKER RHB / RF / R0 / W1 / MVP84

FULL NAME: Stuart Christopher Meaker
BORN: January 21, 1989, Pietermaritzburg, South Africa
SQUAD NO: 18
HEIGHT: 5ft 11in
NICKNAME: Meaks, Ten Bears
EDUCATION: Cranleigh Senior School
TEAMS: England, Surrey
ROLE: Bowler
DEBUT: ODI: 2011; T20I: 2012; First-class: 2008; List A: 2008; T20: 2010

BEST BATTING: 94 Surrey vs Bangladeshis, The Oval, 2010
BEST BOWLING: 8-52 Surrey vs Somerset, The Oval, 2012
COUNTY CAP: 2012

WHAT FIRST GOT YOU INTO CRICKET? Paul and Brian Strang from Zimbabwe
STRANGEST THING SEEN IN A GAME? Grey vervet monkey on the outfield in India
BEST MOMENT IN CRICKET? Making my Surrey and England debuts
HOW WOULD YOUR TEAM-MATES DESCRIBE YOU IN THREE WORDS? Hard-working, compassionate, fast
BEST PLAYER IN COUNTY CRICKET? Kumar Sangakkara (Sur)
MOST UNDERRATED PLAYER IN COUNTY CRICKET? Rory Burns (Sur)
TIP FOR THE TOP? Amar Virdi, Ollie Pope (both Sur)
CRICKETING HEROES? Allan Donald, Dale Steyn – nasty fast bowlers
SURPRISING FACT? I am a science geek and used to be the library monitor at school
TWITTER: @SMeaker18

Batting	Mat	Inns	NO	Runs	HS	Ave	SR	100	50	Ct	St
ODIs	2	2	0	2	1	1.00	12.50	0	0	0	0
T20Is	2	-	-	-	-	-	-	-	-	1	0
First-class	74	97	19	1230	94	15.76	36.98	0	6	13	0
List A	61	30	14	87	21*	5.43	49.43	0	0	14	0
Twenty20	24	6	4	28	17	14.00	147.36	0	0	9	0

Bowling	Mat	Balls	Runs	Wkts	BBI	BBM	Ave	Econ	SR	5w	10
ODIs	2	114	110	2	1/45	1/45	55.00	5.78	57.0	0	0
T20Is	2	47	70	2	1/28	1/28	35.00	8.93	23.5	0	0
First-class	74	11671	7363	252	8/52	11/167	29.21	3.78	46.3	11	2
List A	61	2276	2353	69	4/38	4/38	34.10	6.20	32.9	0	0
Twenty20	24	393	599	20	4/30	4/30	29.95	9.14	19.6	0	0

ALEX MELLOR

LHB / WK / R0 / W0

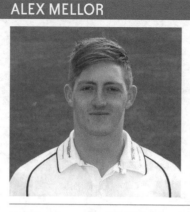

FULL NAME: Alexander James Mellor
BORN: July 22, 1991, Stoke-on-Trent, Staffordshire
SQUAD NO: 15
HEIGHT: 5ft 10in
NICKNAME: Al, Mella
EDUCATION: Westwood College; Staffordshire University
TEAMS: Warwickshire, Derbyshire
ROLE: Wicketkeeper
DEBUT: First-class: 2016; List A: 2016; T20: 2016

BEST BATTING: 44 Derbyshire vs Essex, Derby, 2016

FAMILY TIES? Dad represented Staffordshire age-groups and the senior side. My brother represented Staffordshire age-groups
STRANGEST THING SEEN IN A GAME? A helicopter landing on the pitch during a game
BEST MOMENT IN CRICKET? Playing a part in the RL Cup semi-final against Somerset in 2016
BEST PLAYER IN COUNTY CRICKET? Haseeb Hameed (Lan)
TIP FOR THE TOP? Matthew Lamb (War)
CRICKETING HEROES? Bob Taylor – fantastic person, brilliant keeper. Albie Morkel – I've known him since I was 10, clean striker of the ball, matchwinner. Brian Mellor (my dad) – taught me love for the game. Andrew Flintoff – passion for the game
IF YOU WEREN'T A CRICKETER? I'd be a PE teacher or sports coach
DESERT ISLAND DISC? Oasis – (What's The Story) Morning Glory?
SURPRISING FACT? I'm right-handed and right-footed but I bat left-handed
FANTASY SLIP CORDON? Keeper: Me, 1st: Russell Howard, 2nd: Andrew Flintoff, 3rd: Kumar Sangakarra, Gully: Robbie Savage
TWITTER: @alexmellor22

Batting	Mat	Inns	NO	Runs	HS	Ave	SR	100	50	Ct	St
First-class	5	8	1	164	44	23.42	43.73	0	0	11	0
List A	2	-	-	-	-	-	-	-	-	0	0
Twenty20	1	1	1	10	10*	-	142.85	0	0	0	0

Bowling	Mat	Balls	Runs	Wkts	BBI	BBM	Ave	Econ	SR	5w	10
First-class	5	-	-	-	-	-	-	-	-	-	-
List A	2	-	-	-	-	-	-	-	-	-	-
Twenty20	1	-	-	-	-	-	-	-	-	-	-

JEEVAN MENDIS

LHB / LB / RO / WO

FULL NAME: Balapuwaduge Manukulasuriya Amith Jeevan Mendis
BORN: January 15, 1983, Colombo, Sri Lanka
SQUAD NO: 88
HEIGHT: 5ft 8in
EDUCATION: S Thomas' College, Sri Lanka
TEAMS: SL, Derbyshire, Barbados Tridents, Barisal Bulls, Chittagong Vikings, Delhi Daredevils, Dhaka Division, Kandy Crusaders, Sydney Sixers, Tamil Union
ROLE: Allrounder
DEBUT: ODI: 2010; T20I: 2011; First-class: 2001; List A: 2002; T20: 2004

BEST BATTING: 206* Tamil Union vs Colombo, Colombo, 2013
BEST BOWLING: 6-37 Tamil Union vs Saracens, Colombo, 2011

TWITTER: @jeevanmendis
NOTES: Signed by Derbyshire for the first half of the summer, Mendis will fill the county's overseas role until Imran Tahir's arrival in June. He has played 70 limited-overs matches for Sri Lanka, the last of which came in the 2015 World Cup. A leg-spinner and middle-order batsman, Mendis hit an ODI career-best of 72 from 88 balls against India at Pallekele in 2012. He took 32 wickets at 26.93 and scored 414 runs at 37.63 for Tamil Union in the 2016/17 Sri Lankan domestic season. He has played domestically in Australia, India and West Indies but this will be his first summer in county cricket

Batting	Mat	Inns	NO	Runs	HS	Ave	SR	100	50	Ct	St
ODIs	54	40	10	604	72	20.13	85.07	0	1	13	0
T20Is	16	12	3	197	43*	21.88	124.68	0	0	4	0
First-class	138	216	30	6811	206*	36.61		18	31	113	0
List A	174	148	25	2918	99*	23.72		0	13	59	1
Twenty20	119	102	19	1804	67	21.73	120.26	0	3	33	0

Bowling	Mat	Balls	Runs	Wkts	BBI	BBM	Ave	Econ	SR	5w	10
ODIs	54	1337	1134	28	3/15	3/15	40.50	5.08	47.7	0	0
T20Is	16	108	116	6	3/24	3/24	19.33	6.44	18.0	0	0
First-class	138	12149	6850	257	6/37		26.65	3.38	47.2	13	0
List A	174	4169	3258	109	5/12	5/12	29.88	4.68	38.2	2	0
Twenty20	119	1122	1354	61	4/14	4/14	22.19	7.24	18.3	0	0

CRAIG MESCHEDE RHB / RMF / R0 / W0 / MVP82

GLAMORGAN

FULL NAME: Craig Anthony Joseph Meschede
BORN: November 21, 1991, Johannesburg, South Africa
SQUAD NO: 44
HEIGHT: 6ft 1in
NICKNAME: Mesh, Meshy
EDUCATION: King's College, Taunton
TEAMS: Glamorgan, Somerset
ROLE: Allrounder
DEBUT: First-class: 2011; List A: 2011; T20: 2011

BEST BATTING: 107 Glamorgan vs Northamptonshire, Cardiff, 2015
BEST BOWLING: 5-84 Glamorgan vs Essex, Chelmsford, 2016

STRANGEST THING SEEN IN A GAME? Derbyshire vs Glamorgan, County Championship, Derby, 2016: I'm running in to bowl and it starts to snow
BEST MOMENT IN CRICKET? My maiden first-class wicket – Sachin Tendulkar – and my maiden first-class century for Glamorgan
HOW WOULD YOUR TEAM-MATES DESCRIBE YOU IN THREE WORDS? Gym, fun, annoying
BEST PLAYER IN COUNTY CRICKET? In all formats, Chris Woakes (War) or Ben Stokes (Dur)
MOST UNDERRATED PLAYER IN COUNTY CRICKET? Chris Cooke (Gla)
TIP FOR THE TOP? Tom Abell (Som), David Lloyd (Gla), the Curran brothers (Sur)
CRICKETING HEROES? Jacques Kallis, Sachin Tendulkar
NON-CRICKETING HEROES? Elon Musk, Roger Federer, Leonardo DiCaprio
IF YOU WEREN'T A CRICKETER? I'd be a tennis player, property developer or working in renewable energy
SURPRISING FACT? I'm big into my wildlife – would love to be involved in conservation
FANTASY SLIP CORDON? Keeper: Will Ferrell, 1st: Me, 2nd: Kevin Hart, 3rd: Joe Rogan
TWITTER: @cmeschy

Batting	Mat	Inns	NO	Runs	HS	Ave	SR	100	50	Ct	St
First-class	59	84	12	1803	107	25.04	65.09	2	10	20	0
List A	44	28	4	370	45	15.41	89.80	0	0	10	0
Twenty20	67	50	12	551	53	14.50	123.26	0	1	12	0

Bowling	Mat	Balls	Runs	Wkts	BBI	BBM	Ave	Econ	SR	5w	10
First-class	59	7582	4501	119	5/84	7/80	37.82	3.56	63.7	1	0
List A	44	1521	1391	47	4/5	4/5	29.59	5.48	32.3	0	0
Twenty20	67	734	1064	38	3/9	3/9	28.00	8.69	19.3	0	0

CRAIG MILES
RHB / RFM / RO / W2

FULL NAME: Craig Neil Miles
BORN: July 20, 1994, Swindon, Wiltshire
SQUAD NO: 34
HEIGHT: 6ft 4in
NICKNAME: Milo, Miler
EDUCATION: Bradon Forest School, Purton, Wiltshire; Filton College, Bristol
TEAMS: Gloucestershire
ROLE: Bowler
DEBUT: First-class: 2011; List A: 2011; T20: 2013

BEST BATTING: 62* Gloucestershire vs Worcestershire, Cheltenham, 2014
BEST BOWLING: 6-63 Gloucestershire vs Northamptonshire, Northampton, 2015
COUNTY CAP: 2011

WHAT FIRST GOT YOU INTO CRICKET? Learning how to be a scorer for the second XI at my local cricket club, Purton CC, and trying to get my older brother out in the garden
FAMILY TIES? My older brother Adam has played for Cardiff MCCU and recently played for New Zealand side Otago in the Plunket Shield
BEST MOMENT IN CRICKET? The RL Cup final in 2015, when we beat Surrey despite looking dead and buried. Surely the most surreal game ever
HOW WOULD YOUR TEAM-MATES DESCRIBE YOU IN THREE WORDS? Hates untidy kit
BEST PLAYER IN COUNTY CRICKET? Chris Rushworth (Dur)
TIP FOR THE TOP? George Hankins (Glo), Olly Stone (War)
CRICKETING HEROES? Andrew Flintoff – for the 2005 Ashes. Brett Lee – for his pace
NON-CRICKETING HEROES? My brother – a great bloke who achieved a lot academically
SURPRISING FACT? I played football for Swindon Town Academy until I was 13
DESERT ISLAND DISC? Drake – Take Care
TWITTER: @CMiles34

Batting	Mat	Inns	NO	Runs	HS	Ave	SR	100	50	Ct	St
First-class	44	61	8	1005	62*	18.96	49.28	0	5	11	0
List A	30	12	2	76	16	7.60	64.95	0	0	2	0
Twenty20	11	3	2	5	3*	5.00	100.00	0	0	4	0

Bowling	Mat	Balls	Runs	Wkts	BBI	BBM	Ave	Econ	SR	5w	10
First-class	44	7488	4618	170	6/63	10/121	27.16	3.70	44.0	10	1
List A	30	1240	1262	37	4/29	4/29	34.10	6.10	33.5	0	0
Twenty20	11	217	296	12	3/25	3/25	24.66	8.18	18.0	0	0

TYMAL MILLS

RHB / LF / R0 / W0

SUSSEX

FULL NAME: Tymal Solomon Mills
BORN: August 12, 1992, Dewsbury, Yorkshire
SQUAD NO: 7
HEIGHT: 6ft 2in
NICKNAME: T, Tyrone
EDUCATION: Mildenhall College of
Technology; University of East London
TEAMS: England, Sussex, Auckland,
Brisbane Heat, Chittagong Vikings, Essex,
Quetta Gladiators
ROLE: Bowler
DEBUT: T20I: 2016; First-class: 2011;
List A: 2011; T20: 2012

BEST BATTING: 31* England Lions vs Sri Lanka Emerging Players, Colombo, 2014
BEST BOWLING: 4-25 Essex vs Glamorgan, Cardiff, 2012

WHAT FIRST GOT YOU INTO CRICKET? My friend's team were short when I was 14 and he asked me to help them out
STRANGEST THING SEEN IN A GAME? When I swung a ball in 2012
BEST MOMENT IN CRICKET? Making my England debut in 2016
HOW WOULD YOUR TEAM-MATES DESCRIBE YOU IN THREE WORDS? Fragile, fun, fast
BEST PLAYER IN COUNTY CRICKET? Ed Joyce (Sus)
MOST UNDERRATED PLAYER IN COUNTY CRICKET? Nick Browne (Ess)
TIP FOR THE TOP? Max Holden (Mid)
SURPRISING FACT? I can throw with both arms and I have three toes on each foot that haven't grown since I was 10
DESERT ISLAND DISC? J Cole – 2014 Forest Hills Drive
FANTASY SLIP CORDON? Keeper: Denzel Washington, 2nd: Me, 3rd: Ciara, Gully: Idris Elba
TWITTER: @tmills15

Batting	Mat	Inns	NO	Runs	HS	Ave	SR	100	50	Ct	St
T20Is	4	1	0	0	0	0.00	0.00	0	0	1	0
First-class	32	38	15	260	31*	11.30	57.77	0	0	9	0
List A	23	9	5	7	3*	1.75	31.81	0	0	3	0
Twenty20	58	15	8	31	8*	4.42	93.93	0	0	8	0

Bowling	Mat	Balls	Runs	Wkts	BBI	BBM	Ave	Econ	SR	5w	10
T20Is	4	96	116	3	1/27	1/27	38.66	7.25	32.0	0	0
First-class	32	3531	2008	55	4/25	5/79	36.50	3.41	64.2	0	0
List A	23	790	787	22	3/23	3/23	35.77	5.97	35.9	0	0
Twenty20	58	1191	1487	67	4/22	4/22	22.19	7.49	17.7	0	0

TOM MILNES

RHB / RFM / RO / WO

FULL NAME: Thomas Patrick Milnes
BORN: October 6, 1992, Stourbridge, Worcestershire
SQUAD NO: 8
HEIGHT: 6ft 1in
NICKNAME: Milner
EDUCATION: Heart of England School, West Midlands
TEAMS: Derbyshire, Warwickshire
ROLE: Bowler
DEBUT: First-class: 2011; List A: 2013; T20: 2016

BEST BATTING: 56 Derbyshire vs Gloucestershire, Derby, 2016
BEST BOWLING: 7-39 Warwickshire vs Oxford MCCU, Oxford, 2013

BEST MOMENT IN CRICKET? Being part of Warwickshire's 2012 Championship-winning side, making my Championship debut and taking my first Championship five-wicket haul
HOW WOULD YOUR TEAM-MATES DESCRIBE YOU IN THREE WORDS? Fiery, angry, red
TIP FOR THE TOP? Harvey Hosein (Der)
CRICKETING HEROES? Andrew Flintoff, James Anderson, Dale Steyn, Jacques Kallis
NON-CRICKETING HEROES? Bradley Wiggins, AP McCoy
SURPRISING FACT? I used to play football for Aston Villa, and I love doing impressions
DESERT ISLAND DISC? Oasis – Definitely Maybe
FANTASY SLIP CORDON? Keeper: Alan Partridge, 1st: Me, 2nd: Andrew Flintoff, 3rd: Micky Flanagan, Gully: David Brent
TWITTER: @TPMilnes8

Batting	Mat	Inns	NO	Runs	HS	Ave	SR	100	50	Ct	St
First-class	21	28	4	529	56	22.04	50.23	0	2	4	0
List A	4	3	1	22	16	11.00	64.70	0	0	0	0
Twenty20	1	1	0	0	0	0.00	0.00	0	0	0	0

Bowling	Mat	Balls	Runs	Wkts	BBI	BBM	Ave	Econ	SR	5w	10
First-class	21	2593	1528	42	7/39	9/94	36.38	3.53	61.7	2	0
List A	4	174	242	3	2/73	2/73	80.66	8.34	58.0	0	0
Twenty20	1	18	30	0	-	-	-	10.00	-	0	0

DARYL MITCHELL

RHB / RM / R5 / W0 / MVP43

WORCESTERSHIRE

FULL NAME: Daryl Keith Henry Mitchell
BORN: November 25, 1983, Badsey, Worcestershire
SQUAD NO: 27
HEIGHT: 6ft 2in
NICKNAME: Mitch
EDUCATION: Prince Henry's High School, Evesham; University of Worcester
TEAMS: Worcestershire, Mountaineers
ROLE: Batsman
DEBUT: First-class: 2005; List A: 2005; T20: 2005

BEST BATTING: 298 Worcestershire vs Somerset, Taunton, 2009
BEST BOWLING: 4-49 Worcestershire vs Yorkshire, Headingley, 2009
BENEFIT: 2016

FAMILY TIES? Dad played club cricket and now coaches Worcestershire U13
STRANGEST THING SEEN IN A GAME? Jack Shantry's action
BEST MOMENT IN CRICKET? Winning the Pro40 in 2007
HOW WOULD YOUR TEAM-MATES DESCRIBE YOU IN THREE WORDS? Finds a way
BEST PLAYER IN COUNTY CRICKET? Ben Duckett (Nor)
MOST UNDERRATED PLAYER IN COUNTY CRICKET? Wayne Madsen (Der)
TIP FOR THE TOP? Josh Tongue (Wor)
CRICKETING HEROES? Ian Botham and Graeme Hick – Worcester legends I grew up watching at New Road. Jack Shantry – how does he do it?
NON-CRICKETING HEROES? Paul McGrath – Villa legend
SURPRISING FACT? I'm a member of the Jack Shantry Appreciation Society
UNUSUAL OBJECT AT HOME? 900 Benefit brochures
DESERT ISLAND DISC? Oasis – (What's The Story) Morning Glory?
TWITTER: @mitchwccc

Batting	Mat	Inns	NO	Runs	HS	Ave	SR	100	50	Ct	St
First-class	164	295	34	10284	298	39.40	44.62	24	44	221	0
List A	112	98	16	2787	107	33.98	80.27	2	17	43	0
Twenty20	122	99	22	1872	68*	24.31	119.76	0	7	54	0

Bowling	Mat	Balls	Runs	Wkts	BBI	BBM	Ave	Econ	SR	5w	10
First-class	164	1918	979	22	4/49		44.50	3.06	87.1	0	0
List A	112	2416	2239	62	4/19	4/19	36.11	5.56	38.9	0	0
Twenty20	122	1513	1976	70	5/28	5/28	28.22	7.83	21.6	1	0

TOM MOORES
LHB / WK / R0 / W0

FULL NAME: Thomas James Moores
BORN: September 4, 1996, Brighton
SQUAD NO: 78
NICKNAME: Mooresy
EDUCATION: Loughborough Grammar School; Millfield School, Somerset
TEAMS: Nottinghamshire, Lancashire
ROLE: Wicketkeeper
DEBUT: First-class: 2016; List A: 2016; T20: 2016

NOTTINGHAMSHIRE

BEST BATTING: 41 Nottinghamshire vs Yorkshire, Scarborough, 2016

FAMILY TIES? My father Peter played for Sussex and was England head coach. He's now my coach at Nottinghamshire
BEST MOMENT IN CRICKET? Being Man of the Match for Lancashire in the T20 Blast game against Birmingham Bears in 2016
TIP FOR THE TOP? Aneurin Donald (Gla), Harry Podmore (Mid), Ben Kitt (Not)
CRICKETING HEROES? Adam Gilchrist, AB de Villiers, Virat Kohli
NON-CRICKETING HEROES? Muhammad Ali
IF YOU WEREN'T A CRICKETER? I'd be a DJ
DESERT ISLAND DISC? Ro James – Permission
FANTASY SLIP CORDON? Keeper: Me, 1st: James Corden, 2nd: Kevin Hart, 3rd: Conor McGregor, Gully: Beyoncé
TWITTER: @TJ_Moores_47

Batting	Mat	Inns	NO	Runs	HS	Ave	SR	100	50	Ct	St
First-class	6	10	0	201	41	20.10	42.05	0	0	7	0
List A	4	3	1	22	10	11.00	81.48	0	0	2	1
Twenty20	6	4	2	62	39*	31.00	110.71	0	0	5	1

Bowling	Mat	Balls	Runs	Wkts	BBI	BBM	Ave	Econ	SR	5w	10
First-class	6	-	-	-	-	-	-	-	-	-	-
List A	4	-	-	-	-	-	-	-	-	-	-
Twenty20	6	-	-	-	-	-	-	-	-	-	-

EOIN MORGAN

LHB / RM / R1 / W0

FULL NAME: Eoin Joseph Gerard Morgan
BORN: September 10, 1986, Dublin, Ireland
SQUAD NO: 16
HEIGHT: 5ft 9in
NICKNAME: Moggie, Morgs, Iceman
EDUCATION: Catholic University School,
Dublin; Dulwich College, London
TEAMS: England, Ireland, Middlesex, Kolkata
KR, Peshawar Zalmi, RC Bangalore, Sunrisers
Hyderabad, Sydney Thunder
ROLE: Batsman
DEBUT: Test: 2010; ODI: 2006; T20I: 2009;
First-class: 2004; List A: 2003; T20: 2006

BEST BATTING: 209* Ireland vs UAE, Abu Dhabi, 2007
BEST BOWLING: 2-24 Middlesex vs Nottinghamshire, Lord's, 2007
COUNTY CAP: 2008

TWITTER: @Eoin16
NOTES: An Irishman by birth, Morgan switched his allegiance to England after he was named in England's provisional squad for the 2009 World T20. Made his ODI debut for his adopted nation against West Indies in 2009 at Bristol and his T20I debut a month later in a shock defeat to Netherlands at Lord's. His Test debut followed against Bangladesh in May 2010. After a lean 2013, Morgan rediscovered his form in the away ODI series against Australia in January 2014. Handed the ODI captaincy ahead of the 2015 World Cup and he has turned England into a 50-over force. Also leads the T20I side. Appeared in 14 limited-overs matches for Middlesex in 2016 but has not played first-class cricket for his county since 2015

Batting	Mat	Inns	NO	Runs	HS	Ave	SR	100	50	Ct	St
Tests	16	24	1	700	130	30.43	54.77	2	3	11	0
ODIs	176	165	24	5318	124*	37.71	87.97	10	31	68	0
T20Is	67	66	13	1568	85*	29.58	130.99	0	8	30	0
First-class	93	153	16	4791	209*	34.97	51.35	11	22	71	1
List A	296	273	38	8781	161	37.36	88.62	17	49	106	0
Twenty20	214	201	30	4672	85*	27.32	127.72	0	24	99	0

Bowling	Mat	Balls	Runs	Wkts	BBI	BBM	Ave	Econ	SR	5w	10
Tests	16	-	-	-	-	-	-	-	-	-	-
ODIs	176	-	-	-	-	-	-	-	-	-	-
T20Is	67	-	-	-	-	-	-	-	-	-	-
First-class	93	102	90	2	2/24	2/24	45.00	5.29	51.0	0	0
List A	296	42	49	0	-	-	-	7.00	-	0	0
Twenty20	214	-	-	-	-	-	-	-	-	-	-

OWEN MORGAN

RHB / SLA / R0 / W0

FULL NAME: Alan Owen Morgan
BORN: April 14, 1994, Swansea, Wales
SQUAD NO: 29
HEIGHT: 5ft 11in
NICKNAME: Morgs, Ows, Strawbs
EDUCATION: Ysgol Gyfun Y Strade, Llanelli; Cardiff University
TEAMS: Glamorgan
ROLE: Allrounder
DEBUT: First-class: 2014; List A: 2016

BEST BATTING: 103* Glamorgan vs Worcestershire, Worcester, 2016
BEST BOWLING: 2-37 Glamorgan vs Northamptonshire, Northampton, 2016

WHAT FIRST GOT YOU INTO CRICKET? A local volunteer came into my primary school to start a local village side which I joined
STRANGEST THING SEEN IN A GAME? A match delayed by a session as the kit van was late
BEST MOMENT IN CRICKET? My maiden first-class hundred – as a nightwatchman – against Worcestershire in 2016
SUPERSTITIONS? I scratch my guard eight times. Tap my bat four times before facing a ball
HOW WOULD YOUR TEAM-MATES DESCRIBE YOU IN THREE WORDS? Quiet, focused, chilled
BEST PLAYER IN COUNTY CRICKET? Jeetan Patel (War)
MOST UNDERRATED PLAYER IN COUNTY CRICKET? David Lloyd (Gla)
TIP FOR THE TOP? Lukas Carey (Gla)
CRICKETING HEROES? Ricky Ponting, Shane Warne
NON-CRICKETING HEROES? My grandfather
SURPRISING FACT? I'm fluent in Welsh, grew up on a farm and have a degree in Accounting and Finance
UNUSUAL OBJECT AT HOME? A tractor
TWITTER: @owenmorgan14

Batting	Mat	Inns	NO	Runs	HS	Ave	SR	100	50	Ct	St
First-class	10	18	4	434	103*	31.00	43.70	1	1	3	0
List A	2	1	0	29	29	29.00	80.55	0	0	0	0

Bowling	Mat	Balls	Runs	Wkts	BBI	BBM	Ave	Econ	SR	5w	10
First-class	10	1542	827	15	2/37	3/57	55.13	3.21	102.8	0	0
List A	2	72	67	2	2/49	2/49	33.50	5.58	36.0	0	0

CHARLIE MORRIS
RHB / RMF / R0 / W2

WORCESTERSHIRE

FULL NAME: Charles Andrew John Morris
BORN: July 6, 1992, Hereford
SQUAD NO: 31
HEIGHT: 6ft
NICKNAME: Moz, Tim, Dug, Mr Beige, Tintin
EDUCATION: Kingswood School, Bath; King's College, Taunton; Oxford Brookes University
TEAMS: Worcestershire
ROLE: Bowler
DEBUT: First-class: 2012; List A: 2013; T20: 2013

BEST BATTING: 33* Oxford MCCU vs Warwickshire, Oxford, 2013
BEST BOWLING: 5-54 Worcestershire vs Derbyshire, Derby, 2014

WHAT FIRST GOT YOU INTO CRICKET? I saw a Test match on TV for the first time and then went with my dad to Toys R Us to buy a cricket set
BEST MOMENT IN CRICKET? Beating Surrey in 2014 to gain Championship promotion
HOW WOULD YOUR TEAM-MATES DESCRIBE YOU IN THREE WORDS? Dedicated, pleasant, simple
MOST UNDERRATED PLAYER IN COUNTY CRICKET? Joe Leach (Wor)
TIP FOR THE TOP? Josh Tongue (Wor)
CRICKETING HEROES? Brett Lee and Dale Steyn – two great fast bowlers touching 95mph. They epitomise the attitude necessary for a successful modern fast bowler
IF YOU WEREN'T A CRICKETER? I'd be a Royal Marines commando
SURPRISING FACT? I'm a drummer and hope to join a band in Worcester to start gigging when cricket permits. I eat 42 eggs a week (give or take)
UNUSUAL OBJECT AT HOME? A late Victorian, classic fusee-movement Post Office clock
DESERT ISLAND DISC? Coldplay – Everglow
TWITTER: @morris_9

Batting	Mat	Inns	NO	Runs	HS	Ave	SR	100	50	Ct	St
First-class	44	60	33	274	33*	10.14	28.39	0	0	12	0
List A	17	11	8	43	16*	14.33	68.25	0	0	2	0
Twenty20	4	2	1	5	3	5.00	83.33	0	0	1	0

Bowling	Mat	Balls	Runs	Wkts	BBI	BBM	Ave	Econ	SR	5w	10
First-class	44	7942	4057	127	5/54	9/109	31.94	3.06	62.5	2	0
List A	17	719	694	18	3/46	3/46	38.55	5.79	39.9	0	0
Twenty20	4	84	126	4	2/30	2/30	31.50	9.00	21.0	0	0

STEVEN MULLANEY RHB / RM / R1 / W0 / MVP13

FULL NAME: Steven John Mullaney
BORN: November 19, 1986, Warrington, Cheshire
SQUAD NO: 5
HEIGHT: 5ft 7in
NICKNAME: Mull, Tev
EDUCATION: St Mary's Catholic High School, Astley
TEAMS: Nottinghamshire, Khelaghar Samaj Kallyan Samity, Lancashire
ROLE: Allrounder
DEBUT: First-class: 2006; List A: 2006; T20: 2006

BEST BATTING: 165* Lancashire vs Durham UCCE, Durham University, 2007
BEST BOWLING: 4-31 Nottinghamshire vs Essex, Trent Bridge, 2010
COUNTY CAP: 2013 (Nottinghamshire)

STRANGEST THING SEEN IN A GAME? Samit Patel slipping over. Google it
BEST MOMENT IN CRICKET? Winning the County Championship in 2010, winning a Lord's one-day final in 2013 and scoring a hundred the first time I played at Lord's
HOW WOULD YOUR TEAM-MATES DESCRIBE YOU IN THREE WORDS? Winner, loyal, stubby
BEST PLAYER IN COUNTY CRICKET? Ben Duckett (Nor)
MOST UNDERRATED PLAYER IN COUNTY CRICKET? Steven Patterson (Yor)
TIP FOR THE TOP? Brydon Carse (Dur), Ben Kitt, Tom Moores (both Not)
CRICKETING HEROES? Andrew Flintoff, Luke Fletcher
NON-CRICKETING HEROES? Floyd Mayweather, Conor McGregor
IF YOU WEREN'T A CRICKETER? I did a three-month apprenticeship as an electrician
SURPRISING FACT? I played England schoolboy rugby league
DESERT ISLAND DISC? Westlife – Greatest Hits
TWITTER: @mull05

Batting	Mat	Inns	NO	Runs	HS	Ave	SR	100	50	Ct	St
First-class	99	168	8	5292	165*	33.07	58.36	11	27	91	0
List A	87	60	13	1207	89*	25.68	97.41	0	6	43	0
Twenty20	94	63	18	714	53	15.86	134.97	0	1	48	0

Bowling	Mat	Balls	Runs	Wkts	BBI	BBM	Ave	Econ	SR	5w	10
First-class	99	4479	2376	59	4/31	5/78	40.27	3.18	75.9	0	0
List A	87	2861	2419	78	4/29	4/29	31.01	5.07	36.6	0	0
Twenty20	94	1604	2043	71	4/19	4/19	28.77	7.64	22.5	0	0

DAVID MURPHY

RHB / OB / WK / R0 / W0

FULL NAME: David Murphy
BORN: June 24, 1989, Welwyn Garden City, Hertfordshire
SQUAD NO: 19
HEIGHT: 6ft 1in
NICKNAME: Murph, Smurf
EDUCATION: Richard Hale School, Hertford; Loughborough University; BPP University, London
TEAMS: Scotland, Northamptonshire
ROLE: Wicketkeeper
DEBUT: ODI: 2013; T20I: 2013; First-class: 2009; List A: 2010; T20: 2010

BEST BATTING: 135* Northamptonshire vs Surrey, The Oval, 2015
BEST BOWLING: 1-40 Northamptonshire vs Leicestershire, Northampton, 2016

STRANGEST THING SEEN IN A GAME? A team-mate pick the ball up, take his arm back to throw but release it on the way back. The ball went straight behind him for four
BEST MOMENT IN CRICKET? Winning the T20 Cup in 2013
HOW WOULD YOUR TEAM-MATES DESCRIBE YOU IN THREE WORDS? Untidy, weird, friendly
BEST PLAYER IN COUNTY CRICKET? Ben Duckett (Nor)
MOST UNDERRATED PLAYER IN COUNTY CRICKET? Rob Keogh (Nor)
TIP FOR THE TOP? Joe Clarke (Wor)
CRICKETING HEROES? Jack Russell – the best wicketkeeper stood up I've ever seen
IF YOU WEREN'T A CRICKETER? I'd be a solicitor
SURPRISING FACT? I'm completely deaf in my left ear

Batting	Mat	Inns	NO	Runs	HS	Ave	SR	100	50	Ct	St
ODIs	8	7	2	58	20*	11.60	49.15	0	0	8	3
T20Is	4	4	3	35	20	35.00	100.00	0	0	1	0
First-class	72	97	22	2124	135*	28.32	44.35	1	12	195	16
List A	40	25	13	272	31*	22.66	71.76	0	0	26	12
Twenty20	39	19	7	129	20	10.75	103.20	0	0	18	5

Bowling	Mat	Balls	Runs	Wkts	BBI	BBM	Ave	Econ	SR	5w	10
ODIs	8	-	-	-	-	-	-	-	-	-	-
T20Is	4	-	-	-	-	-	-	-	-	-	-
First-class	72	36	43	1	1/40	1/40	43.00	7.16	36.0	0	0
List A	40	-	-	-	-	-	-	-	-	-	-
Twenty20	39	-	-	-	-	-	-	-	-	-	-

JACK MURPHY

LHB / LFM / RO / WO

FULL NAME: Jack Roger Murphy
BORN: July 15, 1995, Haverfordwest, Pembrokeshire, Wales
SQUAD NO: 7
HEIGHT: 6ft 7in
NICKNAME: Pepe, J Rock
EDUCATION: Ysgol Greenhill School, Pembrokeshire; Cardiff Metropolitan University
TEAMS: Glamorgan
ROLE: Allrounder
DEBUT: First-class: 2015; List A: 2016

BEST BATTING: 22 Cardiff MCCU vs Glamorgan, Cardiff, 2015
BEST BOWLING: 2-90 Cardiff MCCU vs Glamorgan, Cardiff, 2015

FAMILY TIES? My dad likes to think he used to be pretty good because he went on a tour to the West Indies but quite frankly he was rubbish
BEST MOMENT IN CRICKET? Taking four wickets in four balls for my old club Cresselly
HOW WOULD YOUR TEAM-MATES DESCRIBE YOU IN THREE WORDS? Tall, skinny, likeable
BEST PLAYER IN COUNTY CRICKET? Keaton Jennings (Dur) by far – he proved that on his England debut
TIP FOR THE TOP? Kiran Carlson (Gla) – hard-working lad who has a lot of promise
CRICKETING HEROES? Simon Jones and Andrew Flintoff – watching them during the 2005 Ashes was superb
NON-CRICKETING HEROES? My mum and dad. They've sacrificed a lot for me over the years
IF YOU WEREN'T A CRICKETER? I would be in the RAF
SURPRISING FACT? I'm very tall
UNUSUAL OBJECT AT HOME? My brother
DESERT ISLAND DISC? Bob Marley
FANTASY SLIP CORDON? Keeper: Frankie Boyle, 1st: Me, 2nd: Barack Obama, 3rd: James Corden, Gully: Ryan Reynolds
TWITTER: @Jrock6ft7

Batting	Mat	Inns	NO	Runs	HS	Ave	SR	100	50	Ct	St
First-class	2	3	0	39	22	13.00	38.61	0	0	1	0
List A	1	1	0	6	6	6.00	35.29	0	0	0	0

Bowling	Mat	Balls	Runs	Wkts	BBI	BBM	Ave	Econ	SR	5w	10
First-class	2	240	135	2	2/90	2/90	67.50	3.37	120.0	0	0
List A	1	60	64	0	-	-	-	6.40	-	0	0

TIM MURTAGH — LHB / RFM / R0 / W6 / MVP98

MIDDLESEX

FULL NAME: Timothy James Murtagh
BORN: August 2, 1981, Lambeth, London
SQUAD NO: 34
HEIGHT: 6ft
NICKNAME: Murts, Jack, Brow
EDUCATION: The John Fisher School, London; St Mary's College, Twickenham
TEAMS: Ireland, Middlesex, Surrey
ROLE: Bowler
DEBUT: ODI: 2012; T20I: 2012; First-class: 2000; List A: 2000; T20: 2003

BEST BATTING: 74* Surrey vs Middlesex, The Oval, 2004
BEST BOWLING: 7-82 Middlesex vs Derbyshire, Derby, 2009
COUNTY CAP: 2008 (Middlesex) **BENEFIT:** 2015 (Middlesex)

FAMILY TIES? My brother Chris played for Surrey and uncle Andrew played for Hampshire
BEST MOMENT IN CRICKET? Winning the 2016 County Championship
SUPERSTITIONS? I bat with my lucky horseshoe inside my box
HOW WOULD YOUR TEAM-MATES DESCRIBE YOU IN THREE WORDS? Tall, dark, handsome
BEST PLAYER IN COUNTY CRICKET? Ben Stokes (Dur)
MOST UNDERRATED PLAYER IN COUNTY CRICKET? John Simpson (Mid)
TIP FOR THE TOP? Tom Helm, Harry Podmore (both Mid)
NON-CRICKETING HEROES? Jürgen Klopp, followed closely by my wife
IF YOU WEREN'T A CRICKETER? I'd be spotting trains and emptying bins
SURPRISING FACT? I have a famous cousin who is a jockey
TWITTER: @tjmurtagh

Batting	Mat	Inns	NO	Runs	HS	Ave	SR	100	50	Ct	St
ODIs	23	15	5	117	23*	11.70	75.97	0	0	6	0
T20Is	14	5	3	26	12*	13.00	104.00	0	0	3	0
First-class	190	247	72	3559	74*	20.33		0	10	57	0
List A	170	104	38	748	35*	11.33		0	0	43	0
Twenty20	102	38	14	227	40*	9.45	106.57	0	0	22	0

Bowling	Mat	Balls	Runs	Wkts	BBI	BBM	Ave	Econ	SR	5w	10
ODIs	23	1152	885	26	4/32	4/32	34.03	4.60	44.3	0	0
T20Is	14	268	324	13	3/23	3/23	24.92	7.25	20.6	0	0
First-class	190	33197	17436	652	7/82		26.74	3.15	50.9	27	4
List A	170	7616	6544	217	4/14	4/14	30.15	5.15	35.0	0	0
Twenty20	102	1984	2727	106	6/24	6/24	25.72	8.24	18.7	1	0

PHIL MUSTARD
LHB / LB / WK / RO / WO

FULL NAME: Philip Mustard
BORN: October 8, 1982, Sunderland
SQUAD NO: 19
HEIGHT: 5ft 10in
NICKNAME: Colonel
EDUCATION: Usworth Comprehensive, County Durham
TEAMS: England, Gloucestershire, Auckland, Barisal Burners, Durham, Lancashire, Mountaineers
ROLE: Wicketkeeper
DEBUT: ODI: 2007; T20I: 2008; First-class: 2002; List A: 2000; T20: 2003

GLOUCESTERSHIRE

BEST BATTING: 130 Durham vs Kent, Canterbury, 2006
BEST BOWLING: 1-9 Durham vs Sussex, Hove, 2013
BENEFIT: 2016 (Durham)

FAMILY TIES? My father played local cricket, my brother played for Sunderland and Chester-le-Street in the North East Premier League and my cousin is my former Durham team-mate Chris Rushworth
BEST MOMENT IN CRICKET? Playing for England, winning the 2007 FP Trophy with Durham and then following up with two Championship titles in 2008 and 2009
SUPERSTITIONS? I look high to my left when I go out to bat. Not sure why, but it happens
MOST UNDERRATED PLAYER IN COUNTY CRICKET? Keaton Jennings (Dur)
TIP FOR THE TOP? Matt Taylor, George Hankins (both Glo)
CRICKETING HEROES? Adam Gilchrist
TWITTER: @colonel19

Batting	Mat	Inns	NO	Runs	HS	Ave	SR	100	50	Ct	St
ODIs	10	10	0	233	83	23.30	92.46	0	1	9	2
T20Is	2	2	0	60	40	30.00	162.16	0	0	0	0
First-class	195	301	36	8098	130	30.55	60.47	7	49	648	19
List A	198	181	9	5304	143	30.83		7	33	205	47
Twenty20	179	170	8	3999	97*	24.68	123.27	0	21	86	37

Bowling	Mat	Balls	Runs	Wkts	BBI	BBM	Ave	Econ	SR	5w	10
ODIs	10	-	-	-	-	-	-	-	-	-	-
T20Is	2	-	-	-	-	-	-	-	-	-	-
First-class	195	7	9	1	1/9	1/9	9.00	7.71	7.0	0	0
List A	198	-	-	-	-	-	-	-	-	-	-
Twenty20	179	-	-	-	-	-	-	-	-	-	-

JOHANN MYBURGH — RHB / OB / R0 / W0

FULL NAME: Johann Gerhardus Myburgh
BORN: October 22, 1980, Pretoria, South Africa
SQUAD NO: 9
HEIGHT: 5ft 7in
NICKNAME: Mybs, Santi
EDUCATION: Pretoria Boys High School
TEAMS: Somerset, Auckland, Canterbury, Durham, Hampshire, Northerns, Titans
ROLE: Batsman
DEBUT: First-class: 1997; List A: 1999; T20: 2005

BEST BATTING: 203 Northerns B vs Easterns, Pretoria, 1998
BEST BOWLING: 4-56 Canterbury vs Northern Districts, Hamilton, 2008

FAMILY TIES? My brother Stephan is a Dutch international
BEST MOMENT IN CRICKET? Sharing a hundred-run partnership with my brother
HOW WOULD YOUR TEAM-MATES DESCRIBE YOU IN THREE WORDS? Short, easy-going, competitive
TIP FOR THE TOP? Tom Abell (Som)
CRICKETING HEROES? Eric Simons, Brian Lara
NON-CRICKETING HEROES? Boris Becker, Dennis Bergkamp
IF YOU WEREN'T A CRICKETER? Ah that's easy, I'd be a pro-golfer of course
SURPRISING FACT? I might be taller than you think
FANTASY SLIP CORDON? Keeper: Spider-Man, 1st: Matt LeBlanc, 2nd: Matthew Perry, 3rd: David Schwimmer

Batting	Mat	Inns	NO	Runs	HS	Ave	SR	100	50	Ct	St
First-class	108	190	23	6841	203	40.96		16	39	61	0
List A	107	100	10	2611	112	29.01		1	16	24	0
Twenty20	67	59	9	1394	88	27.88	118.43	0	7	16	0

Bowling	Mat	Balls	Runs	Wkts	BBI	BBM	Ave	Econ	SR	5w	10
First-class	108	4345	2160	45	4/56		48.00	2.98	96.5	0	0
List A	107	1772	1497	25	2/22	2/22	59.88	5.06	70.8	0	0
Twenty20	67	374	461	10	3/16	3/16	46.10	7.39	37.4	0	0

CHRIS NASH   RHB / OB / R4 / W0 / MVP66

FULL NAME: Christopher David Nash
BORN: May 19, 1983, Cuckfield, Sussex
SQUAD NO: 23
HEIGHT: 6ft
NICKNAME: Nashy, Knocker, Beaut, Wig
EDUCATION: Collyer's Sixth Form College;
Loughborough University
TEAMS: Sussex, Auckland, England Lions,
Otago, Prime Doleshwar Sporting Club
ROLE: Batsman
DEBUT: First-class: 2002; List A: 2006;
T20: 2006

SUSSEX

BEST BATTING: 184 Sussex vs Leicestershire, Leicester, 2010
BEST BOWLING: 4-12 Sussex vs Glamorgan, Cardiff, 2010
COUNTY CAP: 2008 **BENEFIT:** 2017

WHAT FIRST GOT YOU INTO CRICKET? I was watching my brother hit a ball against a wall when a great man called Dr John Dew got me out on the pitch at the age of two
STRANGEST THING SEEN IN A GAME? Luke Wright running after a ball
BEST MOMENT IN CRICKET? My maiden first-class hundred and maiden T20 hundred
SUPERSTITIONS? I used to have lots but age has meant I don't have enough energy to worry about which pad to put on first
MOST UNDERRATED PLAYER IN COUNTY CRICKET? Ben Brown (Sus)
TIP FOR THE TOP? Harry Finch, George Garton, Stuart Whittingham, Jonty Jenner (all Sus)
NON-CRICKETING HEROES? Richard Hawkes – a great mastermind of modern coaching
IF YOU WEREN'T A CRICKETER? Following Sussex CCC around with my packed lunch asking Luke Wright for cuddles and autographs
SURPRISING FACT? When I was young I had four goldfish: Eenie, Meenie, Minie and Mo
UNUSUAL OBJECT AT HOME? My guitars and my kittens
TWITTER: @chrisnash23

Batting	Mat	Inns	NO	Runs	HS	Ave	SR	100	50	Ct	St
First-class	172	293	19	10846	184	39.58	58.11	22	56	102	0
List A	108	101	4	2944	124*	30.35	89.78	2	18	27	0
Twenty20	140	133	17	2876	112*	24.79	123.01	1	14	42	0

Bowling	Mat	Balls	Runs	Wkts	BBI	BBM	Ave	Econ	SR	5w	10
First-class	172	5521	3139	75	4/12		41.85	3.41	73.6	0	0
List A	108	1525	1399	43	4/40	4/40	32.53	5.50	35.4	0	0
Twenty20	140	1016	1208	49	4/7	4/7	24.65	7.13	20.7	0	0

ROB NEWTON

RHB / LB / RO / WO

FULL NAME: Robert Irving Newton
BORN: January 18, 1990, Taunton
SQUAD NO: 10
HEIGHT: 5ft 8in
NICKNAME: Ewok, KOTL, Newts
EDUCATION: Framlingham College, Suffolk
TEAMS: Northamptonshire
ROLE: Batsman
DEBUT: First-class: 2010; List A: 2009;
T20: 2010

BEST BATTING: 202* Northamptonshire vs Leicestershire, Northampton, 2016

STRANGEST THING SEEN IN A GAME? A streaker kicking down the stumps
BEST MOMENT IN CRICKET? Winning the 'stump game' at Northamptonshire's end-of-season celebrations
HOW WOULD YOUR TEAM-MATES DESCRIBE YOU IN THREE WORDS? Short, round, short
BEST PLAYER IN COUNTY CRICKET? Ben Duckett (Nor)
MOST UNDERRATED PLAYER IN COUNTY CRICKET? Sam Northeast (Ken)
TIP FOR THE TOP? Richard Gleeson (Nor)
CRICKETING HEROES? Ajaz Akhtar
NON-CRICKETING HEROES? Hank Moody, Vincent Chase
IF YOU WEREN'T A CRICKETER? I'd be drinking the profits at my own bar
DESERT ISLAND DISC? The Rolling Stones (any album)
FANTASY SLIP CORDON? Keeper: Noel Fielding, 1st: Me, 2nd: Julian Barratt, 3rd: Sergio García, Gully: Gazza
TWITTER: @robbienewts77

Batting	Mat	Inns	NO	Runs	HS	Ave	SR	100	50	Ct	St
First-class	68	118	11	3765	202*	35.18	57.95	10	13	22	0
List A	32	29	1	760	88*	27.14	94.52	0	3	6	0
Twenty20	20	17	1	206	38	12.87	103.51	0	0	0	0

Bowling	Mat	Balls	Runs	Wkts	BBI	BBM	Ave	Econ	SR	5w	10
First-class	68	19	25	0	-	-	-	7.89	-	0	0
List A	32	-	-	-	-	-	-	-	-	-	-
Twenty20	20	-	-	-	-	-	-	-	-	-	-

ARON NIJJAR

LHB / SLA / R0 / W0

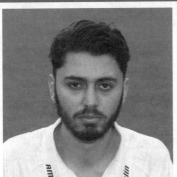

FULL NAME: Aron Stuart Singh Nijjar
BORN: September 24, 1994, Goodmayes, Essex
SQUAD NO: 19
EDUCATION: Ilford County High School
TEAMS: Essex
ROLE: Bowler
DEBUT: First-class: 2015; List A: 2015

ESSEX

BEST BATTING: 53 Essex vs Northamptonshire, Chelmsford, 2015
BEST BOWLING: 2-33 Essex vs Lancashire, Chelmsford, 2015

NOTES: A left-arm orthodox spinner and a fluent left-handed strokemaker, Nijjar has yet to establish himself at his hometown club and, despite having debuted in 2015, didn't feature at all in any format last year. But Nijjar, who plays for the hugely successful Wanstead and Snaresbrook club, is highly regarded at Essex and is expected to feature this term, especially in one-day cricket. A standout unbeaten 170 for Essex Second XI against a Somerset attack featuring Lewis Gregory and Max Waller was his best return in 2016

Batting	Mat	Inns	NO	Runs	HS	Ave	SR	100	50	Ct	St
First-class	7	10	5	155	53	31.00	44.15	0	1	1	0
List A	3	1	0	21	21	21.00	70.00	0	0	4	0

Bowling	Mat	Balls	Runs	Wkts	BBI	BBM	Ave	Econ	SR	5w	10
First-class	7	729	489	12	2/33	3/48	40.75	4.02	60.7	0	0
List A	3	126	107	1	1/39	1/39	107.00	5.09	126.0	0	0

KIERAN NOEMA-BARNETT · LHB / RM / RO / WO

FULL NAME: Kieran Noema-Barnett
BORN: June 4, 1987, Dunedin, New Zealand
SQUAD NO: 11
HEIGHT: 6ft 1in
NICKNAME: Barney, Bear
EDUCATION: Kavanagh College, Dunedin; Massey University, Palmerston North
TEAMS: Gloucestershire, Central Districts, Otago
ROLE: Allrounder
DEBUT: First-class: 2009; List A: 2008; T20: 2007

BEST BATTING: 107 Central Districts vs Auckland, Auckland, 2011
BEST BOWLING: 4-20 Central Districts vs Otago, Dunedin, 2011

FAMILY TIES? Like me, my younger brother Arana has played for New Zealand U19, and my sister Molly also plays at a high level

BEST MOMENT IN CRICKET? I've been involved in winning three championships in New Zealand with Central Stags. Captaining the side to the four-day title was unreal. A 43-ball hundred and a 14-ball fifty in T20 cricket would also be in there, as well as a first-class hat-trick

SUPERSTITIONS? No breakfast on game days – I need to be hungry

CRICKETING HEROES? Brian Lara – he made it look easy

NON-CRICKETING HEROES? My parents for raising my siblings and me. Manny Pacquiao – he does it all: boxer, congressman, basketball player. His fights are always good to watch

IF YOU WEREN'T A CRICKETER? I'd be working in a bank and looking forward to weekends

SURPRISING FACT? I have an unusual laugh, according to some

FANTASY SLIP CORDON? Keeper: Manny Pacquiao (to create a good atmosphere), 1st: Me (best seat in the house), 2nd: Notorious B.I.G. (to provide a few lyrics), 3rd: Craig Herrick (a good friend of mine), Gully: Bruce Lee (for his cat-like reflexes)

Batting	Mat	Inns	NO	Runs	HS	Ave	SR	100	50	Ct	St
First-class	62	93	12	2275	107	28.08	52.02	2	14	29	0
List A	74	58	7	1171	74	22.96	95.82	0	6	32	0
Twenty20	89	77	14	1076	57*	17.07	131.86	0	3	16	0

Bowling	Mat	Balls	Runs	Wkts	BBI	BBM	Ave	Econ	SR	5w	10
First-class	62	7421	3329	97	4/20	6/29	34.31	2.69	76.5	0	0
List A	74	2358	2002	47	3/42	3/42	42.59	5.09	50.1	0	0
Twenty20	89	847	1289	31	2/13	2/13	41.58	9.13	27.3	0	0

SAM NORTHEAST

RHB / OB / R2 / W0 / MVP14

FULL NAME: Sam Alexander Northeast
BORN: October 16, 1989, Ashford, Kent
SQUAD NO: 17
HEIGHT: 5ft 11in
NICKNAME: North, Bam, Nick Knight
EDUCATION: Harrow School, London
TEAMS: Kent
ROLE: Batsman
DEBUT: First-class: 2007; List A: 2007; T20: 2010

BEST BATTING: 191 Kent vs Derbyshire, Canterbury, 2016
BEST BOWLING: 1-60 Kent vs Gloucestershire, Cheltenham, 2013
COUNTY CAP: 2012

TWITTER: @sanortheast
NOTES: Northeast was hotly tipped from the moment he was selected for the Harrow first team at the age of 14. At the end of the 2009 season he scored his maiden first-class hundred but struggled in 2010, averaging 24.57. In 2012 he hit three Championship centuries and finished just short of 1,400 runs in all forms of cricket. He struggled again in 2013 and in 2014 was dropped after scoring 178 runs in his first 12 innings. He returned to the side at No.5 and went on to make four Championship centuries. His excellent form continued last season, scoring over 2,000 runs in all competitions. He was handed the Championship captaincy at the end of 2015 after impressing as leader of the limited-overs teams, and excelled in his first season in charge of all formats, scoring five Championship hundreds as well as 462 runs in the NatWest T20 Blast

Batting	Mat	Inns	NO	Runs	HS	Ave	SR	100	50	Ct	St
First-class	123	210	15	7511	191	38.51	55.28	16	41	64	0
List A	78	71	4	2121	132	31.65	75.72	2	11	24	0
Twenty20	76	69	9	1937	114	32.28	137.08	1	13	18	0

Bowling	Mat	Balls	Runs	Wkts	BBI	BBM	Ave	Econ	SR	5w	10
First-class	123	178	147	1	1/60	1/60	147.00	4.95	178.0	0	0
List A	78	-	-	-	-	-	-	-	-	-	-
Twenty20	76	-	-	-	-	-	-	-	-	-	-

LIAM NORWELL

RHB / RMF / RO / W1

FULL NAME: Liam Connor Norwell
BORN: December 27, 1991, Bournemouth
SQUAD NO: 24
HEIGHT: 6ft 3in
NICKNAME: Pasty
EDUCATION: Redruth School, Cornwall
TEAMS: Gloucestershire
ROLE: Bowler
DEBUT: First-class: 2011; List A: 2012; T20: 2012

BEST BATTING: 102 Gloucestershire vs Derbyshire, Bristol, 2016
BEST BOWLING: 6-33 Gloucestershire vs Essex, Chelmsford, 2015
COUNTY CAP: 2011

WHAT FIRST GOT YOU INTO CRICKET? Watching my dad play in Bournemouth and then Plymouth and being able to have a day off school to play Kwik Cricket
SUPERSTITIONS? I don't like taking my bowling boots off on a bowling day – I'll only take them off if I'm not allowed to wear them for lunch in the pavilion
HOW WOULD YOUR TEAM-MATES DESCRIBE YOU IN THREE WORDS? Boring, ginger, Cornish
BEST PLAYER IN COUNTY CRICKET? Michael Klinger (Glo)
MOST UNDERRATED PLAYER IN COUNTY CRICKET? Chris Dent (Glo)
TIP FOR THE TOP? George Hankins (Glo)
IF YOU WEREN'T A CRICKETER? I'd be a History teacher. I have also looked into firefighting
SURPRISING FACT? My only A in school was in Food Technology. I'm a big fan of NFL and I've been to most of the games played at Wembley
UNUSUAL OBJECT AT HOME? A lightsaber (my mum got me one for Christmas)
TWITTER: @LCNorwell24

Batting	Mat	Inns	NO	Runs	HS	Ave	SR	100	50	Ct	St
First-class	55	71	29	601	102	14.30	41.22	1	1	11	0
List A	11	5	2	28	10	9.33	58.33	0	0	1	0
Twenty20	23	5	5	5	2*	-	71.42	0	0	10	0

Bowling	Mat	Balls	Runs	Wkts	BBI	BBM	Ave	Econ	SR	5w	10
First-class	55	9876	5601	189	6/33	10/65	29.63	3.40	52.2	5	1
List A	11	504	487	18	6/52	6/52	27.05	5.79	28.0	1	0
Twenty20	23	413	631	12	3/27	3/27	52.58	9.16	34.4	0	0

FULL NAME: Graham Onions
BORN: September 9, 1982, Gateshead, County Durham
SQUAD NO: 9
HEIGHT: 6ft 2in
NICKNAME: Bunny, Wills
EDUCATION: St Thomas More Roman Catholic School, Blaydon, Gateshead
TEAMS: England, Durham, Dolphins
ROLE: Bowler
DEBUT: Test: 2009; ODI: 2009; First-class: 2004; List A: 2003; T20: 2004

DURHAM

BEST BATTING: 65 Durham vs Nottinghamshire, Chester-le-Street, 2016
BEST BOWLING: 9-67 Durham vs Nottinghamshire, Trent Bridge, 2012
BENEFIT: 2015

BEST MOMENT IN CRICKET? My Test debut, taking nine wickets against Nottinghamshire and returning to Test cricket against West Indies in 2012 after my serious back injury
SUPERSTITIONS? I lick my fingers before I bowl
CRICKETING HEROES? Darren Gough, Dale Steyn
IF YOU WEREN'T A CRICKETER? I'd be struggling! Maybe a PE teacher
DESERT ISLAND DISC? T-Spoon – Sex On The Beach
FANTASY SLIP CORDON? Keeper: Daniel Radcliffe, 1st: Russell Crowe, 2nd: Paul Gascoigne, 3rd: David Beckham, Gully: George Best
TWITTER: @BunnyOnions

Batting	Mat	Inns	NO	Runs	HS	Ave	SR	100	50	Ct	St
Tests	9	10	7	30	17*	10.00	30.92	0	0	0	0
ODIs	4	1	0	1	1	1.00	50.00	0	0	1	0
First-class	161	209	81	1842	65	14.39	51.10	0	1	32	0
List A	87	32	10	130	19	5.90	68.78	0	0	13	0
Twenty20	44	13	6	61	31	8.71	107.01	0	0	10	0

Bowling	Mat	Balls	Runs	Wkts	BBI	BBM	Ave	Econ	SR	5w	10
Tests	9	1606	957	32	5/38	7/102	29.90	3.57	50.1	1	0
ODIs	4	204	185	4	2/58	2/58	46.25	5.44	51.0	0	0
First-class	161	27824	15702	587	9/67		26.74	3.38	47.4	25	3
List A	87	3616	3073	99	4/45	4/45	31.04	5.09	36.5	0	0
Twenty20	44	936	1034	35	3/15	3/15	29.54	6.62	26.7	0	0

CRAIG OVERTON — RHB / RFM / R0 / W0 / MVP77

SOMERSET

FULL NAME: Craig Overton
BORN: April 10, 1994, Barnstaple, Devon
SQUAD NO: 12
HEIGHT: 6ft 5in
NICKNAME: Goober
EDUCATION: West Buckland School
TEAMS: Somerset, England Lions
ROLE: Allrounder
DEBUT: First-class: 2012; List A: 2012; T20: 2014

BEST BATTING: 138 Somerset vs Hampshire, Taunton, 2016
BEST BOWLING: 6-74 Somerset vs Warwickshire, Edgbaston, 2015
COUNTY CAP: 2016

FAMILY TIES? My father played Minor Counties cricket and my twin brother Jamie also plays for Somerset
BEST MOMENT IN CRICKET? Scoring my maiden first-class hundred for Somerset in 2016
HOW WOULD YOUR TEAM-MATES DESCRIBE YOU IN THREE WORDS? Passionate and hard-working
BEST PLAYER IN COUNTY CRICKET? Keaton Jennings (Dur)
MOST UNDERRATED PLAYER IN COUNTY CRICKET? Jack Leach (Som)
TIP FOR THE TOP? Ben Green (Som)
CRICKETING HEROES? Andrew Flintoff
SURPRISING FACT? Me and my brother don't live with each other
UNUSUAL OBJECT AT HOME? A toy putter which you can use while on the toilet
FANTASY SLIP CORDON? Keeper: James Corden, 1st: Me, 2nd: Michael Jordan, 3rd: Marcus Trescothick, Gully: Jonathan Ross
TWITTER: @craigoverton12

Batting	Mat	Inns	NO	Runs	HS	Ave	SR	100	50	Ct	St
First-class	46	61	9	1318	138	25.34	72.10	1	7	27	0
List A	41	31	6	404	60*	16.16	108.31	0	1	13	0
Twenty20	15	8	3	53	15	10.60	94.64	0	0	8	0

Bowling	Mat	Balls	Runs	Wkts	BBI	BBM	Ave	Econ	SR	5w	10
First-class	46	7054	3818	136	6/74	8/81	28.07	3.24	51.8	2	0
List A	41	1844	1557	40	3/29	3/29	38.92	5.06	46.1	0	0
Twenty20	15	246	416	7	1/23	1/23	59.42	10.14	35.1	0	0

JAMIE OVERTON

RHB / RFM / R0 / W0

FULL NAME: Jamie Overton
BORN: April 10, 1994, Barnstaple, Devon
SQUAD NO: 8
HEIGHT: 6ft 5in
NICKNAME: Goober, J
EDUCATION: West Buckland School
TEAMS: Somerset, England Lions
ROLE: Bowler
DEBUT: First-class: 2012; List A: 2012;
T20: 2015

SOMERSET

BEST BATTING: 56 Somerset vs Warwickshire, Edgbaston, 2014
BEST BOWLING: 6-95 Somerset vs Middlesex, Taunton, 2013

FAMILY TIES? My dad played for Devon and my twin brother Craig also plays for Somerset
BEST MOMENT IN CRICKET? The run-chase against Gloucestershire in the 2016 RL Cup
CRICKETING HEROES? James Anderson – growing up I felt we bowled in similar ways
NON-CRICKETING HEROES? Muhammad Ali – he was a genius. Rory McIlroy – he makes it
look so easy
SURPRISING FACT? I was in a film when I was younger
DESERT ISLAND DISC? MKTO
TWITTER: @JamieOverton

Batting	Mat	Inns	NO	Runs	HS	Ave	SR	100	50	Ct	St
First-class	39	52	16	659	56	18.30	80.75	0	4	2	0
List A	20	12	6	130	40*	21.66	116.07	0	0	10	0
Twenty20	26	14	6	95	31	11.87	148.43	0	0	11	0

Bowling	Mat	Balls	Runs	Wkts	BBI	BBM	Ave	Econ	SR	5w	10
First-class	39	5203	3213	86	6/95	7/134	37.36	3.70	60.5	2	0
List A	20	767	806	28	4/42	4/42	28.78	6.30	27.3	0	0
Twenty20	26	525	786	28	4/22	4/22	28.07	8.98	18.7	0	0

TONY PALLADINO

RHB / RMF / RO / W2

DERBYSHIRE

FULL NAME: Antonio Paul Palladino
BORN: June 29, 1983, Tower Hamlets, London
SQUAD NO: 28
HEIGHT: 6ft 4in
NICKNAME: Battler, Pallas, Dino
EDUCATION: Cardinal Pole Sixth Form, London; Anglia Polytechnic University
TEAMS: Namibia, Derbyshire, Essex
ROLE: Bowler
DEBUT: First-class: 2003; List A: 2003; T20: 2005

BEST BATTING: 106 Derbyshire vs Australia A, Derby, 2012
BEST BOWLING: 7-53 Derbyshire vs Kent, Derby, 2012
COUNTY CAP: 2012 (Derbyshire)

BEST MOMENT IN CRICKET? Winning Division Two of the County Championship in 2012
SUPERSTITIONS? Must wear black socks, sweatband and watch when playing
BEST PLAYER IN COUNTY CRICKET? Kumar Sangakarra (Sur)
MOST UNDERRATED PLAYER IN COUNTY CRICKET? Wayne Madsen (Der)
NON-CRICKETING HEROES? Frank Lampard, John Terry, Didier Drogba and Gianfranco Zola (favourite Chelsea players); Pedro Martínez (favourite baseball player); John Carpenter (love his films); Batman (I collect the graphic comics)
SURPRISING FACT? I'm a Trekkie. In my car I listen exclusively to Classic FM
UNUSUAL OBJECT AT HOME? The complete Sherlock Holmes collectors' hardback
DESERT ISLAND DISC? Beethoven – Moonlight Sonata or Symphony No.7 in A major op. 92
FANTASY SLIP CORDON? Keeper: Batman (safe hands and great reflexes), 1st: Me (I can hide behind Batman), 2nd: Ian Botham (one of the best slippers ever), 3rd: Willy Wonka (I like chocolate), Gully: nobody – it never goes there
TWITTER: @apalladino28

Batting	Mat	Inns	NO	Runs	HS	Ave	SR	100	50	Ct	St
First-class	132	182	39	2303	106	16.10	50.26	1	7	36	0
List A	54	32	7	267	31	10.68	92.06	0	0	6	0
Twenty20	26	12	5	48	14*	6.85	81.35	0	0	5	0

Bowling	Mat	Balls	Runs	Wkts	BBI	BBM	Ave	Econ	SR	5w	10
First-class	132	21732	10674	361	7/53		29.56	2.94	60.1	13	0
List A	54	2153	1913	54	5/49	5/49	35.42	5.33	39.8	1	0
Twenty20	26	490	614	28	4/21	4/21	21.92	7.51	17.5	0	0

GEORGE PANAYI

RHB / RFM / RO / WO

FULL NAME: George David Panayi
BORN: September 23, 1997, Enfield, Middlesex
SQUAD NO: 33
HEIGHT: 6ft 3in
NICKNAME: Poon
EDUCATION: Shrewsbury School
TEAMS: England U19, Warwickshire 2nd XI
ROLE: Bowler
DEBUT: Yet to make first-team debut

WHAT FIRST GOT YOU INTO CRICKET? After failing at football it was the next sport on the list
FAMILY TIES? Dad played village cricket
STRANGEST THING SEEN IN A GAME? An umpire having a cigarette at square-leg
BEST MOMENT IN CRICKET? Taking a wicket on TV
SUPERSTITIONS? I sing my favourite song of the day in my head as I walk out to bat
HOW WOULD YOUR TEAM-MATES DESCRIBE YOU IN THREE WORDS? Asks dumb questions
BEST PLAYER IN COUNTY CRICKET? Jeetan Patel (War)
MOST UNDERRATED PLAYER IN COUNTY CRICKET? Oliver Hannon-Dalby (War)
TIP FOR THE TOP? Sam Hain (War)
CRICKETING HEROES? Andrew Flintoff
NON-CRICKETING HEROES? Buzz Lightyear
IF YOU WEREN'T A CRICKETER? I'd be a musician
SURPRISING FACT? I have a diploma in Saxophone Performance
UNUSUAL OBJECT AT HOME? A fish graveyard
DESERT ISLAND DISC? Oasis – (What's The Story) Morning Glory?
FANTASY SLIP CORDON? Keeper: Michael McIntyre, 1st: Derek Trotter, 2nd: Me,
3rd: Hermione Granger, 4th: John Snow, Gully: Noel Gallagher
TWITTER: @Gpanayi

CALLUM PARKINSON

RHB / SLA / RO / WO

FULL NAME: Callum Francis Parkinson
BORN: October 24, 1996, Bolton, Lancashire
SQUAD NO: 10
HEIGHT: 5ft 9in
NICKNAME: Parko
EDUCATION: Bolton School; Canon Slade, Bolton
TEAMS: Leicestershire, Derbyshire
ROLE: Bowler
DEBUT: First-class: 2016

BEST BATTING: 48* Derbyshire vs Leicestershire, Leicester, 2016
BEST BOWLING: 4-90 Derbyshire vs Leicestershire, Leicester, 2016

FAMILY TIES? My dad played in the Bolton League. My twin brother Matt is at Lancashire
STRANGEST THING SEEN IN A GAME? I saw a bird get hit by a cover-drive (sadly it didn't recover) and a team-mate eat a Subway while at third man
BEST MOMENT IN CRICKET? Making my first-class debut for my former club Derbyshire in 2016 – at the home ground of my new county. Winning the North-East Group with Mount Waverley in Australia last winter
SUPERSTITIONS? I once asked a lad to smell my boots before a game – he was sat next to me – and I did well so I asked him to do it before every match
HOW WOULD YOUR TEAM-MATES DESCRIBE YOU IN THREE WORDS? Aggressive, loud, small
BEST PLAYER IN COUNTY CRICKET? Wayne Madsen (Der) – a hell of a player in all formats
MOST UNDERRATED PLAYER IN COUNTY CRICKET? Nick Browne (Ess) – he got a double hundred in my second game for Derbyshire and could have batted for a week
TIP FOR THE TOP? Dan Lawrence (Ess), Tom Moores (Not), Matt Parkinson (Lan)
NON-CRICKETING HEROES? The late Roy Marland of Heaton CC – a local league legend and a brilliant mentor to me
SURPRISING FACT? I am 16 minutes older than my identical twin brother
TWITTER: @cal_parky

Batting	Mat	Inns	NO	Runs	HS	Ave	SR	100	50	Ct	St
First-class	4	7	2	80	48*	16.00	42.78	0	0	0	0

Bowling	Mat	Balls	Runs	Wkts	BBI	BBM	Ave	Econ	SR	5w	10
First-class	4	1024	531	14	4/90	7/178	37.92	3.11	73.1	0	0

FULL NAME: Matthew William Parkinson
BORN: October 24, 1996, Bolton, Lancashire
SQUAD NO: 28
HEIGHT: 5ft 9in
NICKNAME: Parky
EDUCATION: Canon Slade School, Bolton
TEAMS: Lancashire
ROLE: Bowler
DEBUT: First-class: 2016

LANCASHIRE

BEST BATTING: 9 Lancashire vs Warwickshire, Old Trafford, 2016
BEST BOWLING: 5-49 Lancashire vs Warwickshire, Old Trafford, 2016

WHAT FIRST GOT YOU INTO CRICKET? Going to my local club Heaton CC
FAMILY TIES? Dad played for Lancashire Federation U19 and league cricket in Bolton. My twin Callum played for Derbyshire and recently joined Leicestershire
STRANGEST THING SEEN IN A GAME? On my Lancashire debut we had to come off after three balls of my first over because of a loud PA fault
BEST MOMENT IN CRICKET? My maiden first-class wicket – Jonathan Trott. And winning the Minor Counties Championship with Staffordshire
HOW WOULD YOUR TEAM-MATES DESCRIBE YOU IN THREE WORDS? Competitive, chippy, hungry
BEST PLAYER IN COUNTY CRICKET? Keaton Jennings (Dur)
MOST UNDERRATED PLAYER IN COUNTY CRICKET? Keith Barker (War)
TIP FOR THE TOP? Dom Bess (Som), Saqib Mahmood (Lan), Callum Parkinson (Lei)
CRICKETING HEROES? Shane Warne, Yasir Shah
SURPRISING FACT? I lost my front four teeth in a cricket accident when I was 12 and recently underwent implant surgery
FANTASY SLIP CORDON? Keeper: Peter Kay, 1st: Conor McGregor, 2nd: Thomas Shelby, 3rd: Winston Churchill, Gully: Barack Obama
TWITTER: @mattyparky96

Batting	Mat	Inns	NO	Runs	HS	Ave	SR	100	50	Ct	St
First-class	4	5	1	16	9	4.00	25.00	0	0	1	0

Bowling	Mat	Balls	Runs	Wkts	BBI	BBM	Ave	Econ	SR	5w	10
First-class	4	685	363	10	5/49	6/123	36.30	3.17	68.5	1	0

STEPHEN PARRY

RHB / SLA / RO / WO

LANCASHIRE

FULL NAME: Stephen David Parry
BORN: January 12, 1986, Manchester
SQUAD NO: 4
HEIGHT: 6ft
NICKNAME: Pazza
EDUCATION: Audenshaw High School, Manchester
TEAMS: England, Lancashire, Brisbane Heat
ROLE: Bowler
DEBUT: ODI: 2014; T20I: 2014; First-class: 2007; List A: 2009; T20: 2009

BEST BATTING: 37 Lancashire vs Durham, Old Trafford, 2014
BEST BOWLING: 5-23 Lancashire vs Durham UCCE, Durham University, 2007
COUNTY CAP: 2015

NON-CRICKETING HEROES? Muhammad Ali
IF YOU WEREN'T A CRICKETER? I'd be fishing or travelling the world
SURPRISING FACT? I'm an elite table-tennis player
TWITTER: @SDParry86
NOTES: Left-arm spinner known as a white-ball specialist, Parry played a handful of limited-overs matches for England in 2014 and 2015. Has not played a first-class match for nearly three years, but has well over 200 wickets in List A and T20 cricket combined

Batting	Mat	Inns	NO	Runs	HS	Ave	SR	100	50	Ct	St
ODIs	2	-	-	-	-	-	-	-	-	0	0
T20Is	5	1	0	1	1	1.00	100.00	0	0	2	0
First-class	9	10	1	138	37	15.33	50.36	0	0	2	0
List A	81	38	16	288	31	13.09	73.65	0	0	23	0
Twenty20	109	29	19	114	15	11.40	106.54	0	0	24	0

Bowling	Mat	Balls	Runs	Wkts	BBI	BBM	Ave	Econ	SR	5w	10
ODIs	2	114	92	4	3/32	3/32	23.00	4.84	28.5	0	0
T20Is	5	96	138	3	2/33	2/33	46.00	8.62	32.0	0	0
First-class	9	1276	650	18	5/23	5/46	36.11	3.05	70.8	1	0
List A	81	3465	2862	103	5/17	5/17	27.78	4.95	33.6	1	0
Twenty20	109	2292	2748	113	5/13	5/13	24.31	7.19	20.2	1	0

JEETAN PATEL

RHB / OB / R0 / W5 / MVP1

FULL NAME: Jeetan Shashi Patel
BORN: May 7, 1980, Wellington, New Zealand
SQUAD NO: 5
NICKNAME: Dave
TEAMS: New Zealand, Warwickshire, North Island, Wellington
ROLE: Bowler
DEBUT: Test: 2006; ODI: 2005; T20I: 2005; First-class: 1999; List A: 1999; T20: 2005

WARWICKSHIRE

BEST BATTING: 120 Warwickshire vs Yorkshire, Edgbaston, 2014
BEST BOWLING: 7-38 Somerset vs Warwickshire, Taunton, 2015
COUNTY CAP: 2012

WHAT FIRST GOT YOU INTO CRICKET? My old man – he's a cricket badger
HOW WOULD YOUR TEAM-MATES DESCRIBE YOU IN THREE WORDS? Passionate, sociable, old
BEST PLAYER IN COUNTY CRICKET? Chris Woakes (War)
MOST UNDERRATED PLAYER IN COUNTY CRICKET? Sam Hain (War)
TIP FOR THE TOP? Josh Poysden (War), Sam Curran (Sur)
CRICKETING HEROES? Sir Richard Hadlee, Saqlain Mushtaq
NON-CRICKETING HEROES? Tiger Woods, Jim Furyk
UNUSUAL OBJECT AT HOME? A lot of shoe horns

Batting	Mat	Inns	NO	Runs	HS	Ave	SR	100	50	Ct	St
Tests	22	35	7	359	47	12.82	51.06	0	0	12	0
ODIs	42	14	7	88	34	12.57	56.77	0	0	13	0
T20Is	11	4	1	9	5	3.00	64.28	0	0	4	0
First-class	234	302	69	5175	120	22.21		2	23	115	0
List A	201	106	33	706	50	9.67		0	1	82	0
Twenty20	170	68	22	320	34*	6.95	126.98	0	0	57	0

Bowling	Mat	Balls	Runs	Wkts	BBI	BBM	Ave	Econ	SR	5w	10
Tests	22	5635	2969	62	5/110	6/151	47.88	3.16	90.8	1	0
ODIs	42	1954	1636	47	3/11	3/11	34.80	5.02	41.5	0	0
T20Is	11	199	269	16	3/20	3/20	16.81	8.11	12.4	0	0
First-class	234	48077	23398	677	7/38		34.56	2.92	71.0	25	2
List A	201	9676	7461	245	5/43	5/43	30.45	4.62	39.4	1	0
Twenty20	170	3377	3916	167	4/11	4/11	23.44	6.95	20.2	0	0

RAVI PATEL

RHB / SLA / RO / WO

FULL NAME: Ravi Hasmukh Patel
BORN: August 4, 1991, Harrow, Middlesex
SQUAD NO: 36
HEIGHT: 5ft 9in
NICKNAME: Rav, Ravster
EDUCATION: Merchant Taylors' School, London; Loughborough University
TEAMS: Middlesex, England Lions, Essex
ROLE: Bowler
DEBUT: First-class: 2010; List A: 2010; T20: 2013

BEST BATTING: 26* Middlesex vs Warwickshire, Uxbridge, 2013
BEST BOWLING: 5-69 Middlesex vs Cambridge MCCU, Cambridge, 2013

WHAT FIRST GOT YOU INTO CRICKET? My dad pushed me to play at four years old
FAMILY TIES? Dad played university cricket in India
STRANGEST THING SEEN IN A GAME? A cyclist riding over the cut strip during the middle of an over
BEST MOMENT IN CRICKET? Taking the last Lancashire wicket to send them down in 2012
HOW WOULD YOUR TEAM-MATES DESCRIBE YOU IN THREE WORDS? Honest, funny, outgoing
BEST PLAYER IN COUNTY CRICKET? Toby Roland-Jones (Mid)
MOST UNDERRATED PLAYER IN COUNTY CRICKET? Rob Keogh (Nor)
TIP FOR THE TOP? Harry Podmore, Ryan Higgins (both Mid)
CRICKETING HEROES? Pragyan Ojha – the best left-arm spinner in the world in my opinion. Wish I could bowl like him. Also Monty Panesar. And Sachin
NON-CRICKETING HEROES? My dad for giving me all the opportunities I've wanted in life
SURPRISING FACT? I did German at A-level and got a B
TWITTER: @ravi36patel

Batting	Mat	Inns	NO	Runs	HS	Ave	SR	100	50	Ct	St
First-class	21	28	14	175	26*	12.50	39.06	0	0	5	0
List A	11	2	1	0	0*	0.00	0.00	0	0	1	0
Twenty20	29	5	3	14	11*	7.00	70.00	0	0	5	0

Bowling	Mat	Balls	Runs	Wkts	BBI	BBM	Ave	Econ	SR	5w	10
First-class	21	3884	2036	59	5/69	8/198	34.50	3.14	65.8	1	0
List A	11	546	524	11	3/71	3/71	47.63	5.75	49.6	0	0
Twenty20	29	648	761	31	4/18	4/18	24.54	7.04	20.9	0	0

SAMIT PATEL

RHB / SLA / R4 / W0 / MVP9

FULL NAME: Samit Rohit Patel
BORN: November 30, 1984, Leicester
SQUAD NO: 21
HEIGHT: 5ft 8in
NICKNAME: Sarnie, Slippery
EDUCATION: Worksop College, Nottinghamshire
TEAMS: England, Nottinghamshire, Mohammedan Sporting Club, Rajshahi Kings, Warriors
ROLE: Allrounder
DEBUT: Test: 2012; ODI: 2008; T20I: 2011; First-class: 2002; List A: 2002; T20: 2003

BEST BATTING: 256 Nottinghamshire vs Durham MCCU, Trent Bridge, 2013
BEST BOWLING: 7-68 Nottinghamshire vs Hampshire, Southampton, 2011
COUNTY CAP: 2008 **BENEFIT:** 2017

FAMILY TIES? My dad played league cricket and my brother Akhil played for Notts
BEST MOMENT IN CRICKET? Making my ODI and Test debuts. Taking five wickets against South Africa at The Oval and scoring 70 off 40 balls at Chandigarh against India. Scoring 68 against Sri Lanka in the World T20
SUPERSTITIONS? I always touch the floor before I cross the line as I am walking out to bat
CRICKETING HEROES? Sachin Tendulkar, Stephen Fleming
NON-CRICKETING HEROES? Tiger Woods
IF YOU WEREN'T A CRICKETER? I'd be a sales rep
SURPRISING FACT? I bowl left-handed but throw right-handed

Batting	Mat	Inns	NO	Runs	HS	Ave	SR	100	50	Ct	St
Tests	6	9	0	151	42	16.77	44.67	0	0	3	0
ODIs	36	22	7	482	70*	32.13	93.23	0	1	7	0
T20Is	18	14	2	189	67	15.75	109.24	0	1	3	0
First-class	183	298	15	10418	256	36.81	62.95	24	51	122	0
List A	216	187	30	5260	129*	33.50	84.05	4	29	62	0
Twenty20	183	163	27	3484	90*	25.61	123.24	0	23	52	0

Bowling	Mat	Balls	Runs	Wkts	BBI	BBM	Ave	Econ	SR	5w	10
Tests	6	858	421	7	2/27	3/164	60.14	2.94	122.5	0	0
ODIs	36	1187	1091	24	5/41	5/41	45.45	5.51	49.4	1	0
T20Is	18	252	321	7	2/6	2/6	45.85	7.64	36.0	0	0
First-class	183	21172	10930	277	7/68		39.45	3.09	76.4	3	1
List A	216	7033	6258	198	6/13	6/13	31.60	5.33	35.5	2	0
Twenty20	183	3270	3889	148	4/20	4/20	26.27	7.13	22.0	0	0

STEVEN PATTERSON   RHB / RMF / R0 / W2 / MVP59

FULL NAME: Steven Andrew Patterson
BORN: October 3, 1983, Beverley, Yorkshire
SQUAD NO: 17
HEIGHT: 6ft 4in
NICKNAME: Dead Man, Patto
EDUCATION: Malet Lambert School, Hull; St Mary's Sixth Form College, Hull; University of Leeds
TEAMS: Yorkshire
ROLE: Bowler
DEBUT: First-class: 2005; List A: 2003; T20: 2009

BEST BATTING: 63* Yorkshire vs Warwickshire, Edgbaston, 2016
BEST BOWLING: 6-56 Yorkshire vs Durham, Chester-le-Street, 2016
COUNTY CAP: 2012

FAMILY TIES? My grandad played for Durham before World War II
BEST MOMENT IN CRICKET? Making my Championship debut at Scarborough, receiving my Yorkshire cap, playing in the Champions League T20, winning the County Championship
CRICKETING HEROES? Glenn McGrath, Shaun Pollock
NON-CRICKETING HEROES? My grandad
IF YOU WEREN'T A CRICKETER? I'd be working in finance
SURPRISING FACT? I love my golf
FANTASY SLIP CORDON? Keeper: Morgan Freeman, 1st: Tiger Woods, 2nd: Me, 3rd: Prince Harry, Gully: Alex Ferguson

Batting	Mat	Inns	NO	Runs	HS	Ave	SR	100	50	Ct	St
First-class	122	139	35	1674	63*	16.09	37.30	0	3	18	0
List A	78	33	20	202	25*	15.53		0	0	12	0
Twenty20	38	7	4	9	3*	3.00	50.00	0	0	4	0

Bowling	Mat	Balls	Runs	Wkts	BBI	BBM	Ave	Econ	SR	5w	10
First-class	122	19305	8957	321	6/56	8/94	27.90	2.78	60.1	6	0
List A	78	3287	2736	96	6/32	6/32	28.50	4.99	34.2	2	0
Twenty20	38	751	1062	35	4/30	4/30	30.34	8.48	21.4	0	0

DAVID PAYNE

RHB / LFM / RO / WO

FULL NAME: David Alan Payne
BORN: February 15, 1991, Poole, Dorset
SQUAD NO: 14
HEIGHT: 6ft 2in
NICKNAME: Sid, Payney
EDUCATION: Lytchett Minster Secondary and Sixth Form, Poole
TEAMS: Gloucestershire
ROLE: Bowler
DEBUT: First-class: 2011; List A: 2009; T20: 2010

BEST BATTING: 67* Gloucestershire vs Glamorgan, Cardiff, 2016
BEST BOWLING: 6-26 Gloucestershire vs Leicestershire, Bristol, 2011
COUNTY CAP: 2011

WHAT FIRST GOT YOU INTO CRICKET? Playing down the park with my dad and brother
FAMILY TIES? My brother and dad both played club cricket for Parley CC
BEST MOMENT IN CRICKET? Winning the RL Cup in 2015
HOW WOULD YOUR TEAM-MATES DESCRIBE YOU IN THREE WORDS? Lanky, skinny, Peperami
BEST PLAYER IN COUNTY CRICKET? Chris Rushworth (Dur)
TIP FOR THE TOP? George Hankins (Glo)
CRICKETING HEROES? Andrew Flintoff – he had so much fun when playing
NON-CRICKETING HEROES? David Beckham – an all-round legend
IF YOU WEREN'T A CRICKETER? I'd be doing something in media or coaching
SURPRISING FACT? I cut my own hair
DESERT ISLAND DISC? Usher – Confessions
TWITTER: @sidpayne7

Batting	Mat	Inns	NO	Runs	HS	Ave	SR	100	50	Ct	St
First-class	65	79	23	1099	67*	19.62	45.77	0	5	25	0
List A	58	23	14	102	23	11.33	69.38	0	0	16	0
Twenty20	42	13	7	33	10	5.50	97.05	0	0	8	0

Bowling	Mat	Balls	Runs	Wkts	BBI	BBM	Ave	Econ	SR	5w	10
First-class	65	10311	5683	170	6/26	9/96	33.42	3.30	60.6	3	0
List A	58	2441	2299	101	7/29	7/29	22.76	5.65	24.1	3	0
Twenty20	42	784	1171	48	5/24	5/24	24.39	8.96	16.3	1	0

MARK PETTINI

RHB / RM / R1 / W0

LEICESTERSHIRE

FULL NAME: Mark Lewis Pettini
BORN: August 7, 1983, Brighton
SQUAD NO: 6
HEIGHT: 5ft 11in
NICKNAME: Swampy
EDUCATION: Hills Road Sixth Form College, Cambridge; Cardiff University
TEAMS: Leicestershire, Essex, Kala Bagan Krira Chakra, Mashonaland Eagles, Mountaineers
ROLE: Batsman
DEBUT: First-class: 2001; List A: 2001; T20: 2003

BEST BATTING: 209 Mountaineers vs Matabeleland Tuskers, Bulawayo, 2014
BEST BOWLING: 1-72 Essex vs Leicestershire, Leicester, 2012
COUNTY CAP: 2006 (Essex)

BEST MOMENT IN CRICKET? Winning two Pro40 titles with Essex, being made Essex captain in 2007 and winning the Friends Provident Trophy in 2008
CRICKETING HEROES? Graham Gooch, Andy Flower, Ronnie Irani
DESERT ISLAND DISC? The White Stripes
NOTES: Scored 208* against Derbyshire in 2006. Made England's inaugural 30-man squad for the 2007 World T20, the same month he replaced Ronnie Irani as Essex captain. Led Essex to victory in the 2008 FP Trophy final. Hit his highest score of 209 in 2014 for Mountaineers in Zimbabwe's Logan Cup. Took over the one-day and T20 captaincy when he joined Leicestershire in September 2015 but was replaced as limited-overs skipper by Clint McKay ahead of the 2017 season

Batting	Mat	Inns	NO	Runs	HS	Ave	SR	100	50	Ct	St
First-class	171	284	41	8630	209	35.51	47.82	14	47	119	0
List A	180	166	12	4517	144	29.33	83.26	8	29	66	0
Twenty20	132	128	9	3257	95*	27.36	128.43	0	21	43	0

Bowling	Mat	Balls	Runs	Wkts	BBI	BBM	Ave	Econ	SR	5w	10
First-class	171	132	263	1	1/72	1/72	263.00	11.95	132.0	0	0
List A	180	-	-	-	-	-	-	-	-	-	-
Twenty20	132	-	-	-	-	-	-	-	-	-	-

VERNON PHILANDER   RHB / RFM / R0 / W0

FULL NAME: Vernon Darryl Philander
BORN: June 24, 1985, Bellville, South Africa
NICKNAME: Pro
EDUCATION: Ravensmead High School, Cape Town
TEAMS: South Africa, Sussex, Cape Cobras, Jamaica Tallawahs, Kent, Middlesex, Nottinghamshire, Somerset, Western Districts, Western Province
ROLE: Allrounder
DEBUT: Test: 2011; ODI: 2007; T20I: 2007; First-class: 2004; List A: 2004; T20: 2005

SUSSEX

BEST BATTING: 168 Western Province vs Griqualand West, Kimberley, 2004
BEST BOWLING: 7-61 Cape Cobras vs Knights, Cape Town, 2012

TWITTER: @VDP_24
NOTES: South African seamer who has a stunning Test and ODI record and is also a dangerous lower-order batsman. Joins as an overseas player and is available for Sussex's first six Championship matches, as well as the entire group stage of the RL Cup. Previously played for Middlesex, Somerset, Kent and Nottinghamshire. In November 2016 he took 5-21 to help South Africa bowl out hosts Australia for 85 in Hobart and lead his side to a 2-1 series win

Batting	Mat	Inns	NO	Runs	HS	Ave	SR	100	50	Ct	St
Tests	41	53	12	961	74	23.43	44.71	0	5	11	0
ODIs	30	19	7	151	30*	12.58	70.89	0	0	6	0
T20Is	7	4	0	14	6	3.50	50.00	0	0	1	0
First-class	136	181	32	3671	168	24.63	46.66	2	11	34	0
List A	124	85	28	1343	79*	23.56	75.79	0	5	11	0
Twenty20	95	65	33	801	56*	25.03	133.72	0	1	21	0

Bowling	Mat	Balls	Runs	Wkts	BBI	BBM	Ave	Econ	SR	5w	10
Tests	41	7610	3470	161	6/44	10/102	21.55	2.73	47.2	11	2
ODIs	30	1279	986	41	4/12	4/12	24.04	4.62	31.1	0	0
T20Is	7	83	114	4	2/23	2/23	28.50	8.24	20.7	0	0
First-class	136	23897	10446	488	7/61		21.40	2.62	48.9	22	2
List A	124	5203	4059	126	4/12	4/12	32.21	4.68	41.2	0	0
Twenty20	95	1675	2192	75	5/17	5/17	29.22	7.85	22.3	1	0

KEVIN PIETERSEN — RHB / OB / R3 / W0

FULL NAME: Kevin Peter Pietersen
BORN: June 27, 1980, Pietermaritzburg, South Africa
HEIGHT: 6ft 4in
EDUCATION: University of South Africa
TEAMS: England, Surrey, Delhi Daredevils, Dolphins, Hampshire, KwaZulu-Natal, Melbourne Stars, Natal, Nottinghamshire, St Lucia Zouks, Rising Pune Supergiants, RC Bangalore, Quetta Gladiators
ROLE: Batsman
DEBUT: Test: 2005; ODI: 2004; T20I: 2005; First-class: 1998; List A: 1999; T20: 2003

BEST BATTING: 355* Surrey vs Leicestershire, The Oval, 2015
BEST BOWLING: 4-31 Nottinghamshire vs Durham UCCE, Trent Bridge, 2003
COUNTY CAPS: 2002 (Nottinghamshire); 2005 (Hampshire)

TWITTER: @KP24
NOTES: Surrey have re-signed the former England batsman for this season's NatWest T20 Blast, with Pietersen set to be available from July 19. Now a T20 specialist, in the past year Pietersen has played for Quetta Gladiators in the Pakistan Super League, Melbourne Stars in the Big Bash and Dolphins in South Africa's Ram Slam T20. He is England's third-highest runscorer in T20Is, behind Eoin Morgan and Alex Hales, and was part of the team that won the World T20 final in 2010. Pietersen is also England's fifth-highest runscorer in Test cricket and his tally of 23 centuries is bettered only by Alastair Cook

Batting	Mat	Inns	NO	Runs	HS	Ave	SR	100	50	Ct	St
Tests	104	181	8	8181	227	47.28	61.72	23	35	62	0
ODIs	136	125	16	4440	130	40.73	86.58	9	25	40	0
T20Is	37	36	5	1176	79	37.93	141.51	0	7	14	0
First-class	217	358	26	16522	355*	49.76		50	71	152	0
List A	253	233	34	8112	147	40.76		15	46	85	0
Twenty20	181	175	25	5258	115*	35.05	136.82	3	32	62	0

Bowling	Mat	Balls	Runs	Wkts	BBI	BBM	Ave	Econ	SR	5w	10
Tests	104	1311	886	10	3/52	4/78	88.60	4.05	131.1	0	0
ODIs	136	400	370	7	2/22	2/22	52.85	5.55	57.1	0	0
T20Is	37	30	53	1	1/27	1/27	53.00	10.60	30.0	0	0
First-class	217	6443	3760	73	4/31		51.50	3.50	88.2	0	0
List A	253	2390	2122	41	3/14	3/14	51.75	5.32	58.2	0	0
Twenty20	181	396	534	17	3/33	3/33	31.41	8.09	23.2	0	0

MATHEW PILLANS
RHB / RFM / R0 / W0

FULL NAME: Mathew William Pillans
BORN: July 4, 1991, Pretoria, South Africa
SQUAD NO: 47
HEIGHT: 6ft 4in
NICKNAME: Matty P
EDUCATION: Pretoria Boys High School
TEAMS: Surrey, Dolphins, KwaZulu-Natal, Northerns
ROLE: Bowler
DEBUT: First-class: 2012; List A: 2013; T20: 2014

BEST BATTING: 49 KwaZulu-Natal vs Easterns, Benoni, 2016
BEST BOWLING: 6-67 Dolphins vs Knights, Durban, 2015

FAMILY TIES? My mum played for the Springbok hockey team for 13 years and my dad played rugby in Zimbabwe and represented the World XV
STRANGEST THING SEEN IN A GAME? When a batsman slog-swept a ball into the armpit of a close fielder who had jumped in the air
BEST MOMENT IN CRICKET? Getting my first 10-wicket match haul for the Sunfoil Dolphins in South Africa
SUPERSTITIONS? Right pad first… or was it left? Oh well, I guess we'll see which works and if it doesn't we change it up next time
BEST PLAYER IN COUNTY CRICKET? Kumar Sangakkara (Sur)
CRICKETING HEROES? Adam Gilchrist, Brett Lee, Ricky Ponting, AB de Villiers, David Miller
IF YOU WEREN'T A CRICKETER? I'd be a fly-fisherman
SURPRISING FACT? I had a heart operation when I was 12 years old
FANTASY SLIP CORDON? Keeper: Chuck Norris, 1st: Kevin Hart, 2nd: Roger Federer, 3rd: Nelson Mandela, Gully: Muhammad Ali
TWITTER: @matwilpil

Batting	Mat	Inns	NO	Runs	HS	Ave	SR	100	50	Ct	St
First-class	35	49	5	602	49	13.68	63.70	0	0	19	0
List A	12	8	4	79	20*	19.75	91.86	0	0	3	0
Twenty20	10	5	1	54	23	13.50	98.18	0	0	4	0

Bowling	Mat	Balls	Runs	Wkts	BBI	BBM	Ave	Econ	SR	5w	10
First-class	35	5520	3037	114	6/67	10/129	26.64	3.30	48.4	3	1
List A	12	420	344	16	3/14	3/14	21.50	4.91	26.2	0	0
Twenty20	10	176	196	8	3/15	3/15	24.50	6.68	22.0	0	0

LIAM PLUNKETT   RHB / RFM / R0 / W3 / MVP50

FULL NAME: Liam Edward Plunkett
BORN: April 6, 1985, Middlesbrough, Yorkshire
SQUAD NO: 28
HEIGHT: 6ft 3in
NICKNAME: Pudsy
EDUCATION: Teesside Tertiary College
TEAMS: England, Yorkshire, Dolphins, Durham
ROLE: Allrounder
DEBUT: Test: 2005; ODI: 2005; T20I: 2006; First-class: 2003; List A: 2003; T20: 2003

BEST BATTING: 126 Yorkshire vs Hampshire, Headingley, 2016
BEST BOWLING: 6-33 Durham vs Leeds/Bradford MCCU, Headingley, 2013
COUNTY CAP: 2013 (Yorkshire)

TWITTER: @Liam628
NOTES: Only the second player to record a five-wicket haul on his Championship debut for Durham, 5-53 vs Yorkshire at Headingley in 2003. Made his England Test debut in November 2005 vs Pakistan at Lahore. After missing almost the entire 2012 season for Durham, Plunkett signed for Yorkshire in October of that year. He claimed 42 first-class wickets at 25.35 in 2013. In 2014 he played his first Test for England since 2007 and picked up 18 wickets in four matches before injury ended his summer. Has been a regular member of England's limited-overs teams in recent times. Scored a hundred and three fifties in the Championship in 2016 but managed only 10 wickets at 60.20. Was much more effective with the white ball

Batting	Mat	Inns	NO	Runs	HS	Ave	SR	100	50	Ct	St
Tests	13	20	5	238	55*	15.86	46.75	0	1	3	0
ODIs	49	35	13	483	56	21.95	101.47	0	1	16	0
T20Is	11	4	1	5	4	1.66	71.42	0	0	2	0
First-class	151	209	39	4269	126	25.11		3	22	86	0
List A	164	110	40	1467	72	20.95	101.59	0	3	48	0
Twenty20	106	65	24	656	41	16.00	131.72	0	0	25	0

Bowling	Mat	Balls	Runs	Wkts	BBI	BBM	Ave	Econ	SR	5w	10
Tests	13	2659	1536	41	5/64	9/176	37.46	3.46	64.8	1	0
ODIs	49	2408	2348	73	4/40	4/40	32.16	5.85	32.9	0	0
T20Is	11	239	298	13	3/21	3/21	22.92	7.48	18.3	0	0
First-class	151	23318	14071	445	6/33		31.62	3.62	52.4	11	1
List A	164	7034	6386	210	4/15	4/15	30.40	5.44	33.4	0	0
Twenty20	106	1959	2548	93	5/31	5/31	27.39	7.80	21.0	1	0

HARRY PODMORE

RHB / RMF / R0 / W0

FULL NAME: Harry William Podmore
BORN: July 23, 1994, Hammersmith, Middlesex
SQUAD NO: 23
HEIGHT: 6ft 3in
NICKNAME: Podders, Pods, Pongo, Chav
EDUCATION: Twyford CofE High School, London
TEAMS: Middlesex, Glamorgan
ROLE: Bowler
DEBUT: First-class: 2016; List A: 2014; T20: 2014

MIDDLESEX

BEST BATTING: 21 Middlesex vs Warwickshire, Edgbaston, 2016
BEST BOWLING: 4-54 Middlesex vs Somerset, Taunton, 2016

WHAT FIRST GOT YOU INTO CRICKET? Ealing CC
STRANGEST THING SEEN IN A GAME? Ryan Higgins hit a bird out of the sky
BEST MOMENT IN CRICKET? Playing at Lord's for the first time (on TV), signing for Middlesex, getting on the England fast-bowling programme
SUPERSTITIONS? The volume has to be on 23 on any electrical device
CRICKETING HEROES? Andrew Flintoff
BEST PLAYER IN COUNTY CRICKET? Nick Gubbins (Mid)
TIP FOR THE TOP? Tom Helm, Ravi Patel, Nathan Sowter, Max Holden (all Mid)
CRICKETING HEROES? Ian Botham, Andrew Flintoff
SURPRISING FACT? I have my family crest tattooed on my chest
DESERT ISLAND DISC? Shaggy – Boombastic
FANTASY SLIP CORDON? Keeper: Margot Robbie, 1st: Me, 2nd: Michelle Keegan, 3rd: Keith Lemon, Gully: Andrew Flintoff
TWITTER: @harrypod16

Batting	Mat	Inns	NO	Runs	HS	Ave	SR	100	50	Ct	St
First-class	5	6	2	47	21	11.75	41.96	0	0	1	0
List A	6	1	1	1	1*	-	50	0	0	0	0
Twenty20	19	7	3	26	9	6.5	59.09	0	0	7	0

Bowling	Mat	Balls	Runs	Wkts	BBI	BBM	Ave	Econ	SR	5w	10
First-class	5	867	465	17	4/54	7/143	27.35	3.21	51	0	0
List A	6	236	272	4	2/46	2/46	68	6.91	59	0	0
Twenty20	19	340	513	18	3/13	3/13	28.5	9.05	18.8	0	0
List A	164	7034	6386	210	4/15	4/15	30.40	5.44	33.4	0	0

ED POLLOCK

LHB / OB / R0 / W0

WARWICKSHIRE

FULL NAME: Edward John Pollock
BORN: July 10, 1995, High Wycombe, Buckinghamshire
SQUAD NO: 28
HEIGHT: 5ft 10in
EDUCATION: Royal Grammar School, Worcester; Shrewsbury School; Durham University
TEAMS: Durham MCCU, Warwickshire 2nd XI
ROLE: Batsman
DEBUT: First-class: 2015

BEST BATTING: 22 Durham MCCU vs Gloucestershire, Bristol, 2016

FAMILY TIES? My dad and brother have both captained Cambridge University
BEST MOMENT IN CRICKET? Being in the changing room at Lord's after Warwickshire won the RL Cup in 2016
HOW WOULD YOUR TEAM-MATES DESCRIBE YOU IN THREE WORDS? Rogue, punny, Tinderholic
BEST PLAYER IN COUNTY CRICKET? Jeetan Patel (War)
MOST UNDERRATED PLAYER IN COUNTY CRICKET? Joe Leach (Wor)
TIP FOR THE TOP? Cameron Steel (Dur), Josh Poysden, Mark Adair (both War)
CRICKETING HEROES? Brian Lara – he played the game with such flair
NON-CRICKETING HEROES? My parents – for all the sacrifices they've made for me
SURPRISING FACT? I am a published poet
UNUSUAL OBJECT AT HOME? My first bat – a size three-quarters from Hunts County Bats
DESERT ISLAND DISC? The Beatles – 1. I used to listen to it every year when my family would drive up to Scotland for a holiday
FANTASY SLIP CORDON? Keeper: Emma Watson (so I could spend the day trying to convince her to marry me), 1st: Me, 2nd: Plato (he'd have something interesting to offer when it's a flat pitch), 3rd: Lee Evans (always need a few jokes), Gully: Mihály Csíkszentmihályi
TWITTER: @kcollopde

Batting	Mat	Inns	NO	Runs	HS	Ave	SR	100	50	Ct	St
First-class	3	4	0	61	22	15.25	46.92	0	0	0	0
Bowling	Mat	Balls	Runs	Wkts	BBI	BBM	Ave	Econ	SR	5w	10
First-class	3	-	-	-	-	-	-	-	-	-	-

OLLIE POPE

RHB / WK / R0 / W0

FULL NAME: Oliver John Douglas Pope
BORN: January 2, 1998, Chelsea, London
SQUAD NO: 32
HEIGHT: 5ft 10in
NICKNAME: Pope-dog
EDUCATION: Cranleigh School, Surrey
TEAMS: Surrey
ROLE: Wicketkeeper
DEBUT: List A: 2016

SURREY

STRANGEST THING SEEN IN A GAME? Max Holden having a bowl
BEST MOMENT IN CRICKET? Beating Yorkshire on debut in the Royal London One-Day Cup semi-final in 2016
HOW WOULD YOUR TEAM-MATES DESCRIBE YOU IN THREE WORDS? Wind-up, chirpy
BEST PLAYER IN COUNTY CRICKET? Nick Gubbins (Mid)
MOST UNDERRATED PLAYER IN COUNTY CRICKET? Rory Burns (Sur)
TIP FOR THE TOP? George Hankins (Glo), Max Holden (Mid), Aaron Beard (Ess)
CRICKETING HEROES? Adam Gilchrist, Kumar Sangakkara
NON-CRICKETING HEROES? Thierry Henry, Dan Carter
SURPRISING FACT? I'm good at making scrambled egg
DESERT ISLAND DISC? Quinn XCII – Violins
FANTASY SLIP CORDON? Keeper: Me, 1st: Margot Robbie, 2nd: James Corden, 3rd: Jack Whitehall
TWITTER: @olliepope1015

Batting	Mat	Inns	NO	Runs	HS	Ave	SR	100	50	Ct	St
List A	1	1	0	20	20	20.00	86.95	0	0	0	0

Bowling	Mat	Balls	Runs	Wkts	BBI	BBM	Ave	Econ	SR	5w	10
List A	1	-	-	-	-	-	-	-	-	-	-

JAMIE PORTER

RHB / RMF / R0 / W2

ESSEX

FULL NAME: James Alexander Porter
BORN: May 25, 1993, Leytonstone, Essex
SQUAD NO: 44
HEIGHT: 6ft 1in
NICKNAME: Ports
EDUCATION: Oaks Park High School, Ilford; Epping Forest College, Essex
TEAMS: Essex
ROLE: Bowler
DEBUT: First-class: 2014; List A: 2015

BEST BATTING: 34 Essex vs Glamorgan, Cardiff, 2015
BEST BOWLING: 5-46 Essex vs Northamptonshire, Chelmsford, 2016
COUNTY CAP: 2015

WHAT FIRST GOT YOU INTO CRICKET? Trying to get out of lessons at school! The 2005 Ashes got me hooked
STRANGEST THING SEEN IN A GAME? Team-mate Ashar Zaidi blazing it with his black bat in a T20 against Middlesex in 2016
BEST MOMENT IN CRICKET? Winning Division Two of the Championship in 2016
SUPERSTITIONS? I always sit close to the door in the dressing room
HOW WOULD YOUR TEAM-MATES DESCRIBE YOU IN THREE WORDS? Not very smart
CRICKETING HEROES? Andrew Flintoff, James Anderson, Dale Steyn
NON-CRICKETING HEROES? James Bay
IF YOU WEREN'T A CRICKETER? I'd be selling caravans
SURPRISING FACT? I can cook minute-rice in 59 seconds
UNUSUAL OBJECT AT HOME? My black fridge
DESERT ISLAND DISC? Now That's What I Call Music Vol.1
FANTASY SLIP CORDON? Keeper: Donald Trump, 1st: Theresa May, 2nd: Me, 3rd: Boris Johnson
TWITTER: @jamieporter93

Batting	Mat	Inns	NO	Runs	HS	Ave	SR	100	50	Ct	St
First-class	34	37	14	163	34	7.08	26.03	0	0	13	0
List A	8	2	2	5	5*	-	166.66	0	0	0	0

Bowling	Mat	Balls	Runs	Wkts	BBI	BBM	Ave	Econ	SR	5w	10
First-class	34	5646	3356	121	5/46	8/99	27.73	3.56	46.6	2	0
List A	8	333	301	5	3/39	3/39	60.20	5.42	66.6	0	0

WILL PORTERFIELD

LHB / OB / RO / WO

FULL NAME: William Thomas Stuart Porterfield
BORN: September 6, 1984, Londonderry, NI
SQUAD NO: 10
HEIGHT: 5ft 10in
EDUCATION: Strabane Grammar School, County Tyrone; Leeds Metropolitan University
TEAMS: Ireland, Warwickshire, Gloucestershire
ROLE: Batsman
DEBUT: ODI: 2006; T20I: 2008; First-class: 2006; List A: 2006; T20: 2008

WARWICKSHIRE

BEST BATTING: 186 Ireland vs Namibia, Windhoek, 2015
BEST BOWLING: 1-29 Ireland vs Jamaica, Spanish Town, 2010
COUNTY CAP: 2014 (Warwickshire)

BEST MOMENT IN CRICKET? Playing in the World Cup, captaining Ireland
IF YOU WEREN'T A CRICKETER? I'd be a farmer
FANTASY SLIP CORDON? Keeper: Frankie Boyle, 1st: Jimmy Carr, 2nd: John Bishop, 3rd: Me, Gully: Kerry Katona
TWITTER: @purdy34
NOTES: Joined Warwickshire in 2011 as a well-established top-order batsman and was a valuable member of the sides which won the 2012 County Championship and the NatWest T20 Blast in 2014. He was still Ireland's all-time leading runscorer in ODI and T20I cricket ahead of the series against Afghanistan in March 2017

Batting	Mat	Inns	NO	Runs	HS	Ave	SR	100	50	Ct	St
ODIs	95	94	3	2804	112*	30.81	66.98	8	13	46	0
T20Is	56	54	6	1002	72	20.87	110.96	0	3	22	0
First-class	117	193	7	5729	186	30.80	46.47	8	31	129	0
List A	214	211	7	6589	112*	32.29	72.12	10	38	105	0
Twenty20	162	159	16	3740	127*	26.15	122.98	1	19	70	0

Bowling	Mat	Balls	Runs	Wkts	BBI	BBM	Ave	Econ	SR	5w	10
ODIs	95	-	-	-	-	-	-	-	-	-	-
T20Is	56	-	-	-	-	-	-	-	-	-	-
First-class	117	108	138	2	1/29	1/29	69.00	7.66	54.0	0	0
List A	214	-	-	-	-	-	-	-	-	-	-
Twenty20	162	-	-	-	-	-	-	-	-	-	-

STUART POYNTER

RHB / WK / R0 / W0

FULL NAME: Stuart William Poynter
BORN: October 18, 1990, Hammersmith, London
SQUAD NO: 90
HEIGHT: 5ft 8in
NICKNAME: Stuey, Points
EDUCATION: Teddington School, London
TEAMS: Ireland, Durham, Middlesex, Warwickshire
ROLE: Wicketkeeper
DEBUT: ODI: 2014; T20I: 2015; First-class: 2010; List A: 2012; T20: 2015

BEST BATTING: 125 Ireland vs Zimbabwe A, Harare, 2015

FAMILY TIES? My uncle Deryck and brother Andrew both played for Ireland
BEST MOMENT IN CRICKET? Making my debut for Ireland
CRICKETING HEROES? Jack Russell – just the best keeper I have ever seen and one of the first I saw standing up to pace bowling
NON-CRICKETING HEROES? Rodger Federer – an amazing champion, always so humble and graceful when he is playing
DESERT ISLAND DISC? Ed Sheeran – X
SURPRISING FACT? I play the ukulele
TWITTER: @spoynter_90

Batting	Mat	Inns	NO	Runs	HS	Ave	SR	100	50	Ct	St
ODIs	12	11	1	124	36	12.40	71.67	0	0	15	0
T20Is	14	12	0	152	39	12.66	111.76	0	0	6	1
First-class	15	20	0	514	125	25.70	63.53	1	1	38	2
List A	19	17	4	304	109	23.38	92.68	1	0	23	0
Twenty20	16	13	0	190	39	14.61	117.28	0	0	8	1

Bowling	Mat	Balls	Runs	Wkts	BBI	BBM	Ave	Econ	SR	5w	10
ODIs	12	-	-	-	-	-	-	-	-	-	-
T20Is	14	-	-	-	-	-	-	-	-	-	-
First-class	15	-	-	-	-	-	-	-	-	-	-
List A	19	-	-	-	-	-	-	-	-	-	-
Twenty20	16	-	-	-	-	-	-	-	-	-	-

JOSH POYSDEN
LHB / LB / RO / WO

FULL NAME: Joshua Edward Poysden
BORN: August 8, 1991, Shoreham-by-Sea, Sussex
SQUAD NO: 14
HEIGHT: 5ft 10in
NICKNAME: Dobby, Bendicii
EDUCATION: Cardinal Newman School, Hove; Anglia Ruskin University
TEAMS: Warwickshire, England Lions
ROLE: Bowler
DEBUT: First-class: 2011; List A: 2013; T20: 2014

BEST BATTING: 47 Cambridge MCCU vs Surrey, Cambridge, 2011
BEST BOWLING: 5-53 Warwickshire vs Middlesex, Edgbaston, 2016

WHAT FIRST GOT YOU INTO CRICKET? Going to watch my dad when I was a youngster, then started out playing at Brighton and Hove CC coached by the great man Dick Roberts
STRANGEST THING SEEN IN A GAME? Sam Hain trying to bowl and genuinely yipping-up – a wide that was also a front-foot no-ball and bounced three times
BEST MOMENT IN CRICKET? The atmosphere at Edgbaston when getting on the field as 12th man in the 2015 Ashes
HOW WOULD YOUR TEAM-MATES DESCRIBE YOU IN THREE WORDS? Student of cricket
BEST PLAYER IN COUNTY CRICKET? Jeetan Patel (War)
MOST UNDERRATED PLAYER IN COUNTY CRICKET? Oliver Hannon-Dalby (War)
TIP FOR THE TOP? Ed Pollock, George Panayi (both War), Ollie Pope (Sur), Harry Finch (Sus)
CRICKETING HEROES? Any gun leggies – Shane Warne, Stuart MacGill, Imran Tahir and Mushtaq Ahmed especially
SURPRISING FACT? I'm pretty keen to get a sausage dog called Frank
UNUSUAL OBJECT AT HOME? George Panayi
TWITTER: @JoshPoysden14

Batting	Mat	Inns	NO	Runs	HS	Ave	SR	100	50	Ct	St
First-class	10	8	2	71	47	11.83	42.01	0	0	2	0
List A	18	8	5	22	10*	7.33	61.11	0	0	6	0
Twenty20	19	9	8	13	9*	13.00	130.00	0	0	4	0

Bowling	Mat	Balls	Runs	Wkts	BBI	BBM	Ave	Econ	SR	5w	10
First-class	10	1095	752	21	5/53	8/133	35.80	4.12	52.1	1	0
List A	18	705	674	18	3/33	3/33	37.44	5.73	39.1	0	0
Twenty20	19	306	386	11	4/51	4/51	35.09	7.56	27.8	0	0

SEEKKUGE PRASANNA RHB / LB / R0 / W0

FULL NAME: Seekkuge Prasanna
BORN: June 27, 1985, Balapitiya, Sri Lanka
HEIGHT: 5ft 9in
EDUCATION: Rewatha College, Balapitiya
TEAMS: Sri Lanka, Northamptonshire, Barisal Bulls, Dhaka Dynamites, Hambantota Troopers, Kandurata, Southern Express, Uva Next
ROLE: Bowler
DEBUT: Test: 2011; ODI: 2011; T20I: 2013; First-class: 2006; List A: 2006; T20: 2009

BEST BATTING: 81 Sri Lanka Army vs Colts Cricket Club, Panagoda, 2013
BEST BOWLING: 8-59 Sri Lanka Army vs Bloomfield Cricket Club, Panagoda, 2009

TWITTER: @SekkugeRSL
NOTES: Northamptonshire re-signed Sri Lanka international spinner Prasanna for the 2017 T20 Blast. The leg-spinner played 11 times in the competition last season, taking 12 wickets. Useful lower-order batsman. Made a solitary Test appearance in 2011 but is a regular member of Sri Lanka's ODI and T20I sides. "It's his consistency with the ball – he recently bowled in the powerplay against Australia and did a good job of that," said Northants head coach David Ripley

Batting	Mat	Inns	NO	Runs	HS	Ave	SR	100	50	Ct	St
Tests	1	1	0	5	5	5.00	41.66	0	0	0	0
ODIs	34	31	3	370	95	13.21	103.64	0	2	4	0
T20Is	14	14	4	130	37*	13.00	135.41	0	0	4	0
First-class	98	155	7	3216	81	21.72	97.27	0	18	70	0
List A	129	109	12	1567	95	16.15	106.88	0	7	39	0
Twenty20	97	80	21	1024	53	17.35	164.10	0	2	33	0

Bowling	Mat	Balls	Runs	Wkts	BBI	BBM	Ave	Econ	SR	5w	10
Tests	1	138	80	0	-	-	-	3.47	-	0	0
ODIs	34	1651	1503	28	3/32	3/32	53.67	5.46	58.9	0	0
T20Is	14	228	281	8	2/45	2/45	35.12	7.39	28.5	0	0
First-class	98	18791	10500	488	8/59	14/181	21.51	3.35	38.5	37	8
List A	129	5833	4322	175	6/23	6/23	24.69	4.44	33.3	4	0
Twenty20	97	1736	1984	76	4/19	4/19	26.10	6.85	22.8	0	0

RYAN PRINGLE

RHB / OB / R0 / W0

FULL NAME: Ryan David Pringle
BORN: April 17, 1992, Sunderland
SQUAD NO: 17
HEIGHT: 6ft 1in
NICKNAME: Rhino
EDUCATION: Hetton Comprehensive School, Sunderland; Durham Sixth Form Centre; University of Sunderland
TEAMS: Durham
ROLE: Allrounder
DEBUT: First-class: 2014; List A: 2012; T20: 2013

DURHAM

BEST BATTING: 99 Durham vs Hampshire, Chester-le-Street, 2015
BEST BOWLING: 7-107 Durham vs Hampshire, Southampton, 2016

WHAT FIRST GOT YOU INTO CRICKET? My next-door neighbour made me my first bat, plus the tuck shop at my local club had great mix-up bags
BEST MOMENT IN CRICKET? The ton I scored in the the 2016 RL Cup – my first for Durham
HOW WOULD YOUR TEAM-MATES DESCRIBE YOU IN THREE WORDS? An average bloke
BEST PLAYER IN COUNTY CRICKET? Keaton Jennings (Dur)
TIP FOR THE TOP? Brydon Carse (Dur)
CRICKETING HEROES? Ricky Ponting
NON-CRICKETING HEROES? My grandad – someone I've always looked up to and respected and will continue to do so
IF YOU WEREN'T A CRICKETER? I'd be a psychologist
SURPRISING FACT? I was on the first flight from Teeside airport to Florida
UNUSUAL OBJECT AT HOME? A goat in my downstairs toilet
FANTASY SLIP CORDON? Keeper: Harry Potter, 1st: Severus Snape, 2nd: Draco Malfoy, 3rd: Me, Gully: Hermione Granger (I'm a fan of the Harry Potter series)
TWITTER: @RyanPringle

Batting	Mat	Inns	NO	Runs	HS	Ave	SR	100	50	Ct	St
First-class	23	34	4	796	99	26.53	57.34	0	5	12	0
List A	28	20	0	379	125	18.95	108.90	1	0	9	0
Twenty20	50	36	5	282	33	9.09	120.00	0	0	16	0

Bowling	Mat	Balls	Runs	Wkts	BBI	BBM	Ave	Econ	SR	5w	10
First-class	23	2547	1598	43	7/107	10/260	37.16	3.76	59.2	2	1
List A	28	639	645	9	2/39	2/39	71.66	6.05	71.0	0	0
Twenty20	50	516	736	16	2/13	2/13	46.00	8.55	32.2	0	0

LUKE PROCTER

LHB / RM / R0 / W0

FULL NAME: Luke Anthony Procter
BORN: June 24, 1988, Oldham, Lancashire
SQUAD NO: 2
HEIGHT: 5ft 11in
NICKNAME: Proccy
EDUCATION: Counthill School, Oldham
TEAMS: Lancashire
ROLE: Allrounder
DEBUT: First-class: 2010; List A: 2009;
T20: 2011

BEST BATTING: 137 Lancashire vs Hampshire, Old Trafford, 2016
BEST BOWLING: 7-71 Lancashire vs Surrey, Liverpool, 2012

BEST MOMENT IN CRICKET? Winning the County Championship in 2011
CRICKETING HEROES? Marcus Trescothick
TWITTER: @vvsprocter
NOTES: Procter has flourished in the longer form of the game after developing into a genuine allrounder who bowls left-arm seam and offers solidity with the bat. Scored 822 Championship runs at 34.25 in 2016, including two hundreds, although he struggled with the ball, taking 10 wickets at 50.50

Batting	Mat	Inns	NO	Runs	HS	Ave	SR	100	50	Ct	St
First-class	62	94	6	2799	137	31.80	42.44	3	14	14	0
List A	29	20	6	450	97	32.14	85.22	0	4	4	0
Twenty20	25	13	5	122	25*	15.25	96.06	0	0	7	0

Bowling	Mat	Balls	Runs	Wkts	BBI	BBM	Ave	Econ	SR	5w	10
First-class	62	4194	2388	68	7/71	8/79	35.11	3.41	61.6	2	0
List A	29	510	534	12	3/29	3/29	44.50	6.28	42.5	0	0
Twenty20	25	116	176	8	3/22	3/22	22.00	9.10	14.5	0	0

IMRAN QAYYUM

RHB / SLA / R0 / W0

FULL NAME: Imran Qayyum
BORN: May 23, 1993, Ealing, Middlesex
SQUAD NO: 11
HEIGHT: 5ft 11in
NICKNAME: Imy, IQ
EDUCATION: Villiers High School, Ealing;
Greenford High School, Ealing; City
University of London
TEAMS: Kent
ROLE: Bowler
DEBUT: First-class: 2016; List A: 2017

KENT

BEST BATTING: 0* Kent vs Sussex, Tunbridge Wells, 2016
BEST BOWLING: 3-158 Kent vs Northamptonshire, Northampton, 2016

FAMILY TIES? Dad played in Pakistan, brother plays club cricket in Hertfordshire
BEST MOMENT IN CRICKET? Playing alongside Geraint Jones
HOW WOULD YOUR TEAM-MATES DESCRIBE YOU IN THREE WORDS? Mercurial, loud,
random
BEST PLAYER IN COUNTY CRICKET? Jeetan Patel (War)
MOST UNDERRATED PLAYER IN COUNTY CRICKET? Samit Patel (Not)
TIP FOR THE TOP? Hugh Bernard (Ken)
CRICKETING HEROES? Shoaib Akhtar, Shahid Afridi and Virat Kohli for their extravagance
NON-CRICKETING HEROES? Amir Khan
IF YOU WEREN'T A CRICKETER? I'd be a financial advisor
SURPRISING FACT? I hate sleeping because it makes me feel that I am missing out on life
DESERT ISLAND DISC? Kanye West – Graduation
FANTASY SLIP CORDON? Keeper: Daniel Bell-Drummond, 1st: Me, 2nd: Ivan Thomas,
3rd: Adam Ball, 4th: Alex Blake, Gully: Calum Haggett
TWITTER: @ImranQC

Batting	Mat	Inns	NO	Runs	HS	Ave	SR	100	50	Ct	St
First-class	2	2	1	0	0*	0.00	0.00	0	0	1	0
List A	5	2	0	18	18	9.00	112.50	0	0	2	0

Bowling	Mat	Balls	Runs	Wkts	BBI	BBM	Ave	Econ	SR	5w	10
First-class	2	470	283	6	3/158	3/125	47.16	3.61	78.3	0	0
List A	5	264	192	5	3/42	3/42	38.40	4.36	52.8	0	0

MATT QUINN

RHB / RMF / RO / WO

ESSEX

FULL NAME: Matthew Richard Quinn
BORN: February 28, 1993, Auckland, New Zealand
SQUAD NO: 94
HEIGHT: 6ft 5in
NICKNAME: Quinny, Giraffe
EDUCATION: Sacred Heart College, Auckland; Auckland University of Technology
TEAMS: Essex, Auckland
ROLE: Bowler
DEBUT: First-class: 2013; List A: 2013; T20: 2012

BEST BATTING: 50 Auckland vs Canterbury, Auckland, 2013
BEST BOWLING: 7-76 Essex vs Gloucestershire, Cheltenham, 2016

FAMILY TIES? My great grandad played social cricket in Yorkshire
STRANGEST THING SEEN IN A GAME? A bee-sting up the trouser leg resulting in pants being pulled down in front of a sizeable crowd
HOW WOULD YOUR TEAM-MATES DESCRIBE YOU IN THREE WORDS? The stupid Kiwi
BEST PLAYER IN COUNTY CRICKET? Tom Westley (Ess)
MOST UNDERRATED PLAYER IN COUNTY CRICKET? Dan Lawrence (Ess)
TIP FOR THE TOP? Aaron Beard (Ess)
CRICKETING HEROES? Shane Bond, Martin Crowe
IF YOU WEREN'T A CRICKETER? I'd be driving a forklift
TWITTER: @quinny_cricket

Batting	Mat	Inns	NO	Runs	HS	Ave	SR	100	50	Ct	St
First-class	24	31	5	279	50	10.73	60.25	0	1	4	0
List A	26	17	10	117	36	16.71	71.34	0	0	2	0
Twenty20	39	8	7	23	8*	23.00	135.29	0	0	8	0

Bowling	Mat	Balls	Runs	Wkts	BBI	BBM	Ave	Econ	SR	5w	10
First-class	24	4807	2648	95	7/76	11/163	27.87	3.30	50.6	1	1
List A	26	1290	1256	36	4/71	4/71	34.88	5.84	35.8	0	0
Twenty20	39	790	1178	39	4/35	4/35	30.20	8.94	20.2	0	0

AZEEM RAFIQ — RHB / OB / R0 / W0

FULL NAME: Azeem Rafiq
BORN: February 27, 1991, Karachi, Pakistan
SQUAD NO: 30
NICKNAME: Rafa
EDUCATION: Holgate School, Barnsley; Barnsley College
TEAMS: Yorkshire, Derbyshire
ROLE: Allrounder
DEBUT: First-class: 2009; List A: 2009; T20: 2008

BEST BATTING: 100 Yorkshire vs Worcestershire, Worcester, 2009
BEST BOWLING: 5-50 Yorkshire vs Essex, Chelmsford, 2012
COUNTY CAP: 2016 (Yorkshire)

TWITTER: @AzeemRafiq30
NOTES: Re-joined Yorkshire last season after almost two years away from the professional game. Former captain of England age-group sides – U15, U17 and U19 – and the first player of Asian heritage to captain Yorkshire when he was T20 skipper in 2012. Released by Yorkshire in 2014 after struggling to build on notable early showings but impressed in one-day cricket last season with his intelligent off-breaks and canny batting. Sure to be a useful short-form option again this season, especially with Adil Rashid likely to be on England duty

Batting	Mat	Inns	NO	Runs	HS	Ave	SR	100	50	Ct	St
First-class	32	38	5	812	100	24.60	56.98	1	4	14	0
List A	26	19	8	174	34*	15.81	84.87	0	0	10	0
Twenty20	71	30	19	144	21*	13.09	96.64	0	0	31	0

Bowling	Mat	Balls	Runs	Wkts	BBI	BBM	Ave	Econ	SR	5w	10
First-class	32	4535	2345	61	5/50	8/115	38.44	3.10	74.3	1	0
List A	26	930	867	25	5/30	5/30	34.68	5.59	37.2	1	0
Twenty20	71	1451	1787	77	3/15	3/15	23.20	7.38	18.8	0	0

BEN RAINE

LHB / RMF / R0 / W1 / MVP91

LEICESTERSHIRE

FULL NAME: Benjamin Alexander Raine
BORN: September 14, 1991, Sunderland
SQUAD NO: 44
HEIGHT: 6ft
NICKNAME: Rainger
EDUCATION: St Aidan's Catholic Academy, Sunderland
TEAMS: Leicestershire, Durham
ROLE: Bowler
DEBUT: First-class: 2011; List A: 2011; T20: 2014

BEST BATTING: 72 Leicestershire vs Lancashire, Old Trafford, 2013
BEST BOWLING: 5-43 Leicestershire vs Glamorgan, Cardiff, 2015

WHAT FIRST GOT YOU INTO CRICKET? Watching my dad play local league cricket
BEST MOMENT IN CRICKET? Watching Charlie Shreck take his 500th wicket
HOW WOULD YOUR TEAM-MATES DESCRIBE YOU IN THREE WORDS? Reserved, dependable, relaxed
BEST PLAYER IN COUNTY CRICKET? Chris Rushworth (Dur)
TIP FOR THE TOP? Angus Robson (Lei)
CRICKETING HEROES? Matthew Hayden – he just destroyed bowlers
NON-CRICKETING HEROES? Mike Tyson, Tiger Woods – they're the best at what they do
IF YOU WEREN'T A CRICKETER? I'd be working at the Nissan factory
SURPRISING FACT? I'm not a Newcastle fan, as many seem to think I am
TWITTER: @BenRaine88

Batting	Mat	Inns	NO	Runs	HS	Ave	SR	100	50	Ct	St
First-class	44	71	5	1307	72	19.80	44.38	0	5	9	0
List A	14	10	0	164	43	16.40	110.06	0	0	3	0
Twenty20	34	22	8	273	48	19.50	109.20	0	0	8	0

Bowling	Mat	Balls	Runs	Wkts	BBI	BBM	Ave	Econ	SR	5w	10
First-class	44	7036	3818	123	5/43	8/107	31.04	3.25	57.2	3	0
List A	14	624	656	13	3/62	3/62	50.46	6.30	48.0	0	0
Twenty20	34	698	957	42	3/7	3/7	22.78	8.22	16.6	0	0

RAVI RAMPAUL

LHB / RFM / R0 / W0

FULL NAME: Ravindranath Rampaul
BORN: October 15, 1984, Preysal, Trinidad
SQUAD NO: 14
NICKNAME: Frisco Kid
EDUCATION: Presentation College, Trinidad
TEAMS: West Indies, Surrey, Barbados
Tridents, Ireland, Royal Challengers
Bangalore, Trinidad & Tobago,
ROLE: Bowler
DEBUT: Test: 2009; ODI: 2003; T20I: 2007;
First-class: 2002; List A: 2003; T20: 2007

BEST BATTING: 64* West Indies A vs Sri Lanka A, Basseterre, 2006
BEST BOWLING: 7-51 Trinidad & Tobago vs Barbados, Point-a-Pierre, 2007

TWITTER: @RaviRampaul14
NOTES: Former West Indies seamer who joined Surrey as a Kolpak player on a two-year contract which runs until the end of this season. Rampaul is available to play in all formats, adding consistency and experience to the county's seam attack. Took 21 wickets at 24.28 in six Championship matches last summer, and was also impressive in his fleeting appearances in the short formats. Rampaul made his international debut in 2003 and last played for West Indies in 2015

Batting	Mat	Inns	NO	Runs	HS	Ave	SR	100	50	Ct	St
Tests	18	31	8	335	40*	14.56	53.25	0	0	3	0
ODIs	92	40	11	362	86*	12.48	76.69	0	1	14	0
T20Is	23	6	5	12	8	12.00	57.14	0	0	2	0
First-class	67	98	20	1064	64*	13.64		0	2	20	0
List A	161	78	26	625	86*	12.01		0	1	28	0
Twenty20	114	36	20	155	23*	9.68	101.30	0	0	20	0

Bowling	Mat	Balls	Runs	Wkts	BBI	BBM	Ave	Econ	SR	5w	10
Tests	18	3440	1705	49	4/48	7/75	34.79	2.97	70.2	0	0
ODIs	92	4033	3434	117	5/49	5/49	29.35	5.10	34.4	2	0
T20Is	23	497	705	29	3/16	3/16	24.31	8.51	17.1	0	0
First-class	67	10633	5995	203	7/51		29.53	3.38	52.3	9	1
List A	161	7298	5778	237	5/49	5/49	24.37	4.75	30.7	2	0
Twenty20	114	2446	2994	145	5/9	5/9	20.64	7.34	16.8	1	0

WARWICKSHIRE

FULL NAME: William Boyd Rankin
BORN: July 5, 1984, Londonderry,
Northern Ireland
SQUAD NO: 30
HEIGHT: 6ft 8in
NICKNAME: Boydo
EDUCATION: Strabane Grammar School;
Harper Adams University College
TEAMS: England, Ireland, Warwickshire,
Derbyshire
ROLE: Bowler
DEBUT: Test: 2014; ODI: 2007; T20I: 2009;
First-class: 2007; List A: 2006; T20: 2009

BEST BATTING: 56* Warwickshire vs Worcestershire, Edgbaston, 2015
BEST BOWLING: 6-55 Warwickshire vs Yorkshire, Headingley, 2015
COUNTY CAP: 2013 (Warwickshire)

FAMILY TIES? My dad played club cricket and my brothers Robert and David have played for
Ireland U19, with David also playing for Ireland A. My sister plays for my home club Bready
STRANGEST THING SEEN IN A GAME? Someone run onto the field and take off with the bails
BEST MOMENT IN CRICKET? Beating Pakistan in the 2007 World Cup on St Paddy's Day
HOW WOULD YOUR TEAM-MATES DESCRIBE YOU IN THREE WORDS? Big Friendly Giant
CRICKETING HEROES? I've tried to emulate Curtly Ambrose and Glenn McGrath
NON-CRICKETING HEROES? Steven Gerrard, George Best, Paul O'Connell
IF YOU WEREN'T A CRICKETER? I would be back home in Ireland on the family farm
TWITTER: @boydrankin

Batting	Mat	Inns	NO	Runs	HS	Ave	SR	100	50	Ct	St
Tests	1	2	0	13	13	6.50	54.16	0	0	0	0
ODIs	46	20	14	58	18*	9.66	44.61	0	0	6	0
T20Is	26	6	4	31	16*	15.50	96.87	0	0	9	0
First-class	97	111	46	577	56*	8.87	43.12	0	1	25	0
List A	105	37	20	122	18*	7.17	50.00	0	0	17	0
Twenty20	55	12	7	39	16*	7.80	86.66	0	0	13	0

Bowling	Mat	Balls	Runs	Wkts	BBI	BBM	Ave	Econ	SR	5w	10
Tests	1	125	81	1	1/47	1/81	81.00	3.88	125.0	0	0
ODIs	46	2139	1763	56	4/46	4/46	31.48	4.94	38.1	0	0
T20Is	26	522	537	28	3/16	3/16	19.17	6.17	18.6	0	0
First-class	97	13987	8368	317	6/55	8/115	26.39	3.58	44.1	8	0
List A	105	4412	3658	129	4/34	4/34	28.35	4.97	34.2	0	0
Twenty20	55	1104	1205	63	4/9	4/9	19.12	6.54	17.5	0	0

ADIL RASHID RHB / LB / RO / W2 / MVP74

FULL NAME: Adil Usman Rashid
BORN: February 17, 1988, Bradford, Yorkshire
SQUAD NO: 3
HEIGHT: 5ft 8in
NICKNAME: Dilly, Dilo, Rash
EDUCATION: Heaton School, Bradford; Bellevue Sixth Form College, Bradford
TEAMS: England, Yorkshire, Adelaide Strikers, South Australia
ROLE: Allrounder
DEBUT: Test: 2015; ODI: 2009; T20I: 2009; First-class: 2006; List A: 2006; T20: 2008

YORKSHIRE

BEST BATTING: 180 Yorkshire vs Somerset, Headingley, 2013
BEST BOWLING: 7-107 Yorkshire vs Hampshire, Southampton, 2008
COUNTY CAP: 2008

BEST MOMENT IN CRICKET? Playing for England
CRICKETING HEROES? Sachin Tendulkar, Shane Warne
NON-CRICKETING HEROES? Muhammad Ali
IF YOU WEREN'T A CRICKETER? I'd be a taxi driver
SURPRISING FACT? I have a big FIFA video game rivalry with Moeen Ali
TWITTER: @AdilRashid03

Batting	Mat	Inns	NO	Runs	HS	Ave	SR	100	50	Ct	St
Tests	10	18	2	295	61	18.43	35.28	0	2	3	0
ODIs	41	19	6	336	69	25.84	108.38	0	1	15	0
T20Is	23	9	6	28	9*	9.33	75.67	0	0	8	0
First-class	159	226	37	6366	180	33.68		10	36	78	0
List A	143	92	28	1342	71	20.96	88.46	0	2	46	0
Twenty20	134	72	25	615	36*	13.08	104.06	0	0	39	0

Bowling	Mat	Balls	Runs	Wkts	BBI	BBM	Ave	Econ	SR	5w	10
Tests	10	2544	1626	38	5/64	7/178	42.78	3.83	66.9	1	0
ODIs	41	2068	1945	55	4/43	4/43	35.36	5.64	37.6	0	0
T20Is	23	414	547	16	2/18	2/18	34.18	7.92	25.8	0	0
First-class	159	27981	16685	480	7/107	11/114	34.76	3.57	58.2	19	1
List A	143	6333	5650	178	5/33	5/33	31.74	5.35	35.5	1	0
Twenty20	134	2655	3316	147	4/20	4/20	22.55	7.49	18.0	0	0

DELRAY RAWLINS

LHB / SLA / RO / WO

SUSSEX

FULL NAME: Delray Millard Wendell Rawlins
BORN: September 14, 1997, Bermuda
SQUAD NO: 9
HEIGHT: 6ft 2in
NICKNAME: Del
EDUCATION: St Bede's School, East Sussex
TEAMS: England U19, Sussex 2nd XI
ROLE: Allrounder
DEBUT: Yet to make first-team debut

WHAT FIRST GOT YOU INTO CRICKET? Watching my dad play local league cricket
STRANGEST THING SEEN IN A GAME? Someone picking up the ball with their hat
BEST MOMENT IN CRICKET? Taking five wickets in an U19 World Cup qualifier
SUPERSTITIONS? I tap the crease with my bat a certain number of times before a delivery
HOW WOULD YOUR TEAM-MATES DESCRIBE YOU IN THREE WORDS? Has great potential
BEST PLAYER IN COUNTY CRICKET? Nick Gubbins (Mid)
MOST UNDERRATED PLAYER IN COUNTY CRICKET? David Lloyd (Gla)
TIP FOR THE TOP? Jofra Archer (Sus)
CRICKETING HEROES? Brian Lara
NON-CRICKETING HEROES? Wayne Rooney
IF YOU WEREN'T A CRICKETER? I'd be at university
SURPRISING FACT? I like cheese a lot
DESERT ISLAND DISC? Drake – Nothing Was The Same
FANTASY SLIP CORDON? Keeper: Spider-Man, 1st: Dwayne Leverock, 2nd: Khloé Kardashian,
3rd: Me, Gully: Liam Neeson
TWITTER: @drawlins09

OLLIE RAYNER   RHB/OB/R0/W1/MVP54

FULL NAME: Oliver Philip Rayner
BORN: November 1, 1985, Bad Fallingbostel, Lower Saxony, Germany
SQUAD NO: 2
HEIGHT: 6ft 6in
NICKNAME: Draynes, Vaynes, Great Raynes, Ashton Kutcher
EDUCATION: St Bede's School, East Sussex
TEAMS: Middlesex, England Lions, Mid West Rhinos, Sussex
ROLE: Bowler
DEBUT: First-class: 2006; List A: 2006; T20: 2006

MIDDLESEX

BEST BATTING: 143* Middlesex vs Nottinghamshire, Trent Bridge, 2012
BEST BOWLING: 8-46 Middlesex vs Surrey, The Oval, 2013
COUNTY CAP: 2015 (Middlesex)

WHAT FIRST GOT YOU INTO CRICKET? Playing with my family on the beach when the tide went out in Eastbourne

FAMILY TIES? No family ties – cricket is the only sport not really played in my family, as you can probably tell when watching me!

STRANGEST THING SEEN IN A GAME? Batting with Ryan Higgins when he slog-swept one into a seagull and the gull nearly hitting me. I'm told the bird made a full recovery

BEST PLAYER IN COUNTY CRICKET? Sam Robson (Mid)

MOST UNDERRATED PLAYER IN COUNTY CRICKET? Craig Overton (Som)

TIP FOR THE TOP? Tom Alsop (Ham), Max Holden, Tom Helm (both Mid)

CRICKETING HEROES? Graeme Swann – I was losing faith in bowling conventional off-spin until he tore up the international scene

SURPRISING FACT? I prefer wearing Y-fronts to boxer shorts

UNUSUAL OBJECT AT HOME? Some interesting art prints and a longboard collection

TWITTER: @ollie2rayner

Batting	Mat	Inns	NO	Runs	HS	Ave	SR	100	50	Ct	St
First-class	118	155	26	2805	143*	21.74	50.90	2	12	158	0
List A	60	41	19	500	61	22.72	90.74	0	1	32	0
Twenty20	71	43	16	343	41*	12.70	103.00	0	0	17	0

Bowling	Mat	Balls	Runs	Wkts	BBI	BBM	Ave	Econ	SR	5w	10
First-class	118	18172	8628	266	8/46	15/118	32.43	2.84	68.3	10	1
List A	60	2292	1969	53	4/35	4/35	37.15	5.15	43.2	0	0
Twenty20	71	1323	1620	41	5/18	5/18	39.51	7.34	32.2	1	0

CHRIS READ

RHB / RM / WK / R3 / W0

NOTTINGHAMSHIRE

FULL NAME: Christopher Mark Wells Read
BORN: August 10, 1978, Paignton, Devon
SQUAD NO: 7
HEIGHT: 5ft 8in
NICKNAME: Reados, Readie
EDUCATION: Torquay Boys' Grammar School; University of Bath; Loughborough University
TEAMS: England, Nottinghamshire, Gloucestershire
ROLE: Wicketkeeper
DEBUT: Test: 1999; ODI: 2000; T20I: 2006; First-class: 1998; List A: 1995; T20: 2004

BEST BATTING: 240 Nottinghamshire vs Essex, Chelmsford, 2007
COUNTY CAP: 1999 (Nottinghamshire) BENEFIT: 2009 (Nottinghamshire)

FAMILY TIES? Winning the County Championship with Nottinghamshire twice – first in 2005 and then again in 2010
SUPERSTITIONS? Anything to keep the cricketing gods onside
CRICKETING HEROES? Ian Botham, Ian Healy, Jack Russell
NON-CRICKETING HEROES? Sébastian Loeb
IF YOU WEREN'T A CRICKETER? I'd be racing and road-testing cars or living the dream as a rock star
FANTASY SLIP CORDON? Keeper: Me, 1st: Natalie Portman, 2nd: Noel Gallagher, 3rd: Will Ferrell, Gully: Jeremy Clarkson

Batting	Mat	Inns	NO	Runs	HS	Ave	SR	100	50	Ct	St
Tests	15	23	4	360	55	18.94	39.47	0	1	48	6
ODIs	36	24	7	300	30*	17.64	73.17	0	0	41	2
T20Is	1	1	0	13	13	13.00	118.18	0	0	1	0
First-class	334	507	85	15700	240	37.20		25	89	995	52
List A	321	256	72	5416	135	29.43		2	22	307	73
Twenty20	119	98	36	1441	58*	23.24	124.22	0	1	60	27

Bowling	Mat	Balls	Runs	Wkts	BBI	BBM	Ave	Econ	SR	5w	10
Tests	15	-	-	-	-	-	-	-	-	-	-
ODIs	36	-	-	-	-	-	-	-	-	-	-
T20Is	1	-	-	-	-	-	-	-	-	-	-
First-class	334	96	90	0	-	-	-	5.62	-	0	0
List A	321	-	-	-	-	-	-	-	-	-	-
Twenty20	119	-	-	-	-	-	-	-	-	-	-

LUIS REECE

LHB / LM / RO / WO

FULL NAME: Luis Michael Reece
BORN: August 4, 1990, Taunton
SQUAD NO: 10
HEIGHT: 6ft 1in
NICKNAME: Reecey, Rexy, Red Rum
EDUCATION: St Michael's School;
Myerscough College; Leeds Metropolitan
University
TEAMS: Derbyshire, Lancashire
ROLE: Batsman
DEBUT: First-class: 2012; List A: 2011;
T20: 2016

DERBYSHIRE

BEST BATTING: 114* Leeds/Bradford MCCU vs Leicestershire, Leicester, 2013
BEST BOWLING: 4-28 Leeds/Bradford MCCU vs Leicestershire, Leicester, 2013

STRANGEST THING SEEN IN A GAME? A streaker falling over the stumps after getting his parts stuck
BEST MOMENT IN CRICKET? Walking out at Lord's to play a County Championship game
HOW WOULD YOUR TEAM-MATES DESCRIBE YOU IN THREE WORDS? Guess I'll find out in a few months
BEST PLAYER IN COUNTY CRICKET? Jeetan Patel (War)
MOST UNDERRATED PLAYER IN COUNTY CRICKET? Joe Leach (Wor)
TIP FOR THE TOP? Alex Davies, Liam Livingstone (both Lan), Ben Slater (Der)
CRICKETING HEROES? AB de Villiers, Brett Lee, Brian Lara
IF YOU WEREN'T A CRICKETER? A question I've still not found an answer to…
SURPRISING FACT? I played chess at national level as a kid
DESERT ISLAND DISC? Tenacious D
FANTASY SLIP CORDON? Keeper: Jack Whitehall, 1st: Will Smith, 2nd: Jack Black, 3rd: Me, Gully: Yoda
TWITTER: @lreece17

Batting	Mat	Inns	NO	Runs	HS	Ave	SR	100	50	Ct	St
First-class	29	51	5	1503	114*	32.67	48.59	1	12	17	0
List A	22	20	4	409	59	25.56	84.32	0	2	6	0
Twenty20	4	3	0	48	32	16.00	114.28	0	0	1	0

Bowling	Mat	Balls	Runs	Wkts	BBI	BBM	Ave	Econ	SR	5w	10
First-class	29	888	542	14	4/28	6/67	38.71	3.66	63.4	0	0
List A	22	404	418	6	4/35	4/35	69.66	6.20	67.3	0	0
Twenty20	4	36	65	2	2/29	2/29	32.50	10.83	18.0	0	0

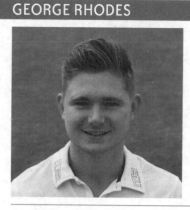

GEORGE RHODES

RHB / OB / R0 / W0

WORCESTERSHIRE

FULL NAME: George Harry Rhodes
BORN: October 26, 1993, Birmingham
SQUAD NO: 34
HEIGHT: 6ft
NICKNAME: Rhodesy, Gnomey, Big Sword
EDUCATION: The Chase School, Malvern; University of Worcester
TEAMS: Worcestershire
ROLE: Allrounder
DEBUT: First-class: 2016; List A: 2016; T20: 2016

BEST BATTING: 59 Worcestershire vs Essex, Chelmsford, 2016
BEST BOWLING: 2-83 Worcestershire vs Kent, Canterbury, 2016

FAMILY TIES? My father (Steve) played for Worcestershire for 20 years and played 11 Tests and nine ODIs for England. Grandfather (William) played first-class cricket for Notts
BEST MOMENT IN CRICKET? Recording my best T20 figures of 4-13 in the victory over Birmingham Bears in 2016
HOW WOULD YOUR TEAM-MATES DESCRIBE YOU IN THREE WORDS? Gnomey round face
BEST PLAYER IN COUNTY CRICKET? Jeetan Patel (War)
MOST UNDERRATED PLAYER IN COUNTY CRICKET? Ben Cox (Wor)
TIP FOR THE TOP? Josh Tongue (Wor)
CRICKETING HEROES? Moeen Ali – inspirational attitude to training and improving
IF YOU WEREN'T A CRICKETER? I'd be an astronaut
SURPRISING FACT? I did a skydive in 2014
UNUSUAL OBJECT AT HOME? Tom Kohler-Cadmore
DESERT ISLAND DISC? Bobby McFerrin – Don't Worry, Be Happy
TWITTER: @Ghrhodes

Batting	Mat	Inns	NO	Runs	HS	Ave	SR	100	50	Ct	St
First-class	6	11	2	274	59	30.44	44.77	0	2	2	0
List A	5	2	1	5	5*	5.00	71.42	0	0	3	0
Twenty20	4	3	0	16	8	5.33	100.00	0	0	1	0

Bowling	Mat	Balls	Runs	Wkts	BBI	BBM	Ave	Econ	SR	5w	10
First-class	6	389	263	3	2/83	2/83	87.66	4.05	129.6	0	0
List A	5	168	162	5	2/34	2/34	32.40	5.78	33.6	0	0
Twenty20	4	42	43	5	4/13	4/13	8.60	6.14	8.4	0	0

392

WILL RHODES
LHB / RMF / R0 / W0

FULL NAME: William Michael Harry Rhodes
BORN: March 2, 1995, Nottingham
SQUAD NO: 35
HEIGHT: 6ft 2in
NICKNAME: Codhead, Besty
EDUCATION: Cottingham High School, Hull
TEAMS: Yorkshire, Essex
ROLE: Allrounder
DEBUT: First-class: 2015; List A: 2013; T20: 2013

BEST BATTING: 95 Yorkshire vs MCC, Abu Dhabi, 2016
BEST BOWLING: 3-42 Yorkshire vs Middlesex, Headingley, 2015

FAMILY TIES? Dad played a bit of Nottinghamshire schoolboy cricket
BEST MOMENT IN CRICKET? Winning a Roses match at Headingley
SUPERSTITIONS? I have to mark my guard 10 times when arriving at the crease
HOW WOULD YOUR TEAM-MATES DESCRIBE YOU IN THREE WORDS? Outgoing, sociable, determined
BEST PLAYER IN COUNTY CRICKET? Jonny Bairstow (Yor)
TIP FOR THE TOP? Matthew Fisher, Matthew Waite (both Yor)
IF YOU WEREN'T A CRICKETER? I'd be a professional footballer
DESERT ISLAND DISC? 5ive – Invincible
FANTASY SLIP CORDON? Keeper: Binky Felstead; 1st: Sarah Rafferty, 2nd: Me, 3rd: Meghan Markle, Gully: Ariana Grande
TWITTER: @will_rhodes152

Batting	Mat	Inns	NO	Runs	HS	Ave	SR	100	50	Ct	St
First-class	19	28	2	693	95	26.65	42.51	0	3	9	0
List A	19	16	2	242	46	17.28	71.38	0	0	6	0
Twenty20	18	16	3	128	45	9.84	105.78	0	0	2	0

Bowling	Mat	Balls	Runs	Wkts	BBI	BBM	Ave	Econ	SR	5w	10
First-class	19	1559	829	25	3/42	4/114	33.16	3.19	62.3	0	0
List A	19	379	344	10	2/22	2/22	34.40	5.44	37.9	0	0
Twenty20	18	187	283	13	3/27	3/27	21.76	9.08	14.3	0	0

MICHAEL RICHARDSON
RHB / WK / R2 / W0

FULL NAME: Michael John Richardson
BORN: October 4, 1986, Port Elizabeth, SA
SQUAD NO: 18
HEIGHT: 5ft 11in
NICKNAME: Richie, Rory, Chelsea
EDUCATION: Rondebosch Boys' High School,
South Africa; Stonyhurst College, Lancashire;
University of Nottingham
TEAMS: Durham, Badureliya Sports Club,
Colombo
ROLE: Wicketkeeper
DEBUT: First-class: 2010; List A: 2012;
T20: 2013

BEST BATTING: 148 Durham vs Yorkshire, Chester-le-Street, 2014

FAMILY TIES? My father David played for South Africa, my grandfather John played for Northern Transvaal, my cousin Matthew played for Border, my uncle Ralph played for Western Province
BEST MOMENT IN CRICKET? Beating Yorkshire in the 2016 T20 semi-final and winning the County Championship in 2013
HOW WOULD YOUR TEAM-MATES DESCRIBE YOU IN THREE WORDS? Just on time
BEST PLAYER IN COUNTY CRICKET? Tim Bresnan (Yor)
MOST UNDERRATED PLAYER IN COUNTY CRICKET? Wayne Madsen (Der)
TIP FOR THE TOP? James Weighell, Brydon Carse (both Dur)
CRICKETING HEROES? Neil McKenzie, AB de Villiers, Brian Lara
NON-CRICKETING HEROES? Rafa Nadal, Rory McIlroy
UNUSUAL OBJECT AT HOME? An egg boiler
DESERT ISLAND DISC? Timo ODV – Dancing Again
FANTASY SLIP CORDON? Keeper: MS Dhoni, 1st: José Mourinho, 2nd: Jennifer Aniston, 3rd: Me, Gully: Dave Roberts
TWITTER: @richo18howu

Batting	Mat	Inns	NO	Runs	HS	Ave	SR	100	50	Ct	St
First-class	82	140	10	3979	148	30.60	53.79	5	21	158	5
List A	9	7	1	273	64	45.50	84.00	0	3	4	0
Twenty20	33	22	6	253	37	15.81	109.52	0	0	18	0

Bowling	Mat	Balls	Runs	Wkts	BBI	BBM	Ave	Econ	SR	5w	10
First-class	82	24	13	0	-	-	-	3.25	-	0	0
List A	9	-	-	-	-	-	-	-	-	-	-
Twenty20	33	-	-	-	-	-	-	-	-	-	-

ADAM RILEY

RHB / OB / R0 / W1

FULL NAME: Adam Edward Nicholas Riley
BORN: March 23, 1992, Sidcup, Kent
SQUAD NO: 33
HEIGHT: 6ft 2in
NICKNAME: MadDog, General, Riles, Gen
EDUCATION: Beths Grammar School, Bexley,
London; Loughborough University
TEAMS: Kent, England Lions
ROLE: Bowler
DEBUT: First-class: 2011; List A: 2011;
T20: 2011

KENT

BEST BATTING: 34 Kent vs Derbyshire, Canterbury, 2015
BEST BOWLING: 7-150 Kent vs Hampshire, Southampton, 2013

WHAT FIRST GOT YOU INTO CRICKET? Learning to be a scorer at my dad's club
BEST MOMENT IN CRICKET? Getting a nine-fer in a Championship win against Surrey and being picked for England Lions
BEST PLAYER IN COUNTY CRICKET? Sam Northeast (Ken)
MOST UNDERRATED PLAYER IN COUNTY CRICKET? Will Gidman (Ken)
TIP FOR THE TOP? Dan Lawrence (Ess), Toby Lester (Lan), Sean Dickson (Ken)
CRICKETING HEROES? Shane Warne and Graeme Swann – just loved watching them bowl
NON-CRICKETING HEROES? Alan Curbishley, Dean Kiely, Clive Mendonca, Richard Rufus, Matt Holland – Charlton legends back when we used to be good
SURPRISING FACT? I didn't disappear off the face of the earth in 2016 – I was injured!
UNUSUAL OBJECT AT HOME? A small home for my two resident tortoises
FANTASY SLIP CORDON? Keeper: Chris Powell, 1st: Alan Curbishley, 2nd: Me, 3rd: Clive Mendonca, Gully: Iain Dowie. We could reminisce about Charlton all day, and when we get bored we could throw sweets at Dowie because we don't like Iain Dowie
TWITTER: @AdamRiley92

Batting	Mat	Inns	NO	Runs	HS	Ave	SR	100	50	Ct	St
First-class	51	65	23	429	34	10.21	27.32	0	0	27	0
List A	27	8	4	45	21*	11.25	56.96	0	0	9	0
Twenty20	29	8	5	18	5*	6.00	85.71	0	0	5	0

Bowling	Mat	Balls	Runs	Wkts	BBI	BBM	Ave	Econ	SR	5w	10
First-class	51	6757	4182	115	7/150	9/123	36.36	3.71	58.7	5	0
List A	27	1014	903	23	2/30	2/30	39.26	5.34	44.0	0	0
Twenty20	29	532	687	23	4/22	4/22	29.86	7.74	23.1	0	0

OLLIE ROBINSON

RHB / RMF / R0 / W0

SUSSEX

FULL NAME: Oliver Edward Robinson
BORN: December 1, 1993, Margate, Kent
SQUAD NO: 25
HEIGHT: 6ft 5in
NICKNAME: Robbo, Rig, Riggy, Ols
EDUCATION: King's School, Canterbury
TEAMS: Sussex, Yorkshire
ROLE: Allrounder
DEBUT: First-class: 2015; List A: 2013; T20: 2014

BEST BATTING: 110 Sussex vs Durham, Chester-le-Street, 2015
BEST BOWLING: 6-33 Sussex vs Warwickshire, Hove, 2015

WHAT FIRST GOT YOU INTO CRICKET? I started with a wind ball in my grandparents' garden at the age of two. I played my first hard-ball game aged six, taking 5-5 (including a hat-trick)
STRANGEST THING SEEN IN A GAME? Match abandoned due to snow
BEST MOMENT IN CRICKET? My debut for Sussex against Durham in April 2015. I scored 110 and took four wickets, but it is more memorable because of the 164 partnership between me and my best friend at Sussex at the time – the late Matthew Hobden. It broke a record that had been standing for 170 years
BEST PLAYER IN COUNTY CRICKET? Ben Duckett (Nor)
MOST UNDERRATED PLAYER IN COUNTY CRICKET? Ben Brown (Sus)
TIP FOR THE TOP? Stuart Whittingham (Sus), Joe Clarke (Wor)
CRICKETING HEROES? Andrew Flintoff, Angelo Mathews, Garry Sobers
SURPRISING FACT? I was held at gunpoint in Australia after being accused of armed robbery
UNUSUAL OBJECT AT HOME? A dressmakers mannequin (my girlfriend is a fashion designer)
TWITTER: @ollierob123

Batting	Mat	Inns	NO	Runs	HS	Ave	SR	100	50	Ct	St
First-class	23	31	7	671	110	27.95	66.30	1	3	7	0
List A	8	6	3	75	30	25.00	82.41	0	0	5	0
Twenty20	20	9	3	29	10	4.83	67.44	0	0	9	0

Bowling	Mat	Balls	Runs	Wkts	BBI	BBM	Ave	Econ	SR	5w	10
First-class	23	3616	2088	65	6/33	8/108	32.12	3.46	55.6	1	0
List A	8	252	259	4	2/61	2/61	64.75	6.16	63.0	0	0
Twenty20	20	338	516	20	3/16	3/16	25.80	9.15	16.9	0	0

ANGUS ROBSON

RHB / LB / R2 / W0

FULL NAME: Angus James Robson
BORN: February 19, 1992, Darlinghurst, Sydney, Australia
SQUAD NO: 8
HEIGHT: 5ft 9in
NICKNAME: Gus, Robbo
EDUCATION: Marcellin College, Sydney; Australian College of Physical Education
TEAMS: Leicestershire
ROLE: Batsman
DEBUT: First-class: 2013; List A: 2014

LEICESTERSHIRE

BEST BATTING: 120 Leicestershire vs Essex, Chelmsford, 2015

WHAT FIRST GOT YOU INTO CRICKET? My dad played a lot throughout his life and was heavily involved so he and my brother first got me involved
FAMILY TIES? My dad Jim played second XI for Worcestershire. My brother Sam is at Middlesex and has played Test cricket for England
BEST EXPERIENCE ON A CRICKET PITCH? My maiden first-class century vs Hampshire, 2014
HOW WOULD YOUR TEAM-MATES DESCRIBE YOU IN THREE WORDS? Enthusiastic, lively, different
SUPERSTITIONS? Pick up the grass to check the wind at the beginning of each over
BEST PLAYER IN COUNTY? Marcus Trescothick (Som)
CRICKETING HEROES? Ian Bell, Michael Clarke, Mike Atherton
NON-CRICKETING HEROES? Jonny Wilkinson, Jamie Carragher
SURPRISING FACT? I am trying to complete a PE Teaching degree
DESERT ISLAND DISC? Blink 182
FANTASY SLIP CORDON? Keeper: Chad Michael Murray, 1st: Me, 2nd: Homer Simpson, 3rd: Ryan Gosling, Gully: Daniel Rootes
TWITTER FEED: @gusrobson92

Batting	Mat	Inns	NO	Runs	HS	Ave	SR	100	50	Ct	St
First-class	53	97	2	2995	120	31.52	51.10	2	27	42	0
List A	15	15	0	333	90	22.20	72.54	0	2	3	0

Bowling	Mat	Balls	Runs	Wkts	BBI	BBM	Ave	Econ	SR	5w	10
First-class	53	153	127	0	-	-	-	4.98	-	0	0
List A	15	-	-	-	-	-	-	-	-	-	-

SAM ROBSON

RHB / LB / R2 / W0

FULL NAME: Samuel David Robson
BORN: July 1, 1989, Sydney, Australia
SQUAD NO: 12
HEIGHT: 6ft
NICKNAME: Robbo, Chum, Mick, Guru
EDUCATION: Marcellin College, Sydney
TEAMS: England, Middlesex
ROLE: Batsman
DEBUT: Test: 2014; First-class: 2009; List A: 2008; T20: 2011

BEST BATTING: 231 Middlesex vs Warwickshire, Lord's, 2016
BEST BOWLING: 1-4 England Lions vs Sri Lanka A, Dambulla, 2014
COUNTY CAP: 2013

FAMILY TIES? My brother Angus plays for Leicestershire and my father Jim played grade cricket in Australia and for Worcestershire Second XI
BEST MOMENT IN CRICKET? My maiden Test century vs Sri Lanka at Headingley in 2014
SUPERSTITIONS? Don't bowl at Jonathan Trott's pads
HOW WOULD YOUR TEAM-MATES DESCRIBE YOU IN THREE WORDS? Witty, charismatic, dapper
BEST PLAYER IN COUNTY CRICKET? Toby Roland-Jones (Mid)
TIP FOR THE TOP? Tom Helm (Mid)
CRICKETING HEROES? Michael Slater, Shane Warne, Michael Vaughan, Nathan Rowe, Daniel Rootes, Jacob Taucher
IF YOU WEREN'T A CRICKETER? I'd be a school teacher and possibly even married or at least in a serious relationship

Batting	Mat	Inns	NO	Runs	HS	Ave	SR	100	50	Ct	St
Tests	7	11	0	336	127	30.54	44.50	1	1	5	0
First-class	115	203	16	7224	231	38.63	51.14	17	29	116	0
List A	15	13	0	395	88	30.38	67.17	0	2	5	0
Twenty20	4	4	2	53	28*	26.50	103.92	0	0	2	0

Bowling	Mat	Balls	Runs	Wkts	BBI	BBM	Ave	Econ	SR	5w	10
Tests	7	-	-	-	-	-	-	-	-	-	-
First-class	115	122	98	2	1/4	1/4	49.00	4.81	61.0	0	0
List A	15	-	-	-	-	-	-	-	-	-	-
Twenty20	4	-	-	-	-	-	-	-	-	-	-

GARETH RODERICK

RHB / WK / RO / WO

FULL NAME: Gareth Hugh Roderick
BORN: August 29, 1991, Durban, South Africa
SQUAD NO: 27
HEIGHT: 6ft
NICKNAME: Roders, Pear
EDUCATION: Maritzburg College, South Africa
TEAMS: Gloucestershire, KwaZulu-Natal
ROLE: Batsman/wicketkeeper
DEBUT: First-class: 2011; List A: 2011; T20: 2011

BEST BATTING: 171 Gloucestershire vs Leicestershire, Bristol, 2014
COUNTY CAP: 2013

STRANGEST THING SEEN IN A GAME? During a club game in South Africa two gun shots went off in the field next to us
BEST EXPERIENCE ON A CRICKET PITCH? The RL Cup win in 2015
HOW WOULD YOUR TEAM-MATES DESCRIBE YOU IN THREE WORDS? Saffa, stubborn, pear
BEST PLAYER IN COUNTY CRICKET? Chris Woakes (War)
MOST UNDERRATED PLAYER IN COUNTY CRICKET? Chris Dent (Glo)
TIP FOR THE TOP? George Hankins (Glo), Josh Shaw (Yor)
CRICKETING HEROES? Steve Waugh – best Test captain and played cricket the way it should be played. Ruthless
IF YOU WEREN'T A CRICKETER? Working with my father in South Africa
SURPRISING FACT? I'm an avid golfer
UNUSUAL OBJECT AT HOME? Shisha pipe
DESERT ISLAND DISC? John Mayer – Free Fallin'
FANTASY SLIP CORDON? Keeper: Me, 1st: Eric Cartman, 2nd: Jimmy Carr, 3rd: Kevin Hart
TWITTER: @Roders369

Batting	Mat	Inns	NO	Runs	HS	Ave	SR	100	50	Ct	St
First-class	60	96	14	3159	171	38.52	51.98	5	21	151	3
List A	37	28	3	727	104	29.08	79.28	1	5	37	4
Twenty20	26	14	5	124	32	13.77	113.76	0	0	9	1

Bowling	Mat	Balls	Runs	Wkts	BBI	BBM	Ave	Econ	SR	5w	10
First-class	60	-	-	-	-	-	-	-	-	-	-
List A	37	-	-	-	-	-	-	-	-	-	-
Twenty20	26	-	-	-	-	-	-	-	-	-	-

TOBY ROLAND-JONES   RHB / RMF / R0 / W2 / MVP7

MIDDLESEX

FULL NAME: Tobias Skelton Roland-Jones
BORN: January 29, 1988, Ashford, Middlesex
SQUAD NO: 21
HEIGHT: 6ft 3in
NICKNAME: Rojo, TRJ
EDUCATION: Hampton School, Greater London; University of Leeds
TEAMS: Middlesex, England Lions
ROLE: Bowler
DEBUT: First-class: 2010; List A: 2010; T20: 2011

BEST BATTING: 103* Middlesex vs Yorkshire, Lord's, 2015
BEST BOWLING: 6-50 Middlesex vs Northamptonshire, Northampton, 2014
COUNTY CAP: 2012

FAMILY TIES? My older brother Olly played for Leeds/Bradford MCCU and Middlesex Second XI. My dad is a coach
BEST MOMENT IN CRICKET? Winning the County Championship in the final session of the 2016 season will take some beating
HOW WOULD YOUR TEAM-MATES DESCRIBE YOU IN THREE WORDS? Moody, sarcastic, angry
BEST PLAYER IN COUNTY CRICKET? Kumar Sangakkara (Sur)
MOST UNDERRATED PLAYER IN COUNTY CRICKET? Paul Stirling (Mid)
TIP FOR THE TOP? Max Holden (Mid)
CRICKETING HEROES? Ian Botham
NON-CRICKETING HEROES? Ricky Gervais, Alan Partridge, Paul Scholes
SURPRISING FACT? I actually live in Surrey
UNUSUAL OBJECT AT HOME? A stuffed panda
TWITTER: @tobyrj21

Batting	Mat	Inns	NO	Runs	HS	Ave	SR	100	50	Ct	St
First-class	84	113	22	2049	103*	22.51	59.72	1	8	28	0
List A	60	34	11	357	31*	15.52	92.48	0	0	11	0
Twenty20	36	20	9	178	30	16.18	141.26	0	0	7	0

Bowling	Mat	Balls	Runs	Wkts	BBI	BBM	Ave	Econ	SR	5w	10
First-class	84	15154	7941	317	6/50	12/105	25.05	3.14	47.8	15	3
List A	60	2732	2388	96	4/40	4/40	24.87	5.24	28.4	0	0
Twenty20	36	704	1002	38	4/25	4/25	26.36	8.53	18.5	0	0

JOE ROOT

RHB / OB / R3 / W0

FULL NAME: Joseph Edward Root
BORN: December 30, 1990, Sheffield
SQUAD NO: 5
HEIGHT: 6ft
NICKNAME: Rooty, Roota, Rootfish
EDUCATION: King Ecgbert School, Sheffield;
Worksop College, Nottinghamshire
TEAMS: England, Yorkshire
ROLE: Batsman
DEBUT: Test: 2012; ODI: 2013; T20I: 2012;
First-class: 2010; List A: 2009; T20: 2011

YORKSHIRE

BEST BATTING: 254 England vs Pakistan, Old Trafford, 2016
BEST BOWLING: 3-33 Yorkshire vs Warwickshire, Headingley, 2011
COUNTY CAP: 2012

FAMILY TIES? My dad played club cricket and represented Nottinghamshire Second XI and
Colts. My brother Billy is at Notts
BEST MOMENT IN CRICKET? Winning the Ashes
TIP FOR THE TOP? Matthew Fisher, Eliot Callis (both Yor), Billy Root (Not)
CRICKETING HEROES? Michael Vaughan
NON-CRICKETING HEROES? Seve Ballesteros, Alan Shearer
IF YOU WEREN'T A CRICKETER? I'd be studying Art and Design at university
SURPRISING FACT? I taught myself to play the ukulele on tour with England
TWITTER: @root66

Batting	Mat	Inns	NO	Runs	HS	Ave	SR	100	50	Ct	St
Tests	53	98	11	4594	254	52.80	55.00	11	27	65	0
ODIs	83	78	8	3344	125	47.77	85.34	9	20	37	0
T20Is	24	22	4	726	90*	40.33	130.10	0	4	12	0
First-class	103	178	20	8122	254	51.40	56.25	20	40	96	0
List A	115	109	12	4279	125	44.11	83.86	10	25	48	0
Twenty20	56	50	10	1308	92*	32.70	126.25	0	7	22	0

Bowling	Mat	Balls	Runs	Wkts	BBI	BBM	Ave	Econ	SR	5w	10
Tests	53	1427	721	15	2/9	2/9	48.06	3.03	95.1	0	0
ODIs	83	936	908	13	2/15	2/15	69.84	5.82	72.0	0	0
T20Is	24	72	128	6	2/9	2/9	21.33	10.66	12.0	0	0
First-class	103	2786	1460	29	3/33	3/33	50.34	3.14	96.0	0	0
List A	115	1427	1316	26	2/10	2/10	50.61	5.53	54.8	0	0
Twenty20	56	246	397	10	2/9	2/9	39.70	9.68	24.6	0	0

BILLY ROOT

NOTTINGHAMSHIRE

FULL NAME: William Thomas Root
BORN: August 5, 1992, Sheffield
SQUAD NO: 71
HEIGHT: 5ft 10in
NICKNAME: Rooty
EDUCATION: Worksop College, Nottinghamshire; Leeds Metropolitan University
TEAMS: Nottinghamshire
ROLE: Batsman
DEBUT: First-class: 2015

BEST BATTING: 133 Leeds/Bradford MCCU vs Sussex, Hove, 2016

WHAT FIRST GOT YOU INTO CRICKET? Watching my father play on the weekends for Sheffield Collegiate
FAMILY TIES? My father was a good cricketer and brother plays the occasional game
STRANGEST THING SEEN IN A GAME? A swarm of bees
BEST MOMENT IN CRICKET? My hundred for Leeds/Bradford MCCU at Lord's in 2015
SUPERSTITIONS? Just the classic Nelson
HOW WOULD YOUR TEAM-MATES DESCRIBE YOU IN THREE WORDS? Good 12th man
TIP FOR THE TOP? Jake Libby, Tom Moores, Ben Kitt (all Not)
CRICKETING HEROES? Matt Root (my father), Graham Thorpe, Marcus Trescothick
NON-CRICKETING HEROES? Micheal van Gerwen, Miguel Ángel Jiménez, Roger Federer, Christian Eriksen, Jamie Hart
IF YOU WEREN'T A CRICKETER? I'd be a greenskeeper
SURPRISING FACT? I've taken five hat-tricks
UNUSUAL OBJECT AT HOME? Elephant decorations
DESERT ISLAND DISC? Muse – Black Holes And Revelations
FANTASY SLIP CORDON? Keeper: Babe Ruth, 1st: Boris Johnson, 2nd: Jack Whitehall, 3rd: Me, Gully: David Attenborough
TWITTER: @Rootdog22

Batting	Mat	Inns	NO	Runs	HS	Ave	SR	100	50	Ct	St
First-class	6	9	1	351	133	43.87	58.69	1	2	0	0

Bowling	Mat	Balls	Runs	Wkts	BBI	BBM	Ave	Econ	SR	5w	10
First-class	6	54	23	0	-	-	-	2.55	-	0	0

ADAM ROSSINGTON   RHB / WK / R0 / W0 / MVP70

FULL NAME: Adam Matthew Rossington
BORN: May 5, 1993, Edgware, Middlesex
SQUAD NO: 7
HEIGHT: 6ft
NICKNAME: Rosso
EDUCATION: Belmont Preparatory School, Surrey; Mill Hill School, London
TEAMS: Northamptonshire, Middlesex
ROLE: Wicketkeeper
DEBUT: First-class: 2010; List A: 2012; T20: 2011

BEST BATTING: 138* Northamptonshire vs Sussex, Arundel, 2016

WHAT FIRST GOT YOU INTO CRICKET? My father and two brothers
STRANGEST THING SEEN IN A GAME? Josh Cobb in whites
BEST MOMENT IN CRICKET? Winning the T20 Blast in 2016
HOW WOULD YOUR TEAM-MATES DESCRIBE YOU IN THREE WORDS? Determined, grumpy, fossil
BEST PLAYER IN COUNTY CRICKET? Josh Cobb (Nor)
MOST UNDERRATED PLAYER IN COUNTY CRICKET? Ben Sanderson (Nor)
TIP FOR THE TOP? Max Holden (Mid)
CRICKETING HEROES? Alec Stewart, Paul Weekes
IF YOU WEREN'T A CRICKETER? I'd be attempting to play golf, or else a property developer
SURPRISING FACT? I support Barnet FC
UNUSUAL OBJECT AT HOME? A dartboard
DESERT ISLAND DISC? Ultimate 80s
FANTASY SLIP CORDON? Keeper: Me, 1st: James Corden, 2nd: Jack Whitehall, 3rd: John Akinde, Gully: Lee Evans
TWITTER: @rossington17

Batting	Mat	Inns	NO	Runs	HS	Ave	SR	100	50	Ct	St
First-class	42	67	8	2074	138*	35.15	72.74	4	14	80	7
List A	28	25	4	713	97	33.95	92.47	0	5	16	4
Twenty20	53	50	5	845	85	18.77	137.39	0	5	24	9

Bowling	Mat	Balls	Runs	Wkts	BBI	BBM	Ave	Econ	SR	5w	10
First-class	42	18	18	0	-	-	-	6.00	-	0	0
List A	28	-	-	-	-	-	-	-	-	-	-
Twenty20	53	-	-	-	-	-	-	-	-	-	-

RILEE ROSSOUW

LHB / OB / R0 / W0

FULL NAME: Rilee Roscoe Rossouw
BORN: October 9, 1989, Bloemfontein, South Africa
NICKNAME: Rudi
EDUCATION: Grey College, Bloemfontein
TEAMS: South Africa, Hampshire, Basnahira Cricket Dundee, Eagles, Free State, Knights, Quetta Gladiators, Royal Challengers Bangalore
ROLE: Batsman
DEBUT: ODI: 2014; T20I: 2014; First-class: 2007; List A: 2007; T20: 2008

BEST BATTING: 319 Eagles vs Titans, Centurion, 2010
BEST BOWLING: 1-1 Knights vs Cape Cobras, Cape Town, 2013

TWITTER: @Rileerr
NOTES: A top-order batsman, Rossouw quit international cricket in 2017 to take up a three-year Kolpak deal with Hampshire and is available across all formats. The left-hander's South Africa career got off to a shaky start in 2014, with ducks in four of his first six ODI innings, but he soon established himself as one of his country's most consistent white-ball performers. His highest first-class score, a 291-ball innings of 319 which included 47 fours and eight sixes, is indicative of his pedigree in the longer format. He had 18 first-class hundreds to his name ahead of the 2017 season

Batting	Mat	Inns	NO	Runs	HS	Ave	SR	100	50	Ct	St
ODIs	36	35	3	1239	132	38.71	94.36	3	7	22	0
T20Is	15	14	3	327	78	29.72	137.97	0	2	9	0
First-class	79	140	6	5940	319	44.32	63.69	18	25	102	0
List A	130	128	7	4668	137	38.57	93.50	9	29	73	0
Twenty20	95	92	8	2344	78	27.90	129.14	0	14	36	0

Bowling	Mat	Balls	Runs	Wkts	BBI	BBM	Ave	Econ	SR	5w	10
ODIs	36	45	44	1	1/17	1/17	44.00	5.86	45.0	0	0
T20Is	15	-	-	-	-	-	-	-	-	-	-
First-class	79	78	70	3	1/1	1/1	23.33	5.38	26.0	0	0
List A	130	45	44	1	1/17	1/17	44.00	5.86	45.0	0	0
Twenty20	95	6	8	1	1/8	1/8	8.00	8.00	6.0	0	0

ADAM ROUSE

RHB / WK / R0 / W0

FULL NAME: Adam Paul Rouse
BORN: June 30, 1992, Harare, Zimbabwe
SQUAD NO: 12
EDUCATION: Perins Community Sports College, Hampshire; Peter Symonds College, Winchester
TEAMS: Kent, Gloucestershire, Hampshire
ROLE: Wicketkeeper
DEBUT: First-class: 2013; List A: 2013; T20: 2014

KENT

BEST BATTING: 65 Kent vs Glamorgan, Cardiff, 2016

TWITTER: @Rousie20
NOTES: A former England U19 wicketkeeper/batsman, Zimbabwean-born Rouse had a trial with Kent in 2015 and also played for their second XI the previous summer. He has had brief spells with Gloucestershire and Hampshire. Agreed a two-year deal with Kent ahead of the 2016 season, in which he played six Championship matches

Batting	Mat	Inns	NO	Runs	HS	Ave	SR	100	50	Ct	St
First-class	12	15	0	298	65	19.86	46.56	0	1	43	3
List A	11	10	3	198	61*	28.28	62.06	0	1	10	2
Twenty20	8	7	2	61	35*	12.20	117.30	0	0	4	4

Bowling	Mat	Balls	Runs	Wkts	BBI	BBM	Ave	Econ	SR	5w	10
First-class	12	-	-	-	-	-	-	-	-	-	-
List A	11	-	-	-	-	-	-	-	-	-	-
Twenty20	8	-	-	-	-	-	-	-	-	-	-

JASON ROY

RHB / RM / R1 / W0 / MVP19

SURREY

FULL NAME: Jason Jonathan Roy
BORN: July 21, 1990, Durban, South Africa
SQUAD NO: 20
HEIGHT: 6ft
NICKNAME: JRoy, Roy the Boy
EDUCATION: Whitgift School, Croydon
TEAMS: England, Surrey, Chittagong Kings, Sydney Sixers, Sydney Thunder
ROLE: Batsman
DEBUT: ODI: 2015; T20I: 2014; First-class: 2010; List A: 2008; T20: 2008

BEST BATTING: 143 Surrey vs Lancashire, The Oval, 2015
BEST BOWLING: 3-9 Surrey vs Gloucestershire, Bristol, 2014
COUNTY CAP: 2014

BEST MOMENT IN CRICKET? Getting promoted with Surrey, my England T20 and ODI debuts and my first century for England in ODI cricket
HOW WOULD YOUR TEAM-MATES DESCRIBE YOU IN THREE WORDS? Charismatic, confident, loyal
BEST PLAYER IN COUNTY CRICKET? Kumar Sangakkara (Sur)
TIP FOR THE TOP? Sam Curran (Sur)
CRICKETING HEROES? Jacques Kallis
IF YOU WEREN'T A CRICKETER? I'd be a professional surfer and living on a beach
DESERT ISLAND DISC? I would take a compilation of chilled vibes
TWITTER: @JasonRoy20

Batting	Mat	Inns	NO	Runs	HS	Ave	SR	100	50	Ct	St
ODIs	38	37	2	1411	162	40.31	104.67	3	9	11	0
T20Is	19	19	0	369	78	19.42	129.92	0	1	2	0
First-class	73	120	10	4119	143	37.44	82.47	8	18	72	0
List A	120	115	7	4040	162	37.40	106.37	10	22	43	0
Twenty20	136	133	7	3585	122*	28.45	144.49	4	22	61	0

Bowling	Mat	Balls	Runs	Wkts	BBI	BBM	Ave	Econ	SR	5w	10
ODIs	38	-	-	-	-	-	-	-	-	-	-
T20Is	19	-	-	-	-	-	-	-	-	-	-
First-class	73	712	495	14	3/9	4/47	35.35	4.17	50.8	0	0
List A	120	6	12	0	-	-	-	12.00	-	0	0
Twenty20	136	18	39	1	1/23	1/23	39.00	13.00	18.0	0	0

JACQUES RUDOLPH

LHB / LB / R4 / W0

FULL NAME: Jacobus Andries Rudolph
BORN: May 4, 1981, Springs, South Africa
SQUAD NO: 4
HEIGHT: 5ft 10in
EDUCATION: Afrikaanse Hoër Seunskool, Pretoria
TEAMS: South Africa, Glamorgan, Eagles, Jamaica Tallawahs, Northerns, Surrey, Titans, Yorkshire
ROLE: Batsman
DEBUT: Test: 2003; ODI: 2003; T20I: 2006; First-class: 1997; List A: 2000; T20: 2004

GLAMORGAN

BEST BATTING: 228* Yorkshire vs Durham, Headingley, 2010
BEST BOWLING: 5-80 Eagles vs Cape Cobras, Newlands, 2007
COUNTY CAPS: 2007 (Yorkshire); 2014 (Glamorgan)

BEST MOMENT IN CRICKET? Making 222 not out on my Test debut in 2003
CRICKETING HEROES? Justin Langer
DESERT ISLAND DISC? U2, Dire Straits or The Killers
NOTES: Scored 222* in his debut Test innings, against Bangladesh at Chittagong in 2003, as part of a record-breaking unbeaten third-wicket stand of 429 with Boeta Dippenaar. Played for Yorkshire between 2007-2011, passing 1,000 runs in four consecutive seasons (2007-2010). Featured for Surrey in 2012 after losing his place in South Africa's Test side and signed with Glamorgan in September 2013, replacing Marcus North as the club's overseas player. Has been Glamorgan captain across all formats since 2015

Batting	Mat	Inns	NO	Runs	HS	Ave	SR	100	50	Ct	St
Tests	48	83	9	2622	222*	35.43	43.81	6	11	29	0
ODIs	45	39	6	1174	81	35.57	68.05	0	7	11	0
T20Is	1	1	1	6	6*	-	85.71	0	0	0	0
First-class	282	487	30	19191	228*	41.99		49	92	241	0
List A	254	239	34	9980	169*	48.68		17	68	89	0
Twenty20	145	131	22	3573	101*	32.77	116.00	1	23	49	0

Bowling	Mat	Balls	Runs	Wkts	BBI	BBM	Ave	Econ	SR	5w	10
Tests	48	664	432	4	1/1	1/1	108.00	3.90	166.0	0	0
ODIs	45	24	26	0	-	-	-	6.50	-	0	0
T20Is	1	-	-	-	-	-	-	-	-	-	-
First-class	282	4789	2696	61	5/80		44.19	3.37	78.5	3	0
List A	254	494	474	13	4/41	4/41	36.46	5.75	38.0	0	0
Twenty20	145	307	406	13	3/16	3/16	31.23	7.93	23.6	0	0

CHRIS RUSHWORTH   RHB / RFM / R0 / W3 / MVP44

DURHAM

FULL NAME: Christopher Rushworth
BORN: July 11, 1986, Sunderland
SQUAD NO: 22
HEIGHT: 6ft 2in
NICKNAME: Rushy, Sponge
EDUCATION: Castle View Comprehensive School, Sunderland
TEAMS: Durham
ROLE: Bowler
DEBUT: First-class: 2010; List A: 2004; T20: 2011

BEST BATTING: 46 Durham vs Somerset, Taunton, 2014
BEST BOWLING: 9-52 Durham vs Northamptonshire, Chester-le-Street, 2014

FAMILY TIES? My father Joe played local cricket, my brother Lee played county age-groups and represented England U17 and U19. My cousin Phil Mustard is now at Gloucestershire
BEST MOMENT IN CRICKET? Winning a Lord's final in the 2014 Royal London One-Day Cup, followed closely by taking 15 wickets in a day against Northants in the same season
HOW WOULD YOUR TEAM-MATES DESCRIBE YOU IN THREE WORDS? Bald, hairy, skilful
BEST PLAYER IN COUNTY CRICKET? Keaton Jennings (Dur), Jeetan Patel (War)
MOST UNDERRATED PLAYER IN COUNTY CRICKET? Mark Stoneman (Sur)
TIP FOR THE TOP? Ed Barnard (Wor), Josh Coughlin (Dur)
CRICKETING HEROES? Shaun Pollock, Darren Gough
NON-CRICKETING HEROES? Tiger Woods, Roger Federer, Phil Taylor
SURPRISING FACT? I once scored 150 not out in school cricket, including 34 off one over
FANTASY SLIP CORDON? Keeper: Tiger Woods, 1st: Lee Evans, 2nd: Michael Jordan, 3rd: Me, Gully: Curtly Ambrose

Batting	Mat	Inns	NO	Runs	HS	Ave	SR	100	50	Ct	St
First-class	87	120	33	1148	46	13.19	65.30	0	0	17	0
List A	58	24	11	108	38*	8.30	75.52	0	0	11	0
Twenty20	61	12	8	16	5	4.00	55.17	0	0	13	0

Bowling	Mat	Balls	Runs	Wkts	BBI	BBM	Ave	Econ	SR	5w	10
First-class	87	14724	7541	312	9/52	15/95	24.16	3.07	47.1	17	2
List A	58	2446	2200	93	5/31	5/31	23.65	5.39	26.3	2	0
Twenty20	61	1197	1538	64	3/14	3/14	24.03	7.70	18.7	0	0

ABI SAKANDE

RHB / RFM / R0 / W0

FULL NAME: Abidine Sakande
BORN: September 22, 1994, Chester, Cheshire
SQUAD NO: 11
HEIGHT: 6ft 4in
NICKNAME: Abi
EDUCATION: Ardingly College, West Sussex; St John's College; University of Oxford
TEAMS: Sussex
ROLE: Bowler
DEBUT: First-class: 2014; List A: 2016

BEST BATTING: 33 Oxford MCCU vs Cambridge MCCU, Cambridge, 2015
BEST BOWLING: 3-38 Oxford MCCU vs Middlesex, Oxford, 2015

STRANGEST THING SEEN IN A GAME? At The Parks during a first-class fixture, a random teenage couple wandered on to the pitch, pausing to busily make out at square-leg, and the guy was then invited by the Middlesex players to bowl a ball at the batsman. After they left the very next ball was a wicket. Dirty tactics?

BEST MOMENT IN CRICKET? Winning the Lord's Varsity one-day match against Cambridge in my first year at Oxford. I came in at 130-9 to chase down 176

HOW WOULD YOUR TEAM-MATES DESCRIBE YOU IN THREE WORDS? Thinker, conscientious, hard-working

BEST PLAYER IN COUNTY CRICKET? Marcus Trescothick (Som)

TIP FOR THE TOP? Rob Jones (Lan), Harvey Hosein (Der), Phil Salt (Sus)

IF YOU WEREN'T A CRICKETER? I'd be studying for a career in academia

SURPRISING FACT? I am half-Burkinabe (from Burkina Faso)

UNUSUAL OBJECT AT HOME? A tub of peanut butter made by my grandmother in Burkina Faso

FANTASY SLIP CORDON? Keeper: CLR James, 1st: Gandalf, 2nd: Beyoncé, 3rd: Me, 4th: Steven Pinker, Gully: Kublai Khan

TWITTER: @AbiSakande

Batting	Mat	Inns	NO	Runs	HS	Ave	SR	100	50	Ct	St
First-class	5	7	1	72	33	12.00	31.44	0	0	3	0
List A	1	-	-	-	-	-	-	-	-	0	0

Bowling	Mat	Balls	Runs	Wkts	BBI	BBM	Ave	Econ	SR	5w	10
First-class	5	830	429	10	3/38	4/82	42.90	3.10	83.0	0	0
List A	1	47	46	1	1/46	1/46	46.00	5.87	47.0	0	0

OLLIE SALE

RHB / RFM / R0 / W0

SOMERSET

FULL NAME: Oliver Richard Trethowan Sale
BORN: September 30, 1995, Newcastle-under-Lyme, Staffordshire
SQUAD NO: 82
HEIGHT: 6ft 2in
NICKNAME: Saler, Salo, Salestorm
EDUCATION: Sherborne School, Dorset; Newcastle University
TEAMS: Somerset
ROLE: Allrounder
DEBUT: T20: 2016

WHAT FIRST GOT YOU INTO CRICKET? I taught myself to bowl by watching it on TV
STRANGEST THING SEEN IN A GAME? A swarm of bees in Zimbabwe. All the locals knew to hit the deck but we stood around with no clue until we were shouted at to lie down
BEST MOMENT IN CRICKET? At Bath CC last year when Jack Leach sprinted to the bowler's end and put in a full-length dive, only to later realise the ball hadn't even been thrown in
BEST PLAYER IN COUNTY CRICKET? Mark Wood (Dur)
MOST UNDERRATED PLAYER IN COUNTY CRICKET? Jack Leach (Som)
TIP FOR THE TOP? Tom Abell, Tim Rouse (both Som)
CRICKETING HEROES? Dale Steyn, Brett Lee
NON-CRICKETING HEROES? I find entrepreneurs very inspiring – Steve Jobs for instance
IF YOU WEREN'T A CRICKETER? I'd be putting more time into the company I set up with some friends at uni. They are all full-time now but I put cricket first
SURPRISING FACT? I'm scared of sponges… when I say 'scared' I mean I literally cannot deal with the feel of them
UNUSUAL OBJECT AT HOME? No sponges, that's for sure
DESERT ISLAND DISC? Jack Johnson – In Between Dreams. I don't usually listen to that type of music but it would suit the mood of a desert island
FANTASY SLIP CORDON? Keeper: Michael McIntyre (chirpser behind the stumps), 1st: Martin Brooke (my school housemaster), 2nd: Gandalf (epic), 3rd: David Beckham (I used to copy his hairstyles, to my mum's delight), Gully: Harry Potter (HP was my childhood)
TWITTER: @olliesale1

Batting	Mat	Inns	NO	Runs	HS	Ave	SR	100	50	Ct	St
Twenty20	1	1	0	1	1	1.00	33.33	0	0	0	0

Bowling	Mat	Balls	Runs	Wkts	BBI	BBM	Ave	Econ	SR	5w	10
Twenty20	1	18	40	0	-	-	-	13.33	-	0	0

PHIL SALT
RHB / OB / R0 / W0

FULL NAME: Philip Dean Salt
BORN: August 28, 1996, Bodelwyddan, Denbighshire, Wales
SQUAD NO: 28
HEIGHT: 6ft
NICKNAME: Salty
EDUCATION: Harrison College, Barbados; Reed's School, Surrey
TEAMS: Sussex
ROLE: Batsman
DEBUT: First-class: 2016; List A: 2015; T20: 2016

BEST BATTING: 42 Sussex vs Gloucestershire, Bristol, 2016

WHAT FIRST GOT YOU INTO CRICKET? Playing Kwik Cricket at school
STRANGEST THING SEEN IN A GAME? When a streaker ran on in a T20 game against Kent a couple of years ago and took out all three stumps with a diving headbutt
BEST MOMENT IN CRICKET? Scoring a double hundred for Sussex Academy
HOW WOULD YOUR TEAM-MATES DESCRIBE YOU IN THREE WORDS? Tall, dark, handsome
BEST PLAYER IN COUNTY CRICKET? Michael Klinger (Glo)
TIP FOR THE TOP? Stuart Whittingham – he bowls quick and is exciting to watch – and George Garton (both Sus)
CRICKETING HEROES? Growing up in Barbados, I didn't look past Sir Garry Sobers
NON-CRICKETING HEROES? Anyone in the emergency services and armed forces
IF YOU WEREN'T A CRICKETER? I'd be in the NBA
SURPRISING FACT? I once picked up Sir Garry Sobers' Indian takeaway by accident
UNUSUAL OBJECT AT HOME? The head of a WW1 bomb
FANTASY SLIP CORDON? Keeper: Me, 1st: Peter Kay, 2nd: Sergio Agüero, 3rd: Geoffrey Boycott, Gully: Shaquille O'Neal
TWITTER: @PhilSalt1

Batting	Mat	Inns	NO	Runs	HS	Ave	SR	100	50	Ct	St
First-class	4	5	1	98	42	24.50	46.88	0	0	0	0
List A	6	6	0	149	81	24.83	88.16	0	1	1	0
Twenty20	10	9	1	151	33	18.87	123.77	0	0	3	0

Bowling	Mat	Balls	Runs	Wkts	BBI	BBM	Ave	Econ	SR	5w	10
First-class	4	-	-	-	-	-	-	-	-	-	-
List A	6	-	-	-	-	-	-	-	-	-	-
Twenty20	10	-	-	-	-	-	-	-	-	-	-

ANDREW SALTER

RHB / OB / RO / WO

FULL NAME: Andrew Graham Salter
BORN: June 1, 1993, Haverfordwest, Pembrokeshire, Wales
SQUAD NO: 21
HEIGHT: 5ft 10in
NICKNAME: Beak, Salty
EDUCATION: Milford Haven School, Pembrokeshire; Cardiff Metropolitan University
TEAMS: Glamorgan
ROLE: Bowler
DEBUT: First-class: 2012; List A: 2012; T20: 2014

BEST BATTING: 73 Glamorgan vs Gloucestershire, Swansea, 2015
BEST BOWLING: 3-5 Glamorgan vs Northamptonshire, Cardiff, 2015

WHAT FIRST GOT YOU INTO CRICKET? Watching my dad hack some through mid-wicket
FAMILY TIES? Father and brother played, mum made teas and scored
STRANGEST THING SEEN IN A GAME? Colin Ingram using Mark Wallace's glove to catch a ball, resulting in five penalty runs
BEST MOMENT IN CRICKET? The 2013 one-day final at Lord's. Although we didn't win, to play in a big game at the home of cricket with a big crowd was special. It was also Simon Jones' last game for Glamorgan and it was great to play alongside a childhood role model
BEST PLAYER IN COUNTY CRICKET? Jeetan Patel (War)
MOST UNDERRATED PLAYER IN COUNTY CRICKET? Timm van der Gugten (Gla)
TIP FOR THE TOP? David Lloyd, Aneurin Donald, Kiran Carlson (all Gla)
CRICKETING HEROES? Glammy spinners Crofty and 'Lurks' (Dean Cosker)
IF YOU WEREN'T A CRICKETER? I'd be riding cafe racer motorcycles around the world
SURPRISING FACT? I'm planning to ride a motorcycle 2,500 km around Europe covering eight countries to raise awareness for men's health
TWITTER: @AndySalts

Batting	Mat	Inns	NO	Runs	HS	Ave	SR	100	50	Ct	St
First-class	31	47	9	755	73	19.86	42.48	0	2	14	0
List A	23	16	7	201	51	22.33	87.01	0	1	7	0
Twenty20	29	18	11	92	17*	13.14	110.84	0	0	10	0

Bowling	Mat	Balls	Runs	Wkts	BBI	BBM	Ave	Econ	SR	5w	10
First-class	31	4413	2592	50	3/5	6/69	51.84	3.52	88.2	0	0
List A	23	808	672	11	2/41	2/41	61.09	4.99	73.4	0	0
Twenty20	29	372	532	16	2/19	2/19	33.25	8.58	23.2	0	0

BEN SANDERSON RHB / RMF / R0 / W1 / MVP99

FULL NAME: Ben William Sanderson
BORN: January 3, 1989, Sheffield
SQUAD NO: 26
HEIGHT: 6ft
NICKNAME: Sando
EDUCATION: Ecclesfield School, Sheffield; Sheffield College
TEAMS: Northamptonshire, Yorkshire
ROLE: Bowler
DEBUT: First-class: 2008; List A: 2010; T20: 2010

BEST BATTING: 42 Northamptonshire vs Kent, Canterbury, 2015
BEST BOWLING: 8-73 Northamptonshire vs Gloucestershire, Northampton, 2016

FAMILY TIES? Dad played club cricket for Whitley Hall CC
STRANGEST THING SEEN IN A GAME? David Murphy throwing the ball
BEST MOMENT IN CRICKET? Taking a wicket in the 2016 T20 final
SUPERSTITIONS? Keep things the same when winning
HOW WOULD YOUR TEAM-MATES DESCRIBE YOU IN THREE WORDS? Tight northern Yorkie
BEST PLAYER IN COUNTY CRICKET? Ben Duckett (Nor)
MOST UNDERRATED PLAYER IN COUNTY CRICKET? Sam Northeast (Ken)
TIP FOR THE TOP? Richard Gleeson (Nor)
CRICKETING HEROES? Darren Gough, Glenn McGrath
NON-CRICKETING HEROES? Chris Waddle, Kevin Pressman
IF YOU WEREN'T A CRICKETER? I'd be working on a building site
UNUSUAL OBJECT AT HOME? Cannonballs
FANTASY SLIP CORDON? Keeper: Peter Kay, 1st: Micky Flanagan, 2nd: Vinnie Jones, 3rd: Me, Gully: Jimmy Bullard
TWITTER: @sando567

Batting	Mat	Inns	NO	Runs	HS	Ave	SR	100	50	Ct	St
First-class	22	23	6	115	42	6.76	35.27	0	0	3	0
List A	14	3	2	18	12*	18.00	112.50	0	0	7	0
Twenty20	7	1	1	1	1*	-	100.00	0	0	0	0

Bowling	Mat	Balls	Runs	Wkts	BBI	BBM	Ave	Econ	SR	5w	10
First-class	22	3323	1617	72	8/73	10/89	22.45	2.91	46.1	5	1
List A	14	336	379	9	2/17	2/17	42.11	6.76	37.3	0	0
Twenty20	7	142	160	14	4/21	4/21	11.42	6.76	10.1	0	0

KUMAR SANGAKKARA   LHB / OB / R1 / W0 / MVP51

FULL NAME: Kumar Chokshanada Sangakkara
BORN: October 27, 1977, Matale, Sri Lanka
SQUAD NO: 11
EDUCATION: Trinity College, Kandy
TEAMS: Sri Lanka, Surrey, Deccan Chargers, Dhaka Dynamites, Durham, Hobart Hurricanes, Jamaica Tallawahs, Kandurata, Kings XI Punjab, Nondescripts, Sunrisers Hyderabad, Udarata Rulers, Warwickshire
ROLE: Batsman
DEBUT: Test: 2000; ODI: 2000; T20I: 2006; First-class: 1997; List A: 1997; T20: 2004

BEST BATTING: 319 Sri Lanka vs Bangladesh, Chittagong, 2014
BEST BOWLING: 1-13 Sri Lankans vs Zimbabwe A, Harare, 2004

TWITTER: @KumarSanga2
NOTES: This is Sangakkara's third stint in English cricket after spells with Warwickshire and Durham. He retired from all international cricket in 2015, finishing with more than 28,000 runs in all formats for Sri Lanka. Only three men have scored more than his 38 Test centuries. He is the second batsman to pass 14,000 ODI runs, after Sachin Tendulkar. This will be his third season at The Oval. In 2015 he hit five Championship centuries in 11 matches and last year passed 1,000 runs in 12 matches, scoring 767 runs at 54.78 in 50-over cricket across both seasons. He will be away for a spell in midsummer while playing in the Caribbean Premier League

Batting	Mat	Inns	NO	Runs	HS	Ave	SR	100	50	Ct	St
Tests	134	233	17	12400	319	57.40	54.19	38	52	182	20
ODIs	404	380	41	14234	169	41.98	78.86	25	93	402	99
T20Is	56	53	9	1382	78	31.40	119.55	0	8	25	20
First-class	250	414	29	19420	319	50.44		56	84	365	33
List A	519	491	52	18908	169	43.07		37	117	514	124
Twenty20	235	229	20	5974	94	28.58	125.79	0	34	143	57

Bowling	Mat	Balls	Runs	Wkts	BBI	BBM	Ave	Econ	SR	5w	10
Tests	134	84	49	0	-	-	-	3.50	-	0	0
ODIs	404	-	-	-	-	-	-	-	-	-	-
T20Is	56	-	-	-	-	-	-	-	-	-	-
First-class	250	246	150	1	1/13		150.00	3.65	246.0	0	0
List A	519	-	-	-	-	-	-	-	-	-	-
Twenty20	235	-	-	-	-	-	-	-	-	-	-

MITCHELL SANTNER

LHB / SLA / R0 / W0

FULL NAME: Mitchell Josef Santner
BORN: February 5, 1992, Hamilton
SQUAD NO: 74
NICKNAME: Flatline
TEAMS: New Zealand, Worcestershire, Northern Districts
ROLE: Allrounder
DEBUT: Test: 2015; ODI: 2015; T20I: 2015; First-class: 2011; List A: 2014; T20: 2014

WORCESTERSHIRE

BEST BATTING: 118 Northern Districts vs Canterbury, Gisborne, 2014
BEST BOWLING: 3-51 Northern Districts vs Auckland, Whangarei, 2014

TWITTER: @MitchellSantner
NOTES: The New Zealander has re-signed for the NatWest T20 Blast after he was restricted to a single appearance for the Rapids in 2016 because of a fractured finger. Persistent, parsimonious and accurate with the ball and more than useful with the bat, the left-arm spinner has two years of international cricket under his belt after making his ODI debut against England in 2015. Impressed in the 2016 World T20 and on New Zealand's tour of India later that year

Batting	Mat	Inns	NO	Runs	HS	Ave	SR	100	50	Ct	St
Tests	14	17	0	427	73	25.11	44.52	0	2	6	0
ODIs	32	26	9	452	48	26.58	85.60	0	0	15	0
T20Is	14	9	1	49	18	6.12	85.96	0	0	7	0
First-class	37	54	4	1435	118	28.70	48.85	2	8	31	0
List A	56	48	10	1079	86	28.39	86.38	0	4	29	0
Twenty20	28	21	6	249	45*	16.60	123.88	0	0	10	0

Bowling	Mat	Balls	Runs	Wkts	BBI	BBM	Ave	Econ	SR	5w	10
Tests	14	2499	1191	30	3/60	5/173	39.70	2.85	83.3	0	0
ODIs	32	1454	1219	35	3/31	3/31	34.82	5.03	41.5	0	0
T20Is	14	295	327	20	4/11	4/11	16.35	6.65	14.7	0	0
First-class	37	5200	2637	55	3/51	5/173	47.94	3.04	94.5	0	0
List A	56	2584	2023	65	4/38	4/38	31.12	4.69	39.7	0	0
Twenty20	28	565	648	29	4/11	4/11	22.34	6.88	19.4	0	0

415

ROB SAYER

RHB / OB / R0 / W0

FULL NAME: Robert John Sayer
BORN: January 25, 1995, Huntingdon, Cambridgeshire
SQUAD NO: 12
HEIGHT: 6ft 2in
NICKNAME: Leo
EDUCATION: Abbey College, Cambridgeshire; Leeds Metropolitan University
TEAMS: Leicestershire
ROLE: Bowler
DEBUT: First-class: 2015; List A: 2015; T20: 2015

BEST BATTING: 34 Leicestershire vs Gloucestershire, Leicester, 2015
BEST BOWLING: 2-41 Leicestershire vs Sri Lankans, Leicester, 2016

WHAT FIRST GOT YOU INTO CRICKET? Indoor cricket with my best mate
BEST MOMENT IN CRICKET? Winning on my first-class debut vs Derbyshire
SUPERSTITIONS? I do everything in twos when I bat
BEST PLAYER IN COUNTY CRICKET? Tim Bresnan (Yor)
MOST UNDERRATED PLAYER IN COUNTY CRICKET? Toby Roland-Jones (Mid)
TIP FOR THE TOP? Zak Chappell (Lei)
CRICKETING HEROES? Andrew Flintoff – he could change a game in minutes. Graeme Swann – an off-spinner like me
NON-CRICKETING HEROES? Muhammad Ali – he was ruthless, self-confident
SURPRISING FACT? I played football for Peterborough Centre of Excellence
UNUSUAL OBJECT AT HOME? An elliptical trainer
DESERT ISLAND DISC? Eminem – Curtain Call
FANTASY SLIP CORDON? Keeper: Peter Kay, 1st: Joey Tribbiani, 2nd: Nicole Scherzinger, 3rd: Me, Gully: Harvey Specter
TWITTER: @Sayer1995

Batting	Mat	Inns	NO	Runs	HS	Ave	SR	100	50	Ct	St
First-class	7	7	2	94	34	18.80	35.47	0	0	1	0
List A	10	9	2	71	26	10.14	71.00	0	0	2	0
Twenty20	8	3	1	14	9	7.00	87.50	0	0	1	0

Bowling	Mat	Balls	Runs	Wkts	BBI	BBM	Ave	Econ	SR	5w	10
First-class	7	1058	713	11	2/41	3/88	64.81	4.04	96.1	0	0
List A	10	486	448	7	1/31	1/31	64.00	5.53	69.4	0	0
Twenty20	8	108	185	6	2/16	2/16	30.83	10.27	18.0	0	0

GEORGE SCOTT

RHB / RM / R0 / W0

FULL NAME: George Frederick Buchan Scott
BORN: November 6, 1995, Hemel Hempstead, Hertfordshire
SQUAD NO: 17
HEIGHT: 6ft 2in
NICKNAME: Scotty
EDUCATION: Beechwood Park School, St Albans; St Albans School; University of Leeds
TEAMS: Middlesex
ROLE: Allrounder
DEBUT: First-class: 2015; List A: 2015; T20: 2015

BEST BATTING: 16* Leeds/Bradford MCCU vs Sussex, Hove, 2016
BEST BOWLING: 2-67 Leeds/Bradford MCCU vs Sussex, Hove, 2015

FAMILY TIES? I have an older brother and younger brother who play Minor Counties cricket for Hertfordshire, and another younger brother in the Middlesex Academy
STRANGEST THING SEEN IN A GAME? A cow at cow corner
BEST MOMENT IN CRICKET? Playing in front of a full house of 28,000 at Lord's
SUPERSTITIONS? Park the car facing away from the ground
BEST PLAYER IN COUNTY CRICKET? Kumar Sangakarra (Sur)
MOST UNDERRATED PLAYER IN COUNTY CRICKET? Michael Klinger (Glo)
TIP FOR THE TOP? Tom Helm (Mid)
CRICKETING HEROES? Kumar Sangakarra. Having a degree in Law and being one of the best cricketers ever shows he must be a very intelligent and well-rounded individual
NON-CRICKETING HEROES? I hope he never reads this, but I look up to my older brother
IF YOU WEREN'T A CRICKETER? I'd be thinking about what to do with a degree in Geography
SURPRISING FACT? I was a music scholar at St Albans School, and I have four cats
UNUSUAL OBJECT AT HOME? A bassoon
TWITTER: @georgefbscott

Batting	Mat	Inns	NO	Runs	HS	Ave	SR	100	50	Ct	St
First-class	4	5	2	37	16*	12.33	22.56	0	0	2	0
List A	1	1	0	4	4	4.00	36.36	0	0	0	0
Twenty20	3	2	1	38	20	38.00	92.68	0	0	0	0

Bowling	Mat	Balls	Runs	Wkts	BBI	BBM	Ave	Econ	SR	5w	10
First-class	4	126	121	2	2/67	2/67	60.50	5.76	63.0	0	0
List A	1	18	28	0	-	-	-	9.33	-	0	0
Twenty20	3	-	-	-	-	-	-	-	-	-	-

GEORGE SCRIMSHAW RHB / RMF / R0 / W0

WORCESTERSHIRE

FULL NAME: George Louis Sheridan Scrimshaw
BORN: February 10, 1998, Burton-on-Trent, Staffordshire
SQUAD NO: 9
HEIGHT: 6ft 6in
NICKNAME: Scrim, Scrimmy, Groot
EDUCATION: Thomas Russel Junior School; John Taylor High School, Burton-on-Trent
TEAMS: Worcestershire 2nd XI
ROLE: Bowler
DEBUT: Yet to make first-team debut

FAMILY TIES? My dad and grandad both played county age-group cricket
STRANGEST THING SEEN IN A GAME? A fielder wearing shinpads to stop the ball
BEST MOMENT IN CRICKET? Taking 4-46 for Worcestershire Second XI against Hampshire Second XI at the Ageas Bowl in 2016
HOW WOULD YOUR TEAM-MATES DESCRIBE YOU IN THREE WORDS? Green, beanpole, big
BEST PLAYER IN COUNTY CRICKET? Ben Duckett (Nor)
MOST UNDERRATED PLAYER IN COUNTY CRICKET? Ben Cox (Wor)
TIP FOR THE TOP? Sam Curran (Sur)
CRICKETING HEROES? Dale Steyn, Andrew Flintoff, Brett Lee, Kevin Pietersen
NON-CRICKETING HEROES? My dad and grandad
SURPRISING FACT? My favourite footballer is Steve Morison – the former Norwich and Leeds United player who is currently at Millwall
UNUSUAL OBJECT AT HOME? A glass-spinning globe
DESERT ISLAND DISC? Hard-Fi – Stars of CCTV
FANTASY SLIP CORDON? Keeper: James Corden, 1st: Jack Whitehall, 2nd: Margot Robbie, 3rd: Me, Gully: Mark Viduka

FULL NAME: Nicholas James Selman
BORN: October 18, 1995, Brisbane, Australia
SQUAD NO: 9
EDUCATION: Matthew Flinders Anglican College, Queensland, Australia
TEAMS: Glamorgan
ROLE: Batsman
DEBUT: First-class: 2016; List A: 2016; T20: 2016

GLAMORGAN

BEST BATTING: 122* Glamorgan vs Northamptonshire, Swansea, 2016

TWITTER: @nickselman22
NOTES: Spent 2015 playing for Kent Second XI before joining Glamorgan in 2016 after an impressive trial for the Welsh county's second XI. After a series of centuries in second XI cricket, the Australian-born batsman was a regular face in the Glamorgan line-up for the second half of the 2016 Championship season. Played Aussie Rules Football at state age-group level. Has dual UK and Australian citizenship

Batting	Mat	Inns	NO	Runs	HS	Ave	SR	100	50	Ct	St
First-class	10	19	2	470	122*	27.64	46.67	2	2	7	0
List A	1	1	0	6	6	6.00	42.85	0	0	1	0
Twenty20	1	-	-	-	-	-	-	-	-	-	-

Bowling	Mat	Balls	Runs	Wkts	BBI	BBM	Ave	Econ	SR	5w	10
First-class	10	18	8	0	-	-	-	2.66	-	0	0
List A	1	-	-	-	-	-	-	-	-	-	-
Twenty20	1	-	-	-	-	-	-	-	-	-	-

AJMAL SHAHZAD

RHB / RFM / R0 / W0

SUSSEX

FULL NAME: Ajmal Shahzad
BORN: July 27, 1985, Huddersfield, Yorkshire
SQUAD NO: 4
HEIGHT: 6ft
NICKNAME: AJ, AJY, Shazza
EDUCATION: Woodhouse Grove Grammar School; Bradford University; Leeds Metropolitan University
TEAMS: England, Sussex, Nottinghamshire, Lancashire, Yorkshire
ROLE: Bowler
DEBUT: Test: 2010; ODI: 2010; T20I: 2010; First-class: 2006; List A: 2004; T20: 2006

BEST BATTING: 88 Yorkshire vs Sussex, Hove, 2009
BEST BOWLING: 5-46 Sussex vs Worcestershire, Hove, 2015
COUNTY CAP: 2010 (Yorkshire)

BEST MOMENT IN CRICKET? Receiving my Yorkshire cap, representing England across all forms, being part of an Ashes-winning squad and the World T20-winning squad
CRICKETING HEROES? Wasim Akram, Waqar Younis, Shoaib Akhtar, James Anderson
IF YOU WEREN'T A CRICKETER? I'd be a pharmacist, accountant or on the front of GQ magazine or Men's Health
FANTASY SLIP CORDON? Keeper: Mike Tyson, 1st: Prince Naseem Hamed, 2nd: Colonel Gaddafi, 3rd: Eddie Murphy, Gully: Me
TWITTER: @AJShahzad

Batting	Mat	Inns	NO	Runs	HS	Ave	SR	100	50	Ct	St
Tests	1	1	0	5	5	5.00	41.66	0	0	2	0
ODIs	11	8	2	39	9	6.50	65.00	0	0	4	0
T20Is	3	1	1	0	0*	-	0.00	0	0	1	0
First-class	95	126	31	2231	88	23.48	42.40	0	6	15	0
List A	84	52	13	511	59*	13.10	90.76	0	1	19	0
Twenty20	54	24	7	165	20	9.70	113.01	0	0	7	0

Bowling	Mat	Balls	Runs	Wkts	BBI	BBM	Ave	Econ	SR	5w	10
Tests	1	102	63	4	3/45	4/63	15.75	3.70	25.5	0	0
ODIs	11	588	490	17	3/41	3/41	28.82	5.00	34.5	0	0
T20Is	3	66	97	3	2/38	2/38	32.33	8.81	22.0	0	0
First-class	95	14635	8418	243	5/46	8/121	34.64	3.45	60.2	4	0
List A	84	3742	3379	118	5/51	5/51	28.63	5.41	31.7	1	0
Twenty20	54	1074	1429	48	3/26	3/26	29.77	7.98	22.3	0	0

JACK SHANTRY

LHB / LM / RO / W2

FULL NAME: Jack David Shantry
BORN: January 29, 1988, Shrewsbury
SQUAD NO: 11
HEIGHT: 6ft 4in
NICKNAME: Shants
EDUCATION: Shrewsbury Sixth Form College;
University of Manchester
TEAMS: Worcestershire
ROLE: Bowler
DEBUT: First-class: 2009; List A: 2009;
T20: 2010

BEST BATTING: 106 Worcestershire vs Gloucestershire, Worcester, 2016
BEST BOWLING: 7-60 Worcestershire vs Oxford MCCU, Oxford, 2013

FAMILY TIES? My brother (Adam) played for Glamorgan, Warwickshire and Northants. My dad (Brian) played for Gloucestershire
STRANGEST THING SEEN IN A GAME? Joe Leach taking a hat-trick with the first three balls of a 50-over match against Northants in 2015 – then a swan swooped down and continuously circled the infield, causing a lengthy delay
BEST MOMENT IN CRICKET? A Championship match against Surrey in 2014. I took 10 wickets and scored 100 to help get us promoted
SUPERSTITIONS? Rub Joe Leach's belly for luck, never get undressed next to Charlie Morris
BEST PLAYER IN COUNTY CRICKET? Mark Wood (Dur)
MOST UNDERRATED PLAYER IN COUNTY CRICKET? Jack Taylor (Glo)
TIP FOR THE TOP? Ben Twohig (Wor)
NON-CRICKETING HEROES? Christopher Hitchens
IF YOU WEREN'T A CRICKETER? I would try to be a goalkeeper for Bristol City
SURPRISING FACT? I went to school with Joe Hart
TWITTER: @JackShantry

Batting	Mat	Inns	NO	Runs	HS	Ave	SR	100	50	Ct	St
First-class	86	110	28	1546	106	18.85	54.30	2	2	27	0
List A	67	32	15	176	31	10.35	68.21	0	0	15	0
Twenty20	84	21	9	76	12*	6.33	90.47	0	0	20	0

Bowling	Mat	Balls	Runs	Wkts	BBI	BBM	Ave	Econ	SR	5w	10
First-class	86	15594	7473	255	7/60	10/26	29.30	2.87	61.1	12	2
List A	67	2705	2529	86	4/29	4/29	29.40	5.60	31.4	0	0
Twenty20	84	1831	2423	90	4/33	4/33	26.92	7.93	20.3	0	0

JOSH SHAW

RHB / RMF / R0 / W0

YORKSHIRE

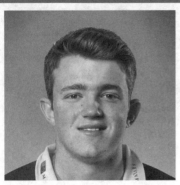

FULL NAME: Joshua Shaw
BORN: January 3, 1996, Wakefield, Yorkshire
SQUAD NO: 25
HEIGHT: 6ft 1in
NICKNAME: Shawy
EDUCATION: Crofton Academy Wakefield;
Skills Exchange College, Wakefield
TEAMS: Yorkshire, Gloucestershire
ROLE: Bowler
DEBUT: First-class: 2016; T20: 2015

BEST BATTING: 29 Gloucestershire vs Leicestershire, Cheltenham, 2016
BEST BOWLING: 5-79 Gloucestershire vs Sussex, Bristol, 2016

WHAT FIRST GOT YOU INTO CRICKET? My father played for Yorkshire. We also lived on the back of Streethouse CC so I was always around cricket from a young age
STRANGEST THING SEEN IN A GAME? Liam Norwell score a hundred for Gloucestershire as a nightwatchman
BEST MOMENT IN CRICKET? Taking my first five-fer in a Championship match in 2016
HOW WOULD YOUR TEAM-MATES DESCRIBE YOU IN THREE WORDS? Standard, simple bloke
BEST PLAYER IN COUNTY CRICKET? Ben Duckett (Nor)
MOST UNDERRATED PLAYER IN COUNTY CRICKET? Matthew Waite (Yor)
TIP FOR THE TOP? George Hankins (Glo)
CRICKETING HEROES? Dale Steyn – he's aggressive and never gives up
NON-CRICKETING HEROES? Anthony Joshua, Conor McGregor – both are really talented and focused on their profession
IF YOU WEREN'T A CRICKETER? I'd be working in the joinery trade
SURPRISING FACT? I passed my driving test with no minors
TWITTER: @joshuashaw1

Batting	Mat	Inns	NO	Runs	HS	Ave	SR	100	50	Ct	St
First-class	15	19	6	168	29	12.92	38.88	0	0	5	0
Twenty20	3	2	1	1	1	1.00	50.00	0	0	1	0

Bowling	Mat	Balls	Runs	Wkts	BBI	BBM	Ave	Econ	SR	5w	10
First-class	15	2433	1537	41	5/79	5/79	37.48	3.79	59.3	1	0
Twenty20	3	36	71	0	-	-	-	11.83	-	0	0

CHARLIE SHRECK

RHB / RFM / R0 / W4

FULL NAME: Charles Edward Shreck
BORN: January 6, 1978, Truro, Cornwall
SQUAD NO: 4
HEIGHT: 6ft 7in
NICKNAME: Shrecker, Ogre, Stoat, Chough
EDUCATION: Truro School
TEAMS: Leicestershire, Kent,
Nottinghamshire, Wellington
ROLE: Bowler
DEBUT: First-class: 2003; List A: 1999;
T20: 2003

LEICESTERSHIRE

BEST BATTING: 56 Leicestershire vs Surrey, The Oval, 2014
BEST BOWLING: 8-31 Nottinghamshire vs Middlesex, Trent Bridge, 2006
COUNTY CAP: 2006 (Nottinghamshire)

BEST MOMENT IN CRICKET? Watching Andrew Parkin-Coates get Phil Mustard out after kicking the stumps down the pitch in his delivery stride
CRICKETING HEROES? Viv Richards, Michael Holding, Ian Botham, Rob Key
DESERT ISLAND DISC? Bob Marley – Catch a Fire
TWITTER: @Shreck
NOTES: Joined Leicestershire in 2014 after taking more than 400 wickets in all competitions during a nine-year spell at Trent Bridge and a further two seasons at Kent, where he was the county's leading Championship wicket-taker in 2012 (55 wickets) and 2013 (33). Has taken 143 Championship wickets in his three seasons at Leicestershire

Batting	Mat	Inns	NO	Runs	HS	Ave	SR	100	50	Ct	St
First-class	173	209	109	775	56	7.75	36.04	0	1	49	0
List A	60	23	14	47	9*	5.22		0	0	15	0
Twenty20	29	8	5	20	10	6.66	68.96	0	0	6	0

Bowling	Mat	Balls	Runs	Wkts	BBI	BBM	Ave	Econ	SR	5w	10
First-class	173	34068	18169	575	8/31		31.59	3.19	59.2	23	2
List A	60	2629	2264	73	5/19	5/19	31.01	5.16	36.0	2	0
Twenty20	29	598	789	30	4/22	4/22	26.30	7.91	19.9	0	0

DOMINIC SIBLEY

RHB / OB / R0 / W0

SURREY

FULL NAME: Dominic Peter Sibley
BORN: September 5, 1995, Epsom, Surrey
SQUAD NO: 45
HEIGHT: 6ft 3in
NICKNAME: Frocko, Big Tree
EDUCATION: Whitgift School, Croydon
TEAMS: Surrey
ROLE: Batsman
DEBUT: First-class: 2013; List A: 2013; T20: 2016

BEST BATTING: 242 Surrey vs Yorkshire, The Oval, 2013
BEST BOWLING: 2-103 Surrey vs Hampshire, Southampton, 2016

STRANGEST THING SEEN IN A GAME? In Australia a fast bowler slid to get the ball and the bottom half of his shoe blew off – the top half was still on
BEST MOMENT IN CRICKET? My T20 debut for Surrey in 2016
SUPERSTITIONS? I take guard every first time I face a ball
HOW WOULD YOUR TEAM-MATES DESCRIBE YOU IN THREE WORDS? Very good diet
BEST PLAYER IN COUNTY CRICKET? Chris Woakes (War)
MOST UNDERRATED PLAYER IN COUNTY CRICKET? Lewis McManus (Ham)
TIP FOR THE TOP? Amar Virdi (Sur)
CRICKETING HEROES? Virat Kohli
NON-CRICKETING HEROES? Lionel Messi
SURPRISING FACT? I'm a UFC fighter
DESERT ISLAND DISC? Kid Ink – Show Me
FANTASY SLIP CORDON? Keeper: Muhammad Ali, 1st: Justin Bieber, 2nd: Me, 3rd: Selena Gomez, Gully: Emily Ratajkowski
TWITTER: @DomSibley

Batting	Mat	Inns	NO	Runs	HS	Ave	SR	100	50	Ct	St
First-class	22	37	2	1039	242	29.68	37.60	1	5	18	0
List A	8	6	2	85	37	21.25	72.64	0	0	4	0
Twenty20	8	6	1	247	74*	49.40	119.90	0	2	1	0

Bowling	Mat	Balls	Runs	Wkts	BBI	BBM	Ave	Econ	SR	5w	10
First-class	22	322	197	3	2/103	2/117	65.66	3.67	107.3	0	0
List A	8	48	53	1	1/20	1/20	53.00	6.62	48.0	0	0
Twenty20	8	36	57	3	2/33	2/33	19.00	9.50	12.0	0	0

RYAN SIDEBOTTOM

LHB / LFM / R0 / W4

FULL NAME: Ryan Jay Sidebottom
BORN: January 15, 1978, Huddersfield, Yorkshire
SQUAD NO: 11
HEIGHT: 6ft 4in
NICKNAME: Siddy
EDUCATION: King James' Grammar School, Huddersfield
TEAMS: England, Yorkshire, Nottinghamshire
ROLE: Bowler
DEBUT: Test: 2001; ODI: 2001; T20I: 2007; First-class: 1997; List A: 1997; T20: 2003

BEST BATTING: 61 Yorkshire vs Worcestershire, Worcester, 2011
BEST BOWLING: 7-37 Yorkshire vs Somerset, Headingley, 2011
COUNTY CAPS: 2000 (Yorkshire); 2004 (Nottinghamshire) BENEFIT: 2010 (Nottinghamshire)

FAMILY TIES? My father Arnie played for Yorkshire and England
BEST MOMENT IN CRICKET? Taking a Test hat-trick against New Zealand and being a World T20 winner in 2010
CRICKETING HEROES? Mark Ealham, Sir Ian Botham, my dad
NON-CRICKETING HEROES? Ryan Giggs, Sam Tomkins, Garreth Carvell
IF YOU WEREN'T A CRICKETER? I'd have been a footballer or a landscape gardener
SURPRISING FACT? I do canvas drawing and I love birdwatching and collecting Steiff bears
TWITTER: @RyanSidebottom

Batting	Mat	Inns	NO	Runs	HS	Ave	SR	100	50	Ct	St
Tests	22	31	11	313	31	15.65	34.66	0	0	5	0
ODIs	25	18	8	133	24	13.30	68.55	0	0	6	0
T20Is	18	1	1	5	5*	-	125.00	0	0	5	0
First-class	222	273	83	2627	61	13.82		0	3	62	0
List A	186	89	39	552	32	11.04		0	0	39	0
Twenty20	85	26	18	140	17*	17.50	101.44	0	0	24	0

Bowling	Mat	Balls	Runs	Wkts	BBI	BBM	Ave	Econ	SR	5w	10
Tests	22	4812	2231	79	7/47	10/139	28.24	2.78	60.9	5	1
ODIs	25	1277	1039	29	3/19	3/19	35.82	4.88	44.0	0	0
T20Is	18	367	437	23	3/16	3/16	19.00	7.14	15.9	0	0
First-class	222	38084	17620	737	7/37		23.90	2.77	51.6	30	4
List A	186	8226	6134	198	6/40	6/40	30.97	4.47	41.5	2	0
Twenty20	85	1797	2149	93	4/25	4/25	23.10	7.17	19.3	0	0

JOHN SIMPSON · LHB / WK / R0 / W0 / MVP60

FULL NAME: John Andrew Simpson
BORN: July 13, 1988, Bury, Lancashire
SQUAD NO: 20
HEIGHT: 5ft 11in
NICKNAME: Simmo
EDUCATION: St Gabriel's RC High School, Bury; Holy Cross College, Bury
TEAMS: Middlesex
ROLE: Wicketkeeper
DEBUT: First-class: 2009; List A: 2009; T20: 2009

BEST BATTING: 143 Middlesex vs Surrey, Lord's, 2011
COUNTY CAP: 2011

FAMILY TIES? Dad played for England Amateurs and Lancashire Cricket Board and holds club and league records in Lancashire/Central Lancashire leagues. Grandad captained the army XI. Uncle plays for Woodbank CC. Two cousins play Lancashire second XI cricket
STRANGEST THING SEEN IN A GAME? A university game at The Parks: a couple walk across the ground, kiss in the middle, and then Tim Murtagh gives the guy the ball to bowl
BEST MOMENT IN CRICKET? Winning the County Championship at Lord's in 2016
BEST PLAYER IN COUNTY CRICKET? Tim Bresnan (Yor) or Toby Roland-Jones (Mid)
TIP FOR THE TOP? Tom Helm, Harry Podmore (both Mid)
CRICKETING HEROES? Jack Russell, Ian Healy, Adam Gilchrist, Brian Lara
NON-CRICKETING HEROES? Tiger Woods, Roger Federer, LeBron James, Michael Jordan
IF YOU WEREN'T A CRICKETER? I'd be a fashion-brand designer
SURPRISING FACT? My great grandad (Walter Gowers) and grandad (Ken Gowers) played rugby league for Great Britain. My dad played lacrosse for England
UNUSUAL OBJECT AT HOME? A Don Bradman porcelain given to me by my grandad
TWITTER: @johnsimpson_88

Batting	Mat	Inns	NO	Runs	HS	Ave	SR	100	50	Ct	St
First-class	115	181	29	4763	143	31.33	46.91	5	29	348	19
List A	65	45	8	881	82	23.81	83.27	0	4	47	9
Twenty20	69	57	13	1043	84*	23.70	128.44	0	5	34	15

Bowling	Mat	Balls	Runs	Wkts	BBI	BBM	Ave	Econ	SR	5w	10
First-class	115	-	-	-	-	-	-	-	-	-	-
List A	65	-	-	-	-	-	-	-	-	-	-
Twenty20	69	-	-	-	-	-	-	-	-	-	-

SUKHJIT SINGH
LHB / SLA / R0 / W0

FULL NAME: Sukhjit Singh
BORN: March 30, 1993, Punjab, India
SQUAD NO: 58
HEIGHT: 5ft 11in
NICKNAME: Sunny
EDUCATION: George Dixon International School, Birmingham; South and City College
TEAMS: Warwickshire 2nd XI
ROLE: Bowler
DEBUT: Yet to make first-team debut

WHAT FIRST GOT YOU INTO CRICKET? My school teachers
BEST MOMENT IN CRICKET? Playing with Varun Chopra
HOW WOULD YOUR TEAM-MATES DESCRIBE YOU IN THREE WORDS? Hard-working, helpful, angry
BEST PLAYER IN COUNTY CRICKET? Jeetan Patel (War)
TIP FOR THE TOP? Joe Clarke (Wor), Andrew Umeed (War), Aneurin Donald (Gla)
CRICKETING HEROES? Eaten Gordon – he helped me a lot when I started playing cricket at the age of 13 for Handsworth CC. He developed me into a better player and got me into the Warwickshire set-up. Recordo Gordon helped me a lot with cricket and other things in life
IF YOU WEREN'T A CRICKETER? I'd be a personal trainer
SURPRISING FACT? I love bhangra music
DESERT ISLAND DISC? Kanye West – The College Dropout
FANTASY SLIP CORDON? Keeper: Kumar Sangakkara, 1st: Alastair Cook, 2nd: Graeme Swann, 3rd: Michael Clarke, Gully: Ravindra Jadeja
TWITTER: @58_sunnyy

BEN SLATER

LHB / OB / RO / WO

FULL NAME: Benjamin Thomas Slater
BORN: August 26, 1991, Chesterfield, Derbyshire
SQUAD NO: 26
HEIGHT: 5ft 11in
NICKNAME: BennySlats, Slats, Slatsy
EDUCATION: Netherthorpe School, Staveley; Leeds Metropolitan University
TEAMS: Derbyshire, Southern Rocks
ROLE: Batsman
DEBUT: First-class: 2012; List A: 2012; T20: 2012

BEST BATTING: 119 Derbyshire vs Leicestershire, Derby, 2014

FAMILY TIES? Both my dad and grandad played to a good standard of league cricket. My sister also used to play for Derbyshire Ladies

STRANGEST THING SEEN IN A GAME? My team in Zimbabwe (Southern Rocks) bowling a side out for 26 when they were set 66 to win in a first-class game which was over in two days. The wicket wasn't even that bad

BEST MOMENT IN CRICKET? Making 148* against Northants last year to break Derbyshire's List A record score against a county side, or back-to-back Championship hundreds in 2014

HOW WOULD YOUR TEAM-MATES DESCRIBE YOU IN THREE WORDS? Charismatic, charming, calm

BEST PLAYER IN COUNTY CRICKET? Wayne Madsen (Der)

TIP FOR THE TOP? Will Davis (Der)

CRICKETING HEROES? Brian Lara, Marcus Trescothick, Matthew Hayden, my grandad (all left-handed batsmen)

FANTASY SLIP CORDON? Keeper: Ryan Gosling, 1st: Margot Robbie, 2nd: Me, 3rd: David Beckham, Gully: Will Smith

TWITTER: @BennySlats

Batting	Mat	Inns	NO	Runs	HS	Ave	SR	100	50	Ct	St
First-class	47	87	2	2422	119	28.49	41.57	3	15	16	0
List A	14	13	2	561	148*	51.00	78.90	3	1	1	0
Twenty20	4	4	0	161	57	40.25	105.22	0	1	0	0
Bowling	Mat	Balls	Runs	Wkts	BBI	BBM	Ave	Econ	SR	5w	10
First-class	47	93	107	0	-	-	-	6.90	-	0	0
List A	14	-	-	-	-	-	-	-	-	-	-
Twenty20	4	-	-	-	-	-	-	-	-	-	-

FULL NAME: Greg Phillip Smith
BORN: November 16, 1988, Leicester
SQUAD NO: 22
HEIGHT: 5ft 11in
EDUCATION: Oundle School,
Northamptonshire; Durham University
TEAMS: Nottinghamshire, Badureliya Sports
Club, Colombo Cricket Club, Kibworth,
Lankan Cricket Club, Leicestershire
ROLE: Batsman
DEBUT: First-class: 2008; List A: 2008;
T20: 2012

NOTTINGHAMSHIRE

BEST BATTING: 158* Leicestershire vs Gloucestershire, Leicester, 2010
BEST BOWLING: 1-64 Leicestershire vs Gloucestershire, Leicester, 2008

FAMILY TIES? My step-grandfather Peter Kelland played for Sussex
STRANGEST THING SEEN IN A GAME? James Sykes trying to field a ball with a wasp in his underpants
BEST MOMENT IN CRICKET? Winning the T20 Cup with Leicestershire in 2010
BEST PLAYER IN COUNTY CRICKET? Angus Robson (Lei)
TIP FOR THE TOP? Ben Kitt (Not)
CRICKETING HEROES? Will Jefferson, Justin Langer
NON-CRICKETING HEROES? Dr Peter Greenfield, Richard Dannatt
IF YOU WEREN'T A CRICKETER? I'd be an Arctic explorer
SURPRISING FACT? I've created my own breed of apple
DESERT ISLAND DISC? Damien Jurado – Ohio
TWITTER: @greg_smith14

Batting	Mat	Inns	NO	Runs	HS	Ave	SR	100	50	Ct	St
First-class	101	188	8	4799	158*	26.66	49.53	8	20	78	0
List A	48	47	5	1130	135*	26.90	80.25	2	5	16	0
Twenty20	48	44	4	1108	102	27.70	124.07	1	7	18	0

Bowling	Mat	Balls	Runs	Wkts	BBI	BBM	Ave	Econ	SR	5w	10
First-class	101	36	73	1	1/64	1/64	73.00	12.16	36.0	0	0
List A	48	-	-	-	-	-	-	-	-	-	-
Twenty20	48	-	-	-	-	-	-	-	-	-	-

RUAIDHRI SMITH

RHB / RM / R0 / W0

GLAMORGAN

FULL NAME: Ruaidhri Alexander James Smith
BORN: August 5, 1994, Glasgow
SQUAD NO: 20
HEIGHT: 6ft 2in
NICKNAME: Trigger
EDUCATION: The Cathedral School, Llandaff; Shrewsbury School; University of Bristol
TEAMS: Scotland, Glamorgan
ROLE: Allrounder
DEBUT: ODI: 2016; First-class: 2013; List A: 2013; T20: 2014

BEST BATTING: 57* Glamorgan vs Gloucestershire, Bristol, 2014
BEST BOWLING: 3-23 Glamorgan vs Derbyshire, Chesterfield, 2015

FAMILY TIES? My dad used to play club cricket and he introduced me to the game
BEST MOMENT IN CRICKET? Taking a wicket with my first ball for Glamorgan
SUPERSTITIONS? Never step on the crease lines while the ball is dead
CRICKETING HEROES? Andrew Flintoff, Jacques Kallis
NON-CRICKETING HEROES? Jonny Wilkinson
IF YOU WEREN'T A CRICKETER? I'd try to be a rugby player
SURPRISING FACT? I'm a Grade 5 pianist and a Harry Potter enthusiast
FANTASY SLIP CORDON? Keeper: Jonny Wilkinson, 1st: Don Bradman, 2nd: Sherlock Holmes, 3rd: Me, Gully: Sir Viv Richards
TWITTER: @RuaidhriSmith

Batting	Mat	Inns	NO	Runs	HS	Ave	SR	100	50	Ct	St
ODIs	2	1	0	10	10	10.00	166.66	0	0	0	0
First-class	15	19	4	285	57*	19.00	52.19	0	1	3	0
List A	13	7	2	33	10	6.60	82.50	0	0	2	0
Twenty20	4	3	2	29	16*	29.00	116.00	0	0	1	0

Bowling	Mat	Balls	Runs	Wkts	BBI	BBM	Ave	Econ	SR	5w	10
ODIs	2	90	97	1	1/34	1/34	97.00	6.46	90.0	0	0
First-class	15	1708	1146	29	3/23	5/87	39.51	4.02	58.8	0	0
List A	13	402	460	12	4/76	4/76	38.33	6.86	33.5	0	0
Twenty20	4	16	35	1	1/11	1/11	35.00	13.12	16.0	0	0

FULL NAME: Thomas Michael John Smith
BORN: August 29, 1987, Eastbourne, Sussex
SQUAD NO: 6
HEIGHT: 5ft 9in
NICKNAME: Smudge
EDUCATION: Seaford Head Community College, East Sussex; Sussex Downs College
TEAMS: Gloucestershire, Middlesex, Surrey, Sussex
ROLE: Bowler
DEBUT: First-class: 2007; List A: 2006; T20: 2007

BEST BATTING: 80 Gloucestershire vs Surrey, Bristol, 2014
BEST BOWLING: 4-35 Gloucestershire vs Kent, Canterbury, 2014
COUNTY CAP: 2013 (Gloucestershire)

WHAT FIRST GOT YOU INTO CRICKET? I discovered a bat in my nan's shed when I was three and I've been hooked ever since. When I was growing up I remember my age-group coach telling us: "There are no traffic jams on the extra mile". A pretty good motto for anyone
BEST MOMENT IN CRICKET? The RL Cup final at Lord's in 2015. What a day!
HOW WOULD YOUR TEAM-MATES DESCRIBE YOU IN THREE WORDS? A cricket badger
BEST PLAYER IN COUNTY CRICKET? Michael Klinger (Glo)
TIP FOR THE TOP? Max Holden (Mid), Miles Hammond (Glo)
CRICKETING HEROES? I grew up watching Shane Warne and was fascinated by spin-bowling
DESERT ISLAND DISC? Kooks – Naive
SURPRISING FACT? I'm a qualified plumber
FANTASY SLIP CORDON? Keeper: David Beckham, 1st: Me, 2nd: Sofia Vergara, 3rd: Michael McIntyre, Gully: Shane Warne

Batting	Mat	Inns	NO	Runs	HS	Ave	SR	100	50	Ct	St
First-class	41	56	11	1024	80	22.75	39.14	0	2	12	0
List A	61	28	11	388	65	22.82	72.65	0	1	29	0
Twenty20	92	35	23	254	36*	21.16	122.11	0	0	29	0

Bowling	Mat	Balls	Runs	Wkts	BBI	BBM	Ave	Econ	SR	5w	10
First-class	41	5935	3378	65	4/35	5/92	51.96	3.41	91.3	0	0
List A	61	2146	1973	50	4/26	4/26	39.46	5.51	42.9	0	0
Twenty20	92	1745	2119	96	5/24	5/24	22.07	7.28	18.1	2	0

WILL SMITH   RHB / OB / R1 / W0

FULL NAME: William Rew Smith
BORN: September 28, 1982, Luton
SQUAD NO: 2
HEIGHT: 5ft 8.5in
NICKNAME: Smudger, Jiggy
EDUCATION: Bedford School; Durham University
TEAMS: Hampshire, Durham, Nottinghamshire
ROLE: Batsman
DEBUT: First-class: 2002; List A: 2002; T20: 2003

BEST BATTING: 210 Hampshire vs Lancashire, Southampton, 2016
BEST BOWLING: 3-34 Durham UCCE vs Leicestershire, Leicester, 2005
COUNTY CAP: 2015 (Hampshire)

WHAT FIRST GOT YOU INTO CRICKET? My brother Ben hurling balls at my head at the tender age of six
STRANGEST THING SEEN IN A GAME? Any time I hit a cover-drive for four
BEST MOMENT IN CRICKET? Winning the County Championship as Durham captain in 2009
BEST PLAYER IN COUNTY CRICKET? Tim Bresnan (Yor)
MOST UNDERRATED PLAYER IN COUNTY CRICKET? Keaton Jennings (Dur)
TIP FOR THE TOP? Brad Wheal, Mason Crane, Tom Alsop, Joe Weatherley (all Ham)
CRICKETING HEROES? Dale Benkenstein, Michael Di Venuto, Graeme Fowler, Jimmy Adams – four very good cricketers and men who I have learnt a great deal from
NON-CRICKETING HEROES? My father Jim and my wife's late father Paul. And every other father in the world who gives and sacrifices anything for their children
IF YOU WEREN'T A CRICKETER? I'd be a horse-racing pundit or professional gambler
UNUSUAL OBJECT AT HOME? A carpet completely buried under kids' toys
TWITTER: @WillSmith_2

Batting	Mat	Inns	NO	Runs	HS	Ave	SR	100	50	Ct	St
First-class	171	290	21	8966	210	33.33	42.62	17	35	109	0
List A	110	94	8	2516	120*	29.25	75.82	2	20	37	0
Twenty20	105	83	21	1006	55	16.22	117.38	0	3	44	0

Bowling	Mat	Balls	Runs	Wkts	BBI	BBM	Ave	Econ	SR	5w	10
First-class	171	2377	1394	28	3/34		49.78	3.51	84.8	0	0
List A	110	443	427	12	2/19	2/19	35.58	5.78	36.9	0	0
Twenty20	105	899	1085	42	3/15	3/15	25.83	7.24	21.4	0	0

FULL NAME: Inderbir Singh Sodhi
BORN: October 31, 1992, Ludhiana, India
TEAMS: New Zealand, Nottinghamshire, Adelaide Strikers, Northern Districts, North Island
ROLE: Bowler
DEBUT: Test: 2013; ODI: 2015; T20I: 2014; First-class: 2012; List A: 2013; T20: 2013

NOTTINGHAMSHIRE

BEST BATTING: 82* Northern Districts vs Otago, Dunedin, 2014
BEST BOWLING: 7-102 Northern Districts vs Otago, Dunedin, 2016

TWITTER: @ish_sodhi
NOTES: Nottinghamshire signed the New Zealand leg-spinner for the duration of the NatWest T20 Blast campaign. "Ish can create pressure and get us some crucial breakthroughs in the middle overs," said head coach Peter Moores. Sodhi impressed during a brief spell with Adelaide Strikers in the 2016/17 Big Bash, taking 6-11 against Sydney Thunder – the sixth-best return in all T20. He was a standout player at the 2016 World T20, claiming 10 wickets at an average of 12

Batting	Mat	Inns	NO	Runs	HS	Ave	SR	100	50	Ct	St
Tests	14	19	3	365	63	22.81	58.87	0	2	8	0
ODIs	15	5	0	6	5	1.20	19.35	0	0	2	0
T20Is	12	1	1	0	0*	-	-	0	0	4	0
First-class	52	77	10	1491	82*	22.25	57.88	0	8	19	0
List A	57	28	6	213	35	9.68	86.58	0	0	14	0
Twenty20	55	13	9	47	19	11.75	109.30	0	0	7	0

Bowling	Mat	Balls	Runs	Wkts	BBI	BBM	Ave	Econ	SR	5w	10
Tests	14	2826	1774	38	4/60	7/79	46.68	3.76	74.3	0	0
ODIs	15	715	668	15	3/38	3/38	44.53	5.60	47.6	0	0
T20Is	12	268	304	21	3/18	3/18	14.47	6.80	12.7	0	0
First-class	52	9231	5953	147	7/102	8/173	40.49	3.86	62.7	6	0
List A	57	2821	2336	77	4/10	4/10	30.33	4.96	36.6	0	0
Twenty20	55	1107	1318	60	6/11	6/11	21.96	7.14	18.4	1	0

NATHAN SOWTER

RHB / LB / RO / WO

FULL NAME: Nathan Adam Sowter
BORN: October 12, 1992, Penrith, New South Wales, Australia
SQUAD NO: 72
HEIGHT: 5ft 10in
NICKNAME: Sowts, Racing Snake, Goblin
EDUCATION: Hills Sport High School, New South Wales
TEAMS: Middlesex
ROLE: Bowler
DEBUT: List A: 2016; T20: 2015

WHAT FIRST GOT YOU INTO CRICKET? Playing with my dad in the backyard
BEST MOMENT IN CRICKET? Being 12th man on the final day of the 2016 season when Middlesex won the County Championship at Lord's
HOW WOULD YOUR TEAM-MATES DESCRIBE YOU IN THREE WORDS? Passionate, angry, competitive
BEST PLAYER IN COUNTY CRICKET? Ben Duckett (Nor)
MOST UNDERRATED PLAYER IN COUNTY CRICKET? Joe Denly (Ken)
TIP FOR THE TOP? Max Holden (Mid)
CRICKETING HEROES? Shane Warne, Ricky Ponting
NON-CRICKETING HEROES? Roger Federer
SURPRISING FACT? I'm also a glazier by trade
UNUSUAL OBJECT AT HOME? A red chicken
FANTASY SLIP CORDON? Keeper: Michael Scofield (Prison Break), 1st: Bart Simpson, 2nd: Me, 3rd: Kerry O'Keefe
TWITTER: @nsowter

Batting	Mat	Inns	NO	Runs	HS	Ave	SR	100	50	Ct	St
List A	2	1	0	0	0	0.00	0.00	0	0	3	0
Twenty20	17	3	2	7	4	7.00	70.00	0	0	4	0

Bowling	Mat	Balls	Runs	Wkts	BBI	BBM	Ave	Econ	SR	5w	10
List A	2	48	62	0	-	-	-	7.75	-	0	0
Twenty20	17	262	338	13	2/2	2/2	26.00	7.74	20.1	0	0

CAMERON STEEL

RHB / LB / R0 / W0

FULL NAME: Cameron Tate Steel
BORN: September 13, 1995, Greenbrae, California, USA
SQUAD NO: 14
HEIGHT: 5ft 10in
NICKNAME: Steely, Lex
EDUCATION: Millfield Prep School, Somerset; Scotch College, Perth, Australia; Durham University
TEAMS: Durham MCCU
ROLE: Batsman
DEBUT: First-class: 2014

DURHAM

BEST BATTING: 80 Durham MCCU vs Somerset, Taunton, 2015
BEST BOWLING: 1-39 Durham MCCU vs Durham, Chester-le-Street, 2014

WHAT FIRST GOT YOU INTO CRICKET? Around the age of seven I was part of the after-school chess club. One day the teacher running the club was off ill, and mum couldn't pick me up until 5pm, so I had to join in with the cricket club instead
FAMILY TIES? My sister played youth representative cricket for Somerset and Western Australia but stopped because of injury
STRANGEST THING SEEN IN A GAME? During a school game in Australia, two local lads rode across the wicket on their bikes. One of the parents from our side chased them with a stump
BEST MOMENT IN CRICKET? Scoring 95 for Durham against Middlesex in the Second XI Championship final in 2016. I was under a lot of pressure playing against my old club
HOW WOULD YOUR TEAM-MATES DESCRIBE YOU IN THREE WORDS? Aussie or English?
BEST PLAYER IN COUNTY CRICKET? Keaton Jennings (Dur)
MOST UNDERRATED PLAYER IN COUNTY CRICKET? Tom Helm (Mid)
TIP FOR THE TOP? Ryan Higgins, Steve Eskinazi (both Mid)
CRICKETING HEROES? Mike Hussey – he is the batsman I'd like to be
IF YOU WEREN'T A CRICKETER? I'd be another unemployed History graduate
SURPRISING FACT? I was the U9 West of England chess champion
UNUSUAL OBJECT AT HOME? A large floating flamingo
TWITTER: @CameronSteel2

Batting	Mat	Inns	NO	Runs	HS	Ave	SR	100	50	Ct	St
First-class	6	9	0	315	80	35.00	39.08	0	3	4	0

Bowling	Mat	Balls	Runs	Wkts	BBI	BBM	Ave	Econ	SR	5w	10
First-class	6	114	118	1	1/39	1/39	118.00	6.21	114.0	0	0

DARREN STEVENS   RHB / RM / R3 / W2 / MVP17

KENT

FULL NAME: Darren Ian Stevens
BORN: April 30, 1976, Leicester
SQUAD NO: 3
HEIGHT: 5ft 11in
NICKNAME: Stevo
EDUCATION: John Cleveland College, Hinckley; Charles Keene College, Leicester
TEAMS: Kent, Comilla Victorians, Dhaka Gladiators, Leicestershire, Mid West Rhinos, Otago
ROLE: Allrounder
DEBUT: First-class: 1997; List A: 1997; T20: 2003

BEST BATTING: 208 Kent vs Middlesex, Canterbury, 2009
BEST BOWLING: 7-21 Kent vs Surrey, Canterbury, 2011
COUNTY CAPS: 2002 (Leicestershire); 2005 (Kent) BENEFIT: 2016 (Kent)

WHAT FIRST GOT YOU INTO CRICKET? My dad pestered me to play. I preferred football but gave in after a year
MOST UNDERRATED PLAYER IN COUNTY CRICKET? Sam Northeast (Ken)
TIP FOR THE TOP? Sean Dickson (Ken)
CRICKETING HEROES? Sir Viv Richards
NON-CRICKETING HEROES? Roger Federer, Fred Couples, Arnold Palmer
IF YOU WEREN'T A CRICKETER? I'd be a professional golfer
SURPRISING FACT? I am colour blind with browns, reds and greens. I struggled when I was with Otago in New Zealand because there were no sightscreens
DESERT ISLAND DISC? Ed Sheeran
TWITTER: @Stevo208

Batting	Mat	Inns	NO	Runs	HS	Ave	SR	100	50	Ct	St
First-class	265	416	23	13899	208	35.36		31	70	190	0
List A	293	271	30	7216	133	29.94		6	45	120	0
Twenty20	194	179	39	3857	90	27.55	137.06	0	17	64	0

Bowling	Mat	Balls	Runs	Wkts	BBI	BBM	Ave	Econ	SR	5w	10
First-class	265	20931	10127	358	7/21		28.28	2.90	58.4	12	1
List A	293	5302	4232	135	5/32	5/32	31.34	4.78	39.2	2	0
Twenty20	194	2114	2766	110	4/14	4/14	25.14	7.85	19.2	0	0

RYAN STEVENSON

RHB / RFM / R0 / W0

FULL NAME: Ryan Anthony Stevenson
BORN: April 2, 1992, Torquay
SQUAD NO: 47
HEIGHT: 6ft 2in
NICKNAME: Raz, Stevo
EDUCATION: King Edward VI Community College, Devon
TEAMS: Hampshire
ROLE: Bowler
DEBUT: First-class: 2015; List A: 2016; T20: 2016

BEST BATTING: 30 Hampshire vs Durham, Chester-le-Street, 2015
BEST BOWLING: 1-15 Hampshire vs Nottinghamshire, Trent Bridge, 2015

FAMILY TIES? My dad has played for Devon Over-50s
BEST MOMENT IN CRICKET? Making my first-class debut against Durham. And fielding as 12th man at Somerset – that's where I watched cricket when I was growing up in Devon
HOW WOULD YOUR TEAM-MATES DESCRIBE YOU IN THREE WORDS? Normal, big, ginger
BEST PLAYER IN COUNTY CRICKET? Roooooot (Yor)
TIP FOR THE TOP? Brad Wheal, Joe Weatherley (both Ham)
CRICKETING HEROES? Brett Lee for his raw pace. But my biggest hero was Shaun Pollock – I always wanted to play like him and loved his bowling action
IF YOU WEREN'T A CRICKETER? I'd be a badminton coach, farmer or running a business
SURPRISING FACT? I played county tennis as a junior
DESERT ISLAND DISC? Toploader – Dancing In The Moonlight
FANTASY SLIP CORDON? Keeper: Jack Whitehall (hilarious), 1st: Andrew Flintoff (hero and a very funny man), 2nd: Me, 3rd: My brother (for the banter and he is a legend), Gully: Odell Beckham Jnr (unbelievable hands – he would catch everything)
TWITTER: @ryanstevenson00

Batting	Mat	Inns	NO	Runs	HS	Ave	SR	100	50	Ct	St
First-class	3	3	0	34	30	11.33	87.17	0	0	0	0
List A	3	1	0	0	0	0.00	0.00	0	0	0	0
Twenty20	1	1	0	3	3	3.00	60.00	0	0	1	0

Bowling	Mat	Balls	Runs	Wkts	BBI	BBM	Ave	Econ	SR	5w	10
First-class	3	341	215	3	1/15	1/46	71.66	3.78	113.6	0	0
List A	3	120	142	2	1/28	1/28	71.00	7.10	60.0	0	0
Twenty20	1	24	40	2	2/40	2/40	20.00	10.00	12.0	0	0

PAUL STIRLING

RHB / OB / R0 / W0

FULL NAME: Paul Robert Stirling
BORN: September 3, 1990, Belfast, Ireland
SQUAD NO: 39
HEIGHT: 5ft 9in
NICKNAME: Stirlo
EDUCATION: Belfast High School
TEAMS: Ireland, Middlesex, Sylhet Royals
ROLE: Allrounder
DEBUT: ODI: 2008; T20I: 2009; First-class: 2008; List A: 2008; T20: 2008

BEST BATTING: 146 Ireland vs UAE, Malahide, 2015
BEST BOWLING: 2-27 Ireland vs Namibia, Windhoek, 2015
COUNTY CAP: 2016

FAMILY TIES? My brother Richard has represented Ireland in an U19 World Cup in Sri Lanka
STRANGEST THING SEEN IN A GAME? A pigeon being hit out of the sky
BEST MOMENT IN CRICKET? Getting a first-class wicket with a flipper, and a Lord's century
SUPERSTITIONS? Don't walk in shadows
HOW WOULD YOUR TEAM-MATES DESCRIBE YOU IN THREE WORDS? Poor man's Inzi
BEST PLAYER IN COUNTY CRICKET? Ed Joyce (Sus)
MOST UNDERRATED PLAYER IN COUNTY CRICKET? Tim Murtagh (Mid)
TIP FOR THE TOP? Stevie Eskinazi (Mid)
CRICKETING HEROES? Damien Martyn – he was the most pleasing to watch
NON-CRICKETING HEROES? George Best – a Belfast legend
TWITTER: @stirlo90

Batting	Mat	Inns	NO	Runs	HS	Ave	SR	100	50	Ct	St
ODIs	73	72	2	2285	177	32.64	91.47	5	9	32	0
T20Is	44	43	4	975	79	25.00	133.37	0	6	13	0
First-class	48	72	4	2003	146	29.45	61.34	4	10	24	0
List A	142	138	7	4276	177	32.64	94.08	10	16	57	0
Twenty20	134	133	7	3235	90	25.67	141.88	0	22	37	0

Bowling	Mat	Balls	Runs	Wkts	BBI	BBM	Ave	Econ	SR	5w	10
ODIs	73	1948	1512	32	4/11	4/11	47.25	4.65	60.8	0	0
T20Is	44	354	413	13	3/21	3/21	31.76	7.00	27.2	0	0
First-class	48	1792	832	19	2/27	3/31	43.78	2.78	94.3	0	0
List A	142	2684	2194	55	4/11	4/11	39.89	4.90	48.8	0	0
Twenty20	134	1086	1249	49	4/10	4/10	25.48	6.90	22.1	0	0

BEN STOKES

LHB / RFM / RO / WO

FULL NAME: Benjamin Andrew Stokes
BORN: June 4, 1991, Christchurch, New Zealand
SQUAD NO: 38
HEIGHT: 6ft 2in
NICKNAME: Stokesy, Benji, Stoker
EDUCATION: Cockermouth School, Cumbria
TEAMS: England, Durham
ROLE: Allrounder
DEBUT: Test: 2013; ODI: 2011; T20I: 2011; First-class: 2010; List A: 2009; T20: 2010

DURHAM

BEST BATTING: 258 England vs South Africa, Cape Town, 2016
BEST BOWLING: 7-67 Durham vs Sussex, Chester-le-Street, 2014

SUPERSTITIONS? Swiping my bat across the crease at the end of every over
CRICKETING HEROES? Herschelle Gibbs
IF YOU WEREN'T A CRICKETER? I'd be on the dole
SURPRISING FACT? My father played one Test match for New Zealand at rugby league. I was a right-handed batsman when I was younger
FANTASY SLIP CORDON? 1st: Michael McIntyre, 2nd: Jordan Belfort, 3rd: Alan (from The Hangover), Gully: Bane (from Batman)
TWITTER: @benstokes38

Batting	Mat	Inns	NO	Runs	HS	Ave	SR	100	50	Ct	St
Tests	32	57	1	1902	258	33.96	63.82	4	8	22	0
ODIs	53	47	5	1244	101	29.61	98.49	1	9	25	0
T20Is	21	18	5	192	38	14.76	136.17	0	0	8	0
First-class	105	174	9	5680	258	34.42		12	27	61	0
List A	120	108	14	3109	164	33.07	100.12	5	16	52	0
Twenty20	77	68	12	1272	77	22.71	134.03	0	5	31	0

Bowling	Mat	Balls	Runs	Wkts	BBI	BBM	Ave	Econ	SR	5w	10
Tests	32	4795	2723	79	6/36	8/161	34.46	3.40	60.6	3	0
ODIs	53	1718	1744	46	5/61	5/61	37.91	6.09	37.3	1	0
T20Is	21	322	485	10	3/26	3/26	48.50	9.03	32.2	0	0
First-class	105	12190	7189	240	7/67	10/121	29.95	3.53	50.7	5	1
List A	120	3207	3054	107	5/61	5/61	28.54	5.71	29.9	1	0
Twenty20	77	812	1165	32	3/26	3/26	36.40	8.60	25.3	0	0

OLLY STONE

RHB / RFM / R0 / W0

FULL NAME: Oliver Peter Stone
BORN: October 9, 1993, Norwich
SQUAD NO: 6
HEIGHT: 6ft 2in
NICKNAME: Stoney
EDUCATION: Thorpe St Andrew High School, Norwich; Moulton College
TEAMS: Warwickshire, Northamptonshire
ROLE: Bowler
DEBUT: First-class: 2012; List A: 2012; T20: 2011

BEST BATTING: 60 Northamptonshire vs Kent, Northampton, 2016
BEST BOWLING: 5-44 Northamptonshire vs Kent, Northampton, 2015

WHAT FIRST GOT YOU INTO CRICKET? Playing down my driveway with my brothers
STRANGEST THING SEEN IN A GAME? David Murphy's fielding
BEST MOMENT IN CRICKET? Making my first-class debut and taking my first wicket
HOW WOULD YOUR TEAM-MATES DESCRIBE YOU IN THREE WORDS? Terrible banter, powerhouse
BEST PLAYER IN COUNTY CRICKET? Ben Duckett (Nor)
MOST UNDERRATED PLAYER IN COUNTY CRICKET? Rob Keogh (Nor)
TIP FOR THE TOP? Saif Zaib (Nor), Tom Helm (Mid)
CRICKETING HEROES? Brett Lee – bowls rapid. Paul Bradshaw – takes lots of wickets
IF YOU WEREN'T A CRICKETER? I'd be a farmer or a butcher
SURPRISING FACT? My great-grandad created the Twix chocolate bar
UNUSUAL OBJECT AT HOME? A wand
TWITTER: @ollystone2

Batting	Mat	Inns	NO	Runs	HS	Ave	SR	100	50	Ct	St
First-class	25	32	7	407	60	16.28	46.62	0	1	14	0
List A	17	11	7	90	24*	22.50	65.69	0	0	7	0
Twenty20	30	8	4	15	6*	3.75	78.94	0	0	6	0

Bowling	Mat	Balls	Runs	Wkts	BBI	BBM	Ave	Econ	SR	5w	10
First-class	25	4055	2210	72	5/44	6/90	30.69	3.27	56.3	2	0
List A	17	634	556	11	3/34	3/34	50.54	5.26	57.6	0	0
Twenty20	30	474	706	17	2/18	2/18	41.52	8.93	27.8	0	0

MARK STONEMAN
LHB / OB / R4 / W0 / MVP15

FULL NAME: Mark Daniel Stoneman
BORN: June 26, 1987, Newcastle
SQUAD NO: 23
HEIGHT: 5ft 10in
NICKNAME: Rocky
EDUCATION: Whickham Comprehensive School, Newcastle Upon Tyne
TEAMS: Surrey, Durham
ROLE: Batsman
DEBUT: First-class: 2007; List A: 2008; T20: 2010

BEST BATTING: 187 Durham vs Middlesex, Chester-le-Street, 2014

WHAT FIRST GOT YOU INTO CRICKET? Following my dad everywhere as soon as I could, carrying my little plastic bat along with me
FAMILY TIES? My grandfather played and umpired locally for many years
BEST MOMENT IN CRICKET? Captaining the Durham side which won the 2014 RL Cup
SUPERSTITIONS? Nervous wee box goes on first
HOW WOULD YOUR TEAM-MATES DESCRIBE YOU IN THREE WORDS? Vocal, grumpy, passionate
TIP FOR THE TOP? Mason Crane (Ham), Ryan Pringle, Paul Coughlin (both Dur)
CRICKETING HEROES? Michael Di Venuto – the best role model for a young county cricketer
IF YOU WEREN'T A CRICKETER? I'd be a fisherman
SURPRISING FACT? The Lion King makes me cry
DESERT ISLAND DISC? Red Hot Chili Peppers – Stadium Arcadium
FANTASY SLIP CORDON? Keeper: Jennifer Lopez (she's a keeper!), 1st: Me, 2nd: Conor McGregor (he would be the best sledger ever), 3rd: Dwayne Johnson (everyone loves the rock), Gully: Don Bradman (to see what he thought of modern standards)
TWITTER: @mark23stone

Batting	Mat	Inns	NO	Runs	HS	Ave	SR	100	50	Ct	St
First-class	135	238	6	7659	187	33.01	57.81	16	37	70	0
List A	60	57	4	2119	136*	39.98	92.41	5	12	18	0
Twenty20	57	55	4	1085	89*	21.27	121.36	0	6	21	0

Bowling	Mat	Balls	Runs	Wkts	BBI	BBM	Ave	Econ	SR	5w	10
First-class	135	204	150	0	-	-	-	4.41	-	0	0
List A	60	4	8	1	1/8	1/8	8.00	12.00	4.0	0	0
Twenty20	57	-	-	-	-	-	-	-	-	-	-

JAMES SYKES

LHB / SLA / R0 / W0

LEICESTERSHIRE

FULL NAME: James Stuart Sykes
BORN: April 26, 1992, Huntingdon, Cambridgeshire
SQUAD NO: 60
HEIGHT: 6ft 2in
NICKNAME: Sykesy
EDUCATION: St Ivo School, Cambridgeshire
TEAMS: Leicestershire
ROLE: Bowler
DEBUT: First-class: 2013; List A: 2012; T20: 2012

BEST BATTING: 34 Leicestershire vs Lancashire, Old Trafford, 2013
BEST BOWLING: 4-176 Leicestershire vs Essex, Chelmsford, 2013

BEST MOMENT IN CRICKET? Making my debut and playing at Lord's
CRICKETING HEROES? Shane Warne – because he was the king of spin
NON-CRICKETING HEROES? David Beckham – just an absolute hero
IF YOU WEREN'T A CRICKETER? I'd be trying to cut people's hair
SURPRISING FACT? I'm planning on becoming a barber after cricket
DESERT ISLAND DISC? Kanye West – The College Dropout
FANTASY SLIP CORDON? Keeper: Micky Flanagan, 1st: Kanye West, 2nd: Scott Disick, 3rd: David Beckham, Gully: Me
TWITTER: @Sykesy20

Batting	Mat	Inns	NO	Runs	HS	Ave	SR	100	50	Ct	St
First-class	12	19	4	186	34	12.40	36.75	0	0	6	0
List A	20	11	4	46	15	6.57	64.78	0	0	3	0
Twenty20	5	1	1	2	2*	-	50.00	0	0	0	0

Bowling	Mat	Balls	Runs	Wkts	BBI	BBM	Ave	Econ	SR	5w	10
First-class	12	1995	1166	21	4/176	5/180	55.52	3.50	95.0	0	0
List A	20	709	666	15	3/34	3/34	44.40	5.63	47.2	0	0
Twenty20	5	90	107	3	2/24	2/24	35.66	7.13	30.0	0	0

IMRAN TAHIR RHB / LB / RO / W2

FULL NAME: Mohammad Imran Tahir
BORN: March 27, 1979, Lahore, Pakistan
SQUAD NO: 99
EDUCATION: Pak Angels High School, Lahore
TEAMS: South Africa, Derbyshire, Delhi Daredevils, Dolphins, Easterns, Hampshire, Lahore, Lions, Middlesex, Nottinghamshire, Sialkot, Sui Gas Corporation, Titans, Warwickshire, Water & Power Development Authority, Yorkshire
ROLE: Bowler
DEBUT: Test: 2011; ODI: 2011; T20I: 2013; First-class: 1996; List A: 1998; T20: 2006

BEST BATTING: 77* Hampshire vs Somerset, Southampton, 2009
BEST BOWLING: 8-42 Dolphins vs Knights, Kimberley, 2015
COUNTY CAPS: 2009 (Hampshire); 2010 (Warwickshire)

NOTES: Tahir is expected to be available for Derbyshire from June depending on his international commitments. This will be the South African leg-spinner's sixth county – equalling Marcus North's record for an overseas player. At the time of writing he is ranked No.1 in the ICC ODI and T20I bowling rankings. He took 25 first-class wickets at 37.20 for Nottinghamshire last season. His best county campaign came in 2010 when he claimed 56 first-class wickets at 24.57 for Warwickshire

Batting	Mat	Inns	NO	Runs	HS	Ave	SR	100	50	Ct	St
Tests	20	23	9	130	29*	9.28	55.31	0	0	8	0
ODIs	74	23	11	117	29	9.75	75.97	0	0	14	0
T20Is	31	3	2	18	9*	18.00	105.88	0	0	5	0
First-class	190	240	61	2576	77*	14.39		0	4	80	0
List A	188	57	20	424	41*	11.45		0	0	39	0
Twenty20	148	28	13	131	17*	8.73	114.91	0	0	35	0

Bowling	Mat	Balls	Runs	Wkts	BBI	BBM	Ave	Econ	SR	5w	10
Tests	20	3925	2294	57	5/32	8/130	40.24	3.50	68.8	2	0
ODIs	74	3892	3004	127	7/45	7/45	23.65	4.63	30.6	2	0
T20Is	31	695	740	54	5/24	5/24	13.70	6.38	12.8	1	0
First-class	190	37552	20475	771	8/42		26.55	3.27	48.7	51	11
List A	188	8775	6751	287	7/45	7/45	23.52	4.61	30.5	5	0
Twenty20	148	3131	3628	173	5/24	5/24	20.97	6.95	18.0	1	0

WILLIAM TAVARÉ

RHB / RM / R1 / W0

FULL NAME: William Andrew Tavaré
BORN: January 1, 1990, Bristol
SQUAD NO: 4
HEIGHT: 6ft 1in
NICKNAME: Tav, Tekkers, Postman, Mezut, Zukkers
EDUCATION: Bristol Grammar School; Loughborough University
TEAMS: Gloucestershire, Tamil Union Cricket and Athletic Club
ROLE: Batsman
DEBUT: First-class: 2010; List A 2014

BEST BATTING: 139 Gloucestershire vs Hampshire, Bristol, 2014

FAMILY TIES? My dad played for Gloucestershire Second XI and my uncle Chris played for England
BEST MOMENT IN CRICKET? Winning the 2015 Lord's one-day final
HOW WOULD YOUR TEAM-MATES DESCRIBE YOU IN THREE WORDS? Determined, hard-working, quiet
BEST PLAYER IN COUNTY CRICKET? James Vince (Ham)
MOST UNDERRATED PLAYER IN COUNTY CRICKET? Chris Dent (Glo)
TIP FOR THE TOP? George Hankins (Glo)
CRICKETING HEROES? My uncle, plus any England player from the 2005 Ashes
NON-CRICKETING HEROES? Jonny Wilkinson – I loved how determined he was and I will never forget his drop goal to win the World Cup
SURPRISING FACT? I lived in Dallas just after I was born
UNUSUAL OBJECT AT HOME? Lots of mould
DESERT ISLAND DISC? Bombay Bicycle Club – Flaws
FANTASY SLIP CORDON? Keeper: David Attenborough, 1st: Me, 2nd: Andrew Flintoff, 3rd: Hamish Marshall, Gully: Simon Lee
TWITTER: @wtav90

Batting	Mat	Inns	NO	Runs	HS	Ave	SR	100	50	Ct	St
First-class	43	74	5	2189	139	31.72	46.22	4	12	29	0
List A	8	8	0	221	77	27.62	72.22	0	2	1	0

Bowling	Mat	Balls	Runs	Wkts	BBI	BBM	Ave	Econ	SR	5w	10
First-class	43	54	30	0	-	-	-	3.33	-	0	0
List A	8	-	-	-	-	-	-	-	-	-	-

FULL NAME: Bradley Jacob Taylor
BORN: March 14, 1997, Winchester, Hampshire
SQUAD NO: 93
HEIGHT: 6ft
NICKNAME: Bradders
EDUCATION: Alton College, Hampshire
TEAMS: Hampshire
ROLE: Bowler
DEBUT: First-class: 2013; List A: 2013; T20: 2014

BEST BATTING: 36 Hampshire vs Cardiff MCCU, Southampton, 2016
BEST BOWLING: 4-64 Hampshire vs Lancashire, Southport, 2013

FAMILY TIES? My dad is a Level 3 coach
BEST MOMENT IN CRICKET? Taking four wickets on my first-class debut, getting Simon Katich on my one-day debut and being Man of the Match for England U19 against South Africa U19 on TV
CRICKETING HEROES? Daniel Vettori, Graeme Swann
NON-CRICKETING HEROES? LeBron James – he works hard and is always motivated to become better even though he is the best in the world at his sport
SURPRISING FACT? I'm a Southampton fan and go to the home games whenever possible
DESERT ISLAND DISC? Ed Sheeran – X
TWITTER: @bradtay93

Batting	Mat	Inns	NO	Runs	HS	Ave	SR	100	50	Ct	St
First-class	3	4	1	57	36	19.00	50.89	0	0	2	0
List A	2	1	1	2	2*	-	50.00	0	0	0	0
Twenty20	6	3	1	21	9*	10.50	84.00	0	0	2	0

Bowling	Mat	Balls	Runs	Wkts	BBI	BBM	Ave	Econ	SR	5w	10
First-class	3	318	219	7	4/64	4/106	31.28	4.13	45.4	0	0
List A	2	90	73	4	2/23	2/23	18.25	4.86	22.5	0	0
Twenty20	6	68	84	3	2/20	2/20	28.00	7.41	22.6	0	0

BRENDAN TAYLOR RHB / OB / R1 / W0

FULL NAME: Brendan Ross Murray Taylor
BORN: February 6, 1986, Harare, Zimbabwe
SQUAD NO: 1
EDUCATION: St John's College, Harare, Zimbabwe
TEAMS: Zimbabwe, Nottinghamshire, Barisal Bulls, Chittagong Kings, Mashonaland, Mid West Rhinos, Northerns, Prime Bank Cricket Club, Sunrisers Hyderabad, Uthura Rudras, Wellington
ROLE: Batsman
DEBUT: Test: 2004; ODI: 2004; T20I: 2006; First-class: 2001; List A: 2003; T20: 2006

BEST BATTING: 217 Mid West Rhinos vs Southern Rocks, Masvingo, 2010
BEST BOWLING: 2-36 Mashonaland vs Manicaland, Mutare, 2003

TWITTER: @BrendanTaylor86
NOTES: The Zimbabwean enjoyed a productive 2015 county season after quitting international cricket, hitting three Championship centuries for Nottinghamshire. He followed that up with two more first-class hundreds in 2016, although he struggled in the short formats. Taylor played 23 Tests, 167 ODIs and 26 T20Is for Zimbabwe, standing out as the country's classiest batsman

Batting	Mat	Inns	NO	Runs	HS	Ave	SR	100	50	Ct	St
Tests	23	46	3	1493	171	34.72	51.09	4	7	23	0
ODIs	167	166	15	5258	145*	34.82	74.47	8	32	98	20
T20Is	26	26	5	594	75*	28.28	123.75	0	5	10	1
First-class	117	214	12	8208	217	40.63		28	29	131	4
List A	265	258	25	7794	145*	33.45		13	44	162	32
Twenty20	116	111	15	2558	101*	26.64	120.83	1	20	45	11

Bowling	Mat	Balls	Runs	Wkts	BBI	BBM	Ave	Econ	SR	5w	10
Tests	23	42	38	0	-	-	-	5.42	-	0	0
ODIs	167	396	406	9	3/54	3/54	45.11	6.15	44.0	0	0
T20Is	26	30	17	1	1/16	1/16	17.00	3.40	30.0	0	0
First-class	117	384	225	4	2/36		56.25	3.51	96.0	0	0
List A	265	606	604	20	5/28	5/28	30.20	5.98	30.3	1	0
Twenty20	116	150	152	8	3/38	3/38	19.00	6.08	18.7	0	0

CALLUM TAYLOR

RHB / RM / RO / WO

FULL NAME: Callum John Taylor
BORN: June 26, 1997, Norwich
SQUAD NO: 67
HEIGHT: 5ft 10in
NICKNAME: Chappy
EDUCATION: Cromer Academy, Norfolk;
Eastern College, Norwich
TEAMS: Essex
ROLE: Allrounder
DEBUT: First-class: 2015; T20: 2015

ESSEX

BEST BATTING: 26 Essex vs Glamorgan, Cardiff, 2015
BEST BOWLING: 1-6 Essex vs Cambridge MCCU, Cambridge, 2016

BEST MOMENT IN CRICKET? Scoring 212 runs and taking six wickets in one day for Mount Lawley District CC in Australian grade cricket last December
SUPERSTITIONS? Mark my guard by dragging my bat five times down and three times across
HOW WOULD YOUR TEAM-MATES DESCRIBE YOU IN THREE WORDS? Aggressive, fun, sociable
BEST PLAYER IN COUNTY CRICKET? Keaton Jennings (Dur)
MOST UNDERRATED PLAYER IN COUNTY CRICKET? Rob Newton (Nor)
TIP FOR THE TOP? George Garton (Sus), Matt Parkinson (Lan), Aaron Beard (Ess), Tom Abell (Som), Rob Jones (Lan)
CRICKETING HEROES? Andrew Flintoff, Jaques Kallis
NON-CRICKETING HEROES? Dad, Ryan Giggs
SURPRISING FACT? I always shave the day before a game
UNUSUAL OBJECT AT HOME? A cocktail shaker
FANTASY SLIP CORDON? Keeper: Jack Whitehall, 1st: Andrew Flintoff, 2nd: Me, 3rd: James Corden, 4th: Mark Wahlberg, Gully: Jennifer Anniston
TWITTER: @Callumjtaylor12

Batting	Mat	Inns	NO	Runs	HS	Ave	SR	100	50	Ct	St
First-class	2	3	0	49	26	16.33	46.66	0	0	1	0
Twenty20	7	5	1	19	14	4.75	70.37	0	0	1	0

Bowling	Mat	Balls	Runs	Wkts	BBI	BBM	Ave	Econ	SR	5w	10
First-class	2	15	6	1	1/6	1/6	6.00	2.40	15.0	0	0
Twenty20	7	6	19	0	-	-	-	19.00	-	0	0

JACK TAYLOR

RHB / OB / R0 / W0 / MVP97

GLOUCESTERSHIRE

FULL NAME: Jack Martin Robert Taylor
BORN: November 12, 1991, Banbury, Oxfordshire
SQUAD NO: 10
HEIGHT: 6ft
NICKNAME: Tails, Tringale, Jacko
EDUCATION: Chipping Norton School, Oxfordshire
TEAMS: Gloucestershire
ROLE: Allrounder
DEBUT: First-class: 2010; List A: 2011; T20: 2011

BEST BATTING: 156 Gloucestershire vs Northamptonshire, Cheltenham, 2015
BEST BOWLING: 4-16 Gloucestershire vs Glamorgan, Bristol, 2016
COUNTY CAP: 2010

FAMILY TIES? My grandad and dad both played Minor Counties for Oxfordshire. My younger brother Matt also plays for Gloucestershire
STRANGEST THING SEEN IN A GAME? Mark Ramprakash run out obstructing the ball at Cheltenham. He wasn't too happy about it
BEST MOMENT IN CRICKET? Taking the winning catch in the 2015 Lord's final against Surrey
HOW WOULD YOUR TEAM-MATES DESCRIBE YOU IN THREE WORDS? Loud, competitive, moaner
BEST PLAYER IN COUNTY CRICKET? Micheal Klinger (Glo)
MOST UNDERRATED PLAYER IN COUNTY CRICKET? Chris Dent (Glo)
TIP FOR THE TOP? George Hankins (Glo)
CRICKETING HEROES? Jacques Kallis, Shane Warne
NON-CRICKETING HEROES? Justin Timberlake – he can act, sing and dance
SURPRISING FACT? I am unbelievably ticklish
TWITTER: @jacktaylor141

Batting	Mat	Inns	NO	Runs	HS	Ave	SR	100	50	Ct	St
First-class	42	64	4	1801	156	30.01	73.30	4	6	22	0
List A	29	21	5	388	53	24.25	128.47	0	1	12	0
Twenty20	41	28	7	348	80	16.57	146.21	0	1	7	0

Bowling	Mat	Balls	Runs	Wkts	BBI	BBM	Ave	Econ	SR	5w	10
First-class	42	4747	2657	61	4/16	5/140	43.55	3.35	77.8	0	0
List A	29	902	757	27	4/38	4/38	28.03	5.03	33.4	0	0
Twenty20	41	574	774	22	4/16	4/16	35.18	8.09	26.0	0	0

MATT TAYLOR

RHB / LMF / R0 / W0

FULL NAME: Matthew David Taylor
BORN: July 8, 1994, Banbury, Oxfordshire
SQUAD NO: 36
HEIGHT: 6ft 2in
NICKNAME: MT, Tayls, Melon, Swede, Balloon
EDUCATION: Chipping Norton Secondary School, Oxfordshire
TEAMS: Gloucestershire
ROLE: Bowler
DEBUT: First-class: 2013; List A: 2011; T20: 2015

BEST BATTING: 32* Gloucestershire vs Essex, Chelmsford, 2014
BEST BOWLING: 5-75 Gloucestershire vs Hampshire, Bristol, 2014
COUNTY CAP: 2013

WHAT FIRST GOT YOU INTO CRICKET? My grandfather, father and brother all played so I was around cricket from an early age
FAMILY TIES? My older brother Jack also plays for Gloucestershire
BEST MOMENT IN CRICKET? Taking my maiden first-class wicket in 2013
BEST PLAYER IN COUNTY CRICKET? Michael Klinger (Glo)
TIP FOR THE TOP? Miles Hammond, George Hankins (both Glo)
CRICKETING HEROES? Darren Gough – for his yorker-bowling
NON-CRICKETING HEROES? Cristiano Ronaldo – for his drive to be the best
DESERT ISLAND DISC? Ed Sheeran – X
FANTASY SLIP CORDON? Keeper: Michelle Keegan, 1st: Ed Sheeran, 2nd: Sara Sampaio, 3rd: Me, Gully: Leonardo DiCaprio
TWITTER: @matt_taylor94

Batting	Mat	Inns	NO	Runs	HS	Ave	SR	100	50	Ct	St
First-class	23	31	15	215	32*	13.43	41.10	0	0	3	0
List A	10	5	4	32	16	32.00	118.51	0	0	1	0
Twenty20	15	2	2	2	6	5*	-	200.00	0	0	2	0

Bowling	Mat	Balls	Runs	Wkts	BBI	BBM	Ave	Econ	SR	5w	10
First-class	23	3645	2296	52	5/75	6/101	44.15	3.77	70.0	2	0
List A	10	425	411	10	2/33	2/33	41.10	5.80	42.5	0	0
Twenty20	15	282	362	16	3/16	3/16	22.62	7.70	17.6	0	0

ROSS TAYLOR

RHB / OB / RO / WO

FULL NAME: Luteru Ross Poutoa Lote Taylor
BORN: March 8, 1984, Lower Hutt, NZ
SQUAD NO: 16
HEIGHT: 6ft 1in
NICKNAME: Rosco, Pallekele Plunderer
EDUCATION: Wairarapa College, Masterton
TEAMS: NZ, Sussex, Central Districts, Delhi Daredevils, Durham, North Island, Pune Warriors, Rajasthan Royals, RC Bangalore, St Lucia Zouks, T&T Red Steel, Victoria
ROLE: Batsman
DEBUT: Test: 2007; ODI: 2006; T20I: 2006; First-class: 2003; List A: 2003; T20: 2006

BEST BATTING: 290 New Zealand vs Australia, Perth, 2015
BEST BOWLING: 2-4 New Zealand vs India, Ahmedabad, 2010

TWITTER: @RossLTaylor
NOTES: Taylor has been re-signed by Sussex for the NatWest T20 Blast. He was the county's leading runscorer in the competition last summer, with 394 runs at 56.28 from 10 matches. A vastly experienced international batsman across all formats for New Zealand, he made his best Test score of 290 at Perth in November 2015. Captained New Zealand to Test victories in Australia and Sri Lanka

Batting	Mat	Inns	NO	Runs	HS	Ave	SR	100	50	Ct	St
Tests	81	146	18	6030	290	47.10	59.56	16	27	123	0
ODIs	183	169	28	6144	131*	43.57	82.06	17	33	115	0
T20Is	73	65	13	1256	63	24.15	120.07	0	5	42	0
First-class	146	246	21	9812	290	43.60		23	50	184	0
List A	235	221	32	8123	132*	42.97		21	49	146	0
Twenty20	224	209	47	5090	111*	31.41	134.47	1	27	108	0

Bowling	Mat	Balls	Runs	Wkts	BBI	BBM	Ave	Econ	SR	5w	10
Tests	81	96	48	2	2/4	2/4	24.00	3.00	48.0	0	0
ODIs	183	42	35	0	-	-	-	5.00	-	0	0
T20Is	73	-	-	-	-	-	-	-	-	-	-
First-class	146	684	378	6	2/4	2/4	63.00	3.31	114.0	0	0
List A	235	318	242	3	1/13	1/13	80.66	4.56	106.0	0	0
Twenty20	224	186	280	8	3/28	3/28	35.00	9.03	23.2	0	0

TOM TAYLOR

RHB / RMF / R0 / W0

FULL NAME: Thomas Alexander Ian Taylor
BORN: December 21, 1994, Stoke-on-Trent, Staffordshire
SQUAD NO: 15
HEIGHT: 6ft 3in
NICKNAME: Audi, Anne Robinson
EDUCATION: Trentham High School, Stoke-on-Trent; Newcastle-under-Lyme College; Leeds Metropolitan University
TEAMS: Derbyshire
ROLE: Bowler
DEBUT: First-class: 2014; List A: 2014

BEST BATTING: 80 Derbyshire vs Kent, Derby, 2016
BEST BOWLING: 6-61 Derbyshire vs Lancashire, Derby, 2015

FAMILY TIES? Father, cousins, uncles all play cricket; other family members used to run my home club
STRANGEST THING SEEN IN A GAME? Match abandoned because all the balls were lost
BEST MOMENT IN CRICKET? Probably my maiden first-class five-wicket haul, against Lancashire. Getting Hashim Amla as my maiden first-class wicket wasn't bad either
HOW WOULD YOUR TEAM-MATES DESCRIBE YOU IN THREE WORDS? Surprisingly strong legs
BEST PLAYER IN COUNTY CRICKET? Jeetan Patel (War)
MOST UNDERRATED PLAYER IN COUNTY CRICKET? Wayne Madsen (Der)
CRICKETING HEROES? Shane Warne, Andrew Flintoff, Brett Lee, James Anderson
SURPRISING FACT? I drink a lot of milk
DESERT ISLAND DISC? Arctic Monkeys – AM
FANTASY SLIP CORDON? Keeper: Tom Cruise, 1st: Kendall Jenner, 2nd: Cameron Diaz, 3rd: Justin Bieber, Gully: Me
TWITTER: @TomTaylor43

Batting	Mat	Inns	NO	Runs	HS	Ave	SR	100	50	Ct	St
First-class	18	28	5	395	80	17.17	41.84	0	1	3	0
List A	4	-	-	-	-	-	-	-	-	0	0

Bowling	Mat	Balls	Runs	Wkts	BBI	BBM	Ave	Econ	SR	5w	10
First-class	18	2678	1647	47	6/61	8/116	35.04	3.69	56.9	2	0
List A	4	176	174	5	3/48	3/48	34.80	5.93	35.2	0	0

RYAN TEN DOESCHATE RHB / RM / R1 / W0 / MVP36

ESSEX

FULL NAME: Ryan Neil ten Doeschate
BORN: June 30, 1980, Port Elizabeth, SA
SQUAD NO: 27
HEIGHT: 5ft 11in
EDUCATION: University of Cape Town
TEAMS: Netherlands, Essex, Adelaide Strikers, Canterbury, Chittagong Kings, Comilla Victorians, Dhaka Dynamites, Impi, Kolkata Knight Riders, Mashonaland Eagles, Otago, Tasmania, Western Province
ROLE: Allrounder
DEBUT: ODI: 2006; T20I: 2008; First-class: 2003; List A: 2003; T20: 2003

BEST BATTING: 259* Netherlands vs Canada, Pretoria, 2006
BEST BOWLING: 6-20 Netherlands vs Canada, Pretoria, 2006
COUNTY CAP: 2006

NOTES: Netherlands international who won the inaugural ICC Associate ODI Player of the Year in 2007 and the ICC Affiliate Player of the Year award in 2010. Scored 686 runs at an average of 228.66 in the ICC Intercontinental Cup in 2006, recording four consecutive hundreds, including a competition record 259* vs Canada in Pretoria. Made a century (119) against England at Nagpur in the World Cup 2011, becoming the first batsman from the Netherlands to make a hundred in the World Cup finals, and scored a second century against Ireland at Kolkata. He was handed the Essex Championship captaincy ahead of the 2016 season and will lead in all formats in 2017

Batting	Mat	Inns	NO	Runs	HS	Ave	SR	100	50	Ct	St
ODIs	33	32	9	1541	119	67.00	87.70	5	9	13	0
T20Is	9	9	4	214	56	42.80	128.91	0	1	3	0
First-class	145	213	33	8864	259*	49.24		25	40	89	0
List A	194	162	48	5219	180	45.78		9	28	59	0
Twenty20	285	250	58	5642	121*	29.38	135.82	2	24	111	0

Bowling	Mat	Balls	Runs	Wkts	BBI	BBM	Ave	Econ	SR	5w	10
ODIs	33	1580	1327	55	4/31	4/31	24.12	5.03	28.7	0	0
T20Is	9	204	241	12	3/23	3/23	20.08	7.08	17.0	0	0
First-class	145	10735	7069	208	6/20		33.98	3.95	51.6	7	0
List A	194	5116	4913	162	5/50	5/50	30.32	5.76	31.5	1	0
Twenty20	285	2053	2774	108	4/24	4/24	25.68	8.10	19.0	0	0

SHIV THAKOR

RHB / RM / R0 / W0 / MVP71

FULL NAME: Shivsinh Jaysinh Thakor
BORN: October 22, 1993, Leicester
SQUAD NO: 57
HEIGHT: 5ft 11in
NICKNAME: Shiva, Shivy, Shivametimbers
EDUCATION: Uppingham School, Rutland
TEAMS: Derbyshire, Leicestershire
ROLE: Allrounder
DEBUT: First-class: 2011; List A: 2011;
T20: 2013

BEST BATTING: 134 Leicestershire vs Loughborough MCCU, Leicester, 2011
BEST BOWLING: 5-63 Derbyshire vs Kent, Derby, 2016

BEST MOMENT IN CRICKET? Captaining England U19, becoming the youngest centurion for Leicestershire and scoring 134 on my first-class debut
SUPERSTITIONS? Far too many…
TIP FOR THE TOP? Tom Taylor, Harvey Hosein, Greg Cork, Will Davis, Ben Cotton (all Der)
CRICKETING HEROES? Sachin Tendulkar has always been a hero of mine for his achievements both on and off the field for 20 years. Jacques Kallis – because he was undoubtedly one of the greatest allrounders in the game
SURPRISING FACT? I can't swim
FANTASY SLIP CORDON? Keeper: Paul Chowdhry, 1st: Jessica Alba, 2nd: Me, 3rd: Cristiano Ronaldo, Gully: Leonardo DiCaprio
TWITTER: @thakor57

Batting	Mat	Inns	NO	Runs	HS	Ave	SR	100	50	Ct	St
First-class	45	69	11	2243	134	38.67	52.76	4	12	10	0
List A	39	33	6	537	83*	19.88	80.63	0	4	6	0
Twenty20	34	27	5	270	42	12.27	120.53	0	0	7	0

Bowling	Mat	Balls	Runs	Wkts	BBI	BBM	Ave	Econ	SR	5w	10
First-class	45	3401	2150	51	5/63	5/78	42.15	3.79	66.6	1	0
List A	39	1111	1109	38	4/49	4/49	29.18	5.98	29.2	0	0
Twenty20	34	561	762	32	3/17	3/17	23.81	8.14	17.5	0	0

IVAN THOMAS

RHB / RMF / R0 / W0

FULL NAME: Ivan Alfred Astley Thomas
BORN: September 25, 1991, Greenwich, Kent
SQUAD NO: 5
HEIGHT: 6ft 4in
NICKNAME: Blade, Big Iv, Big Red, Backpacker, The Viking, Goober
EDUCATION: The John Roan School, Greenwich; University of Leeds
TEAMS: Kent
ROLE: Bowler
DEBUT: First-class: 2012; List A: 2014; T20: 2015

BEST BATTING: 13 Kent vs Australians, Canterbury, 2015
BEST BOWLING: 4-48 Kent vs Leicestershire, Canterbury, 2015

WHAT FIRST GOT YOU INTO CRICKET? A Kwik Cricket tournament in primary school
BEST MOMENT IN CRICKET? Knuckleballing Jesse Ryder on my T20 debut
MOST UNDERRATED PLAYER IN COUNTY CRICKET? Alex Blake (Ken)
TIP FOR THE TOP? Hugh Bernard (Ken)
CRICKETING HEROES? Andrew Flintoff
NON-CRICKETING HEROES? Sean Conway and Mark Beaumont – both are fantastic adventurers
IF YOU WEREN'T A CRICKETER? I'd be struggling
SURPRISING FACT? I have clicking bones, and I can tear an apple in half
DESERT ISLAND DISC? Wu-Tang Clan
TWITTER: @ivanthomas_5

Batting	Mat	Inns	NO	Runs	HS	Ave	SR	100	50	Ct	St
First-class	19	30	14	97	13	6.06	26.72	0	0	3	0
List A	10	4	2	8	5*	4.00	24.24	0	0	6	0
Twenty20	8	3	2	3	3*	3.00	60.00	0	0	1	0

Bowling	Mat	Balls	Runs	Wkts	BBI	BBM	Ave	Econ	SR	5w	10
First-class	19	2851	1390	43	4/48	6/75	32.32	2.92	66.3	0	0
List A	10	468	446	15	4/51	4/51	29.73	5.71	31.2	0	0
Twenty20	8	168	245	7	2/42	2/42	35.00	8.75	24.0	0	0

AARON THOMASON

RHB / RFM / R0 / W0

FULL NAME: Aaron Dean Thomason
BORN: June 26, 1997, Birmingham
SQUAD NO: 26
HEIGHT: 5ft 10in
NICKNAME: Thomo
EDUCATION: Barr Beacon School, Walsall
TEAMS: Warwickshire
ROLE: Allrounder
DEBUT: List A: 2014; T20: 2016

WARWICKSHIRE

FAMILY TIES? We are members of Sutton Coldfield CC, where my brother plays and my whole family go and watch each Saturday
BEST MOMENT IN CRICKET? Making my Warwickshire debut at Lord's
HOW WOULD YOUR TEAM-MATES DESCRIBE YOU IN THREE WORDS? Childish, determined, demanding
BEST PLAYER IN COUNTY CRICKET? Joe Root (Yor)
TIP FOR THE TOP? Mason Crane (Ham), Joe Clarke (Wor), Josh Poysden (War)
CRICKETING HEROES? Andrew Flintoff – bats, bowls, fields well and has a great laugh off the field
NON-CRICKETING HEROES? My great-grandad watched us all the time. He left me some medals he was awarded for service in the war which I treasure
IF YOU WEREN'T A CRICKETER? I'd be window-cleaning with my dad
SURPRISING FACT? I went to the same school as Chris Woakes – a non-cricket school
DESERT ISLAND DISC? The Killers – Mr Brightside
FANTASY SLIP CORDON? Keeper: Ricky Gervais, 1st: Karl Pilkinton, 2nd: Me, 3rd: Andrew Flintoff, Gully: Peter Kay

Batting	Mat	Inns	NO	Runs	HS	Ave	SR	100	50	Ct	St
List A	1	1	1	0	0*	-	-	0	0	0	0
Twenty20	5	3	0	12	6	4.00	70.58	0	0	1	0

Bowling	Mat	Balls	Runs	Wkts	BBI	BBM	Ave	Econ	SR	5w	10
List A	1	24	23	0	-	-	-	5.75	-	0	0
Twenty20	5	36	68	2	2/24	2/24	34.00	11.33	18.0	0	0

JOSH TONGUE

RHB / RMF / R0 / W0

WORCESTERSHIRE

FULL NAME: Joshua Charles Tongue
BORN: November 15, 1997, Redditch, Worcestershire
SQUAD NO: 24
HEIGHT: 6ft 4in
NICKNAME: Tonguey
EDUCATION: King's School, Worcester; Christopher Whitehead Language College, Worcester
TEAMS: Worcestershire
ROLE: Bowler
DEBUT: First-class: 2016

BEST BOWLING: 3-35 Worcestershire vs Oxford MCCU, Oxford, 2016

FAMILY TIES? My dad is a coach and my mum used to be manager for different age-groups in Worcester

BEST MOMENT IN CRICKET? Getting six wickets against Hampshire in second XI cricket, scoring 150 in Birmingham League cricket and making my first-class debut in 2016

HOW WOULD YOUR TEAM-MATES DESCRIBE YOU IN THREE WORDS? Polite, friendly, talkative

BEST PLAYER IN COUNTY CRICKET? Joe Leach (Wor)

TIP FOR THE TOP? Joe Clarke (Wor)

CRICKETING HEROES? Andrew Flintoff

NON-CRICKETING HEROES? Cristiano Ronaldo – he played for the football club I supported and I always watch him when Real Madrid are on

DESERT ISLAND DISC? Drake (any album)

FANTASY SLIP CORDON? Keeper: Conor McGregor, 1st: Cristiano Ronaldo, 2nd: Me, 3rd: Keith Lemon, Gully: Anthony Joshua

TWITTER: @JoshTongue

Batting	Mat	Inns	NO	Runs	HS	Ave	SR	100	50	Ct	St
First-class	1	-	-	-	-	-	-	-	-	0	0

Bowling	Mat	Balls	Runs	Wkts	BBI	BBM	Ave	Econ	SR	5w	10
First-class	1	150	49	4	3/35	4/49	12.25	1.96	37.5	0	0

REECE TOPLEY

RHB / LFM / R0 / W0

FULL NAME: Reece James William Topley
BORN: February 21, 1994, Ipswich
SQUAD NO: 6
HEIGHT: 6ft 6in
NICKNAME: Toppers, Smash, Neil, Zlatan
EDUCATION: Royal Hospital School, Suffolk
TEAMS: England, Hampshire, Essex
ROLE: Bowler
DEBUT: ODI: 2015; T20I: 2015; First-class:
2011; List A: 2011; T20: 2012

HAMPSHIRE

BEST BATTING: 15 Hampshire vs Warwickshire, Southampton, 2016
BEST BOWLING: 6-29 Essex vs Worcestershire, Chelmsford, 2013
COUNTY CAP: 2013 (Essex)

FAMILY TIES? My father Don played for Essex and Surrey and also coached Zimbabwe. My
uncle Peter played for Kent
BEST MOMENT IN CRICKET? Taking 4-50 for England in an ODI against South Africa
TIP FOR THE TOP? Brad Wheal (Ham)
CRICKETING HEROES? Wasim Akram, Zaheer Khan, Mitchell Starc
NON-CRICKETING HEROES? David Beckham, Johnny Knoxville, David Jason, LeBron James
IF YOU WEREN'T A CRICKETER? I'd be an actor
SURPRISING FACT? I speak Spanish to a very good standard
UNUSUAL OBJECT AT HOME? Mike Tyson's boxing glove
DESERT ISLAND DISC? Kanye West – Life Of Pablo
TWITTER: @reece_topley

Batting	Mat	Inns	NO	Runs	HS	Ave	SR	100	50	Ct	St
ODIs	10	5	4	7	6	7.00	17.50	0	0	2	0
T20Is	6	1	1	1	1*	-	50.00	0	0	1	0
First-class	32	38	17	71	15	3.38	18.20	0	0	8	0
List A	40	13	7	41	19	6.83	41.83	0	0	9	0
Twenty20	56	9	6	14	5*	4.66	58.33	0	0	15	0

Bowling	Mat	Balls	Runs	Wkts	BBI	BBM	Ave	Econ	SR	5w	10
ODIs	10	463	410	16	4/50	4/50	25.62	5.31	28.9	0	0
T20Is	6	103	173	5	3/24	3/24	34.60	10.07	20.6	0	0
First-class	32	5700	3223	125	6/29	11/85	25.78	3.39	45.6	7	2
List A	40	1801	1637	69	4/26	4/26	23.72	5.45	26.1	0	0
Twenty20	56	1179	1634	77	4/26	4/26	21.22	8.31	15.3	0	0

JAMES TREDWELL

LHB / OB / RO / W1

FULL NAME: James Cullum Tredwell
BORN: February 27, 1982, Ashford, Kent
SQUAD NO: 15
HEIGHT: 5ft 11in
NICKNAME: Tredders, Treddy, Pingu, Chad
EDUCATION: Dymchurch Primary School, Kent; Southlands Community Comprehensive, Kent
TEAMS: England, Kent, Sussex
ROLE: Bowler
DEBUT: Test: 2010; ODI: 2010; T20I: 2012; First-class: 2001; List A: 2000; T20: 2003

BEST BATTING: 124 Kent vs Essex, Chelmsford, 2016
BEST BOWLING: 8-66 Kent vs Glamorgan, Canterbury, 2009
COUNTY CAP: 2007 (Kent)

FAMILY TIES? Dad played to a good club level for Ashford and Folkestone in the Kent League
BEST MOMENT IN CRICKET? Receiving my cap to play for England
HOW WOULD YOUR TEAM-MATES DESCRIBE YOU IN THREE WORDS? Quiet, solid, committed
MOST UNDERRATED PLAYER IN COUNTY CRICKET? Sam Northeast (Ken)
TIP FOR THE TOP? Jack Leaning (Yor)
CRICKETING HEROES? Shane Warne, David Gower
SURPRISING FACT? I enjoy growing my own fruit and veg, and make my own chutney/jam

Batting	Mat	Inns	NO	Runs	HS	Ave	SR	100	50	Ct	St
Tests	2	2	0	45	37	22.50	51.72	0	0	2	0
ODIs	45	25	11	163	30	11.64	67.35	0	0	14	0
T20Is	17	6	3	32	22	10.66	160.00	0	0	2	0
First-class	170	237	28	4544	124	21.74	43.89	4	16	189	0
List A	258	166	60	1820	88	17.16		0	4	105	0
Twenty20	158	70	24	497	34*	10.80	108.51	0	0	46	0

Bowling	Mat	Balls	Runs	Wkts	BBI	BBM	Ave	Econ	SR	5w	10
Tests	2	786	321	11	4/47	6/181	29.18	2.45	71.4	0	0
ODIs	45	2104	1666	60	4/41	4/41	27.76	4.75	35.0	0	0
T20Is	17	317	416	7	1/16	1/16	59.42	7.87	45.2	0	0
First-class	170	30046	15166	419	8/66		36.19	3.02	71.7	12	3
List A	258	11012	8645	270	6/27	6/27	32.01	4.71	40.7	1	0
Twenty20	158	3080	3748	124	4/21	4/21	30.22	7.30	24.8	0	0

PETER TREGO

RHB / RM / R1 / W1 / MVP18

FULL NAME: Peter David Trego
BORN: June 12, 1981, Weston-super-Mare
SQUAD NO: 7
HEIGHT: 6ft
NICKNAME: Tregs, Pirate, Big Tone
EDUCATION: Wyvern School, Weston-super-Mare
TEAMS: Somerset, Central Districts, England Lions, Kent, Mashonaland Eagles, Middlesex, Sylhet Royals
ROLE: Allrounder
DEBUT: First-class: 2000; List A: 1999; T20: 2003

SOMERSET

BEST BATTING: 154* Somerset vs Lancashire, Old Trafford, 2016
BEST BOWLING: 7-84 Somerset vs Yorkshire, Headingley, 2014
COUNTY CAP: 2007 (Somerset) **BENEFIT:** 2015 (Somerset)

BEST MOMENT IN CRICKET? Winning the PCA MVP award, all of my England Lions appearances and playing in the Hong Kong Sixes
HOW WOULD YOUR TEAM-MATES DESCRIBE YOU IN THREE WORDS? Pain in arse
CRICKETING HEROES? Graham Rose, Ian Botham, Justin Langer
IF YOU WEREN'T A CRICKETER? Something manual
SURPRISING FACT? My house is full of pets – it's like a bloody zoo and it drives me crackers
DESERT ISLAND DISC? Green Day – Dookie
FANTASY SLIP CORDON? Keeper: Tiger Woods, 1st: John Cleese, 2nd: Me, 3rd: Iron Man, 4th: Wolverine, Gully: Spider-Man
TWITTER: @tregs140

Batting	Mat	Inns	NO	Runs	HS	Ave	SR	100	50	Ct	St
First-class	207	306	37	9207	154*	34.22		15	52	85	0
List A	171	149	25	3884	147	31.32		7	19	52	0
Twenty20	171	158	18	3328	94*	23.77	124.92	0	17	48	0

Bowling	Mat	Balls	Runs	Wkts	BBI	BBM	Ave	Econ	SR	5w	10
First-class	207	23576	13562	372	7/84		36.45	3.45	63.3	4	1
List A	171	5683	5294	164	5/40	5/40	32.28	5.58	34.6	2	0
Twenty20	171	1704	2404	77	4/27	4/27	31.22	8.46	22.1	0	0

MARCUS TRESCOTHICK LHB / RM / R8 / W0 / MVP85

FULL NAME: Marcus Edward Trescothick
BORN: December 25, 1975, Keynsham, Somerset
SQUAD NO: 2
HEIGHT: 6ft 3in
NICKNAME: Banger, Tresco
EDUCATION: Sir Bernard Lovell School, Bristol
TEAMS: England, Somerset
ROLE: Batsman
DEBUT: Test: 2000; ODI: 2000; T20I: 2005; First-class: 1993; List A: 1993; T20: 2004

BEST BATTING: 284 Somerset vs Northamptonshire, Northampton, 2007
BEST BOWLING: 4-36 Somerset vs Young Australia, Taunton, 1995
COUNTY CAP: 1999 BENEFIT: 2008

TWITTER: @Trescricket
NOTES: Trescothick's maiden Test appearance came against West Indies at Old Trafford in 2000. His highest Test score was 219 against South Africa in a decisive nine-wicket victory at The Oval. Played his last Test against Pakistan at the same ground in 2006. Wisden Cricketer of the Year in 2005 and PCA Player of the Year in 2000, 2009 and 2011. Has the English record for ODI hundreds, scoring 12. Passed 1,000 first-class runs five years in a row between 2007 and 2011, with 1,673 runs in 2011 alone. After a rare blip in 2013, he has passed 1,000 Championship runs in each of the last three seasons. Stood down as captain in January 2016 after six years in charge. This summer is his 25th as a Somerset player

Batting	Mat	Inns	NO	Runs	HS	Ave	SR	100	50	Ct	St
Tests	76	143	10	5825	219	43.79	54.51	14	29	95	0
ODIs	123	122	6	4335	137	37.37	85.21	12	21	49	0
T20Is	3	3	0	166	72	55.33	126.71	0	2	2	0
First-class	361	620	34	24884	284	42.46		63	122	513	0
List A	372	357	29	12229	184	37.28		28	63	149	0
Twenty20	89	87	5	2363	108*	28.81	150.60	2	17	29	0

Bowling	Mat	Balls	Runs	Wkts	BBI	BBM	Ave	Econ	SR	5w	10
Tests	76	300	155	1	1/34	1/34	155.00	3.10	300.0	0	0
ODIs	123	232	219	4	2/7	2/7	54.75	5.66	58.0	0	0
T20Is	3	-	-	-	-	-	-	-	-	-	-
First-class	361	2704	1551	36	4/36		43.08	3.44	75.1	0	0
List A	372	2010	1644	57	4/50	4/50	28.84	4.90	35.2	0	0
Twenty20	89	-	-	-	-	-	-	-	-	-	-

JONATHAN TROTT — RHB / RM / R7 / W0 / MVP61

FULL NAME: Ian Jonathan Leonard Trott
BORN: April 22, 1981, Cape Town, South Africa
SQUAD NO: 9
HEIGHT: 6ft
NICKNAME: Booger, Trotters, Trotty
EDUCATION: Rondebosch Boys' High School; Stellenbosch University
TEAMS: England, Warwickshire, Boland, Otago, Western Province
ROLE: Batsman
DEBUT: Test: 2009; ODI: 2009; T20I: 2007; First-class: 2000; List A: 2000; T20: 2003

BEST BATTING: 226 England vs Bangladesh, Lord's, 2010
BEST BOWLING: 7-39 Warwickshire vs Kent, Canterbury, 2003
COUNTY CAP: 2005 **BENEFIT:** 2014

TWITTER: @Trotty
NOTES: Represented South Africa A. Scored 245 on debut for Warwickshire Second XI, 134 on his Championship debut in 2003, and 119 on Test debut for England in the deciding match of the 2009 Ashes at The Oval. One of the four Wisden Cricketers of the Year for 2011. ICC Cricketer of the Year for 2011. Played in three Ashes-winning England sides. Quit international cricket in 2015 following stress-related problems. Returned to his best form last summer, averaging 44.31 in the Championship and scoring 515 runs at 85.83 to guide Warwickshire to the RL Cup, making 82* in the final

Batting	Mat	Inns	NO	Runs	HS	Ave	SR	100	50	Ct	St
Tests	52	93	6	3835	226	44.08	47.18	9	19	29	0
ODIs	68	65	10	2819	137	51.25	77.06	4	22	14	0
T20Is	7	7	1	138	51	23.00	95.83	0	1	0	0
First-class	251	417	43	16519	226	44.16		39	81	202	0
List A	258	240	43	9477	137	48.10		20	64	73	0
Twenty20	79	74	16	2122	86*	36.58	114.27	0	13	18	0

Bowling	Mat	Balls	Runs	Wkts	BBI	BBM	Ave	Econ	SR	5w	10
Tests	52	708	400	5	1/5	1/5	80.00	3.38	141.6	0	0
ODIs	68	183	166	2	2/31	2/31	83.00	5.44	91.5	0	0
T20Is	7	-	-	-	-	-	-	-	-	-	-
First-class	251	5990	3376	69	7/39		48.92	3.38	86.8	1	0
List A	258	1684	1582	54	4/55	4/55	29.29	5.63	31.1	0	0
Twenty20	79	144	234	8	2/19	2/19	29.25	9.75	18.0	0	0

BEN TWOHIG

RHB / SLA / RO / WO

FULL NAME: Benjamin Jake Twohig
BORN: April 13, 1998, Dewsbury, Yorkshire
SQUAD NO: 42
HEIGHT: 5ft 9in
NICKNAME: Twiggy, The Owl, Twiglet
EDUCATION: Malvern College
TEAMS: England U19, Worcestershire 2nd XI
ROLE: Bowler
DEBUT: Yet to make first-team debut

WHAT FIRST GOT YOU INTO CRICKET? It was a big part of my life at a young age as I grew up five minutes away from the local cricket club
FAMILY TIES? My dad played a lot of club cricket when I was younger and so did my brother
STRANGEST THING SEEN IN A GAME? Coming off the field because of a sand storm. The match was abandoned
BEST MOMENT IN CRICKET? Representing England U19
HOW WOULD YOUR TEAM-MATES DESCRIBE YOU IN THREE WORDS? Little northern sod
MOST UNDERRATED PLAYER IN COUNTY CRICKET? Jack Leach (Som)
TIP FOR THE TOP? Dom Bess (Som)
CRICKETING HEROES? Kevin Pietersen – for the way he played his cricket without any fear. Daniel Vettori – someone I look up to as a fellow slow left-armer
NON-CRICKETING HEROES? Muhammad Ali – he stood up for what he believed in
IF YOU WEREN'T A CRICKETER? I'd be an actor
SURPRISING FACT? I played Dorothy in The Wizard of Oz for a school play
UNUSUAL OBJECT AT HOME? A circular saw
DESERT ISLAND DISC? The Stone Roses
FANTASY SLIP CORDON? Keeper: Dynamo, 1st: Me, 2nd: Jennifer Aniston, 3rd: Benedict Cumberbatch, Gully: Bob Marley
TWITTER: @Ben_Twohig

ANDREW TYE

RHB / RFM / R0 / W0

FULL NAME: Andrew James Tye
BORN: December 12, 1986, Perth, Australia
SQUAD NO: 68
HEIGHT: 6ft 3in
NICKNAME: AJ
EDUCATION: Padbury Senior High School, Western Australia
TEAMS: Australia, Gloucestershire, Perth Scorchers, Sydney Thunder, Western Australia
ROLE: Bowler
DEBUT: T20I: 2016; First-class: 2014; List A: 2013; T20: 2014

BEST BATTING: 10 Western Australia vs Tasmania, Hobart, 2014
BEST BOWLING: 3-47 Western Australia vs Queensland, Brisbane, 2015

TWITTER: @aj191
NOTES: A team-mate of Gloucestershire's white-ball captain Michael Klinger for the Perth Scorchers, Tye was a key component of the Scorchers' Big Bash wins in 2015 and 2016. He is returning for his second T20 stint at Gloucestershire, having taken 18 wickets last summer. A bit of a late developer, he made his Australia debut in January 2016 aged 29. Has had second XI stints in England with Durham, Northamptonshire and Somerset

Batting	Mat	Inns	NO	Runs	HS	Ave	SR	100	50	Ct	St
T20Is	5	3	1	4	4	2.00	66.66	0	0	0	0
First-class	8	8	0	39	10	4.87	41.05	0	0	1	0
List A	20	14	6	135	28*	16.87	109.75	0	0	7	0
Twenty20	51	18	7	137	42	12.45	102.23	0	0	8	0

Bowling	Mat	Balls	Runs	Wkts	BBI	BBM	Ave	Econ	SR	5w	10
T20Is	5	110	188	5	3/37	3/37	37.60	10.25	22.0	0	0
First-class	8	1475	810	22	3/47	6/159	36.81	3.29	67.0	0	0
List A	20	963	910	41	5/46	5/46	22.19	5.66	23.4	1	0
Twenty20	51	1125	1453	62	4/18	4/18	23.43	7.74	18.1	0	0

ANDY UMEED

RHB / LB / RO / WO

FULL NAME: Andrew Robert Isaac Umeed
BORN: April 19, 1996, Glasgow, Scotland
SQUAD NO: 23
HEIGHT: 6ft 1in
EDUCATION: The High School of Glasgow
TEAMS: Scotland, Warwickshire
ROLE: Batsman
DEBUT: First-class: 2015

BEST BATTING: 101 Warwickshire vs Durham, Edgbaston, 2016

WHAT FIRST GOT YOU INTO CRICKET? My father's passion for the game
STRANGEST THING SEEN IN A GAME? A bowler chasing a fielder with a stump
BEST MOMENT IN CRICKET? Scoring a hundred on my Championship debut against Durham at Edgbaston in 2016
BEST PLAYER IN COUNTY CRICKET? Jeetan Patel (War)
MOST UNDERRATED PLAYER IN COUNTY CRICKET? Varun Chopra (Ess)
CRICKETING HEROES? Sachin Tendulkar, Mahela Jayawardene, Younis Khan, Rahul Dravid
NON-CRICKETING HEROES? Michael Jordan, Barack Obama, Muhammad Ali
DESERT ISLAND DISC? Notorious B.I.G. – Ready To Die
FANTASY SLIP CORDON? Keeper: Barack Obama, 1st: Michael Jordan, 2nd: Me, 3rd: Will Smith, Gully: Denzel Washington
TWITTER: @andyumeed

Batting	Mat	Inns	NO	Runs	HS	Ave	SR	100	50	Ct	St
First-class	7	11	1	172	101	17.20	42.26	1	0	4	0

Bowling	Mat	Balls	Runs	Wkts	BBI	BBM	Ave	Econ	SR	5w	10
First-class	7	-	-	-	-	-	-	-	-	-	-

GRAEME VAN BUUREN

RHB / SLA / RO / WO

FULL NAME: Graeme Lourens van Buuren
BORN: August 22, 1990, Pretoria, South Africa
SQUAD NO: 12
NICKNAME: GVB
EDUCATION: Pretoria Boys High School, South Africa
TEAMS: Gloucestershire, Northerns, Titans
ROLE: Allrounder
DEBUT: First-class: 2010; List A: 2010; T20: 2011

BEST BATTING: 235 Northerns vs Eastern Province, Centurion, 2015
BEST BOWLING: 4-12 Northerns vs South Western Districts, Oudtshoorn, 2013

BEST MOMENT IN CRICKET? Scoring 172 not out for Gloucestershire in 2016 – my maiden first-class century for the club
HOW WOULD YOUR TEAM-MATES DESCRIBE YOU IN THREE WORDS? Energetic, fun, laugh
BEST PLAYER IN COUNTY CRICKET? Ben Duckett (Nor) or Michael Klinger (Glo)
MOST UNDERRATED PLAYER IN COUNTY CRICKET? Chris Dent (Glo)
TIP FOR THE TOP? Matt Taylor, George Hankins (both Glo)
CRICKETING HEROES? AB de Villiers
NON-CRICKETING HEROES? Novak Djokovic
IF YOU WEREN'T A CRICKETER? I'd be a golfer
UNUSUAL OBJECT AT HOME? A hippopotamus on the dinning-room table
DESERT ISLAND DISC? Mumford And Sons – Wilder Mind
TWITTER: @GraemeGVB

Batting	Mat	Inns	NO	Runs	HS	Ave	SR	100	50	Ct	St
First-class	59	91	16	3753	235	50.04	65.88	10	21	37	0
List A	58	52	11	1248	119*	30.43	82.97	1	5	16	0
Twenty20	42	32	10	525	64	23.86	110.75	0	3	22	0

Bowling	Mat	Balls	Runs	Wkts	BBI	BBM	Ave	Econ	SR	5w	10
First-class	59	4006	1863	71	4/12	6/87	26.23	2.79	56.4	0	0
List A	58	1752	1343	47	5/35	5/35	28.57	4.59	37.2	1	0
Twenty20	42	559	580	27	5/8	5/8	21.48	6.22	20.7	1	0

FREDDIE VAN DEN BERGH

RHB / SLA / RO / WO

SURREY

FULL NAME: Freddie Oliver Edward van den Bergh
BORN: June 14, 1992, Bickley, Kent
SQUAD NO: 5
HEIGHT: 6ft 4in
NICKNAME: Vanders, Frube
EDUCATION: Whitgift School, Croydon; Durham University
TEAMS: Surrey
ROLE: Bowler
DEBUT: First-class: 2011; List A: 2014

BEST BATTING: 34 Surrey vs Nottinghamshire, Trent Bridge, 2013
BEST BOWLING: 4-84 Surrey vs Nottinghamshire, Trent Bridge, 2013

FAMILY TIES? My dad used to play as a youngster and then worked for the ECB
STRANGEST THING SEEN IN A GAME? Arriving at the ground in Durham in March to find the whole ground covered in a layer of frost. Fair to say it was a cold day in the field
BEST MOMENT IN CRICKET? Making my first-class debut for Surrey when Kevin Pietersen was captain and then taking three wickets
HOW WOULD YOUR TEAM-MATES DESCRIBE YOU IN THREE WORDS? Competitive, organised, team-man
BEST PLAYER IN COUNTY CRICKET? Kumar Sangakkara (Sur) – he is one of the best players in the world in all formats. Great to chat to – his knowledge of the game is tremendous
MOST UNDERRATED PLAYER IN COUNTY CRICKET? Arun Harinath, Rory Burns (both Sur)
TIP FOR THE TOP? Ollie Pope (Sur)
CRICKETING HEROES? Freddie Flintoff – watching the 2005 Ashes and seeing him perform so well was inspiring. Shane Warne – was incredible to see him perform all his variations
IF YOU WEREN'T A CRICKETER? Hopefully I'd be putting my university degree to good use in the City
TWITTER: @freddievdb15

Batting	Mat	Inns	NO	Runs	HS	Ave	SR	100	50	Ct	St
First-class	6	8	1	57	34	8.14	54.80	0	0	1	0
List A	3	1	1	29	29*	-	107.40	0	0	0	0

Bowling	Mat	Balls	Runs	Wkts	BBI	BBM	Ave	Econ	SR	5w	10
First-class	6	817	522	11	4/84	5/145	47.45	3.83	74.2	0	0
List A	3	156	122	0	-	-	-	4.69	-	0	0

TIMM VAN DER GUGTEN RHB / RFM / R0 / W1 / MVP26

FULL NAME: Timm van der Gugten
BORN: February 25, 1991, Sydney, Australia
SQUAD NO: 64
HEIGHT: 6ft 1in
EDUCATION: St Pius X College, Sydney
TEAMS: Netherlands, Glamorgan, Hobart
Hurricanes, New South Wales, Northern
Districts, Tasmania
ROLE: Bowler
DEBUT: ODI: 2012; T20I: 2012; First-class:
2011; List A: 2011; T20: 2012

GLAMORGAN

BEST BATTING: 57 Netherlands vs Papua New Guinea, Amstelveen, 2015
BEST BOWLING: 7-68 Netherlands vs Namibia, Windhoek, 2013

NOTES: Australian-born van der Gugten has represented Netherlands as well as playing in Australia and New Zealand. He took 1-11 in Netherlands' win over England at the 2014 World T20. The seamer signed a three-year deal with Glamorgan in February 2016 and enjoyed an outstanding first summer with the Welsh county, claiming 82 wickets in all formats and deservedly being voted the club's Player of the Year

Batting	Mat	Inns	NO	Runs	HS	Ave	SR	100	50	Ct	St
ODIs	4	2	0	4	2	2.00	66.66	0	0	0	0
T20Is	25	7	3	45	12*	11.25	102.27	0	0	2	0
First-class	20	27	6	236	57	11.23	45.12	0	1	4	0
List A	31	17	6	181	36	16.45	110.36	0	0	3	0
Twenty20	54	20	6	95	13	6.78	95.95	0	0	8	0

Bowling	Mat	Balls	Runs	Wkts	BBI	BBM	Ave	Econ	SR	5w	10
ODIs	4	126	85	8	5/24	5/24	10.62	4.04	15.7	1	0
T20Is	25	455	529	25	3/18	3/18	21.16	6.97	18.2	0	0
First-class	20	3665	1958	73	7/68	10/121	26.82	3.20	50.2	7	1
List A	31	1379	1195	45	5/24	5/24	26.55	5.19	30.6	1	0
Twenty20	54	991	1201	63	5/21	5/21	19.06	7.27	15.7	1	0

ROELOF VAN DER MERWE RHB / SLA / RO / WO / MVP73

SOMERSET

FULL NAME: Roelof Erasmus van der Merwe
BORN: December 31, 1984, Johannesburg, South Africa
SQUAD NO: 52
HEIGHT: 5ft 8in
NICKNAME: Roela
EDUCATION: Pretoria High School
TEAMS: Netherlands, South Africa, Somerset, Brisbane Heat, Delhi Daredevils, Northerns, RC Bangalore, St Lucia Zouks, Titans
ROLE: Allrounder
DEBUT: ODIs: 2009; T20I: 2009; First-class: 2006; List A: 2006; T20: 2008

BEST BATTING: 205* Titans vs Warriors, Benoni, 2014
BEST BOWLING: 4-45 Somerset vs Durham, Taunton, 2016

STRANGEST THING SEEN IN A GAME? Shots fired... our coach chased off some guys on quad bikes
BEST MOMENT IN CRICKET? My debut for South Africa on my home ground, Centurion
HOW WOULD YOUR TEAM-MATES DESCRIBE YOU IN THREE WORDS? Short, sensible, calm
BEST PLAYER IN COUNTY CRICKET? Marcus Trescothick (Som)
MOST UNDERRATED PLAYER IN COUNTY CRICKET? James Hildreth (Som)
TIP FOR THE TOP? Jack Leach (Som)
CRICKETING HEROES? Jonty Rhodes
NON-CRICKETING HEROES? The All Blacks
SURPRISING FACT? I love cheese
DESERT ISLAND DISC? Roxette – Greatest Hits
TWITTER: @Roela52

Batting	Mat	Inns	NO	Runs	HS	Ave	SR	100	50	Ct	St
ODIs	13	7	3	39	12	9.75	95.12	0	0	3	0
T20Is	24	15	6	174	48	19.33	131.81	0	0	12	0
First-class	58	94	14	2833	205*	35.41	69.11	5	18	43	0
List A	144	116	36	1992	93	24.90	100.05	0	8	51	0
Twenty20	158	117	30	1775	89*	20.40	128.99	0	8	61	0

Bowling	Mat	Balls	Runs	Wkts	BBI	BBM	Ave	Econ	SR	5w	10
ODIs	13	705	561	17	3/27	3/27	33.00	4.77	41.4	0	0
T20Is	24	480	546	29	2/3	2/3	18.82	6.82	16.5	0	0
First-class	58	7720	3904	102	4/45	8/104	38.27	3.03	75.6	0	0
List A	144	6356	5040	194	5/26	5/26	25.97	4.75	32.7	4	0
Twenty20	158	3006	3534	145	3/16	3/16	24.37	7.05	20.7	0	0

PAUL VAN MEEKEREN

RHB / RFM / RO / WO

FULL NAME: Paul Adriaan van Meekeren
BORN: January 15, 1993, Amsterdam, Netherlands
SQUAD NO: 47
HEIGHT: 6ft 4in
NICKNAME: Meerkat, Smacky, Meeks
TEAMS: Netherlands, Somerset
ROLE: Bowler
DEBUT: ODI: 2013; T20I: 2013; First-class: 2013; List A: 2013; T20: 2013

SOMERSET

BEST BATTING: 34 Netherlands vs Papua New Guinea, Amstelveen, 2015
BEST BOWLING: 3-44 Netherlands vs Papua New Guinea, Amstelveen, 2015

WHAT FIRST GOT YOU INTO CRICKET? My dad dragged me around to the cricket every weekend, made me watch all the old men play. I was convinced I was better than them
STRANGEST THING SEEN IN A GAME? Oblivious people back in Holland continuously crossing the field to get to a football game, rather than walking around the boundary
BEST MOMENT IN CRICKET? My first ODI wicket (Mr Amla)
HOW WOULD YOUR TEAM-MATES DESCRIBE YOU IN THREE WORDS? A crazy Dutchman
TIP FOR THE TOP? I'm still getting to know my own team-mates!
CRICKETING HEROES? I didn't really grow up watching cricket
NON-CRICKETING HEROES? Dennis Bergkamp
SURPRISING FACT? I'm very proud to call myself Dutch. The first thing I do in the morning is turn on the radio and get dressed while dancing
TWITTER: @paulvanmeekeren

Batting	Mat	Inns	NO	Runs	HS	Ave	SR	100	50	Ct	St
ODIs	2	1	1	15	15*	-	88.23	0	0	0	0
T20Is	18	4	0	21	18	5.25	110.52	0	0	4	0
First-class	6	10	1	99	34	11.00	34.73	0	0	1	0
List A	23	11	4	56	15*	8.00	62.22	0	0	7	0
Twenty20	27	10	3	37	18	5.28	102.77	0	0	8	0

Bowling	Mat	Balls	Runs	Wkts	BBI	BBM	Ave	Econ	SR	5w	10
ODIs	2	66	79	1	1/54	1/54	79.00	7.18	66.0	0	0
T20Is	18	324	330	18	4/11	4/11	18.33	6.11	18.0	0	0
First-class	6	1022	586	16	3/44	5/75	36.62	3.44	63.8	0	0
List A	23	756	643	18	3/42	3/42	35.72	5.10	42.0	0	0
Twenty20	27	480	564	21	4/11	4/11	26.85	7.05	22.8	0	0

STIAAN VAN ZYL

LHB / RM / RO / WO

FULL NAME: Stiaan van Zyl
BORN: September 19, 1987, Cape Town, South Africa
SQUAD NO: 74
EDUCATION: Kenridge Primary School, Western Cape; Boland Agricultural School
TEAMS: South Africa, Sussex, Boland, Cape Cobras, Western Province
ROLE: Allrounder
DEBUT: Test: 2014; First-class: 2006; List A: 2006; T20: 2008

BEST BATTING: 172 Cape Cobras vs Titans, Benoni, 2010
BEST BOWLING: 5-32 Boland vs Northerns, Paarl, 2011

TWITTER: @laggies74
NOTES: In Stiaan van Zyl Sussex are getting an accomplished cross-format batting allrounder who began 2016 as South Africa's Test-match opener. Signed as a Kolpak on a three-year deal, the left-hander – who made a Test century on debut – adds steel to Sussex's top order and brings a wealth of experience across all formats. "To have a top-order batsman who is able to bowl seam is a very important element in balancing our team ahead of the new season," said Sussex head coach Mark Davis

Batting	Mat	Inns	NO	Runs	HS	Ave	SR	100	50	Ct	St
Tests	12	17	2	395	101*	26.33	50.77	1	0	6	0
First-class	138	230	36	8377	172	43.18	51.57	21	38	85	0
List A	108	99	12	3131	114*	35.98	73.73	5	16	30	0
Twenty20	52	47	5	1093	86*	26.02	112.91	0	7	15	0

Bowling	Mat	Balls	Runs	Wkts	BBI	BBM	Ave	Econ	SR	5w	10
Tests	12	403	148	6	3/20	3/22	24.66	2.20	67.1	0	0
First-class	138	4393	1958	53	5/32	7/82	36.94	2.67	82.8	1	0
List A	108	906	779	19	4/24	4/24	41.00	5.15	47.6	0	0
Twenty20	52	96	116	5	2/19	2/19	23.20	7.25	19.2	0	0

KISHEN VELANI

FULL NAME: Kishen Shailesh Velani
BORN: September 2, 1994, Newham, London
SQUAD NO: 8
NICKNAME: Joggy, Bruno
EDUCATION: Brentwood School, Essex
TEAMS: Essex
ROLE: Batsman
DEBUT: First-class: 2013; List A: 2014; T20: 2014

BEST BATTING: 58 Essex vs Gloucestershire, Chelmsford, 2015

BEST MOMENT IN CRICKET? Playing for England U19 and making my first-class debut
CRICKETING HEROES? Sachin Tendulkar
NON-CRICKETING HEROES? Kobe Bryant
IF YOU WEREN'T A CRICKETER? I'd be a golfer
DESERT ISLAND DISC? Drake – Take Care
FANTASY SLIP CORDON? Keeper: Sachin Tendulkar, 1st: Kobe Bryant, 2nd: James Corden, 3rd: Drake, Gully: Me
TWITTER: @kishenvelani8

Batting	Mat	Inns	NO	Runs	HS	Ave	SR	100	50	Ct	St
First-class	11	16	1	351	58	23.40	55.27	0	1	3	0
List A	10	6	0	79	27	13.16	100.00	0	0	6	0
Twenty20	16	14	0	172	34	12.28	111.68	0	0	2	0

Bowling	Mat	Balls	Runs	Wkts	BBI	BBM	Ave	Econ	SR	5w	10
First-class	11	57	62	0	-	-	-	6.52	-	0	0
List A	10	12	14	1	1/14	1/14	14.00	7.00	12.0	0	0
Twenty20	16	-	-	-	-	-	-	-	-	-	-

DANE VILAS

RHB / WK / R0 / W0

FULL NAME: Dane James Vilas
BORN: June 10, 1985, Johannesburg, South Africa
HEIGHT: 6ft
NICKNAME: Vili
EDUCATION: King Edward VII School, Johannesburg
TEAMS: South Africa, Lancashire, Cape Cobras, Gauteng, Lions, South Western Districts, Western Province
ROLE: Wicketkeeper
DEBUT: Test: 2015; T20I: 2012; First-class: 2006; List A: 2006; T20: 2009

BEST BATTING: 216* Cape Cobras vs Lions, Paarl, 2016

TWITTER: @DaneVilas

NOTES: The former Test wicketkeeper was another South African cricketer to announce his international retirement in early 2017 to take up a two-year Kolpak deal with Lancashire. He will play across all formats. "Signing a player of Dane's undoubted calibre and experience is a great boost," said Lancashire head coach Glen Chapple. The last of his six Tests came against England in 2016, with his final innings ended by James Taylor's miraculous catch at short-leg. The emergence of Quinton de Kock had pushed him down the pecking order

Batting	Mat	Inns	NO	Runs	HS	Ave	SR	100	50	Ct	St
Tests	6	9	0	94	26	10.44	44.76	0	0	13	0
T20Is	1	-	-	-	-	-	-	-	-	0	0
First-class	100	152	17	5239	216*	38.80	67.38	12	25	291	14
List A	122	112	19	3115	120	33.49	95.14	5	14	132	23
Twenty20	84	70	19	1720	71*	33.72	122.68	0	10	48	13

Bowling	Mat	Balls	Runs	Wkts	BBI	BBM	Ave	Econ	SR	5w	10
Tests	6	-	-	-	-	-	-	-	-	-	-
T20Is	1	-	-	-	-	-	-	-	-	-	-
First-class	100	6	3	0	-	-	-	3.00	-	0	0
List A	122	-	-	-	-	-	-	-	-	-	-
Twenty20	84	-	-	-	-	-	-	-	-	-	-

HARDUS VILJOEN

RHB / RF / R0 / W0

FULL NAME: GC Viljoen
BORN: March 6, 1989, Witbank, South Africa
SQUAD NO: 7
HEIGHT: 6ft 4in
TEAMS: South Africa, Derbyshire, Easterns, Kent, Lions, Titans
ROLE: Bowler
DEBUT: Test: 2016; First-class: 2008; List A: 2009; T20: 2011

BEST BATTING: 72 Lions vs Titans, Centurion, South Africa
BEST BOWLING: 8-105 Easterns vs Northerns, Benoni, South Africa

TWITTER: @Hardus_Vijl
NOTES: The South African fast bowler has signed for Derbyshire as a Kolpak player on a three-year deal. "He's a strike bowler who can bowl over 90 miles an hour and has experience both internationally and here in England," said Kim Barnett, Derbyshire's director of cricket. He represented Kent as an overseas player last summer, taking 20 first-class wickets at 19.25, including figures of 5-55 against Gloucestershire on his debut. Viljoen dismissed Alastair Cook with his first ball in Test cricket last January in his only international appearance. His most productive campaign to date came in 2010/11 when he claimed 68 wickets at 24.58 for Easterns in South Africa's domestic four-day competition

Batting	Mat	Inns	NO	Runs	HS	Ave	SR	100	50	Ct	St
Tests	1	2	1	26	20*	26.00	83.87	0	0	0	0
First-class	94	127	16	1642	72	14.79	57.49	0	6	29	0
List A	71	41	12	459	54*	15.82	77.53	0	2	17	0
Twenty20	54	30	15	262	41*	17.46	120.18	0	0	15	0

Bowling	Mat	Balls	Runs	Wkts	BBI	BBM	Ave	Econ	SR	5w	10
Tests	1	114	94	1	1/79	1/94	94.00	4.94	114.0	0	0
First-class	94	16388	9817	370	8/105	10/114	26.53	3.59	44.2	22	4
List A	71	3177	3114	103	6/19	6/19	30.23	5.88	30.8	1	0
Twenty20	54	1175	1456	64	5/16	5/16	22.75	7.43	18.3	1	0

JAMES VINCE

RHB / RM / R2 / W0

HAMPSHIRE

FULL NAME: James Michael Vince
BORN: March 14, 1991, Cuckfield, Sussex
SQUAD NO: 14
HEIGHT: 6ft 2in
NICKNAME: Vincey
EDUCATION: Warminster School, Wiltshire
TEAMS: England, Hampshire, Karachi Kings, Sydney Thunder
ROLE: Batsman
DEBUT: Test: 2016; ODI: 2015; T20I: 2015; First-class: 2009; List A: 2009; T20: 2010

BEST BATTING: 240 Hampshire vs Essex, Southampton, 2014
BEST BOWLING: 5-41 Hampshire vs Loughborough MCCU, Southampton, 2013
COUNTY CAP: 2013

WHAT FIRST GOT YOU INTO CRICKET? A Kwik Cricket day at school
STRANGEST THING SEEN IN A GAME? James Tomlinson taking a one-handed diving catch while eating a banana at fine-leg
SUPERSTITIONS? Do not eat duck, calamari or onion rings on the day before a game (blame Neil McKenzie)
BEST PLAYER IN COUNTY CRICKET? Kumar Sangakkara (Sur)
MOST UNDERRATED PLAYER IN COUNTY CRICKET? James Hildreth (Som)
TIP FOR THE TOP? The Currans (Sur), Joe Clarke (Wor), Mason Crane, Tom Alsop (both Ham)
TWITTER: @vincey14

Batting	Mat	Inns	NO	Runs	HS	Ave	SR	100	50	Ct	St
Tests	7	11	0	212	42	19.27	52.21	0	0	3	0
ODIs	5	4	0	104	51	26.00	84.55	0	1	4	0
T20Is	5	5	0	163	46	32.60	118.97	0	0	0	0
First-class	120	198	18	7064	240	39.24	63.45	18	28	106	0
List A	99	94	6	3117	131	35.42	92.90	5	15	35	0
Twenty20	122	117	12	3068	107*	29.21	128.96	1	19	65	0

Bowling	Mat	Balls	Runs	Wkts	BBI	BBM	Ave	Econ	SR	5w	10
Tests	7	24	13	0	-	-	-	3.25	-	0	0
ODIs	5	-	-	-	-	-	-	-	-	-	-
T20Is	5	-	-	-	-	-	-	-	-	-	-
First-class	120	1538	945	21	5/41	6/56	45.00	3.68	73.2	1	0
List A	99	84	84	1	1/18	1/18	84.00	6.00	84.0	0	0
Twenty20	122	72	81	3	1/5	1/5	27.00	6.75	24.0	0	0

AMAR VIRDI

FULL NAME: Guramar Singh Virdi
BORN: July 19, 1998, Chiswick, Middlesex
SQUAD NO: 19
HEIGHT: 5ft 10in
NICKNAME: Virds
EDUCATION: Guru Nanak Sikh Academy, Middlesex
TEAMS: England U19, Surrey 2nd XI
ROLE: Bowler
DEBUT: Yet to make first-team debut

SURREY

STRANGEST THING SEEN IN A GAME? When a batsman broke out on the floor just before the ball was delivered because he had terrible cramp
BEST MOMENT IN CRICKET? My five-fer on debut for England U19 against Sri Lanka U19
SUPERSTITIONS? I walk around the stumps when I get on strike
HOW WOULD YOUR TEAM-MATES DESCRIBE YOU IN THREE WORDS? Funny and young
BEST PLAYER IN COUNTY CRICKET? Kumar Sangakkara (Sur)
MOST UNDERRATED PLAYER IN COUNTY CRICKET? Arun Harinath (Sur)
CRICKETING HEROES? Saqlain Mushtaq, Harbhajan Singh
NON-CRICKETING HEROES? My dad
SURPRISING FACT? I fractured my wrist a few years ago just before a training camp – I cut the cast off my wrist just so I could attend the session
UNUSUAL OBJECT AT HOME? A dartboard
FANTASY SLIP CORDON? Keeper: Mike Tyson, 1st: Saqlain Mushtaq, 2nd: Denzel Washington, 3rd: Me, Gully: Sachin Tendulkar

ADAM VOGES

RHB / SLA / R0 / W0

FULL NAME: Adam Charles Voges
BORN: October 4, 1979, Perth, Australia
SQUAD NO: 32
HEIGHT: 6ft 1in
NICKNAME: V, Vogesy, Happy
EDUCATION: Edith Cowan University, Perth
TEAMS: Australia, Middlesex, Hampshire, Jamaica Tallawahs, Melbourne Stars, Nottinghamshire, Perth Scorchers, Rajasthan Royals, Western Australia
ROLE: Batsman
DEBUT: Test: 2015; ODI: 2007; T20I: 2007; First-class: 2002; List A: 2004; T20: 2006

BEST BATTING: 269* Australia vs West Indies, Hobart, 2015
BEST BOWLING: 4-92 Western Australia vs South Australia, Adelaide, 2007
COUNTY CAPS: 2008 (Nottinghamshire); 2016 (Middlesex)

FAMILY TIES? My dad played and umpired
CRICKETING HEROES? I loved watching Dean Jones bat. He revolutionised one-day cricket in Australia
IF YOU WEREN'T A CRICKETER? I'd be a sports teacher
SURPRISING FACT? I stick my tongue out when concentrating
DESERT ISLAND DISC? Pearl Jam – Elderly Woman Behind The Counter In A Small Town
TWITTER: @acvoges

Batting	Mat	Inns	NO	Runs	HS	Ave	SR	100	50	Ct	St
Tests	20	31	7	1485	269*	61.87	55.68	5	4	15	0
ODIs	31	28	9	870	112*	45.78	87.17	1	4	7	0
T20Is	7	5	2	139	51	46.33	121.92	0	1	3	0
First-class	201	335	48	13390	269*	46.65	51.41	32	68	268	0
List A	184	176	42	5883	112*	43.90	79.72	5	46	74	0
Twenty20	167	155	33	3785	82*	31.02	126.58	0	17	67	0

Bowling	Mat	Balls	Runs	Wkts	BBI	BBM	Ave	Econ	SR	5w	10
Tests	20	76	44	0	-	-	-	3.47	-	0	0
ODIs	31	301	276	6	1/3	1/3	46.00	5.50	50.1	0	0
T20Is	7	12	5	2	2/5	2/5	2.50	2.50	6.0	0	0
First-class	201	3644	1928	54	4/92		35.70	3.17	67.4	0	0
List A	184	1881	1604	39	3/20	3/20	41.12	5.11	48.2	0	0
Twenty20	167	554	731	27	2/4	2/4	27.07	7.91	20.5	0	0

GARETH WADE

RHB / RMF / R0 / W0

FULL NAME: Gareth Wade
BORN: January 11, 1991, Hexham, Northumberland
SQUAD NO: 9
HEIGHT: 6ft 2in
NICKNAME: Gwade, Wadey
EDUCATION: Prudhoe Community High School, Northumberland; Sunderland University
TEAMS: Northumberland, Worcestershire 2nd XI
ROLE: Bowler
DEBUT: Yet to make first-team debut

NORTHAMPTONSHIRE

WHAT FIRST GOT YOU INTO CRICKET? It was a good way to meet people

STRANGEST THING SEEN IN A GAME? Me scoring a run

BEST MOMENT IN CRICKET? My first game for Chester-le-Street CC away to Hetton Lyons in the North East Premier League

SUPERSTITIONS? I won't go onto the pitch until all the players are out of the changing room

HOW WOULD YOUR TEAM-MATES DESCRIBE YOU IN THREE WORDS? Sit down Wadey

BEST PLAYER IN COUNTY CRICKET? Mark Wood, Ben Stokes (both Dur), Alastair Cook (Ess)

MOST UNDERRATED PLAYER IN COUNTY CRICKET? Ben Sanderson (Nor)

TIP FOR THE TOP? Max Holden (Mid)

CRICKETING HEROES? Mark Wood, Alastair Cook, Ben Stokes, Mitchell Starc, Andrew Flintoff, Paul Collingwood, Simon Birtwisle, Jacques du Toit, Quentin Hughes, Chris Youldon and Chris Catnach

NON-CRICKETING HEROES? Alan Shearer. My parents, sister and the whole family who have backed me since day one

IF YOU WEREN'T A CRICKETER? I'd be living in Australia or New Zealand

SURPRISING FACT? My first Minor Counties season was in 2015 for Northumberland under Geoff Cook, Stewart Tiffin and Jacques du Toit

UNUSUAL OBJECT AT HOME? Muhammad Azharullah

DESERT ISLAND DISC? Chris Brown (any album)

FANTASY SLIP CORDON? Keeper: Chris Martin, 1st: Andrew Smith, 2nd: Chris Youlden, 3rd: Me, 4th: Simon Birtwisle, Gully: Max Morley

TWITTER: @gareth_wade

GRAHAM WAGG

RHB / LM / R0 / W2 / MVP33

GLAMORGAN

FULL NAME: Graham Grant Wagg
BORN: April 28, 1983, Rugby, Warwickshire
SQUAD NO: 8
HEIGHT: 6ft
NICKNAME: Waggy
EDUCATION: Ashlawn School, Rugby
TEAMS: Glamorgan, Derbyshire, Warwickshire
ROLE: Allrounder
DEBUT: First-class: 2002; List A: 2000; T20: 2003

BEST BATTING: 200 Glamorgan vs Surrey, Guildford, 2015
BEST BOWLING: 6-29 Glamorgan vs Surrey, The Oval, 2014
COUNTY CAPS: 2007 (Derbyshire); 2013 (Glamorgan)

FAMILY TIES? My dad played second XI cricket, Minor Counties and a good standard of Premier League – he could bowl a heavy ball and hit a long ball. My little man Brayden Wagg is just learning, so watch out for his name
BEST MOMENT IN CRICKET? Getting my first contract at Warwickshire and playing for England Schools in all the age-groups
CRICKETING HEROES? Ian Botham, Allan Donald, Viv Richards
IF YOU WEREN'T A CRICKETER? I'd be a full-time dad
SURPRISING FACT? I'm a dark horse on the snooker table
TWITTER: @GGWagg

Batting	Mat	Inns	NO	Runs	HS	Ave	SR	100	50	Ct	St
First-class	144	210	21	5191	200	27.46	66.09	4	31	47	0
List A	124	102	15	1643	62*	18.88		0	3	42	0
Twenty20	102	79	23	981	62	17.51	120.96	0	2	32	0

Bowling	Mat	Balls	Runs	Wkts	BBI	BBM	Ave	Econ	SR	5w	10
First-class	144	24884	14511	422	6/29		34.38	3.49	58.9	12	1
List A	124	4760	4706	138	4/35	4/35	34.10	5.93	34.4	0	0
Twenty20	102	1730	2369	98	5/14	5/14	24.17	8.21	17.6	1	0

NEIL WAGNER

LHB / LMF / RO / WO

FULL NAME: Neil Wagner
BORN: March 13, 1986, Pretoria, South Africa
SQUAD NO: 13
HEIGHT: 5ft 9in
NICKNAME: Wags
EDUCATION: Afrikaans Boys High School, Pretoria, South Africa
TEAMS: New Zealand, Essex, Lancashire, Northerns, Otago
ROLE: Bowler
DEBUT: Test: 2012; First-class: 2006; List A: 2006; T20: 2009

BEST BATTING: 70 Otago vs Wellington, Queenstown, 2009
BEST BOWLING: 7-46 Otago vs Wellington, Dunedin, 2012

STRANGEST THING SEEN IN A GAME? My run-out against Bangladesh at Christchurch earlier this year. I grounded my bat in time and was well inside the crease but was given out because my whole body and bat were in mid-air when the bails came off
BEST MOMENT IN CRICKET? Taking five wickets in one over for Otago in 2011
HOW WOULD YOUR TEAM-MATES DESCRIBE YOU IN THREE WORDS? Humble, competitive, determined
BEST PLAYER IN COUNTY CRICKET? Alastair Cook (Ess)
TIP FOR THE TOP? Liam Livingstone (Lan)
CRICKETING HEROES? Allan Donald, Brett Lee, Brian Lara, Jacques Kallis, Shane Bond
NON-CRICKETING HEROES? Richie McCaw, Dan Carter, Usain Bolt
IF YOU WEREN'T A CRICKETER? I'd be a rugby player
SURPRISING FACT? I play golf right-handed
TWITTER: @NeilWagner13

Batting	Mat	Inns	NO	Runs	HS	Ave	SR	100	50	Ct	St
Tests	30	38	9	384	37	13.24	44.03	0	0	6	0
First-class	128	168	33	2125	70	15.74	50.29	0	6	34	0
List A	85	46	8	467	42	12.28	82.65	0	0	15	0
Twenty20	61	26	10	104	14	6.50	102.97	0	0	11	0

Bowling	Mat	Balls	Runs	Wkts	BBI	BBM	Ave	Econ	SR	5w	10
Tests	30	6683	3518	123	6/41	8/103	28.60	3.15	54.3	4	0
First-class	128	26357	14282	538	7/46	11/111	26.54	3.25	48.9	27	2
List A	85	4092	3601	135	5/34	5/34	26.67	5.28	30.3	2	0
Twenty20	61	1255	1778	68	4/33	4/33	26.14	8.50	18.4	0	0

JAMES WAINMAN

RHB / LM / R0 / W0

YORKSHIRE

FULL NAME: James Charles Wainman
BORN: January 25, 1993, Harrogate, Yorkshire
SQUAD NO: 15
HEIGHT: 6ft 4in
NICKNAME: Wainers
EDUCATION: Leeds Grammar School
TEAMS: Yorkshire
ROLE: Bowler
DEBUT: List A: 2014; T20: 2016

FAMILY TIES? My dad played a good standard of club cricket and coached me as a junior
BEST MOMENT IN CRICKET? My first List A game against Sri Lanka A, when I took 3-51 and scored 33 runs
CRICKETING HEROES? Glenn McGrath
NON-CRICKETING HEROES? Leonardo DiCaprio
TWITTER: @jcwainman
NOTES: Left-arm seamer with a reputation for putting a squeeze on the run-rate. Claimed 42 wickets from 24 appearances in all forms of second XI cricket in 2016, including two five-wicket hauls in the three-day Championship. Made his List A debut in 2014 and played two matches in last season's NatWest T20 Blast

Batting	Mat	Inns	NO	Runs	HS	Ave	SR	100	50	Ct	St
List A	1	1	0	33	33	33.00	122.22	0	0	1	0
Twenty20	2	1	1	12	12*	-	100.00	0	0	0	0

Bowling	Mat	Balls	Runs	Wkts	BBI	BBM	Ave	Econ	SR	5w	10
List A	1	48	51	3	3/51	3/51	17.00	6.37	16.0	0	0
Twenty20	2	30	49	1	1/27	1/27	49.00	9.80	30.0	0	0

MATTHEW WAITE

RHB / RFM / RO / WO

FULL NAME: Matthew James Waite
BORN: December 24, 1995, Leeds
SQUAD NO: 6
NICKNAME: Pingu
EDUCATION: Brigshaw High School, West Yorkshire
TEAMS: Yorkshire
ROLE: Allrounder
DEBUT: List A: 2014; T20: 2015

TWITTER: @mat_waite
NOTES: A seam-bowling allrounder, Waite signed a two-year junior professional contract with Yorkshire at the end of 2015. He made his senior debut in the RL Cup in 2014, and played his first NatWest T20 Blast game the following year. In 2016 he made two appearances for Yorkshire in white-ball cricket, impressing on both occasions. He hit 19* and took 1-6 from two overs in the T20 quarter-final against Glamorgan at Cardiff, and then 38 and 3-48 from 10 overs in the RL Cup semi-final against Surrey at Headingley. More opportunities in limited-overs cricket beckon in 2017

Batting	Mat	Inns	NO	Runs	HS	Ave	SR	100	50	Ct	St
List A	3	3	1	61	38	30.50	73.49	0	0	0	0
Twenty20	3	2	2	33	19*	-	150.00	0	0	2	0

Bowling	Mat	Balls	Runs	Wkts	BBI	BBM	Ave	Econ	SR	5w	10
List A	3	120	117	3	3/48	3/48	39.00	5.85	40.0	0	0
Twenty20	3	42	51	1	1/6	1/6	51.00	7.28	42.0	0	0

ALEX WAKELY

RHB / RM / RO / WO

FULL NAME: Alex George Wakely
BORN: November 3, 1988, London
SQUAD NO: 8
HEIGHT: 6ft 2in
NICKNAME: Wakers, Baby Seal
EDUCATION: Bedford School
TEAMS: Northamptonshire
ROLE: Batsman
DEBUT: First-class: 2007; List A: 2005; T20: 2009

BEST BATTING: 123 Northamptonshire vs Leicestershire, Northampton, 2015
BEST BOWLING: 2-62 Northamptonshire vs Somerset, Taunton, 2007
COUNTY CAP: 2012

WHAT FIRST GOT YOU INTO CRICKET? My grandad made me a bat when I was five. Then watching my dad play for Ampthill Town CC for many years
STRANGEST THING SEEN IN A GAME? A streaker fist-pumping Rob Keogh
BEST MOMENT IN CRICKET? Winning the T20 Cup in 2013 and 2016 and scoring a hundred at Lord's
BEST PLAYER IN COUNTY CRICKET? Ben Duckett (Nor)
MOST UNDERRATED PLAYER IN COUNTY CRICKET? Rob Newton (Nor)
TIP FOR THE TOP? Saif Zaib (Nor)
CRICKETING HEROES? David Sales, Ricky Ponting
NON-CRICKETING HEROES? Michael Jordan, Bruce Wayne, Bill Gates, my grandad
IF YOU WEREN'T A CRICKETER? I would work in the City or in journalism
SURPRISING FACT? I play the piano and love the CityIndex
UNUSUAL OBJECT AT HOME? A gekko
TWITTER: @AlexWakely1

Batting	Mat	Inns	NO	Runs	HS	Ave	SR	100	50	Ct	St
First-class	108	169	10	4941	123	31.07	46.55	5	29	66	0
List A	67	63	7	1664	102	29.71	84.50	1	11	20	0
Twenty20	88	82	17	1768	64	27.20	118.81	0	11	28	0

Bowling	Mat	Balls	Runs	Wkts	BBI	BBM	Ave	Econ	SR	5w	10
First-class	108	453	351	6	2/62	2/62	58.50	4.64	75.5	0	0
List A	67	136	131	5	2/14	2/14	26.20	5.77	27.2	0	0
Twenty20	88	12	29	0	-	-	-	14.50	-	0	0

MAX WALLER

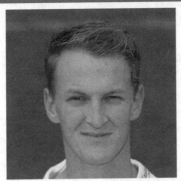

FULL NAME: Maximilian Thomas Charles Waller
BORN: March 3, 1988, Salisbury, Wiltshire
SQUAD NO: 10
HEIGHT: 6ft
NICKNAME: Goose, Jun Jun, Maxy
EDUCATION: Millfield School, Somerset; Bournemouth University
TEAMS: Somerset
ROLE: Bowler
DEBUT: First-class: 2009; List A: 2009; T20: 2009

SOMERSET

BEST BATTING: 28 Somerset vs Hampshire, Southampton, 2009
BEST BOWLING: 3-33 Somerset vs Cambridge MCCU, Taunton, 2012

WHAT FIRST GOT YOU INTO CRICKET? My grandad took me to cricket camps at Lord's
STRANGEST THING SEEN IN A GAME? Roelof van der Merwe eating a worm
BEST MOMENT IN CRICKET? The T20 Champions League 2009 and 2011, and Finals Day in the Caribbean T20 2009-12
SUPERSTITIONS? I have to be holding the ball before handing my cap to the umpire at the start of my over
BEST PLAYER IN COUNTY CRICKET? Kumar Sangakarra (Sur)
MOST UNDERRATED PLAYER IN COUNTY CRICKET? John Simpson (Mid)
TIP FOR THE TOP? Dan Lawrence (Ess)
CRICKETING HEROES? Shane Warne, Jonty Rhodes, Damien Martyn
NON-CRICKETING HEROES? Ayrton Senna – for his flair and his fearless approach
IF YOU WEREN'T A CRICKETER? I'd be a struggling artist
SURPRISING FACT? I've sold some paintings
UNUSUAL OBJECT AT HOME? An ostrich-egg-shell lamp
TWITTER: @MaxTCWaller

Batting	Mat	Inns	NO	Runs	HS	Ave	SR	100	50	Ct	St
First-class	8	9	1	91	28	11.37	42.92	0	0	5	0
List A	50	19	13	97	25*	16.16	69.78	0	0	23	0
Twenty20	81	22	13	56	11*	6.22	70.88	0	0	40	0

Bowling	Mat	Balls	Runs	Wkts	BBI	BBM	Ave	Econ	SR	5w	10
First-class	8	840	493	10	3/33	3/57	49.30	3.52	84.0	0	0
List A	50	1574	1477	38	3/39	3/39	38.86	5.63	41.4	0	0
Twenty20	81	1473	1808	79	4/16	4/16	22.88	7.36	18.6	0	0

PAUL WALTER

ESSEX

FULL NAME: Paul Ian Walter
BORN: May 28, 1994, Basildon, Essex
SQUAD NO: 22
HEIGHT: 6ft 7in
EDUCATION: Billericay School, Essex
TEAMS: Essex
ROLE: Allrounder
DEBUT: First-class: 2016; T20 2016

BEST BATTING: 47 Essex vs Derbyshire, Derby, 2016
BEST BOWLING: 3-44 Essex vs Derbyshire, Derby, 2016

TWITTER: @PWalter_22
NOTES: Walter signed a professional contract with his hometown club midway through last summer after impressing in club cricket for Hornchurch and for Essex Second XI. An allrounder with Premier League hundreds under his belt allied to a series of thrusting spells of high-quality pace bowling, Walter offers Essex options, especially in one-day cricket, as the club looks to move on from the Napier-Masters era. At 6ft 7in, he brings considerable presence to the Essex attack

Batting	Mat	Inns	NO	Runs	HS	Ave	SR	100	50	Ct	St
First-class	2	2	0	75	47	37.50	67.56	0	0	0	0
Twenty20	7	3	1	15	8	7.50	136.36	0	0	1	0

Bowling	Mat	Balls	Runs	Wkts	BBI	BBM	Ave	Econ	SR	5w	10
First-class	2	300	214	4	3/44	4/112	53.50	4.28	75.0	0	0
Twenty20	7	108	178	4	3/26	3/26	44.50	9.88	27.0	0	0

FULL NAME: Jared David Warner
BORN: November 14, 1996, Wakefield, Yorkshire
SQUAD NO: 45
HEIGHT: 6ft 1in
NICKNAME: Jazz
EDUCATION: Silcoates School, West Yorkshire; Kettlethorpe High School, Wakefield
TEAMS: England U19, Yorkshire 2nd XI
ROLE: Bowler
DEBUT: Yet to make first-team debut

YORKSHIRE

WHAT FIRST GOT YOU INTO CRICKET? Wakefield Thornes CC

BEST MOMENT IN CRICKET? Winning the double with Yorkshire Academy. Taking figures of 9-19 from 10.2 overs for Yorkshire Academy against Castleford in a Yorkshire Premier League North match in 2016. Representing England U19

HOW WOULD YOUR TEAM-MATES DESCRIBE YOU IN THREE WORDS? Joker, competitive, trustworthy

BEST PLAYER IN COUNTY CRICKET? Joe Root (Yor)

TIP FOR THE TOP? Sam Curran (Sur)

CRICKETING HEROES? Andrew Flintoff – I love the way he played the game

NON-CRICKETING HEROES? Michael Owen – he got me into football as a kid

SURPRISING FACT? I'm a Sheffield United supporter

DESERT ISLAND DISC? 90s Greatest Hits

TWITTER? @jaredwarner96

JOE WEATHERLEY

RHB / OB / R0 / W0

FULL NAME: Joe James Weatherley
BORN: January 19, 1997, Winchester, Hampshire
SQUAD NO: 5
EDUCATION: King Edward VI School, Southampton
TEAMS: Hampshire, Kent
ROLE: Batsman
DEBUT: First-class: 2016; List A: 2016; T20: 2016

BEST BATTING: 83 Hampshire vs Cardiff MCCU, Southampton, 2016

TWITTER: @Joe_Weatherley
NOTES: A product of the Hampshire Academy, Weatherley is a top-order batsman who bowls off-spin. He has captained Hampshire age-groups and England U19. Made his County Championship debut in 2016 and also featured in two RL Cup matches and five NatWest T20 Blast matches last summer. He joined Kent on loan ahead of the 2017 season

Batting	Mat	Inns	NO	Runs	HS	Ave	SR	100	50	Ct	St
First-class	2	3	0	96	83	32.00	53.03	0	1	0	0
List A	2	2	0	29	27	14.50	76.31	0	0	0	0
Twenty20	5	4	0	81	43	20.25	132.78	0	0	3	0

Bowling	Mat	Balls	Runs	Wkts	BBI	BBM	Ave	Econ	SR	5w	10
First-class	2	24	41	0	-	-	-	10.25	-	0	0
List A	2	18	17	0	-	-	-	5.66	-	0	0
Twenty20	5	6	9	0	-	-	-	9.00	-	0	0

JAMES WEIGHELL LHB / RMF / R0 / W0

FULL NAME: William James Weighell
BORN: January 28, 1994, Middlesbrough, Yorkshire
SQUAD NO: 28
HEIGHT: 6ft 3in
EDUCATION: Stokesley School, North Yorkshire
TEAMS: Durham
ROLE: Allrounder
DEBUT: First-class: 2015

BEST BATTING: 25 Durham vs Middlesex, Chester-le-Street, 2015
BEST BOWLING: 5-33 Durham vs Warwickshire, Edgbaston, 2016

WHAT FIRST GOT YOU INTO CRICKET? Watching my dad play from a young age
BEST MOMENT IN CRICKET? My maiden first-class five-wicket haul at Edgbaston last season
HOW WOULD YOUR TEAM-MATES DESCRIBE YOU IN THREE WORDS? Strong hair-line
BEST PLAYER IN COUNTY CRICKET? Keaton Jennings (Dur)
TIP FOR THE TOP? Brydon Carse, Graham Clark (both Dur)
CRICKETING HEROES? Andrew Flintoff
DESERT ISLAND DISC? Sandi Thom – I Wish I Was a Punk Rocker
TWITTER: @jamesweighell

Batting	Mat	Inns	NO	Runs	HS	Ave	SR	100	50	Ct	St
First-class	5	8	1	122	25	17.42	61.92	0	0	2	0

Bowling	Mat	Balls	Runs	Wkts	BBI	BBM	Ave	Econ	SR	5w	10
First-class	5	896	508	17	5/33	9/130	29.88	3.40	52.7	1	0

LUKE WELLS

LHB / OB / R1 / W0

SUSSEX

FULL NAME: Luke William Peter Wells
BORN: December 29, 1990, Eastbourne, Sussex
SQUAD NO: 31
HEIGHT: 6ft 4in
NICKNAME: Dave, Rinser
EDUCATION: St Bede's, Hailsham; Loughborough University
TEAMS: Sussex, Colombo Cricket Club
ROLE: Batsman
DEBUT: First-class: 2010; List A: 2010; T20: 2011

BEST BATTING: 208 Sussex vs Surrey, The Oval, 2013
BEST BOWLING: 3-35 Sussex vs Durham, Arundel, 2015

FAMILY TIES? My father Alan played for Sussex, Kent and England. My uncle Colin played for Sussex, Derbyshire and England
BEST MOMENT IN CRICKET? Scoring a double hundred in the 2013 season. Scoring a matchwinning hundred against Surrey in 2012
SUPERSTITIONS? I only bat in one particular pair of Gray-Nicolls whites
HOW WOULD YOUR TEAM-MATES DESCRIBE YOU IN THREE WORDS? Stubborn, fighter, confident
TIP FOR THE TOP? Phil Salt (Sus) – an explosive batsman
CRICKETING HEROES? Sachin Tendulkar, Brian Lara. But probably my favourite was Matt Hayden. I loved the way he played as an opening left-handed batter. And my old man
IF YOU WEREN'T A CRICKETER? I'd be studying full-time and looking to start out as a teacher and coach
TWITTER: @luke_wells07

Batting	Mat	Inns	NO	Runs	HS	Ave	SR	100	50	Ct	St
First-class	98	161	9	5254	208	34.56	44.18	13	22	50	0
List A	17	12	0	110	23	9.16	60.10	0	0	1	0
Twenty20	5	5	0	18	11	3.60	66.66	0	0	1	0

Bowling	Mat	Balls	Runs	Wkts	BBI	BBM	Ave	Econ	SR	5w	10
First-class	98	3574	2202	46	3/35	5/119	47.86	3.69	77.6	0	0
List A	17	209	178	6	3/19	3/19	29.66	5.11	34.8	0	0
Twenty20	5	1	4	0	-	-	-	24.00	-	0	0

TOM WELLS

RHB / RMF / RO / WO

FULL NAME: Thomas Joshua Wells
BORN: March 15, 1993, Grantham, Lincolnshire
SQUAD NO: 48
HEIGHT: 6ft 2in
NICKNAME: Wellsy
EDUCATION: Gartree High School, Leicester; Beauchamp College, Leicester
TEAMS: Leicestershire
ROLE: Allrounder
DEBUT: First-class: 2013; List A: 2012; T20: 2013

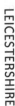

LEICESTERSHIRE

BEST BATTING: 87* Leicestershire vs Sri Lankans, Leicester, 2016
BEST BOWLING: 3-68 Leicestershire vs Lancashire, Leicester, 2015

WHAT FIRST GOT YOU INTO CRICKET? Paul Nixon was my next-door neighbour
STRANGEST THING SEEN IN A GAME? The batsman hits the ball to short extra-cover, hits him flush on the head, and mid-off takes a catch diving forward
BEST MOMENT IN CRICKET? Playing in the Championship win over Essex a few years ago
HOW WOULD YOUR TEAM-MATES DESCRIBE YOU IN THREE WORDS? Very large head
BEST PLAYER IN COUNTY CRICKET? Keaton Jennings (Dur)
MOST UNDERRATED PLAYER IN COUNTY CRICKET? Angus Robson (Lei)
TIP FOR THE TOP? Aadil Ali, Rob Sayer (both Lei)
CRICKETING HEROES? Paul Nixon, Andrew Flintoff
NON-CRICKETING HEROES? My old man was the Leicester Tigers rugby captain and coach, and he has been a big influence on my career
IF YOU WEREN'T A CRICKETER? I'd be an ice-road trucker or gardener
SURPRISING FACT? I hate flying
TWITTER: @t_wells15

Batting	Mat	Inns	NO	Runs	HS	Ave	SR	100	50	Ct	St
First-class	14	23	2	412	87*	19.61	52.02	0	2	7	0
List A	16	14	4	230	32*	23.00	88.46	0	0	5	0
Twenty20	39	28	10	433	64*	24.05	133.23	0	2	19	0

Bowling	Mat	Balls	Runs	Wkts	BBI	BBM	Ave	Econ	SR	5w	10
First-class	14	1008	692	13	3/68	3/88	53.23	4.11	77.5	0	0
List A	16	198	266	5	2/45	2/45	53.20	8.06	39.6	0	0
Twenty20	39	114	192	2	1/17	1/17	96.00	10.10	57.0	0	0

RIKI WESSELS

RHB / WK / R2 / W0 / MVP45

NOTTINGHAMSHIRE

FULL NAME: Mattheus Hendrik Wessels
BORN: November 12, 1985, Australia
SQUAD NO: 9
HEIGHT: 5ft 11in
NICKNAME: Blood, Weasel, Bobby
EDUCATION: Woodridge College, Port Elizabeth; University of Northampton
TEAMS: Nottinghamshire, Karachi Kings, Mid West Rhinos, Nondescripts, Northamptonshire, Sydney Sixers
ROLE: Batsman/wicketkeeper
DEBUT: First-class: 2004; List A: 2005; T20: 2005

BEST BATTING: 199 Nottinghamshire vs Sussex, Hove, 2012
BEST BOWLING: 1-10 Mid West Rhinos vs Matabeleland Tuskers, Bulawayo, 2009

BEST MOMENT IN CRICKET? That has to be my maiden first-class hundred, and also the finals I've taken part in
CRICKETING HEROES? Michael Slater, Justin Langer
NON-CRICKETING HEROES? All the soldiers fighting currently, having lost a few friends to war myself
IF YOU WEREN'T A CRICKETER? I'd probably be in the army on the front line
SURPRISING FACT? I've bungee-jumped at Victoria Falls, I lived in Colombo for six months and I love hunting
TWITTER: @rikiwessels

Batting	Mat	Inns	NO	Runs	HS	Ave	SR	100	50	Ct	St
First-class	170	284	24	9259	199	35.61	63.04	19	48	274	16
List A	151	141	14	3877	146	30.52	99.25	4	20	106	0
Twenty20	164	151	20	3755	97	28.66	135.16	0	19	62	15

Bowling	Mat	Balls	Runs	Wkts	BBI	BBM	Ave	Econ	SR	5w	10
First-class	170	210	115	3	1/10	1/10	38.33	3.28	70.0	0	0
List A	151	49	48	1	1/0	1/0	48.00	5.87	49.0	0	0
Twenty20	164	-	-	-	-	-	-	-	-	-	-

OLLIE WESTBURY

RHB / OB / R0 / W0

FULL NAME: Oliver Edward Westbury
BORN: July 2, 1997, Dudley, West Midlands
SQUAD NO: 19
HEIGHT: 5ft 11in
NICKNAME: Wes, Westy
EDUCATION: Ellowes Hall Sports College, Dudley; Shrewsbury School
TEAMS: England U19, Shropshire
ROLE: Batsman
DEBUT: Yet to make first-team debut

WHAT FIRST GOT YOU INTO CRICKET? The 2005 Ashes
BEST MOMENT IN CRICKET? Scoring a century on my England U19 debut against Sri Lanka U19 in 2016
BEST PLAYER IN COUNTY CRICKET? Kumar Sangakkara (Sur)
TIP FOR THE TOP? Josh Tongue (Wor), George Hankins (Glo)
CRICKETING HEROES? Andrew Flintoff, Alastair Cook, Michael Vaughan, AB de Villiers
NON-CRICKETING HEROES? Dad, Jamie Turner, Morgan Freeman, Chris Martin
IF YOU WEREN'T A CRICKETER? I'd be on a ski season somewhere in Europe, working in a bar or restaurant by night and skiing during the day. Or I'd be at university (whichever one would have me)
SURPRISING FACT? I know all the lyrics to We Didn't Start The Fire by Billy Joel
UNUSUAL OBJECT AT HOME? A turbo trainer
DESERT ISLAND DISC? Oasis – Don't Look Back In Anger
FANTASY SLIP CORDON? Keeper: John Bishop, 1st: Margot Robbie, 2nd: Bumble, 3rd: Del Boy, Gully: Me
TWITTER: @ollywestbury

TOM WESTLEY

RHB / OB / R1 / W0 / MVP32

ESSEX

FULL NAME: Thomas Westley
BORN: March 13, 1989, Cambridge
SQUAD NO: 21
HEIGHT: 6ft 2in
NICKNAME: Westie, Shellsy, Wezzo
EDUCATION: Linton Valley College, South Cambridgeshire; Hills Road College, Cambridge; Durham University
TEAMS: Essex, Bloomfield Cricket and Athletic Club, England Lions
ROLE: Batsman
DEBUT: First-class: 2007; List A: 2006; T20: 2010

BEST BATTING: 254 Essex vs Worcestershire, Chelmsford, 2016
BEST BOWLING: 4-55 Durham MCCU vs Durham, Durham University, 2010
COUNTY CAP: 2013

FAMILY TIES? My dad, uncle and brother all play for Weston Colville CC. My dad harbours ambitions to play for England Over-50s
TIP FOR THE TOP? Kishen Velani (Ess)
CRICKETING HEROES? Jacques Kallis, Sachin Tendulkar, Ben Matthews, Max Nolan, Dave Babbage, James Bunbury, Ben Lawrence
NON-CRICKETING HEROES? Giovanni Colussi
SURPRISING FACT? I was part of the first group of students to study Harry Potter academically
DESERT ISLAND DISC? Swedish House Mafia – Don't You Worry Child
TWITTER: @Westley21

Batting	Mat	Inns	NO	Runs	HS	Ave	SR	100	50	Ct	St
First-class	131	219	15	7432	254	36.43	53.15	15	38	93	0
List A	62	56	3	1778	111*	33.54	84.70	3	14	12	0
Twenty20	54	48	6	1395	109*	33.21	131.35	2	5	21	0

Bowling	Mat	Balls	Runs	Wkts	BBI	BBM	Ave	Econ	SR	5w	10
First-class	131	4642	2466	52	4/55	5/122	47.42	3.18	89.2	0	0
List A	62	988	818	20	4/60	4/60	40.90	4.96	49.4	0	0
Twenty20	54	246	311	7	2/27	2/27	44.42	7.58	35.1	0	0

IAN WESTWOOD

LHB / OB / R0 / W0

FULL NAME: Ian James Westwood
BORN: July 13, 1982, Birmingham
SQUAD NO: 22
HEIGHT: 5ft 7in
NICKNAME: Westy, Wezzo
EDUCATION: Solihull Sixth Form College
TEAMS: Warwickshire
ROLE: Batsman
DEBUT: First-class: 2003; List A: 2001; T20: 2005

BEST BATTING: 196 Warwickshire vs Yorkshire, Headingley, 2015
BEST BOWLING: 2-39 Warwickshire vs Hampshire, Southampton, 2009
COUNTY CAP: 2008; **BENEFIT:** 2015

WHAT FIRST GOT YOU INTO CRICKET? My grandad was a member at Edgbaston
FAMILY TIES? My brother played Warwickshire schools
BEST MOMENT IN CRICKET? Winning the County Championship at New Road in 2012
HOW WOULD YOUR TEAM-MATES DESCRIBE YOU IN THREE WORDS? Small, stirrer, competitive
BEST PLAYER IN COUNTY CRICKET? Jonny Bairstow (Yor)
TIP FOR THE TOP? Sam Hain (War)
CRICKETING HEROES? Warwickshire's 1994 squad, especially Brian Lara. Great to watch
IF YOU WEREN'T A CRICKETER? I'd be a banker
SURPRISING FACT? I'm the tallest in my family
DESERT ISLAND DISC? Fleetwood Mac – Rumours
FANTASY SLIP CORDON? Keeper: Stevie Nicks, 1st: Phil Mickelson, 2nd: Tom Jones, 3rd: Lionel Richie
TWITTER: @ianwestwood08

Batting	Mat	Inns	NO	Runs	HS	Ave	SR	100	50	Ct	St
First-class	155	259	22	7824	196	33.01	44.98	15	41	82	0
List A	60	50	9	940	65	22.92		0	3	7	0
Twenty20	38	27	12	342	49*	22.80	114.00	0	0	5	0

Bowling	Mat	Balls	Runs	Wkts	BBI	BBM	Ave	Econ	SR	5w	10
First-class	155	604	337	7	2/39		48.14	3.34	86.2	0	0
List A	60	264	227	3	1/28	1/28	75.66	5.15	88.0	0	0
Twenty20	38	54	91	5	3/29	3/29	18.20	10.11	10.8	0	0

BRAD WHEAL

RHB / RFM / R0 / W0

FULL NAME: Bradley Thomas James Wheal
BORN: August 28, 1996, Durban, South Africa
SQUAD NO: 58
EDUCATION: Clifton School, Durban
TEAMS: Scotland, Hampshire
ROLE: Bowler
DEBUT: ODI: 2016; T20I: 2016; First-class: 2015; List A: 2016; T20: 2016

BEST BATTING: 14 Hampshire vs Surrey, Southampton, 2016
BEST BOWLING: 6-51 Hampshire vs Nottinghamshire, Trent Bridge, 2016

TWITTER: @Brad_wheal
NOTES: Born in South Africa, Wheal holds a British passport because his mother is Scottish. Made his Hampshire debut in 2015 after signing a two-year-deal with the county and his Scotland debut in January 2016, aged 19. The fast bowler chipped in with key contributions with the ball in one-day and Championship cricket for Hampshire during the 2016 summer, taking a career-best 6-51 against Nottinghamshire

Batting	Mat	Inns	NO	Runs	HS	Ave	SR	100	50	Ct	St
ODIs	5	4	3	2	2*	2.00	10.00	0	0	0	0
T20Is	5	2	2	2	2*	-	100.00	0	0	1	0
First-class	13	15	5	54	14	5.40	18.06	0	0	2	0
List A	9	7	5	21	13	10.50	60.00	0	0	0	0
Twenty20	11	4	2	20	16	10.00	100.00	0	0	1	0

Bowling	Mat	Balls	Runs	Wkts	BBI	BBM	Ave	Econ	SR	5w	10
ODIs	5	259	218	7	2/31	2/31	31.14	5.05	37.0	0	0
T20Is	5	104	143	5	3/20	3/20	28.60	8.25	20.8	0	0
First-class	13	1938	1142	30	6/51	7/71	38.06	3.53	64.6	1	0
List A	9	430	361	14	4/38	4/38	25.78	5.03	30.7	0	0
Twenty20	11	200	272	10	3/20	3/20	27.20	8.16	20.0	0	0

ADAM WHEATER

RHB / WK / R0 / W0 / MVP80

FULL NAME: Adam Jack Aubrey Wheater
BORN: February 13, 1990, Whipps Cross Hospital, London
SQUAD NO: 31
EDUCATION: Millfield School, Somerset; Anglia Ruskin University
TEAMS: Essex, Badureliya Sports Club, Hampshire, Matabeleland Tuskers
ROLE: Batsman/wicketkeeper
DEBUT: First-class: 2008; List A: 2010; T20: 2009

BEST BATTING: 204* Hampshire vs Warwickshire, Edgbaston, 2016
BEST BOWLING: 1-86 Essex vs Leicestershire, Leicester, 2012

BEST MOMENT IN CRICKET? On a broader scale, having the opportunity to see the world through cricket
CRICKETING HEROES? Alec Stewart, Nasser Hussain, Adam Gilchrist
IF YOU WEREN'T A CRICKETER? I'd find myself a very wealthy girlfriend I could sponge off
DESERT ISLAND DISC? Snow Patrol – Greatest Hits
FANTASY SLIP CORDON? Keeper: Spider-Man (he's taking everyone's catches), 1st: Anthony Kiedis (he would have some stories to tell), 2nd: Micky Flanagan (just in case you had a long time in the field), 3rd: Me, Gully: Shakira (to teach me Spanish)

Batting	Mat	Inns	NO	Runs	HS	Ave	SR	100	50	Ct	St
First-class	108	161	20	5321	204*	37.73	68.41	10	29	167	8
List A	66	51	5	1252	135	27.21	97.88	2	5	24	8
Twenty20	80	59	12	825	78	17.55	115.22	0	2	30	18

Bowling	Mat	Balls	Runs	Wkts	BBI	BBM	Ave	Econ	SR	5w	10
First-class	108	24	86	1	1/86	1/86	86.00	21.50	24.0	0	0
List A	66	-	-	-	-	-	-	-	-	-	-
Twenty20	80	-	-	-	-	-	-	-	-	-	-

GRAEME WHITE

RHB / SLA / RO / WO

FULL NAME: Graeme Geoffrey White
BORN: April 18, 1987, Milton Keynes, Buckinghamshire
SQUAD NO: 87
HEIGHT: 5ft 10in
NICKNAME: Whitey, G
EDUCATION: Royal Latin School, Buckinghamshire; Stowe School
TEAMS: Northamptonshire
ROLE: Bowler
DEBUT: First-class: 2006; List A: 2007; T20: 2007

BEST BATTING: 65 Northamptonshire vs Glamorgan, Colwyn Bay, 2007
BEST BOWLING: 6-44 Northamptonshire vs Glamorgan, Northampton, 2016

WHAT FIRST GOT YOU INTO CRICKET? Playing with my dad on the beach in France
FAMILY TIES? My dad played club cricket, my sister played England Women U17 and my brother played Northants age-group cricket
STRANGEST THING SEEN IN A GAME? David Murphy fielding
BEST MOMENT IN CRICKET? Winning the T20 Cup in 2016
HOW WOULD YOUR TEAM-MATES DESCRIBE YOU IN THREE WORDS? Hilarious, grumpy, ripped
BEST PLAYER IN COUNTY CRICKET? Ben Stokes (Dur)
MOST UNDERRATED PLAYER IN COUNTY CRICKET? Chris Rushworth (Dur)
TIP FOR THE TOP? Richard Gleeson, Adam Rossington (both Nor)
CRICKETING HEROES? Phil Tufnell, Shane Warne, Daniel Vettori
NON-CRICKETING HEROES? David Beckham, Lionel Messi, Cristiano Ronaldo
IF YOU WEREN'T A CRICKETER? I'd be a model or businessman
SURPRISING FACT? I'm currently taking my Level 3 coaching course
UNUSUAL OBJECT AT HOME? A Nintendo 64

Batting	Mat	Inns	NO	Runs	HS	Ave	SR	100	50	Ct	St
First-class	36	51	5	571	65	12.41	46.99	0	2	12	0
List A	65	36	15	335	40	15.95	85.67	0	0	26	0
Twenty20	82	28	13	188	34	12.53	134.28	0	0	32	0

Bowling	Mat	Balls	Runs	Wkts	BBI	BBM	Ave	Econ	SR	5w	10
First-class	36	4344	2425	62	6/44	7/89	39.11	3.34	70.0	1	0
List A	65	2286	1940	76	6/37	6/37	25.52	5.09	30.0	2	0
Twenty20	82	1199	1589	64	5/22	5/22	24.82	7.95	18.7	1	0

FULL NAME: Robert George White
BORN: September 15, 1995, Ealing, London
SQUAD NO: 14
HEIGHT: 5ft 10in
NICKNAME: Whitey
EDUCATION: Harrow School, London;
Loughborough University
TEAMS: Loughborough MCCU, Middlesex
2nd XI
ROLE: Batsman/wicketkeeper
DEBUT: First-class: 2015

MIDDLESEX

BEST BATTING: 30 Loughborough MCCU vs Kent, Canterbury, 2016

WHAT FIRST GOT YOU INTO CRICKET? Playing in the garden (and lounge) with my brother
BEST MOMENT IN CRICKET? Winning the second XI T20 for two consecutive years
HOW WOULD YOUR TEAM-MATES DESCRIBE YOU IN THREE WORDS? Sarcastic, good
footballer
BEST PLAYER IN COUNTY CRICKET? Sam Northeast (Ken)
MOST UNDERRATED PLAYER IN COUNTY CRICKET? Stevie Eskinazi (Mid)
TIP FOR THE TOP? Max Holden (Mid)
CRICKETING HEROES? Matt Prior, Alec Stewart, Michael Vaughan
NON-CRICKETING HEROES? Roger Federer, Tiger Woods
IF YOU WEREN'T A CRICKETER? I'd be a professional golfer
SURPRISING FACT? I am related to Jessica Ennis-Hill
UNUSUAL OBJECT AT HOME? A putting-rebounder machine
DESERT ISLAND DISC? Oasis – (What's The Story) Morning Glory?
FANTASY SLIP CORDON? Keeper: Anthony Joshua, 1st: Jürgen Klopp, 2nd: Me, 3rd: Rachel
Riley, 4th: Hugh Grant, Gully: Ant and Dec
TWITTER: @Rwhitey15

Batting	Mat	Inns	NO	Runs	HS	Ave	SR	100	50	Ct	St
First-class	4	4	0	34	30	8.50	38.63	0	0	3	0

Bowling	Mat	Balls	Runs	Wkts	BBI	BBM	Ave	Econ	SR	5w	10
First-class	4	-	-	-	-	-	-	-	-	-	-

WORCESTERSHIRE

FULL NAME: Ross Andrew Whiteley
BORN: September 13, 1988, Sheffield
SQUAD NO: 44
HEIGHT: 6ft 2in
NICKNAME: Rossco, Pico, Shaggy
EDUCATION: Repton School, Derbyshire;
Leeds Metropolitan University
TEAMS: Worcestershire, Derbyshire,
England Lions
ROLE: Batsman
DEBUT: First-class: 2008; List A: 2008;
T20: 2011

BEST BATTING: 130* Derbyshire vs Kent, Derby, 2011
BEST BOWLING: 2-6 Derbyshire vs Hampshire, Derby, 2012
COUNTY CAP: 2013 (Worcestershire)

FAMILY TIES? My brother played for Derbyshire Academy and a handful of second XI games
STRANGEST THING SEEN IN A GAME? Snow
BEST MOMENT IN CRICKET? Hitting a six to win Division Two of the County Championship
HOW WOULD YOUR TEAM-MATES DESCRIBE YOU IN THREE WORDS? Tough but fair
BEST PLAYER IN COUNTY CRICKET? Rikki Clarke (War)
MOST UNDERRATED PLAYER IN COUNTY CRICKET? Joe Leach (Wor)
TIP FOR THE TOP? Joe Clarke (Wor)
CRICKETING HEROES? Matthew Hayden – I loved watching him bully attacks
NON-CRICKETING HEROES? Soldiers fighting for our country
SURPRISING FACT? I have 11 sheep with each squad number of the Derbyshire side which
won Division Two shaved onto them
FANTASY SLIP CORDON? Keeper: Tiger Woods, 1st: Me, 2nd: Emily Ratajkowski, 3rd: Ricky
Hatton, Gully: Donald Trump
TWITTER: @rosswhiteley44

Batting	Mat	Inns	NO	Runs	HS	Ave	SR	100	50	Ct	St
First-class	66	106	11	2618	130*	27.55	48.62	3	13	41	0
List A	52	43	5	844	77	22.21	83.56	0	5	12	0
Twenty20	65	61	20	1173	91*	28.60	146.44	0	2	23	0

Bowling	Mat	Balls	Runs	Wkts	BBI	BBM	Ave	Econ	SR	5w	10
First-class	66	2245	1626	29	2/6	4/43	56.06	4.34	77.4	0	0
List A	52	381	423	8	1/17	1/17	52.87	6.66	47.6	0	0
Twenty20	65	54	87	2	1/12	1/12	43.50	9.66	27.0	0	0

STUART WHITTINGHAM

RHB / RFM / RO / WO

FULL NAME: Stuart Gordon Whittingham
BORN: February 10, 1994, Derby
SQUAD NO: 29
HEIGHT: 6ft 2in
NICKNAME: The Jug
EDUCATION: Christ's Hospital, Horsham;
Loughborough University
TEAMS: Sussex
ROLE: Bowler
DEBUT: First-class: 2015

BEST BATTING: 8* Sussex vs Worcestershire, Worcester, 2016
BEST BOWLING: 4-58 Sussex vs Glamorgan, Hove, 2016

WHAT FIRST GOT YOU INTO CRICKET? Playing in the garden
BEST MOMENT IN CRICKET? Making my Sussex first-class debut at Derby in 2016
SUPERSTITIONS? I have to do my run-up in a loop
BEST PLAYER IN COUNTY CRICKET? Steve Magoffin (Sus)
MOST UNDERRATED PLAYER IN COUNTY CRICKET? Ben Brown (Sus)
TIP FOR THE TOP? George Garton, Jofra Archer (both Sus)
CRICKETING HEROES? Brett Lee
NON-CRICKETING HEROES? Brian Clough, Richard Keogh, George Thorne, Will Hughes
IF YOU WEREN'T A CRICKETER? I'd be a pilot
FANTASY SLIP CORDON? Keeper: Gary Barlow, 1st: Me, 2nd: Robbie Williams, 3rd: Howard
Donald, 4th: Mark Owen, Gully: Jason Orange
TWITTER: @Stuartwhitt10

Batting	Mat	Inns	NO	Runs	HS	Ave	SR	100	50	Ct	St
First-class	7	5	2	20	8*	6.66	27.77	0	0	1	0

Bowling	Mat	Balls	Runs	Wkts	BBI	BBM	Ave	Econ	SR	5w	10
First-class	7	1030	685	19	4/58	5/116	36.05	3.99	54.2	0	0

DAVID WIESE

RHB / RMF / RO / WO

FULL NAME: David Wiese
BORN: May 18, 1985, Roodepoort, Transvaal, South Africa
SQUAD NO: 96
EDUCATION: Witbank High School, South Africa
TEAMS: South Africa, Sussex, Barbados Tridents, Easterns, Guyana Amazon Warriors, Royal Challengers Bangalore, Titans
ROLE: Allrounder
DEBUT: ODI: 2015; T20I: 2013; First-class: 2005; List A: 2005; T20: 2008

BEST BATTING: 208 Easterns vs Griqualand West, Benoni, 2008
BEST BOWLING: 6-58 Titans vs Knights, Centurion, 2015

TWITTER: @David_Wiese
NOTES: Seam-bowling allrounder who returns to Sussex in 2017 after two spells as an overseas player last year. He has now signed a three-year contract as a Kolpak cricketer, so ruling him out of selection for South Africa and making him available to Sussex for all formats for the whole season. Wiese, who made his international debut in 2013, will join up with compatriot Stiaan van Zyl, who also signed a long-term Kolpak deal with Sussex over the off-season

Batting	Mat	Inns	NO	Runs	HS	Ave	SR	100	50	Ct	St
ODIs	6	6	1	102	41*	20.40	88.69	0	0	0	0
T20Is	20	11	4	92	28	13.14	122.66	0	0	9	0
First-class	85	136	16	4145	208	34.54	70.60	9	22	63	0
List A	116	99	20	2764	106	34.98	116.03	1	15	40	0
Twenty20	140	94	40	1191	71*	22.05	152.10	0	3	42	0

Bowling	Mat	Balls	Runs	Wkts	BBI	BBM	Ave	Econ	SR	5w	10
ODIs	6	294	316	9	3/50	3/50	35.11	6.44	32.6	0	0
T20Is	20	392	497	24	5/23	5/23	20.70	7.60	16.3	1	0
First-class	85	12390	6654	249	6/58	10/111	26.72	3.22	49.7	7	1
List A	116	4159	3706	100	5/25	5/25	37.06	5.34	41.5	1	0
Twenty20	140	2037	2772	118	5/19	5/19	23.49	8.16	17.2	3	0

DAVID WILLEY

LHB / LFM / RO / WO

FULL NAME: David Jonathan Willey
BORN: February 28, 1990, Northampton
SQUAD NO: 72
HEIGHT: 6ft 1in
NICKNAME: Will, Wills, Wildman
EDUCATION: Northampton School For Boys
TEAMS: England, Yorkshire,
Northamptonshire, Perth Scorchers
ROLE: Allrounder
DEBUT: ODI: 2015; T20I: 2015; First-class:
2009; List A: 2009; T20: 2009

YORKSHIRE

BEST BATTING: 104* Northamptonshire vs Gloucestershire, Northampton, 2015
BEST BOWLING: 5-29 Northamptonshire vs Gloucestershire, Northampton, 2011
COUNTY CAPS: 2013 (Northamptonshire); 2016 (Yorkshire)

FAMILY TIES? My dad Peter played for England, Northamptonshire and Leicestershire
BEST MOMENT IN CRICKET? Representing England
TIP FOR THE TOP? Olly Stone (War)
CRICKETING HEROES? My dad – I always wanted to follow in his footsteps as a child
SURPRISING FACT? My wife Carolynne is a country singer and was a two-time X Factor
contestant
FANTASY SLIP CORDON? Keeper: Karl Pilkington (I'd like to hear his opinions on everything),
1st: Dad (he'd probably bounce off Pilkington and be sour together), 2nd: Me, 3rd: Michael
McIntyre
TWITTER: @david_willey

Batting	Mat	Inns	NO	Runs	HS	Ave	SR	100	50	Ct	St
ODIs	25	14	7	99	13*	14.14	70.21	0	0	14	0
T20Is	12	8	3	73	21	14.60	123.72	0	0	6	0
First-class	62	87	10	2110	104*	27.40	64.82	2	14	14	0
List A	97	70	14	1256	167	22.42	94.01	2	3	37	0
Twenty20	121	87	20	1478	100	22.05	139.17	1	5	48	0

Bowling	Mat	Balls	Runs	Wkts	BBI	BBM	Ave	Econ	SR	5w	10
ODIs	25	1120	1048	32	4/34	4/34	32.75	5.61	35.0	0	0
T20Is	12	236	325	18	3/20	3/20	18.05	8.26	13.1	0	0
First-class	62	8560	4735	157	5/29	10/75	30.15	3.31	54.5	5	1
List A	97	3463	3243	98	5/62	5/62	33.09	5.61	35.3	1	0
Twenty20	121	1875	2342	119	4/9	4/9	19.68	7.49	15.7	0	0

GARY WILSON

RHB / WK / R0 / W0 / MVP78

FULL NAME: Gary Craig Wilson
BORN: February 5, 1986, Dundonald, Northern Ireland
SQUAD NO: 5
HEIGHT: 5ft 9in
NICKNAME: Wils
EDUCATION: Methodist College, Belfast
TEAMS: Ireland, Derbyshire, Surrey
ROLE: Wicketkeeper
DEBUT: ODI: 2007; T20I: 2008; First-class: 2005; List A: 2006; T20: 2008

BEST BATTING: 160* Surrey vs Leicestershire, The Oval, 2014
COUNTY CAP: 2014 (Surrey)

STRANGEST THING SEEN IN A GAME? William Porterfield and Andre Botha involved in a mix-up against Scotland. Google it
BEST MOMENT IN CRICKET? Beating England in the 2011 World Cup
HOW WOULD YOUR TEAM-MATES DESCRIBE YOU IN THREE WORDS? Patriotic, passionate, loud
BEST PLAYER IN COUNTY CRICKET? Kumar Sangakkara (Sur)
TIP FOR THE TOP? Sam Curran (Sur)
CRICKETING HEROES? Alec Stewart
NON-CRICKETING HEROES? A.P. McCoy, Brian O'Driscoll – any Irish sportsperson doing well
IF YOU WEREN'T A CRICKETER? I'd be a policeman or fireman
SURPRISING FACT? I like numbers
TWITTER: @gwilson14

Batting	Mat	Inns	NO	Runs	HS	Ave	SR	100	50	Ct	St
ODIs	73	69	7	1575	113	25.40	74.15	1	11	53	10
T20Is	53	46	6	891	65*	22.27	104.57	0	2	28	4
First-class	82	125	19	3822	160*	36.05		3	23	148	5
List A	166	149	13	3155	113	23.19	70.89	1	20	124	26
Twenty20	145	125	28	2483	65*	25.59	112.86	0	9	77	19

Bowling	Mat	Balls	Runs	Wkts	BBI	BBM	Ave	Econ	SR	5w	10
ODIs	73	-	-	-	-	-	-	-	-	-	-
T20Is	53	-	-	-	-	-	-	-	-	-	-
First-class	82	108	89	0	-	-	-	4.94	-	0	0
List A	166	-	-	-	-	-	-	-	-	-	-
Twenty20	145	-	-	-	-	-	-	-	-	-	-

CHRIS WOAKES

RHB / RFM / R0 / W3

FULL NAME: Christopher Roger Woakes
BORN: March 2, 1989, Birmingham
SQUAD NO: 19
HEIGHT: 6ft 1in
NICKNAME: Woaksy, Woako, Wiz, GB
EDUCATION: Barr Beacon Language College
TEAMS: England, Warwickshire, Sydney Thunder, Wellington
ROLE: Allrounder
DEBUT: Test: 2013; ODI: 2011; T20I: 2011; First-class: 2006; List A: 2007; T20: 2008

WARWICKSHIRE

BEST BATTING: 152* Warwickshire vs Derbyshire, Derby, 2013
BEST BOWLING: 9-36 Warwickshire vs Durham, Edgbaston, 2016
COUNTY CAP: 2009

FAMILY TIES? My brothers played Birmingham League cricket
STRANGEST THING SEEN IN A GAME? Jonathan Trott catching a ball in his pocket (not on purpose)
BEST MOMENT IN CRICKET? Receiving my first England cap
SUPERSTITIONS? I always turn off my left shoulder at the end of my run-up
BEST PLAYER IN COUNTY CRICKET? Kumar Sangakkara (Sur)
TIP FOR THE TOP? Sam Curran (Sur), Sam Hain (War)
SURPRISING FACT? I won a keep-uppy competition when I was 10 (70 keepy-ups)
TWITTER: @chriswoakes

Batting	Mat	Inns	NO	Runs	HS	Ave	SR	100	50	Ct	St
Tests	17	28	8	591	66	29.55	46.02	0	2	9	0
ODIs	61	47	15	794	95*	24.81	86.77	0	2	28	0
T20Is	8	7	4	91	37	30.33	144.44	0	0	1	0
First-class	124	180	45	4899	152*	36.28		9	19	55	0
List A	137	95	31	1443	95*	22.54	87.50	0	2	41	0
Twenty20	87	54	29	656	55*	26.24	138.39	0	1	31	0

Bowling	Mat	Balls	Runs	Wkts	BBI	BBM	Ave	Econ	SR	5w	10
Tests	17	2750	1408	48	6/70	11/102	29.33	3.07	57.2	2	1
ODIs	61	2964	2771	85	6/45	6/45	32.60	5.60	34.8	2	0
T20Is	8	162	253	7	2/40	2/40	36.14	9.37	23.1	0	0
First-class	124	20793	10612	424	9/36	11/97	25.02	3.06	49.0	18	4
List A	137	5934	5475	158	6/45	6/45	34.65	5.53	37.5	2	0
Twenty20	87	1662	2245	86	4/21	4/21	26.10	8.10	19.3	0	0

CHRIS WOOD

RHB / LMF / RO / WO

FULL NAME: Christopher Philip Wood
BORN: June 27, 1990, Basingstoke, Hampshire
SQUAD NO: 25
HEIGHT: 6ft 3in
NICKNAME: Woody, Nuts
EDUCATION: St Lawrence CofE Primary School; Amery Hill School; Alton College, Hampshire
TEAMS: Hampshire
ROLE: Bowler
DEBUT: First-class: 2010; List A: 2010; T20: 2010

BEST BATTING: 105* Hampshire vs Leicestershire, Leicester, 2012
BEST BOWLING: 5-39 Hampshire vs Kent, Canterbury, 2014

STRANGEST THING SEEN IN A GAME? The final over of the 2010 T20 Cup final
BEST MOMENT IN CRICKET? Winning the 2012 one-day final at Lord's
HOW WOULD YOUR TEAM-MATES DESCRIBE YOU IN THREE WORDS? Loud, mad, competitive
BEST PLAYER IN COUNTY CRICKET? Ben Duckett (Nor)
TIP FOR THE TOP? Saqib Mahmood (Lan), Mason Crane (Ham)
CRICKETING HEROES? Nathan Bracken, Andrew Flintoff
NON-CRICKETING HEROES? Novak Djokovic
SURPRISING FACT? I played football at semi-professional level
DESERT ISLAND DISC? Red Hot Chili Peppers (any album)
FANTASY SLIP CORDON? Keeper: James Corden, 1st: David Beckham, 2nd: Miley Cyrus, 3rd: Tiger Woods, Gully: Jennifer Aniston
TWITTER: @CWoody27

Batting	Mat	Inns	NO	Runs	HS	Ave	SR	100	50	Ct	St
First-class	39	55	5	1265	105*	25.30	66.40	1	6	12	0
List A	62	35	10	311	41	12.44	95.98	0	0	20	0
Twenty20	86	28	11	204	27	12.00	110.27	0	0	25	0

Bowling	Mat	Balls	Runs	Wkts	BBI	BBM	Ave	Econ	SR	5w	10
First-class	39	5719	2894	99	5/39	7/49	29.23	3.03	57.7	3	0
List A	62	2465	2256	88	5/22	5/22	25.63	5.49	28.0	1	0
Twenty20	86	1754	2448	89	4/16	4/16	27.50	8.37	19.7	0	0

LUKE WOOD

LHB / LMF / RO / WO

FULL NAME: Luke Wood
BORN: August 2, 1995, Sheffield
SQUAD NO: 14
HEIGHT: 5ft 9in
NICKNAME: Biscuit
EDUCATION: Portland Comprehensive School, Worksop; Outwood Post 16 Centre Worksop
TEAMS: Nottinghamshire
ROLE: Bowler
DEBUT: First-class: 2014; List A: 2016; T20: 2016

BEST BATTING: 100 Nottinghamshire vs Sussex, Trent Bridge, 2015
BEST BOWLING: 5-40 Nottinghamshire vs Cambridge MCCU, Cambridge, 2016

WHAT FIRST GOT YOU INTO CRICKET? My neighbour took me down to the local club
STRANGEST THING SEEN IN A GAME? A batsman given out then called back by the umpire
BEST MOMENT IN CRICKET? Definitely my maiden hundred against Sussex in my fifth first-class game – I will never forget it
HOW WOULD YOUR TEAM-MATES DESCRIBE YOU IN THREE WORDS? Funny, stupid, loud
BEST PLAYER IN COUNTY CRICKET? Jake Ball (Not)
MOST UNDERRATED PLAYER IN COUNTY CRICKET? Steve Patterson (Yor)
TIP FOR THE TOP? Jake Libby, Tom Moores (both Not), George Garton (Sus)
CRICKETING HEROES? Ryan Sidebottom, Wasim Akram
SURPRISING FACT? I like grime/hip-hop
UNUSUAL OBJECT AT HOME? An artificial tree plant
DESERT ISLAND DISC? 2 Chainz – Good Drank
FANTASY SLIP CORDON? Keeper: Gordon Ramsey, 1st: Will Ferrell, 2nd: Conor McGregor, 3rd: Me, Gully: Chris Brown
TWITTER: @lwood_95

Batting	Mat	Inns	NO	Runs	HS	Ave	SR	100	50	Ct	St
First-class	16	25	5	539	100	26.95	66.62	1	2	4	0
List A	2	2	1	56	52	56.00	160.00	0	1	0	0
Twenty20	1	1	0	0	0	0.00	0.00	0	0	0	0

Bowling	Mat	Balls	Runs	Wkts	BBI	BBM	Ave	Econ	SR	5w	10
First-class	16	2311	1437	43	5/40	6/53	33.41	3.73	53.7	1	0
List A	2	78	76	3	2/44	2/44	25.33	5.84	26.0	0	0
Twenty20	1	12	22	0	-	-	-	11.00	-	0	0

MARK WOOD

RHB / RF / R0 / W0

DURHAM

FULL NAME: Mark Andrew Wood
BORN: January 11, 1990, Ashington, Northumberland
SQUAD NO: 33
HEIGHT: 6ft
NICKNAME: Woody
EDUCATION: Ashington High School; Newcastle College
TEAMS: England, Durham
ROLE: Bowler
DEBUT: Test: 2015; ODI: 2015; List A: 2015; First-class: 2011; List A: 2011; T20: 2013

BEST BATTING: 66 Durham vs Nottinghamshire, Chester-le-Street, 2015
BEST BOWLING: 5-32 England Lions vs Sri Lanka A Emerging Players, Colombo, 2014

FAMILY TIES? My dad Derek and uncle Neil played for Ashington CC and Northumberland
CRICKETING HEROES? Graham Onions, Stephen Harmison, Ben Harmison, Michael Holding, Ian Botham
DESERT ISLAND DISC? Celine Dion – All By Myself
SURPRISING FACT? I was in the Newcastle United Academy
FANTASY SLIP CORDON? Keeper: Denis Cyplenkov (Russian wrestler with the biggest hands in the world), 1st: Sanka Coffie (from Cool Runnings – because he'd be a top sledger), 2nd: Leslie Nielsen (to keep morale up in the field), 3rd: Vinnie Jones (famous for getting his hands around balls), Gully: Jason Bourne (because he lived on the edge)
TWITTER: @MAWood33

Batting	Mat	Inns	NO	Runs	HS	Ave	SR	100	50	Ct	St
Tests	8	14	5	185	32*	20.55	54.73	0	0	2	0
ODIs	11	4	3	34	13	34.00	106.25	0	0	3	0
T20Is	1	-	-	-	-	-	-	-	-	0	0
First-class	36	58	12	953	66	20.71	53.03	0	2	9	0
List A	33	13	7	62	15*	10.33	92.53	0	0	10	0
Twenty20	15	5	2	29	12	9.66	100.00	0	0	2	0

Bowling	Mat	Balls	Runs	Wkts	BBI	BBM	Ave	Econ	SR	5w	10
Tests	8	1527	860	25	3/39	5/83	34.40	3.37	61.0	0	0
ODIs	11	594	578	12	3/46	3/46	48.16	5.83	49.5	0	0
T20Is	1	18	26	3	3/26	3/26	8.66	8.66	6.0	0	0
First-class	36	5562	3145	116	5/32	6/47	27.11	3.39	47.9	5	0
List A	33	1440	1262	43	3/23	3/23	29.34	5.25	33.4	0	0
Twenty20	15	282	377	15	4/25	4/25	25.13	8.02	18.8	0	0

TOM WOOD

RHB / R0 / W0

FULL NAME: Thomas Andrew Wood
BORN: May 11, 1994, Derby
SQUAD NO: 23
HEIGHT: 6ft
NICKNAME: Woody, Woodster
EDUCATION: Heanor Gate Science College, Derbyshire
TEAMS: Derbyshire
ROLE: Batsman
DEBUT: First-class: 2016; List A: 2016

BEST BATTING: 14 Derbyshire vs Leicestershire, Derby, 2016

WHAT FIRST GOT YOU INTO CRICKET? Dad played at the local club and I used to go down on Saturday to play in the nets with my brother
STRANGEST THING SEEN IN A GAME? A fielder running in to kick the stumps out the ground when his team took a wicket
BEST MOMENT IN CRICKET? Walking out to bat on my debut
BEST PLAYER IN COUNTY CRICKET? Wayne Madsen (Der)
MOST UNDERRATED PLAYER IN COUNTY CRICKET? Tony Palladino (Der)
CRICKETING HEROES? Andrew Flintoff and Kevin Pietersen. I grew up watching them, particularly in the 2005 Ashes
NON-CRICKETING HEROES? Tiger Woods. He's the best golfer of all time and has transformed the game into what it is now
IF YOU WEREN'T A CRICKETER? I'd be working for my dad selling cars
SURPRISING FACT? I was born and bred in Derby but support Newcastle FC
UNUSUAL OBJECT AT HOME? A shotgun hanging above the fireplace
DESERT ISLAND DISC? Drake – Views
FANTASY SLIP CORDON? Keeper: Adam Gilchrist, 1st: Tiger Woods, 2nd: Andrew Flintoff, 3rd: Me, Gully: James Corden
TWITTER: @tom_wood

Batting	Mat	Inns	NO	Runs	HS	Ave	SR	100	50	Ct	St
First-class	2	4	0	32	14	8.00	33.33	0	0	1	0
List A	1	1	0	44	44	44.00	107.31	0	0	0	0

Bowling	Mat	Balls	Runs	Wkts	BBI	BBM	Ave	Econ	SR	5w	10
First-class	2	-	-	-	-	-	-	-	-	-	-
List A	1	-	-	-	-	-	-	-	-	-	-

CHRIS WRIGHT

RHB / RFM / R0 / W1 /

WARWICKSHIRE

FULL NAME: Christopher Julian Clement Wright
BORN: July 14, 1985, Chipping Norton, Oxfordshire
SQUAD NO: 31
HEIGHT: 6ft 3in
NICKNAME: Wrighty, Dog, Wrightdog
EDUCATION: Eggars Grammar School, Alton
TEAMS: Warwickshire, England Lions, Essex, Middlesex, Tamil Union
ROLE: Bowler
DEBUT: First-class: 2004; List A: 2004; T20: 2004

BEST BATTING: 77 Essex vs Cambridge MCCU, Cambridge, 2011
BEST BOWLING: 6-22 Essex vs Leicestershire, Leicester, 2008
COUNTY CAP: 2013 (Warwickshire)

BEST MOMENT IN CRICKET? Bowling out Worcestershire for 60 in a session. Keith Barker and I each got five wickets and effectively sealed the 2012 title for Warwickshire
SUPERSTITIONS? Sometimes handing my hat to Will Porterfield to give to the umpire at the start of my over. This gets me a wicket 60 per cent of the time
BEST PLAYER IN COUNTY CRICKET? Jeetan Patel (War)
MOST UNDERRATED PLAYER IN COUNTY CRICKET? Keith Barker (War) – gets the best batsmen out regularly and scores important runs
CRICKETING HEROES? Jason Gillespie – amazing action, quick, moved it away, long hair
NON-CRICKETING HEROES? James Richardson – former presenter of Gazzetta Football Italia
SURPRISING FACT? A long time ago I missed a pre-season game to play in the Irish Open Poker tournament. I was knocked out, got drunk, and missed my flight home. I was £10,000 poorer and ill but it was a good life experience. The coach of the club didn't see it that way
UNUSUAL OBJECT AT HOME? A unicorn's head and a golden gnome
TWITTER: @chriswright1985

Batting	Mat	Inns	NO	Runs	HS	Ave	SR	100	50	Ct	St
First-class	122	153	37	2116	77	18.24	50.42	0	9	20	0
List A	97	38	17	219	42	10.42	78.49	0	0	16	0
Twenty20	58	14	9	28	6*	5.60	103.70	0	0	13	0

Bowling	Mat	Balls	Runs	Wkts	BBI	BBM	Ave	Econ	SR	5w	10
First-class	122	19529	11559	345	6/22		33.50	3.55	56.6	9	0
List A	97	3767	3493	99	4/20	4/20	35.28	5.56	38.0	0	0
Twenty20	58	1167	1739	52	4/24	4/24	33.44	8.94	22.4	0	0

FULL NAME: Luke James Wright
BORN: March 7, 1985, Grantham, Lincolnshire
SQUAD NO: 10
HEIGHT: 5ft 10in
EDUCATION: Loughborough University
TEAMS: England, Sussex, Abhani Limited, Auckland, Dhaka Gladiators, Impi, Leicestershire, Melbourne Stars, Pune Warriors, Quetta Gladiators, Wellington
ROLE: Allrounder
DEBUT: ODI: 2007; T20I: 2007; First-class: 2003; List A 2002; T20: 2004

BEST BATTING: 226* Sussex vs Worcestershire, Worcester, 2015
BEST BOWLING: 5-65 Sussex vs Derbyshire, Derby, 2010
COUNTY CAP: 2007

FAMILY TIES? My brother Ashley was a pro at Leicestershire
STRANGEST THING SEEN IN A GAME? Insects stop play during a match between England and South Africa
BEST MOMENT IN CRICKET? Winning the World T20 with England. Scoring a T20 hundred for Melbourne Stars against Melbourne Renegades in front of 85,000 spectators at the MCG
SUPERSTITIONS? Do not mess with Mother Cricket
BEST PLAYER IN COUNTY CRICKET? Ed Joyce (Sus)
MOST UNDERRATED PLAYER IN COUNTY CRICKET? Chris Nash (Sus)
TIP FOR THE TOP? Jofra Archer (Sus)
SURPRISING FACT? I help stick Chris Nash's wig on before each match
TWITTER: @lukewright204

Batting	Mat	Inns	NO	Runs	HS	Ave	SR	100	50	Ct	St
ODIs	50	39	4	707	52	20.20	86.21	0	2	18	0
T20Is	51	45	5	759	99*	18.97	137.00	0	4	14	0
First-class	122	185	22	6531	226*	40.06	65.11	16	33	51	0
List A	191	157	21	4243	143*	31.19		9	14	59	0
Twenty20	266	246	26	6296	153*	28.61	144.80	6	31	89	0

Bowling	Mat	Balls	Runs	Wkts	BBI	BBM	Ave	Econ	SR	5w	10
ODIs	50	1038	884	15	2/34	2/34	58.93	5.10	69.2	0	0
T20Is	51	330	465	18	2/24	2/24	25.83	8.45	18.3	0	0
First-class	122	8264	4862	120	5/65		40.51	3.53	68.8	3	0
List A	191	4752	4231	111	4/12	4/12	38.11	5.34	42.8	0	0
Twenty20	266	1799	2563	79	3/17	3/17	32.44	8.54	22.7	0	0

SAIF ZAIB

LHB / SLA / RO / WO

FULL NAME: Saif Ali Zaib
BORN: May 22, 1998, High Wycombe, Buckinghamshire
SQUAD NO: 5
HEIGHT: 5ft 9in
NICKNAME: Saify, Zaiby
EDUCATION: Royal Grammar School, High Wycombe
TEAMS: Northamptonshire
ROLE: Bowler
DEBUT: First-class: 2015; List A: 2014

BEST BATTING: 65* Northamptonshire vs Glamorgan, Swansea, 2016
BEST BOWLING: 5-148 Northamptonshire vs Leicestershire, Northampton, 2016

FAMILY TIES? Dad played Minor Counties
STRANGEST THING SEEN IN A GAME? A batsman arguing with the umpire about whether he was out – and winning the argument
BEST MOMENT IN CRICKET? Even though I didn't play, being part of the team which won the T20 Blast in 2016
BEST PLAYER IN COUNTY CRICKET? Ben Duckett (Nor)
MOST UNDERRATED PLAYER IN COUNTY CRICKET? Alex Wakely (Nor)
TIP FOR THE TOP? Adam Rossington (Nor)
CRICKETING HEROES? Brian Lara
NON-CRICKETING HEROES? Muhammad Ali
SURPRISING FACT? I can throw with both arms
DESERT ISLAND DISC? The Weekend – Starboy
FANTASY SLIP CORDON? Keeper: Muhammad Ali, 1st: Brian Lara, 2nd: David Warner, 3rd: Me
TWITTER: @zaib_05

Batting	Mat	Inns	NO	Runs	HS	Ave	SR	100	50	Ct	St
First-class	5	7	1	148	65*	24.66	46.98	0	1	3	0
List A	3	2	0	27	16	13.50	100.00	0	0	0	0

Bowling	Mat	Balls	Runs	Wkts	BBI	BBM	Ave	Econ	SR	5w	10
First-class	5	258	230	5	5/148	5/174	46.00	5.34	51.6	1	0
List A	3	18	30	0	-	-	-	10.00	-	0	0

ASHAR ZAIDI

LHB / SLA / RO / WO

FULL NAME: Syed Ashar Ahmed Zaidi
BORN: July 13, 1981, Karachi, Sind
SQUAD NO: 99
HEIGHT: 5ft 7in
NICKNAME: Ashi
TEAMS: Essex, Comilla Victorians, Federal Areas, Gazi Tank Cricketers, Islamabad, Khan Research Laboratories, Pakistan Telecommunication Company Limited, Rawalpindi, Sussex
ROLE: Allrounder
DEBUT: First-class: 1999; List A: 1999; T20: 2006

BEST BATTING: 202 Islamabad vs Sialkot, Sialkot, 2009
BEST BOWLING: 4-50 Islamabad vs Hyderabad, Hyderabad, 2009

BEST MOMENT IN CRICKET? Representing Pakistan U19 and Pakistan A, and playing county cricket in England
TIP FOR THE TOP? Harry Finch (Sus)
CRICKETING HEROES? Saeed Anwar, Brian Lara
IF YOU WEREN'T A CRICKETER? I'd be an air-force pilot
TWITTER: @Asharzaidi1981

Batting	Mat	Inns	NO	Runs	HS	Ave	SR	100	50	Ct	St
First-class	110	177	13	5986	202	36.50		12	29	82	0
List A	89	83	10	2540	141	34.79		4	11	31	0
Twenty20	48	38	9	830	59*	28.62	138.79	0	4	12	0

Bowling	Mat	Balls	Runs	Wkts	BBI	BBM	Ave	Econ	SR	5w	10
First-class	110	5873	2760	91	4/50		30.32	2.81	64.5	0	0
List A	89	2801	2004	67	4/39	4/39	29.91	4.29	41.8	0	0
Twenty20	48	666	746	31	4/11	4/11	24.06	6.72	21.4	0	0

THE BIGGEST TEST IS YET TO COME

REAL PEOPLE, REAL NEEDS

The pressure is on, and the whole world feels like it's against you...
only this time it's not a game. Sometimes the greatest challenges cricketers
face are not on the pitch. This is when they need our support more than ever.
With your help, the PCA Benevolent fund safeguards our players against
illness or at a time of crisis, while we provide the care and support that's
always been at the heart of the game.

For more information, or to get involved
Ian Thomas, *Head of Development and Welfare* **ithomas@thepca.co.uk**
Emily Lewis, *Head of Events & Fundraising* **elewis@thepca.co.uk**

thepca.co.uk/benevolent_fund
www.twitter.com/pcabenevolent

PCA
BENEVOLENT
FUND
Legacy Year Appeal

Supported by

ROYAL
LONDON

England
Women

FIXTURES

CAPTAIN: Heather Knight
HEAD COACH: Mark Robinson

2017 SUMMER FIXTURES

June 24
England vs India
ICC Women's World Cup
Derby

June 27
England vs Pakistan
ICC Women's World Cup
Leicester

July 2
England vs Sri Lanka
ICC Women's World Cup
Taunton

July 5
England vs South Africa
ICC Women's World Cup
Bristol

July 9
England vs Australia
ICC Women's World Cup
Bristol

July 12
England vs New Zealand
ICC Women's World Cup
Derby

July 15
England vs West Indies
ICC Women's World Cup
Bristol

TAMMY BEAUMONT

RHB / WK

FULL NAME: Tamsin Tilley Beaumont
BORN: March 11, 1991, Dover, Kent
SQUAD NO: 12
HEIGHT: 5ft 3in
NICKNAME: Tambo, Little Mitts
EDUCATION: Sir Roger Manwood's School;
Loughborough University
TEAMS: England, Kent, Surrey Stars,
Adelaide Strikers, Emeralds, Sapphires,
Diamonds
ROLE: Batsman
DEBUT: Test: 2013; ODI: 2009; T20I: 2009

BEST ODI BATTING: 168* England vs Pakistan, Taunton, 2016

WHAT FIRST GOT YOU INTO CRICKET? My older brother and dad used to play for Sandwich Town CC every weekend when I was growing up. I soon got bored of just watching
STRANGEST THING SEEN IN A GAME? We once had a horse stop play, as it galloped onto the square with its owner frantically running after it
BEST MOMENT IN CRICKET? Diving in to get my first ODI hundred at Worcester (I'm still relieved the fielder missed the stumps)
HOW WOULD YOUR TEAM-MATES DESCRIBE YOU IN THREE WORDS? Lively, clumsy, badger
BEST PLAYER IN COUNTY CRICKET? Heather Knight (Ber)
MOST UNDERRATED PLAYER IN COUNTY CRICKET? Beth Langston (Yor)
TIP FOR THE TOP? Alice Davidson-Richards (Ken)
CRICKETING HEROES? Justin Langer, Graham Thorpe
NON-CRICKETING HEROES? My late grandad – even at 80 years old he would still take my brother and I down the park and throw balls to us for hours on end
IF YOU WEREN'T A CRICKETER? I'd be a chemist
SURPRISING FACT? I once won a national school gymnastics competition
TWITTER: @Tammy_Beaumont

Batting	Mat	Inns	NO	Runs	HS	Ave	SR	100	50	Ct	St
Tests	2	3	0	25	12	8.33	35.71	0	0	1	0
ODIs	35	28	5	818	168*	35.56	68.16	2	3	9	4
T20Is	44	30	4	439	82	16.88	95.02	0	2	7	4

Bowling	Mat	Balls	Runs	Wkts	BBI	BBM	Ave	Econ	SR	5w	10
Tests	2	-	-	-	-	-	-	-	-	-	-
ODIs	35	-	-	-	-	-	-	-	-	-	-
T20Is	44	-	-	-	-	-	-	-	-	-	-

KATHERINE BRUNT

RHB / RFM

FULL NAME: Katherine Helen Brunt
BORN: July 2, 1985, Barnsley
SQUAD NO: 26
HEIGHT: 5ft 5in
NICKNAME: Brunty, Nunny
EDUCATION: Penistone Grammar School
TEAMS: England, Yorkshire, Yorkshire Diamonds, Braves, Knight Riders, Perth Scorchers, Sapphires
ROLE: Bowler
DEBUT: Test: 2004; ODI: 2005; T20I: 2005

BEST ODI BATTING: 31 England vs Australia, Worcester, 2015
BEST ODI BOWLING: 5-18 England vs Australia, Wormsley, 2011

WHAT FIRST GOT YOU INTO CRICKET? My brother and my father. My brother Daniel is nearly four years older than me and he would make me watch cricket videos of Darren Gough and Curtly Ambrose and then bowl at him outside in the garden
FAMILY TIES? My brother Daniel played to a good standard in the Yorkshire leagues and my dad played in the Barnsley seconds
BEST MOMENT IN CRICKET? Winning the Ashes back in 2005
BEST PLAYER IN COUNTY CRICKET? Tammy Beaumont (Ken), Nat Sciver (Sur). Previously there were always one or two people who were above the rest but there are a lot more competing for that position now
MOST UNDERRATED PLAYER IN COUNTY CRICKET? Holly Armitage (Yor) – a hard-hitting top-order batsman and a decent leg-spinner. She's also got buckets for hands
TIP FOR THE TOP? Emma Lamb (Lan), Fran Wilson (Mid), Georgia Hennessy (War)
CRICKETING HEROES? Darren Gough, Curtly Ambrose, Courtney Walsh, Brian Lara
SURPRISING FACT? I seem like a nut case on the field but off it I'm actually a softy
TWITTER: @KBrunt26

Batting	Mat	Inns	NO	Runs	HS	Ave	SR	100	50	Ct	St
Tests	10	13	4	155	52	17.22	30.87	0	1	3	0
ODIs	94	44	12	376	31	11.75	77.52	0	0	24	0
T20Is	57	28	14	197	35	14.07	94.71	0	0	18	0

Bowling	Mat	Balls	Runs	Wkts	BBI	BBM	Ave	Econ	SR	5w	10
Tests	10	1950	808	38	6/69	9/111	21.26	2.48	51.3	2	0
ODIs	94	4685	2624	120	5/18	5/18	21.86	3.36	39.0	4	0
T20Is	57	1248	1042	51	3/6	3/6	20.43	5.00	24.4	0	0

KATE CROSS RHB / RMF

FULL NAME: Kathryn Laura Cross
BORN: October 3, 1991, Manchester
SQUAD NO: 16
HEIGHT: 5ft 8in
NICKNAME: Crossy, Sunny
EDUCATION: Bury Grammar School; University of Leeds
TEAMS: England, Lancashire, Lancashire Thunder, Brisbane Heat, Emeralds, Sapphires
ROLE: Bowler
DEBUT: Test: 2014; ODI: 2013; T20I: 2013

BEST ODI BATTING: 4* England vs India, Scarborough, 2014
BEST ODI BOWLING: 5-24 England vs New Zealand, Lincoln, 2015

FAMILY TIES? My uncle was the U11 coach at Heywood CC, where I first played boys' cricket. My brother had a year on the books at Lancashire and my sister played for Lancashire
STRANGEST THING SEEN IN A GAME? Alex Hartley dancing
BEST MOMENT IN CRICKET? Winning the Ashes at Hobart in 2014
HOW WOULD YOUR TEAM-MATES DESCRIBE YOU IN THREE WORDS? Sarcastic, sleepy, northern
BEST PLAYER IN COUNTY CRICKET? Natalie Sciver (Sur)
MOST UNDERRATED PLAYER IN COUNTY CRICKET? Amy Jones (War)
TIP FOR THE TOP? Sophie Ecclestone, Emma Lamb (both Lan)
CRICKETING HEROES? Andrew Flintoff – loved his fiery temperament. And he's a Lanky
IF YOU WEREN'T A CRICKETER? My degree is in Psychology but I would love to branch out into Criminal Psychology or Forensics
SURPRISING FACT? I can make my tongue look like a four-leaf clover
UNUSUAL OBJECT AT HOME? A few lucky pigs
TWITTER: @katecross16

Batting	Mat	Inns	NO	Runs	HS	Ave	SR	100	50	Ct	St
Tests	3	6	3	15	4*	5.00	24.19	0	0	0	0
ODIs	14	4	2	7	4*	3.50	33.33	0	0	3	0
T20Is	4	-	-	-	-	-	-	-	-	0	0

Bowling	Mat	Balls	Runs	Wkts	BBI	BBM	Ave	Econ	SR	5w	10
Tests	3	554	209	14	3/29	6/70	14.92	2.26	39.5	0	0
ODIs	14	636	476	16	5/24	5/24	29.75	4.49	39.7	1	0
T20Is	4	72	83	3	2/27	2/27	27.66	6.91	24.0	0	0

SOPHIE ECCLESTONE

RHB / SLA

ENGLAND WOMEN

FULL NAME: Sophie Ecclestone
BORN: May 6, 1999, Chester, Cheshire
SQUAD NO: 71
HEIGHT: 5ft 10in
NICKNAME: Eccles
EDUCATION: Helsby High School
TEAMS: England, Lancashire, Lancashire Thunder, Cheshire
ROLE: Bowler
DEBUT: ODI: 2016; T20I: 2016

BEST ODI BATTING: 3 England vs West Indies, Florence Hall, 2016
BEST ODI BOWLING: 2-28 England vs West Indies, Florence Hall, 2016

WHAT FIRST GOT YOU INTO CRICKET? My brother and my dad played at my local club and they taught me all I know
FAMILY TIES? I play in the same team as my brother on Saturdays
BEST MOMENT IN CRICKET? Receiving my T20 England cap and then getting my first international wicket
HOW WOULD YOUR TEAM-MATES DESCRIBE YOU IN THREE WORDS? Dipsy and stupid
MOST UNDERRATED PLAYER IN COUNTY CRICKET? Rebecca Duckworth (Lan) – top-order bat and can bowl off-spin. Definitely one for the future
TIP FOR THE TOP? Emma Lamb (Lan) – she had a class 2016 season and was brilliant in the T20 Super League
CRICKETING HEROES? James Anderson, Andrew Flintoff
NON-CRICKETING HEROES? My brother James. I always looked up to him and followed him round saying I'm his sister
SURPRISING FACT? I have been known to go clay-pigeon shooting in my spare time
UNUSUAL OBJECT AT HOME? My mum still has my brownie outfit with my sash and all my badges on it
TWITTER: @sophecc223

Batting	Mat	Inns	NO	Runs	HS	Ave	SR	100	50	Ct	St
ODIs	2	2	0	3	3	1.50	23.07	0	0	0	0
T20Is	2	-	-	-	-	-	-	-	-	0	0

Bowling	Mat	Balls	Runs	Wkts	BBI	BBM	Ave	Econ	SR	5w	10
ODIs	2	84	48	3	2/28	2/28	16.00	3.42	28.0	0	0
T20Is	2	48	47	3	2/26	2/26	15.66	5.87	16.0	0	0

GEORGIA ELWISS

RHB / RMF

FULL NAME: Georgia Amanda Elwiss
BORN: May 31, 1991, Wolverhampton
SQUAD NO: 34
HEIGHT: 5ft 7in
NICKNAME: G, George, G Dog
EDUCATION: Wolverhampton Girls' High School; Loughborough University
TEAMS: England, Sussex, Loughborough Lightning, Diamonds, Emeralds, Knight Riders, Rubies, Sapphires, Staffordshire
ROLE: Allrounder
DEBUT: Test: 2015; ODI: 2011; T20I: 2011

BEST ODI BATTING: 77 England vs Pakistan, Taunton, 2016
BEST ODI BOWLING: 3-17 England vs India, Wormsley, 2012

WHAT FIRST GOT YOU INTO CRICKET? My older brother used to make me bowl at him in the back garden
STRANGEST THING SEEN IN A GAME? Donkey stops play
BEST MOMENT IN CRICKET? The Pakistan home series in 2016 was very special – we had a lot to prove as a young team, so to play the way we did was amazing
HOW WOULD YOUR TEAM-MATES DESCRIBE YOU IN THREE WORDS? Happy, positive, loving
BEST PLAYER IN COUNTY CRICKET? Natalie Sciver (Sur)
MOST UNDERRATED PLAYER IN COUNTY CRICKET? Sonia Odedra (Not)
TIP FOR THE TOP? Georgia Adams (Sus), Sophie Ecclestone (Lan)
CRICKETING HEROES? I always used to look up to Allan Donald and Lucy Pearson. They were both incredible fast bowlers
SURPRISING FACT? I actually bowl quicker with my left arm
UNUSUAL OBJECT AT HOME? A model tuk-tuk
TWITTER: @gelwiss

Batting	Mat	Inns	NO	Runs	HS	Ave	SR	100	50	Ct	St
Tests	1	2	0	63	46	31.50	36.41	0	0	0	0
ODIs	25	17	3	308	77	22.00	78.77	0	2	7	0
T20Is	13	4	2	24	18	12.00	100.00	0	0	3	0

Bowling	Mat	Balls	Runs	Wkts	BBI	BBM	Ave	Econ	SR	5w	10
Tests	1	18	11	0	-	-	-	3.66	-	0	0
ODIs	25	688	389	16	3/17	3/17	24.31	3.39	43.0	0	0
T20Is	13	151	139	8	2/9	2/9	17.37	5.52	18.8	0	0

TASH FARRANT

LHB / LMF

FULL NAME: Natasha Eleni Farrant
BORN: May 29, 1996, Athens, Greece
SQUAD NO: 53
HEIGHT: 5ft 5in
NICKNAME: Faz
EDUCATION: Sevenoaks School; Loughborough University
TEAMS: England, Kent, Southern Vipers, Sapphires, Western Australia
ROLE: Bowler
DEBUT: ODI: 2013; T20I: 2013

BEST ODI BATTING: 1* England vs West Indies, Port of Spain, 2013
BEST ODI BOWLING: 1-14 England vs West Indies, Port of Spain, 2013

WHAT FIRST GOT YOU INTO CRICKET? Playing in the garden with my two brothers. Then playing for Kent U11 when I was eight
BEST MOMENT IN CRICKET? Running out West Indies' Stafanie Taylor off my own bowling and being mauled by most of the team
SUPERSTITIONS? I have to touch the floor when walking back to my mark, and throw the ball up twice
HOW WOULD YOUR TEAM-MATES DESCRIBE YOU IN THREE WORDS? Joker, diva, posh
BEST PLAYER IN COUNTY CRICKET? Heather Knight (Ber)
MOST UNDERRATED PLAYER IN COUNTY CRICKET? Carla Rudd (Ber)
TIP FOR THE TOP? Alice Davidson-Richards (Ken), Linsey Smith (Ber)
CRICKETING HEROES? Wasim Akram, Charlotte Edwards
NON-CRICKETING HEROES? Jessica Ennis-Hill
IF YOU WEREN'T A CRICKETER? I'd be a hockey player
SURPRISING FACT? I've lived in four countries (Greece, Italy, Singapore, England)
UNUSUAL OBJECT AT HOME? A didgeridoo
DESERT ISLAND DISC? The Weeknd – Starboy
TWITTER: @tashfarrant

Batting	Mat	Inns	NO	Runs	HS	Ave	SR	100	50	Ct	St
ODIs	1	1	1	1	1*	-	12.50	0	0	0	0
T20Is	9	1	1	1	1*	-	100.00	0	0	1	0

Bowling	Mat	Balls	Runs	Wkts	BBI	BBM	Ave	Econ	SR	5w	10
ODIs	1	42	14	1	1/14	1/14	14.00	2.00	42.0	0	0
T20Is	9	209	174	6	2/15	2/15	29.00	4.99	34.8	0	0

JENNY GUNN RHB / RMF

FULL NAME: Jennifer Louise Gunn
BORN: May 9, 1986, Nottingham
SQUAD NO: 24
HEIGHT: 5ft 10in
NICKNAME: Chuckie
EDUCATION: Rushcliffe School; South Nottingham College
TEAMS: England, Warwickshire, Yorkshire Diamonds, Diamonds, Emeralds, Knight Riders, Nottinghamshire, Rubies, South Australia, Super Strikers, Western Australia
ROLE: Allrounder
DEBUT: Test: 2004; ODI: 2004; T20I: 2004

BEST ODI BATTING: 73 England vs New Zealand, Taunton, 2007
BEST ODI BOWLING: 5-22 England vs Pakistan, Louth, 2013

WHAT FIRST GOT YOU INTO CRICKET? My family played so I wanted to give it a go
FAMILY TIES? Dad was a professional footballer and, no, I'm not related to the Gunns that played for Notts years ago
BEST MOMENT IN CRICKET? Winning the Ashes in Australia or the World Cup in 2009
HOW WOULD YOUR TEAM-MATES DESCRIBE YOU IN THREE WORDS? Laid-back, approachable, talkative
BEST PLAYER IN COUNTY CRICKET? Natalie Sciver (Sur)
MOST UNDERRATED PLAYER IN COUNTY CRICKET? Becky Grundy (War)
TIP FOR THE TOP? Amy Jones (War)
NON-CRICKETING HEROES? I looked up to Alan Shearer as I wanted to play football for England
IF YOU WEREN'T A CRICKETER? Singing and dancing on the West End, or a chef
DESERT ISLAND DISC? Best of Motown
TWITTER: @GunnJenny

Batting	Mat	Inns	NO	Runs	HS	Ave	SR	100	50	Ct	St
Tests	11	19	2	391	62*	23.00	30.38	0	1	6	0
ODIs	132	100	25	1467	73	19.56	56.51	0	5	45	0
T20Is	95	62	16	658	69	14.30	100.61	0	1	55	0

Bowling	Mat	Balls	Runs	Wkts	BBI	BBM	Ave	Econ	SR	5w	10
Tests	11	2189	645	29	5/19	5/59	22.24	1.76	75.4	1	0
ODIs	132	5396	3397	123	5/22	5/22	27.61	3.77	43.8	2	0
T20Is	95	1217	1240	66	5/18	5/18	18.78	6.11	18.4	1	0

ALEX HARTLEY

RHB / SLA

FULL NAME: Alexandra Hartley
BORN: September 26, 1993, Blackburn, Lancashire
SQUAD NO: 65
HEIGHT: 5ft 4in
EDUCATION: Ribbledale High School; Loughborough College
TEAMS: England, Middlesex, Surrey Stars, Emeralds, Lancashire, Rubies
ROLE: Bowler
DEBUT: ODI: 2016; T20I: 2016

BEST ODI BATTING: 2* England vs West Indies, Florence Hall, 2016
BEST ODI BOWLING: 4-24 England vs West Indies, Kingston, 2016

WHAT FIRST GOT YOU INTO CRICKET? The lads on my estate all started going up to the local club on a Friday evening so I asked my mum if I could join them as there was no one to play football with after school on a Friday

STRANGEST THING SEEN IN A GAME? Cows on the pitch

HOW WOULD YOUR TEAM-MATES DESCRIBE YOU IN THREE WORDS? Confident, lively, fighter

BEST PLAYER IN COUNTY CRICKET? Heather Knight (Ber) – I'd be in trouble if I said anyone else, right?

MOST UNDERRATED PLAYER IN COUNTY CRICKET? Sophia Dunkley (Mid)

TIP FOR THE TOP? Emma Lamb (Lan)

CRICKETING HEROES? Monty Panesar

IF YOU WEREN'T A CRICKETER? I'd most likely be working for my dad as a receptionist

SURPRISING FACT? I was an extra on Made In Chelsea

UNUSUAL OBJECT AT HOME? A life-size Buddha. I've no idea why it's there

FANTASY SLIP CORDON? Keeper: Adele, 1st: Justin Bieber, 2nd: James Corden, 3rd: Me, Gully: Tom Hardy

TWITTER: @alexhartley93

Batting	Mat	Inns	NO	Runs	HS	Ave	SR	100	50	Ct	St
ODIs	9	5	5	3	2*	-	16.66	0	0	1	0
T20Is	1	-	-	-	-	-	-	-	-	0	0

Bowling	Mat	Balls	Runs	Wkts	BBI	BBM	Ave	Econ	SR	5w	10
ODIs	9	456	276	17	4/24	4/24	16.23	3.63	26.8	0	0
T20Is	1	18	19	2	2/19	2/19	9.50	6.33	9.0	0	0

DANIELLE HAZELL RHB / OB

FULL NAME: Danielle Hazell
BORN: May 13, 1988, Durham
SQUAD NO: 17
HEIGHT: 5ft 3in
NICKNAME: Pet
EDUCATION: Deerness Valley School
TEAMS: England, Yorkshire, Yorkshire Diamonds, Diamonds, Durham, Emeralds, Melbourne Stars, Sapphires
ROLE: Bowler
DEBUT: Test: 2011; ODI: 2009; T20I: 2009

ENGLAND WOMEN

BEST ODI BATTING: 45 England vs Sri Lanka, Colombo, 2016
BEST ODI BOWLING: 3-21 England vs Sri Lanka, Colombo, 2016

FAMILY TIES? Dad coaches at Durham City and my mum does the scoring for the first team
BEST MOMENT IN CRICKET? Winning the Ashes in 2013 and 2014
HOW WOULD YOUR TEAM-MATES DESCRIBE YOU IN THREE WORDS? Competitive, northern, fiery
BEST PLAYER IN COUNTY CRICKET? Natalie Sciver (Sur)
MOST UNDERRATED PLAYER IN COUNTY CRICKET? Katie Thompson (Yor)
TIP FOR THE TOP? Emma Lamb (Lan)
CRICKETING HEROES? Ricky Ponting
NON-CRICKETING HEROES? Rebel Wilson – she is very funny
IF YOU WEREN'T A CRICKETER? I'd be a lollipop lady
SURPRISING FACT? I have a dog called Maverick
DESERT ISLAND DISC? Savage Garden – Greatest Hits
FANTASY SLIP CORDON? Keeper: Superman, 1st: Rebel Wilson, 2nd: The Queen, 3rd: Batman, Gully: Bobby Robson
TWITTER: @dhazell17

Batting	Mat	Inns	NO	Runs	HS	Ave	SR	100	50	Ct	St
Tests	3	5	1	28	15	7.00	17.17	0	0	1	0
ODIs	45	23	5	309	45	17.16	85.83	0	0	8	0
T20Is	70	25	8	161	18*	9.47	84.73	0	0	10	0

Bowling	Mat	Balls	Runs	Wkts	BBI	BBM	Ave	Econ	SR	5w	10
Tests	3	390	204	2	2/32	2/52	102.00	3.13	195.0	0	0
ODIs	45	2169	1367	47	3/21	3/21	29.08	3.78	46.1	0	0
T20Is	70	1596	1384	73	4/12	4/12	18.95	5.20	21.8	0	0

AMY JONES   RHB / WK

FULL NAME: Amy Ellen Jones
BORN: June 13, 1993, Solihull, Warwickshire
SQUAD NO: 40
HEIGHT: 5ft 9in
NICKNAME: Jonesy
EDUCATION: John Willmott School;
Loughborough College
TEAMS: England, Warwickshire,
Loughborough Lightning, Diamonds,
Emeralds, Rubies, Sydney Sixers
ROLE: Wicketkeeper/batsman
DEBUT: ODI: 2013; T20I: 2013

BEST ODI BATTING: 41 England vs Sri Lanka, Mumbai, 2013

WHAT FIRST GOT YOU INTO CRICKET? I played in a local football team and a lot of the boys played cricket so I went along with them to Walmley CC
FAMILY TIES? Only my younger sister has ever played – she played for Warwickshire U13 but doesn't play anymore. My mum played two games for Walmley when we were short
BEST MOMENT IN CRICKET? Retaining the Ashes in Australia at Hobart at the start of 2015
HOW WOULD YOUR TEAM-MATES DESCRIBE YOU IN THREE WORDS? Laid-back, friendly, competitive
BEST PLAYER IN COUNTY CRICKET? Heather Knight (Ber)
TIP FOR THE TOP? Evelyn Jones (Sta), Thea Brookes (Wor), Paige Scholfield (Sus) – they all performed well in the T20 Super League for Loughborough Lightning so 2017 could be a big year for them
CRICKETING HEROES? AB de Villiers – he's such an exciting player to watch
IF YOU WEREN'T A CRICKETER? I'd be trying to play football for England
SURPRISING FACT? I used to play football for Aston Villa until I was 16
UNUSUAL OBJECT AT HOME? Juggling balls – a brilliant Secret Santa present from Jenny Gunn. Keeps me entertained whenever I'm bored
DESERT ISLAND DISC? James Bay – Chaos And The Calm
TWITTER: @amyjones313

Batting	Mat	Inns	NO	Runs	HS	Ave	SR	100	50	Ct	St
ODIs	20	14	2	185	41	15.41	68.51	0	0	12	5
T20Is	15	9	0	60	14	6.66	89.55	0	0	7	1
Bowling	Mat	Balls	Runs	Wkts	BBI	BBM	Ave	Econ	SR	5w	10
ODIs	20	-	-	-	-	-	-	-	-	-	-
T20Is	15	-	-	-	-	-	-	-	-	-	-

HEATHER KNIGHT   RHB / OB

FULL NAME: Heather Clare Knight
BORN: December 26, 1990, Plymouth
SQUAD NO: 5
HEIGHT: 5ft 7in
NICKNAME: Trev
EDUCATION: Plymstock School; Cardiff University
TEAMS: England, Berkshire, Western Storm, Devon, Emeralds, Hobart Hurricanes, Rubies, Sapphires, Tasmania
ROLE: Allrounder
DEBUT: Test: 2011; ODI: 2010; T20I: 2010

ENGLAND WOMEN

BEST ODI BATTING: 79 England vs New Zealand, Mount Maunganui, 2015
BEST ODI BOWLING: 5-26 England vs Pakistan, Leicester, 2016

WHAT FIRST GOT YOU INTO CRICKET? My brother – I always had to bat because if I bowled he would whack me over the fence and we'd lose the ball
FAMILY TIES? My brother played for Devon
STRANGEST THING SEEN IN A GAME? Fran Wilson's bowling action
BEST MOMENT IN CRICKET? Scoring my first Test hundred for England
HOW WOULD YOUR TEAM-MATES DESCRIBE YOU IN THREE WORDS? Sarcastic, energetic, competitive
BEST PLAYER IN COUNTY CRICKET? Natalie Sciver (Sur)
MOST UNDERRATED PLAYER IN COUNTY CRICKET? Carla Rudd (Ber)
TIP FOR THE TOP? Lauren Bell (Ber), Hannah Jones (Sur)
CRICKETING HEROES? Michael Atherton – I loved watching him grind out an innings
NON-CRICKETING HEROES? Denise Lewis – she always competed with a smile on her face
SURPRISING FACT? I've got a degree in Biomedical Science
UNUSUAL OBJECT AT HOME? A yo-yo
TWITTER: @heatherknight55

Batting	Mat	Inns	NO	Runs	HS	Ave	SR	100	50	Ct	St
Tests	5	10	0	217	157	21.70	40.63	1	0	6	0
ODIs	66	62	14	1564	79	32.58	64.49	0	11	26	0
T20Is	36	31	5	363	30	13.96	103.41	0	0	11	0

Bowling	Mat	Balls	Runs	Wkts	BBI	BBM	Ave	Econ	SR	5w	10
Tests	5	131	59	2	1/7	1/7	29.50	2.70	65.5	0	0
ODIs	66	1091	758	35	5/26	5/26	21.65	4.16	31.1	1	0
T20Is	36	291	259	12	3/10	3/10	21.58	5.34	24.2	0	0

EMMA LAMB
RHB / RM

FULL NAME: Emma Louise Lamb
BORN: December 16, 1997, Preston, Lancashire
SQUAD NO: 67
HEIGHT: 5ft 7in
NICKNAME: Lamby
EDUCATION: Cardinal Newman College; Edge Hill University
TEAMS: Lancashire, Lancashire Thunder
ROLE: Batsman
DEBUT: Yet to make England debut

FAMILY TIES? My brother Danny plays for Lancashire
STRANGEST THING SEEN IN A GAME? Ball hits bird
BEST MOMENT IN CRICKET? Scoring 150 for Lancashire at Scarborough
HOW WOULD YOUR TEAM-MATES DESCRIBE YOU IN THREE WORDS? Blonde, humorous, team-player
BEST PLAYER IN COUNTY CRICKET? Tammy Beaumont (Ken)
TIP FOR THE TOP? Sophia Dunkley (Mid)
CRICKETING HEROES? Andrew Flintoff, Kevin Pietersen
NON-CRICKETING HEROES? Alan Sugar, Kate Middleton
IF YOU WEREN'T A CRICKETER? I'd be at university studying Sport and Exercise Science
SURPRISING FACT? I used to play county-level netball and badminton. I like going to Blackburn Rovers, mainly to eat the food in the Premier Suit
UNUSUAL OBJECT AT HOME? A buddha
DESERT ISLAND DISC? Gorillaz – Feel Good Inc
FANTASY SLIP CORDON? Keeper: Conor McGregor, 1st: Matt Lucas, 2nd: The Wealdstone Raider, 3rd: James Corden, Gully: Jo Brand
TWITTER: @EmmaLamb236

BETH LANGSTON

RHB / RFM

FULL NAME: Bethany Alicia Langston
BORN: September 6, 1992, Harold Wood, Essex
SQUAD NO: 42
HEIGHT: 5ft 7in
NICKNAME: Langers
EDUCATION: Hall Mead School;
Coopers' Company and Coborn School;
Loughborough University
TEAMS: England, Yorkshire, Loughborough Lightning, Diamonds, Emeralds, Essex, Otago
ROLE: Bowler
DEBUT: ODI: 2016; T20I: 2013

BEST ODI BATTING: 21 England vs Sri Lanka, Colombo, 2016
BEST ODI BOWLING: 1-23 England vs Sri Lanka, Colombo, 2016

STRANGEST THING SEEN IN A GAME? Not being able to start my run-up for a ball a number of times because a whole load of crows wouldn't get out of the way
BEST MOMENT IN CRICKET? Making my ODI debut with all four of my house-mates playing in the same game
HOW WOULD YOUR TEAM-MATES DESCRIBE YOU IN THREE WORDS? Hard-working, shy, goofy
BEST PLAYER IN COUNTY CRICKET? Katherine Brunt (Yor)
MOST UNDERRATED PLAYER IN COUNTY CRICKET? Sonia Odedra (Not)
TIP FOR THE TOP? Sophia Dunkley (Mid)
CRICKETING HEROES? I admire James Anderson and the variation and control he has with both the new and old ball
NON-CRICKETING HEROES? JK Rowling
IF YOU WEREN'T A CRICKETER? I would be training to be a zookeeper
SURPRISING FACT? I have a large appetite and occasionally take part in eating challenges
UNUSUAL OBJECT AT HOME? A pair of onion-chopping glasses that wouldn't look out of place on Dame Edna Everage
TWITTER: @B_Langers92

Batting	Mat	Inns	NO	Runs	HS	Ave	SR	100	50	Ct	St
ODIs	4	2	1	21	21	21.00	100.00	0	0	2	0
T20Is	2	-	-	-	-	-	-	-	-	1	0

Bowling	Mat	Balls	Runs	Wkts	BBI	BBM	Ave	Econ	SR	5w	10
ODIs	4	186	94	2	1/23	1/23	47.00	3.03	93.0	0	0
T20Is	2	48	44	1	1/16	1/16	44.00	5.50	48.0	0	0

LAURA MARSH

RHB / OB

FULL NAME: Laura Alexandra Marsh
BORN: December 5, 1986, Pembury, Kent
SQUAD NO: 7
HEIGHT: 5ft 5in
NICKNAME: Boggy
EDUCATION: Brighton College; Loughborough University
TEAMS: England, Kent, Surrey Stars, Braves, Emeralds, New South Wales, Otago, Rubies, Sapphires, Sussex, Sydney Sixers
ROLE: Bowler
DEBUT: Test: 2006; ODI: 2006; T20I: 2007

BEST ODI BATTING: 67 England vs Ireland, Kibworth, 2010
BEST ODI BOWLING: 5-15 England vs Pakistan, Sydney, 2009

STRANGEST THING SEEN IN A GAME? An ice-cream van come onto the pitch in the West Indies in 2016
BEST MOMENT IN CRICKET? Winning the T20 and 50-over World Cups in 2009
HOW WOULD YOUR TEAM-MATES DESCRIBE YOU IN THREE WORDS? Quiet, cheeky, determined
BEST PLAYER IN COUNTY CRICKET? Sarah Bartlett (Her)
TIP FOR THE TOP? Bryony Smith (Sur)
CRICKETING HEROES? Jonty Rhodes, AB de Villiers, Daniel Vettori
NON-CRICKETING HEROES? Andy Murray
SURPRISING FACT? I was national U13 javelin champion
UNUSUAL OBJECT AT HOME? A workbench and tools – I like to make things like wine racks and coffee tables when I have time
FANTASY SLIP CORDON? Keeper: AB de Villiers, 1st: Me, 2nd: Michael McIntyre, 3rd: Dan Carter, Gully: Andy Murray
TWITTER: @lauramarsh7

Batting	Mat	Inns	NO	Runs	HS	Ave	SR	100	50	Ct	St
Tests	7	10	0	110	55	11.00	21.48	0	1	4	0
ODIs	83	49	8	550	67	13.41	64.70	0	1	19	0
T20Is	60	51	6	729	54	16.20	99.31	0	1	6	0

Bowling	Mat	Balls	Runs	Wkts	BBI	BBM	Ave	Econ	SR	5w	10
Tests	7	1499	570	17	3/44	4/83	33.52	2.28	88.1	0	0
ODIs	83	4282	2706	103	5/15	5/15	26.27	3.79	41.5	1	0
T20Is	60	1347	1169	60	3/12	3/12	19.48	5.20	22.4	0	0

NATALIE SCIVER

RHB / RM

FULL NAME: Natalie Ruth Sciver
BORN: August 20, 1992, Tokyo, Japan
SQUAD NO: 39
HEIGHT: 5ft 10in
NICKNAME: Sciv
EDUCATION: Epsom College; Loughborough University
TEAMS: England, Surrey, Surrey Stars, Emeralds, Melbourne Stars, Rubies
ROLE: Allrounder
DEBUT: Test: 2014; ODI: 2013; T20I: 2013

BEST ODI BATTING: 80 England vs Pakistan, Worcester, 2016
BEST ODI BOWLING: 3-19 England vs West Indies, Port of Spain, 2013

BEST MOMENT IN CRICKET? Winning the Ashes in 2013 in England and running on to the pitch to celebrate
HOW WOULD YOUR TEAM-MATES DESCRIBE YOU IN THREE WORDS? Quiet, fun, hard-working
BEST PLAYER IN COUNTY CRICKET? Heather Knight (Ber)
MOST UNDERRATED PLAYER IN COUNTY CRICKET? Sophia Dunkley (Mid)
TIP FOR THE TOP? Emma Lamb (Lan)
CRICKETING HEROES? Andrew Flintoff – he was an allrounder like me
NON-CRICKETING HEROES? Serena Williams, Jessica Ennis-Hill
IF YOU WEREN'T A CRICKETER? I'd pursue a career in dance
UNUSUAL OBJECT AT HOME? Katherine Brunt's dog Bailey
DESERT ISLAND DISC? Frank Ocean – Channel Orange
FANTASY SLIP CORDON? Keeper: Miranda, 1st: Rebel Wilson, 2nd: Hugh Grant, 3rd: Me, Gully: Sonny Bill Williams
TWITTER: @natsciver

Batting	Mat	Inns	NO	Runs	HS	Ave	SR	100	50	Ct	St
Tests	3	6	0	122	49	20.33	30.50	0	0	1	0
ODIs	32	26	7	837	80	44.05	102.19	0	8	14	0
T20Is	37	34	7	470	47	17.40	96.31	0	0	18	0

Bowling	Mat	Balls	Runs	Wkts	BBI	BBM	Ave	Econ	SR	5w	10
Tests	3	149	71	1	1/30	1/30	71.00	2.85	149.0	0	0
ODIs	32	736	516	23	3/19	3/19	22.43	4.20	32.0	0	0
T20Is	37	551	585	35	4/15	4/15	16.71	6.37	15.7	0	0

ANYA SHRUBSOLE RHB / RFM

FULL NAME: Anya Shrubsole
BORN: December 7, 1991, Bath
SQUAD NO: 41
HEIGHT: 5ft 10in
NICKNAME: Hoof
EDUCATION: Hayesfield School;
Loughborough University
TEAMS: England, Somerset, Western Storm,
Braves, Emeralds, Perth Scorchers, Rubies
ROLE: Bowler
DEBUT: Test: 2013; ODI: 2008; T20I: 2008

BEST ODI BATTING: 29 England vs New Zealand, Mount Maunganui, 2015
BEST ODI BOWLING: 5-17 England vs South Africa, Cuttack, 2013

FAMILY TIES? Dad played for Bath CC for many years and a bit of Minor Counties
STRANGEST THING SEEN IN A GAME? Two streakers running round the outfield at Hove during an Ashes match
BEST MOMENT IN CRICKET? Winning an Ashes Test at the WACA – best game I've played in
HOW WOULD YOUR TEAM-MATES DESCRIBE YOU IN THREE WORDS? Intelligent, logical, reliable
BEST PLAYER IN COUNTY CRICKET? Alex Hartley (Mid)
MOST UNDERRATED PLAYER IN COUNTY CRICKET? Beth Morgan (Mid)
TIP FOR THE TOP? Beth Langston (Yor)
CRICKETING HEROES? Any of the old West Indies quicks but particularly Michael Holding
NON-CRICKETING HEROES? Karen Brady – to achieve what she has in a male-dominated environment is amazing
SURPRISING FACT? I have a cat that I trained to sit and do paw high-fives like a dog would
UNUSUAL OBJECT AT HOME? A bright green toy horse that was won at the local fair
TWITTER: @Anya_shrubsole

Batting	Mat	Inns	NO	Runs	HS	Ave	SR	100	50	Ct	St
Tests	4	7	0	31	14	4.42	19.87	0	0	1	0
ODIs	37	12	5	109	29	15.57	96.46	0	0	11	0
T20Is	47	10	5	33	10*	6.60	97.05	0	0	14	0

Bowling	Mat	Balls	Runs	Wkts	BBI	BBM	Ave	Econ	SR	5w	10
Tests	4	966	360	16	4/51	7/99	22.50	2.23	60.3	0	0
ODIs	37	1781	1231	48	5/17	5/17	25.64	4.14	37.1	1	0
T20Is	47	957	870	68	5/11	5/11	12.79	5.45	14.0	1	0

SARAH TAYLOR   RHB / WK

FULL NAME: Sarah Jane Taylor
BORN: May 20, 1989, London
SQUAD NO: 17
HEIGHT: 5ft 8in
NICKNAME: Sezzie, Squirt, Staylor
EDUCATION: St Bede's School; Brighton College
TEAMS: England, Sussex, Adelaide Strikers, Emeralds, Rubies, South Australia, Super Strikers, Wellington
ROLE: Wicketkeeper/batsman
DEBUT: Test: 2006; ODI: 2006; T20I: 2006

BEST ODI BATTING: 129 England vs South Africa, Lord's, 2008

WHAT FIRST GOT YOU INTO CRICKET? It was an after-school club at my primary school and, seeing as I used to play football at lunch with the boys, I was convinced to give cricket a go
FAMILY TIES? None. My dad caught a ball once. Apparently
STRANGEST THING SEEN IN A GAME? An old woman walking straight across the middle of the field with her dog. She had no clue we were playing
BEST MOMENT IN CRICKET? Watching Charlotte Edwards hit the winning runs at Hobart to win the Ashes. And keeping next to Mark Cosgrove at first slip for Northern Districts in the men's A-Grade in Australia
HOW WOULD YOUR TEAM-MATES DESCRIBE YOU IN THREE WORDS? Bubbly, caring, messy
CRICKETING HEROES? Graham Thorpe – I loved how gutsy he was and how he kept his cricket so simple. Ironically, I bat nothing like him
NON-CRICKETING HEROES? Steffi Graf – I admired her elegance on and off the field
IF YOU WEREN'T A CRICKETER? A photographer for National Geographic or an archaeologist
SURPRISING FACT? I travel with a teddy bear called Bephy
TWITTER: @Sarah_Taylor30

Batting	Mat	Inns	NO	Runs	HS	Ave	SR	100	50	Ct	St
Tests	8	15	1	266	40	19.00	49.71	0	0	17	2
ODIs	101	94	12	3261	129	39.76	80.08	5	16	75	40
T20Is	81	79	11	2054	77	30.20	109.60	0	15	22	46
Bowling	Mat	Balls	Runs	Wkts	BBI	BBM	Ave	Econ	SR	5w	10
Tests	8	-	-	-	-	-	-	-	-	-	-
ODIs	101	-	-	-	-	-	-	-	-	-	-
T20Is	81	-	-	-	-	-	-	-	-	-	-

FRAN WILSON

RHB / OB

FULL NAME: Frances Claire Wilson
BORN: November 7, 1991, Farnham, Surrey
SQUAD NO: 18
HEIGHT: 5ft 4in
EDUCATION: University of Bath; Loughborough University
TEAMS: England, Middlesex, Western Storm, Diamonds, Emeralds, Rubies, Somerset, Wellington
ROLE: Batsman
DEBUT: ODI: 2010; T20I: 2010

BEST ODI BATTING: 30 England vs Sri Lanka, Colombo, 2010

WHAT FIRST GOT YOU INTO CRICKET? Playing in the garden with my family and friends
BEST MOMENT IN CRICKET? Being Man of the Match against Pakistan in 2016 after a five-year absence from international cricket
HOW WOULD YOUR TEAM-MATES DESCRIBE YOU IN THREE WORDS? Easily wound-up
BEST PLAYER IN COUNTY CRICKET? Heather Knight (Ber)
MOST UNDERRATED PLAYER IN COUNTY CRICKET? Fi Morris (Ber)
TIP FOR THE TOP? Georgia Hennessy (War)
CRICKETING HEROES? AB de Villiers, Brett Lee
IF YOU WEREN'T A CRICKETER? I would be an entrepreneur
SURPRISING FACT? I have an MSc in Sport and Exercise Nutrition and run a business delivering nutrition workshops in schools
UNUSUAL OBJECT AT HOME? A violin from year three (I stopped playing in year four)
DESERT ISLAND DISC? Maroon 5 – Songs About Jane
FANTASY SLIP CORDON? Keeper: The Queen, 1st: Dalai Lama, 2nd: Me, 3rd: Jennifer Saunders
TWITTER: @fwilson07

Batting	Mat	Inns	NO	Runs	HS	Ave	SR	100	50	Ct	St
ODIs	6	4	0	41	30	10.25	83.67	0	0	3	0
T20Is	7	6	3	81	43*	27.00	98.78	0	0	3	0

Bowling	Mat	Balls	Runs	Wkts	BBI	BBM	Ave	Econ	SR	5w	10
ODIs	6	-	-	-	-	-	-	-	-	-	-
T20Is	7	-	-	-	-	-	-	-	-	-	-

LAUREN WINFIELD

RHB / WK

FULL NAME: Lauren Winfield
BORN: August 16, 1990, York
SQUAD NO: 19
HEIGHT: 5ft 7in
NICKNAME: Loz
EDUCATION: Lougborough University
TEAMS: England, Yorkshire, Yorkshire Diamonds, Brisbane Heat, Diamonds, Rubies, Sapphires
ROLE: Batsman
DEBUT: Test: 2014; ODI: 2013; T20I: 2013

BEST ODI BATTING: 123 England vs Pakistan, Worcester, 2016

WHAT FIRST GOT YOU INTO CRICKET? My dad plays and we spent many a Saturday afternoon down at my local club, Stamford Bridge

BEST MOMENT IN CRICKET? Sharing England's highest opening-partnership stand with Tammy Beaumont and making my first international hundred

HOW WOULD YOUR TEAM-MATES DESCRIBE YOU IN THREE WORDS? Joker, hard-working, passionate

BEST PLAYER IN COUNTY CRICKET? Georgia Hennessy (War)

MOST UNDERRATED PLAYER IN COUNTY CRICKET? Sonia Odedra (Not)

TIP FOR THE TOP? Emma Lamb (Lan)

CRICKETING HEROES? Alec Stewart – he was the England batter/keeper when I was growing up. Graham Dilley – my coach, hero, mentor and friend. Kane Williamson – can watch him bat all day

IF YOU WEREN'T A CRICKETER? Part-time police officer or in the army

UNUSUAL OBJECT AT HOME? A ukulele

DESERT ISLAND DISC? Lighthouse Family – High

TWITTER: @lozwinfield

Batting	Mat	Inns	NO	Runs	HS	Ave	SR	100	50	Ct	St
Tests	2	4	0	56	35	14.00	32.18	0	0	0	0
ODIs	25	25	2	606	123	26.34	65.37	1	3	8	0
T20Is	18	18	1	404	74	23.76	112.53	0	3	6	0
Bowling	Mat	Balls	Runs	Wkts	BBI	BBM	Ave	Econ	SR	5w	10
Tests	2	-	-	-	-	-	-	-	-	-	-
ODIs	25	-	-	-	-	-	-	-	-	-	-
T20Is	18	-	-	-	-	-	-	-	-	-	-

DANIELLE WYATT

RHB / OB

FULL NAME: Danielle Nicole Wyatt
BORN: April 22, 1991, Stoke-on-Trent, Staffordshire
SQUAD NO: 20
HEIGHT: 5ft 4in
NICKNAME: Chesney, Waggy
EDUCATION: St Peter's High School; Stoke-On-Trent Sixth Form College
TEAMS: England, Sussex, Lancashire Thunder, Emeralds, Melbourne Renegades, Nottinghamshire, Sapphires, Staffordshire, Victoria
ROLE: Allrounder
DEBUT: ODI: 2010; T20I: 2010

BEST ODI BATTING: 44 England vs West Indies, Florence Hall, 2016
BEST ODI BOWLING: 3-7 England vs South Africa, Cuttack, 2013

FAMILY TIES? My older brother Ryan played but then he quit when I got better than him – whoops! Dad still rolls them over on a Sunday for the mighty Whitmore Third XI

STRANGEST THING SEEN IN A GAME? Myself stood at point in Sri Lanka during the 4th ODI – then realising I was in my training trousers. Watta wally

BEST MOMENT IN CRICKET? Celebrating my first Ashes win at the Ageas Bowl

SUPERSTITIONS? Two poached eggs with a Yorkshire Tea before a game

HOW WOULD YOUR TEAM-MATES DESCRIBE YOU IN THREE WORDS? Weird, crazy, caring

BEST PLAYER IN COUNTY CRICKET? Georgia Hennessy (War)

MOST UNDERRATED PLAYER IN COUNTY CRICKET? Sonia Odedra (Not)

TIP FOR THE TOP? Paige Schofield (Sus)

NON-CRICKETING HEROES? My grandad Baggaley. He fought in the war, ran marathons all his life while being the best dad, husband and grandad

SURPRISING FACT? I studied World Development at sixth form and got a D (which is a pass). I know a lot of capital cities

UNUSUAL OBJECT AT HOME? An elephant in my conservatory. I have a collection. Every time I go to Sri Lanka or India I come back with an elephant

TWITTER: @Danni_Wyatt

Batting	Mat	Inns	NO	Runs	HS	Ave	SR	100	50	Ct	St
ODIs	48	38	5	521	44	15.78	69.74	0	0	9	0
T20Is	70	49	8	488	41	11.90	104.72	0	0	15	0

Bowling	Mat	Balls	Runs	Wkts	BBI	BBM	Ave	Econ	SR	5w	10
ODIs	48	864	718	27	3/7	3/7	26.59	4.98	32.0	0	0
T20Is	70	711	671	46	4/11	4/11	14.58	5.66	15.4	0	0

The
Umpires

ROB BAILEY

NAME: Robert John Bailey
BORN: October 28, 1963, Biddulph, Staffordshire
HEIGHT: 6ft 3in **NICKNAME:** Bailers
APPOINTED TO FIRST-CLASS LIST: 2006
INTERNATIONAL PANEL: 2011-
ELITE PANEL: 2014
TESTS UMPIRED: 1 (1 as TV umpire)
ODIS UMPIRED: 20 (4 as TV umpire)
T20IS UMPIRED: 19 (6 as TV umpire)
COUNTIES AS PLAYER: Northamptonshire, Derbyshire
ROLE: Right-hand bat; off-spin bowler
COUNTY DEBUT: 1982 (Northamptonshire), 2000 (Derbyshire)
TEST DEBUT: 1988 **ODI DEBUT:** 1985

FAVOURITE OUTGROUND? North Marine Road, Scarborough
BEST PERFORMANCE WITNESSED LAST SEASON? Keaton Jennings scoring a century in both innings of the match between Durham and Somerset at Chester-le-Street
TRICKS TO MAINTAIN CONCENTRATION? Sometimes in Championship matches I count the crowd when standing at square-leg. Easier at some grounds than others!
UNUSUAL OBJECT AT HOME? A kiln or two
UNUSUAL ITEM RECEIVED FROM A BOWLER? An asthma inhaler
STRANGEST LOCATION WHERE UMPIRED? In Calgary on an MCC tour to Canada. The pitch was solid ice
FAVOURITE UMPIRE AS A PLAYER? Neil Mallender, even though he always gave me out lbw

Batting	Mat	Inns	NO	Runs	HS	Ave	SR	100	50	Ct	St
Tests	4	8	0	119	43	14.87	36.50	0	0	0	0
ODIs	4	4	2	137	43*	68.50	69.89	0	0	1	0
First-class	374	628	89	21844	224*	40.52		47	111	272	0
List A	396	376	65	12076	153*	38.82		10	79	111	0

Bowling	Mat	Balls	Runs	Wkts	BBI	BBM	Ave	Econ	SR	5w	10
Tests	4	-	-	-	-	-	-	-	-	-	-
ODIs	4	36	25	0	-	-	-	4.16	-	0	0
First-class	374	9713	5144	121	5/54		42.51	3.17	80.2	2	0
List A	396	3092	2564	72	5/45	5/45	35.61	4.97	42.9	1	0

NEIL BAINTON

NAME: Neil Laurence Bainton
BORN: October 2, 1970, Romford, Essex
HEIGHT: 5ft 8in
APPOINTED TO FIRST-CLASS LIST: 2006

FAVOURITE OUTGROUND? Colwyn Bay. Lovely little ground, great pitch, friendly people
BEST PERFORMANCE WITNESSED LAST SEASON? Marcus Trescothick at Trent Bridge in the Championship – he was on the pitch the whole game in 30-plus degrees, having to wipe his glasses after every ball
TRICKS TO MAINTAIN CONCENTRATION? Split sessions into 15-minute segments
STRANGEST LOCATION WHERE UMPIRED? I'm lucky to have umpired in Mozambique and Uganda on MCC tours
FAVOURITE UMPIRE AS A PLAYER? As a non-player, I always looked up to Nigel Plews – he was a great help to recreational umpires
HIGHLIGHT OF YOUR PLAYING CAREER? I kept wicket for South of England U15 at the England Schools Festival in 1986
FAVOURITE PASTIMES OUTSIDE OF CRICKET? Playing golf badly
SURPRISING FACT? I still work for the Royal Mail as a postman during the winter months

PAUL BALDWIN

NAME: Paul Kerr Baldwin
BORN: July 18, 1973, Epsom, Surrey
APPOINTED TO FIRST-CLASS LIST: 2015
ODIS UMPIRED: 20 (2 as TV umpire)
T20IS UMPIRED: 9

FAVOURITE OUTGROUND? Colwyn Bay – a lovely ground and the catering is spectacular
BEST PERFORMANCE WITNESSED LAST SEASON? Haseeb Hameed in the County
Championship Roses match at Old Trafford. Two fantastic innings. Composure far beyond
his years
TRICKS TO MAINTAIN CONCENTRATION? Yes, but I'm not going to say in case the players
cotton on and try to distract me. My only quirk is that I count the over with coins and they
have to be in a certain order, ranked by size, largest on the bottom, smallest on the top
UNUSUAL OBJECT AT HOME? A trophy for winning an episode of Fifteen To One (on
Channel 4). It belongs to my partner Emma – she's incredibly intelligent and even more
competitive than I am
UNUSUAL ITEM RECEIVED FROM A BOWLER? Teeth
CHEEKIEST PLAYER IN COUNTY CRICKET? Mark Footitt at Surrey is certainly up there, along
with Tom Milnes at Derbyshire
FAVOURITE UMPIRE AS A PLAYER? David Shepherd – he was respected by everyone and a
real character
HIGHLIGHT OF YOUR PLAYING CAREER? Being selected to captain RAF Brüggen, my club
side in Germany in 1996, which I captained for the next four years
FAVOURITE PASTIMES OUTSIDE OF CRICKET? Equestrian photography – mostly when our
horses compete. And walking for miles with our two black labs across the Lincolnshire
countryside
IF YOU COULD CHANGE ONE RULE ABOUT CRICKET? The tea interval should be longer. In
club cricket it isn't enough time to get through the amazing selection of cakes
SURPRISING FACT? I was the English voice on BFBS Forces radio of DJ Ötzi who sung Hey
Baby! in the '90s

MIKE BURNS

NAME: Michael Burns
BORN: February 6, 1969, Barrow-in-Furness, Lancashire
APPOINTED TO FIRST-CLASS LIST: 2016
COUNTIES AS PLAYER: Warwickshire, Somerset
ROLE: Right-hand bat; wicketkeeper
COUNTY DEBUT: 1992 (Warwickshire), 1997 (Somerset)

FAVOURITE COUNTY GROUND? Trent Bridge – a really good stadium which still feels like a cricket ground even with the relatively new stands

BEST PERFORMANCE WITNESSED LAST SEASON? Nick Gubbins' 145 versus Durham at Lord's, against a bowling attack of Wood, Rushworth and Onions on a difficult pitch

CHEEKIEST PLAYER IN COUNTY CRICKET? Not sure that cheeky is the right description but Mark Wood usually comes out with a few decent chirps

STRANGEST LOCATION WHERE UMPIRED? The Singapore Cricket Club in the middle of the city – spectacular

FAVOURITE UMPIRE AS A PLAYER? Peter Willey was always good value – he just used to stand there shaking his head when I was keeping wicket. Fair enough! It was great to stand with him in his last season

HIGHLIGHT OF YOUR PLAYING CAREER? Three home semi-final wins at Taunton. Standing on the balcony spraying champagne, the field full of fans – that's why we play the game

Batting	Mat	Inns	NO	Runs	HS	Ave	SR	100	50	Ct	St
First-class	154	248	14	7648	221	32.68		8	51	142	7
List A	221	207	21	4802	115*	25.81		3	31	101	15
Twenty20	9	7	0	108	36	15.42	108.00	0	0	3	0
Bowling	Mat	Balls	Runs	Wkts	BBI	BBM	Ave	Econ	SR	5w	10
First-class	154	4751	2885	68	6/54		42.42	3.64	69.8	1	0
List A	221	1844	1769	58	4/39	4/39	30.50	5.75	31.7	0	0
Twenty20	9	36	55	2	1/15	1/15	27.50	9.16	18.0	0	0

NICK COOK

NAME: Nicholas Grant Billson Cook
BORN: June 17, 1956, Leicester
HEIGHT: 6ft
NICKNAME: Beast
APPOINTED TO FIRST-CLASS LIST: 2009
COUNTIES AS PLAYER: Leicestershire,
Northamptonshire
ROLE: Right-hand bat; slow left-arm bowler
COUNTY DEBUT: 1978 (Leicestershire),
1986 (Northamptonshire)
TEST DEBUT: 1983
ODI DEBUT: 1984

FAVOURITE OUTGROUND? Scarborough – always a good cricket pitch, good atmosphere, best crowds for four-day cricket, lovely fish and chips at close of play
BEST PERFORMANCE WITNESSED LAST SEASON? Ben Duckett in a T20 vs Yorkshire – he only got 70-odd but hit eight consecutive balls to the boundary and played with so much time and confidence. Tim Bresnan and Liam Plunkett just shrugged shoulders as he walked off – that was brilliant
UNUSUAL OBJECT AT HOME? A hare made out of pliers, horse shoes, a spring from a motor car and various other metal components welded together
CHEEKIEST PLAYER IN COUNTY CRICKET? There's a few who are barking mad. Ollie Rayner is always a touch optimistic with his lbw shouts! Sam Billings loves a chat
FAVOURITE UMPIRE AS A PLAYER? Mervyn Kitchen – outstanding umpire who had upmost respect. You could laugh and joke with him at his expense and he'd take it all in good heart
SURPRISING FACT? I have two Siamese cats

Batting	Mat	Inns	NO	Runs	HS	Ave	SR	100	50	Ct	St
Tests	15	25	4	179	31	8.52	23.58	0	0	5	0
ODIs	3	-	-	-	-	-	-	-	-	2	0
First-class	356	365	96	3137	75	11.66		0	4	197	0
List A	223	89	36	491	23	9.26		0	0	74	0

Bowling	Mat	Balls	Runs	Wkts	BBI	BBM	Ave	Econ	SR	5w	10
Tests	15	4174	1689	52	6/65	11/83	32.48	2.42	80.2	4	1
ODIs	3	144	95	5	2/18	2/18	19.00	3.95	28.8	0	0
First-class	356	64460	25507	879	7/34		29.01	2.37	73.3	31	4
List A	223	10077	6812	200	4/22	4/22	34.06	4.05	50.3	0	0

NAME: Nigel Geoffrey Charles Cowley
BORN: March 1, 1953, Shaftesbury, Dorset
HEIGHT: 5ft 7in
NICKNAME: Dougall
APPOINTED TO FIRST-CLASS LIST: 2000
COUNTIES AS PLAYER: Hampshire, Glamorgan
ROLE: Right-hand bat; off-spin bowler
COUNTY DEBUT: 1974 (Hampshire), 1990 (Glamorgan)

FAVOURITE OUTGROUND? Cheltenham College
BEST PERFORMANCE WITNESSED LAST SEASON? Keaton Jennings scoring a century in both innings at Chester-le-Street in April
UNUSUAL ITEM RECEIVED FROM A BOWLER? An asthma inhaler
FAVOURITE UMPIRE AS A PLAYER? Barrie Meyer – just a great man
NOTES: Has stood as a reserve umpire in four Tests and three ODIs and officiated in one women's ODI and one women's T20I. As an allrounder he passed 1,000 runs and took 56 wickets in 1984 for Hampshire. In 1988 he took 1-17 from his 11 overs to help Hampshire win the Benson & Hedges Cup against Derbyshire

Batting	Mat	Inns	NO	Runs	HS	Ave	SR	100	50	Ct	St
First-class	271	375	62	7309	109*	23.35		2	36	105	0
List A	305	226	45	3022	74	16.69		0	5	69	0

Bowling	Mat	Balls	Runs	Wkts	BBI	BBM	Ave	Econ	SR	5w	10
First-class	271	32662	14879	437	6/48		34.04	2.73	74.7	5	0
List A	305	11704	8038	248	5/24	5/24	32.41	4.12	47.1	1	0

JEFF EVANS

NAME: Jeffrey Howard Evans
BORN: August 7, 1954, Llanelli, Carmarthenshire, Wales
HEIGHT: 5ft 8in
APPOINTED TO FIRST-CLASS LIST: 2001

FAVOURITE OUTGROUND? Scarborough for its atmosphere and excellent support

BEST PERFORMANCE WITNESSED LAST SEASON? Tom Kohler-Cadmore's 120 for Worcestershire against Durham in the T20 Blast

TRICKS TO MAINTAIN CONCENTRATION? Maintain a good level of fitness in general. Healthy body, healthy mind

UNUSUAL OBJECT AT HOME? Some old driftwood made into shelving

FUNNIEST THING HEARD IN THE MIDDLE? "Bowl him a piano and see if he can play that" (after a batsman had continually played and missed)

MOST MEMORABLE DISMISSAL? Giving Brian Lara out first ball in the Indian Cricket League. Thankfully the replays showed the decision was correct

FUNNIEST MOMENT AS AN UMPIRE? Watching the band of the Royal Gurkha Regiment march towards the boundary in Canterbury only for them to immediately turn around and march towards the pitch. At this point my colleague Vanburn Holder called "play" with the band situated at mid-off

SURPRISING FACT ABOUT YOURSELF? I shared a beer with Liam Neeson at a friend's BBQ some years ago. The friend happened to have been Liam Neeson's best man at his wedding

NAME: Russell John Evans
BORN: October 1, 1995, Calverton, Nottinghamshire
APPOINTED TO FIRST-CLASS LIST: 2015
COUNTIES AS PLAYER: Nottinghamshire
ROLE: Right-hand bat; right-arm medium bowler
COUNTY DEBUT: 1987

BEST PERFORMANCE WITNESSED LAST SEASON? Keaton Jennings on a number of occasions

TRICKS TO MAINTAIN CONCENTRATION? Clearly marked footmarks – once the batsman and bowler is ready, move into the footmarks

FUNNIEST THING HEARD IN THE MIDDLE? Ryan Sidebottom asking if his three-point disciplinary penalty could be transferred to his wife

FAVOURITE UMPIRE AS A PLAYER? They were all good, but John Holder was great to talk to

HIGHLIGHT OF YOUR PLAYING CAREER? Making my first-class debut or scoring 209* in New Zealand

FAVOURITE PASTIMES OUTSIDE OF CRICKET? It has been golf but I've simply not had time recently. I enjoy keeping fit, running, swimming and cycling

Batting	Mat	Inns	NO	Runs	HS	Ave	SR	100	50	Ct	St
First-class	7	11	3	201	59	25.12		0	2	5	0
List A	16	14	1	211	56	16.23		0	1	1	0

Bowling	Mat	Balls	Runs	Wkts	BBI	BBM	Ave	Econ	SR	5w	10
First-class	7	198	97	3	3/40		32.33	2.93	66.0	0	0
List A	16	-	-	-	-	-	-	-	-	-	-

STEVE GALE

NAME: Stephen Clifford Gale
BORN: June 3, 1952, Shrewsbury, Shropshire
APPOINTED TO FIRST-CLASS LIST: 2001
COUNTIES AS PLAYER: Shropshire
ROLE: Right-hand bat; leg-spin bowler

FAVOURITE OUTGROUND? Arundel
BEST PERFORMANCE WITNESSED LAST SEASON? Nottinghamshire scoring 445 in 50 overs
TRICKS TO MAINTAIN CONCENTRATION? Sleep well
STRANGEST LOCATION WHERE UMPIRED? Ventnor on the Isle of Wight – unique bowl-shaped ground
FAVOURITE UMPIRE AS A PLAYER? Mervyn Kitchen – top cricket man
RITUALS OR QUIRKS? I use six pound coins to count the number of deliveries
FUNNIEST MOMENT AS AN UMPIRE? During an England Lions vs Australia match a bail flew about 50 yards – a fielder went to pick it up but a large seagull got there first and then sat on the pavilion for five minutes with the bail in its beak
HIGHLIGHT OF YOUR PLAYING CAREER? Captaining my club Shrewsbury to success at Lord's
FAVOURITE PASTIMES OUTSIDE OF CRICKET? Coastal walks in Cornwall
SURPRISING FACT? I'm the first person from Shropshire to become a first-class umpire

Batting	Mat	Inns	NO	Runs	HS	Ave	SR	100	50	Ct	St
List A	5	5	0	156	68	31.20		0	1	0	0
Bowling	Mat	Balls	Runs	Wkts	BBI	BBM	Ave	Econ	SR	5w	10
List A	5	-	-	-	-	-	-	-	-	-	-

STEVE GARRATT

NAME: Steven Arthur Garratt
BORN: July 5, 1953, Nottingham
HEIGHT: 6ft 2in
NICKNAME: Trigger
APPOINTED TO FIRST-CLASS LIST: 2008

FAVOURITE OUTGROUND? Scarborough – always a large crowd and proximity of spectators to the playing area creates a great atmosphere

BEST PERFORMANCE WITNESSED LAST SEASON? The partnership between Joe Root and Jonny Bairstow against Surrey at Headingley in the County Championship, early season

TRICKS TO MAINTAIN CONCENTRATION? Count the crowd

UNUSUAL ITEM RECEIVED FROM A BOWLER? Hemorrhoid cream

CHEEKIEST PLAYER IN COUNTY CRICKET? Sam Billings

STRANGEST LOCATION WHERE UMPIRED? On a game reserve in South Africa. We had to stop the game so that rhinos could cross the outfield to get to the water hole

FAVOURITE UMPIRE AS A PLAYER? Nigel Plews – Mr Cool, Calm, Collected

FUNNIEST MOMENT AS AN UMPIRE? Seeing a seagull fly off with one of the bails at Canterbury in 2011 will take some beating

IF YOU COULD CHANGE ONE RULE ABOUT CRICKET? The third umpire in televised matches should be able to rectify (overrule) any decision where the evidence is clear and conclusive

SURPRISING FACT? In 1980 I played rugby union at Murrayfield in the National Police Knockout Cup final

MICHAEL GOUGH

NAME: Michael Andrew Gough
BORN: December 18, 1978, Hartlepool
HEIGHT: 6ft 5in
NICKNAME: Goughy
APPOINTED TO FIRST-CLASS LIST: 2009
INTERNATIONAL PANEL: 2013-
ELITE PANEL: 2014
TESTS UMPIRED: 5 (1 as TV umpire)
ODIS UMPIRED: 45 (14 as TV umpire)
T20IS UMPIRED: 12 (4 as TV umpire)
COUNTIES AS PLAYER: Durham
ROLE: Right-hand bat; off-spin bowler
COUNTY DEBUT: 1998

FAVOURITE OUTGROUND? Colchester – I scored my first Championship hundred and umpired my first Championship match at the ground

BEST PERFORMANCE WITNESSED LAST SEASON? Michael Lumb (184 off 150 balls) and Rory Kleinveldt (128 off 63 balls) in the Notts vs Northants RL Cup match at Trent Bridge. Aggregate of 870 runs in the match

UNUSUAL OBJECT AT HOME? U19 World Cup Winner's Medal from South Africa, 1998

CHEEKIEST PLAYER IN COUNTY CRICKET? Luke Fletcher and Mark Wood are always good value

MOST MEMORABLE DISMISSAL? I was at the bowler's end for the Jos Buttler Mankad dismissal at Edgbaston in 2014

FAVOURITE UMPIRE AS A PLAYER? John Hampshire – I enjoyed many conversations with John when I played at Durham. If I was fielding at square-leg or stood at the non-striker's end I would enjoy his stories and he would always offer some words of encouragement

SURPRISING FACT? I'm a qualified football referee and season-ticket holder at Hartlepool United FC

Batting	Mat	Inns	NO	Runs	HS	Ave	SR	100	50	Ct	St
First-class	67	119	3	2952	123	25.44		2	15	57	0
List A	49	45	4	974	132	23.75		1	3	14	0

Bowling	Mat	Balls	Runs	Wkts	BBI	BBM	Ave	Econ	SR	5w	10
First-class	67	2486	1350	30	5/66		45.00	3.25	82.8	1	0
List A	49	1136	947	21	3/26		45.09	5.00	54.0	0	0

G

IAN GOULD

NAME: Ian James Gould
BORN: August 19, 1957, Taplow,
Buckinghamshire
HEIGHT: 5ft 7in
NICKNAME: Gunner
APPOINTED TO FIRST-CLASS LIST: 2002
INTERNATIONAL PANEL: 2006-
ELITE PANEL: 2009-
TESTS UMPIRED: 77 (19 as TV umpire)
ODIS UMPIRED: 146 (32 as TV umpire)
T20IS UMPIRED: 55 (18 as TV umpire)
COUNTIES AS PLAYER: Middlesex, Sussex
ROLE: Left-hand bat; wicketkeeper
COUNTY DEBUT: 1975 (Middlesex), 1981 (Sussex)
ODI DEBUT: 1983

UMPIRES

NOTES: Made his debut as an international umpire in 2006. PCA Umpire of the Year in 2005 and 2007. Umpired at the 2007, 2011 and 2015 World Cups and the 2009, 2010, 2012, 2014 and 2016 World T20s. As a player he kept wicket for England at the 1983 World Cup and captained Sussex to victory in the 1986 NatWest Trophy

Batting	Mat	Inns	NO	Runs	HS	Ave	SR	100	50	Ct	St
ODIs	18	14	2	155	42	12.91	63.78	0	0	15	3
First-class	298	399	63	8756	128	26.05		4	47	536	67
List A	315	270	41	4377	88	19.11		0	20	242	37
Bowling	Mat	Balls	Runs	Wkts	BBI	BBM	Ave	Econ	SR	5w	10
ODIs	18	-	-	-	-	-	-	-	-	-	
First-class	298	478	365	7	3/10		52.14	4.58	68.2	0	0
List A	315	20	16	1	1/0	1/0	16.00	4.80	20.0	0	0

PETER HARTLEY

NAME: Peter John Hartley
BORN: April 18, 1960, Keighley, Yorkshire
HEIGHT: 6ft
NICKNAME: Jack
APPOINTED TO FIRST-CLASS LIST: 2003
INTERNATIONAL PANEL: 2006-2009
TESTS UMPIRED: 9 (9 as TV umpire)
ODIS UMPIRED: 16 (10 as TV umpire)
T20IS UMPIRED: 7 (4 as TV umpire)
COUNTIES AS PLAYER: Warwickshire, Yorkshire, Hampshire
ROLE: Right-hand bat; right-arm fast-medium bowler
COUNTY DEBUT: 1982 (Warwickshire), 1985 (Yorkshire), 1998 (Hampshire)

BEST PERFORMANCE WITNESSED LAST SEASON? Steven Finn's fast and intimidating spell for Middlesex against Yorkshire at Scarborough – it changed the game
CHEEKIEST PLAYER IN COUNTY CRICKET? Azeem Rafiq
STRANGEST LOCATION WHERE UMPIRED? An army camp in Kuala Lumpur
FAVOURITE UMPIRE AS A PLAYER? Kevin Lyons
CAREER HIGHLIGHT AS AN UMPIRE? Standing in T20 Finals Day
IF YOU COULD CHANGE ONE RULE ABOUT CRICKET, WHAT WOULD IT BE? Any ball that passes above the height of the stumps (without bouncing) should be a no-ball

Batting	Mat	Inns	NO	Runs	HS	Ave	SR	100	50	Ct	St
First-class	232	283	66	4321	127*	19.91		2	14	68	0
List A	269	170	62	1765	83	16.34		0	4	46	0

Bowling	Mat	Balls	Runs	Wkts	BBI	BBM	Ave	Econ	SR	5w	10
First-class	232	37108	20635	683	9/41		30.21	3.33	54.3	23	3
List A	269	12636	9069	356	5/20	5/20	25.47	4.30	35.4	5	0

NAME: Richard Keith Illingworth
BORN: August 23, 1963, Bradford
HEIGHT: 5ft 11in
NICKNAME: Harry, Lucy
APPOINTED TO FIRST-CLASS LIST: 2006
INTERNATIONAL PANEL: 2009-
ELITE PANEL: 2013-
TESTS UMPIRED: 37 (11 as TV umpire)
ODIS UMPIRED: 89 (38 as TV umpire)
T20IS UMPIRED: 23 (7 as TV umpire)
COUNTIES AS PLAYER: Worcestershire, Derbyshire
ROLE: Right-hand bat; slow left-arm bowler
COUNTY DEBUT: 1982 (Worcestershire), 2001 (Derbyshire)
TEST DEBUT: 1991 ODI DEBUT: 1991

UMPIRES

FAVOURITE OUTGROUND? Tunbridge Wells – beautiful when the flowers are in full bloom
BEST PERFORMANCE WITNESSED LAST SEASON? Azhar Ali's 300*in the Dubai day-night Test – a great deal of physical and mental strength, skill and concentration
CHEEKIEST PLAYER IN COUNTY CRICKET? Niall O'Brien
RITUALS OR QUIRKS? I use old penny coins (dated 1967) to count balls in the over
CAREER HIGHLIGHT AS AN UMPIRE? Australia vs New Zealand at Adelaide – the first day-night Test
FUNNIEST MOMENT AS AN UMPIRE? Being complimented by David Warner – at least I think it was a compliment
HIGHLIGHT OF YOUR PLAYING CAREER? Realising a dream of playing for England and winning trophies with my adopted county Worcestershire
IF YOU COULD CHANGE ONE RULE ABOUT CRICKET? Leg-byes should go to the batsman

Batting	Mat	Inns	NO	Runs	HS	Ave	SR	100	50	Ct	St
Tests	9	14	7	128	28	18.28	32.08	0	0	5	0
ODIs	25	11	5	68	14	11.33	57.14	0	0	8	0
First-class	376	435	122	7027	120*	22.45		4	21	161	0
List A	381	185	87	1458	53*	14.87		0	1	93	0

Bowling	Mat	Balls	Runs	Wkts	BBI	BBM	Ave	Econ	SR	5w	10
Tests	13	1485	615	19	4/96	6/150	32.36	2.48	78.1	0	0
ODIs	25	1501	1059	30	3/33	3/33	35.30	4.23	50.0	0	0
First-class	376	65868	26213	831	7/50		31.54	2.38	79.2	27	6
List A	381	16918	11157	412	5/24	5/24	27.08	3.95	41.0	2	0

RICHARD KETTLEBOROUGH

NAME: Richard Allan Kettleborough
BORN: March 15, 1973, Sheffield
HEIGHT: 5ft 10in
NICKNAME: Ketts
APPOINTED TO FIRST-CLASS LIST: 2006
INTERNATIONAL PANEL: 2008-
ELITE PANEL: 2011-
TESTS UMPIRED: 57 (15 as TV umpire)
ODIS UMPIRED: 98 (30 as TV umpire)
T20IS UMPIRED: 31 (9 as TV umpire)
COUNTIES AS PLAYER: Yorkshire, Middlesex
ROLE: Left-hand bat; right-arm medium bowler
COUNTY DEBUT: 1994 (Yorkshire), 1998 (Middlesex)

FAVOURITE COUNTY GROUND? Trent Bridge – I used to go there when I was young and it's quite close to home
CAREER HIGHLIGHT AS AN UMPIRE? Standing in the World Cup final at the MCG in front of 95,000 people and in Sachin Tendulkar's final Test match in Mumbai. Also saw Brendon McCullum hit the quickest century in Test cricket at Christchurch
RITUALS OR QUIRKS? I always take a picture of my children out to the middle with me
UNUSUAL OBJECT AT HOME? A signed Sheffield Wednesday shirt from the 1991 League Cup-winning team – unusual because we don't win that much
FAVOURITE UMPIRE AS A PLAYER? John Hampshire – he was a family friend but also because he was the person who got me into umpiring
MOST MEMORABLE DISMISSAL? Giving Sachin Tendulkar out lbw in both innings of a Test match in Delhi
FUNNIEST MOMENT AS AN UMPIRE? Most days standing with Neil Mallender
HIGHLIGHT OF YOUR PLAYING CAREER? Scoring my maiden first-class century in 1996
IF YOU COULD CHANGE ONE RULE ABOUT CRICKET? Allow home umpires in Test matches

Batting	Mat	Inns	NO	Runs	HS	Ave	SR	100	50	Ct	St
First-class	33	56	6	1258	108	25.16		1	7	20	0
List A	21	16	4	290	58	24.16		0	1	6	0

Bowling	Mat	Balls	Runs	Wkts	BBI	BBM	Ave	Econ	SR	5w	10
First-class	33	378	243	3	2/26		81.00	3.85	126.0	0	0
List A	21	270	230	6	2/43	2/43	38.33	5.11	45.0	0	0

NAME: Nigel James Llong
BORN: February 11, 1969, Ashford, Kent
HEIGHT: 6ft
NICKNAME: Nidge
APPOINTED TO FIRST-CLASS LIST: 2002
INTERNATIONAL PANEL: 2004-2006 (TV umpire), 2006-present (full member)
ELITE PANEL: 2012-
TESTS UMPIRED: 63 (21 as TV umpire)
ODIS UMPIRED: 166 (59 as TV umpire)
T20IS UMPIRED: 44 (12 as TV umpire)
COUNTIES AS PLAYER: Kent
ROLE: Left-hand bat; off-spin bowler
COUNTY DEBUT: 1990

FAVOURITE OUTGROUND? Tunbridge Wells – a beautiful ground with the rhododendrons in flower. Cheltenham College has wonderful buildings
CAREER HIGHLIGHT AS AN UMPIRE? My first Test match and reaching 100 ODIs
UNUSUAL OBJECT AT HOME? Me. Pretty unusual I'm home, given my year-round schedule!
UNUSUAL ITEM RECEIVED FROM A BOWLER? Cigarette lighter
FUNNIEST THING HEARD IN THE MIDDLE? Umpiring with Neil Mallender is hilarious
STRANGEST LOCATION WHERE UMPIRED? Dharamsala under the Himalayas in India
RITUALS OR QUIRKS? I pray that the umpiring gods will be kind to me and give me easy decisions on the day
FUNNIEST MOMENT AS AN UMPIRE? Do we still have fun on a cricket field?
MOST MEMORABLE DISMISSAL? As a batsman Wasim Akram snapped my stump in two
HIGHLIGHT OF YOUR PLAYING CAREER? Kent vs Glamorgan at Canterbury in 1995. One-day match, with the winning team becoming league champions. Best atmosphere I've played in
FAVOURITE PASTIMES OUTSIDE OF CRICKET? I try and fish in various parts of the world

Batting	Mat	Inns	NO	Runs	HS	Ave	SR	100	50	Ct	St
First-class	68	108	11	3024	130	31.17		6	16	59	0
List A	136	115	24	2302	123	25.29		2	8	41	0

Bowling	Mat	Balls	Runs	Wkts	BBI	BBM	Ave	Econ	SR	5w	10
First-class	68	2273	1259	35	5/21		35.97	3.32	64.9	2	0
List A	136	1317	1210	40	4/24	4/24	30.25	5.51	32.9	0	0

GRAHAM LLOYD

NAME: Graham David Lloyd
BORN: July 1, 1969, Accrington, Lancashire
APPOINTED TO FIRST-CLASS LIST: 2014
COUNTY AS PLAYER: Lancashire
ROLE: Right-hand bat; right-arm medium bowler
COUNTY DEBUT: 1988
ODI DEBUT: 1996

FAVOURITE OUTGROUND? Colwyn Bay
BEST PERFORMANCE WITNESSED LAST SEASON? Keaton Jennings scoring a double hundred
CAREER HIGHLIGHT AS AN UMPIRE? Umpiring the Somerset vs India tour match a few years ago
UNUSUAL ITEM RECEIVED FROM A BOWLER? A packet of Marlboro Lights
FAVOURITE UMPIRE AS A PLAYER? Nigel Plews – great bloke and a top umpire
FUNNIEST MOMENT AS AN UMPIRE? Ian Austin doing his Bob Willis impression and losing his footing in his delivery stride, resulting in him rolling uncontrollably down the wicket
FAVOURITE PASTIMES OUTSIDE OF CRICKET? Horse-racing and football
SURPRISING FACT? As a teenager I represented Lancashire and North of England at tennis

Batting	Mat	Inns	NO	Runs	HS	Ave	SR	100	50	Ct	St
ODIs	6	5	1	39	22	9.75	48.75	0	0	2	0
First-class	203	323	28	11279	241	38.23		24	64	140	0
List A	295	258	48	6117	134	29.12		4	29	67	0

Bowling	Mat	Balls	Runs	Wkts	BBI	BBM	Ave	Econ	SR	5w	10
ODIs	6	-	-	-	-	-	-	-	-	-	-
First-class	203	339	440	2	1/4		220.00	7.78	169.5	0	0
List A	295	72	103	1	1/23	1/23	103.00	8.58	72.0	0	0

NAME: Jeremy William Lloyds
BORN: November 17, 1954, Penang, Malaysia
HEIGHT: 5ft 11in
NICKNAME: Jerry
APPOINTED TO FIRST-CLASS LIST: 1998
INTERNATIONAL PANEL: 2002-2004 (TV umpire); 2004-2006 (full member)
TESTS UMPIRED: 15 (10 as TV umpire)
ODIS UMPIRED: 40 (22 as TV umpire)
T20IS UMPIRED: 1
COUNTIES AS PLAYER: Somerset, Gloucestershire
ROLE: Left-hand bat; off-spin bowler
COUNTY DEBUT: 1979 (Somerset), 1985 (Gloucestershire)

FAVOURITE OUTGROUND? Difficult to choose between these four: Scarborough, Chesterfield, Cheltenham and Southport. It's always about the fantastic people who look after you

BEST PERFORMANCE WITNESSED LAST SEASON? Keating Jennings scoring a double hundred in the Durham vs Yorkshire Championship fixture. It seemed like a different pitch for him

TRICKS TO MAINTAIN CONCENTRATION? That would be telling

UNUSUAL ITEM RECEIVED FROM A BOWLER? You really don't want to know

FUNNIEST THING HEARD IN THE MIDDLE? Not for this publication

FAVOURITE UMPIRE AS A PLAYER? John Hampshire and all the Somerset and Gloucestershire guys!

HIGHLIGHT OF YOUR PLAYING CAREER? Winning the NatWest Trophy final in 1983 with Somerset

SURPRISING FACT? I'm probably a better rugby player than a cricketer, or so my friends at Taunton RFC tell me

Batting	Mat	Inns	NO	Runs	HS	Ave	SR	100	50	Ct	St
First-class	267	408	64	10679	132*	31.04		10	62	229	0
List A	177	150	26	1982	73*	15.98		0	5	58	0

Bowling	Mat	Balls	Runs	Wkts	BBI	BBM	Ave	Econ	SR	5w	10
First-class	267	24175	12943	333	7/88		38.86	3.21	72.5	13	1
List A	177	1522	1129	26	3/14	3/14	44.42	4.45	58.5	0	0

NEIL MALLENDER

NAME: Neil Alan Mallender
BORN: August 13, 1961, Kirk Sandall, Yorkshire
HEIGHT: 6ft
NICKNAME: Ghostie
APPOINTED TO FIRST-CLASS LIST: 1999
INTERNATIONAL PANEL: 2002-2004
TESTS UMPIRED: 8 (5 as TV umpire)
ODIS UMPIRED: 32 (10 as TV umpire)
COUNTIES AS PLAYER: Northamptonshire, Somerset
ROLE: Right-hand bat; right-arm fast-medium bowler
COUNTY DEBUT: 1980 (Northamptonshire), 1987 (Somerset)
TEST DEBUT: 1992

BEST PERFORMANCE WITNESSED LAST SEASON? Keaton Jennings scoring a double century vs Surrey on a sporting Durham pitch. One of the best innings I have seen during my umpiring career
CAREER HIGHLIGHT AS AN UMPIRE? The 2003 World Cup
UNUSUAL OBJECT AT HOME? A persimmon-headed driver
CHEEKIEST PLAYER IN COUNTY CRICKET? Tim Bresnan has a very dry sense of humour
FAVOURITE UMPIRE AS A PLAYER? Ken Palmer and Peter Willey
RITUALS OR QUIRKS? I will never pick an end. I always toss up or flick a bail up to decide
MOST MEMORABLE DISMISSAL? Giving Sachin Tendulkar out lbw to Ronnie Irani at Lord's
FUNNIEST MOMENT AS AN UMPIRE? Watching Mark Davies of Durham come in as nightwatchman to face Andrew Flintoff at Old Trafford
HIGHLIGHT OF YOUR PLAYING CAREER? My Test debut at Headingley
SURPRISING FACT ABOUT YOURSELF? I enjoy rock/metal music. My favourite group is a Dutch group called Within Temptation – highly recommended

Batting	Mat	Inns	NO	Runs	HS	Ave	SR	100	50	Ct	St
Tests	2	3	0	8	4	2.66	36.36	0	0	0	0
First-class	345	396	122	4709	100*	17.18		1	10	111	0
List A	325	163	75	1146	38*	13.02		0	0	60	0

Bowling	Mat	Balls	Runs	Wkts	BBI	BBM	Ave	Econ	SR	5w	10
Tests	2	449	215	10	5/50	8/122	21.50	2.87	44.49	1	0
First-class	345	53215	24654	937	7/27		26.31	2.77	56.7	36	5
List A	325	15488	9849	387	7/37	7/37	25.44	3.81	40.0	3	0

DAVID MILLNS

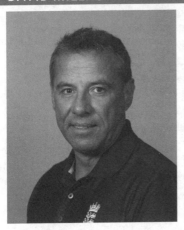

NAME: David James Millns
BORN: February 7, 1965, Clipstone, Nottinghamshire
HEIGHT: 6ft 3in
NICKNAME: Rocket Man
APPOINTED TO FIRST-CLASS LIST: 2009
COUNTIES AS A PLAYER: Nottinghamshire, Leicestershire
ROLE: Left-hand bat; right-arm fast bowler
COUNTY DEBUT: 1988 (Nottinghamshire), 1990 (Leicestershire)

BEST PERFORMANCE WITNESSED LAST SEASON? Jeetan Patel's spell for Warwickshire in the RL Cup semi-final against Somerset at Edgbaston
UNUSUAL OBJECT AT HOME? An African tapestry of the cave man paintings at Bushmans Kloof (Cape Town) dated 8000BC
UNUSUAL ITEM RECEIVED FROM A BOWLER? Tino Best gave me his gold chain to hold in Barbados when the clasp broke – must have weighed at least two pounds. Proper bling
FUNNIEST THING HEARD IN THE MIDDLE? Abu Dhabi, MCC vs Yorkshire, 2016: Jake Ball tells everyone he is Jonty Rhodes after a great bit of fielding at backward point. Next ball he drops a very easy catch
STRANGEST LOCATION WHERE UMPIRED? Palam Station Air Force Base in Delhi, India. Had a plane taking off or landing every five minutes and flying less than 300ft over the ground
HIGHLIGHT OF YOUR PLAYING CAREER? Being part of the Leicestershire Championship-winning sides of 1996 and 1998
IF YOU COULD CHANGE ONE RULE ABOUT CRICKET? Tea in the Championship would be 30 minutes
SURPRISING FACT? I still can't tie a dickie-bow at 52 years old

Batting	Mat	Inns	NO	Runs	HS	Ave	SR	100	50	Ct	St
First-class	171	203	63	3082	121	22.01		3	8	76	0
List A	91	49	26	338	39*	14.69		0	0	18	0

Bowling	Mat	Balls	Runs	Wkts	BBI	BBM	Ave	Econ	SR	5w	10
First-class	171	26571	15129	553	9/37		27.35	3.41	48.0	23	4
List A	91	3931	3144	83	4/26	4/26	37.87	4.79	47.3	0	0

STEVE O'SHAUGHNESSY

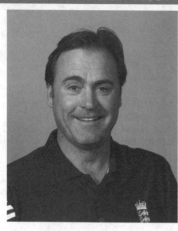

NAME: Steven Joseph O'Shaughnessy
BORN: September 9, 1961, Bury, Lancashire
APPOINTED TO FIRST-CLASS LIST: 2011
COUNTIES AS PLAYER: Lancashire, Worcestershire
ROLE: Right-hand bat; right-arm medium bowler
COUNTY DEBUT: 1980 (Lancashire), 1988 (Worcestershire)

NOTES: O'Shaughnessy started umpiring in 2007 and was appointed to the full list for the 2011 season. He has officiated in four women's ODIs, including in the 2013 Ashes series. As a player he won the Walter Lawrence Trophy for the fastest hundred of the 1983 season – a 35-minute blitz for Lancashire against Leicestershire at Old Trafford

Batting	Mat	Inns	NO	Runs	HS	Ave	SR	100	50	Ct	St
First-class	112	181	28	3720	159*	24.31		5	16	57	0
List A	176	151	23	2999	101*	23.42		1	15	44	0

Bowling	Mat	Balls	Runs	Wkts	BBI	BBM	Ave	Econ	SR	5w	10
First-class	112	7179	4108	114	4/66		36.03	3.43	62.9	0	0
List A	176	5389	4184	115	4/17	4/17	36.38	4.65	46.8	0	0

R

TIM ROBINSON

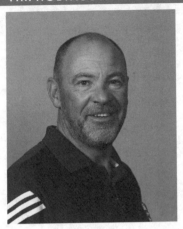

NAME: Robert Timothy Robinson
BORN: November 21, 1958, Sutton-in-Ashfield, Nottinghamshire
HEIGHT: 6ft
NICKNAME: Robbo, Chop
APPOINTED TO FIRST-CLASS LIST: 2007
INTERNATIONAL PANEL: 2013-
TESTS UMPIRED: 1 (1 as TV umpire)
ODIS UMPIRED: 11 (1 as TV umpire)
T20IS UMPIRED: 13 (6 as TV umpire)
COUNTIES AS PLAYER: Nottinghamshire
ROLE: Right-hand bat; right-arm medium bowler
COUNTY DEBUT: 1978
TEST DEBUT: 1984
ODI DEBUT: 1984

UMPIRES

BEST PERFORMANCE WITNESSED LAST SEASON? Toby Roland-Jones bowling in the tense and deciding final Championship game between Middlesex and Yorkshire at Lord's
UNUSUAL OBJECT AT HOME? My dad's old lawnmower which was so special to him
UNUSUAL ITEM RECEIVED FROM A BOWLER? An Afghanistan bowler's false teeth
FUNNIEST THING HEARD IN THE MIDDLE? A captain telling his opening bowler to bounce Kevin Pietersen and then having to fetch the ball from halfway up the stand
CHEEKIEST PLAYER IN COUNTY CRICKET? Adam Wheater. It's always the smaller guys
STRANGEST LOCATION WHERE UMPIRED? The middle of the national football stadium in Oman – the wicket was a carpet rolled out on top of the grass
FAVOURITE UMPIRE AS A PLAYER? David Shepherd – a competent umpire who was so approachable and friendly and whose international fame never changed him
HIGHLIGHT OF YOUR PLAYING CAREER? Captaining Nottinghamshire to a one-day final victory and being Man of the Match

Batting	Mat	Inns	NO	Runs	HS	Ave	SR	100	50	Ct	St
Tests	29	49	5	1601	175	36.38	41.62	4	6	8	0
ODIs	26	26	0	597	83	22.96	58.18	0	3	6	0
First-class	425	739	85	27571	220*	42.15		63	141	257	0
List A	397	386	40	11879	139	34.33		9	75	120	0

Bowling	Mat	Balls	Runs	Wkts	BBI	BBM	Ave	Econ	SR	5w	10
Tests	29	6	0	0	-	-	-	0.00	-	0	0
ODIs	26	-	-	-	-	-	-	-	-	-	-
First-class	425	259	289	4	1/22		72.25	6.69	64.7	0	0
List A	397	-	-	-	-	-	-	-	-	-	-

MARTIN SAGGERS

NAME: Martin John Saggers
BORN: May 23, 1972, King's Lynn, Norfolk
HEIGHT: 6ft 2in
NICKNAME: Saggs
APPOINTED TO FIRST-CLASS LIST: 2012
COUNTIES AS PLAYER: Durham, Kent
ROLE: Right-hand bat; right-arm fast-medium bowler
COUNTY DEBUT: 1996 (Durham), 1999 (Kent)
TEST DEBUT: 2003

FAVOURITE OUTGROUND? Chesterfield – typical English country park with a pavilion
BEST PERFORMANCE WITNESSED LAST SEASON? The white ball can sometimes be difficult to control, but Northants seamer Richard Gleeson blew away the top order of Warwickshire in a T20 match at Edgbaston
CHEEKIEST PLAYER IN COUNTY CRICKET? Neil Dexter – I've known him for years
STRANGEST LOCATION WHERE UMPIRED? I organised a game of cricket in the middle of the African bush, where a herd of buffalos stopped play
MOST MEMORABLE DISMISSAL? Giving out my friend and former room-mate, Jon Batty. He told me that he wasn't going to walk
FAVOURITE UMPIRE AS A PLAYER? Ray Julian was always a bowler's favourite
HIGHLIGHT OF YOUR PLAYING CAREER? Getting a wicket with my first delivery in my debut home Test
FAVOURITE PASTIMES OUTSIDE OF CRICKET? I dabble a little bit in wildlife photography

Batting	Mat	Inns	NO	Runs	HS	Ave	SR	100	50	Ct	St
Tests	3	3	0	1	1	0.33	3.33	0	0	1	0
First-class	119	147	43	1165	64	11.20		0	2	27	0
List A	124	68	34	313	34*	9.20		0	0	23	0
Twenty20	10	1	0	5	5	5.00	62.50	0	0	2	0

Bowling	Mat	Balls	Runs	Wkts	BBI	BBM	Ave	Econ	SR	5w	10
Tests	3	493	247	7	2/29	3/62	35.28	3.00	70.4	0	0
First-class	119	20676	10513	415	7/79		25.33	3.05	49.8	18	0
List A	124	5622	4229	166	5/22	5/22	25.47	4.51	33.8	2	0
Twenty20	9	186	256	6	2/14	2/14	42.66	8.25	31.0	0	0

BILLY TAYLOR

NAME: Billy Victor Taylor
BORN: January 11, 1977, Southampton, Hampshire
APPOINTED TO FIRST-CLASS LIST: 2016
COUNTIES AS PLAYER: Sussex, Hampshire
ROLE: Left-hand bat; right medium-fast
COUNTY DEBUT: 1999 (Sussex), 2004 (Hampshire)

FAVOURITE OUTGROUND? Arundel – I made my debut there as a player and you are always looked after well there as an umpire

UNUSUAL OBJECT AT HOME? A jellyfish paperweight that glows in the dark

STRANGEST LOCATION WHERE UMPIRED? I umpire the American College Cricket National finals in Fort Lauderdale (Florida) every March – people are surprised they play cricket in America

FAVOURITE UMPIRE AS A PLAYER? Peter Willey – dry sense of humour, really good man

RITUALS OR QUIRKS? I have a golden eagle feather on my hat

HIGHLIGHT OF YOUR PLAYING CAREER? Winning the Championship with Sussex in 2003. Taking the first-ever domestic first-class hat-trick at the Rose Bowl in 2006

IF YOU COULD CHANGE ONE RULE ABOUT CRICKET? I would rather add a regulation: no play below 10 degrees

SURPRISING FACT? I once trained and flew a golden eagle

Batting	Mat	Inns	NO	Runs	HS	Ave	SR	100	50	Ct	St
First-class	54	68	26	431	40	10.26		0	0	6	0
List A	142	58	28	191	21*	6.36		0	0	26	0
Twenty20	37	9	8	22	12*	22.00	84.61	0	0	3	0

Bowling	Mat	Balls	Runs	Wkts	BBI	BBM	Ave	Econ	SR	5w	10
First-class	54	8412	4535	136	6/32		33.34	3.23	61.8	4	0
List A	142	6311	4699	182	5/28	5/28	25.81	4.46	34.6	1	0
Twenty20	37	713	883	30	2/9	2/9	29.43	7.43	23.7	0	0

ALEX WHARF

NAME: Alexander George Wharf
BORN: June 4, 1975, Bradford, Yorkshire
HEIGHT: 6ft 4in
NICKNAME: Gangster
APPOINTED TO FIRST-CLASS LIST: 2014
COUNTIES AS PLAYER: Yorkshire,
Nottinghamshire, Glamorgan
ROLE: Right-hand bat; right-arm medium-
fast bowler
COUNTY DEBUT: 1994 (Yorkshire), 1998
(Nottinghamshire), 2000 (Glamorgan)
ODI DEBUT: 2004

NOTES: As a player Wharf was called up to the England ODI side in 2004 after impressing
for Glamorgan. He took a wicket with his fifth ball, removing India's Sourav Ganguly at
Trent Bridge. He retired in 2009 because of a knee injury and moved into umpiring soon
after. He was added to the ECB's reserve list of umpires in 2011 and was promoted to the
full first-class list for the 2014 season

Batting	Mat	Inns	NO	Runs	HS	Ave	SR	100	50	Ct	St
ODIs	13	5	3	19	9	9.50	67.85	0	0	1	0
First-class	121	184	29	3570	128*	23.03		6	14	63	0
List A	155	109	22	1411	72	16.21		0	1	42	0
Twenty20	34	20	7	157	19	12.07	120.76	0	0	5	0

Bowling	Mat	Balls	Runs	Wkts	BBI	BBM	Ave	Econ	SR	5w	10
ODIs	13	584	428	18	4/24	4/24	23.77	4.39	32.4	0	0
First-class		16825	10941	293	6/59		37.34	3.90	57.4	5	1
List A		6497	5552	192	6/5	6/5	28.91	5.12	33.8	1	0
Twenty20	32	644	1028	39	4/39	4/39	26.35	9.57	16.5	0	0

Roll *of* Honour

Division One

Team	Mat	Won	Lost	Tied	Draw	Aban	Pts
Middlesex	16	6	0	0	10	0	230
Somerset	16	6	1	0	9	0	226
Yorkshire	16	5	3	0	8	0	211
Durham	16	5	3	0	8	0	200
Surrey	16	4	6	0	6	0	182
Warwickshire	16	3	4	0	9	0	176
Lancashire	16	3	5	0	8	0	165
Hampshire	16	2	4	0	10	0	155
Nottinghamshire	16	1	9	0	6	0	124

Division Two

Team	Mat	Won	Lost	Tied	Draw	Aban	Pts
Essex	16	6	3	0	7	0	235
Kent	16	5	2	0	8	1	212
Worcestershire	16	6	4	0	5	1	203
Sussex	16	4	2	0	10	0	192
Northamptonshire	16	4	3	0	8	1	184
Gloucestershire	16	4	5	0	7	0	183
Leicestershire	16	4	4	0	8	0	182
Glamorgan	16	3	8	0	5	0	148
Derbyshire	16	0	5	0	10	1	119

North Group

Team	Mat	Won	Lost	Tied	N/R	Pts	Net RR
Northamptonshire	8	4	3	0	1	9	0.784
Warwickshire	8	4	3	0	1	9	0.74
Yorkshire	8	4	3	0	1	9	0.596
Worcestershire	8	4	3	0	1	9	0.04
Durham	8	4	3	0	1	9	-0.634
Nottinghamshire	8	3	4	0	1	7	0.228
Derbyshire	8	2	3	0	3	7	-0.335
Leicestershire	8	2	3	0	3	7	-0.486
Lancashire	8	2	4	0	2	6	-1.328

South Group

Team	Mat	Won	Lost	Tied	N/R	Pts	Net RR
Somerset	8	6	1	1	0	13	-0.087
Kent	8	5	3	0	0	10	0.587
Essex	8	4	2	1	1	10	-0.119
Surrey	8	4	3	0	1	9	0.992
Hampshire	8	4	4	0	0	8	0.393
Middlesex	8	4	4	0	0	8	0.117
Glamorgan	8	3	4	0	1	7	-0.32
Gloucestershire	8	2	5	0	1	5	-0.709
Sussex	8	1	7	0	0	2	-0.679

QUARTER-FINALS

Somerset v Worcestershire at Taunton
August 17 – *Somerset won by 9 wickets*
Worcestershire 210 (42.5/50 ov); Somerset 214-1 (36.5/50 ov)

Warwickshire v Essex at Edgbaston
August 17 – *Warwickshire won by 70 runs*
Warwickshire 283-7 (50/50 ov); Essex 213 (42.1/50 ov)

Northamptonshire v Surrey at Northampton
August 18 – *Surrey won by 1 wicket*
Northamptonshire 276 (49/50 ov); Surrey 279-9 (50/50 ov)

Kent v Yorkshire at Canterbury
August 18 – *Yorkshire won by 11 runs*
Yorkshire 256-9 (50/50 ov); Kent 245 (47.5/50 ov)

SEMI-FINALS

Yorkshire v Surrey at Headingley
August 28 – *Surrey won by 19 runs*
Surrey 255-7 (50/50 ov); Yorkshire 236 (48.5/50 ov)

Warwickshire v Somerset at Edgbaston
August 29 – *Warwickshire won by 8 runs*
Warwickshire 284-4 (50/50 ov); Somerset 276-9 (50/50 ov)

FINAL

Surrey v Warwickshire at Lord's
September 17 – *Warwickshire won by 8 wickets*
Surrey 136 (40.1/50 ov); Warwickshire 137-2 (30.2/50 ov)

North Group

Team	Mat	Won	Lost	Tied	N/R	Pts	Net RR
Nottinghamshire	14	8	2	0	4	20	0.741
Northamptonshire	14	7	5	0	2	16	0.265
Yorkshire	14	7	5	0	2	16	0.223
Durham	14	6	6	0	2	14	-0.05
Lancashire	14	6	7	0	1	13	0.2
Warwickshire	14	6	7	0	1	13	-0.215
Derbyshire	14	5	7	0	2	12	0.021
Worcestershire	14	5	7	0	2	12	-0.862
Leicestershire	14	4	8	0	2	10	-0.18

South Group

Team	Mat	Won	Lost	Tied	N/R	Pts	Net RR
Gloucestershire	14	10	3	0	1	21	0.518
Glamorgan	14	8	3	0	3	19	1.005
Middlesex	14	7	6	0	1	15	0.395
Essex	14	7	6	0	1	15	0.174
Surrey	14	7	7	0	0	14	0.153
Sussex	14	5	6	0	3	13	-0.053
Kent	14	6	8	0	0	12	-0.643
Hampshire	14	4	8	0	2	10	-0.691
Somerset	14	3	10	0	1	7	-0.66

QUARTER-FINALS

Nottinghamshire v Essex at Trent Bridge
August 8 – *Nottinghamshire won by 39 runs*
Nottinghamshire 162-7 (20/20 ov); Essex 123 (18.4/20 ov)

Northamptonshire v Middlesex at Northampton
August 9 – *Northamptonshire won by 7 wickets*
Middlesex 132-7 (20/20 ov); Northamptonshire 135-3 (18.1/20 ov)

Gloucestershire v Durham at Bristol
August 10 – *Durham won by 19 runs*
Durham 180-5 (20/20 ov); Gloucestershire 161 (19/20 ov)

Glamorgan v Yorkshire at Cardiff
August 11 – *Yorkshire won by 90 runs*
Yorkshire 180-8 (20/20 ov); Glamorgan 90 (13/20 ov)

SEMI-FINALS

Nottinghamshire v Northamptonshire at Edgbaston
August 20 – *Northamptonshire won by 8 runs*
Northamptonshire 161-8 (20/20 ov);
Nottinghamshire 153-9 (20/20 ov)

Durham v Yorkshire at Edgbaston
August 20 – *Durham won by 7 runs*
Durham 156-6 (20/20 ov); Yorkshire 149-9 (20/20 ov)

FINAL

Durham v Northamptonshire at Edgbaston
August 20 – *Northamptonshire won by 4 wickets*
Durham 153-8 (20/20 ov); Northamptonshire 155-6 (19.1/20 ov)

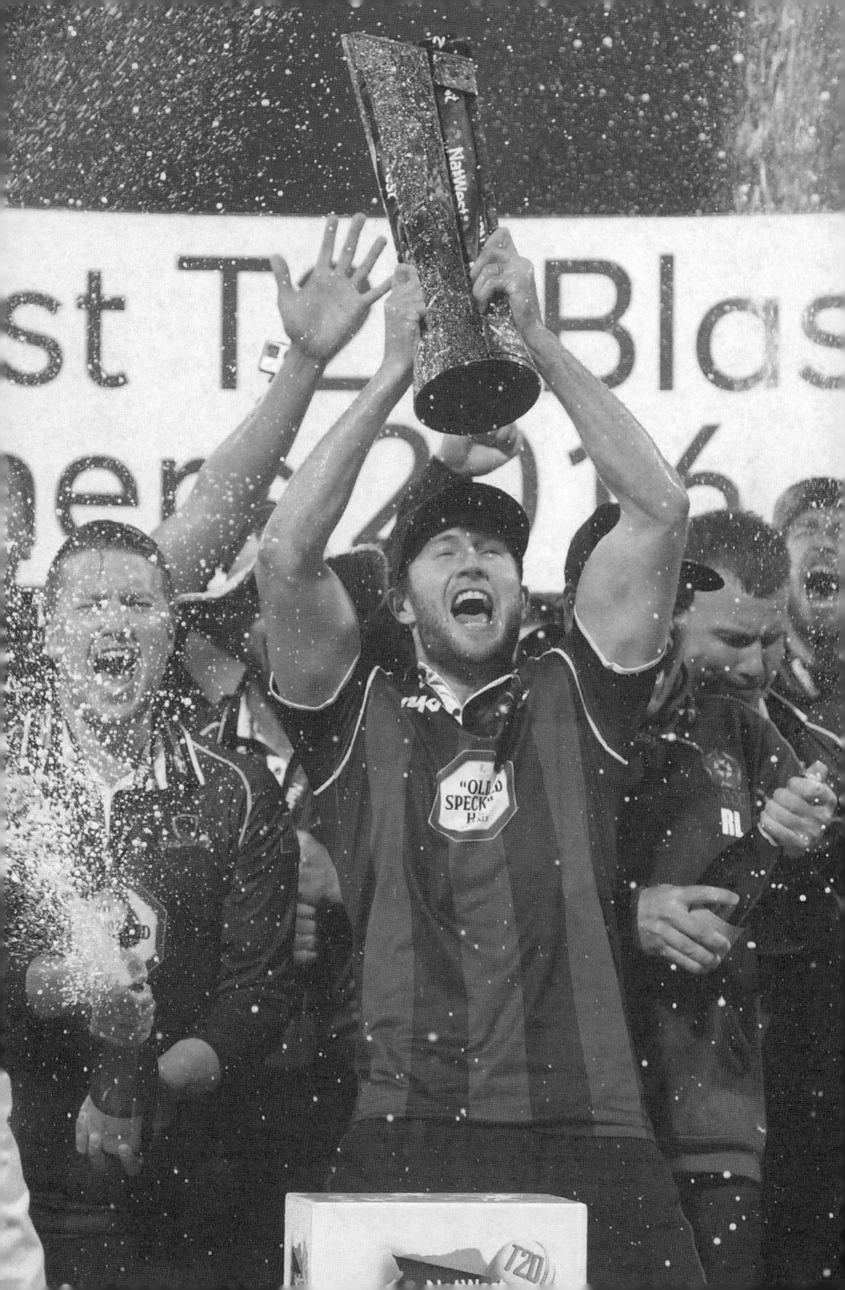
NatWest
"OLD
SPECK"
RL
T20

FIRST-CLASS AVERAGES

Name	Mat	Inns	NO	Runs	HS	Ave	BF	SR	100	50	0	4s	6s
SA Northeast	16	23	6	1402	191	82.47	2056	68.19	5	4	0	167	7
AN Cook	14	24	7	1278	142	75.17	2352	54.33	4	6	0	167	2
RN ten Doeschate	17	23	5	1226	145	68.11	1674	73.23	4	6	0	132	8
DJ Bell-Drummond	13	20	6	953	206*	68.07	1610	59.19	2	6	3	127	3
KK Jennings	17	29	4	1602	221*	64.08	2950	54.3	7	3	2	225	2
NRT Gubbins	16	24	1	1409	201*	61.26	2694	52.3	4	9	2	187	10
WL Madsen	15	26	4	1292	163	58.72	2447	52.79	6	3	3	171	2
BM Duckett	15	25	2	1338	282*	58.17	1686	79.35	4	5	3	190	7
T Westley	18	25	0	1435	254	57.4	2449	58.59	5	7	3	219	1
SM Ervine	13	23	4	1090	158*	57.36	1953	55.81	4	5	1	129	11
CD Nash	15	24	1	1256	144	54.6	2407	52.18	3	9	0	188	0
BC Brown	18	24	6	980	159*	54.44	1416	69.2	4	4	2	122	4
ME Trescothick	17	29	3	1353	218	52.03	2291	59.05	5	4	1	214	6
R McLaren	16	26	9	869	100	51.11	1706	50.93	1	6	1	116	6
JM Clarke	16	27	1	1325	194	50.96	2149	61.65	6	4	4	179	2
LS Livingstone	15	23	7	815	108*	50.93	1405	58	2	6	2	89	8
NLJ Browne	18	28	3	1262	255	50.48	2256	55.93	3	6	1	173	4
JC Hildreth	17	25	3	1107	166	50.31	1690	65.5	4	2	2	143	3
H Hameed	16	27	3	1198	122	49.91	3071	39.01	4	7	2	143	1
KC Sangakkara	12	22	1	1039	171	49.47	1552	66.94	1	7	2	142	9
AN Petersen	15	24	1	1134	191	49.3	1761	64.39	3	6	0	125	10
MJ Cosgrove	16	27	1	1279	146	49.19	2078	61.54	5	5	2	182	5
RI Newton	11	20	3	827	202*	48.64	1529	54.08	3	2	2	115	2
DW Lawrence	17	24	2	1070	154	48.63	1839	58.18	3	6	1	132	9
CDJ Dent	17	31	3	1336	180	47.71	2516	53.1	3	8	2	180	7
MD Stoneman	17	29	1	1317	141*	47.03	2068	63.68	2	6	0	175	6
IJL Trott	17	26	3	1051	219*	45.69	1830	57.43	2	6	0	142	2
AJA Wheater	15	25	4	948	204*	45.14	1573	60.26	2	4	2	118	8
SD Robson	14	21	1	899	231	44.95	1759	51.1	3	4	5	121	3
PD Trego	17	26	2	1070	154*	44.58	1512	70.76	2	6	3	131	12
SM Davies	16	28	2	1147	117	44.11	1852	61.93	3	5	2	153	3
BT Foakes	16	26	7	836	141*	44	1786	46.8	1	4	1	104	2
CJL Rogers	16	25	2	1010	132	43.91	1963	51.45	3	6	4	124	0
LWP Wells	17	23	1	955	181	43.4	2143	44.56	4	2	1	118	3
JA Simpson	16	23	5	779	100*	43.27	1544	50.45	1	7	1	105	12
DJ Malan	15	23	1	951	147	43.22	1673	56.84	3	5	2	130	4
RJ Burns	17	32	2	1248	122	41.6	2436	51.23	2	8	0	178	3
TR Ambrose	15	20	4	653	104	40.81	1418	46.05	1	7	3	73	2
A Lyth	16	30	2	1133	202	40.46	1993	56.84	4	3	2	142	13
SG Borthwick	17	29	2	1084	188*	40.14	2031	53.37	3	5	2	150	2
AZ Lees	17	32	2	1199	132	39.96	2401	49.93	3	7	3	142	6
AG Wakely	13	20	3	678	104	39.88	1426	47.54	1	4	1	82	8
JS Foster	16	20	3	677	113	39.82	1035	65.41	1	3	0	76	13
DKH Mitchell	16	29	2	1069	155	39.59	1944	54.98	3	5	3	129	1
SJ Mullaney	17	31	2	1148	165	39.58	1874	61.25	4	3	2	173	11
RS Bopara	17	24	2	870	99	39.54	1815	47.93	0	7	1	103	2
SR Dickson	15	21	3	701	207*	38.94	1483	47.26	1	4	2	80	6
BA Godleman	13	24	0	934	204	38.91	1756	53.18	3	2	1	124	6
HJH Marshall	17	27	0	1046	135	38.74	1911	54.73	4	5	3	136	4
JL Denly	15	21	2	733	206*	38.57	1472	49.79	1	4	3	94	3

FIRST-CLASS AVERAGES

Player	Mat	Overs	Mdns	Runs	Wkts	BBI	BBM	Ave	Econ	SR	5	10
JM Anderson	10	334.4	103	765	45	5/16	10/45	17	2.28	44.6	3	1
CR Woakes	12	351.1	85	1052	59	9/36	11/102	17.83	2.99	35.7	3	1
SJ Magoffin	16	523.1	144	1249	62	5/32	10/70	20.14	2.38	50.6	5	1
BW Sanderson	15	420.5	98	1204	55	8/73	10/89	21.89	2.86	45.9	4	1
GR Napier	15	470.3	100	1539	69	5/29	8/78	22.3	3.27	40.9	5	0
CJ McKay	15	411.1	78	1260	56	6/73	8/84	22.5	3.06	44	1	0
MJ Leach	16	561.3	123	1536	68	6/42	9/115	22.58	2.73	49.5	5	0
KHD Barker	17	540.4	156	1426	62	5/53	7/86	23	2.63	52.3	1	0
JT Ball	13	390	80	1257	54	6/57	9/120	23.27	3.22	43.3	3	0
OP Rayner	13	444.5	108	1202	51	6/79	9/102	23.56	2.7	52.3	3	0
JS Patel	16	616.4	168	1658	69	5/32	10/123	24.02	2.68	53.6	4	1
JA Brooks	14	432.2	105	1501	60	6/65	8/77	25.01	3.47	43.2	3	0
RS Bopara	17	355.2	69	1171	45	5/49	7/120	26.02	3.29	47.3	2	0
T van der Gugten	14	461	74	1485	56	5/52	9/133	26.51	3.22	49.3	5	0
TD Groenewald	13	369	91	1071	40	5/90	7/187	26.77	2.9	55.3	2	0
MG Hogan	16	512.4	140	1322	49	5/36	6/106	26.97	2.57	62.7	2	0
J Leach	16	519.4	81	1842	67	5/60	9/109	27.49	3.54	46.5	5	0
SCJ Broad	11	356.3	95	979	35	4/21	6/109	27.97	2.74	61.1	0	0
TS Roland-Jones	15	482.2	95	1524	54	6/54	10/127	28.22	3.15	53.5	2	1
JA Porter	15	478.2	80	1683	59	5/46	8/99	28.52	3.51	48.6	2	0
TJ Murtagh	14	457.2	116	1227	43	5/53	7/86	28.53	2.68	63.8	1	0
CN Miles	14	404.2	62	1641	57	5/54	8/112	28.78	4.05	42.5	2	0
LC Norwell	12	413.5	94	1271	44	4/65	8/140	28.88	3.07	56.4	0	0
R Clarke	16	430.3	103	1223	42	4/20	5/44	29.11	2.84	61.5	0	0
SA Patterson	15	440.5	138	1146	39	6/56	8/133	29.38	2.59	67.8	1	0
HF Gurney	14	426.5	79	1326	45	6/61	9/136	29.46	3.1	56.9	2	0
DI Stevens	15	415.1	105	1172	39	4/74	5/77	30.05	2.82	63.8	0	0
AP Palladino	14	453.5	110	1201	39	5/74	7/91	30.79	2.64	69.8	2	0
C Rushworth	14	355.2	74	1071	34	5/93	5/75	31.5	3.01	62.7	1	0
G Onions	17	561	99	1736	55	5/90	8/152	31.56	3.09	61.2	1	0
BA Raine	14	338	77	1108	35	5/66	7/111	31.65	3.27	57.9	1	0
ME Claydon	15	416.4	76	1600	50	5/42	8/156	32	3.84	50	2	0
GJ Batty	17	444.1	93	1325	41	7/32	10/115	32.31	2.98	65	2	1
KM Jarvis	16	545.2	130	1673	51	6/70	11/119	32.8	3.06	64.1	2	1
DA Payne	15	461	84	1412	43	5/36	8/132	32.83	3.06	64.3	1	0
CE Shreck	14	442.3	85	1455	44	4/33	6/92	33.06	3.28	60.3	0	0
ST Finn	14	423.1	64	1461	43	4/54	7/111	33.97	3.45	59	0	0
C Overton	13	380.5	83	1168	34	4/54	6/91	34.35	3.06	67.2	0	0
SR Patel	17	356.5	64	1163	32	4/71	5/100	36.34	3.25	66.9	0	0
J Shaw	13	405.3	79	1537	41	5/79	5/79	37.48	3.79	59.3	1	0
SC Kerrigan	13	498.4	106	1326	35	6/86	10/166	37.88	2.65	85.4	2	1
GG Wagg	14	434	73	1426	37	5/90	7/127	38.54	3.28	70.3	1	0
R McLaren	16	387	83	1249	32	5/104	5/61	39.03	3.22	72.5	1	0
EG Barnard	15	382.2	76	1423	35	4/62	4/72	40.65	3.72	65.5	0	0
TK Curran	14	469.2	93	1565	37	4/58	7/156	42.29	3.33	76.1	0	0
MS Crane	13	399	55	1498	35	3/19	6/89	42.8	3.75	68.4	0	0
CAJ Meschede	14	360.5	67	1199	27	5/84	6/162	44.4	3.32	80.1	1	0
DR Briggs	13	381.5	71	1176	26	5/93	5/108	45.23	3.07	88.1	2	0
JD Shantry	12	384.3	98	1114	23	5/46	5/75	48.43	2.89	100.3	1	0

Name	Mat	Inns	Dis	Ct	St	Max Dis Inns	Dis/Inn
TR Ambrose	15	28	59	55	4	6 (5ct 1st)	2.107
MA Wallace	15	26	54	53	1	5 (5ct 0st)	2.076
JS Foster	16	30	49	48	1	5 (5ct 0st)	1.633
BT Foakes	16	24	48	45	3	5 (5ct 0st)	2
JA Simpson	16	28	46	45	1	5 (5ct 0st)	1.642
BC Brown	18	29	43	43	0	3 (3ct 0st)	1.482
JM Bairstow	11	20	40	38	2	5 (5ct 0st)	2
CMW Read	13	25	40	38	2	3 (3ct 0st)	1.6
OB Cox	16	29	40	38	2	4 (4ct 0st)	1.379
AJ Hodd	12	22	38	35	3	4 (4ct 0st)	1.727
D Murphy	12	17	35	33	2	5 (5ct 0st)	2.058
MJ Richardson	16	22	34	33	1	3 (3ct 0st)	1.545
RC Davies	15	27	33	27	6	4 (4ct 0st)	1.222
AP Rouse	7	11	31	30	1	5 (5ct 0st)	2.818
NJ O'Brien	9	17	30	30	0	5 (5ct 0st)	1.764

Name	Mat	Inns	Ct	Max	Ct/Inn
ME Trescothick	17	31	34	4	1.096
R Clarke	16	30	31	3	1.033
LS Livingstone	15	26	26	4	1
SG Borthwick	17	29	26	3	0.896
A Lyth	16	28	25	3	0.892
V Chopra	17	32	23	2	0.718
JE Root	9	18	20	4	1.111
J Allenby	12	22	20	3	0.909
CD Nash	15	25	20	3	0.8
T Kohler-Cadmore	14	26	20	2	0.769
SJ Mullaney	17	31	20	3	0.645
SR Hain	16	30	19	2	0.633
T Westley	18	34	19	3	0.558
OP Rayner	13	24	18	3	0.75
CDJ Dent	17	27	18	3	0.666
KK Jennings	17	29	18	3	0.62
SD Robson	14	24	16	2	0.666
RJ Burns	17	27	16	2	0.592
AN Cook	14	27	15	2	0.555
HJH Marshall	17	29	15	3	0.517
DKH Mitchell	16	29	15	2	0.517

#	Name	County	Batting	Bowling	Field	Capt.	Wins	Pld	Pts	Average
1	Patel, Jeetan	Warks	51.62	476.49	20	0	16	40	564	14.1
2	Bresnan, Tim	Yorks	229.8	251.19	22	0	17	35	520	14.86
3	Jennings, Keaton	Durham	395.78	70.65	24	0	17	41	507	12.38
4	Leach, Joe	Worcs	134.05	345.04	8	2	15	36	504	14.01
5	Dawson, Liam	Hants	242.9	217.46	15	2	10	33	487	14.77
6	Lyth, Adam	Yorks	400.08	23.73	39	0	18	38	481	12.65
7	Roland-Jones, Toby	Middx	69.6	381.59	12	0	13	34	476	14.01
8	Clarke, Rikki	Warks	89.22	312.28	41	0	15	37	458	12.36
9	Patel, Samit	Notts	220.61	204.13	19	0	13	37	457	12.34
10	Borthwick, Scott	Durham	235.63	162.4	39	0	17	41	454	11.07
11	Duckett, Ben	Northants	423.45	-2.4	15	0	16	36	452	12.56
12	Barker, Keith	Warks	100.41	310.36	10	0	5	20	426	21.29
13	Mullaney, Steven	Notts	248.64	130.05	31	0	13	37	423	11.42
14	Northeast, Sam	Kent	361.51	-0.2	13	16	16	38	406	10.69
15	Stoneman, Mark	Durham	364.82	-2.53	20	7	17	41	406	9.91
16	Bopara, Ravinder	Essex	156.28	191.15	21	11	17	39	397	10.17
17	Stevens, Darren	Kent	165.56	200.36	12	0	15	37	393	10.62
18	Trego, Peter	Somerset	287.05	73.72	13	0	16	39	390	9.99
19	Roy, Jason	Surrey	347.17	0	25	0	14	33	386	11.7
20	Batty, Gareth	Surrey	83.93	251.4	9	17	17	40	378	9.46
21	McLaren, Ryan	Hants	163.18	199.84	7	0	5	22	375	17.05
22	Petersen, Alviro	Lancs	345.09	0	16	0	11	35	372	10.63
23	Allenby, James	Somerset	217.78	100.03	27	10	14	35	369	10.54
24	Napier, Graham	Essex	45.4	293.74	9	0	13	32	361	11.27
25	Ball, Jake	Notts	33.8	303.15	11	0	11	27	359	13.29
26	van der Gugten, Timm	Glamorgan	43.82	296.71	6	0	11	32	357	11.16
27	Lees, Alex	Yorks	296.89	7.72	23	12	17	40	357	8.92
28	Gurney, Harry	Notts	9.08	333.14	2	0	12	33	356	10.79
29	Coles, Matt	Kent	77.05	250.78	13	0	12	27	353	13.07
30	Gregory, Lewis	Somerset	89.94	238.87	11	0	13	32	353	11.03
31	Curran, Tom	Surrey	94.34	228.13	14	0	15	38	351	9.25
32	Westley, Tom	Essex	270.99	37.63	25	0	17	40	350	8.76
33	Wagg, Graham	Glamorgan	118.72	198.96	18	0	13	35	348	9.96
34	Klinger, Michael	Gloucs	303.49	0	17	12	14	30	347	11.56
35	Cosgrove, Mark	Leics	316.41	3.19	14	4	9	34	347	10.19
36	ten Doeschate, Ryan	Essex	232.06	64.32	19	6	17	39	338	8.67
37	Madsen, Wayne	Derbyshire	254.84	46.42	27	0	7	34	335	9.85
38	Hogan, Michael	Glamorgan	38.06	264.44	16	0	14	36	333	9.25
39	Kleinveldt, Rory	Northants	135.13	170.97	10	1	14	27	331	12.26
40	McKay, Clint	Leics	43.47	273.3	4	0	8	32	329	10.27
41	Gubbins, Nick	Middx	300.76	-0.54	12	0	15	35	327	9.35
42	Curran, Samuel	Surrey	124.08	179.47	9	0	14	32	327	10.2
43	Bell, Ian	Warks	277.96	-0.21	18	15	15	39	326	8.35
44	Rushworth, Chris	Durham	17.81	286.21	9	0	12	34	325	9.56
45	Wessels, Riki	Notts	265.27	0	45	0	13	33	323	9.8
46	D'Oliveira, Brett	Worcs	189.89	98.29	20	0	15	34	323	9.49
47	Burns, Rory	Surrey	280.75	-0.13	23	0	17	39	321	8.22
48	Franklin, James	Middx	135.94	135.31	20	10	17	37	318	8.6
49	Malan, Dawid	Middx	285.27	4.69	9	6	13	33	318	9.64
50	Plunkett, Liam	Yorks	108.12	179.26	14	0	14	30	315	10.51

#	Name	County	Batting	Bowling	Field	Capt.	Wins	Pld	Pts	Average
51	Sangakkara, Kumar	Surrey	287.1	0	16	0	10	27	313	11.6
52	Jarvis, Kyle	Lancs	49.26	252.45	5	0	4	20	311	15.54
53	Foakes, Ben	Surrey	188.33	0	107	0	14	34	309	9.1
54	Rayner, Ollie	Middx	20.62	251.58	26	0	10	24	308	12.84
55	Brooks, Jack	Yorks	36.92	259.77	6	0	5	15	308	20.51
56	Bell-Drummond, Daniel	Kent	287.86	0	7	0	13	29	308	10.61
57	Ingram, Colin	Glamorgan	222.38	59.6	14	0	11	22	307	13.95
58	Dent, Chris	Gloucs	256.17	11.86	24	0	15	35	307	8.76
59	Patterson, Steven	Yorks	45.26	244.06	4	0	12	31	305	9.85
60	Simpson, John	Middx	187.71	0	99	0	17	39	304	7.79
61	Trott, Jonathan	Warks	280.55	6.06	7	0	9	24	303	12.61
62	Dexter, Neil	Leics	141.65	145.01	6	0	8	31	301	9.71
63	Hain, Samuel	Warks	253.5	-0.8	32	0	15	38	300	7.89
64	Leach, Jack	Somerset	17.31	270.54	5	0	6	15	299	19.92
65	Lumb, Michael	Notts	274.24	0	7	0	13	37	294	7.95
66	Nash, Chris	Sussex	267.74	-3.65	19	0	10	35	293	8.37
67	Denly, Joe	Kent	252.62	7.1	15	0	16	38	290	7.64
68	Groenewald, Tim	Somerset	40.41	229.56	8	0	12	26	290	11.15
69	Mitchell, Daryl	Worcs	214.12	31.21	16	13	13	34	288	8.46
70	Rossington, Adam	Northants	204.63	-0.48	68	0	15	36	287	7.97
71	Thakor, Shivsinh	Derbyshire	115.6	161.5	2	0	7	28	286	10.22
72	Ervine, Sean	Hants	252.62	7.21	15	4	7	30	286	9.53
73	van der Merwe, Roelof	Somerset	90.33	162.87	20	0	12	28	285	10.19
74	Rashid, Adil	Yorks	65.52	194.12	12	0	13	27	285	10.54
75	Marshall, Hamish	Gloucs	250.74	-1.58	19	0	16	39	285	7.3
76	Lloyd, David	Glamorgan	242.66	14.8	12	0	14	37	283	7.66
77	Overton, Craig	Somerset	79.36	174.44	16	0	13	26	283	10.88
78	Ambrose, Tim	Warks	159.47	4.1	104	0	10	24	278	11.57
79	Onions, Graham	Durham	40.43	227.95	3	0	5	16	276	17.27
80	Wheater, Adam	Essex	222.85	0	46	0	7	28	276	9.84
81	White, Graeme	Northants	29.89	213.44	14	0	17	29	275	9.47
82	Meschede, Craig	Glamorgan	73.75	179.56	7	0	14	35	275	7.85
83	Livingstone, Liam	Lancs	223.5	7.44	32	0	11	35	274	7.83
84	Meaker, Stuart	Surrey	15.45	239.75	8	0	10	22	273	12.42
85	Trescothick, Marcus	Somerset	231.86	0	33	0	6	16	271	16.93
86	Lawrence, Dan	Essex	155.24	79.12	20	0	16	38	271	7.13
87	Croft, Steven	Lancs	175.05	28.64	44	11	11	37	270	7.29
88	Magoffin, Steve	Sussex	11.43	248.96	3	0	4	17	268	15.74
89	Browne, Nick	Essex	236.61	-0.64	18	0	12	31	266	8.59
90	Clarke, Joe	Worcs	242.31	-0.88	9	0	15	33	265	8.04
91	Raine, Ben	Leics	59.8	188.28	8	0	9	30	265	8.82
92	Davies, Steven	Surrey	236.65	0	14	0	13	34	264	7.75
93	Ansari, Zafar	Surrey	98.11	147.14	7	0	9	26	261	10.05
94	Howell, Benny	Gloucs	70.76	169.02	9	0	12	28	261	9.31
95	Hildreth, James	Somerset	236.49	0	11	0	13	30	260	8.68
96	Cobb, Josh	Northants	201.23	31.1	11	1	14	30	258	8.6
97	Taylor, Jack	Gloucs	169.98	68.42	11	0	7	26	256	9.86
98	Murtagh, Tim	Middx	26.97	210.96	6	0	9	19	253	13.31
99	Sanderson, Ben	Northants	7.18	234.12	3	0	6	20	250	12.5
100	Jordan, Chris	Sussex	82.51	145.04	16	0	5	22	248	11.29

SPREADING THE POWER OF CRICKET

Chance to Shine is a national charity on a mission to spread the power of cricket throughout schools and communities.

We take cricket to new places and use it to ignite new passions, teach vital skills, unite diverse groups and educate young people from Cardiff to Cornwall to County Durham.

Since 2005 we have given over 3 million children, in more than 12,000 state schools, the opportunity to play and learn through cricket.

Go to chancetoshine.org to find out more.

 **CHANCE TO SHINE**
Spreading the power of cricket

Late
Arrivals

MATT HENRY

RHB / RFM

FULL NAME: Matthew James Henry
BORN: December 14, 1991, Christchurch, New Zealand
HEIGHT: 6ft 2in
TEAMS: New Zealand, Derbyshire, Canterbury, Worcestershire
ROLE: Bowler
DEBUT: Test: 2015; ODI: 2014; T20I: 2014; First-class: 2011; List A: 2011; T20: 2011

BEST BATTING: 75* Canterbury vs Central Districts, Rangiora, 2015
BEST BOWLING: 5-18 New Zealand A vs Surrey, The Oval, 2014

TWITTER: @Matthenry014
NOTES: Derbyshire have signed the Kiwi international paceman for this summer's NatWest T20 Blast and he is expected to be available for the whole competition. Kim Barnett, Derbyshire's director of cricket, said: "I've been liaising with John Wright (Derbyshire's T20 coach) and Matt was one of his first picks. He came highly recommended as a fast bowler and also someone with a high strike-rate with the bat down the order." This will be Henry's second stint in county cricket, having played for Worcestershire in the 2016 campaign when he took 27 first-class wickets at 26.51

Batting	Mat	Inns	NO	Runs	HS	Ave	SR	100	50	Ct	St
Tests	7	12	3	200	66	22.22	80.64	0	1	4	0
ODIs	30	13	5	165	48*	20.62	104.43	0	0	9	0
T20Is	6	2	1	10	10	10.00	200.00	0	0	1	0
First-class	42	52	11	969	75*	23.63	77.70	0	3	19	0
List A	71	41	14	422	48*	15.62	103.17	0	0	22	0
Twenty20	59	31	13	248	42	13.77	166.44	0	0	21	0

Bowling	Mat	Balls	Runs	Wkts	BBI	BBM	Ave	Econ	SR	5w	10
Tests	7	1735	954	17	4/93	6/105	56.11	3.29	102.0	0	0
ODIs	30	1535	1456	58	5/30	5/30	25.10	5.69	26.4	2	0
T20Is	6	132	191	7	3/44	3/44	27.28	8.68	18.8	0	0
First-class	42	8599	4481	156	5/18	9/137	28.72	3.12	55.1	7	0
List A	71	3356	3079	120	6/45	6/45	25.65	5.50	27.9	4	0
Twenty20	59	1107	1521	52	4/43	4/43	29.25	8.24	21.2	0	0

JAMES PATTINSON

LHB / RFM

FULL NAME: James Lee Pattinson
BORN: May 3, 1990, Melbourne, Victoria, Australia
HEIGHT: 6ft 1in
NICKNAME: Patto
TEAMS: Australia, Nottinghamshire, Dandenong, Kolkata Knight Riders, Melbourne Renegades, Victoria
ROLE: Bowler
DEBUT: Test: 2011; ODI: 2011; T20I: 2011; First-class: 2008; List A: 2009; T20: 2010

BEST BATTING: 66 Australia A vs Ireland, Belfast, 2013
BEST BOWLING: 6-32 Victoria vs Queensland, Brisbane, 2012

TWITTER: @_jamespattinson
NOTES: Nottinghamshire have signed Pattinson as a replacement for the injured Peter Siddle, and the Australian quick will be available to play first-class and 50-over cricket through to the end of June. He was named Man of the Match on his Test debut in 2011 after taking 5-27 in the second innings of Australia's victory over New Zealand in Brisbane. Pattinson's Test bowling strike-rate is the fifth-best of any Australian (minimum 2,000 balls) but his progress has been hampered by a succession of injuries. After a successful return to first-class cricket in the 2016/17 Australian domestic season (14 wickets at 19.71) he will hope an impressive showing for Notts puts him in contention for the 2017/18 Ashes. His older brother Darren, a former Notts seamer, played a single Test for England in 2008

Batting	Mat	Inns	NO	Runs	HS	Ave	SR	100	50	Ct	St
Tests	17	19	7	332	42	27.66	39.80	0	0	4	0
ODIs	15	8	4	42	13	10.50	52.50	0	0	3	0
T20Is	4	2	2	5	5*	-	166.66	0	0	3	0
First-class	44	52	12	869	66	21.72	40.10	0	2	14	0
List A	45	26	7	245	44	12.89	71.22	0	0	9	0
Twenty20	28	12	5	44	13	6.28	83.01	0	0	10	0

Bowling	Mat	Balls	Runs	Wkts	BBI	BBM	Ave	Econ	SR	5w	10
Tests	17	3279	1831	70	5/27	8/105	26.15	3.35	46.8	4	0
ODIs	15	727	681	16	4/51	4/51	42.56	5.62	45.4	0	0
T20Is	4	78	104	3	2/17	2/17	34.66	8.00	26.0	0	0
First-class	44	7981	4316	178	6/32	8/61	24.24	3.24	44.8	6	0
List A	45	2298	1948	68	6/48	6/48	28.64	5.08	33.7	1	0
Twenty20	28	585	837	34	4/24	4/24	24.61	8.58	17.2	0	0

LUKE RONCHI

RHB / WK

FULL NAME: Luke Ronchi
BORN: April 23, 1981, Dannevirke, Manawatu, New Zealand
HEIGHT: 5ft 9in
NICKNAME: Rock
EDUCATION: Kent Street Senior High School, Perth, Australia
TEAMS: Australia, NZ, Leicestershire, Mumbai Indians, Perth Scorchers, Somerset, Warwickshire, Wellington, WA
ROLE: Wicketkeeper
DEBUT: Test: 2015; ODI: 2008; T20I: 2008; First-class: 2002; List A: 2002; T20: 2006

BEST BATTING: 148 Western Australia vs New South Wales, Sydney, 2009

TWITTER: @ronchi04
NOTES: Leicestershire signed the New Zealand keeper-batsman for the NatWest T20 Blast as a replacement for Sharjeel Khan after the Pakistan opener was charged with corruption by the PCB. Ronchi is expected to be available for the duration of the tournament. "We're delighted to sign Luke, who will offer power and dynamism to our batting line-up," said Leicestershire head coach Pierre de Bruyn. Ronchi has previously had spells in county cricket with Somerset in 2015 and last summer with Warwickshire. He made his international debut in 2008 for Australia but switched his allegiance to the country of his birth in 2013 and played every match in the Black Caps' run to the 2015 World Cup final

Batting	Mat	Inns	NO	Runs	HS	Ave	SR	100	50	Ct	St
Tests	4	8	0	319	88	39.87	73.84	0	2	5	0
ODIs	78	61	9	1215	170*	23.36	113.65	1	3	99	10
T20Is	32	25	6	359	51*	18.89	141.33	0	1	24	5
First-class	98	155	15	5598	148	39.98	84.15	16	23	333	17
List A	183	164	20	4012	170*	27.86	106.47	7	20	243	30
Twenty20	114	99	15	1619	79	19.27	141.89	0	6	73	24

Bowling	Mat	Balls	Runs	Wkts	BBI	BBM	Ave	Econ	SR	5w	10
Tests	4	-	-	-	-	-	-	-	-	-	-
ODIs	78	-	-	-	-	-	-	-	-	-	-
T20Is	32	-	-	-	-	-	-	-	-	-	-
First-class	98	-	-	-	-	-	-	-	-	-	-
List A	183	-	-	-	-	-	-	-	-	-	-
Twenty20	114	-	-	-	-	-	-	-	-	-	-

DARYN SMIT

RHB / LB / WK

FULL NAME: Daryn Smit
BORN: January 28, 1984, Durban,
South Africa
NICKNAME: Smitty
EDUCATION: Northwood School, Durban;
University of South Africa
TEAMS: Derbyshire, Dolphins,
KwaZulu-Natal
ROLE: Batsman
DEBUT: First-class: 2004; List A: 2004;
T20: 2004

BEST BATTING: 156* KwaZulu-Natal vs North West, Durban, 2015
BEST BOWLING: 7-27 KwaZulu-Natal vs South Western Districts, Durban, 2014

TWITTER: @DarynSmit
NOTES: Derbyshire have signed Smit, a batsman capable of keeping wicket and bowling leg-spin, on a two-year deal as a non-overseas player. He has played Lancashire League cricket for the past three seasons and impressed for Derbyshire's second XI last season. Scored 625 runs at 52.08 including three centuries in the 2016/17 South African first-class campaign. "He has over 14 years as a professional and will strengthen the depth to our batting line-up," said Kim Barnett, Derbyshire's director of cricket

Batting	Mat	Inns	NO	Runs	HS	Ave	SR	100	50	Ct	St
First-class	125	187	34	5711	156*	37.32	46.94	9	33	332	19
List A	107	80	21	1870	109	31.69	76.89	1	10	95	11
Twenty20	80	46	17	701	57	24.17	121.28	0	2	46	7

Bowling	Mat	Balls	Runs	Wkts	BBI	BBM	Ave	Econ	SR	5w	10
First-class	125	6684	3444	106	7/27		32.49	3.09	63.0	3	0
List A	107	2107	1718	45	4/39	4/39	38.17	4.89	46.8	0	0
Twenty20	80	630	721	28	3/19	3/19	25.75	6.86	22.5	0	0